GNU Emacs Manual

GNU Emacs Manual

Sixteenth Edition, Updated for Emacs Version 22.

Richard Stallman

This is the Sixteenth edition of the *GNU Emacs Manual*,
updated for Emacs version 22.

Published by the Free Software Foundation
51 Franklin Street, Fifth Floor
Boston, MA 02110-1301 USA
ISBN 1-882114-86-8

Cover art by Etienne Suvasa.

Short Contents

Table of Contents

13   Commands for Fixing Typos 105

14   Keyboard Macros 111

15   File Handling 119

33   Dealing with Common Problems 440

Appendix A   GNU GENERAL PUBLIC LICENSE 455

Appendix B   GNU Free Documentation License 463

Appendix G   Emacs and Microsoft Windows/MS-DOS

Preface

This manual documents the use and simple customization of the Emacs editor. Simple Emacs customizations do not require you to be a programmer, but if you are not interested in customizing, you can ignore the customization hints.

This is primarily a reference manual, but can also be used as a primer. If you are new to Emacs, we recommend you start with the on-line, learn-by-doing tutorial, before reading the manual. To run the tutorial, start Emacs and type C-h t. The tutorial describes commands, tells you when to try them, and explains the results.

On first reading, just skim chapters 1 and 2, which describe the notational conventions of the manual and the general appearance of the Emacs display screen. Note which questions are answered in these chapters, so you can refer back later. After reading chapter 4, you should practice the commands shown there. The next few chapters describe fundamental techniques and concepts that are used constantly. You need to understand them thoroughly, so experiment with them until you are fluent.

Chapters 14 through 19 describe intermediate-level features that are useful for many kinds of editing. Chapter 20 and following chapters describe optional but useful features; read those chapters when you need them.

Read the Trouble chapter if Emacs does not seem to be working properly. It explains how to cope with several common problems (see Section 33.2 [Lossage], page 441), as well as when and how to report Emacs bugs (see Section 33.3 [Bugs], page 445).

To find the documentation of a particular command, look in the index. Keys (character commands) and command names have separate indexes. There is also a glossary, with a cross reference for each term.

This manual is available as a printed book and also as an Info file. The Info file is for on-line perusal with the Info program, which is the principal means of accessing on-line documentation in the GNU system. Both the Emacs Info file and an Info reader are included with GNU Emacs. The Info file and the printed book contain substantially the same text and are generated from the same source files, which are also distributed with GNU Emacs.

GNU Emacs is a member of the Emacs editor family. There are many Emacs editors, all sharing common principles of organization. For information on the underlying philosophy of Emacs and the lessons learned from its development, see *Emacs, the Extensible, Customizable Self-Documenting Display Editor*, available from `ftp://publications.ai.mit.edu/ai-publications/pdf/AIM-519A.pdf`.

This edition of the manual is intended for use with GNU Emacs installed on GNU and Unix systems. GNU Emacs can also be used on VMS, MS-DOS (also called MS-DOG), Microsoft Windows, and Macintosh systems. Those systems use different file name syntax; in addition, VMS and MS-DOS do not support all GNU Emacs features. See Appendix G [Microsoft Windows], page 506, for information about using Emacs on Windows. See Appendix F [Mac OS], page 500, for information about using Emacs on Macintosh. We don't try to describe VMS usage in this manual.

Distribution

GNU Emacs is *free software*; this means that everyone is free to use it and free to redistribute it on certain conditions. GNU Emacs is not in the public domain; it is copyrighted and there are restrictions on its distribution, but these restrictions are designed to permit everything that a good cooperating citizen would want to do. What is not allowed is to try to prevent others from further sharing any version of GNU Emacs that they might get from you. The precise conditions are found in the GNU General Public License that comes with Emacs and also appears in this manual[1]. See Appendix A [Copying], page 455.

One way to get a copy of GNU Emacs is from someone else who has it. You need not ask for our permission to do so, or tell any one else; just copy it. If you have access to the Internet, you can get the latest distribution version of GNU Emacs by anonymous FTP; see `http://www.gnu.org/software/emacs` on our website for more information.

You may also receive GNU Emacs when you buy a computer. Computer manufacturers are free to distribute copies on the same terms that apply to everyone else. These terms require them to give you the full sources, including whatever changes they may have made, and to permit you to redistribute the GNU Emacs received from them under the usual terms of the General Public License. In other words, the program must be free for you when you get it, not just free for the manufacturer.

You can also order copies of GNU Emacs from the Free Software Foundation. This is a convenient and reliable way to get a copy; it is also a good way to help fund our work. We also sell hardcopy versions of this manual and *An Introduction to Programming in Emacs Lisp*, by Robert J. Chassell. You can find an order form on our web site at `http://www.gnu.org/order/order.html`. For further information, write to

> Free Software Foundation
> 51 Franklin Street, Fifth Floor
> Boston, MA 02110-1301
> USA

The income from distribution fees goes to support the foundation's purpose: the development of new free software, and improvements to our existing programs including GNU Emacs.

If you find GNU Emacs useful, please **send a donation** to the Free Software Foundation to support our work. Donations to the Free Software Foundation are tax deductible in the US. If you use GNU Emacs at your workplace, please suggest that the company make a donation. If company policy is unsympathetic to the idea of donating to charity, you might instead suggest ordering a CD-ROM from the Foundation occasionally, or subscribing to periodic updates.

---

[1] This manual is itself covered by the GNU Free Documentation License. This license is similar in spirit to the General Public License, but is more suitable for documentation. See Appendix B [GNU Free Documentation License], page 463.

Acknowledgments

Contributors to GNU Emacs include Jari Aalto, Per Abrahamsen, Tomas Abrahamsson, Jay K. Adams, Michael Albinus, Nagy Andras, Ralf Angeli, Joe Arceneaux, Miles Bader, David Bakhash, Juanma Barranquero, Eli Barzilay, Steven L. Baur, Jay Belanger, Alexander L. Belikoff, Boaz Ben-Zvi, Karl Berry, Anna M. Bigatti, Ray Blaak, Jim Blandy, Johan Bockgård, Per Bothner, Terrence Brannon, Frank Bresz, Peter Breton, Emmanuel Briot, Kevin Broadey, Vincent Broman, David M. Brown, Georges Brun-Cottan, Joe Buehler, Włodek Bzyl, Bill Carpenter, Per Cederqvist, Hans Chalupsky, Chris Chase, Bob Chassell, Andrew Choi, Sacha Chua, James Clark, Mike Clarkson, Glynn Clements, Andrew Csillag, Doug Cutting, Mathias Dahl, Satyaki Das, Michael DeCorte, Gary Delp, Matthieu Devin, Eri Ding, Jan Djärv, Carsten Dominik, Scott Draves, Benjamin Drieu, Viktor Dukhovni, John Eaton, Rolf Ebert, Paul Eggert, Stephen Eglen, Torbjörn Einarsson, Tsugutomo Enami, Hans Henrik Eriksen, Michael Ernst, Ata Etemadi, Frederick Farnbach, Oscar Figueiredo, Fred Fish, Karl Fogel, Gary Foster, Romain Francoise, Noah Friedman, Andreas Fuchs, Hallvard Furuseth, Keith Gabryelski, Peter S. Galbraith, Kevin Gallagher, Kevin Gallo, Juan León Lahoz García, Howard Gayle, Stephen Gildea, Julien Gilles, David Gillespie, Bob Glickstein, Deepak Goel, Boris Goldowsky, Michelangelo Grigni, Odd Gripenstam, Kai Großjohann, Michael Gschwind, Henry Guillaume, Doug Gwyn, Ken'ichi Handa, Lars Hansen, Chris Hanson, K. Shane Hartman, John Heidemann, Jon K. Hellan, Jesper Harder, Markus Heritsch, Karl Heuer, Manabu Higashida, Anders Holst, Jeffrey C. Honig, Kurt Hornik, Tom Houlder, Joakim Hove, Denis Howe, Lars Ingebrigtsen, Andrew Innes, Seiichiro Inoue, Pavel Janik, Paul Jarc, Ulf Jasper, Michael K. Johnson, Kyle Jones, Terry Jones, Simon Josefsson, Arne Jørgensen, Tomoji Kagatani, Brewster Kahle, Lute Kamstra, David Kastrup, David Kaufman, Henry Kautz, Taichi Kawabata, Howard Kaye, Michael Kifer, Richard King, Peter Kleiweg, Shuhei Kobayashi, Pavel Kobiakov, Larry K. Kolodney, David M. Koppelman, Koseki Yoshinori, Robert Krawitz, Sebastian Kremer, Ryszard Kubiak, Geoff Kuenning, David Kågedal, Daniel LaLiberte, Mario Lang, Aaron Larson, James R. Larus, Vinicius Jose Latorre, Werner Lemberg, Frederic Lepied, Peter Liljenberg, Lars Lindberg, Chris Lindblad, Anders Lindgren, Thomas Link, Juri Linkov, Francis Litterio, Emilio C. Lopes, Dave Love, Sascha Lüdecke, Eric Ludlam, Alan Mackenzie, Christopher J. Madsen, Neil M. Mager, Ken Manheimer, Bill Mann, Brian Marick, Simon Marshall, Bengt Martensson, Charlie Martin, Thomas May, Roland McGrath, Will Mengarini, David Megginson, Ben A. Mesander, Wayne Mesard, Brad Miller, Lawrence Mitchell, Richard Mlynarik, Gerd Moellmann, Stefan Monnier, Morioka Tomohiko, Keith Moore, Glenn Morris, Diane Murray, Sen Nagata, Erik Naggum, Thomas Neumann, Thien-Thi Nguyen, Mike Newton, Jurgen Nickelsen, Dan Nicolaescu, Hrvoje Niksic, Jeff Norden, Andrew Norman, Alexandre Oliva, Bob Olson, Michael Olson, Takaaki Ota, Pieter E. J. Pareit, David Pearson, Jeff Peck, Damon Anton Permezel, Tom Perrine, William M. Perry, Per Persson, Jens Petersen, Daniel Pfeiffer, Richard L. Pieri, Fred Pierresteguy, Christian Plaunt, David Ponce, Francesco A. Potorti, Michael D. Prange, Mukesh Prasad, Ken Raeburn, Marko Rahamaa, Ashwin Ram, Eric S. Raymond, Paul Reilly, Edward M. Reingold, Alex Rezinsky, Rob Riepel, David Reitter, Nick Roberts, Roland B. Roberts, John Robinson, Danny Roozendaal, William Rosenblatt, Guillermo J. Rozas, Martin Rudalics, Ivar Rummelhoff, Jason Rumney, Wolfgang Rupprecht, Kevin Ryde, James B. Salem, Masahiko Sato, Jorgen Schaefer, Holger Schauer, William Schelter, Ralph Schleicher, Gregor Schmid, Michael Schmidt, Ronald S. Schnell, Philippe Schnoebelen, Jan Schormann, Alex Schroeder, Stephen Schoef, Raymond Scholz, Randal Schwartz, Oliver Seidel, Manuel Serrano, Hovav Shacham, Stanislav Shalunov, Marc Shapiro, Richard Sharman, Olin Shivers, Espen Skoglund, Rick Sladkey, Lynn Slater, Chris Smith, David Smith, Paul D. Smith, Andre Spiegel, Michael Staats, William Sommerfeld, Michael Staats, Reiner Steib, Sam Steingold, Ake Stenhoff, Peter Stephenson, Ken Stevens, Jonathan Stigelman, Martin Stjernholm, Kim F. Storm, Steve Strassman, Olaf Sylvester, Naoto Takahashi, Steven Tamm, Jean-Philippe Theberge, Jens T. Berger Thielemann, Spencer Thomas, Jim Thompson, Luc Teirlinck, Tom Tromey, Enami Tsugutomo, Eli Tziperman, Daiki Ueno, Masanobu Umeda, Rajesh Vaidheeswarran, Neil W. Van Dyke, Didier Verna, Ulrik Vieth, Geoffrey Voelker, Johan Vromans, Inge Wallin, John Paul Wallington, Colin Walters, Barry Warsaw, Morten Welinder, Joseph Brian Wells, Rodney Whitby, John Wiegley, Ed Wilkinson, Mike Williams, Bill Wohler, Steven A. Wood, Dale R. Worley, Francis J. Wright, Felix S. T. Wu, Tom Wurgler, Katsumi Yamaoka, Masatake Yamato, Jonathan Yavner, Ryan Yeske, Chong Yidong, Ilya Zakharevich, Milan Zamazal, Victor Zandy, Eli Zaretskii, Jamie Zawinski, Shenghuo Zhu, Ian T. Zimmermann, Reto Zimmermann, Neal Ziring, Teodor Zlatanov, and Detlev Zundel.

Introduction

You are reading about GNU Emacs, the GNU incarnation of the advanced, self-documenting, customizable, extensible editor Emacs. (The 'G' in 'GNU' is not silent.)

We call Emacs advanced because it provides much more than simple insertion and deletion. It can control subprocesses, indent programs automatically, show two or more files at once, and edit formatted text. Emacs editing commands operate in terms of characters, words, lines, sentences, paragraphs, and pages, as well as expressions and comments in various programming languages.

Self-documenting means that at any time you can type a special character, Control-h, to find out what your options are. You can also use it to find out what any command does, or to find all the commands that pertain to a topic. See Chapter 7 [Help], page 40.

Customizable means that you can alter Emacs commands' behavior in simple ways. For example, if you use a programming language in which comments start with '<**' and end with '**>', you can tell the Emacs comment manipulation commands to use those strings (see Section 23.5 [Comments], page 260). Another sort of customization is rearrangement of the command set. For example, you can rebind the basic cursor motion commands (up, down, left and right) to any keys on the keyboard that you find comfortable. See Chapter 32 [Customization], page 406.

Extensible means that you can go beyond simple customization and write entirely new commands—programs in the Lisp language to be run by Emacs's own Lisp interpreter. Emacs is an "on-line extensible" system, which means that it is divided into many functions that call each other, any of which can be redefined in the middle of an editing session. Almost any part of Emacs can be replaced without making a separate copy of all of Emacs. Most of the editing commands of Emacs are written in Lisp; the few exceptions could have been written in Lisp but use C instead for efficiency. Writing an extension is programming, but non-programmers can use it afterwards. See section "Preface" in *An Introduction to Programming in Emacs Lisp*, if you want to learn Emacs Lisp programming.

When running on a graphical display, Emacs provides its own menus and convenient handling of mouse buttons. In addition, Emacs provides many of the benefits of a graphical display even on a text-only terminal. For instance, it can highlight parts of a file, display and edit several files at once, move text between files, and edit files while running shell commands.

1 The Organization of the Screen

On a text-only terminal, the Emacs display occupies the whole screen. On a graphical display, such as on GNU/Linux using the X Window System, Emacs creates its own windows to use. We use the term *frame* to mean the entire text-only screen or an entire system-level window used by Emacs. Emacs uses both kinds of frames, in the same way, to display your editing. Emacs normally starts out with just one frame, but you can create additional frames if you wish. See Chapter 18 [Frames], page 171.

When you start Emacs, the main central area of the frame, all except for the top and bottom and sides, displays the text you are editing. This area is called *the window*. At the top there is normally a *menu bar* where you can access a series of menus; then there may be a *tool bar*, a row of icons that perform editing commands if you click on them. Below this, the window begins, often with a *scroll bar* on one side. Below the window comes the last line of the frame, a special *echo area* or *minibuffer window*, where prompts appear and you enter information when Emacs asks for it. See following sections for more information about these special lines.

You can subdivide the window horizontally or vertically to make multiple text windows, each of which can independently display some file or text (see Chapter 17 [Windows], page 165). In this manual, the word "window" refers to the initial large window if not subdivided, or any one of the multiple windows you have subdivided it into.

At any time, one window is the *selected window*. On graphical displays, the selected window normally shows a more prominent cursor (usually solid and blinking) while other windows show a weaker cursor (such as a hollow box). Text terminals have just one cursor, so it always appears in the selected window.

Most Emacs commands implicitly apply to the text in the selected window; the text in unselected windows is mostly visible for reference. However, mouse commands generally operate on whatever window you click them in, whether selected or not. If you use multiple frames on a graphical display, then giving the input focus to a particular frame selects a window in that frame.

Each window's last line is a *mode line*, which describes what is going on in that window. It appears in different color and/or a "3D" box if the terminal supports them; its contents normally begin with '`--:-- *scratch*`' when Emacs starts. The mode line displays status information such as what buffer is being displayed above it in the window, what major and minor modes are in use, and whether the buffer contains unsaved changes.

1.1 Point

Within Emacs, the active cursor shows the location at which editing commands will take effect. This location is called *point*. Many Emacs commands move point through the text, so that you can edit at different places in it. You can also place point by clicking mouse button 1 (normally the left button).

While the cursor appears to be *on* a character, you should think of point as *between* two characters; it points *before* the character that appears under the cursor.

For example, if your text looks like 'frob' with the cursor over the 'b', then point is between the 'o' and the 'b'. If you insert the character '!' at that position, the result is 'fro!b', with point between the '!' and the 'b'. Thus, the cursor remains over the 'b', as before.

Sometimes people speak of "the cursor" when they mean "point," or speak of commands that move point as "cursor motion" commands.

If you are editing several files in Emacs, each in its own buffer, each buffer has its own point location. A buffer that is not currently displayed remembers its point location in case you display it again later. When Emacs displays multiple windows, each window has its own point location. If the same buffer appears in more than one window, each window has its own point position in that buffer, and (when possible) its own cursor.

A text-only terminal has just one cursor, in the selected window. The other windows do not show a cursor, even though they do have their own position of point. When Emacs updates the screen on a text-only terminal, it has to put the cursor temporarily at the place the output goes. This doesn't mean point is there, though. Once display updating finishes, Emacs puts the cursor where point is.

On graphical displays, Emacs shows a cursor in each window; the selected window's cursor is solid and blinking, and the other cursors are just hollow. Thus, the most prominent cursor always shows you the selected window, on all kinds of terminals.

See Section 11.15 [Cursor Display], page 83, for customizable variables that control display of the cursor or cursors.

The term "point" comes from the character '.', which was the command in TECO (the language in which the original Emacs was written) for accessing the value now called "point."

1.2 The Echo Area

The line at the bottom of the frame (below the mode line) is the *echo area*. It is used to display small amounts of text for various purposes.

Echoing means displaying the characters that you type. At the command line, the operating system normally echoes all your input. Emacs handles echoing differently.

Single-character commands do not echo in Emacs, and multi-character commands echo only if you pause while typing them. As soon as you pause for more than a second in the middle of a command, Emacs echoes all the characters of the command so far. This is to *prompt* you for the rest of the command. Once echoing has started, the rest of the command echoes immediately as you type it. This behavior is designed to give confident users fast response, while giving hesitant users maximum feedback. You can change this behavior by setting a variable (see Section 11.17 [Display Custom], page 85).

If a command cannot do its job, it may display an *error message* in the echo area. Error messages are accompanied by beeping or by flashing the screen. The error also discards any input you have typed ahead.

Some commands display informative messages in the echo area. These messages look much like error messages, but they are not announced with a beep and do not throw away input. Sometimes the message tells you what the command has done, when this is not obvious from looking at the text being edited. Sometimes the sole purpose of a command is to show you a message giving you specific information— for example, C-x = (hold down CTRL and type x, then let go of CTRL and type =) displays a message describing the character position of point in the text and its current column in the window. Commands that take a long time often display messages ending in '...' while they are working, and add 'done' at the end when they are finished. They may also indicate progress with percentages.

Echo-area informative messages are saved in an editor buffer named '*Messages*'. (We have not explained buffers yet; see Chapter 16 [Buffers], page 156, for more information about them.) If you miss a message that appears briefly on the screen, you can switch to the '*Messages*' buffer to see it again. (Successive progress messages are often collapsed into one in that buffer.)

The size of '*Messages*' is limited to a certain number of lines. The variable message-log-max specifies how many lines. Once the buffer has that many lines, adding lines at the end deletes lines from the beginning, to keep the size constant. See Section 32.3 [Variables], page 416, for how to set variables such as message-log-max.

The echo area is also used to display the *minibuffer*, a window where you can input arguments to commands, such as the name of a file to be edited. When the minibuffer is in use, the echo area begins with a prompt string that usually ends with a colon; also, the cursor appears in that line because it is the selected window. You can always get out of the minibuffer by typing C-g. See Chapter 5 [Minibuffer], page 31.

1.3 The Mode Line

Each text window's last line is a *mode line*, which describes what is going on in that window. The mode line starts and ends with dashes. When there is only one text window, the mode line appears right above the echo area; it is the next-to-last line in the frame. On a text-only terminal, the mode line is in inverse video if the terminal supports that; on a graphics display, the mode line has a 3D box appearance to help it stand out. The mode line of the selected window is highlighted if possible; see Section 11.13 [Optional Mode Line], page 81, for more information.

Normally, the mode line looks like this:

```
-cs:ch-fr  buf        pos line. (major minor)------
```

This gives information about the window and the buffer it displays: the buffer's name, what major and minor modes are in use, whether the buffer's text has been changed, and how far down the buffer you are currently looking.

ch contains two stars '**' if the text in the buffer has been edited (the buffer is "modified"), or '--' if the buffer has not been edited. For a read-only buffer, it is '%*' if the buffer is modified, and '%%' otherwise.

fr gives the selected frame name (see Chapter 18 [Frames], page 171). It appears only on text-only terminals. The initial frame's name is 'F1'.

buf is the name of the window's *buffer*. Usually this is the same as the name of a file you are editing. See Chapter 16 [Buffers], page 156.

The buffer displayed in the selected window (the window with the cursor) is the *current buffer*, where editing happens. When a command's effect applies to "the buffer," we mean it does those things to the current buffer.

pos tells you whether there is additional text above the top of the window, or below the bottom. If your buffer is small and it is all visible in the window, *pos* is 'All'. Otherwise, it is 'Top' if you are looking at the beginning of the buffer, 'Bot' if you are looking at the end of the buffer, or 'nn%', where *nn* is the percentage of the buffer above the top of the window. With Size Indication mode, you can display the size of the buffer as well. See Section 11.13 [Optional Mode Line], page 81.

line is 'L' followed by the current line number of point. This is present when Line Number mode is enabled (it normally is). You can display the current column number too, by turning on Column Number mode. It is not enabled by default because it is somewhat slower. See Section 11.13 [Optional Mode Line], page 81.

major is the name of the *major mode* in effect in the buffer. A buffer can only be in one major mode at a time. The major modes available include Fundamental mode (the least specialized), Text mode, Lisp mode, C mode, Texinfo mode, and many others. See Chapter 20 [Major Modes], page 207, for details of how the modes differ and how to select them.

Some major modes display additional information after the major mode name. For example, Rmail buffers display the current message number and the total number of messages. Compilation buffers and Shell buffers display the status of the subprocess.

minor is a list of some of the *minor modes* that are turned on at the moment in the window's chosen buffer. For example, 'Fill' means that Auto Fill mode is on. 'Abbrev' means that Word Abbrev mode is on. 'Ovwrt' means that Overwrite mode is on. See Section 32.1 [Minor Modes], page 406, for more information.

'Narrow' means that the buffer being displayed has editing restricted to only a portion of its text. (This is not really a minor mode, but is like one.) See Section 31.9 [Narrowing], page 396. 'Def' means that a keyboard macro is being defined. See Chapter 14 [Keyboard Macros], page 111.

In addition, if Emacs is inside a recursive editing level, square brackets ('[...]') appear around the parentheses that surround the modes. If Emacs is in one recursive editing level within another, double square brackets appear, and so on. Since recursive editing levels affect Emacs globally, not just one buffer, the square brackets appear in every window's mode line or not in any of them. See Section 31.13 [Recursive Edit], page 399.

cs states the coding system used for the file you are editing. A dash indicates the default state of affairs: no code conversion, except for end-of-line translation if the file contents call for that. '=' means no conversion whatsoever. Nontrivial code conversions are represented by various letters—for example, '1' refers to ISO Latin-1. See Section 19.7 [Coding Systems], page 193, for more information.

On a text-only terminal, *cs* includes two additional characters which describe the coding system for keyboard input and the coding system for terminal output. They come right before the coding system used for the file you are editing.

If you are using an input method, a string of the form '*i* >' is added to the beginning of *cs*; *i* identifies the input method. (Some input methods show '+' or '@' instead of '>'.) See Section 19.4 [Input Methods], page 190.

When multibyte characters are not enabled, *cs* does not appear at all. See Section 19.2 [Enabling Multibyte], page 187.

The colon after *cs* changes to another string in some cases. Emacs uses newline characters to separate lines in the buffer. Some files use different conventions for separating lines: either carriage-return linefeed (the MS-DOS convention) or just carriage-return (the Macintosh convention). If the buffer's file uses carriage-return linefeed, the colon changes to either a backslash ('\') or '(DOS)', depending on the operating system. If the file uses just carriage-return, the colon indicator changes to either a forward slash ('/') or '(Mac)'. On some systems, Emacs displays '(Unix)' instead of the colon for files that use newline as the line separator.

See Section 11.13 [Optional Mode Line], page 81, to add other handy information to the mode line, such as the size of the buffer, the current column number of point, and whether new mail for you has arrived.

The mode line is mouse-sensitive; when you move the mouse across various parts of it, Emacs displays help text to say what a click in that place will do. See Section 18.4 [Mode Line Mouse], page 176.

1.4 The Menu Bar

Each Emacs frame normally has a *menu bar* at the top which you can use to perform common operations. There's no need to list them here, as you can more easily see them yourself.

On a graphical display, you can use the mouse to choose a command from the menu bar. A right-arrow at the end of the menu item means it leads to a subsidiary menu; '...' at the end means that the command invoked will read arguments (further input from you) before it actually does anything.

You can also invoke the first menu bar item by pressing F10 (to run the command menu-bar-open). You can then navigate the menus with the arrow keys. You select an item by pressing RET and cancel menu navigation with ESC.

To view the full command name and documentation for a menu item, type C-h k, and then select the menu bar with the mouse in the usual way (see Section 7.1 [Key Help], page 42).

On text-only terminals with no mouse, you can use the menu bar by typing M-' or F10 (these run the command tmm-menubar). This lets you select a menu item with the keyboard. A provisional choice appears in the echo area. You can use the up and down arrow keys to move through the menu to different items, and then you can type RET to select the item.

Each menu item also has an assigned letter or digit which designates that item; it is usually the initial of some word in the item's name. This letter or digit is separated from the item name by '=>'. You can type the item's letter or digit to select the item.

Some of the commands in the menu bar have ordinary key bindings as well; one such binding is shown in parentheses after the item itself.

2 Characters, Keys and Commands

This chapter explains the character sets used by Emacs for input commands and for the contents of files, and the fundamental concepts of *keys* and *commands*, whereby Emacs interprets your keyboard and mouse input.

2.1 Kinds of User Input

GNU Emacs is designed for use with keyboard commands because that is the most efficient way to edit. You can do editing with the mouse, as in other editors, and you can give commands with the menu bar and tool bar, and scroll with the scroll bar. But if you keep on editing that way, you won't get the benefits of Emacs. Therefore, this manual documents primarily how to edit with the keyboard. You can force yourself to practice using the keyboard by using the shell command 'emacs -nw' to start Emacs, so that the mouse won't work.

Emacs uses an extension of the ASCII character set for keyboard input; it also accepts non-character input events including function keys and mouse button actions.

ASCII consists of 128 character codes. Some of these codes are assigned graphic symbols such as 'a' and '='; the rest are control characters, such as `Control-a` (usually written `C-a` for short). `C-a` gets its name from the fact that you type it by holding down the CTRL key while pressing a.

Some ASCII control characters have special names, and most terminals have special keys you can type them with: for example, RET, TAB, DEL and ESC. The space character is usually known as SPC, even though strictly speaking it is a graphic character that is blank.

Emacs extends the ASCII character set with thousands more printing characters (see Chapter 19 [International], page 186), additional control characters, and a few more modifiers that can be combined with any character.

On ASCII terminals, there are only 32 possible control characters. These are the control variants of letters and '@[]\^_'. In addition, the shift key is meaningless with control characters: `C-a` and `C-A` are the same character, and Emacs cannot distinguish them.

The Emacs character set has room for control variants of all printing characters, and distinguishes `C-A` from `C-a`. Graphical terminals make it possible to enter all these characters. For example, `C--` (that's Control-Minus) and `C-5` are meaningful Emacs commands on a graphical terminal.

Another Emacs character-set extension is additional modifier bits. Only one modifier bit is commonly used; it is called Meta. Every character has a Meta variant; examples include `Meta-a` (normally written `M-a`, for short), `M-A` (different from `M-a`, but they are normally equivalent in Emacs), `M-RET`, and `M-C-a`. That last means a with both the CTRL and META modifiers. We usually write it as `C-M-a` rather than `M-C-a`, for reasons of tradition.

Some terminals have a META key, and allow you to type Meta characters by holding this key down. Thus, you can type `Meta-a` by holding down META and pressing a. The META key works much like the SHIFT key. In fact, this key is more often labeled ALT or EDIT, instead of META; on a Sun keyboard, it may have a diamond on it.

If there is no META key, you can still type Meta characters using two-character sequences starting with ESC. Thus, you can enter M-a by typing ESC a. You can enter C-M-a by typing ESC C-a. Unlike META, which modifies other characters, ESC is a separate character. You don't hold down ESC while typing the next character; instead, you press it and release it, then you enter the next character. ESC is allowed on terminals with META keys, too, in case you have formed a habit of using it.

Emacs defines several other modifier keys that can be applied to any input character. These are called SUPER, HYPER and ALT. We write 's-', 'H-' and 'A-' to say that a character uses these modifiers. Thus, s-H-C-x is short for Super-Hyper-Control-x. Not all graphical terminals actually provide keys for these modifier flags—in fact, many terminals have a key labeled ALT which is really a META key. The standard key bindings of Emacs do not include any characters with these modifiers. But you can assign them meanings of your own by customizing Emacs.

If your keyboard lacks one of these modifier keys, you can enter it using C-x @: C-x @ h adds the "hyper" flag to the next character, C-x @ s adds the "super" flag, and C-x @ a adds the "alt" flag. For instance, C-x @ h C-a is a way to enter Hyper-Control-a. (Unfortunately there is no way to add two modifiers by using C-x @ twice for the same character, because the first one goes to work on the C-x.)

Keyboard input includes keyboard keys that are not characters at all, such as function keys and arrow keys. Mouse buttons are also not characters. However, you can modify these events with the modifier keys CTRL, META, SUPER, HYPER and ALT, just like keyboard characters.

Input characters and non-character inputs are collectively called *input events*. See section "Input Events" in *The Emacs Lisp Reference Manual*, for the full Lisp-level details. If you are not doing Lisp programming, but simply want to redefine the meaning of some characters or non-character events, see Chapter 32 [Customization], page 406.

ASCII terminals cannot really send anything to the computer except ASCII characters. These terminals use a sequence of characters to represent each function key. But that is invisible to the Emacs user, because the keyboard input routines catch these special sequences and convert them to function key events before any other part of Emacs gets to see them.

On graphical displays, the window manager is likely to block the character Meta-TAB before Emacs can see it. It may also block Meta-SPC, C-M-d and C-M-l. If you have these problems, we recommend that you customize your window manager to turn off those commands, or put them on key combinations that Emacs does not use.

2.2 Keys

A *key sequence* (*key*, for short) is a sequence of input events that is meaningful as a unit—a "single command." Some Emacs command sequences are invoked by just one character or one event; for example, just C-f moves forward one character in the buffer. But Emacs also has commands that take two or more events to invoke.

If a sequence of events is enough to invoke a command, it is a *complete key*. Examples of complete keys include C-a, X, RET, NEXT (a function key), DOWN (an arrow key), C-x C-f, and C-x 4 C-f. If it isn't long enough to be complete, we call it a *prefix key*. The above examples show that C-x and C-x 4 are prefix keys. Every key sequence is either a complete key or a prefix key.

Most single characters constitute complete keys in the standard Emacs command bindings. A few of them are prefix keys. A prefix key combines with the following input event to make a longer key sequence, which may itself be complete or a prefix. For example, C-x is a prefix key, so C-x and the next input event combine to make a two-event key sequence. Most of these key sequences are complete keys, including C-x C-f and C-x b. A few, such as C-x 4 and C-x r, are themselves prefix keys that lead to three-event key sequences. There's no limit to the length of a key sequence, but in practice people rarely use sequences longer than four events.

You can't add input events onto a complete key. For example, the two-event sequence C-f C-k is not a key, because the C-f is a complete key in itself. It's impossible to give C-f C-k an independent meaning as a command. C-f C-k is two key sequences, not one.

All told, the prefix keys in Emacs are C-c, C-h, C-x, C-x RET, C-x @, C-x a, C-x n, C-x r, C-x v, C-x 4, C-x 5, C-x 6, ESC, M-g, and M-o. (F1 and F2 are aliases for C-h and C-x 6.) This list is not cast in stone; it describes the standard key bindings. If you customize Emacs, you can make new prefix keys, or eliminate some of the standard ones (not recommended for most users). See Section 32.4 [Key Bindings], page 423.

If you make or eliminate prefix keys, that changes the set of possible key sequences. For example, if you redefine C-f as a prefix, C-f C-k automatically becomes a key (complete, unless you define that too as a prefix). Conversely, if you remove the prefix definition of C-x 4, then C-x 4 f and C-x 4 *anything* are no longer keys.

Typing the help character (C-h or F1) after a prefix key displays a list of the commands starting with that prefix. There are a few prefix keys after which C-h does not work—for historical reasons, they define other meanings for C-h which are painful to change. F1 works after all prefix keys.

2.3 Keys and Commands

This manual is full of passages that tell you what particular keys do. But Emacs does not assign meanings to keys directly. Instead, Emacs assigns meanings to named *commands*, and then gives keys their meanings by *binding* them to commands.

Every command has a name chosen by a programmer. The name is usually made of a few English words separated by dashes; for example, next-line or forward-word. A command also has a *function definition* which is a Lisp program; this is how the command does its work. In Emacs Lisp, a command is a Lisp function with special options to read arguments and for interactive use. For more information on commands and functions, see section "What Is a Function" in *The Emacs Lisp Reference Manual*. (The definition here is simplified slightly.)

The bindings between keys and commands are recorded in tables called *keymaps*. See Section 32.4.1 [Keymaps], page 423.

When we say that "C-n moves down vertically one line" we are glossing over a subtle distinction that is irrelevant in ordinary use, but vital for Emacs customization. The command `next-line` does a vertical move downward. C-n has this effect *because* it is bound to `next-line`. If you rebind C-n to the command `forward-word`, C-n will move forward one word instead. Rebinding keys is an important method of customization.

In the rest of this manual, we usually ignore this distinction to keep things simple. We will often speak of keys like C-n as commands, even though strictly speaking the key is bound to a command. Usually we state the name of the command which really does the work in parentheses after mentioning the key that runs it. For example, we will say that "The command C-n (`next-line`) moves point vertically down," meaning that the command `next-line` moves vertically down, and the key C-n is normally bound to it.

Since we are discussing customization, we should tell you about *variables*. Often the description of a command will say, "To change this, set the variable `mumble-foo`." A variable is a name used to store a value. Most of the variables documented in this manual are meant for customization; some command or other part of Emacs examines the variable and behaves differently according to the value that you set. You can ignore the information about variables until you are interested in customizing them. Then read the basic information on variables (see Section 32.3 [Variables], page 416) and the information about specific variables will make sense.

2.4 Character Set for Text

Text in Emacs buffers is a sequence of characters. In the simplest case, these are ASCII characters, each stored in one 8-bit byte. Both ASCII control characters (octal codes 000 through 037, and 0177) and ASCII printing characters (codes 040 through 0176) are allowed. The other modifier flags used in keyboard input, such as Meta, are not allowed in buffers.

Non-ASCII printing characters can also appear in buffers, when multibyte characters are enabled. They have character codes starting at 256, octal 0400, and each one is represented as a sequence of two or more bytes. See Chapter 19 [International], page 186. Single-byte characters with codes 128 through 255 can also appear in multibyte buffers. However, non-ASCII control characters cannot appear in a buffer.

Some ASCII control characters serve special purposes in text, and have special names. For example, the newline character (octal code 012) is used in the buffer to end a line, and the tab character (octal code 011) is used for indenting to the next tab stop column (normally every 8 columns). See Section 11.14 [Text Display], page 82.

If you disable multibyte characters, then you can use only one alphabet of non-ASCII characters, which all fit in one byte. They use octal codes 0200 through 0377. See Section 19.18 [Unibyte Mode], page 204.

3 Entering and Exiting Emacs

The usual way to invoke Emacs is with the shell command `emacs`. Emacs clears the screen, then displays an initial help message and copyright notice. Some operating systems discard your type-ahead when Emacs starts up; they give Emacs no way to prevent this. On those systems, wait for Emacs to clear the screen before you start typing.

From a shell window under the X Window System, run Emacs in the background with `emacs&`. This way, Emacs won't tie up the shell window, so you can use it to run other shell commands while Emacs is running. You can type Emacs commands as soon as you direct your keyboard input to an Emacs frame.

When Emacs starts up, it creates a buffer named '`*scratch*`'. That's the buffer you start out in. The '`*scratch*`' buffer uses Lisp Interaction mode; you can use it to type Lisp expressions and evaluate them. You can also ignore that capability and just write notes there. You can specify a different major mode for this buffer by setting the variable `initial-major-mode` in your init file. See Section 32.6 [Init File], page 433.

It is possible to specify files to be visited, Lisp files to be loaded, and functions to be called through Emacs command-line arguments. See Appendix C [Emacs Invocation], page 471. The feature exists mainly for compatibility with other editors, and for scripts.

Many editors are designed to edit one file. When done with that file, you exit the editor. The next time you want to edit a file, you must start the editor again. Working this way, it is convenient to use a command line argument to say which file to edit.

However, killing Emacs after editing one each and starting it afresh for the next file is both unnecessary and harmful, since it denies you the full power of Emacs. Emacs can visit more than one file in a single editing session, and that is the right way to use it. Exiting the Emacs session loses valuable accumulated context, such as the kill ring, registers, undo history, and mark ring. These features are useful for operating on multiple files, or even continuing to edit one file. If you kill Emacs after each file, you don't take advantage of them.

The recommended way to use GNU Emacs is to start it only once, just after you log in, and do all your editing in the same Emacs session. Each time you edit a file, you visit it with the existing Emacs, which eventually has many files in it ready for editing. Usually you do not kill Emacs until you are about to log out. See Chapter 15 [Files], page 119, for more information on visiting more than one file.

To edit a file from another program while Emacs is running, you can use the `emacsclient` helper program to open a file in the already running Emacs. See Section 31.3 [Emacs Server], page 389.

3.1 Exiting Emacs

There are two commands for exiting Emacs, and three kinds of exiting: *iconifying* Emacs, *suspending* Emacs, and *killing* Emacs.

Iconifying means replacing the Emacs frame with a small box or "icon" on the screen. This is the usual way to exit Emacs when you're using a graphical display—if you bother to "exit" at all. (Just switching to another application is usually sufficient.)

Suspending means stopping Emacs temporarily and returning control to its parent process (usually a shell), allowing you to resume editing later in the same Emacs job. This is the usual way to exit Emacs when running it on a text terminal.

Killing Emacs means destroying the Emacs job. You can run Emacs again later, but you will get a fresh Emacs; there is no way to resume the same editing session after it has been killed.

C-z   Suspend Emacs (`suspend-emacs`) or iconify a frame (`iconify-or-deiconify-frame`).

C-x C-c   Kill Emacs (`save-buffers-kill-emacs`).

On graphical displays, C-z runs the command `iconify-or-deiconify-frame`, which temporarily iconifies (or "minimizes") the selected Emacs frame (see Chapter 18 [Frames], page 171). You can then use the window manager to select some other application. (You could select another application without iconifying Emacs first, but getting the Emacs frame out of the way can make it more convenient to find the other application.)

On a text terminal, C-z runs the command `suspend-emacs`. Suspending Emacs takes you back to the shell from which you invoked Emacs. You can resume Emacs with the shell command `%emacs` in most common shells. On systems that don't support suspending programs, C-z starts an inferior shell that communicates directly with the terminal, and Emacs waits until you exit the subshell. (The way to do that is probably with C-d or `exit`, but it depends on which shell you use.) On these systems, you can only get back to the shell from which Emacs was run (to log out, for example) when you kill Emacs.

Suspending can fail if you run Emacs under a shell that doesn't support suspension of its subjobs, even if the system itself does support it. In such a case, you can set the variable `cannot-suspend` to a non-`nil` value to force C-z to start an inferior shell.

To exit and kill Emacs, type C-x C-c (`save-buffers-kill-emacs`). A two-character key is used to make it harder to type by accident. This command first offers to save any modified file-visiting buffers. If you do not save them all, it asks for confirmation with `yes` before killing Emacs, since any changes not saved now will be lost forever. Also, if any subprocesses are still running, C-x C-c asks for confirmation about them, since killing Emacs will also kill the subprocesses.

If the value of the variable `confirm-kill-emacs` is non-`nil`, C-x C-c assumes that its value is a predicate function, and calls that function. If the result is non-`nil`, the session is killed, otherwise Emacs continues to run. One convenient function to use as the value of `confirm-kill-emacs` is the function `yes-or-no-p`. The default value of `confirm-kill-emacs` is `nil`.

You can't resume an Emacs session after killing it. Emacs can, however, record certain session information when you kill it, such as which files you visited, so the

next time you start Emacs it will try to visit the same files. See Section 31.12
[Saving Emacs Sessions], page 399.

   The operating system usually listens for certain special characters whose meaning is to kill or suspend the program you are running. **This operating system feature
is turned off while you are in Emacs.** The meanings of C-z and C-x C-c as keys
in Emacs were inspired by the use of C-z and C-c on several operating systems as
the characters for stopping or killing a program, but that is their only relationship
with the operating system. You can customize these keys to run any commands of
your choice (see Section 32.4.1 [Keymaps], page 423).

4 Basic Editing Commands

Here we explain the basics of how to enter text, make corrections, and save the text in a file. If this material is new to you, we suggest you first run the Emacs learn-by-doing tutorial, by typing `Control-h t` inside Emacs. (`help-with-tutorial`).

To clear and redisplay the screen, type `C-l` (`recenter`).

4.1 Inserting Text

Typing printing characters inserts them into the text you are editing. It inserts them into the buffer at the cursor; more precisely, it inserts them at *point*, but the cursor normally shows where point is. See Section 1.1 [Point], page 6.

Insertion moves the cursor forward, and the following text moves forward with the cursor. If the text in the buffer is 'FOOBAR', with the cursor before the 'B', and you type XX, you get 'FOOXXBAR', with the cursor still before the 'B'.

To *delete* text you have just inserted, use the large key labeled DEL, BACKSPACE or DELETE which is a short distance above the RET or ENTER key. Regardless of the label on that key, Emacs thinks of it as DEL, and that's what we call it in this manual. DEL is the key you normally use outside Emacs to erase the last character that you typed.

The DEL key deletes the character *before* the cursor. As a consequence, the cursor and all the characters after it move backwards. If you type a printing character and then type DEL, they cancel out.

On most computers, Emacs sets up DEL automatically. In some cases, especially with text-only terminals, Emacs may guess wrong. If the key that ought to erase the last character doesn't do it in Emacs, see Section 33.2.1 [DEL Does Not Delete], page 441.

Most PC keyboards have both a BACKSPACE key a little ways above RET or ENTER, and a DELETE key elsewhere. On these keyboards, Emacs tries to set up BACKSPACE as DEL. The DELETE key deletes "forwards" like `C-d` (see below), which means it deletes the character underneath the cursor (after point).

To end a line and start typing a new one, type RET. (This key may be labeled RETURN or ENTER, but in Emacs we call it RET.) This inserts a newline character in the buffer. If point is at the end of the line, this creates a new blank line after it. If point is in the middle of a line, the effect is to split that line. Typing DEL when the cursor is at the beginning of a line deletes the preceding newline character, thus joining the line with the one before it.

Emacs can split lines automatically when they become too long, if you turn on a special minor mode called *Auto Fill* mode. See Section 22.5 [Filling], page 217, for Auto Fill mode and other methods of *filling* text.

If you prefer printing characters to replace (overwrite) existing text, rather than shove it to the right, you should enable Overwrite mode, a minor mode. See Section 32.1 [Minor Modes], page 406.

Only printing characters and SPC insert themselves in Emacs. Other characters act as editing commands and do not insert themselves. These include control characters, and characters with codes above 200 octal. If you need to insert one of these characters in the buffer, you must *quote* it by typing the character `Control-q` (`quoted-insert`) first. (This character's name is normally written `C-q` for short.) There are two ways to use `C-q`:

- `C-q` followed by any non-graphic character (even `C-g`) inserts that character.
- `C-q` followed by a sequence of octal digits inserts the character with the specified octal character code. You can use any number of octal digits; any non-digit terminates the sequence. If the terminating character is RET, it serves only to terminate the sequence. Any other non-digit terminates the sequence and then acts as normal input—thus, `C-q 1 0 1 B` inserts 'AB'.

  The use of octal sequences is disabled in ordinary non-binary Overwrite mode, to give you a convenient way to insert a digit instead of overwriting with it.

When multibyte characters are enabled, if you specify a code in the range 0200 through 0377 octal, `C-q` assumes that you intend to use some ISO 8859-*n* character set, and converts the specified code to the corresponding Emacs character code. See Section 19.2 [Enabling Multibyte], page 187. You select *which* of the ISO 8859 character sets to use through your choice of language environment (see Section 19.3 [Language Environments], page 188).

To use decimal or hexadecimal instead of octal, set the variable `read-quoted-char-radix` to 10 or 16. If the radix is greater than 10, some letters starting with a serve as part of a character code, just like digits.

A numeric argument tells `C-q` how many copies of the quoted character to insert (see Section 4.10 [Arguments], page 28).

Customization information: DEL in most modes runs the command `delete-backward-char`; RET runs the command `newline`, and self-inserting printing characters run the command `self-insert`, which inserts whatever character you typed. Some major modes rebind DEL to other commands.

4.2 Changing the Location of Point

To do more than insert characters, you have to know how to move point (see Section 1.1 [Point], page 6). The simplest way to do this is with arrow keys, or by clicking the left mouse button where you want to move to.

There are also control and meta characters for cursor motion. Some are equivalent to the arrow keys (it is faster to use these control keys than move your hand over to the arrow keys). Others do more sophisticated things.

`C-a`   Move to the beginning of the line (`move-beginning-of-line`).

`C-e`   Move to the end of the line (`move-end-of-line`).

`C-f`   Move forward one character (`forward-char`). The right-arrow key does the same thing.

`C-b`   Move backward one character (`backward-char`). The left-arrow key has the same effect.

`M-f`   Move forward one word (`forward-word`).

M-b   Move backward one word (`backward-word`).

C-n   Move down one line vertically (`next-line`). This command attempts
             to keep the horizontal position unchanged, so if you start in the middle
             of one line, you move to the middle of the next. The down-arrow key
             does the same thing.

C-p   Move up one line, vertically (`previous-line`). The up-arrow key has
             the same effect. This command preserves position within the line, like
             C-n.

M-r   Move point to left margin, vertically centered in the window (`move-to-window-line`). Text does not move on the screen. A numeric
             argument says which screen line to place point on, counting downward
             from the top of the window (zero means the top line). A negative
             argument counts lines up from the bottom (−1 means the bottom
             line).

M-<   Move to the top of the buffer (`beginning-of-buffer`). With numeric
             argument n, move to $n/10$ of the way from the top. See Section 4.10
             [Arguments], page 28, for more information on numeric arguments.

M->   Move to the end of the buffer (`end-of-buffer`).

C-v
PAGEDOWN
PRIOR   Scroll the display one screen forward, and move point if necessary to
             put it on the screen (`scroll-up`). This doesn't always move point, but
             it is commonly used to do so. If your keyboard has a PAGEDOWN
             or PRIOR key, it does the same thing.

             Scrolling commands are described further in Section 11.1 [Scrolling],
             page 69.

M-v
PAGEUP
NEXT   Scroll one screen backward, and move point if necessary to put it on
             the screen (`scroll-down`). This doesn't always move point, but it is
             commonly used to do so. If your keyboard has a PAGEUP or NEXT
             key, it does the same thing.

M-x goto-char
             Read a number n and move point to buffer position n. Position 1 is
             the beginning of the buffer.

M-g M-g
M-g g
M-x goto-line
             Read a number n and move point to the beginning of line number n.
             Line 1 is the beginning of the buffer. If point is on or just after a
             number in the buffer, and you type RET with the minibuffer empty,
             that number is used for n.

C-x C-n   Use the current column of point as the *semipermanent goal column*
                 for C-n and C-p (set-goal-column). When a semipermanent goal
                 column is in effect, those commands always try to move to this column,
                 or as close as possible to it, after moving vertically. The goal column
                 remains in effect until canceled.

C-u C-x C-n
                 Cancel the goal column. Henceforth, C-n and C-p try to preserve the
                 horizontal position, as usual.

If you set the variable track-eol to a non-nil value, then C-n and C-p, when
starting at the end of the line, move to the end of another line. Normally, track-
eol is nil. See Section 32.3 [Variables], page 416, for how to set variables such as
track-eol.

C-n normally stops at the end of the buffer when you use it on the last line of
the buffer. However, if you set the variable next-line-add-newlines to a non-nil
value, C-n on the last line of a buffer creates an additional line at the end and moves
down into it.

4.3 Erasing Text

DEL   Delete the character before point (delete-backward-char).

C-d   Delete the character after point (delete-char).

DELETE
BACKSPACE
                 One of these keys, whichever is the large key above the RET or ENTER
                 key, deletes the character before point—it is DEL. If BACKSPACE
                 is DEL, and your keyboard also has DELETE, then DELETE deletes
                 forwards, like C-d.

C-k   Kill to the end of the line (kill-line).

M-d   Kill forward to the end of the next word (kill-word).

M-DEL   Kill back to the beginning of the previous word (backward-kill-
                 word).

You already know about the DEL key which deletes the character before point
(that is, before the cursor). Another key, Control-d (C-d for short), deletes the
character after point (that is, the character that the cursor is on). This shifts the
rest of the text on the line to the left. If you type C-d at the end of a line, it joins
that line with the following line.

To erase a larger amount of text, use the C-k key, which erases (kills) a line at
a time. If you type C-k at the beginning or middle of a line, it kills all the text up
to the end of the line. If you type C-k at the end of a line, it joins that line with
the following line.

See Chapter 9 [Killing], page 55, for more flexible ways of killing text.

4.4 Undoing Changes

Emacs records a list of changes made in the buffer text, so you can you can undo recent changes, as far as the records go. Usually each editing command makes a separate entry in the undo records, but sometimes an entry covers just part of a command, and very simple commands may be grouped.

C-x u   Undo one entry of the undo records—usually, one command worth (undo).

C-_
C-/   The same.

The command C-x u (or C-_ or C-/) is how you undo. Normally this command undoes the last change, and moves point back to where it was before the change.

If you repeat C-x u (or its aliases), each repetition undoes another, earlier change, back to the limit of the undo information available. If all recorded changes have already been undone, the undo command displays an error message and does nothing.

The undo command applies only to changes in the buffer; you can't use it to undo mere cursor motion. However, some cursor motion commands set the mark, so if you use these commands from time to time, you can move back to the neighborhoods you have moved through by popping the mark ring (see Section 8.6 [Mark Ring], page 54).

4.5 Files

Text that you insert in an Emacs buffer lasts only as long as the Emacs session. To keep any text permanently you must put it in a file. Files are named units of text which are stored by the operating system for you to retrieve later by name. To use the contents of a file in any way, you must specify the file name. That includes editing the file with Emacs.

Suppose there is a file named 'test.emacs' in your home directory. To begin editing this file in Emacs, type

    C-x C-f test.emacs RET

Here the file name is given as an *argument* to the command C-x C-f (find-file). That command uses the *minibuffer* to read the argument, and you type RET to terminate the argument (see Chapter 5 [Minibuffer], page 31).

Emacs obeys this command by *visiting* the file: it creates a buffer, it copies the contents of the file into the buffer, and then displays the buffer for editing. If you alter the text, you can *save* the new text in the file by typing C-x C-s (save-buffer). This copies the altered buffer contents back into the file 'test.emacs', making them permanent. Until you save, the changed text exists only inside Emacs, and the file 'test.emacs' is unaltered.

To create a file, just visit it with C-x C-f as if it already existed. This creates an empty buffer, in which you can insert the text you want to put in the file. Emacs actually creates the file the first time you save this buffer with C-x C-s.

To learn more about using files in Emacs, see Chapter 15 [Files], page 119.

4.6 Help

If you forget what a key does, you can find out with the Help character, which is
C-h (or F1, which is an alias for C-h). Type C-h k followed by the key of interest;
for example, C-h k C-n tells you what C-n does. C-h is a prefix key; C-h k is just
one of its subcommands (the command describe-key). The other subcommands
of C-h provide different kinds of help. Type C-h twice to get a description of all the
help facilities. See Chapter 7 [Help], page 40.

4.7 Blank Lines

Here are special commands and techniques for inserting and deleting blank lines.

C-o   Insert one or more blank lines after the cursor (open-line).

C-x C-o   Delete all but one of many consecutive blank lines (delete-blank-
             lines).

To insert a new line of text before an existing line, type the new line of text,
followed by RET. However, it may be easier to see what you are doing if you first
make a blank line and then insert the desired text into it. This is easy to do using
the key C-o (open-line), which inserts a newline after point but leaves point in
front of the newline. After C-o, type the text for the new line. C-o F O O has the
same effect as F O O RET, except for the final location of point.

You can make several blank lines by typing C-o several times, or by giving it
a numeric argument specifying how many blank lines to make. See Section 4.10
[Arguments], page 28, for how. If you have a fill prefix, the C-o command inserts
the fill prefix on the new line, if typed at the beginning of a line. See Section 22.5.3
[Fill Prefix], page 219.

The easy way to get rid of extra blank lines is with the command C-x C-o
(delete-blank-lines). C-x C-o in a run of several blank lines deletes all but one
of them. C-x C-o on a lone blank line deletes that one. When point is on a nonblank
line, C-x C-o deletes all following blank lines (if any).

4.8 Continuation Lines

When a text line is too long to fit in one screen line, Emacs displays it on two
or more screen lines. This is called *continuation* or *line wrapping*. On graphical
displays, Emacs indicates line wrapping with small bent arrows in the left and right
window fringes. On text-only terminals, Emacs displays a '\' character at the right
margin of a screen line if it is not the last in its text line. This '\' character says
that the following screen line is not really a new text line.

When line wrapping occurs just before a character that is wider than one column,
some columns at the end of the previous screen line may be "empty." In this case,
Emacs displays additional '\' characters in the "empty" columns before the '\'
character that indicates continuation.

Continued lines can be difficult to read, since lines can break in the middle of a
word. If you prefer, you can make Emacs insert a newline automatically when a line

gets too long, by using Auto Fill mode. Or enable Long Lines mode, which ensures that wrapping only occurs between words. See Section 22.5 [Filling], page 217.

Emacs can optionally *truncate* long lines—this means displaying just one screen line worth, and the rest of the long line does not appear at all. '$' in the last column or a small straight arrow in the window's right fringe indicates a truncated line.

See Section 11.16 [Line Truncation], page 84, for more about line truncation, and other variables that control how text is displayed.

4.9 Cursor Position Information

Here are commands to get information about the size and position of parts of the buffer, and to count lines.

M-x what-page
> Display the page number of point, and the line number within that page.

M-x what-line
> Display the line number of point in the whole buffer.

M-x line-number-mode
M-x column-number-mode
> Toggle automatic display of the current line number or column number. See Section 11.13 [Optional Mode Line], page 81.

M-=
> Display the number of lines in the current region (count-lines-region). See Chapter 8 [Mark], page 49, for information about the region.

C-x =
> Display the character code of character after point, character position of point, and column of point (what-cursor-position).

M-x hl-line-mode
> Enable or disable highlighting of the current line. See Section 11.15 [Cursor Display], page 83.

M-x size-indication-mode
> Toggle automatic display of the size of the buffer. See Section 11.13 [Optional Mode Line], page 81.

M-x what-line displays the current line number in the echo area. You can also see the current line number in the mode line; see Section 1.3 [Mode Line], page 8; but if you narrow the buffer, the line number in the mode line is relative to the accessible portion (see Section 31.9 [Narrowing], page 396). By contrast, what-line shows both the line number relative to the narrowed region and the line number relative to the whole buffer.

M-x what-page counts pages from the beginning of the file, and counts lines within the page, showing both numbers in the echo area. See Section 22.4 [Pages], page 216.

Use M-= (`count-lines-region`) to displays the number of lines in the region (see Chapter 8 [Mark], page 49). See Section 22.4 [Pages], page 216, for the command C-x l which counts the lines in the current page.

The command C-x = (`what-cursor-position`) shows what cursor's column position, and other information about point and the character after it. It displays a line in the echo area that looks like this: ·

    Char: c (99, #o143, #x63) point=28062 of 36168 (78%) column=53

The four values after 'Char:' describe the character that follows point, first by showing it and then by giving its character code in decimal, octal and hex. For a non-ASCII multibyte character, these are followed by '`file`' and the character's representation, in hex, in the buffer's coding system, if that coding system encodes the character safely and with a single byte (see Section 19.7 [Coding Systems], page 193). If the character's encoding is longer than one byte, Emacs shows '`file` ...'.

However, if the character displayed is in the range 0200 through 0377 octal, it may actually stand for an invalid UTF-8 byte read from a file. In Emacs, that byte is represented as a sequence of 8-bit characters, but all of them together display as the original invalid byte, in octal code. In this case, C-x = shows '`part of display` ...' instead of '`file`'.

'`point=`' is followed by the position of point expressed as a character count. The start of the buffer is position 1, one character later is position 2, and so on. The next, larger, number is the total number of characters in the buffer. Afterward in parentheses comes the position expressed as a percentage of the total size.

'`column=`' is followed by the horizontal position of point, in columns from the left edge of the window.

If the buffer has been narrowed, making some of the text at the beginning and the end temporarily inaccessible, C-x = displays additional text describing the currently accessible range. For example, it might display this:

    Char: C (67, #o103, #x43) point=252 of 889 (28%) <231-599> column=0

where the two extra numbers give the smallest and largest character position that point is allowed to assume. The characters between those two positions are the accessible ones. See Section 31.9 [Narrowing], page 396.

If point is at the end of the buffer (or the end of the accessible part), the C-x = output does not describe a character after point. The output might look like this:

    point=36169 of 36168 (EOB) column=0

C-u C-x = displays the following additional information about a character.

- The character set name, and the codes that identify the character within that character set; ASCII characters are identified as belonging to the `ascii` character set.

- The character's syntax and categories.

- The character's encodings, both internally in the buffer, and externally if you were to save the file.

- What keys to type to input the character in the current input method (if it supports the character).

- If you are running Emacs on a graphical display, the font name and glyph code for the character. If you are running Emacs on a text-only terminal, the code(s) sent to the terminal.

- The character's text properties (see section "Text Properties" in *the Emacs Lisp Reference Manual*), and any overlays containing it (see section "Overlays" in *the same manual*).

Here's an example showing the Latin-1 character A with grave accent, in a buffer whose coding system is `iso-latin-1`, whose terminal coding system is `iso-latin-1` (so the terminal actually displays the character as 'À'), and which has font-lock-mode (see Section 11.7 [Font Lock], page 76) enabled:

```
  character: À (2240, #o4300, #x8c0, U+00C0)
    charset: latin-iso8859-1
             (Right-Hand Part of Latin Alphabet 1...
 code point: #x40
     syntax: w  which means: word
   category: l:Latin
   to input: type "'A" with latin-1-prefix
buffer code: #x81 #xC0
  file code: #xC0 (encoded by coding system iso-latin-1)
    display: terminal code #xC0

There are text properties here:
  fontified            t
```

4.10 Numeric Arguments

In mathematics and computer usage, *argument* means "data provided to a function or operation." You can give any Emacs command a *numeric argument* (also called a *prefix argument*). Some commands interpret the argument as a repetition count. For example, `C-f` with an argument of ten moves forward ten characters instead of one. With these commands, no argument is equivalent to an argument of one. Negative arguments tell most such commands to move or act in the opposite direction.

If your terminal keyboard has a META key (labeled ALT on PC keyboards), the easiest way to specify a numeric argument is to type digits and/or a minus sign while holding down the META key. For example,

```
    M-5 C-n
```

moves down five lines. The characters `Meta-1`, `Meta-2`, and so on, as well as `Meta--`, do this because they are keys bound to commands (`digit-argument` and `negative-argument`) that are defined to set up an argument for the next command. `Meta--` without digits normally means -1. Digits and - modified with Control, or Control and Meta, also specify numeric arguments.

You can also specify a numeric argument by typing `C-u` (`universal-argument`) followed by the digits. The advantage of `C-u` is that you can type the digits without modifier keys; thus, `C-u` works on all terminals. For a negative argument, type a minus sign after `C-u`. A minus sign without digits normally means -1.

C-u alone has the special meaning of "four times": it multiplies the argument for the next command by four. C-u C-u multiplies it by sixteen. Thus, C-u C-u C-f moves forward sixteen characters. This is a good way to move forward "fast," since it moves about 1/5 of a line in the usual size screen. Other useful combinations are C-u C-n, C-u C-u C-n (move down a good fraction of a screen), C-u C-u C-o (make "a lot" of blank lines), and C-u C-k (kill four lines).

Some commands care whether there is an argument, but ignore its value. For example, the command M-q (**fill-paragraph**) fills text; with an argument, it justifies the text as well. (See Section 22.5 [Filling], page 217, for more information on M-q.) Plain C-u is a handy way of providing an argument for such commands.

Some commands use the value of the argument as a repeat count, but do something peculiar when there is no argument. For example, the command C-k (**kill-line**) with argument n kills n lines, including their terminating newlines. But C-k with no argument is special: it kills the text up to the next newline, or, if point is right at the end of the line, it kills the newline itself. Thus, two C-k commands with no arguments can kill a nonblank line, just like C-k with an argument of one. (See Chapter 9 [Killing], page 55, for more information on C-k.)

A few commands treat a plain C-u differently from an ordinary argument. A few others may treat an argument of just a minus sign differently from an argument of −1. These unusual cases are described when they come up; they exist to make an individual command more convenient, and they are documented in that command's documentation string.

You can use a numeric argument before a self-inserting character to insert multiple copies of it. This is straightforward when the character is not a digit; for example, C-u 6 4 a inserts 64 copies of the character 'a'. But this does not work for inserting digits; C-u 6 4 1 specifies an argument of 641. You can separate the argument from the digit to insert with another C-u; for example, C-u 6 4 C-u 1 does insert 64 copies of the character '1'.

We use the term "prefix argument" as well as "numeric argument," to emphasize that you type these argument before the command, and to distinguish them from minibuffer arguments that come after the command.

4.11 Repeating a Command

Many simple commands, such as those invoked with a single key or with M-x *command-name* RET, can be repeated by invoking them with a numeric argument that serves as a repeat count (see Section 4.10 [Arguments], page 28). However, if the command you want to repeat prompts for input, or uses a numeric argument in another way, that method won't work.

The command C-x z (**repeat**) provides another way to repeat an Emacs command many times. This command repeats the previous Emacs command, whatever that was. Repeating a command uses the same arguments that were used before; it does not read new arguments each time.

To repeat the command more than once, type additional z's: each z repeats the command one more time. Repetition ends when you type a character other than z, or press a mouse button.

For example, suppose you type C-u 2 0 C-d to delete 20 characters. You can repeat that command (including its argument) three additional times, to delete a total of 80 characters, by typing C-x z z z. The first C-x z repeats the command once, and each subsequent z repeats it once again.

5 The Minibuffer

The *minibuffer* is where Emacs commands read complicated arguments (anything more a single number). We call it the "minibuffer" because it's a special-purpose buffer with a small amount of screen space. Minibuffer arguments can be file names, buffer names, Lisp function names, Emacs command names, Lisp expressions, and many other things—whatever the command wants to read. You can use the usual Emacs editing commands in the minibuffer to edit the argument text.

When the minibuffer is in use, it appears in the echo area, with a cursor. The minibuffer display starts with a *prompt* in a distinct color; it says what kind of input is expected and how it will be used. Often the prompt is derived from the name of the command that is reading the argument. The prompt normally ends with a colon.

Sometimes a *default argument* appears in the prompt, inside parentheses before the colon. The default will be used as the argument value if you just type RET. For example, commands that read buffer names show a buffer name as the default. You can type RET to operate on that default buffer.

The simplest way to enter a minibuffer argument is to type the text, then RET to exit the minibuffer. You can cancel the minibuffer, and the command that wants the argument, by typing C-g.

Since the minibuffer appears in the echo area, it can conflict with other uses of the echo area. Here is how Emacs handles such conflicts:

- An error occurs while the minibuffer is active.

  The error message hides the minibuffer for a few seconds, or until you type something. Then the minibuffer comes back.

- A command such as C-x = needs to display a message in the echo area.

  The message hides the minibuffer for a few seconds, or until you type something. Then the minibuffer comes back.

- Keystrokes don't echo while the minibuffer is in use.

5.1 Minibuffers for File Names

When you use the minibuffer to enter a file name, it starts out with some initial text—the *default directory*, ending in a slash. The file you specify will be in this directory unless you alter or replace it.

For example, if the minibuffer starts out with these contents:

    Find File: /u2/emacs/src/

(where 'Find File: ' is the prompt), and you type buffer.c as input, that specifies the file '/u2/emacs/src/buffer.c'. You can specify the parent directory by adding '..'; thus, if you type ../lisp/simple.el, you will get '/u2/emacs/lisp/simple.el'. Alternatively, you can use M-DEL to kill the directory names you don't want (see Section 22.1 [Words], page 213).

You can kill the entire default with C-a C-k, but there's no need to do that. It's easier to ignore the default, and enter an absolute file name starting with a slash or a tilde after the default directory. For example, to specify '`/etc/termcap`', just type that name:

    Find File: /u2/emacs/src//etc/termcap

GNU Emacs interprets a double slash (which is not normally useful in file names) as, "ignore everything before the second slash in the pair." In the example above, '`/u2/emacs/src/`' is ignored, so you get '`/etc/termcap`'. The ignored part of the file name is dimmed if the terminal allows it; to disable this dimming, turn off File Name Shadow mode (a minor mode) with the command `M-x file-name-shadow-mode`.

If the variable `insert-default-directory` is `nil`, the default directory is never inserted in the minibuffer—so the minibuffer starts out empty. Nonetheless, relative file name arguments are still interpreted based on the same default directory.

5.2 Editing in the Minibuffer

The minibuffer is an Emacs buffer (albeit a peculiar one), and the usual Emacs commands are available for editing the argument text.

Since RET in the minibuffer is defined to exit the minibuffer, you can't use it to insert a newline in the minibuffer. To do that, type `C-o` or `C-q C-j`. (The newline character is really the ASCII character control-J.)

The minibuffer has its own window, which normally has space in the frame at all times, but it only acts like an Emacs window when the minibuffer is active. When active, this window is much like any other Emacs window; for instance, you can switch to another window (with `C-x o`), edit text there, then return to the minibuffer window to finish the argument. You can even kill text in another window, return to the minibuffer window, and then yank the text into the argument. See Chapter 17 [Windows], page 165.

There are some restrictions on the minibuffer window, however: you cannot kill it, or split it, or switch buffers in it—the minibuffer and its window are permanently attached.

The minibuffer window expands vertically as necessary to hold the text that you put in the minibuffer. If `resize-mini-windows` is `t` (the default), the window always resizes as needed by its contents. If its value is the symbol `grow-only`, the window grows automatically as needed, but shrinks (back to the normal size) only when the minibuffer becomes inactive. If its value is `nil`, you have to adjust the height yourself.

The variable `max-mini-window-height` controls the maximum height for re-sizing the minibuffer window: a floating-point number specifies a fraction of the frame's height; an integer specifies the maximum number of lines; `nil` means do not resize the minibuffer window automatically. The default value is 0.25.

The `C-M-v` command in the minibuffer scrolls the help text from commands that display help text of any sort in another window. `M-PAGEUP` and `M-PAGEDOWN` also operate on that help text. This is especially useful with long lists of possible completions. See Section 17.3 [Other Window], page 166.

Emacs normally disallows most commands that use the minibuffer while the minibuffer is active. (Entering the minibuffer from the minibuffer can be confusing.)

To allow such commands in the minibuffer, set the variable `enable-recursive-minibuffers` to `t`.

5.3 Completion

Some arguments allow *completion* to enter their value. This means that after you type part of the argument, Emacs can fill in the rest, or some of it, based on what you have typed so far.

When completion is available, certain keys—TAB, RET, and SPC—are rebound to complete the text in the minibuffer before point into a longer string chosen from a set of *completion alternatives* provided by the command that requested the argument. (SPC does not do completion in reading file names, because it is common to use spaces in file names on some systems.) ? displays a list of the possible completions at any time.

For example, M-x uses the minibuffer to read the name of a command, so it provides a list of all Emacs command names for completion candidates. The completion keys match the minibuffer text against these candidates, find any additional name characters implied by the text already present in the minibuffer, and add those characters. This makes it possible to type `M-x ins SPC b RET` instead of `M-x insert-buffer RET`, for example.

Case is significant in completion when it is significant in the argument you are entering (buffer names, file names, command names, for instance). Thus, 'fo' does not complete to 'Foo'. Completion ignores case distinctions for certain arguments in which case does not matter.

Completion acts only on the text before point. If there is text in the minibuffer after point—i.e., if you move point backward after typing some text into the minibuffer—it remains unchanged.

5.3.1 Completion Example

A concrete example may help here. If you type `M-x au TAB`, the TAB looks for alternatives (in this case, command names) that start with 'au'. There are several, including `auto-fill-mode` and `auto-save-mode`, but they all begin with `auto-`, so the 'au' in the minibuffer completes to 'auto-'.

If you type TAB again immediately, it cannot determine the next character; it could be any of 'cfilrs'. So it does not add any characters; instead, TAB displays a list of all possible completions in another window.

Now type `f TAB`. This TAB sees 'auto-f'. The only command name starting with that is `auto-fill-mode`, so completion fills in the rest of that. You have been able to enter 'auto-fill-mode' by typing just `au TAB f TAB`.

5.3.2 Completion Commands

Here is a list of the completion commands defined in the minibuffer when completion is allowed.

TAB   Complete the text before point in the minibuffer as much as possible
           (`minibuffer-complete`).

SPC   Complete up to one word from the minibuffer text before point (`minibuffer-complete-word`). SPC for completion is not available when entering a file name, since file names often include spaces.

RET   Submit the text in the minibuffer as the argument, possibly completing first as described in the next subsection (`minibuffer-complete-and-exit`).

?   Display a list of possible completions of the text before point (`minibuffer-completion-help`).

SPC completes like TAB, but only up to the next hyphen or space. If you have 'auto-f' in the minibuffer and type SPC, it finds that the completion is 'auto-fill-mode', but it only inserts 'ill-', giving 'auto-fill-'. Another SPC at this point completes all the way to 'auto-fill-mode'. The command that implements this behavior is called `minibuffer-complete-word`.

When you display a list of possible completions, you can choose one from it:

Mouse-1
Mouse-2   Clicking mouse button 1 or 2 on a completion possibility chooses that completion (`mouse-choose-completion`). You must click in the list of completions, not in the minibuffer.

PRIOR
M-v   Typing PRIOR or PAGE-UP, or M-v, while in the minibuffer, selects the window showing the completion list buffer (`switch-to-completions`). This paves the way for using the commands below. (Selecting that window in other ways has the same effect.)

RET   Typing RET *in the completion list buffer* chooses the completion that point is in or next to (`choose-completion`). To use this command, you must first switch to the completion list window.

RIGHT   Typing the right-arrow key RIGHT *in the completion list buffer* moves point to the following completion possibility (`next-completion`).

LEFT   Typing the left-arrow key LEFT *in the completion list buffer* moves point to the previous completion possibility (`previous-completion`).

5.3.3 Strict Completion

There are three different ways that RET can do completion, depending on how the argument will be used.

- *Strict* completion accepts only known completion candidates. For example, when C-x k reads the name of a buffer to kill, only the name of an existing buffer makes sense. In strict completion, RET refuses to exit if the text in the minibuffer does not complete to an exact match.

- *Cautious* completion is similar to strict completion, except that RET exits only if the text is an already exact match. Otherwise, RET does not exit, but it does complete the text. If that completes to an exact match, a second RET will exit.

Cautious completion is used for reading file names for files that must already exist, for example.

- *Permissive* completion allows any input; the completion candidates are just suggestions. For example, when C-x C-f reads the name of a file to visit, any file name is allowed, including nonexistent file (in case you want to create a file). In permissive completion, RET does not complete, it just submits the argument as you have entered it.

The completion commands display a list of all possible completions whenever they can't determine even one more character by completion. Also, typing ? explicitly requests such a list. You can scroll the list with C-M-v (see Section 17.3 [Other Window], page 166).

5.3.4 Completion Options

When completing file names, certain file names are usually ignored. The variable completion-ignored-extensions contains a list of strings; a file name ending in any of those strings is ignored as a completion candidate. The standard value of this variable has several elements including ".o", ".elc", ".dvi" and "~". The effect is that, for example, 'foo' can complete to 'foo.c' even though 'foo.o' exists as well. However, if *all* the possible completions end in "ignored" strings, then they are not ignored. Displaying a list of possible completions disregards completion-ignored-extensions; it shows them all.

If an element of completion-ignored-extensions ends in a slash ('/'), it's a subdirectory name; then that directory and its contents are ignored. Elements of completion-ignored-extensions which do not end in a slash are ordinary file names, and do not apply to names of directories.

If completion-auto-help is set to nil, the completion commands never display a list of possibilities; you must type ? to display the list.

Partial Completion mode implements a more powerful kind of completion that can complete multiple words in parallel. For example, it can complete the command name abbreviation p-b into print-buffer if no other command starts with two words whose initials are 'p' and 'b'.

To enable this mode, use M-x partial-completion-mode, or customize the variable partial-completion-mode. This mode binds special partial completion commands to TAB, SPC, RET, and ? in the minibuffer. The usual completion commands are available on M-TAB (or C-M-i), M-SPC, M-RET and M-?.

Partial completion of directories in file names uses '*' to indicate the places for completion; thus, '/u*/b*/f*' might complete to '/usr/bin/foo'. For remote files, partial completion enables completion of methods, user names and host names. See Section 15.14 [Remote Files], page 152.

Partial Completion mode also extends find-file so that '<include>' looks for the file named *include* in the directories in the path PC-include-file-path. If you set PC-disable-includes to non-nil, this feature is disabled.

Icomplete mode presents a constantly-updated display that tells you what completions are available for the text you've entered so far. The command to enable or disable this minor mode is M-x icomplete-mode.

5.4 Minibuffer History

Every argument that you enter with the minibuffer is saved on a *minibuffer history list* so you can easily use it again later. Special commands fetch the text of an earlier argument into the minibuffer, replacing the old minibuffer contents. You can think of them as moving through the history of previous arguments.

UP
M-p   Move to the previous item in the minibuffer history, an earlier argument (previous-history-element).

DOWN
M-n   Move to the next item in the minibuffer history (next-history-element).

M-r *regexp* RET
             Move to an earlier item in the minibuffer history that matches *regexp* (previous-matching-history-element).

M-s *regexp* RET
             Move to a later item in the minibuffer history that matches *regexp* (next-matching-history-element).

To move through the minibuffer history list one item at a time, use M-p or up-arrow (previous-history-element) to fetch the next earlier minibuffer input, and use M-n or down-arrow (next-history-element) to fetch the next later input. These commands don't move the cursor, they pull different saved strings into the minibuffer. But you can think of them as "moving" through the history list.

The input that you fetch from the history entirely replaces the contents of the minibuffer. To use it again unchanged, just type RET. You can also edit the text before you reuse it; this does not change the history element that you "moved" to, but your new argument does go at the end of the history list in its own right.

For many minibuffer arguments there is a "default" value. You can insert the default value into the minibuffer as text by using M-n. You can think of this as moving "into the future" in the history.

There are also commands to search forward or backward through the history; they search for history elements that match a regular expression. M-r (previous-matching-history-element) searches older elements in the history, while M-s (next-matching-history-element) searches newer elements. These commands are unusual; they use the minibuffer to read the regular expression even though they are invoked from the minibuffer. As with incremental searching, an uppercase letter in the regular expression makes the search case-sensitive (see Section 12.8 [Search Case], page 98).

All uses of the minibuffer record your input on a history list, but there are separate history lists for different kinds of arguments. For example, there is a list for file names, used by all the commands that read file names. (As a special feature, this history list records the absolute file name, even if the name you entered was not absolute.)

There are several other specific history lists, including one for buffer names, one for arguments of commands like `query-replace`, one used by M-x for command names, and one used by `compile` for compilation commands. Finally, there is one "miscellaneous" history list that most minibuffer arguments use.

The variable `history-length` specifies the maximum length of a minibuffer history list; adding a new element deletes the oldest element if the list gets too long. If the value of `history-length` is `t`, though, there is no maximum length.

The variable `history-delete-duplicates` specifies whether to delete duplicates in history. If it is `t`, adding a new element deletes from the list all other elements that are equal to it.

5.5 Repeating Minibuffer Commands

Every command that uses the minibuffer once is recorded on a special history list, the *command history*, together with the values of its arguments, so that you can repeat the entire command. In particular, every use of M-x is recorded there, since M-x uses the minibuffer to read the command name.

C-x ESC ESC
>   Re-execute a recent minibuffer command from the command history
>   (`repeat-complex-command`).

M-x list-command-history
>   Display the entire command history, showing all the commands C-x
>   ESC ESC can repeat, most recent first.

C-x ESC ESC is used to re-execute a recent command that used the minibuffer. With no argument, it repeats the last such command. A numeric argument specifies which command to repeat; 1 means the last one, 2 the previous, and so on.

C-x ESC ESC works by turning the previous command into a Lisp expression and then entering a minibuffer initialized with the text for that expression. Even if you don't understand Lisp syntax, it will probably be obvious which command is displayed for repetition. If you type just RET, that repeats the command unchanged. You can also change the command by editing the Lisp expression before you execute it. The repeated command is added to the front of the command history unless it is identical to the most recently item.

Once inside the minibuffer for C-x ESC ESC, you can use the minibuffer history commands (M-p, M-n, M-r, M-s; see Section 5.4 [Minibuffer History], page 36) to move through the history list of saved entire commands. After finding the desired previous command, you can edit its expression as usual and then repeat it by typing RET.

Incremental search does not, strictly speaking, use the minibuffer. Therefore, although it behaves like a complex command, it normally does not appear in the history list for C-x ESC ESC. You can make incremental search commands appear in the history by setting `isearch-resume-in-command-history` to a non-`nil` value. See Section 12.1 [Incremental Search], page 86.

The list of previous minibuffer-using commands is stored as a Lisp list in the variable `command-history`. Each element is a Lisp expression which describes one command and its arguments. Lisp programs can re-execute a command by calling `eval` with the `command-history` element.

6 Running Commands by Name

Every Emacs command has a name that you can use to run it. For convenience, many commands also have key bindings. You can run those commands by typing the keys, or run them by name. Most Emacs commands have no key bindings, so the only way to run them is by name. (See Section 32.4 [Key Bindings], page 423, for how to set up key bindings.)

By convention, a command name consists of one or more words, separated by hyphens; for example, `auto-fill-mode` or `manual-entry`. Command names mostly use complete English words to make them easier to remember.

To run a command by name, start with M-x, type the command name, then terminate it with RET. M-x uses the minibuffer to read the command name. The string 'M-x' appears at the beginning of the minibuffer as a *prompt* to remind you to enter a command name to be run. RET exits the minibuffer and runs the command. See Chapter 5 [Minibuffer], page 31, for more information on the minibuffer.

You can use completion to enter the command name. For example, to invoke the command `forward-char`, you can type

    M-x forward-char RET

or

    M-x forw TAB c RET

Note that `forward-char` is the same command that you invoke with the key C-f. The existence of a key binding does not stop you from running the command by name.

To cancel the M-x and not run a command, type C g instead of entering the command name. This takes you back to command level.

To pass a numeric argument to the command you are invoking with M-x, specify the numeric argument before M-x. The argument value appears in the prompt while the command name is being read, and finally M-x passes the argument to that command.

When the command you run with M-x has a key binding, Emacs mentions this in the echo area after running the command. For example, if you type M-x forward-word, the message says that you can run the same command by typing M-f. You can turn off these messages by setting the variable `suggest-key-bindings` to `nil`.

In this manual, when we speak of running a command by name, we often omit the RET that terminates the name. Thus we might say M-x `auto-fill-mode` rather than M-x `auto-fill-mode` RET. We mention the RET only for emphasis, such as when the command is followed by arguments.

M-x works by running the command `execute-extended-command`, which is responsible for reading the name of another command and invoking it.

7 Help

Emacs provides extensive help features, all accessible through the *help character*, C-h. This is a prefix key that is used for commands that display documentation; the next character you type should be a *help options*, to ask for a particular kind of help. You can cancel the C-h command with C-g. The function key F1 is equivalent to C-h.

C-h itself is one of the help options; C-h C-h displays a list of help options, with a brief description of each one (help-for-help). You can scroll the list with SPC and DEL, then type the help option you want. To cancel, type C-g.

C-h or F1 means "help" in various other contexts as well. For instance, you can type them after a prefix key to display list of the keys that can follow the prefix key. (A few prefix keys don't support C-h in this way, because they define other meanings for it, but they all support F1 for help.)

Most help buffers use a special major mode, Help mode, which lets you scroll conveniently with SPC and DEL. You can also follow hyperlinks to URLs, and to other facilities including Info nodes and customization buffers. See Section 7.4 [Help Mode], page 45.

If you are looking for a certain feature, but don't know what it is called or where to look, we recommend three methods. First, try an apropos command, then try searching the manual index, then look in the FAQ and the package keywords.

C-h a *topics* RET

> This searches for commands whose names match the argument *topics*. The argument can be a keyword, a list of keywords, or a regular expression (see Section 12.5 [Regexps], page 92). This command displays all the matches in a new buffer. See Section 7.3 [Apropos], page 43.

C-h i d m emacs RET i *topic* RET

> This searches for *topic* in the indices of the on-line Emacs manual, and displays the first match found. Press , to see subsequent matches. You can use a regular expression as *topic*.

C-h i d m emacs RET s *topic* RET

> Similar, but searches the *text* of the manual rather than the indices.

C-h C-f   This displays the Emacs FAQ. You can use the Info commands to browse it.

C-h p   This displays the available Emacs packages based on keywords. See Section 7.5 [Library Keywords], page 46.

Here is a summary of the Emacs interactive help commands. (The character that follows C-h is the "help option.") See Section 7.8 [Help Files], page 48, for other help commands that display fixed files of information.

C-h a *topics* RET

> Display a list of commands whose names match *topics* (apropos-command; see Section 7.3 [Apropos], page 43).

C-h b   Display all active key bindings; minor mode bindings first, then those of the major mode, then global bindings (`describe-bindings`).

C-h c *key* Given a key sequence *key*, show the name of the command that it runs (`describe-key-briefly`). Here c stands for "character." For more extensive information on *key*, use C-h k.

C-h d *topics* RET
             Display the commands and variables whose documentation matches *topics* (`apropos-documentation`).

C-h e   Display the *Messages* buffer (`view-echo-area-messages`).

C-h f *function* RET
             Display documentation on the Lisp function named *function* (`describe-function`). Since commands are Lisp functions, this works for commands too.

C-h h   Display the 'HELLO' file, which shows examples of various character sets.

C-h i   Run Info, the GNU documentation browser (`info`). The complete Emacs manual is available on-line in Info.

C-h k *key* Display the name and documentation of the command that *key* runs (`describe-key`).

C-h l   Display a description of the last 100 characters you typed (`view-lossage`).

C-h m   Display documentation of the current major mode (`describe-mode`).

C-h p   Find packages by topic keyword (`finder-by-keyword`).

C-h s   Display the current contents of the syntax table, with an explanation of what they mean (`describe-syntax`). See Section 32.5 [Syntax], page 433.

C-h t   Enter the Emacs interactive tutorial (`help-with-tutorial`).

C-h v *var* RET
             Display the documentation of the Lisp variable *var* (`describe-variable`).

C-h w *command* RET
             Show which keys run the command named *command* (`where-is`).

C-h C *coding* RET
             Describe the coding system *coding* (`describe-coding-system`).

C-h C RET   Describe the coding systems currently in use.

C-h I *method* RET
             Describe the input method *method* (`describe-input-method`).

C-h L *language-env* RET

> Display information on the character sets, coding systems, and input methods used in language environment *language-env* (describe-language-environment).

C-h F *function* RET

> Enter Info and goes to the node that documents the Emacs function *function* (Info-goto-emacs-command-node).

C-h K *key*   Enter Info and goes to the node that documents the key sequence *key* (Info-goto-emacs-key-command-node).

C-h S *symbol* RET

> Display the Info documentation on symbol *symbol* according to the programming language you are editing (info-lookup-symbol).

C-h .   Display the help message for a special text area, if point is in one (display-local-help). (These include, for example, links in '*Help*' buffers.)

7.1 Documentation for a Key

The help commands to get information about a key sequence are C-h c and C-h k. C-h c *key* displays in the echo area the name of the command that *key* is bound to. For example, C-h c C-f displays 'forward-char'. Since command names are chosen to describe what the commands do, this gives you a very brief description of what *key* does.

C-h k *key* is similar but gives more information: it displays the documentation string of the command as well as its name. It displays this information in a window, since it may not fit in the echo area.

To find the documentation of a key sequence *key*, type C-h K *key*. This displays the appropriate manual section which contains the documentation of *key*.

C-h c, C-h k and C-h K work for any sort of key sequences, including function keys, menus, and mouse events. For instance, after C-h k you can select a menu item from the menu bar, to view the documentation string of the command it runs.

C-h w *command* RET lists the keys that are bound to *command*. It displays the list in the echo area. If it says the command is not on any key, that means you must use M-x to run it. C-h w runs the command where-is.

7.2 Help by Command or Variable Name

C-h f *function* RET (describe-function) displays the documentation of Lisp function *function*, in a window. Since commands are Lisp functions, you can use this method to view the documentation of any command whose name you know. For example,

> C-h f auto-fill-mode RET

displays the documentation of auto-fill-mode. This is the only way to get the documentation of a command that is not bound to any key (one which you would normally run using M-x).

C-h f is also useful for Lisp functions that you use in a Lisp program. For example, if you have just written the expression (make-vector len) and want to check that you are using make-vector properly, type C-h f make-vector RET. Because C-h f allows all function names, not just command names, you may find that some of your favorite completion abbreviations that work in M-x don't work in C-h f. An abbreviation that is unique among command names may not be unique among all function names.

If you type C-h f RET, it describes the function called by the innermost Lisp expression in the buffer around point, *provided* that function name is a valid, defined Lisp function. (That name appears as the default while you enter the argument.) For example, if point is located following the text '(make-vector (car x)', the innermost list containing point is the one that starts with '(make-vector', so C-h f RET will describe the function make-vector.

C-h f is also useful just to verify that you spelled a function name correctly. If the minibuffer prompt for C-h f shows the function name from the buffer as the default, it means that name is defined as a Lisp function. Type C-g to cancel the C-h f command if you don't really want to view the documentation.

C-h v (describe variable) is like C h f but describes Lisp variables instead of Lisp functions. Its default is the Lisp symbol around or before point, if that is the name of a defined Lisp variable. See Section 32.3 [Variables], page 416.

Help buffers that describe Emacs variables and functions normally have hyperlinks to the corresponding source definition, if you have the source files installed. (See Section 31.15 [Hyperlinking], page 402.) If you know Lisp (or C), this provides the ultimate documentation. If you don't know Lisp, you should learn it. (The Introduction to Emacs Lisp Programming, available from the FSF through fsf.org, is a good way to get started.) If Emacs feels you are just *using* it, treating it as an object program, its feelings may be hurt. For real intimacy, read the Emacs source code.

To find a function's documentation in a manual, use C-h F (Info-goto-emacs-command-node). This knows about various manuals, not just the Emacs manual, and finds the right one.

7.3 Apropos

The *apropos* commands answer questions like, "What are the commands for working with files?" More precisely, you specify an *apropos pattern*, which means either a word, a list of words, or a regular expression. Each apropos command displays a list of items that match the pattern, in a separate buffer.

C-h a *pattern* RET

> Search for commands whose names match *pattern*.

M-x apropos RET *pattern* RET

> Search for functions and variables whose names match *pattern*. Both interactive functions (commands) and noninteractive functions can be found by this command.

M-x apropos-variable RET *pattern* RET
> Search for user-option variables whose names match *pattern*.

M-x apropos-value RET *pattern* RET
> Search for functions whose definitions *pattern*, and variables whose values match *pattern*.

C-h d *pattern* RET
> Search for functions and variables whose **documentation strings** match *pattern*.

The simplest kind of apropos pattern is one word. Anything which contains that word matches the pattern. Thus, to find the commands that work on files, type C-h a file RET. This displays a list of all command names that contain 'file', including copy-file, find-file, and so on. Each command name comes with a brief description and a list of keys you can currently invoke it with. In our example, it would say that you can invoke find-file by typing C-x C-f.

The a in C-h a stands for "Apropos"; C-h a runs the command apropos-command. This command normally checks only commands (interactive functions); if you specify a prefix argument, it checks noninteractive functions as well.

For more information about a function definition, variable or symbol property listed in the apropos buffer, you can click on it with Mouse-1 or Mouse-2, or move there and type RET.

When you specify more than one word in the apropos pattern, a name must contain at least two of the words in order to match. Thus, if you are looking for commands to kill a chunk of text before point, you could try C-h a kill back backward behind before RET. The real command name kill-backward will match that; if there were a command kill-text-before, it would also match, since it contains two of the specified words.

For even greater flexibility, you can specify a regular expression (see Section 12.5 [Regexps], page 92). An apropos pattern is interpreted as a regular expression if it contains any of the regular expression special characters, '^$*+?.\['.

Following the conventions for naming Emacs commands, here are some words that you'll find useful in apropos patterns. By using them in C-h a, you will also get a feel for the naming conventions.

> char, line, word, sentence, paragraph, region, page, sexp, list, defun, rect, buffer, frame, window, face, file, dir, register, mode, beginning, end, forward, backward, next, previous, up, down, search, goto, kill, delete, mark, insert, yank, fill, indent, case, change, set, what, list, find, view, describe, default.

Use M-x apropos instead of C-h a to list all the Lisp symbols that match an apropos pattern, not just the symbols that are commands. This command does not list key bindings by default; specify a numeric argument if you want it to list them.

Use M-x apropos-variable to list user-customizable variables that match an apropos pattern. If you specify a prefix argument, it lists all matching variables.

The apropos-documentation command is like apropos except that it searches documentation strings instead of symbol names for matches.

The `apropos-value` command is like `apropos` except that it searches variables' values for matches for the apropos pattern. With a prefix argument, it also checks symbols' function definitions and property lists.

If the variable `apropos-do-all` is non-`nil`, the apropos commands always behave as if they had been given a prefix argument.

By default, apropos lists the search results in alphabetical order. If the variable `apropos-sort-by-scores` is non-`nil`, the apropos commands try to guess the relevance of each result, and display the most relevant ones first.

By default, apropos lists the search results for `apropos-documentation` in order of relevance of the match. If the variable `apropos-documentation-sort-by-scores` is `nil`, apropos lists the symbols found in alphabetical order.

7.4 Help Mode Commands

Help buffers provide the same commands as View mode (see Section 15.11 [Misc File Ops], page 150), plus a few special commands of their own.

SPC   Scroll forward.

DEL   Scroll backward.

RET   Follow a cross reference at point.

TAB   Move point forward to the next cross reference.

S-TAB   Move point back to the previous cross reference.

Mouse-1
Mouse-2   Follow a cross reference that you click on.

C-c C-c   Show all documentation about the symbol at point.

When a function name (see Chapter 6 [Running Commands by Name], page 39), variable name (see Section 32.3 [Variables], page 416), or face name (see Section 11.5 [Faces], page 72) appears in the documentation, it normally appears inside paired single-quotes. To view the documentation of that command, variable or face, you can click on the name with `Mouse-1` or `Mouse-2`, or move point there and type RET. Use `C-c C-b` to retrace your steps.

You can follow cross references to URLs (web pages) also. This uses the `browse-url` command to view the page in the browser you choose. See Section 31.15.1 [Browse-URL], page 402.

There are convenient commands to move point to cross references in the help text. TAB (`help-next-ref`) moves point down to the next cross reference. S-TAB moves up to the previous cross reference (`help-previous-ref`).

To view all documentation about any symbol name that appears in the text, move point to the symbol name and type `C-c C-c` (`help-follow-symbol`). This shows all available documentation about the symbol as a variable, function and/or face. As above, use `C-c C-b` to retrace your steps.

7.5 Keyword Search for Lisp Libraries

The C-h p command lets you search the standard Emacs Lisp libraries by topic keywords. Here is a partial list of keywords you can use:

abbrev	abbreviation handling, typing shortcuts, macros.
bib	code related to the bib bibliography processor.
c	support for the C language and related languages.
calendar	calendar and time management support.
comm	communications, networking, remote access to files.
convenience	convenience features for faster editing.
data	support for editing files of data.
docs	support for Emacs documentation.
emulations	emulations of other editors.
extensions	Emacs Lisp language extensions.
faces	support for multiple fonts.
files	support for editing and manipulating files.
frames	support for Emacs frames and window systems.
games	games, jokes and amusements.
hardware	support for interfacing with exotic hardware.
help	support for on-line help systems.
hypermedia	support for links between text or other media types.
i18n	internationalization and alternate character-set support.
internal	code for Emacs internals, build process, defaults.
languages	specialized modes for editing programming languages.
lisp	Lisp support, including Emacs Lisp.
local	code local to your site.
maint	maintenance aids for the Emacs development group.
mail	modes for electronic-mail handling.
matching	various sorts of searching and matching.
mouse	mouse support.
multimedia	images and sound support.
news	support for netnews reading and posting.
oop	support for object-oriented programming.
outlines	support for hierarchical outlining.
processes	process, subshell, compilation, and job control support.
terminals	support for terminal types.
tex	supporting code for the TEX formatter.
tools	programming tools.
unix	front-ends/assistants for, or emulators of, UNIX-like features.
wp	word processing.

7.6 Help for International Language Support

You can use the command C-h L (describe-language-environment) to get information about a specific language environment. See Section 19.3 [Language Environments], page 188. This tells you which languages this language environment supports. It also lists the character sets, coding systems, and input methods that work with this language environment, and finally shows some sample text to illustrate scripts.

The command C-h h (view-hello-file) displays the file 'etc/HELLO', which shows how to say "hello" in many languages.

The command C-h I (describe-input-method) describes an input method—either a specified input method, or by default the input method currently in use. See Section 19.4 [Input Methods], page 190.

The command C-h C (describe-coding-system) describes coding systems—either a specified coding system, or the ones currently in use. See Section 19.7 [Coding Systems], page 193.

7.7 Other Help Commands

C-h i (info) runs the Info program, which browses structured documentation files. The entire Emacs manual is available within Info, along with many other manuals for the GNU system. Type h after entering Info to run a tutorial on using Info.

With a numeric argument n, C-h i selects the Info buffer '*info*<n>'. This is useful if you want to browse multiple Info manuals simultaneously. If you specify just C-u as the prefix argument, C-h i prompts for the name of a documentation file, so you can browse a file which doesn't have an entry in the top-level Info menu.

The help commands C-h F *function* RET and C-h K *key*, described above, enter Info and go straight to the documentation of *function* or *key*.

When editing a program, if you have an Info version of the manual for the programming language, you can use C-h S (info-lookup-symbol) to find symbol (keyword, function or variable) in the proper manual. The details of how this command works depend on the major mode.

If something surprising happens, and you are not sure what you typed, use C-h l (view-lossage). C-h l displays the last 100 characters you typed in Emacs. If you see commands that you don't know, you can use C-h c to find out what they do.

To review recent echo area messages, use C-h e (view-echo-area-messages). This displays the buffer *Messages*, where those messages are kept.

Each Emacs major mode typically redefines a few keys and makes other changes in how editing works. C-h m (describe-mode) displays documentation on the current major mode, which normally describes the commands and features that are changed in this mode.

C-h b (describe-bindings) and C-h s (describe-syntax) show other information about the current environment within Emacs. C-h b displays a list of all the key bindings now in effect: first the local bindings of the current minor modes, then the local bindings defined by the current major mode, and finally the global bindings (see Section 32.4 [Key Bindings], page 423). C-h s displays the contents of the syntax table, with explanations of each character's syntax (see Section 32.5 [Syntax], page 433).

You can get a list of subcommands for a particular prefix key by typing C-h after the prefix key. (There are a few prefix keys for which this does not work—those that provide their own bindings for C-h. One of these is ESC, because ESC C-h is actually C-M-h, which marks a defun.)

7.8 Help Files

The Emacs help commands described above display dynamic help based on the current state within Emacs, or refer to manuals. Other help commands display pre-written, static help files. These commands all have the form C-h C-*char*; that is, C-h followed by a control character.

C-h C-c   Display the Emacs copying conditions (describe-copying). These are the rules under which you can copy and redistribute Emacs.

C-h C-d   Display how to download or order the latest version of Emacs and other GNU software (describe-distribution).

C-h C-e   Display the list of known Emacs problems, sometimes with suggested workarounds (view-emacs-problems).

C-h C-f   Display the Emacs frequently-answered-questions list (view-emacs-FAQ).

C-h C-n   Display the Emacs "news" file, which lists new features in the most recent version of Emacs (view-emacs-news).

C-h C-p   Display general information about the GNU Project (describe-project).

C-h C-t   Display the Emacs to-do list (view-todo).

C-h C-w   Display the full details on the complete absence of warranty for GNU Emacs (describe-no-warranty).

7.9 Help on Active Text and Tooltips

When a region of text is "active," so that you can select it with the mouse or a key like RET, it often has associated help text. For instance, most parts of the mode line have help text. On graphical displays, the help text is displayed as a "tooltip" (sometimes known as "balloon help"), when you move the mouse over the active text. See Section 18.17 [Tooltips], page 184. On some systems, it is shown in the echo area. On text-only terminals, if Emacs cannot follow the mouse, it cannot show the help text on mouse-over.

You can also access text region help info using the keyboard. The command C-h . (display-local-help) displays any help text associated with the text at point, using the echo area. If you want help text to be displayed automatically whenever it is available at point, set the variable help-at-pt-display-when-idle to t.

8 The Mark and the Region

Many Emacs commands operate on an arbitrary contiguous part of the current buffer. To specify the text for such a command to operate on, you set *the mark* at one end of it, and move point to the other end. The text between point and the mark is called *the region*. Emacs highlights the region whenever there is one, if you enable Transient Mark mode (see Section 8.2 [Transient Mark], page 50).

Certain Emacs commands set the mark; other editing commands do not affect it, so the mark remains where you set it last. Each Emacs buffer has its own mark, and setting the mark in one buffer has no effect on other buffers' marks. When you return to a buffer that was current earlier, its mark is at the same place as before.

The ends of the region are always point and the mark. It doesn't matter which of them was put in its current place first, or which one comes earlier in the text—the region starts from point or the mark (whichever comes first), and ends at point or the mark (whichever comes last). Every time you move point, or set the mark in a new place, the region changes.

Many commands that insert text, such as `C-y` (yank) and `M-x insert-buffer`, position point and the mark at opposite ends of the inserted text, so that the region consists of the text just inserted.

Aside from delimiting the region, the mark is also useful for remembering a spot that you may want to go back to. To make this feature more useful, each buffer remembers 16 previous locations of the mark in the *mark ring*.

8.1 Setting the Mark

Here are some commands for setting the mark:

C-SPC   Set the mark where point is (`set-mark-command`).

C-@   The same.

C-x C-x   Interchange mark and point (`exchange-point-and-mark`).

Drag-Mouse-1
             Set point and the mark around the text you drag across.

Mouse-3   Set the mark where point is, then move point to where you click (`mouse-save-then-kill`).

For example, suppose you wish to convert part of the buffer to upper case, using the `C-x C-u` (upcase-region) command, which operates on the text in the region. You can first go to the beginning of the text to be capitalized, type `C-SPC` to put the mark there, move to the end, and then type `C-x C-u`. Or, you can set the mark at the end of the text, move to the beginning, and then type `C-x C-u`.

The most common way to set the mark is with the `C-SPC` command (`set-mark-command`). This sets the mark where point is. Then you can move point away, leaving the mark behind.

There are two ways to set the mark with the mouse. You can drag mouse button one across a range of text; that puts point where you release the mouse button, and sets the mark at the other end of that range. Or you can click mouse button three, which sets the mark at point (like C-SPC) and then moves point where you clicked (like Mouse-1).

Using the mouse to mark a region copies the region into the kill ring in addition to setting the mark; that gives behavior consistent with other window-driven applications. If you don't want to modify the kill ring, you must use keyboard commands to set the mark. See Section 18.1.1 [Mouse Commands], page 171.

When Emacs was developed, terminals had only one cursor, so Emacs does not show where the mark is located–you have to remember. If you enable Transient Mark mode (see below), then the region is highlighted when it is active; you can tell mark is at the other end of the highlighted region. But this only applies when the mark is active.

The usual solution to this problem is to set the mark and then use it soon, before you forget where it is. Alternatively, you can see where the mark is with the command C-x C-x (exchange-point-and-mark) which puts the mark where point was and point where the mark was. The extent of the region is unchanged, but the cursor and point are now at the previous position of the mark. In Transient Mark mode, this command also reactivates the mark.

C-x C-x is also useful when you are satisfied with the position of point but want to move the other end of the region (where the mark is); do C-x C-x to put point at that end of the region, and then move it. Using C-x C-x a second time, if necessary, puts the mark at the new position with point back at its original position.

For more facilities that allow you to go to previously set marks, see Section 8.6 [Mark Ring], page 54.

There is no such character as C-SPC in ASCII; when you type SPC while holding down CTRL on a text terminal, what you get is the character C-@. This key is also bound to set-mark-command–so unless you are unlucky enough to have a text terminal where typing C-SPC does not produce C-@, you might as well think of this character as C-SPC.

8.2 Transient Mark Mode

On a terminal that supports colors, Emacs has the ability to highlight the current region. But normally it does not. Why not?

In the normal mode of use, every command that sets the mark also activates it, and nothing ever deactivates it. Thus, once you have set the mark in a buffer, there is *always* a region in that buffer. Highlighting the region all the time would be a nuisance. So normally Emacs highlights the region only immediately after you have selected one with the mouse.

If you want region highlighting, you can use Transient Mark mode. This is a more rigid mode of operation in which the region "lasts" only until you use it; operating on the region text deactivates the mark, so there is no region any more. Therefore, you must explicitly set up a region for each command that uses one.

When Transient Mark mode is enabled, Emacs highlights the region, whenever there is a region. In Transient Mark mode, most of the time there is no region; therefore, highlighting the region when it exists is useful and not annoying.

To enable Transient Mark mode, type M-x transient-mark-mode. This command toggles the mode; you can use the same command to turn the mode off again.

Here are the details of Transient Mark mode:

- To set the mark, type C-SPC (set-mark-command). This makes the mark active and thus begins highlighting of the region. As you move point, you will see the highlighted region grow and shrink.

- The mouse commands for specifying the mark also make it active. So do keyboard commands whose purpose is to specify a region, including M-@, C-M-@, M-h, C-M-h, C-x C-p, and C-x h.

- You can tell that the mark is active because the region is highlighted.

- When the mark is active, you can execute commands that operate on the region, such as killing, indenting, or writing to a file.

- Any change to the buffer, such as inserting or deleting a character, deactivates the mark. This means any subsequent command that operates on a region will get an error and refuse to operate. You can make the region active again by typing C-x C-x.

- If Delete Selection mode is also enabled, some commands delete the region when used while the mark is active. See Section 18.1.1 [Mouse Commands], page 171.

- Quitting with C-g deactivates the mark.

- Commands like M-> and C-s, that "leave the mark behind" in addition to some other primary purpose, do not activate the new mark. You can activate the new region by executing C-x C-x (exchange-point-and-mark).

- Commands that normally set the mark before moving long distances (like M-< and C-s) do not alter the mark in Transient Mark mode when the mark is active.

- Some commands operate on the region if a region is active. For instance, C-x u in Transient Mark mode operates on the region, when there is a region. (Outside Transient Mark mode, you must type C-u C-x u if you want it to operate on the region.) See Section 13.1 [Undo], page 105. Other commands that act this way are identified in their own documentation.

The highlighting of the region uses the region face; you can customize the appearance of the highlighted region by changing this face. See Section 32.2.5 [Face Customization], page 413.

When multiple windows show the same buffer, they can have different regions, because they can have different values of point (though they all share one common mark position). Ordinarily, only the selected window highlights its region (see Chapter 17 [Windows], page 165). However, if the variable highlight-nonselected-windows is non-nil, then each window highlights its own region (provided that Transient Mark mode is enabled and the mark in the window's buffer is active).

If the variable `mark-even-if-inactive` is non-`nil` in Transient Mark mode, then commands can use the mark and the region even when it is inactive. Region highlighting appears and disappears just as it normally does in Transient Mark mode, but the mark doesn't really go away when the highlighting disappears, so you can still use region commands.

Transient Mark mode is also sometimes known as "Zmacs mode" because the Zmacs editor on the MIT Lisp Machine handled the mark in a similar way.

8.3 Using Transient Mark Mode Momentarily

If you don't like Transient Mark mode in general, you might still want to use it once in a while. To do this, type `C-SPC C-SPC` or `C-u C-x C-x`. These commands set or activate the mark, and enable Transient Mark mode only until the mark is deactivated.

`C-SPC C-SPC`

> Set the mark at point (like plain `C-SPC`), and enable Transient Mark mode just once until the mark is deactivated. (This is not really a separate command; you are using the `C-SPC` command twice.)

`C-u C-x C-x`

> Activate the mark without changing it; enable Transient Mark mode just once, until the mark is deactivated. (This is the `C-x C-x` command, `exchange-point-and-mark`, with a prefix argument.)

One of the secondary features of Transient Mark mode is that certain commands operate only on the region, when there is an active region. If you don't use Transient Mark mode, the region once set never becomes inactive, so there is no way for these commands to make such a distinction. Enabling Transient Mark mode momentarily gives you a way to use these commands on the region.

Momentary use of Transient Mark mode is also a way to highlight the region for the time being.

8.4 Operating on the Region

Once you have a region and the mark is active, here are some of the ways you can operate on the region:

- Kill it with `C-w` (see Chapter 9 [Killing], page 55).
- Save it in a register with `C-x r s` (see Chapter 10 [Registers], page 65).
- Save it in a buffer or a file (see Section 9.3 [Accumulating Text], page 60).
- Convert case with `C-x C-l` or `C-x C-u` (see Section 22.6 [Case], page 223).
- Indent it with `C-x TAB` or `C-M-\` (see Chapter 21 [Indentation], page 210).
- Fill it as text with `M-x fill-region` (see Section 22.5 [Filling], page 217).
- Print hardcopy with `M-x print-region` (see Section 31.4 [Printing], page 391).
- Evaluate it as Lisp code with `M-x eval-region` (see Section 24.9 [Lisp Eval], page 289).

- Undo changes within it using `C-u C-x u` (see Section 13.1 [Undo], page 105).

Most commands that operate on the text in the region have the word `region` in their names.

8.5 Commands to Mark Textual Objects

Here are the commands for placing point and the mark around a textual object such as a word, list, paragraph or page.

`M-@`   Set mark after end of next word (`mark-word`). This command and the following one do not move point.

`C-M-@`   Set mark after end of following balanced expression (`mark-sexp`).

`M-h`   Put region around current paragraph (`mark-paragraph`).

`C-M-h`   Put region around current defun (`mark-defun`).

`C-x h`   Put region around the entire buffer (`mark-whole-buffer`).

`C-x C-p`   Put region around current page (`mark-page`).

`M-@` (`mark-word`) puts the mark at the end of the next word, while `C-M-@` (`mark-sexp`) puts it at the end of the next balanced expression (see Section 23.4.1 [Expressions], page 257). These commands handle arguments just like `M-f` and `C-M-f`. Repeating these commands extends the region. For example, you can type either `C-u 2 M-@` or `M-@ M-@` to mark the next two words. These commands also extend the region in Transient Mark mode, regardless of the last command.

Other commands set both point and mark, to delimit an object in the buffer. For example, `M-h` (`mark-paragraph`) moves point to the beginning of the paragraph that surrounds or follows point, and puts the mark at the end of that paragraph (see Section 22.3 [Paragraphs], page 215). It prepares the region so you can indent, case-convert, or kill a whole paragraph. With a prefix argument, if the argument's value is positive, `M-h` marks that many paragraphs starting with the one surrounding point. If the prefix argument is −n, `M-h` also marks n paragraphs, running back form the one surrounding point. In that last case, point moves forward to the end of that paragraph, and the mark goes at the start of the region. Repeating the `M-h` command extends the region to subsequent paragraphs.

`C-M-h` (`mark-defun`) similarly puts point before, and the mark after, the current (or following) major top-level definition, or defun (see Section 23.2.2 [Moving by Defuns], page 252). Repeating `C-M-h` extends the region to subsequent defuns.

`C-x C-p` (`mark-page`) puts point before the current page, and mark at the end (see Section 22.4 [Pages], page 216). The mark goes after the terminating page delimiter (to include it in the region), while point goes after the preceding page delimiter (to exclude it). A numeric argument specifies a later page (if positive) or an earlier page (if negative) instead of the current page.

Finally, `C-x h` (`mark-whole-buffer`) sets up the entire buffer as the region, by putting point at the beginning and the mark at the end. (In some programs this is called "select all.")

In Transient Mark mode, all of these commands activate the mark.

8.6 The Mark Ring

Aside from delimiting the region, the mark is also useful for remembering a spot that you may want to go back to. To make this feature more useful, each buffer remembers 16 previous locations of the mark, in the *mark ring*. Commands that set the mark also push the old mark onto this ring. To return to a marked location, use C-u C-SPC (or C-u C-@); this is the command `set-mark-command` given a numeric argument. It moves point to where the mark was, and restores the mark from the ring of former marks.

If you set `set-mark-command-repeat-pop` to non-`nil`, then when you repeat the character C-SPC after typing C-u C-SPC, each repetition moves point to a previous mark position from the ring. The mark positions you move through in this way are not lost; they go to the end of the ring.

Each buffer has its own mark ring. All editing commands use the current buffer's mark ring. In particular, C-u C-SPC always stays in the same buffer.

Many commands that can move long distances, such as M-< (`beginning-of-buffer`), start by setting the mark and saving the old mark on the mark ring. This is to make it easier for you to move back later. Searches set the mark if they move point. However, in Transient Mark mode, these commands do not set the mark when the mark is already active. You can tell when a command sets the mark because it displays '`Mark set`' in the echo area.

If you want to move back to the same place over and over, the mark ring may not be convenient enough. If so, you can record the position in a register for later retrieval (see Section 10.1 [Saving Positions in Registers], page 65).

The variable `mark-ring-max` specifies the maximum number of entries to keep in the mark ring. If that many entries exist and another one is pushed, the earliest one in the list is discarded. Repeating C-u C-SPC cycles through the positions currently in the ring.

The variable `mark-ring` holds the mark ring itself, as a list of marker objects, with the most recent first. This variable is local in every buffer.

8.7 The Global Mark Ring

In addition to the ordinary mark ring that belongs to each buffer, Emacs has a single *global mark ring*. It records a sequence of buffers in which you have recently set the mark, so you can go back to those buffers.

Setting the mark always makes an entry on the current buffer's mark ring. If you have switched buffers since the previous mark setting, the new mark position makes an entry on the global mark ring also. The result is that the global mark ring records a sequence of buffers that you have been in, and, for each buffer, a place where you set the mark.

The command C-x C-SPC (`pop-global-mark`) jumps to the buffer and position of the latest entry in the global ring. It also rotates the ring, so that successive uses of C-x C-SPC take you to earlier and earlier buffers.

9 Killing and Moving Text

Killing means erasing text and copying it into the *kill ring*, from which you can bring it back into the buffer by *yanking* it. (Some systems use the terms "cutting" and "pasting" for these operations.) This is the most common way of moving or copying text within Emacs. Killing and yanking is very safe because Emacs remembers several recent kills, not just the last one. It is versatile, because the many commands for killing syntactic units can also be used for moving those units. But there are other ways of copying text for special purposes.

9.1 Deletion and Killing

Most commands which erase text from the buffer save it in the kill ring. These commands are known as *kill* commands. The commands that erase text but do not save it in the kill ring are known as *delete* commands. The C-x u (`undo`) command (see Section 13.1 [Undo], page 105) can undo both kill and delete commands; the importance of the kill ring is that you can also yank the text in a different place or places. Emacs has only one kill ring for all buffers, so you can kill text in one buffer and yank it in another buffer.

The delete commands include C-d (`delete-char`) and DEL (`delete-backward-char`), which delete only one character at a time, and those commands that delete only spaces or newlines. Commands that can erase significant amounts of nontrivial data generally do a kill operation instead. The commands' names and individual descriptions use the words '`kill`' and '`delete`' to say which kind of operation they perform.

You cannot kill read-only text, since such text does not allow any kind of modification. But some users like to use the kill commands to copy read-only text into the kill ring, without actually changing it. Therefore, the kill commands work specially in a read-only buffer: they move over text, and copy it to the kill ring, without actually deleting it from the buffer. Normally, kill commands beep and display an error message when this happens. But if you set the variable `kill-read-only-ok` to a non-`nil` value, they just print a message in the echo area to explain why the text has not been erased.

You can also use the mouse to kill and yank. See Section 18.1 [Cut and Paste], page 171.

9.1.1 Deletion

Deletion means erasing text and not saving it in the kill ring. For the most part, the Emacs commands that delete text are those that erase just one character or only whitespace.

C-d
DELETE   Delete next character (`delete-char`). If your keyboard has a
                DELETE function key (usually located in the edit keypad), Emacs
                binds it to `delete-char` as well.

DEL

BS   Delete previous character (`delete-backward-char`).

M-\   Delete spaces and tabs around point (`delete-horizontal-space`).

M-SPC   Delete spaces and tabs around point, leaving one space (`just-one-space`).

C-x C-o   Delete blank lines around the current line (`delete-blank-lines`).

M-^   Join two lines by deleting the intervening newline, along with any indentation following it (`delete-indentation`).

The most basic delete commands are `C-d` (`delete-char`) and DEL (`delete-backward-char`). `C-d` deletes the character after point, the one the cursor is "on top of." This doesn't move point. DEL deletes the character before the cursor, and moves point back. You can delete newlines like any other characters in the buffer; deleting a newline joins two lines. Actually, `C-d` and DEL aren't always delete commands; when given arguments, they kill instead, since they can erase more than one character this way.

Every keyboard has a large key which is a short distance above the RET or ENTER key and is normally used for erasing what you have typed. It may be labeled DEL, BACKSPACE, BS, DELETE, or even with a left arrow. Regardless of the label on the key, in Emacs it called DEL, and it should delete one character backwards.

Many keyboards (including standard PC keyboards) have a BACKSPACE key a short ways above RET or ENTER, and a DELETE key elsewhere. In that case, the BACKSPACE key is DEL, and the DELETE key is equivalent to `C-d`—or it should be.

Why do we say "or it should be"? When Emacs starts up using a graphical display, it determines automatically which key or keys should be equivalent to DEL. As a result, BACKSPACE and/or DELETE keys normally do the right things. But in some unusual cases Emacs gets the wrong information from the system. If these keys don't do what they ought to do, you need to tell Emacs which key to use for DEL. See Section 33.2.1 [DEL Does Not Delete], page 441, for how to do this.

On most text-only terminals, Emacs cannot tell which keys the keyboard really has, so it follows a uniform plan which may or may not fit your keyboard. The uniform plan is that the ASCII DEL character deletes, and the ASCII BS (backspace) character asks for help (it is the same as `C-h`). If this is not right for your keyboard, such as if you find that the key which ought to delete backwards enters Help instead, see Section 33.2.1 [DEL Does Not Delete], page 441.

The other delete commands are those which delete only whitespace characters: spaces, tabs and newlines. `M-\` (`delete-horizontal-space`) deletes all the spaces and tab characters before and after point. With a prefix argument, this only deletes spaces and tab characters before point. `M-SPC` (`just-one-space`) does likewise but leaves a single space after point, regardless of the number of spaces that existed previously (even if there were none before). With a numeric argument n, it leaves n spaces after point.

`C-x C-o` (`delete-blank-lines`) deletes all blank lines after the current line. If the current line is blank, it deletes all blank lines preceding the current line as well (leaving one blank line, the current line). On a solitary blank line, it deletes that line.

`M-^` (`delete-indentation`) joins the current line and the previous line, by deleting a newline and all surrounding spaces, usually leaving a single space. See Chapter 21 [Indentation], page 210.

9.1.2 Killing by Lines

`C-k`   Kill rest of line or one or more lines (`kill-line`).

`C-S-backspace`
               Kill an entire line at once (`kill-whole-line`)

The simplest kill command is `C-k`. If given at the beginning of a line, it kills all the text on the line, leaving it blank. When used on a blank line, it kills the whole line including its newline. To kill an entire non-blank line, go to the beginning and type `C-k` twice.

More generally, `C-k` kills from point up to the end of the line, unless it is at the end of a line. In that case it kills the newline following point, thus merging the next line into the current one. Spaces and tabs that you can't see at the end of the line are ignored when deciding which case applies, so if point appears to be at the end of the line, you can be sure `C-k` will kill the newline.

When `C-k` is given a positive argument, it kills that many lines and the newlines that follow them (however, text on the current line before point is not killed). With a negative argument −n, it kills n lines preceding the current line (together with the text on the current line before point). Thus, `C-u - 2 C-k` at the front of a line kills the two previous lines.

`C-k` with an argument of zero kills the text before point on the current line.

If the variable `kill-whole-line` is non-nil, `C-k` at the very beginning of a line kills the entire line including the following newline. This variable is normally `nil`.

`C-S-backspace` (`kill-whole-line`) will kill a whole line including its newline regardless of the position of point within the line. Note that many character terminals will prevent you from typing the key sequence `C-S-backspace`.

9.1.3 Other Kill Commands

`C-w`   Kill region (from point to the mark) (`kill-region`).

`M-d`   Kill word (`kill-word`). See Section 22.1 [Words], page 213.

`M-DEL`   Kill word backwards (`backward-kill-word`).

`C-x DEL`   Kill back to beginning of sentence (`backward-kill-sentence`). See Section 22.2 [Sentences], page 214.

`M-k`   Kill to end of sentence (`kill-sentence`).

C-M-k   Kill the following balanced expression (`kill-sexp`). See Section 23.4.1
               [Expressions], page 257.

M-z *char*   Kill through the next occurrence of *char* (`zap-to-char`).

   The most general kill command is C-w (`kill-region`), which kills everything
between point and the mark. With this command, you can kill any contiguous
sequence of characters, if you first set the region around them.

   A convenient way of killing is combined with searching: M-z (`zap-to-char`)
reads a character and kills from point up to (and including) the next occurrence
of that character in the buffer. A numeric argument acts as a repeat count. A
negative argument means to search backward and kill text before point.

   Other syntactic units can be killed: words, with M-DEL and M-d (see Section 22.1
[Words], page 213); balanced expressions, with C-M-k (see Section 23.4.1 [Expres-
sions], page 257); and sentences, with C-x DEL and M-k (see Section 22.2 [Sentences],
page 214).

9.2 Yanking

Yanking means reinserting text previously killed. This is what some systems call
"pasting." The usual way to move or copy text is to kill it and then yank it elsewhere
one or more times. This is very safe because Emacs remembers many recent kills,
not just the last one.

C-y   Yank last killed text (`yank`).

M-y   Replace text just yanked with an earlier batch of killed text (`yank-`
               `pop`).

M-w   Save region as last killed text without actually killing it (`kill-ring-`
               `save`). Some systems call this "copying."

C-M-w   Append next kill to last batch of killed text (`append-next-kill`).

   On graphical displays with window systems, if there is a current selection in
some other application, and you selected it more recently than you killed any text
in Emacs, C-y copies the selection instead of text killed within Emacs.

9.2.1 The Kill Ring

All killed text is recorded in the *kill ring*, a list of blocks of text that have been
killed. There is only one kill ring, shared by all buffers, so you can kill text in one
buffer and yank it in another buffer. This is the usual way to move text from one file
to another. (See Section 9.3 [Accumulating Text], page 60, for some other ways.)

   The command C-y (`yank`) reinserts the text of the most recent kill. It leaves
the cursor at the end of the text. It sets the mark at the beginning of the text. See
Chapter 8 [Mark], page 49.

   C-u C-y leaves the cursor in front of the text, and sets the mark after it. This
happens only if the argument is specified with just a C-u, precisely. Any other
sort of argument, including C-u and digits, specifies an earlier kill to yank (see
Section 9.2.3 [Earlier Kills], page 59).

The yank commands discard certain text properties from the text that is yanked, those that might lead to annoying results. For instance, they discard text properties that respond to the mouse or specify key bindings. The variable `yank-excluded-properties` specifies the properties to discard. Yanking of register contents and rectangles also discard these properties.

To copy a block of text, you can use `M-w` (`kill-ring-save`), which copies the region into the kill ring without removing it from the buffer. This is approximately equivalent to `C-w` followed by `C-x u`, except that `M-w` does not alter the undo history and does not temporarily change the screen.

9.2.2 Appending Kills

Normally, each kill command pushes a new entry onto the kill ring. However, two or more kill commands in a row combine their text into a single entry, so that a single `C-y` yanks all the text as a unit, just as it was before it was killed.

Thus, if you want to yank text as a unit, you need not kill all of it with one command; you can keep killing line after line, or word after word, until you have killed it all, and you can still get it all back at once.

Commands that kill forward from point add onto the end of the previous killed text. Commands that kill backward from point add text onto the beginning. This way, any sequence of mixed forward and backward kill commands puts all the killed text into one entry without rearrangement. Numeric arguments do not break the sequence of appending kills. For example, suppose the buffer contains this text:

    This is a line *of sample text.

with point shown by *. If you type M d M DEL M-d M-DEL, killing alternately forward and backward, you end up with 'a line of sample' as one entry in the kill ring, and 'This is text.' in the buffer. (Note the double space between 'is' and 'text', which you can clean up with `M-SPC` or `M-q`.)

Another way to kill the same text is to move back two words with `M-b M-b`, then kill all four words forward with `C-u M-d`. This produces exactly the same results in the buffer and in the kill ring. `M-f M-f C-u M-DEL` kills the same text, all going backward; once again, the result is the same. The text in the kill ring entry always has the same order that it had in the buffer before you killed it.

If a kill command is separated from the last kill command by other commands (not just numeric arguments), it starts a new entry on the kill ring. But you can force it to append by first typing the command `C-M-w` (`append-next-kill`) right before it. The `C-M-w` tells the following command, if it is a kill command, to append the text it kills to the last killed text, instead of starting a new entry. With `C-M-w`, you can kill several separated pieces of text and accumulate them to be yanked back in one place.

A kill command following `M-w` does not append to the text that `M-w` copied into the kill ring.

9.2.3 Yanking Earlier Kills

To recover killed text that is no longer the most recent kill, use the `M-y` command (`yank-pop`). It takes the text previously yanked and replaces it with the text from an earlier kill. So, to recover the text of the next-to-the-last kill, first use C-y to yank the last kill, and then use M-y to replace it with the previous kill. M-y is allowed only after a C-y or another M-y.

You can understand M-y in terms of a "last yank" pointer which points at an entry in the kill ring. Each time you kill, the "last yank" pointer moves to the newly made entry at the front of the ring. C-y yanks the entry which the "last yank" pointer points to. M-y moves the "last yank" pointer to a different entry, and the text in the buffer changes to match. Enough M-y commands can move the pointer to any entry in the ring, so you can get any entry into the buffer. Eventually the pointer reaches the end of the ring; the next M-y loops back around to the first entry again.

M-y moves the "last yank" pointer around the ring, but it does not change the order of the entries in the ring, which always runs from the most recent kill at the front to the oldest one still remembered.

M-y can take a numeric argument, which tells it how many entries to advance the "last yank" pointer by. A negative argument moves the pointer toward the front of the ring; from the front of the ring, it moves "around" to the last entry and continues forward from there.

Once the text you are looking for is brought into the buffer, you can stop doing M-y commands and it will stay there. It's just a copy of the kill ring entry, so editing it in the buffer does not change what's in the ring. As long as no new killing is done, the "last yank" pointer remains at the same place in the kill ring, so repeating C-y will yank another copy of the same previous kill.

If you know how many M-y commands it would take to find the text you want, you can yank that text in one step using C-y with a numeric argument. C-y with an argument restores the text from the specified kill ring entry, counting back from the most recent as 1. Thus, C-u 2 C-y gets the next-to-the-last block of killed text—it is equivalent to C-y M-y. C-y with a numeric argument starts counting from the "last yank" pointer, and sets the "last yank" pointer to the entry that it yanks.

The length of the kill ring is controlled by the variable kill-ring-max; no more than that many blocks of killed text are saved.

The actual contents of the kill ring are stored in a variable named kill-ring; you can view the entire contents of the kill ring with the command C-h v kill-ring.

9.3 Accumulating Text

Usually we copy or move text by killing it and yanking it, but there are other convenient methods for copying one block of text in many places, or for copying many scattered blocks of text into one place. To copy one block to many places, store it in a register (see Chapter 10 [Registers], page 65). Here we describe the commands to accumulate scattered pieces of text into a buffer or into a file.

M-x append-to-buffer
> Append region to the contents of a specified buffer.

M-x prepend-to-buffer
> Prepend region to the contents of a specified buffer.

`M-x copy-to-buffer`
> Copy region into a specified buffer, deleting that buffer's old contents.

`M-x insert-buffer`
> Insert the contents of a specified buffer into current buffer at point.

`M-x append-to-file`
> Append region to the contents of a specified file, at the end.

To accumulate text into a buffer, use `M-x append-to-buffer`. This reads a buffer name, then inserts a copy of the region into the buffer specified. If you specify a nonexistent buffer, `append-to-buffer` creates the buffer. The text is inserted wherever point is in that buffer. If you have been using the buffer for editing, the copied text goes into the middle of the text of the buffer, starting from wherever point happens to be at that moment.

Point in that buffer is left at the end of the copied text, so successive uses of `append-to-buffer` accumulate the text in the specified buffer in the same order as they were copied. Strictly speaking, `append-to-buffer` does not always append to the text already in the buffer—it appends only if point in that buffer is at the end. However, if `append-to-buffer` is the only command you use to alter a buffer, then point is always at the end.

`M-x prepend-to-buffer` is just like `append-to-buffer` except that point in the other buffer is left before the copied text, so successive prependings add text in reverse order. `M-x copy-to-buffer` is similar, except that any existing text in the other buffer is deleted, so the buffer is left containing just the text newly copied into it.

To retrieve the accumulated text from another buffer, use the command `M-x insert-buffer`; this too takes *buffername* as an argument. It inserts a copy of the whole text in buffer *buffername* into the current buffer at point, and sets the mark after the inserted text. Alternatively, you can select the other buffer for editing, then copy text from it by killing. See Chapter 16 [Buffers], page 156, for background information on buffers.

Instead of accumulating text within Emacs, in a buffer, you can append text directly into a file with `M-x append-to-file`, which takes *filename* as an argument. It adds the text of the region to the end of the specified file. The file is changed immediately on disk.

You should use `append-to-file` only with files that are *not* being visited in Emacs. Using it on a file that you are editing in Emacs would change the file behind Emacs's back, which can lead to losing some of your editing.

9.4 Rectangles

The rectangle commands operate on rectangular areas of the text: all the characters between a certain pair of columns, in a certain range of lines. Commands are provided to kill rectangles, yank killed rectangles, clear them out, fill them with blanks or text, or delete them. Rectangle commands are useful with text in multicolumn formats, and for changing text into or out of such formats.

When you must specify a rectangle for a command to work on, you do it by putting the mark at one corner and point at the opposite corner. The rectangle thus specified is called the *region-rectangle* because you control it in much the same way as the region is controlled. But remember that a given combination of point and mark values can be interpreted either as a region or as a rectangle, depending on the command that uses them.

If point and the mark are in the same column, the rectangle they delimit is empty. If they are in the same line, the rectangle is one line high. This asymmetry between lines and columns comes about because point (and likewise the mark) is between two columns, but within a line.

C-x r k   Kill the text of the region-rectangle, saving its contents as the "last killed rectangle" (`kill-rectangle`).

C-x r d   Delete the text of the region-rectangle (`delete-rectangle`).

C-x r y   Yank the last killed rectangle with its upper left corner at point (`yank-rectangle`).

C-x r o   Insert blank space to fill the space of the region-rectangle (`open-rectangle`). This pushes the previous contents of the region-rectangle rightward.

C-x r c   Clear the region-rectangle by replacing all of its contents with spaces (`clear-rectangle`).

M-x delete-whitespace-rectangle
            Delete whitespace in each of the lines on the specified rectangle, starting from the left edge column of the rectangle.

C-x r t *string* RET
            Replace rectangle contents with *string* on each line (`string-rectangle`).

M-x string-insert-rectangle RET *string* RET
            Insert *string* on each line of the rectangle.

The rectangle operations fall into two classes: commands for deleting and inserting rectangles, and commands for blank rectangles.

There are two ways to get rid of the text in a rectangle: you can discard the text (delete it) or save it as the "last killed" rectangle. The commands for these two ways are C-x r d (`delete-rectangle`) and C-x r k (`kill-rectangle`). In either case, the portion of each line that falls inside the rectangle's boundaries is deleted, causing any following text on the line to move left into the gap.

Note that "killing" a rectangle is not killing in the usual sense; the rectangle is not stored in the kill ring, but in a special place that can only record the most recent rectangle killed. This is because yanking a rectangle is so different from yanking linear text that different yank commands have to be used. It is hard to define yank-popping for rectangles, so we do not try.

To yank the last killed rectangle, type C-x r y (`yank-rectangle`). Yanking a rectangle is the opposite of killing one. Point specifies where to put the rectangle's upper left corner. The rectangle's first line is inserted there, the rectangle's second line is inserted at the same horizontal position, but one line vertically down, and so on. The number of lines affected is determined by the height of the saved rectangle.

You can convert single-column lists into double-column lists using rectangle killing and yanking; kill the second half of the list as a rectangle and then yank it beside the first line of the list. See Section 31.10 [Two-Column], page 397, for another way to edit multi-column text.

You can also copy rectangles into and out of registers with `C-x r r r` and `C-x r i r`. See Section 10.3 [Rectangle Registers], page 66.

There are two commands you can use for making blank rectangles: `C-x r c` (`clear-rectangle`) which blanks out existing text, and `C-x r o` (`open-rectangle`) which inserts a blank rectangle. Clearing a rectangle is equivalent to deleting it and then inserting a blank rectangle of the same size.

The command `M-x delete-whitespace-rectangle` deletes horizontal white-space starting from a particular column. This applies to each of the lines in the rectangle, and the column is specified by the left edge of the rectangle. The right edge of the rectangle does not make any difference to this command.

The command `C-x r t` (`string-rectangle`) replaces the contents of a region-rectangle with a string on each line. The string's width need not be the same as the width of the rectangle. If the string's width is less, the text after the rectangle shifts left; if the string is wider than the rectangle, the text after the rectangle shifts right.

The command `M-x string-insert-rectangle` is similar to `string-rectangle`, but inserts the string on each line, shifting the original text to the right.

9.5 CUA Bindings

The command `M-x cua-mode` sets up key bindings that are compatible with the Common User Access (CUA) system used in many other applications. `C-x` means cut (kill), `C-c` copy, `C-v` paste (yank), and `C-z` undo. Standard Emacs commands like `C-x C-c` still work, because `C-x` and `C-c` only take effect when the mark is active (and the region is highlighted). However, if you don't want to override these bindings in Emacs at all, set `cua-enable-cua-keys` to `nil`.

In CUA mode, using `Shift` together with the movement keys activates and highlights the region over which they move. The standard (unshifted) movement keys deactivate the mark, and typed text replaces the active region as in Delete-Selection mode (see Section 18.1.1 [Mouse Commands], page 171).

To enter an Emacs command like `C-x C-f` while the mark is active, use one of the following methods: either hold `Shift` together with the prefix key, e.g. `S-C-x C-f`, or quickly type the prefix key twice, e.g. `C-x C-x C-f`.

CUA mode provides enhanced rectangle support with visible rectangle high-lighting. Use `C-RET` to start a rectangle, extend it using the movement commands, and cut or copy it using `C-x` or `C-c`. `RET` moves the cursor to the next (clockwise) corner of the rectangle, so you can easily expand it in any direction. Normal text you type is inserted to the left or right of each line in the rectangle (on the same side as the cursor).

With CUA you can easily copy text and rectangles into and out of registers by providing a one-digit numeric prefix to the kill, copy, and yank commands, e.g. C-1 C-c copies the region into register 1, and C-2 C-v yanks the contents of register 2.

CUA mode also has a global mark feature which allows easy moving and copying of text between buffers. Use C-S-SPC to toggle the global mark on and off. When the global mark is on, all text that you kill or copy is automatically inserted at the global mark, and text you type is inserted at the global mark rather than at the current position.

For example, to copy words from various buffers into a word list in a given buffer, set the global mark in the target buffer, then navigate to each of the words you want in the list, mark it (e.g. with S-M-f), copy it to the list with C-c or M-w, and insert a newline after the word in the target list by pressing RET.

10 Registers

Emacs *registers* are compartments where you can save text, rectangles, positions, and other things for later use. Once you save text or a rectangle in a register, you can copy it into the buffer once, or many times; you can move point to a position saved in a register once, or many times.

Each register has a name, which consists of a single character. A register can store a number, a piece of text, a rectangle, a position, a window configuration, or a file name, but only one thing at any given time. Whatever you store in a register remains there until you store something else in that register. To see what a register *r* contains, use M-x view-register.

M-x view-register RET *r*
> Display a description of what register *r* contains.

Bookmarks record files and positions in them, so you can return to those positions when you look at the file again. Bookmarks are similar enough in spirit to registers that they seem to belong in this chapter.

10.1 Saving Positions in Registers

Saving a position records a place in a buffer so that you can move back there later. Moving to a saved position switches to that buffer and moves point to that place in it.

C-x r SPC *r*
> Save position of point in register *r* (point-to-register).

C-x r j *r*   Jump to the position saved in register *r* (jump-to-register).

To save the current position of point in a register, choose a name *r* and type C-x r SPC *r*. The register *r* retains the position thus saved until you store something else in that register.

The command C-x r j *r* moves point to the position recorded in register *r*. The register is not affected; it continues to hold the same position. You can jump to the saved position any number of times.

If you use C-x r j to go to a saved position, but the buffer it was saved from has been killed, C-x r j tries to create the buffer again by visiting the same file. Of course, this works only for buffers that were visiting files.

10.2 Saving Text in Registers

When you want to insert a copy of the same piece of text several times, it may be inconvenient to yank it from the kill ring, since each subsequent kill moves that entry further down the ring. An alternative is to store the text in a register and later retrieve it.

C-x r s *r*   Copy region into register *r* (copy-to-register).

C-x r i *r*   Insert text from register *r* (insert-register).

`M-x append-to-register RET` *r*
> Append region to text in register *r*.

`M-x prepend-to-register RET` *r*
> Prepend region to text in register *r*.

`C-x r s` *r* stores a copy of the text of the region into the register named *r*. `C-u` `C-x r s` *r*, the same command with a numeric argument, deletes the text from the buffer as well; you can think of this as "moving" the region text into the register.

`M-x append-to-register RET` *r* appends the copy of the text in the region to the text already stored in the register named *r*. If invoked with a numeric argument, it deletes the region after appending it to the register. The command `prepend-to-register` is similar, except that it *prepends* the region text to the text in the register, rather than *appending* it.

`C-x r i` *r* inserts in the buffer the text from register *r*. Normally it leaves point before the text and places the mark after, but with a numeric argument (`C-u`) it puts point after the text and the mark before.

10.3 Saving Rectangles in Registers

A register can contain a rectangle instead of linear text. The rectangle is represented as a list of strings. See Section 9.4 [Rectangles], page 61, for basic information on how to specify a rectangle in the buffer.

`C-x r r` *r*   Copy the region-rectangle into register *r* (`copy-rectangle-to-register`). With numeric argument, delete it as well.

`C-x r i` *r*   Insert the rectangle stored in register *r* (if it contains a rectangle) (`insert-register`).

The `C-x r i` *r* command inserts a text string if the register contains one, and inserts a rectangle if the register contains one.

See also the command `sort-columns`, which you can think of as sorting a rectangle. See Section 31.8 [Sorting], page 394.

10.4 Saving Window Configurations in Registers

You can save the window configuration of the selected frame in a register, or even the configuration of all windows in all frames, and restore the configuration later.

`C-x r w` *r*   Save the state of the selected frame's windows in register *r* (`window-configuration-to-register`).

`C-x r f` *r*   Save the state of all frames, including all their windows, in register *r* (`frame-configuration-to-register`).

Use `C-x r j` *r* to restore a window or frame configuration. This is the same command used to restore a cursor position. When you restore a frame configuration, any existing frames not included in the configuration become invisible. If you wish to delete these frames instead, use `C-u C-x r j` *r*.

10.5 Keeping Numbers in Registers

There are commands to store a number in a register, to insert the number in the buffer in decimal, and to increment it. These commands can be useful in keyboard macros (see Chapter 14 [Keyboard Macros], page 111).

C-u *number* C-x r n *r*
> Store *number* into register *r* (number-to-register).

C-u *number* C-x r + *r*
> Increment the number in register *r* by *number* (increment-register).

C-x r i *r*   Insert the number from register *r* into the buffer.

C-x r i is the same command used to insert any other sort of register contents into the buffer. C-x r + with no numeric argument increments the register value by 1; C-x r n with no numeric argument stores zero in the register.

10.6 Keeping File Names in Registers

If you visit certain file names frequently, you can visit them more conveniently if you put their names in registers. Here's the Lisp code used to put a file name in a register:

```
(set-register ?r '(file . name))
```

For example,

```
(set-register ?z '(file . "/gd/gnu/emacs/19.0/src/ChangeLog"))
```

puts the file name shown in register 'z'.

To visit the file whose name is in register *r*, type C-x r j *r*. (This is the same command used to jump to a position or restore a frame configuration.)

10.7 Bookmarks

Bookmarks are somewhat like registers in that they record positions you can jump to. Unlike registers, they have long names, and they persist automatically from one Emacs session to the next. The prototypical use of bookmarks is to record "where you were reading" in various files.

C-x r m RET
> Set the bookmark for the visited file, at point.

C-x r m *bookmark* RET
> Set the bookmark named *bookmark* at point (bookmark-set).

C-x r b *bookmark* RET
> Jump to the bookmark named *bookmark* (bookmark-jump).

C-x r l   List all bookmarks (list-bookmarks).

M-x bookmark-save
> Save all the current bookmark values in the default bookmark file.

The prototypical use for bookmarks is to record one current position in each of several files. So the command C-x r m, which sets a bookmark, uses the visited file name as the default for the bookmark name. If you name each bookmark after the file it points to, then you can conveniently revisit any of those files with C-x r b, and move to the position of the bookmark at the same time.

To display a list of all your bookmarks in a separate buffer, type C-x r l (list-bookmarks). If you switch to that buffer, you can use it to edit your bookmark definitions or annotate the bookmarks. Type C-h m in the bookmark buffer for more information about its special editing commands.

When you kill Emacs, Emacs offers to save your bookmark values in your default bookmark file, '~/.emacs.bmk', if you have changed any bookmark values. You can also save the bookmarks at any time with the M-x bookmark-save command. The bookmark commands load your default bookmark file automatically. This saving and loading is how bookmarks persist from one Emacs session to the next.

If you set the variable bookmark-save-flag to 1, then each command that sets a bookmark will also save your bookmarks; this way, you don't lose any bookmark values even if Emacs crashes. (The value, if a number, says how many bookmark modifications should go by between saving.)

Bookmark position values are saved with surrounding context, so that bookmark-jump can find the proper position even if the file is modified slightly. The variable bookmark-search-size says how many characters of context to record on each side of the bookmark's position.

Here are some additional commands for working with bookmarks:

M-x bookmark-load RET *filename* RET

> Load a file named *filename* that contains a list of bookmark values. You can use this command, as well as bookmark-write, to work with other files of bookmark values in addition to your default bookmark file.

M-x bookmark-write RET *filename* RET

> Save all the current bookmark values in the file *filename*.

M-x bookmark-delete RET *bookmark* RET

> Delete the bookmark named *bookmark*.

M-x bookmark-insert-location RET *bookmark* RET

> Insert in the buffer the name of the file that bookmark *bookmark* points to.

M-x bookmark-insert RET *bookmark* RET

> Insert in the buffer the *contents* of the file that bookmark *bookmark* points to.

11 Controlling the Display

Since only part of a large buffer fits in the window, Emacs tries to show a part that is likely to be interesting. Display-control commands allow you to specify which part of the text you want to see, and how to display it. Many variables also affect the details of redisplay. Unless otherwise stated, the variables described in this chapter have their effect by customizing redisplay itself; therefore, their values only make a difference at the time of redisplay.

11.1 Scrolling

If a buffer contains text that is too large to fit entirely within a window that is displaying the buffer, Emacs shows a contiguous portion of the text. The portion shown always contains point.

Scrolling means moving text up or down in the window so that different parts of the text are visible. Scrolling "forward" or "up" means that text moves up, and new text appears at the bottom. Scrolling "backward" or "down" moves text down, and new text appears at the top.

Scrolling happens automatically if you move point past the bottom or top of the window. You can also scroll explicitly with the commands in this section.

C-l   Clear screen and redisplay, scrolling the selected window to center point vertically within it (`recenter`).

C-v   Scroll forward (a windowful or a specified number of lines) (`scroll-up`).

NEXT
PAGEDOWN
            Likewise, scroll forward.

M-v   Scroll backward (`scroll-down`).

PRIOR
PAGEUP   Likewise, scroll backward.

arg C-l   Scroll so point is on line *arg* (`recenter`).

C-M-l   Scroll heuristically to bring useful information onto the screen (`reposition-window`).

The most basic scrolling command is C-l (`recenter`) with no argument. It scrolls the selected window so that point is halfway down from the top of the window. On a text terminal, it also clears the screen and redisplays all windows. That is useful in case the screen is garbled (see Section 33.2.3 [Screen Garbled], page 443).

To read the buffer a windowful at a time, use C-v (`scroll-up`) with no argument. This scrolls forward by nearly the whole window height. The effect is to take the two lines at the bottom of the window and put them at the top, followed by nearly a whole windowful of lines that were not previously visible. If point was in the text that scrolled off the top, it ends up at the new top of the window.

M-v (`scroll-down`) with no argument scrolls backward in a similar way, also with overlap. The number of lines of overlap that the C-v or M-v commands leave is controlled by the variable `next-screen-context-lines`; by default, it is 2. The function keys NEXT and PRIOR, or PAGEDOWN and PAGEUP, are equivalent to C-v and M-v.

The commands C-v and M-v with a numeric argument scroll the text in the selected window up or down a few lines. C-v with an argument moves the text and point up, together, that many lines; it brings the same number of new lines into view at the bottom of the window. M-v with numeric argument scrolls the text downward, bringing that many new lines into view at the top of the window. C-v with a negative argument is like M-v and vice versa.

The names of scroll commands are based on the direction that the text moves in the window. Thus, the command to scroll forward is called `scroll-up` because it moves the text upward on the screen. The keys PAGEDOWN and PAGEUP derive their names and customary meanings from a different convention that developed elsewhere; hence the strange result that PAGEDOWN runs `scroll-up`.

Some users like the full-screen scroll commands to keep point at the same screen line. To enable this behavior, set the variable `scroll-preserve-screen-position` to a non-`nil` value. In this mode, when these commands would scroll the text around point off the screen, or within `scroll-margin` lines of the edge, they move point to keep the same vertical position within the window. This mode is convenient for browsing through a file by scrolling by screenfuls; if you come back to the screen where you started, point goes back to the line where it started. However, this mode is inconvenient when you move to the next screen in order to move point to the text there.

Another way to do scrolling is with C-l with a numeric argument. C-l does not clear the screen when given an argument; it only scrolls the selected window. With a positive argument n, it repositions text to put point n lines down from the top. An argument of zero puts point on the very top line. Point does not move with respect to the text; rather, the text and point move rigidly on the screen. C-l with a negative argument puts point that many lines from the bottom of the window. For example, C-u - 1 C-l puts point on the bottom line, and C-u - 5 C-l puts it five lines from the bottom. C-u C-l scrolls to put point at the center (vertically) of the selected window.

The C-M-l command (`reposition-window`) scrolls the current window heuristically in a way designed to get useful information onto the screen. For example, in a Lisp file, this command tries to get the entire current defun onto the screen if possible.

11.2 Automatic Scrolling

Redisplay scrolls the buffer automatically when point moves out of the visible portion of the text. The purpose of automatic scrolling is to make point visible, but you can customize many aspects of how this is done.

Normally, automatic scrolling centers point vertically within the window. However, if you set `scroll-conservatively` to a small number n, then if you move point just a little off the screen—less than n lines—then Emacs scrolls the text just far enough to bring point back on screen. By default, `scroll-conservatively` is 0.

When the window does scroll by a longer distance, you can control how aggressively it scrolls, by setting the variables `scroll-up-aggressively` and `scroll-down-aggressively`. The value of `scroll-up-aggressively` should be either `nil`, or a fraction f between 0 and 1. A fraction specifies where on the screen to put point when scrolling upward. More precisely, when a window scrolls up because point is above the window start, the new start position is chosen to put point f part of the window height from the top. The larger f, the more aggressive the scrolling.

`nil`, which is the default, scrolls to put point at the center. So it is equivalent to .5.

Likewise, `scroll-down-aggressively` is used for scrolling down. The value, f, specifies how far point should be placed from the bottom of the window; thus, as with `scroll-up-aggressively`, a larger value is more aggressive.

The variable `scroll-margin` restricts how close point can come to the top or bottom of a window. Its value is a number of screen lines; if point comes within that many lines of the top or bottom of the window, Emacs recenters the window. By default, `scroll-margin` is 0.

11.3 Horizontal Scrolling

Horizontal scrolling means shifting all the lines sideways within a window—so that some of the text near the left margin is not displayed at all. When the text in a window is scrolled horizontally, text lines are truncated rather than continued (see Section 11.16 [Line Truncation], page 84). Whenever a window shows truncated lines, Emacs automatically updates its horizontal scrolling whenever point moves off the left or right edge of the screen. You can also use these commands to do explicit horizontal scrolling.

C-x <   Scroll text in current window to the left (`scroll-left`).

C-x >   Scroll to the right (`scroll-right`).

The command C-x < (`scroll-left`) scrolls the selected window to the left by n columns with argument n. This moves part of the beginning of each line off the left edge of the window. With no argument, it scrolls by almost the full width of the window (two columns less, to be precise).

C-x > (`scroll-right`) scrolls similarly to the right. The window cannot be scrolled any farther to the right once it is displayed normally (with each line starting at the window's left margin); attempting to do so has no effect. This means that you don't have to calculate the argument precisely for C-x >; any sufficiently large argument will restore the normal display.

If you use those commands to scroll a window horizontally, that sets a lower bound for automatic horizontal scrolling. Automatic scrolling will continue to scroll the window, but never farther to the right than the amount you previously set by `scroll-left`.

The value of the variable `hscroll-margin` controls how close to the window's edges point is allowed to get before the window will be automatically scrolled. It is measured in columns. If the value is 5, then moving point within 5 columns of the edge causes horizontal scrolling away from that edge.

The variable `hscroll-step` determines how many columns to scroll the window when point gets too close to the edge. If it's zero, horizontal scrolling centers point horizontally within the window. If it's a positive integer, it specifies the number of columns to scroll by. If it's a floating-point number, it specifies the fraction of the window's width to scroll by. The default is zero.

To disable automatic horizontal scrolling, set the variable `auto-hscroll-mode` to `nil`.

11.4 Follow Mode

Follow mode is a minor mode that makes two windows, both showing the same buffer, scroll as a single tall "virtual window." To use Follow mode, go to a frame with just one window, split it into two side-by-side windows using `C-x 3`, and then type `M-x follow-mode`. From then on, you can edit the buffer in either of the two windows, or scroll either one; the other window follows it.

In Follow mode, if you move point outside the portion visible in one window and into the portion visible in the other window, that selects the other window—again, treating the two as if they were parts of one large window.

To turn off Follow mode, type `M-x follow-mode` a second time.

11.5 Using Multiple Typefaces

You can specify various styles for displaying text using *faces*. Each face can specify various *face attributes*, such as the font family, the height, weight and slant of the characters, the foreground and background color, and underlining or overlining. A face does not have to specify all of these attributes; often it inherits most of them from another face.

On graphical display, all the Emacs face attributes are meaningful. On a text-only terminal, only some of them work. Some text-only terminals support inverse video, bold, and underline attributes; some support colors. Text-only terminals generally do not support changing the height and width or the font family.

Emacs uses faces automatically for highlighting, through the work of Font Lock mode. See Section 11.7 [Font Lock], page 76, for more information about Font Lock mode and syntactic highlighting. You can print out the buffer with the highlighting that appears on your screen using the command `ps-print-buffer-with-faces`. See Section 31.5 [PostScript], page 392.

You control the appearance of a part of the text in the buffer by specifying the face or faces to use for it. The style of display used for any given character is determined by combining the attributes of all the applicable faces specified for that character. Any attribute that isn't specified by these faces is taken from the `default` face, whose attributes reflect the default settings of the frame itself.

Enriched mode, the mode for editing formatted text, includes several commands and menus for specifying faces for text in the buffer. See Section 22.12.4 [Format

Faces], page 238, for how to specify the font for text in the buffer. See Section 22.12.5 [Format Colors], page 239, for how to specify the foreground and background color.

To alter the appearance of a face, use the customization buffer. See Section 32.2.5 [Face Customization], page 413. You can also use X resources to specify attributes of particular faces (see Section D.1 [Resources], page 489). Alternatively, you can change the foreground and background colors of a specific face with M-x `set-face-foreground` and M-x `set-face-background`. These commands prompt in the minibuffer for a face name and a color name, with completion, and then set that face to use the specified color. Changing the colors of the `default` face also changes the foreground and background colors on all frames, both existing and those to be created in the future. (You can also set foreground and background colors for the current frame only; see Section 18.10 [Frame Parameters], page 180.)

If you want to alter the appearance of all Emacs frames, you need to customize the frame parameters in the variable `default-frame-alist`; see Section 18.5 [Creating Frames], page 177.

Emacs can correctly display variable-width fonts, but Emacs commands that calculate width and indentation do not know how to calculate variable widths. This can sometimes lead to incorrect results when you use variable-width fonts. In particular, indentation commands can give inconsistent results, so we recommend you avoid variable-width fonts for editing program source code. Filling will sometimes make lines too long or too short. We plan to address these issues in future Emacs versions.

11.6 Standard Faces

To see what faces are currently defined, and what they look like, type M-x `list-faces-display`. It's possible for a given face to look different in different frames; this command shows the appearance in the frame in which you type it. With a prefix argument, this prompts for a regular expression, and displays only faces with names matching that regular expression.

Here are the standard faces for specifying text appearance. You can apply them to specific text when you want the effects they produce.

default   This face is used for ordinary text that doesn't specify any face.

bold   This face uses a bold variant of the default font, if it has one. It's up to you to choose a default font that has a bold variant, if you want to use one.

italic   This face uses an italic variant of the default font, if it has one.

bold-italic
             This face uses a bold italic variant of the default font, if it has one.

underline   This face underlines text.

fixed-pitch
             This face forces use of a particular fixed-width font.

`variable-pitch`

> This face forces use of a particular variable-width font. It's reasonable to customize this face to use a different variable-width font, if you like, but you should not make it a fixed-width font.

`shadow`
> This face is used for making the text less noticeable than the surrounding ordinary text. Usually this can be achieved by using shades of gray in contrast with either black or white default foreground color.

Here's an incomplete list of faces used to highlight parts of the text temporarily for specific purposes. (Many other modes define their own faces for this purpose.)

`highlight`
> This face is used for highlighting portions of text, in various modes. For example, mouse-sensitive text is highlighted using this face.

`isearch`
> This face is used for highlighting the current Isearch match.

`query-replace`
> This face is used for highlighting the current Query Replace match.

`lazy-highlight`

> This face is used for lazy highlighting of Isearch and Query Replace matches other than the current one.

`region`
> This face is used for displaying a selected region (when Transient Mark mode is enabled—see below).

`secondary-selection`

> This face is used for displaying a secondary X selection (see Section 18.1.4 [Secondary Selection], page 174).

`trailing-whitespace`

> The face for highlighting excess spaces and tabs at the end of a line when `show-trailing-whitespace` is non-`nil`; see Section 11.11 [Useless Whitespace], page 80.

`nobreak-space`

> The face for displaying the character "nobreak space."

`escape-glyph`

> The face for highlighting the '\' or '^' that indicates a control character. It's also used when '\' indicates a nobreak space or nobreak (soft) hyphen.

When Transient Mark mode is enabled, the text of the region is highlighted when the mark is active. This uses the face named `region`; you can control the style of highlighting by changing the style of this face (see Section 32.2.5 [Face Customization], page 413). See Section 8.2 [Transient Mark], page 50, for more information about Transient Mark mode and activation and deactivation of the mark.

These faces control the appearance of parts of the Emacs frame. They exist as faces to provide a consistent way to customize the appearance of these parts of the frame.

mode-line
modeline   This face is used for the mode line of the currently selected window,
              and for menu bars when toolkit menus are not used. By default, it's
              drawn with shadows for a "raised" effect on graphical displays, and
              drawn as the inverse of the default face on non-windowed terminals.
              modeline is an alias for the mode-line face, for compatibility with
              old Emacs versions.

mode-line-inactive
              Like mode-line, but used for mode lines of the windows other than the
              selected one (if mode-line-in-non-selected-windows is non-nil).
              This face inherits from mode-line, so changes in that face affect mode
              lines in all windows.

mode-line-highlight
              Like highlight, but used for portions of text on mode lines.

mode-line-buffer-id
              This face is used for buffer identification parts in the mode line.

header-line
              Similar to mode-line for a window's header line, which appears at the
              top of a window just as the mode line appears at the bottom. Most
              windows do not have a header line—only some special modes, such
              Info mode, create one.

vertical-border
              This face is used for the vertical divider between windows. By default
              this face inherits from the mode-line-inactive face on character ter-
              minals. On graphical displays the foreground color of this face is used
              for the vertical line between windows without scrollbars.

minibuffer-prompt
              This face is used for the prompt strings displayed in the minibuf-
              fer. By default, Emacs automatically adds this face to the value of
              minibuffer-prompt-properties, which is a list of text properties
              used to display the prompt text. (This variable takes effect when you
              enter the minibuffer.)

fringe   The face for the fringes to the left and right of windows on graphic
              displays. (The fringes are the narrow portions of the Emacs frame
              between the text area and the window's right and left borders.) See
              Section 11.9 [Fringes], page 79.

scroll-bar
              This face determines the visual appearance of the scroll bar. See Sec-
              tion 18.11 [Scroll Bars], page 181.

border   This face determines the color of the frame border.

cursor   This face determines the color of the cursor.

mouse   This face determines the color of the mouse pointer.

tool-bar   This face determines the color of tool bar icons. See Section 18.15
               [Tool Bars], page 183.

tooltip   This face is used for tooltips. See Section 18.17 [Tooltips], page 184.

menu   This face determines the colors and font of Emacs's menus. See Sec-
               tion 18.14 [Menu Bars], page 183. Setting the font of LessTif/Motif
               menus is currently not supported; attempts to set the font are ignored
               in this case. Likewise, attempts to customize this face in Emacs built
               with GTK and in the MS-Windows/Mac ports are ignored by the re-
               spective GUI toolkits; you need to use system-wide styles and options
               to change the appearance of the menus.

11.7 Font Lock mode

Font Lock mode is a minor mode, always local to a particular buffer, which highlights
(or "fontifies") the buffer contents according to the syntax of the text you are editing. It can recognize comments and strings in most languages; in several languages,
it can also recognize and properly highlight various other important constructs—
for example, names of functions being defined or reserved keywords. Some special
modes, such as Occur mode and Info mode, have completely specialized ways of
assigning fonts for Font Lock mode.

Font Lock mode is turned on by default in all modes which support it. You can
toggle font-lock for each buffer with the command M-x font-lock-mode. Using a
positive argument unconditionally turns Font Lock mode on, and a negative or zero
argument turns it off.

If you do not wish Font Lock mode to be turned on by default, customize the
variable global-font-lock-mode using the Customize interface (see Section 32.2
[Easy Customization], page 408), or use the function global-font-lock-mode in
your '.emacs' file, like this:

    (global-font-lock-mode 0)

This variable, like all the variables that control Font Lock mode, take effect whenever
fontification is done; that is, potentially at any time.

If you have disabled Global Font Lock mode, you can still enable Font Lock
for specific major modes by adding the function turn-on-font-lock to the mode
hooks (see Section 32.3.2 [Hooks], page 418). For example, to enable Font Lock
mode for editing C files, you can do this:

    (add-hook 'c-mode-hook 'turn-on-font-lock)

Font Lock mode uses several specifically named faces to do its job, including
font-lock-string-face, font-lock-comment-face, and others. The easiest way
to find them all is to use M-x customize-group RET font-lock-faces RET. You
can then use that customization buffer to customize the appearance of these faces.
See Section 32.2.5 [Face Customization], page 413.

You can also customize these faces using M-x set-face-foreground or M-x
set-face-background. See Section 11.5 [Faces], page 72.

The variable `font-lock-maximum-decoration` specifies the preferred level of fontification, for modes that provide multiple levels. Level 1 is the least amount of fontification; some modes support levels as high as 3. The normal default is "as high as possible." You can specify an integer, which applies to all modes, or you can specify different numbers for particular major modes; for example, to use level 1 for C/C++ modes, and the default level otherwise, use this:

```
(setq font-lock-maximum-decoration
      '((c-mode . 1) (c++-mode . 1)))
```

Fontification can be too slow for large buffers, so you can suppress it for buffers above a certain size. The variable `font-lock-maximum-size` specifies a buffer size, beyond which buffer fontification is suppressed.

Comment and string fontification (or "syntactic" fontification) relies on analysis of the syntactic structure of the buffer text. For the sake of speed, some modes, including Lisp mode, rely on a special convention: an open-parenthesis or open-brace in the leftmost column always defines the beginning of a defun, and is thus always outside any string or comment. (See Section 23.2.1 [Left Margin Paren], page 251.) If you don't follow this convention, Font Lock mode can misfontify the text that follows an open-parenthesis or open-brace in the leftmost column that is inside a string or comment.

The variable `font-lock-beginning-of-syntax-function` (always buffer-local) specifies how Font Lock mode can find a position guaranteed to be outside any comment or string. In modes which use the leftmost column parenthesis convention, the default value of the variable is `beginning-of-defun`—that tells Font Lock mode to use the convention. If you set this variable to `nil`, Font Lock no longer relies on the convention. This avoids incorrect results, but the price is that, in some cases, fontification for a changed text must rescan buffer text from the beginning of the buffer. This can considerably slow down redisplay while scrolling, particularly if you are close to the end of a large buffer.

Font Lock highlighting patterns already exist for many modes, but you may want to fontify additional patterns. You can use the function `font-lock-add-keywords`, to add your own highlighting patterns for a particular mode. For example, to highlight 'FIXME:' words in C comments, use this:

```
(font-lock-add-keywords
 'c-mode
 '(("\\<\\(FIXME\\):" 1 font-lock-warning-face t)))
```

To remove keywords from the font-lock highlighting patterns, use the function `font-lock-remove-keywords`. See section "Search-based Fontification" in *The Emacs Lisp Reference Manual*, for documentation of the format of this list.

Fontifying large buffers can take a long time. To avoid large delays when a file is visited, Emacs fontifies only the visible portion of a buffer. As you scroll through the buffer, each portion that becomes visible is fontified as soon as it is displayed. The parts of the buffer that are not displayed are fontified "stealthily," in the background, i.e. when Emacs is idle. You can control this background fontification, also called *Just-In-Time* (or *JIT*) Lock, by customizing variables in the customization group 'jit-lock'. See Section 32.2.6 [Specific Customization], page 414.

11.8 Interactive Highlighting

Use M-x `highlight-changes-mode` to enable (or disable) Highlight Changes mode, a minor mode that uses faces (colors, typically) to indicate which parts of the buffer were changed most recently.

Hi Lock mode highlights text that matches regular expressions you specify. For example, you might wish to see all the references to a certain variable in a program source file, highlight certain parts in a voluminous output of some program, or make certain names stand out in an article. Use the M-x `hi-lock-mode` command to enable (or disable) Hi Lock mode. To enable Hi Lock mode for all buffers, use M-x `global-hi-lock-mode` or place `(global-hi-lock-mode 1)` in your '.emacs' file.

Hi Lock mode works like Font Lock mode (see Section 11.7 [Font Lock], page 76), except that you specify explicitly the regular expressions to highlight. You control them with these commands:

C-x w h *regexp* RET *face* RET

> Highlight text that matches *regexp* using face *face* (`highlight-regexp`). The highlighting will remain as long as the buffer is loaded. For example, to highlight all occurrences of the word "whim" using the default face (a yellow background) C-x w h whim RET RET. Any face can be used for highlighting, Hi Lock provides several of its own and these are pre-loaded into a history list. While being prompted for a face use M-p and M-n to cycle through them.

> You can use this command multiple times, specifying various regular expressions to highlight in different ways.

C-x w r *regexp* RET

> Unhighlight *regexp* (`unhighlight-regexp`).

> If you invoke this from the menu, you select the expression to unhighlight from a list. If you invoke this from the keyboard, you use the minibuffer. It will show the most recently added regular expression; use M-p to show the next older expression and M-n to select the next newer expression. (You can also type the expression by hand, with completion.) When the expression you want to unhighlight appears in the minibuffer, press RET to exit the minibuffer and unhighlight it.

C-x w l *regexp* RET *face* RET

> Highlight entire lines containing a match for *regexp*, using face *face* (`highlight-lines-matching-regexp`).

C-x w b

> Insert all the current highlighting regexp/face pairs into the buffer at point, with comment delimiters to prevent them from changing your program. (This key binding runs the `hi-lock-write-interactive-patterns` command.)

> These patterns are extracted from the comments, if appropriate, if you invoke M-x `hi-lock-find-patterns`, or if you visit the file while Hi Lock mode is enabled (since that runs `hi-lock-find-patterns`).

C-x w i   Extract regexp/face pairs from comments in the current buffer (`hi-lock-find-patterns`). Thus, you can enter patterns interactively with `highlight-regexp`, store them into the file with `hi-lock-write-interactive-patterns`, edit them (perhaps including different faces for different parenthesized parts of the match), and finally use this command (`hi-lock-find-patterns`) to have Hi Lock highlight the edited patterns.

The variable `hi-lock-file-patterns-policy` controls whether Hi Lock mode should automatically extract and highlight patterns found in a file when it is visited. Its value can be `nil` (never highlight), `t` (highlight the patterns), `ask` (query the user), or a function. If it is a function, `hi-lock-find-patterns` calls it with the patterns as argument; if the function returns non-`nil`, the patterns are used. The default is `nil`. Note that patterns are always highlighted if you call `hi-lock-find-patterns` directly, regardless of the value of this variable.

Also, `hi-lock-find-patterns` does nothing if the current major mode's symbol is a member of the list `hi-lock-exclude-modes`.

11.9 Window Fringes

On a graphical display, each Emacs window normally has narrow *fringes* on the left and right edges. The fringes display indications about the text in the window.

The most common use of the fringes is to indicate a continuation line, when one line of text is split into multiple lines on the screen. The left fringe shows a curving arrow for each screen line except the first, indicating that "this is not the real beginning." The right fringe shows a curving arrow for each screen line except the last, indicating that "this is not the real end."

The fringes indicate line truncation with short horizontal arrows meaning "there's more text on this line which is scrolled horizontally out of view;" clicking the mouse on one of the arrows scrolls the display horizontally in the direction of the arrow. The fringes can also indicate other things, such as empty lines, or where a program you are debugging is executing (see Section 24.6 [Debuggers], page 278).

You can enable and disable the fringes for all frames using `M-x fringe-mode`. To enable and disable the fringes for the selected frame, use `M-x set-fringe-style`.

11.10 Displaying Boundaries

On a graphical display, Emacs can indicate the buffer boundaries in the fringes. It indicates the first line and the last line with angle images in the fringes. This can be combined with up and down arrow images which say whether it is possible to scroll the window up and down.

The buffer-local variable `indicate-buffer-boundaries` controls how the buffer boundaries and window scrolling is indicated in the fringes. If the value is `left` or `right`, both angle and arrow bitmaps are displayed in the left or right fringe, respectively.

If value is an alist, each element (*indicator* . *position*) specifies the position of one of the indicators. The *indicator* must be one of `top`, `bottom`, `up`, `down`, or `t` which specifies the default position for the indicators not present in the alist. The *position* is one of `left`, `right`, or `nil` which specifies not to show this indicator.

For example, `((top . left) (t . right))` places the top angle bitmap in left fringe, the bottom angle bitmap in right fringe, and both arrow bitmaps in right fringe. To show just the angle bitmaps in the left fringe, but no arrow bitmaps, use `((top . left) (bottom . left))`.

The value of the variable `default-indicate-buffer-boundaries` is the default value for `indicate-buffer-boundaries` in buffers that do not override it.

11.11 Useless Whitespace

It is easy to leave unnecessary spaces at the end of a line, or empty lines at the end of a file, without realizing it. In most cases, this *trailing whitespace* has no effect, but there are special circumstances where it matters. It can also be a nuisance that the line has "changed," when the change is just spaces added or removed at the end.

You can make trailing whitespace at the end of a line visible on the screen by setting the buffer-local variable `show-trailing-whitespace` to `t`. Then Emacs displays trailing whitespace in the face `trailing-whitespace`.

This feature does not apply when point is at the end of the line containing the whitespace. Strictly speaking, that is "trailing whitespace" nonetheless, but displaying it specially in that case looks ugly while you are typing in new text. In this special case, the location of point is enough to show you that the spaces are present.

To delete all trailing whitespace within the current buffer's accessible portion (see Section 31.9 [Narrowing], page 396), type `M-x delete-trailing-whitespace RET`. (This command does not remove the form-feed characters.)

Emacs can indicate unused lines at the end of the window with a small image in the left fringe (see Section 11.9 [Fringes], page 79). The image appears for window lines that do not correspond to any buffer text. Blank lines at the end of the buffer then stand out because they do not have this image in the fringe.

To enable this feature, set the buffer-local variable `indicate-empty-lines` to a non-`nil` value. The default value of this variable is controlled by the variable `default-indicate-empty-lines`; by setting that variable, you can enable or disable this feature for all new buffers. (This feature currently doesn't work on text-only terminals.)

11.12 Selective Display

Emacs has the ability to hide lines indented more than a certain number of columns (you specify how many columns). You can use this to get an overview of a part of a program.

To hide lines in the current buffer, type C-x $ (set-selective-display) with a numeric argument n. Then lines with at least n columns of indentation disappear from the screen. The only indication of their presence is that three dots ('...') appear at the end of each visible line that is followed by one or more hidden ones.

The commands C-n and C-p move across the hidden lines as if they were not there.

The hidden lines are still present in the buffer, and most editing commands see them as usual, so you may find point in the middle of the hidden text. When this happens, the cursor appears at the end of the previous line, after the three dots. If point is at the end of the visible line, before the newline that ends it, the cursor appears before the three dots.

To make all lines visible again, type C-x $ with no argument.

If you set the variable selective-display-ellipses to nil, the three dots do not appear at the end of a line that precedes hidden lines. Then there is no visible indication of the hidden lines. This variable becomes local automatically when set.

See also Section 22.8 [Outline Mode], page 224 for another way to hide part of the text in a buffer.

11.13 Optional Mode Line Features

The buffer percentage *pos* indicates the percentage of the buffer above the top of the window. You can additionally display the size of the buffer by typing M-x size-indication-mode to turn on Size Indication mode. The size will be displayed immediately following the buffer percentage like this:

   POS of *SIZE*

Here *SIZE* is the human readable representation of the number of characters in the buffer, which means that 'k' for 10^3, 'M' for 10^6, 'G' for 10^9, etc., are used to abbreviate.

If you have narrowed the buffer (see Section 31.9 [Narrowing], page 396), the size of the accessible part of the buffer is shown.

The current line number of point appears in the mode line when Line Number mode is enabled. Use the command M-x line-number-mode to turn this mode on and off; normally it is on. The line number appears after the buffer percentage *pos*, with the letter 'L' to indicate what it is. See Section 32.1 [Minor Modes], page 406, for more information about minor modes and about how to use this command.

If you have narrowed the buffer (see Section 31.9 [Narrowing], page 396), the displayed line number is relative to the accessible portion of the buffer. Thus, it isn't suitable as an argument to goto-line. (Use what-line command to see the line number relative to the whole file.)

If the buffer is very large (larger than the value of line-number-display-limit), then the line number doesn't appear. Emacs doesn't compute the line number when the buffer is large, because that would be too slow. Set it to nil to remove the limit.

Line-number computation can also be slow if the lines in the buffer are too long. For this reason, Emacs normally doesn't display line numbers if the average width, in characters, of lines near point is larger than the value of the variable `line-number-display-limit-width`. The default value is 200 characters.

You can also display the current column number by turning on Column Number mode. It displays the current column number preceded by the letter 'C'. Type `M-x column-number-mode` to toggle this mode.

Emacs can optionally display the time and system load in all mode lines. To enable this feature, type `M-x display-time` or customize the option `display-time-mode`. The information added to the mode line usually appears after the buffer name, before the mode names and their parentheses. It looks like this:

   hh:*mm*pm *l.ll*

Here *hh* and *mm* are the hour and minute, followed always by 'am' or 'pm'. *l.ll* is the average number of running processes in the whole system recently. (Some fields may be missing if your operating system cannot support them.) If you prefer time display in 24-hour format, set the variable `display-time-24hr-format` to t.

The word 'Mail' appears after the load level if there is mail for you that you have not read yet. On a graphical display you can use an icon instead of 'Mail' by customizing `display-time-use-mail-icon`; this may save some space on the mode line. You can customize `display-time-mail-face` to make the mail indicator prominent. Use `display-time-mail-file` to specify the mail file to check, or set `display-time-mail-directory` to specify the directory to check for incoming mail (any nonempty regular file in the directory is considered as "newly arrived mail").

By default, the mode line is drawn on graphics displays with 3D-style highlighting, like that of a button when it is not being pressed. If you don't like this effect, you can disable the 3D highlighting of the mode line, by customizing the attributes of the `mode-line` face. See Section 32.2.5 [Face Customization], page 413.

By default, the mode line of nonselected windows is displayed in a different face, called `mode-line-inactive`. Only the selected window is displayed in the `mode-line` face. This helps show which window is selected. When the minibuffer is selected, since it has no mode line, the window from which you activated the minibuffer has its mode line displayed using `mode-line`; as a result, ordinary entry to the minibuffer does not change any mode lines.

You can disable use of `mode-line-inactive` by setting variable `mode-line-in-non-selected-windows` to `nil`; then all mode lines are displayed in the `mode-line` face.

You can customize the mode line display for each of the end-of-line formats by setting each of the variables `eol-mnemonic-unix`, `eol-mnemonic-dos`, `eol-mnemonic-mac`, and `eol-mnemonic-undecided` to the strings you prefer.

11.14 How Text Is Displayed

ASCII printing characters (octal codes 040 through 0176) in Emacs buffers are displayed with their graphics, as are non-ASCII multibyte printing characters (octal codes above 0400).

Some ASCII control characters are displayed in special ways. The newline character (octal code 012) is displayed by starting a new line. The tab character (octal code 011) is displayed by moving to the next tab stop column (normally every 8 columns).

Other ASCII control characters are normally displayed as a caret ('^') followed by the non-control version of the character; thus, control-A is displayed as '^A'. The caret appears in face escape-glyph.

Non-ASCII characters 0200 through 0237 (octal) are displayed with octal escape sequences; thus, character code 0230 (octal) is displayed as '\230'. The backslash appears in face escape-glyph.

If the variable ctl-arrow is nil, control characters in the buffer are displayed with octal escape sequences, except for newline and tab. Altering the value of ctl-arrow makes it local to the current buffer; until that time, the default value is in effect. The default is initially t.

The display of character codes 0240 through 0377 (octal) may be either as escape sequences or as graphics. They do not normally occur in multibyte buffers, but if they do, they are displayed as Latin-1 graphics. In unibyte mode, if you enable European display they are displayed using their graphics (assuming your terminal supports them), otherwise as escape sequences. See Section 19.18 [Unibyte Mode], page 204.

Some character sets define "no-break" versions of the space and hyphen characters, which are used where a line should not be broken. Emacs normally displays these characters with special faces (respectively, nobreak-space and escape-glyph) to distinguish them from ordinary spaces and hyphens. You can turn off this feature by setting the variable nobreak-char-display to nil. If you set the variable to any other value, that means to prefix these characters with an escape character.

Normally, a tab character in the buffer is displayed as whitespace which extends to the next display tab stop position, and display tab stops come at intervals equal to eight spaces. The number of spaces per tab is controlled by the variable tab-width, which is made local by changing it. Note that how the tab character in the buffer is displayed has nothing to do with the definition of TAB as a command. The variable tab-width must have an integer value between 1 and 1000, inclusive. The variable default-tab-width controls the default value of this variable for buffers where you have not set it locally.

You can customize the way any particular character code is displayed by means of a display table. See section "Display Tables" in *The Emacs Lisp Reference Manual*.

11.15 Displaying the Cursor

You can customize the cursor's color, and whether it blinks, using the cursor Custom group (see Section 32.2 [Easy Customization], page 408). On a graphical display, the command M-x blink-cursor-mode enables or disables the blinking of the cursor. (On text terminals, the terminal itself blinks the cursor, and Emacs has no control over it.) You can control how the cursor appears when it blinks off by setting the variable blink-cursor-alist.

Some text terminals offer two different cursors: the normal cursor and the very visible cursor, where the latter may be e.g. bigger or blinking. By default Emacs uses the very visible cursor, and switches to it when you start or resume Emacs. If the variable visible-cursor is nil when Emacs starts or resumes, it doesn't switch, so it uses the normal cursor.

Normally, the cursor appears in non-selected windows in the "off" state, with the same appearance as when the blinking cursor blinks "off." For a box cursor, this is a hollow box; for a bar cursor, this is a thinner bar. To turn off cursors in non-selected windows, customize the variable cursor-in-non-selected-windows and assign it a nil value.

On graphical displays, Emacs can optionally draw the block cursor as wide as the character under the cursor—for example, if the cursor is on a tab character, it would cover the full width occupied by that tab character. To enable this feature, set the variable x-stretch-cursor to a non-nil value.

To make the cursor even more visible, you can use HL Line mode, a minor mode that highlights the line containing point. Use M-x hl-line-mode to enable or disable it in the current buffer. M-x global-hl-line-mode enables or disables the same mode globally.

11.16 Truncation of Lines

As an alternative to continuation, Emacs can display long lines by *truncation*. This means that all the characters that do not fit in the width of the screen or window do not appear at all. On graphical displays, a small straight arrow in the fringe indicates truncation at either end of the line. On text-only terminals, '$' appears in the first column when there is text truncated to the left, and in the last column when there is text truncated to the right.

Horizontal scrolling automatically causes line truncation (see Section 11.3 [Horizontal Scrolling], page 71). You can explicitly enable line truncation for a particular buffer with the command M-x toggle-truncate-lines. This works by locally changing the variable truncate-lines. If that variable is non-nil, long lines are truncated; if it is nil, they are continued onto multiple screen lines. Setting the variable truncate-lines in any way makes it local to the current buffer; until that time, the default value is in effect. The default value is normally nil.

If the variable truncate-partial-width-windows is non-nil, it forces truncation rather than continuation in any window less than the full width of the screen or frame, regardless of the value of truncate-lines. For information about side-by-side windows, see Section 17.2 [Split Window], page 165. See also section "Display" in *The Emacs Lisp Reference Manual*.

If the variable overflow-newline-into-fringe is non-nil on a graphical display, then Emacs does not continue or truncate a line which is exactly as wide as the window. Instead, the newline overflows into the right fringe, and the cursor appears in the fringe when positioned on that newline.

11.17 Customization of Display

This section describes variables (see Section 32.3 [Variables], page 416) that you can change to customize how Emacs displays. Beginning users can skip it.

If the variable `inverse-video` is non-`nil`, Emacs attempts to invert all the lines of the display from what they normally are.

If the variable `visible-bell` is non-`nil`, Emacs attempts to make the whole screen blink when it would normally make an audible bell sound. This variable has no effect if your terminal does not have a way to make the screen blink.

The variable `echo-keystrokes` controls the echoing of multi-character keys; its value is the number of seconds of pause required to cause echoing to start, or zero, meaning don't echo at all. The value takes effect when there is someting to echo. See Section 1.2 [Echo Area], page 7.

The variable `baud-rate` holds the output speed of the terminal, as far as Emacs knows. Setting this variable does not change the speed of actual data transmission, but the value is used for calculations. On text-only terminals, it affects padding, and decisions about whether to scroll part of the screen or redraw it instead. It also affects the behavior of incremental search.

On graphical displays, `baud-rate` is only used to determine how frequently to look for pending input during display updating. A higher value of `baud-rate` means that check for pending input will be done less frequently.

On graphical display, Emacs can optionally display the mouse pointer in a special shape to say that Emacs is busy. To turn this feature on or off, customize the group `cursor`. You can also control the amount of time Emacs must remain busy before the busy indicator is displayed, by setting the variable `hourglass delay`.

On graphical display, this variables specifies the vertical position of an overline above the text, including the height of the overline itself (1 pixel). The default value is 2 pixels.

On graphical display, Emacs normally draws an underline at the baseline level of the font. If `x-underline-at-descent-line` is non-`nil`, Emacs draws the underline at the same height as the font's descent line.

On some text-only terminals, bold face and inverse video together result in text that is hard to read. Call the function `tty-suppress-bold-inverse-default-colors` with a non-`nil` argument to suppress the effect of bold-face in this case.

On a text-only terminal, when you reenter Emacs after suspending, Emacs normally clears the screen and redraws the entire display. On some terminals with more than one page of memory, it is possible to arrange the termcap entry so that the 'ti' and 'te' strings (output to the terminal when Emacs is entered and exited, respectively) switch between pages of memory so as to use one page for Emacs and another page for other output. On such terminals, you might want to set the variable `no-redraw-on-reenter` non-`nil`; this tells Emacs to assume, when resumed, that the screen page it is using still contains what Emacs last wrote there.

12 Searching and Replacement

Like other editors, Emacs has commands for searching for occurrences of a string. The principal search command is unusual in that it is *incremental*; it begins to search before you have finished typing the search string. There are also nonincremental search commands more like those of other editors.

Besides the usual `replace-string` command that finds all occurrences of one string and replaces them with another, Emacs has a more flexible replacement command called `query-replace`, which asks interactively which occurrences to replace. There are also commands to find and operate on all matches for a pattern.

You can also search multiple files under control of a tags table (see Section 25.3.6 [Tags Search], page 301) or through the Dired `A` command (see Section 29.7 [Operating on Files], page 344), or ask the `grep` program to do it (see Section 24.4 [Grep Searching], page 277).

12.1 Incremental Search

An incremental search begins searching as soon as you type the first character of the search string. As you type in the search string, Emacs shows you where the string (as you have typed it so far) would be found. When you have typed enough characters to identify the place you want, you can stop. Depending on what you plan to do next, you may or may not need to terminate the search explicitly with RET.

C-s   Incremental search forward (`isearch-forward`).

C-r   Incremental search backward (`isearch-backward`).

12.1.1 Basics of Incremental Search

C-s starts a forward incremental search. It reads characters from the keyboard, and moves point past the next occurrence of those characters. If you type C-s and then F, that puts the cursor after the first 'F' (the first following the starting point, since this is a forward search). Then if you type an O, you will see the cursor move to just after the first 'FO' (the 'F' in that 'FO' may or may not be the first 'F'). After another O, the cursor moves to just after the first 'FOO' after the place where you started the search. At each step, the buffer text that matches the search string is highlighted, if the terminal can do that; the current search string is always displayed in the echo area.

If you make a mistake in typing the search string, you can cancel characters with DEL. Each DEL cancels the last character of search string. This does not happen until Emacs is ready to read another input character; first it must either find, or fail to find, the character you want to erase. If you do not want to wait for this to happen, use C-g as described below.

When you are satisfied with the place you have reached, you can type RET, which stops searching, leaving the cursor where the search brought it. Also, any command not specially meaningful in searches stops the searching and is then executed. Thus, typing C-a would exit the search and then move to the beginning of the line. RET is necessary only if the next command you want to type is a printing character, DEL, RET, or another character that is special within searches (C-q, C-w, C-r, C-s, C-y, M-y, M-r, M-c, M-e, and some other meta-characters).

When you exit the incremental search, it sets the mark where point *was* before the search. That is convenient for moving back there. In Transient Mark mode, incremental search sets the mark without activating it, and does so only if the mark is not already active.

12.1.2 Repeating Incremental Search

Sometimes you search for 'FOO' and find one, but not the one you expected to find. There was a second 'FOO' that you forgot about, before the one you were aiming for. In this event, type another C-s to move to the next occurrence of the search string. You can repeat this any number of times. If you overshoot, you can cancel some C-s characters with DEL.

After you exit a search, you can search for the same string again by typing just C-s C-s: the first C-s is the key that invokes incremental search, and the second C-s means "search again."

If a search is failing and you ask to repeat it by typing another C-s, it starts again from the beginning of the buffer. Repeating a failing reverse search with C-r starts again from the end. This is called *wrapping around*, and 'Wrapped' appears in the search prompt once this has happened. If you keep on going past the original starting point of the search, it changes to 'Overwrapped', which means that you are revisiting matches that you have already seen.

To reuse earlier search strings, use the *search ring*. The commands M-p and M-n move through the ring to pick a search string to reuse. These commands leave the selected search ring element in the minibuffer, where you can edit it. To edit the current search string in the minibuffer without replacing it with items from the search ring, type M-e. Type C-s or C-r to terminate editing the string and search for it.

You can change to searching backwards with C-r. For instance, if you are searching forward but you realize you were looking for something above the starting point, you can do this. Repeated C-r keeps looking for more occurrences backwards. A C-s starts going forwards again. C-r in a search can be canceled with DEL.

If you know initially that you want to search backwards, you can use C-r instead of C-s to start the search, because C-r as a key runs a command (isearch-backward) to search backward. A backward search finds matches that end before the starting point, just as a forward search finds matches that begin after it.

12.1.3 Errors in Incremental Search

If your string is not found at all, the echo area says 'Failing I-Search'. The cursor is after the place where Emacs found as much of your string as it could. Thus, if you search for 'FOOT', and there is no 'FOOT', you might see the cursor after the 'FOO' in 'FOOL'. At this point there are several things you can do. If your string was mistyped, you can rub some of it out and correct it. If you like the place you have found, you can type RET or some other Emacs command to remain there. Or you can type C-g, which removes from the search string the characters that could not be found (the 'T' in 'FOOT'), leaving those that were found (the 'FOO' in 'FOOT'). A second C-g at that point cancels the search entirely, returning point to where it was when the search started.

The C-g "quit" character does special things during searches; just what it does depends on the status of the search. If the search has found what you specified and is waiting for input, C-g cancels the entire search. The cursor moves back to where you started the search. If C-g is typed when there are characters in the search string that have not been found—because Emacs is still searching for them, or because it has failed to find them—then the search string characters which have not been found are discarded from the search string. With them gone, the search is now successful and waiting for more input, so a second C-g will cancel the entire search.

12.1.4 Special Input for Incremental Search

An upper-case letter in the search string makes the search case-sensitive. If you delete the upper-case character from the search string, it ceases to have this effect. See Section 12.8 [Search Case], page 98.

To search for a newline, type C-j. To search for another control character, such as control-S or carriage return, you must quote it by typing C-q first. This function of C-q is analogous to its use for insertion (see Section 4.1 [Inserting Text], page 20): it causes the following character to be treated the way any "ordinary" character is treated in the same context. You can also specify a character by its octal code: enter C-q followed by a sequence of octal digits.

M-% typed in incremental search invokes `query-replace` or `query-replace-regexp` (depending on search mode) with the current search string used as the string to replace. See Section 12.9.4 [Query Replace], page 101.

Entering RET when the search string is empty launches nonincremental search (see Section 12.2 [Nonincremental Search], page 90).

To customize the special characters that incremental search understands, alter their bindings in the keymap `isearch-mode-map`. For a list of bindings, look at the documentation of `isearch-mode` with C-h f isearch-mode RET.

12.1.5 Isearch for Non-ASCII Characters

To enter non-ASCII characters in an incremental search, you can use C-q (see the previous section), but it is easier to use an input method (see Section 19.4 [Input Methods], page 190). If an input method is enabled in the current buffer when you start the search, you can use it in the search string also. Emacs indicates that by including the input method mnemonic in its prompt, like this:

    I-search [*im*]:

where *im* is the mnemonic of the active input method.

You can toggle (enable or disable) the input method while you type the search string with C-\ (`isearch-toggle-input-method`). You can turn on a certain (non-default) input method with C-^ (`isearch-toggle-specified-input-method`), which prompts for the name of the input method. The input method you enable during incremental search remains enabled in the current buffer afterwards.

12.1.6 Isearch Yanking

The characters C-w and C-y can be used in incremental search to grab text from the buffer into the search string. This makes it convenient to search for another occurrence of text at point. C-w copies the character or word after point as part of the search string, advancing point over it. (The decision, whether to copy a character or a word, is heuristic.) Another C-s to repeat the search will then search for a string including that character or word.

C-y is similar to C-w but copies all the rest of the current line into the search string. If point is already at the end of a line, it grabs the entire next line. Both C-y and C-w convert the text they copy to lower case if the search is currently not case-sensitive; this is so the search remains case-insensitive.

C-M-w and C-M-y modify the search string by only one character at a time: C-M-w deletes the last character from the search string and C-M-y copies the character after point to the end of the search string. An alternative method to add the character after point into the search string is to enter the minibuffer by M-e and to type C-f at the end of the search string in the minibuffer.

The character M-y copies text from the kill ring into the search string. It uses the same text that C-y as a command would yank. Mouse-2 in the echo area does the same. See Section 9.2 [Yanking], page 58.

12.1.7 Lazy Search Highlighting

When you pause for a little while during incremental search, it highlights all other possible matches for the search string. This makes it easier to anticipate where you can get to by typing C-s or C-r to repeat the search. The short delay before highlighting other matches helps indicate which match is the current one. If you don't like this feature, you can turn it off by setting isearch-lazy-highlight to nil.

You can control how this highlighting looks by customizing the faces isearch (used for the current match) and lazy-highlight (for all the other matches).

12.1.8 Scrolling During Incremental Search

You can enable the use of vertical scrolling during incremental search (without exiting the search) by setting the customizable variable isearch-allow-scroll to a non-nil value. This applies to using the vertical scroll-bar and to certain keyboard commands such as PRIOR (scroll-down), NEXT (scroll-up) and C-l (recenter). You must run these commands via their key sequences to stay in the search—typing M-x will terminate the search. You can give prefix arguments to these commands in the usual way.

This feature won't let you scroll the current match out of visibility, however.

The feature also affects some other commands, such as C-x 2 (split-window-vertically) and C-x ^ (enlarge-window) which don't exactly scroll but do affect where the text appears on the screen. In general, it applies to any command whose name has a non-nil isearch-scroll property. So you can control which commands are affected by changing these properties.

For example, to make C-h l usable within an incremental search in all future Emacs sessions, use C-h c to find what command it runs. (You type C-h c C-h l; it says view-lossage.) Then you can put the following line in your '.emacs' file (see Section 32.6 [Init File], page 133):

```
(put 'view-lossage 'isearch-scroll t)
```

This feature can be applied to any command that doesn't permanently change point, the buffer contents, the match data, the current buffer, or the selected window and frame. The command must not itself attempt an incremental search.

12.1.9 Slow Terminal Incremental Search

Incremental search on a slow terminal uses a modified style of display that is designed to take less time. Instead of redisplaying the buffer at each place the search gets to, it creates a new single-line window and uses that to display the line that the search has found. The single-line window comes into play as soon as point moves outside of the text that is already on the screen.

When you terminate the search, the single-line window is removed. Emacs then redisplays the window in which the search was done, to show its new position of point.

The slow terminal style of display is used when the terminal baud rate is less than or equal to the value of the variable search-slow-speed, initially 1200. See also the discussion of the variable baud-rate (see [Customization of Display], page 85).

The number of lines to use in slow terminal search display is controlled by the variable search-slow-window-lines. Its normal value is 1.

12.2 Nonincremental Search

Emacs also has conventional nonincremental search commands, which require you to type the entire search string before searching begins.

C-s RET *string* RET
> Search for *string*.

C-r RET *string* RET
> Search backward for *string*.

To do a nonincremental search, first type C-s RET. This enters the minibuffer to read the search string; terminate the string with RET, and then the search takes place. If the string is not found, the search command signals an error.

When you type C-s RET, the C-s invokes incremental search as usual. That command is specially programmed to invoke nonincremental search, search-forward, if the string you specify is empty. (Such an empty argument would otherwise be useless.) But it does not call search-forward right away. First it checks the next input character to see if is C-w, which specifies a word search. C-r RET does likewise, for a reverse incremental search.

Forward and backward nonincremental searches are implemented by the commands search-forward and search-backward. These commands may be bound to keys in the usual manner. The feature that you can get to them via the incremental search commands exists for historical reasons, and to avoid the need to find separate key sequences for them.

12.3 Word Search

Word search searches for a sequence of words without regard to how the words are separated. More precisely, you type a string of many words, using single spaces to separate them, and the string can be found even if there are multiple spaces, newlines, or other punctuation characters between these words.

Word search is useful for editing a printed document made with a text formatter. If you edit while looking at the printed, formatted version, you can't tell where the line breaks are in the source file. With word search, you can search without having to know them.

C-s RET C-w *words* RET
>   Search for *words*, ignoring details of punctuation.

C-r RET C-w *words* RET
>   Search backward for *words*, ignoring details of punctuation.

Word search as a special case of nonincremental search is invoked with C-s RET C-w. This is followed by the search string, which must always be terminated with RET. Being nonincremental, this search does not start until the argument is terminated. It works by constructing a regular expression and searching for that; see Section 12.4 [Regexp Search], page 91.

Use C-r RET C-w to do backward word search.

You can also invoke word search with C-s M-e C-w or C-r M-e C-w followed by the search string and terminated with RET, C-s or C-r. This puts word search into incremental mode where you can use all keys available for incremental search. However, when you type more words in incremental word search, it will fail until you type complete words.

Forward and backward word searches are implemented by the commands word-search-forward and word-search-backward. These commands may be bound to keys in the usual manner. They are available via the incremental search commands both for historical reasons and to avoid the need to find separate key sequences for them.

12.4 Regular Expression Search

A *regular expression* (*regexp*, for short) is a pattern that denotes a class of alternative strings to match, possibly infinitely many. GNU Emacs provides both incremental and nonincremental ways to search for a match for a regexp. The syntax of regular expressions is explained in the following section.

Incremental search for a regexp is done by typing C-M-s (isearch-forward-regexp), by invoking C-s with a prefix argument (whose value does not matter), or by typing M-r within a forward incremental search. This command reads a search string incrementally just like C-s, but it treats the search string as a regexp rather than looking for an exact match against the text in the buffer. Each time you add text to the search string, you make the regexp longer, and the new regexp is searched for. To search backward for a regexp, use C-M-r (`isearch-backward-regexp`), C-r with a prefix argument, or M-r within a backward incremental search.

All of the control characters that do special things within an ordinary incremental search have the same function in incremental regexp search. Typing C-s or C-r immediately after starting the search retrieves the last incremental search regexp used; that is to say, incremental regexp and non-regexp searches have independent defaults. They also have separate search rings that you can access with M-p and M-n.

If you type SPC in incremental regexp search, it matches any sequence of whitespace characters, including newlines. If you want to match just a space, type C-q SPC. You can control what a bare space matches by setting the variable `search-whitespace-regexp` to the desired regexp.

In some cases, adding characters to the regexp in an incremental regexp search can make the cursor move back and start again. For example, if you have searched for 'foo' and you add '\|bar', the cursor backs up in case the first 'bar' precedes the first 'foo'.

Forward and backward regexp search are not symmetrical, because regexp matching in Emacs always operates forward, starting with the beginning of the regexp. Thus, forward regexp search scans forward, trying a forward match at each possible starting position. Backward regexp search scans backward, trying a forward match at each possible starting position. These search methods are not mirror images.

Nonincremental search for a regexp is done by the functions `re-search-forward` and `re-search-backward`. You can invoke these with M-x, or bind them to keys, or invoke them by way of incremental regexp search with C-M-s RET and C-M-r RET.

If you use the incremental regexp search commands with a prefix argument, they perform ordinary string search, like `isearch-forward` and `isearch-backward`. See Section 12.1 [Incremental Search], page 86.

12.5 Syntax of Regular Expressions

This manual describes regular expression features that users typically want to use. There are additional features that are mainly used in Lisp programs; see section "Regular Expressions" in *The Emacs Lisp Reference Manual*.

Regular expressions have a syntax in which a few characters are special constructs and the rest are *ordinary*. An ordinary character is a simple regular expression which matches that same character and nothing else. The special characters are '$', '^', '.', '*', '+', '?', '[', and '\'. The character ']' is special if it ends a character alternative (see later). The character '-' is special inside a character alternative. Any other character appearing in a regular expression is ordinary, unless a '\' precedes it. (When you use regular expressions in a Lisp program, each '\' must be doubled, see the example near the end of this section.)

For example, 'f' is not a special character, so it is ordinary, and therefore 'f' is a regular expression that matches the string 'f' and no other string. (It does *not* match the string 'ff'.) Likewise, 'o' is a regular expression that matches only 'o'. (When case distinctions are being ignored, these regexps also match 'F' and 'O', but we consider this a generalization of "the same string," rather than an exception.)

Any two regular expressions *a* and *b* can be concatenated. The result is a regular expression which matches a string if *a* matches some amount of the beginning of that string and *b* matches the rest of the string.

As a simple example, we can concatenate the regular expressions 'f' and 'o' to get the regular expression 'fo', which matches only the string 'fo'. Still trivial. To do something nontrivial, you need to use one of the special characters. Here is a list of them.

. (Period)   is a special character that matches any single character except a newline. Using concatenation, we can make regular expressions like 'a.b', which matches any three-character string that begins with 'a' and ends with 'b'.

*   is not a construct by itself; it is a postfix operator that means to match the preceding regular expression repetitively as many times as possible. Thus, 'o*' matches any number of 'o's (including no 'o's).

'*' always applies to the *smallest* possible preceding expression. Thus, 'fo*' has a repeating 'o', not a repeating 'fo'. It matches 'f', 'fo', 'foo', and so on.

The matcher processes a '*' construct by matching, immediately, as many repetitions as can be found. Then it continues with the rest of the pattern. If that fails, backtracking occurs, discarding some of the matches of the '*'-modified construct in case that makes it possible to match the rest of the pattern. For example, in matching 'ca*ar' against the string 'caaar', the 'a*' first tries to match all three 'a's; but the rest of the pattern is 'ar' and there is only 'r' left to match, so this try fails. The next alternative is for 'a*' to match only two 'a's. With this choice, the rest of the regexp matches successfully.

\+   is a postfix operator, similar to '*' except that it must match the preceding expression at least once. So, for example, 'ca+r' matches the strings 'car' and 'caaaar' but not the string 'cr', whereas 'ca*r' matches all three strings.

?   is a postfix operator, similar to '*' except that it can match the preceding expression either once or not at all. For example, 'ca?r' matches 'car' or 'cr'; nothing else.

?, +?, ?? are non-greedy variants of the operators above. The normal operators '', '+', '?' are *greedy* in that they match as much as they can, as long as the overall regexp can still match. With a following '?', they are non-greedy: they will match as little as possible.

Thus, both 'ab*' and 'ab*?' can match the string 'a' and the string 'abbbb'; but if you try to match them both against the text 'abbb', 'ab*' will match it all (the longest valid match), while 'ab*?' will match just 'a' (the shortest valid match).

Non-greedy operators match the shortest possible string starting at a given starting point; in a forward search, though, the earliest possible starting point for match is always the one chosen. Thus, if you search for 'a.*?$' against the text 'abbab' followed by a newline, it matches the whole string. Since it *can* match starting at the first 'a', it does.

\{*n*\}   is a postfix operator that specifies repetition *n* times—that is, the preceding regular expression must match exactly *n* times in a row. For example, 'x\{4\}' matches the string 'xxxx' and nothing else.

\{*n*,*m*\}   is a postfix operator that specifies repetition between *n* and *m* times— that is, the preceding regular expression must match at least *n* times, but no more than *m* times. If *m* is omitted, then there is no upper limit, but the preceding regular expression must match at least *n* times. '\{0,1\}' is equivalent to '?'.
'\{0,\}' is equivalent to '*'.
'\{1,\}' is equivalent to '+'.

[...]   is a *character set*, which begins with '[' and is terminated by ']'. In the simplest case, the characters between the two brackets are what this set can match.

Thus, '[ad]' matches either one 'a' or one 'd', and '[ad]*' matches any string composed of just 'a's and 'd's (including the empty string), from which it follows that 'c[ad]*r' matches 'cr', 'car', 'cdr', 'caddaar', etc.

You can also include character ranges in a character set, by writing the starting and ending characters with a '-' between them. Thus, '[a-z]' matches any lower-case ASCII letter. Ranges may be intermixed freely with individual characters, as in '[a-z$%.]', which matches any lower-case ASCII letter or '$', '%' or period.

Note that the usual regexp special characters are not special inside a character set. A completely different set of special characters exists inside character sets: ']', '-' and '^'.

To include a ']' in a character set, you must make it the first character. For example, '[]a]' matches ']' or 'a'. To include a '-', write '-' as the first or last character of the set, or put it after a range. Thus, '[]-]' matches both ']' and '-'.

To include '^' in a set, put it anywhere but at the beginning of the set. (At the beginning, it complements the set—see below.)

When you use a range in case-insensitive search, you should write both ends of the range in upper case, or both in lower case, or both should be non-letters. The behavior of a mixed-case range such as 'A-z' is somewhat ill-defined, and it may change in future Emacs versions.

[^ ...]   '[^' begins a *complemented character set*, which matches any char-
            acter except the ones specified. Thus, '[^a-z0-9A-Z]' matches all
            characters *except* ASCII letters and digits.

            '^' is not special in a character set unless it is the first character. The
            character following the '^' is treated as if it were first (in other words,
            '-' and ']' are not special there).

            A complemented character set can match a newline, unless newline is
            mentioned as one of the characters not to match. This is in contrast
            to the handling of regexps in programs such as `grep`.

^   is a special character that matches the empty string, but only at the
            beginning of a line in the text being matched. Otherwise it fails to
            match anything. Thus, '^foo' matches a 'foo' that occurs at the
            beginning of a line.

            For historical compatibility reasons, '^' can be used with this meaning
            only at the beginning of the regular expression, or after '\(' or '\|'.

$ is similar to '^' but matches only at the end of a line. Thus, 'x+$'
            matches a string of one 'x' or more at the end of a line.

            For historical compatibility reasons, '$' can be used with this meaning
            only at the end of the regular expression, or before '\)' or '\|'.

\   has two functions: it quotes the special characters (including '\'), and
            it introduces additional special constructs.

            Because '\' quotes special characters, '\$' is a regular expression that
            matches only '$', and '\[' is a regular expression that matches only
            '[', and so on.

            See the following section for the special constructs that begin with '\'.

Note: for historical compatibility, special characters are treated as ordinary ones
if they are in contexts where their special meanings make no sense. For example,
'*foo' treats '*' as ordinary since there is no preceding expression on which the '*'
can act. It is poor practice to depend on this behavior; it is better to quote the
special character anyway, regardless of where it appears.

As a '\' is not special inside a character alternative, it can never remove the
special meaning of '-' or ']'. So you should not quote these characters when they
have no special meaning either. This would not clarify anything, since backslashes
can legitimately precede these characters where they *have* special meaning, as in
'[^\]' ("[^\\]" for Lisp string syntax), which matches any single character except
a backslash.

12.6 Backslash in Regular Expressions

For the most part, '\' followed by any character matches only that character. However, there are several exceptions: two-character sequences starting with '\' that
have special meanings. The second character in the sequence is always an ordinary
character when used on its own. Here is a table of '\' constructs.

\|

specifies an alternative. Two regular expressions *a* and *b* with '\|' in between form an expression that matches some text if either *a* matches it or *b* matches it. It works by trying to match *a*, and if that fails, by trying to match *b*.

Thus, 'foo\|bar' matches either 'foo' or 'bar' but no other string.

'\|' applies to the largest possible surrounding expressions. Only a surrounding '\(... \)' grouping can limit the grouping power of '\|'.

Full backtracking capability exists to handle multiple uses of '\|'.

\(... \)

is a grouping construct that serves three purposes:

1. To enclose a set of '\|' alternatives for other operations. Thus, '\(foo\|bar\)x' matches either 'foox' or 'barx'.

2. To enclose a complicated expression for the postfix operators '*', '+' and '?' to operate on. Thus, 'ba\(na\)*' matches 'bananana', etc., with any (zero or more) number of 'na' strings.

3. To record a matched substring for future reference.

This last application is not a consequence of the idea of a parenthetical grouping; it is a separate feature that is assigned as a second meaning to the same '\(... \)' construct. In practice there is usually no conflict between the two meanings; when there is a conflict, you can use a "shy" group.

\(?: ... \)

specifies a "shy" group that does not record the matched substring; you can't refer back to it with '\d'. This is useful in mechanically combining regular expressions, so that you can add groups for syntactic purposes without interfering with the numbering of the groups that are meant to be referred to.

\d

matches the same text that matched the *d*th occurrence of a '\(... \)' construct. This is called a *back reference*.

After the end of a '\(... \)' construct, the matcher remembers the beginning and end of the text matched by that construct. Then, later on in the regular expression, you can use '\' followed by the digit *d* to mean "match the same text matched the *d*th time by the '\(... \)' construct."

The strings matching the first nine '\(... \)' constructs appearing in a regular expression are assigned numbers 1 through 9 in the order that the open-parentheses appear in the regular expression. So you can use '\1' through '\9' to refer to the text matched by the corresponding '\(... \)' constructs.

For example, '\(.*\)\1' matches any newline-free string that is composed of two identical halves. The '\(.*\)' matches the first half, which may be anything, but the '\1' that follows must match the same exact text.

If a particular '\(... \)' construct matches more than once (which can easily happen if it is followed by '*'), only the last match is recorded.

\`   matches the empty string, but only at the beginning of the string or buffer (or its accessible portion) being matched against.

\'   matches the empty string, but only at the end of the string or buffer (or its accessible portion) being matched against.

\=   matches the empty string, but only at point.

\b   matches the empty string, but only at the beginning or end of a word. Thus, '\bfoo\b' matches any occurrence of 'foo' as a separate word. '\bballs?\b' matches 'ball' or 'balls' as a separate word.

             '\b' matches at the beginning or end of the buffer regardless of what text appears next to it.

\B   matches the empty string, but *not* at the beginning or end of a word.

\<   matches the empty string, but only at the beginning of a word. '\<' matches at the beginning of the buffer only if a word-constituent character follows.

\>   matches the empty string, but only at the end of a word. '\>' matches at the end of the buffer only if the contents end with a word-constituent character.

\w   matches any word-constituent character. The syntax table determines which characters these are. See Section 32.5 [Syntax], page 433.

\W   matches any character that is not a word-constituent.

<   matches the empty string, but only at the beginning of a symbol. A symbol is a sequence of one or more symbol-constituent characters. A symbol constituent character is a character whose syntax is either 'w' or ''. '_<' matches at the beginning of the buffer only if a symbol-constituent character follows.

>   matches the empty string, but only at the end of a symbol. '>' matches at the end of the buffer only if the contents end with a symbol-constituent character.

\s*c*   matches any character whose syntax is *c*. Here *c* is a character that designates a particular syntax class: thus, 'w' for word constituent, '-' or ' ' for whitespace, '.' for ordinary punctuation, etc. See Section 32.5 [Syntax], page 433.

\S*c*   matches any character whose syntax is not *c*.

\c*c*   matches any character that belongs to the category *c*. For example, '\cc' matches Chinese characters, '\cg' matches Greek characters, etc. For the description of the known categories, type M-x describe-categories RET.

`\Cc`   matches any character that does *not* belong to category *c*.

The constructs that pertain to words and syntax are controlled by the setting of the syntax table (see Section 32.5 [Syntax], page 433).

12.7 Regular Expression Example

Here is a complicated regexp—a simplified version of the regexp that Emacs uses, by default, to recognize the end of a sentence together with any whitespace that follows. We show its Lisp syntax to distinguish the spaces from the tab characters. In Lisp syntax, the string constant begins and ends with a double-quote. '\"' stands for a double-quote as part of the regexp, '\\' for a backslash as part of the regexp, '\t' for a tab, and '\n' for a newline.

```
"[.?!][]\"')]*\\($\\| $\\|\t\\|  \\)[ \t\n]*"
```

This contains four parts in succession: a character set matching period, '?', or '!'; a character set matching close-brackets, quotes, or parentheses, repeated zero or more times; a set of alternatives within backslash-parentheses that matches either end-of-line, a space at the end of a line, a tab, or two spaces; and a character set matching whitespace characters, repeated any number of times.

To enter the same regexp in incremental search, you would type TAB to enter a tab, and C-j to enter a newline. You would also type single backslashes as themselves, instead of doubling them for Lisp syntax. In commands that use ordinary minibuffer input to read a regexp, you would quote the C-j by preceding it with a C-q to prevent C-j from exiting the minibuffer.

12.8 Searching and Case

Incremental searches in Emacs normally ignore the case of the text they are searching through, if you specify the text in lower case. Thus, if you specify searching for 'foo', then 'Foo' and 'foo' are also considered a match. Regexps, and in particular character sets, are included: '[ab]' would match 'a' or 'A' or 'b' or 'B'.

An upper-case letter anywhere in the incremental search string makes the search case-sensitive. Thus, searching for 'Foo' does not find 'foo' or 'FOO'. This applies to regular expression search as well as to string search. The effect ceases if you delete the upper-case letter from the search string.

Typing M-c within an incremental search toggles the case sensitivity of that search. The effect does not extend beyond the current incremental search to the next one, but it does override the effect of including an upper-case letter in the current search.

If you set the variable `case-fold-search` to `nil`, then all letters must match exactly, including case. This is a per-buffer variable; altering the variable affects only the current buffer, but there is a default value in `default-case-fold-search` that you can also set. See Section 32.3.3 [Locals], page 419. This variable applies to nonincremental searches also, including those performed by the replace commands (see Section 12.9 [Replace], page 99) and the minibuffer history matching commands (see Section 5.4 [Minibuffer History], page 36).

Several related variables control case-sensitivity of searching and matching for specific commands or activities. For instance, `tags-case-fold-search` controls case sensitivity for `find-tag`. To find these variables, do `M-x apropos-variable RET case-fold-search RET`.

12.9 Replacement Commands

Global search-and-replace operations are not needed often in Emacs, but they are available. In addition to the simple `M-x replace-string` command which replaces all occurrences, there is `M-%` (`query-replace`), which presents each occurrence of the pattern and asks you whether to replace it.

The replace commands normally operate on the text from point to the end of the buffer; however, in Transient Mark mode (see Section 8.2 [Transient Mark], page 50), when the mark is active, they operate on the region. The basic replace commands replace one string (or regexp) with one replacement string. It is possible to perform several replacements in parallel using the command `expand-region-abbrevs` (see Section 26.3 [Expanding Abbrevs], page 304).

12.9.1 Unconditional Replacement

`M-x replace-string RET` *string* `RET` *newstring* `RET`
        Replace every occurrence of *string* with *newstring*.

To replace every instance of 'foo' after point with 'bar', use the command `M-x replace-string` with the two arguments 'foo' and 'bar'. Replacement happens only in the text after point, so if you want to cover the whole buffer you must go to the beginning first. All occurrences up to the end of the buffer are replaced; to limit replacement to part of the buffer, narrow to that part of the buffer before doing the replacement (see Section 31.9 [Narrowing], page 396). In Transient Mark mode, when the region is active, replacement is limited to the region (see Section 8.2 [Transient Mark], page 50).

When `replace-string` exits, it leaves point at the last occurrence replaced. It sets the mark to the prior position of point (where the `replace-string` command was issued); use `C-u C-SPC` to move back there.

A numeric argument restricts replacement to matches that are surrounded by word boundaries. The argument's value doesn't matter.

See Section 12.9.3 [Replacement and Case], page 101, for details about case-sensitivity in replace commands.

What if you want to exchange 'x' and 'y': replace every 'x' with a 'y' and vice versa? You can do it this way:

```
M-x replace-string RET x RET @TEMP@ RET
M-< M-x replace-string RET y RET x RET
M-< M-x replace-string RET @TEMP@ RET y RET
```

This works provided the string '@TEMP@' does not appear in your text.

12.9.2 Regexp Replacement

The M-x `replace-string` command replaces exact matches for a single string. The similar command M-x `replace-regexp` replaces any match for a specified pattern.

M-x replace-regexp RET *regexp* RET *newstring* RET
> Replace every match for *regexp* with *newstring*.

In `replace-regexp`, the *newstring* need not be constant: it can refer to all or part of what is matched by the *regexp*. '\&' in *newstring* stands for the entire match being replaced. '\d' in *newstring*, where *d* is a digit, stands for whatever matched the *d*th parenthesized grouping in *regexp*. (This is called a "back reference.") '\#' refers to the count of replacements already made in this command, as a decimal number. In the first replacement, '\#' stands for '0'; in the second, for '1'; and so on. For example,

    M-x replace-regexp RET c[ad]+r RET \&-safe RET

replaces (for example) 'cadr' with 'cadr-safe' and 'cddr' with 'cddr-safe'.

    M-x replace-regexp RET \(c[ad]+r\)-safe RET \1 RET

performs the inverse transformation. To include a '\' in the text to replace with, you must enter '\\'.

If you want to enter part of the replacement string by hand each time, use '\?' in the replacement string. Each replacement will ask you to edit the replacement string in the minibuffer, putting point where the '\?' was.

The remainder of this subsection is intended for specialized tasks and requires knowledge of Lisp. Most readers can skip it.

You can use Lisp expressions to calculate parts of the replacement string. To do this, write '\,' followed by the expression in the replacement string. Each replacement calculates the value of the expression and converts it to text without quoting (if it's a string, this means using the string's contents), and uses it in the replacement string in place of the expression itself. If the expression is a symbol, one space in the replacement string after the symbol name goes with the symbol name, so the value replaces them both.

Inside such an expression, you can use some special sequences. '\&' and '\n' refer here, as usual, to the entire match as a string, and to a submatch as a string. *n* may be multiple digits, and the value of '\n' is `nil` if subexpression *n* did not match. You can also use '\#&' and '\#n' to refer to those matches as numbers (this is valid when the match or submatch has the form of a numeral). '\#' here too stands for the number of already-completed replacements.

Repeating our example to exchange 'x' and 'y', we can thus do it also this way:

    M-x replace-regexp RET \(x\)\|y RET
    \,(if \1 "y" "x") RET

For computing replacement strings for '\,', the `format` function is often useful (see section "Formatting Strings" in *The Emacs Lisp Reference Manual*). For example, to add consecutively numbered strings like 'ABC00042' to columns 73 to 80 (unless they are already occupied), you can use

    M-x replace-regexp RET ^.\{0,72\}$ RET
    \,(format "%-72sABC%05d" \& \#) RET

12.9.3 Replace Commands and Case

If the first argument of a replace command is all lower case, the command ignores case while searching for occurrences to replace—provided `case-fold-search` is non-nil. If `case-fold-search` is set to `nil`, case is always significant in all searches.

In addition, when the *newstring* argument is all or partly lower case, replacement commands try to preserve the case pattern of each occurrence. Thus, the command

        M-x replace-string RET foo RET bar RET

replaces a lower case 'foo' with a lower case 'bar', an all-caps 'FOO' with 'BAR', and a capitalized 'Foo' with 'Bar'. (These three alternatives—lower case, all caps, and capitalized, are the only ones that `replace-string` can distinguish.)

If upper-case letters are used in the replacement string, they remain upper case every time that text is inserted. If upper-case letters are used in the first argument, the second argument is always substituted exactly as given, with no case conversion. Likewise, if either `case-replace` or `case-fold-search` is set to `nil`, replacement is done without case conversion.

12.9.4 Query Replace

M-% *string* RET *newstring* RET
M-x query-replace RET *string* RET *newstring* RET
                Replace some occurrences of *string* with *newstring*.

C-M-% *regexp* RET *newstring* RET
M-x query-replace-regexp RET *regexp* RET *newstring* RET
                Replace some matches for *regexp* with *newstring*.

If you want to change only some of the occurrences of 'foo' to 'bar', not all of them, then you cannot use an ordinary `replace-string`. Instead, use M-% (query-replace). This command finds occurrences of 'foo' one by one, displays each occurrence and asks you whether to replace it. Aside from querying, `query-replace` works just like `replace-string`. It preserves case, like `replace-string`, provided `case-replace` is non-nil, as it normally is (see Section 12.9.3 [Replacement and Case], page 101). A numeric argument means consider only occurrences that are bounded by word-delimiter characters.

C-M-% performs regexp search and replace (`query-replace-regexp`). It works like `replace-regexp` except that it queries like `query-replace`.

These commands highlight the current match using the face `query-replace`. They highlight other matches using `lazy-highlight` just like incremental search (see Section 12.1 [Incremental Search], page 86).

The characters you can type when you are shown a match for the string or regexp are:

SPC   to replace the occurrence with *newstring*.

DEL   to skip to the next occurrence without replacing this one.

, (Comma)   to replace this occurrence and display the result. You are then asked for another input character to say what to do next. Since the replacement has already been made, DEL and SPC are equivalent in this situation; both move to the next occurrence.

You can type C-r at this point (see below) to alter the replaced text. You can also type C-x u to undo the replacement; this exits the query-replace, so if you want to do further replacement you must use C-x ESC ESC RET to restart (see Section 5.5 [Repetition], page 37).

RET   to exit without doing any more replacements.

. (Period)   to replace this occurrence and then exit without searching for more occurrences.

!   to replace all remaining occurrences without asking again.

^   to go back to the position of the previous occurrence (or what used to be an occurrence), in case you changed it by mistake or want to reexamine it.

C-r   to enter a recursive editing level, in case the occurrence needs to be edited rather than just replaced with *newstring*. When you are done, exit the recursive editing level with C-M-c to proceed to the next occurrence. See Section 31.13 [Recursive Edit], page 399.

C-w   to delete the occurrence, and then enter a recursive editing level as in C-r. Use the recursive edit to insert text to replace the deleted occurrence of *string*. When done, exit the recursive editing level with C-M-c to proceed to the next occurrence.

e   to edit the replacement string in the minibuffer. When you exit the minibuffer by typing RET, the minibuffer contents replace the current occurrence of the pattern. They also become the new replacement string for any further occurrences.

C-l   to redisplay the screen. Then you must type another character to specify what to do with this occurrence.

C-h   to display a message summarizing these options. Then you must type another character to specify what to do with this occurrence.

Some other characters are aliases for the ones listed above: y, n and q are equivalent to SPC, DEL and RET.

Aside from this, any other character exits the query-replace, and is then reread as part of a key sequence. Thus, if you type C-k, it exits the query-replace and then kills to end of line.

To restart a query-replace once it is exited, use C-x ESC ESC, which repeats the query-replace because it used the minibuffer to read its arguments. See Section 5.5 [Repetition], page 37.

See Section 29.7 [Operating on Files], page 344, for the Dired Q command which performs query replace on selected files. See also Section 29.9 [Transforming File Names], page 347, for Dired commands to rename, copy, or link files by replacing regexp matches in file names.

12.10 Other Search-and-Loop Commands

Here are some other commands that find matches for a regular expression. They all ignore case in matching, if the pattern contains no upper-case letters and `case-fold-search` is non-nil. Aside from `occur` and its variants, all operate on the text from point to the end of the buffer, or on the active region in Transient Mark mode.

`M-x occur RET` *regexp* `RET`

> Display a list showing each line in the buffer that contains a match for *regexp*. To limit the search to part of the buffer, narrow to that part (see Section 31.9 [Narrowing], page 396). A numeric argument *n* specifies that *n* lines of context are to be displayed before and after each matching line. Currently, `occur` can not correctly handle multiline matches.
>
> The buffer '`*Occur*`' containing the output serves as a menu for finding the occurrences in their original context. Click `Mouse-2` on an occurrence listed in '`*Occur*`', or position point there and type RET; this switches to the buffer that was searched and moves point to the original of the chosen occurrence. `o` and `C-o` display the match in another window; `C o` does not select it.
>
> After using `M-x occur`, you can use `next-error` to visit the occurrences found, one by one. Section 24.2 [Compilation Mode], page 274.

`M-x list-matching-lines`

> Synonym for `M-x occur`.

`M-x multi-occur RET` *buffers* `RET` *regexp* `RET`

> This function is just like `occur`, except it is able to search through multiple buffers. It asks you to specify the buffer names one by one.

`M-x multi-occur-in-matching-buffers RET` *bufregexp* `RET` *regexp* `RET`

> This function is similar to `multi-occur`, except the buffers to search are specified by a regular expression that matches visited file names. With a prefix argument, it uses the regular expression to match buffer names instead.

`M-x how-many RET` *regexp* `RET`

> Print the number of matches for *regexp* that exist in the buffer after point. In Transient Mark mode, if the region is active, the command operates on the region instead.

`M-x flush-lines RET` *regexp* `RET`

> This command deletes each line that contains a match for *regexp*, operating on the text after point; it deletes the current line if it contains a match starting after point. In Transient Mark mode, if the region is active, the command operates on the region instead; it deletes a line partially contained in the region if it contains a match entirely contained in the region.
>
> If a match is split across lines, `flush-lines` deletes all those lines. It deletes the lines before starting to look for the next match; hence,

it ignores a match starting on the same line at which another match ended.

`M-x keep-lines RET` *regexp* `RET`

This command deletes each line that *does not* contain a match for *regexp*, operating on the text after point; if point is not at the beginning of a line, it always keeps the current line. In Transient Mark mode, if the region is active, the command operates on the region instead; it never deletes lines that are only partially contained in the region (a newline that ends a line counts as part of that line).

If a match is split across lines, this command keeps all those lines.

13 Commands for Fixing Typos

In this chapter we describe the commands that are especially useful for the times when you catch a mistake in your text just after you have made it, or change your mind while composing text on the fly.

The most fundamental command for correcting erroneous editing is the undo command, C-x u or C-_ or C-/. This command undoes a single command (usually), a part of a command (in the case of query-replace), or several consecutive self-inserting characters. Consecutive repetitions of the undo command undo earlier and earlier changes, back to the limit of the undo information available. See Section 13.1 [Undo], page 105, for more information.

13.1 Undo

The *undo* commands undo recent changes in the buffer's text. Each buffer records changes individually, and the undo command always applies to the current buffer. You can undo all the changes in a buffer for as far as back these records go. Usually each editing command makes a separate entry in the undo records, but some commands such as query-replace divide their changes into multiple entries for flexibility in undoing. Meanwhile, self-inserting characters are usually grouped to make undoing less tedious.

```
C-x u
C-_
C-/              Undo one entry in the current buffer's undo records (undo).
```

To begin to undo, type the command C-x u (or its aliases, C-_ or C-/). This undoes the most recent change in the buffer, and moves point back to where it was before that change.

Consecutive repetitions of C-x u (or its aliases) undo earlier and earlier changes in the current buffer, back to the limit of the current buffer's undo records. If all the recorded changes have already been undone, the undo command just signals an error.

If you notice that a buffer has been modified accidentally, the easiest way to recover is to type C-_ repeatedly until the stars disappear from the front of the mode line. At this time, all the modifications you made have been canceled. Whenever an undo command makes the stars disappear from the mode line, it means that the buffer contents are the same as they were when the file was last read in or saved.

If you do not remember whether you changed the buffer deliberately, type C-_ once. When you see the last change you made undone, you will see whether it was an intentional change. If it was an accident, leave it undone. If it was deliberate, redo the change as described below.

Any command other than an undo command breaks the sequence of undo commands. Starting from that moment, the previous undo commands become ordinary changes that you can undo. Thus, to redo changes you have undone, type C-f or any other command that will harmlessly break the sequence of undoing, then type undo commands again. On the other hand, if you want to resume undoing, without redoing previous undo commands, use M-x undo-only. This is like undo, but will not redo changes you have just undone.

Ordinary undo applies to all changes made in the current buffer. You can also perform *selective undo*, limited to the region.

To do this, specify the region you want, then run the undo command with a prefix argument (the value does not matter): C-u C-x u or C-u C-_. This undoes the most recent change in the region. To undo further changes in the same region, repeat the undo command (no prefix argument is needed). In Transient Mark mode (see Section 8.2 [Transient Mark], page 50), any use of undo when there is an active region performs selective undo; you do not need a prefix argument.

Some specialized buffers do not make undo records. Buffers whose names start with spaces never do; these buffers are used internally by Emacs and its extensions to hold text that users don't normally look at or edit.

When the undo records for a buffer becomes too large, Emacs discards the oldest undo records from time to time (during garbage collection). You can specify how much undo records to keep by setting three variables: undo-limit, undo-strong-limit, and undo-outer-limit. Their values are expressed in units of bytes of space.

The variable undo-limit sets a soft limit: Emacs keeps undo data for enough commands to reach this size, and perhaps exceed it, but does not keep data for any earlier commands beyond that. Its default value is 20000. The variable undo-strong-limit sets a stricter limit: a previous command (not the most recent one) which pushes the size past this amount is itself forgotten. The default value of undo-strong-limit is 30000.

Regardless of the values of those variables, the most recent change is never discarded unless it gets bigger than undo-outer-limit (normally 3,000,000). At that point, Emacs discards the undo data and warns you about it. This is the only situation in which you cannot undo the last command. If this happens, you can increase the value of undo-outer-limit to make it even less likely to happen in the future. But if you didn't expect the command to create such large undo data, then it is probably a bug and you should report it. See Section 33.3 [Reporting Bugs], page 445.

The reason the undo command has three key bindings, C-x u, C-_ and C-/, is that it is worthy of a single-character key, but C-x u is more straightforward for beginners to remember and type. Meanwhile, C-- on a text-only terminal is really C-_, which makes it a natural and easily typed binding for undoing.

13.2 Killing Your Mistakes

DEL   Delete last character (delete-backward-char).

M-DEL   Kill last word (backward-kill-word).

C-x DEL   Kill to beginning of sentence (backward-kill-sentence).

The DEL character (delete-backward-char) is the most important correction command. It deletes the character before point. When DEL follows a self-inserting character command, you can think of it as canceling that command. However, avoid the confusion of thinking of DEL as a general way to cancel a command!

When your mistake is longer than a couple of characters, it might be more convenient to use M-DEL or C-x DEL. M-DEL kills back to the start of the last word, and C-x DEL kills back to the start of the last sentence. C-x DEL is particularly useful when you change your mind about the phrasing of the text you are writing. M-DEL and C-x DEL save the killed text for C-y and M-y to retrieve. See Section 9.2 [Yanking], page 58.

M-DEL is often useful even when you have typed only a few characters wrong, if you know you are confused in your typing and aren't sure exactly what you typed. At such a time, you cannot correct with DEL except by looking at the screen to see what you did. Often it requires less thought to kill the whole word and start again.

13.3 Transposing Text

C-t   Transpose two characters (transpose-chars).

M-t   Transpose two words (transpose-words).

C-M-t   Transpose two balanced expressions (transpose-sexps).

C-x C-t   Transpose two lines (transpose-lines).

The common error of transposing two characters can be fixed, when they are adjacent, with the C-t command (transpose-chars). Normally, C-t transposes the two characters on either side of point. When given at the end of a line, rather than transposing the last character of the line with the newline, which would be useless, C-t transposes the last two characters on the line. So, if you catch your transposition error right away, you can fix it with just a C-t. If you don't catch it so fast, you must move the cursor back between the two transposed characters before you type C-t. If you transposed a space with the last character of the word before it, the word motion commands are a good way of getting there. Otherwise, a reverse search (C-r) is often the best way. See Chapter 12 [Search], page 86.

M-t transposes the word before point with the word after point (transpose-words). It moves point forward over a word, dragging the word preceding or containing point forward as well. The punctuation characters between the words do not move. For example, 'FOO, BAR' transposes into 'BAR, FOO' rather than 'BAR FOO,'.

C-M-t (transpose-sexps) is a similar command for transposing two expressions (see Section 23.4.1 [Expressions], page 257), and C-x C-t (transpose-lines) exchanges lines. They work like M-t except as regards what units of text they transpose.

A numeric argument to a transpose command serves as a repeat count: it tells the transpose command to move the character (word, expression, line) before or containing point across several other characters (words, expressions, lines). For example, C-u 3 C-t moves the character before point forward across three other characters. It would change 'f*oobar' into 'oobf*ar'. This is equivalent to repeating C-t three times. C-u - 4 M-t moves the word before point backward across four words. C-u - C-M-t would cancel the effect of plain C-M-t.

A numeric argument of zero is assigned a special meaning (because otherwise a command with a repeat count of zero would do nothing): to transpose the character (word, expression, line) ending after point with the one ending after the mark.

13.4 Case Conversion

M-- M-l   Convert last word to lower case. Note `Meta--` is Meta-minus.

M-- M-u   Convert last word to all upper case.

M-- M-c   Convert last word to lower case with capital initial.

A very common error is to type words in the wrong case. Because of this, the word case-conversion commands M-l, M-u and M-c have a special feature when used with a negative argument: they do not move the cursor. As soon as you see you have mistyped the last word, you can simply case-convert it and go on typing. See Section 22.6 [Case], page 223.

13.5 Checking and Correcting Spelling

This section describes the commands to check the spelling of a single word or of a portion of a buffer. These commands work with the spelling checker programs Aspell and Ispell, which are not part of Emacs.

M-x flyspell-mode
>   Enable Flyspell mode, which highlights all misspelled words.

M-x flyspell-prog-mode
>   Enable Flyspell mode for comments and strings only.

M-$ Check and correct spelling of the word at point (`ispell-word`).

M-TAB
ESC TAB   Complete the word before point based on the spelling dictionary (`ispell-complete-word`).

M-x ispell Spell-check the active region or the current buffer.

M-x ispell-buffer
>   Check and correct spelling of each word in the buffer.

M-x ispell-region
>   Check and correct spelling of each word in the region.

M-x ispell-message
>   Check and correct spelling of each word in a draft mail message, excluding cited material.

M-x ispell-change-dictionary RET *dict* RET
>   Restart the Aspell or Ispell process, using *dict* as the dictionary.

M-x ispell-kill-ispell
>   Kill the Aspell or Ispell subprocess.

Flyspell mode is a fully-automatic way to check spelling as you edit in Emacs. It operates by checking words as you change or insert them. When it finds a word that it does not recognize, it highlights that word. This does not interfere with your editing, but when you see the highlighted word, you can move to it and fix it. Type M-x flyspell-mode to enable or disable this mode in the current buffer.

When Flyspell mode highlights a word as misspelled, you can click on it with Mouse-2 to display a menu of possible corrections and actions. You can also correct the word by editing it manually in any way you like.

Flyspell Prog mode works just like ordinary Flyspell mode, except that it only checks words in comments and string constants. This feature is useful for editing programs. Type M-x flyspell-prog-mode to enable or disable this mode in the current buffer.

The other Emacs spell-checking features check or look up words when you give an explicit command to do so.

To check the spelling of the word around or before point, and optionally correct it as well, use the command M-$ (ispell-word). If the word is not correct, the command offers you various alternatives for what to do about it.

To check the entire current buffer, use M-x ispell-buffer. Use M-x ispell-region to check just the current region. To check spelling in an email message you are writing, use M-x ispell-message; that command checks the whole buffer, except for material that is indented or appears to be cited from other messages.

The M-x ispell command spell-checks the active region if the Transient Mark mode is on (see Section 8.2 [Transient Mark], page 50), otherwise it spell-checks the current buffer.

Each time these commands encounter an incorrect word, they ask you what to do. They display a list of alternatives, usually including several "near misses" — words that are close to the word being checked. Then you must type a single-character response. Here are the valid responses:

SPC   Skip this word—continue to consider it incorrect, but don't change it here.

r *new* RET   Replace the word (just this time) with *new*. (The replacement string will be rescanned for more spelling errors.)

R *new* RET   Replace the word with *new*, and do a query-replace so you can replace it elsewhere in the buffer if you wish. (The replacements will be rescanned for more spelling errors.)

digit   Replace the word (just this time) with one of the displayed near-misses. Each near-miss is listed with a digit; type that digit to select it.

a   Accept the incorrect word—treat it as correct, but only in this editing session.

A   Accept the incorrect word—treat it as correct, but only in this editing session and for this buffer.

i   Insert this word in your private dictionary file so that Aspell or Ispell
             will consider it correct from now on, even in future sessions.

u   Insert the lower-case version of this word in your private dictionary
             file.

m   Like i, but you can also specify dictionary completion information.

l *word* RET Look in the dictionary for words that match *word*. These words be-
             come the new list of "near-misses"; you can select one of them as the
             replacement by typing a digit. You can use '*' in *word* as a wildcard.

C-g   Quit interactive spell checking, leaving point at the word that was
             being checked. You can restart checking again afterward with C-u
             M-$.

X   Same as C-g.

x   Quit interactive spell checking and move point back to where it was
             when you started spell checking.

q   Quit interactive spell checking and kill the Ispell subprocess.

C-l   Refresh the screen.

C-z   This key has its normal command meaning (suspend Emacs or iconify
             this frame).

?   Show the list of options.

The command ispell-complete-word, which is bound to the key M-TAB in Text
mode and related modes, shows a list of completions based on spelling correction.
Insert the beginning of a word, and then type M-TAB; the command displays a
completion list window. (If your window manager intercepts M-TAB, type ESC TAB
or C-M-i.) To choose one of the completions listed, click Mouse-2 or Mouse-1 fast
on it, or move the cursor there in the completions window and type RET. See
Section 22.7 [Text Mode], page 224.

Once started, the Aspell or Ispell subprocess continues to run (waiting for something to do), so that subsequent spell checking commands complete more quickly.
If you want to get rid of the process, use M-x ispell-kill-ispell. This is not
usually necessary, since the process uses no time except when you do spelling correction.

Ispell and Aspell use two dictionaries together for spell checking: the standard
dictionary and your private dictionary. The variable ispell-dictionary specifies
the file name to use for the standard dictionary; a value of nil selects the default
dictionary. The command M-x ispell-change-dictionary sets this variable and
then restarts the subprocess, so that it will use a different standard dictionary.

Aspell and Ispell use a separate dictionary for word completion. The variable
ispell-complete-word-dict specifies the file name of this dictionary. The completion dictionary must be different because it cannot use root and affix information.
For some languages there is a spell checking dictionary but no word completion
dictionary.

14 Keyboard Macros

In this chapter we describe how to record a sequence of editing commands so you can repeat it conveniently later.

A *keyboard macro* is a command defined by an Emacs user to stand for another sequence of keys. For example, if you discover that you are about to type C-n M-d C-d forty times, you can speed your work by defining a keyboard macro to do C-n M-d C-d, and then executing it 39 more times.

You define a keyboard macro by executing and recording the commands which are its definition. Put differently, as you define a keyboard macro, the definition is being executed for the first time. This way, you can see the effects of your commands, so that you don't have to figure them out in your head. When you close the definition, the keyboard macro is defined and also has been, in effect, executed once. You can then do the whole thing over again by invoking the macro.

Keyboard macros differ from ordinary Emacs commands in that they are written in the Emacs command language rather than in Lisp. This makes it easier for the novice to write them, and makes them more convenient as temporary hacks. However, the Emacs command language is not powerful enough as a programming language to be useful for writing anything intelligent or general. For such things, Lisp must be used.

14.1 Basic Use

F3
C-x (Start defining a keyboard macro (kmacro-start-macro).

F4   If a keyboard macro is being defined, end the definition; otherwise, execute the most recent keyboard macro (kmacro-end-or-call-macro).

C-x)   End the definition of a keyboard macro (kmacro-end-macro).

C-x e   Execute the most recent keyboard macro (kmacro-end-and-call-macro). First end the definition of the keyboard macro, if currently defining it. To immediately execute the keyboard macro again, just repeat the e.

C-u C-x (Re-execute last keyboard macro, then add more keys to its definition.

C-u C-u C-x (
             Add more keys to the last keyboard macro without re-executing it.

C-x C-k r   Run the last keyboard macro on each line that begins in the region (apply-macro-to-region-lines).

To start defining a keyboard macro, type the F3 or C-x (command (kmacro-start-macro). From then on, your keys continue to be executed, but also become part of the definition of the macro. 'Def' appears in the mode line to remind you of what is going on. When you are finished, the F4 or C-x) command (kmacro-end-macro) terminates the definition (without becoming part of it!). For example,

```
C-x ( M-f foo C-x )
```
defines a macro to move forward a word and then insert 'foo'.

The macro thus defined can be invoked again with the C-x e command (kmacro-end-and-call-macro), which may be given a repeat count as a numeric argument to execute the macro many times. If you enter C-x e while defining a macro, the macro is terminated and executed immediately.

After executing the macro with C-x e, you can use e repeatedly to immediately repeat the macro one or more times. For example,

```
C-x ( xyz C-x e e e
```
inserts 'xyzxyzxyzxyz' in the current buffer.

C-x) can also be given a repeat count as an argument, in which case it repeats the macro that many times right after defining it, but defining the macro counts as the first repetition (since it is executed as you define it). Therefore, giving C-x) an argument of 4 executes the macro immediately 3 additional times. An argument of zero to C-x e or C-x) means repeat the macro indefinitely (until it gets an error or you type C-g or, on MS-DOS, C-BREAK).

The key F4 is like a combination of C-x) and C-x e. If you're defining a macro, F4 ends the definition. Otherwise it executes the last macro. For example,

```
F3 xyz F4 F4 F4
```
inserts 'xyzxyzxyz' in the current buffer.

If you wish to repeat an operation at regularly spaced places in the text, define a macro and include as part of the macro the commands to move to the next place you want to use it. For example, if you want to change each line, you should position point at the start of a line, and define a macro to change that line and leave point at the start of the next line. Then repeating the macro will operate on successive lines.

When a command reads an argument with the minibuffer, your minibuffer input becomes part of the macro along with the command. So when you replay the macro, the command gets the same argument as when you entered the macro. For example,

```
C-x ( C-a C-SPC C-n M-w C-x b f o o RET C-y C-x b RET C-x )
```
defines a macro that copies the current line into the buffer 'foo', then returns to the original buffer.

You can use function keys in a keyboard macro, just like keyboard keys. You can even use mouse events, but be careful about that: when the macro replays the mouse event, it uses the original mouse position of that event, the position that the mouse had while you were defining the macro. The effect of this may be hard to predict. (Using the current mouse position would be even less predictable.)

One thing that sometimes works badly in a keyboard macro is the command C-M-c (exit-recursive-edit). When this command exits a recursive edit that started within the macro, it works as you'd expect. But if it exits a recursive edit that started before you invoked the keyboard macro, it also necessarily exits the keyboard macro as part of the process.

After you have terminated the definition of a keyboard macro, you can add to the end of its definition by typing C-u F3 or C-u C-x (. This is equivalent to plain C-x (followed by retyping the whole definition so far. As a consequence it re-executes the macro as previously defined.

You can also add to the end of the definition of the last keyboard macro without re-executing it by typing C-u C-u C-x (.

The variable kmacro-execute-before-append specifies whether a single C-u prefix causes the existing macro to be re-executed before appending to it.

The command C-x C-k r (apply-macro-to-region-lines) repeats the last defined keyboard macro on each line that begins in the region. It does this line by line, by moving point to the beginning of the line and then executing the macro.

14.2 The Keyboard Macro Ring

All defined keyboard macros are recorded in the "keyboard macro ring," a list of sequences of keys. There is only one keyboard macro ring, shared by all buffers.

C-x C-k C-k

> Execute the keyboard macro at the head of the ring (kmacro-end-or-call-macro-repeat).

C-x C-k C-n

> Rotate the keyboard macro ring to the next macro (defined earlier) (kmacro-cycle-ring-next).

C-x C-k C-p

> Rotate the keyboard macro ring to the previous macro (defined later) (kmacro-cycle-ring-previous).

All commands which operate on the keyboard macro ring use the same C-x C-k prefix. Most of these commands can be executed and repeated immediately after each other without repeating the C-x C-k prefix. For example,

   C-x C-k C-p C-p C-k C-k C-k C-n C-n C-k C-p C-k C-d

will rotate the keyboard macro ring to the "second previous" macro, execute the resulting head macro three times, rotate back to the original head macro, execute that once, rotate to the "previous" macro, execute that, and finally delete it from the macro ring.

The command C-x C-k C-k (kmacro-end-or-call-macro-repeat) executes the keyboard macro at the head of the macro ring. You can repeat the macro immediately by typing another C-k, or you can rotate the macro ring immediately by typing C-n or C-p.

When a keyboard macro is being defined, C-x C-k C-k behaves like C-x) except that, immediately afterward, you can use most key bindings of this section without the C-x C-k prefix. For instance, another C-k will re-execute the macro.

The commands C-x C-k C-n (kmacro-cycle-ring-next) and C-x C-k C-p (kmacro-cycle-ring-previous) rotate the macro ring, bringing the next or previous keyboard macro to the head of the macro ring. The definition of the new head macro is displayed in the echo area. You can continue to rotate the macro ring immediately by repeating just C-n and C-p until the desired macro is at the head of the ring. To execute the new macro ring head immediately, just type C-k.

Note that Emacs treats the head of the macro ring as the "last defined keyboard macro." For instance, C-x e will execute that macro, and C-x C-k n will give it a name.

The maximum number of macros stored in the keyboard macro ring is determined by the customizable variable `kmacro-ring-max`.

14.3 The Keyboard Macro Counter

C-x C-k C-i

> Insert the keyboard macro counter value in the buffer (`kmacro-insert-counter`).

C-x C-k C-c

> Set the keyboard macro counter (`kmacro-set-counter`).

C-x C-k C-a

> Add the prefix arg to the keyboard macro counter (`kmacro-add-counter`).

C-x C-k C-f

> Specify the format for inserting the keyboard macro counter (`kmacro-set-format`).

Each keyboard macro has an associated counter. Normally, the macro counter is initialized to 0 when you start defining the macro, and incremented by 1 after each insertion of the counter value; that is, if you insert the macro counter twice while defining the macro, the counter will increase by 2 on each repetition of the macro.

The command C-x C-k C-i (`kmacro-insert-counter`) inserts the current value of the current keyboard macro's counter, and increments the counter by 1. You can use a numeric prefix argument to specify a different increment. If you just specify a C-u prefix, then the increment is zero, so it repeats the last inserted counter value. For example, if you enter the following sequence while defining a macro

> C-x C-k C-i C-x C-k C-i C-u C-x C-k C-i C-x C-k C-i

it inserts '0112' in the buffer. The next two iterations of the macro will insert '3445' and '6778'.

This command usually only makes sense while defining a keyboard macro. But its behavior when no keyboard macro is being defined or executed is predictable: it inserts and increments the counter of the macro at the head of the keyboard macro ring.

The command C-x C-k C-c (`kmacro-set-counter`) sets the current macro counter to the value of the numeric argument. If you use it inside the macro, it operates on each repetition of the macro. If you specify just C-u as the prefix, while executing the macro, that resets the counter to the value it had at the beginning of the current repetition of the macro (undoing any increments so far in this repetition).

The command C-x C-k C-a (`kmacro-add-counter`) adds the prefix argument to the current macro counter. With just C-u as argument, it resets the counter to the last value inserted by any keyboard macro. (Normally, when you use this, the last insertion will be in the same macro and it will be the same counter.)

The command C-x C-k C-f (kmacro-set-format) prompts for the format to use when inserting the macro counter. The default format is '%d', which means to insert the number in decimal without any padding. You can exit with empty minibuffer to reset the format to this default. You can specify any format string that the format function accepts and that makes sense with a single integer extra argument (see section "Formatting Strings" in *The Emacs Lisp Reference Manual*). Do not put the format string inside double quotes when you insert it in the minibuffer.

If you use this command while no keyboard macro is being defined or executed, the new format affects all subsequent macro definitions. Existing macros continue to use the format in effect when they were defined. If you set the format while defining a keyboard macro, this affects the macro being defined from that point on, but it does not affect subsequent macros. Execution of the macro will, at each step, use the format in effect at that step during its definition. Changes to the macro format during execution of a macro, like the corresponding changes during its definition, have no effect on subsequent macros.

The format set by C-x C-k C-f does not affect insertion of numbers stored in registers.

14.4 Executing Macros with Variations

C-x q   When this point is reached during macro execution, ask for confirma-
                 tion (kbd-macro-query).

Using C-x q (kbd-macro-query), you can get an effect similar to that of query-replace, where the macro asks you each time around whether to make a change. While defining the macro, type C-x q at the point where you want the query to occur. During macro definition, the C-x q does nothing, but when you run the macro later, C-x q asks you interactively whether to continue

The valid responses when C-x q asks are SPC (or y), DEL (or n), RET (or q), C-l and C-r. The answers are the same as in query-replace, though not all of the query-replace options are meaningful.

These responses include SPC to continue, and DEL to skip the remainder of this repetition of the macro and start right away with the next repetition. RET means to skip the remainder of this repetition and cancel further repetitions. C-l redraws the screen and asks you again for a character to say what to do.

C-r enters a recursive editing level, in which you can perform editing which is not part of the macro. When you exit the recursive edit using C-M-c, you are asked again how to continue with the keyboard macro. If you type a SPC at this time, the rest of the macro definition is executed. It is up to you to leave point and the text in a state such that the rest of the macro will do what you want.

C-u C-x q, which is C-x q with a numeric argument, performs a completely different function. It enters a recursive edit reading input from the keyboard, both when you type it during the definition of the macro, and when it is executed from the macro. During definition, the editing you do inside the recursive edit does not become part of the macro. During macro execution, the recursive edit gives you a chance to do some particularized editing on each repetition. See Section 31.13 [Recursive Edit], page 399.

Another way to vary the behavior of a keyboard macro is to use a register as a counter, incrementing it on each repetition of the macro. See Section 10.5 [RegNumbers], page 67.

14.5 Naming and Saving Keyboard Macros

C-x C-k n   Give a command name (for the duration of the Emacs session) to the most recently defined keyboard macro (`kmacro-name-last-macro`).

C-x C-k b   Bind the most recently defined keyboard macro to a key sequence (for the duration of the session) (`kmacro-bind-to-key`).

M-x insert-kbd-macro
              Insert in the buffer a keyboard macro's definition, as Lisp code.

If you wish to save a keyboard macro for later use, you can give it a name using C-x C-k n (`kmacro-name-last-macro`). This reads a name as an argument using the minibuffer and defines that name to execute the last keyboard macro, in its current form. (If you later add to the definition of this macro, that does not alter the name's definition as a macro.) The macro name is a Lisp symbol, and defining it in this way makes it a valid command name for calling with M-x or for binding a key to with `global-set-key` (see Section 32.4.1 [Keymaps], page 423). If you specify a name that has a prior definition other than a keyboard macro, an error message is shown and nothing is changed.

You can also bind the last keyboard macro (in its current form) to a key, using C-x C-k b (`kmacro-bind-to-key`) followed by the key sequence you want to bind. You can bind to any key sequence in the global keymap, but since most key sequences already have other bindings, you should select the key sequence carefully. If you try to bind to a key sequence with an existing binding (in any keymap), this command asks you for confirmation before replacing the existing binding.

To avoid problems caused by overriding existing bindings, the key sequences C-x C-k 0 through C-x C-k 9 and C-x C-k A through C-x C-k Z are reserved for your own keyboard macro bindings. In fact, to bind to one of these key sequences, you only need to type the digit or letter rather than the whole key sequences. For example,

      C-x C-k b 4

will bind the last keyboard macro to the key sequence C-x C-k 4.

Once a macro has a command name, you can save its definition in a file. Then it can be used in another editing session. First, visit the file you want to save the definition in. Then use this command:

      M-x insert-kbd-macro RET *macroname* RET

This inserts some Lisp code that, when executed later, will define the same macro with the same definition it has now. (You need not understand Lisp code to do this, because `insert-kbd-macro` writes the Lisp code for you.) Then save the file. You can load the file later with `load-file` (see Section 24.8 [Lisp Libraries], page 288). If the file you save in is your init file '`~/.emacs`' (see Section 32.6 [Init File], page 433) then the macro will be defined each time you run Emacs.

If you give `insert-kbd-macro` a numeric argument, it makes additional Lisp code to record the keys (if any) that you have bound to *macroname*, so that the macro will be reassigned the same keys when you load the file.

14.6 Editing a Keyboard Macro

C-x C-k C-e
> Edit the last defined keyboard macro (`kmacro-edit-macro`).

C-x C-k e *name* RET
> Edit a previously defined keyboard macro *name* (`edit-kbd-macro`).

C-x C-k l   Edit the last 100 keystrokes as a keyboard macro (`kmacro-edit-lossage`).

You can edit the last keyboard macro by typing C-x C-k C-e or C-x C-k RET (`kmacro-edit-macro`). This formats the macro definition in a buffer and enters a specialized major mode for editing it. Type C-h m once in that buffer to display details of how to edit the macro. When you are finished editing, type C-c C-c.

You can edit a named keyboard macro or a macro bound to a key by typing C-x C-k e (`edit-kbd-macro`). Follow that with the keyboard input that you would use to invoke the macro — C-x e or M-x *name* or some other key sequence.

You can edit the last 100 keystrokes as a macro by typing C-x C-k l (`kmacro-edit-lossage`).

14.7 Stepwise Editing a Keyboard Macro

You can interactively replay and edit the last keyboard macro, one command at a time, by typing C-x C-k SPC (`kmacro-step-edit-macro`). Unless you quit the macro using q or C-g, the edited macro replaces the last macro on the macro ring.

This macro editing feature shows the last macro in the minibuffer together with the first (or next) command to be executed, and prompts you for an action. You can enter ? to get a summary of your options. These actions are available:

- SPC and y execute the current command, and advance to the next command in the keyboard macro.

- n, d, and DEL skip and delete the current command.

- f skips the current command in this execution of the keyboard macro, but doesn't delete it from the macro.

- TAB executes the current command, as well as all similar commands immediately following the current command; for example, TAB may be used to insert a sequence of characters (corresponding to a sequence of `self-insert-command` commands).

- c continues execution (without further editing) until the end of the keyboard macro. If execution terminates normally, the edited macro replaces the original keyboard macro.

- C-k skips and deletes the rest of the keyboard macro, terminates step-editing, and replaces the original keyboard macro with the edited macro.

- q and C-g cancels the step-editing of the keyboard macro; discarding any changes made to the keyboard macro.

- i KEY... C-j reads and executes a series of key sequences (not including the final C-j), and inserts them before the current command in the keyboard macro, without advancing over the current command.

- I KEY... reads one key sequence, executes it, and inserts it before the current command in the keyboard macro, without advancing over the current command.

- r KEY... C-j reads and executes a series of key sequences (not including the final C-j), and replaces the current command in the keyboard macro with them, advancing over the inserted key sequences.

- R KEY... reads one key sequence, executes it, and replaces the current command in the keyboard macro with that key sequence, advancing over the inserted key sequence.

- a KEY... C-j executes the current command, then reads and executes a series of key sequences (not including the final C-j), and inserts them after the current command in the keyboard macro; it then advances over the current command and the inserted key sequences.

- A KEY... C-j executes the rest of the commands in the keyboard macro, then reads and executes a series of key sequences (not including the final C-j), and appends them at the end of the keyboard macro; it then terminates the step-editing and replaces the original keyboard macro with the edited macro.

15 File Handling

The operating system stores data permanently in named *files*, so most of the text you edit with Emacs comes from a file and is ultimately stored in a file.

To edit a file, you must tell Emacs to read the file and prepare a buffer containing a copy of the file's text. This is called *visiting* the file. Editing commands apply directly to text in the buffer; that is, to the copy inside Emacs. Your changes appear in the file itself only when you *save* the buffer back into the file.

In addition to visiting and saving files, Emacs can delete, copy, rename, and append to files, keep multiple versions of them, and operate on file directories.

15.1 File Names

Most Emacs commands that operate on a file require you to specify the file name. (Saving and reverting are exceptions; the buffer knows which file name to use for them.) You enter the file name using the minibuffer (see Chapter 5 [Minibuffer], page 31). *Completion* is available (see Section 5.3 [Completion], page 33) to make it easier to specify long file names. When completing file names, Emacs ignores those whose file-name extensions appear in the variable `completion-ignored-extensions`; see Section 5.3.4 [Completion Options], page 35.

For most operations, there is a *default file name* which is used if you type just RET to enter an empty argument. Normally the default file name is the name of the file visited in the current buffer; this makes it easy to operate on that file with any of the Emacs file commands.

Each buffer has a default directory which is normally the same as the directory of the file visited in that buffer. When you enter a file name without a directory, the default directory is used. If you specify a directory in a relative fashion, with a name that does not start with a slash, it is interpreted with respect to the default directory. The default directory is kept in the variable `default-directory`, which has a separate value in every buffer.

The command M-x pwd displays the current buffer's default directory, and the command M-x cd sets it (to a value read using the minibuffer). A buffer's default directory changes only when the cd command is used. A file-visiting buffer's default directory is initialized to the directory of the file it visits. If you create a buffer with C-x b, its default directory is copied from that of the buffer that was current at the time.

For example, if the default file name is '/u/rms/gnu/gnu.tasks' then the default directory is normally '/u/rms/gnu/'. If you type just 'foo', which does not specify a directory, it is short for '/u/rms/gnu/foo'. '../.login' would stand for '/u/rms/.login'. 'new/foo' would stand for the file name '/u/rms/gnu/new/foo'.

The default directory actually appears in the minibuffer when the minibuffer becomes active to read a file name. This serves two purposes: it *shows* you what the default is, so that you can type a relative file name and know with certainty what it will mean, and it allows you to *edit* the default to specify a different directory. This insertion of the default directory is inhibited if the variable `insert-default-directory` is set to `nil`.

Note that it is legitimate to type an absolute file name after you enter the minibuffer, ignoring the presence of the default directory name as part of the text. The final minibuffer contents may look invalid, but that is not so. For example, if the minibuffer starts out with '/usr/tmp/' and you add '/x1/rms/foo', you get '/usr/tmp//x1/rms/foo'; but Emacs ignores everything through the first slash in the double slash; the result is '/x1/rms/foo'. See Section 5.1 [Minibuffer File], page 31.

You can use '~/' in a file name to mean your home directory, or '~user-id/' to mean the home directory of a user whose login name is user-id[1].

'$' in a file name is used to substitute an environment variable. The environment variable name consists of all the alphanumeric characters after the '$'; alternatively, it can be enclosed in braces after the '$'. For example, if you have used the shell command export FOO=rms/hacks to set up an environment variable named FOO, then you can use '/u/$FOO/test.c' or '/u/${FOO}/test.c' as an abbreviation for '/u/rms/hacks/test.c'. If the environment variable is not defined, no substitution occurs: '/u/$notdefined' stands for itself (assuming the environment variable notdefined is not defined).

Note that shell commands to set environment variables affect Emacs only when done before Emacs is started.

To access a file with '$' in its name, if the '$' causes expansion, type '$$'. This pair is converted to a single '$' at the same time as variable substitution is performed for a single '$'. Alternatively, quote the whole file name with '/:' (see Section 15.15 [Quoted File Names], page 153). File names which begin with a literal '~' should also be quoted with '/:'.

The Lisp function that performs the '$'-substitution is called substitute-in-file-name. The substitution is performed only on file names read as such using the minibuffer.

You can include non-ASCII characters in file names if you set the variable file-name-coding-system to a non-nil value. See Section 19.13 [File Name Coding], page 200.

15.2 Visiting Files

C-x C-f   Visit a file (find-file).

C-x C-r   Visit a file for viewing, without allowing changes to it (find-file-read-only).

C-x C-v   Visit a different file instead of the one visited last (find-alternate-file).

C-x 4 f   Visit a file, in another window (find-file-other-window). Don't alter what is displayed in the selected window.

---

[1] On MS-Windows and MS-DOS systems, where a user doesn't have a home directory, Emacs replaces '~/' with the value of the environment variable HOME; see Section C.5.1 [General Variables], page 476. On these systems, the '~user-id/' construct is supported only for the current user, i.e., only if user-id is the current user's login name.

C-x 5 f   Visit a file, in a new frame (`find-file-other-frame`). Don't alter
             what is displayed in the selected frame.

M-x find-file-literally
             Visit a file with no conversion of the contents.

Visiting a file means reading its contents into an Emacs buffer so you can edit
them. Emacs makes a new buffer for each file that you visit. We often say that this
buffer "is visiting" that file, or that the buffer's "visited file" is that file. Emacs
constructs the buffer name from the file name by throwing away the directory,
keeping just the name proper. For example, a file named '`/usr/rms/emacs.tex`'
would get a buffer named '`emacs.tex`'. If there is already a buffer with that name,
Emacs constructs a unique name—the normal method is to append '`<2>`', '`<3>`', and
so on, but you can select other methods (see Section 16.7.1 [Uniquify], page 163).

Each window's mode line shows the name of the buffer that is being displayed
in that window, so you can always tell what buffer you are editing.

The changes you make with editing commands are made in the Emacs buffer.
They do not take effect in the file that you visited, or any permanent place, until
you *save* the buffer. Saving the buffer means that Emacs writes the current contents
of the buffer into its visited file. See Section 15.3 [Saving], page 123.

If a buffer contains changes that have not been saved, we say the buffer is
modified. This is important because it implies that some changes will be lost if
the buffer is not saved. The mode line displays two stars near the left margin to
indicate that the buffer is modified.

To visit a file, use the command C-x C-f (`find-file`) Follow the command
with the name of the file you wish to visit, terminated by a RET.

The file name is read using the minibuffer (see Chapter 5 [Minibuffer], page 31),
with defaulting and completion in the standard manner (see Section 15.1 [File
Names], page 119). While in the minibuffer, you can abort C-x C-f by typing
C-g. File-name completion ignores certain file names; for more about this, see
Section 5.3.4 [Completion Options], page 35.

Your confirmation that C-x C-f has completed successfully is the appearance of
new text on the screen and a new buffer name in the mode line. If the specified file
does not exist and you could not create it, or exists but you can't read it, then you
get an error, with an error message displayed in the echo area.

If you visit a file that is already in Emacs, C-x C-f does not make another copy.
It selects the existing buffer containing that file. However, before doing so, it checks
whether the file itself has changed since you visited or saved it last. If the file has
changed, Emacs offers to reread it.

If you try to visit a file larger than `large-file-warning-threshold` (the default
is 10000000, which is about 10 megabytes), Emacs will ask you for confirmation
first. You can answer y to proceed with visiting the file. Note, however, that Emacs
cannot visit files that are larger than the maximum Emacs buffer size, which is
around 256 megabytes on 32-bit machines (see Chapter 16 [Buffers], page 156). If
you try, Emacs will display an error message saying that the maximum buffer size
has been exceeded.

On graphical displays there are two additional methods for visiting files. Firstly, when Emacs is built with a suitable GUI toolkit, commands invoked with the mouse (by clicking on the menu bar or tool bar) use the toolkit's standard File Selection dialog instead of prompting for the file name in the minibuffer. On Unix and GNU/Linux platforms, Emacs does that when built with GTK, LessTif, and Motif toolkits; on MS-Windows and Mac, the GUI version does that by default. For information on how to customize this, see Section 18.16 [Dialog Boxes], page 183.

Secondly, Emacs supports "drag and drop"; dropping a file into an ordinary Emacs window visits the file using that window. However, dropping a file into a window displaying a Dired buffer moves or copies the file into the displayed directory. For details, see Section 18.13 [Drag and Drop], page 182, and Section 29.18 [Misc Dired Features], page 353.

What if you want to create a new file? Just visit it. Emacs displays '(New file)' in the echo area, but in other respects behaves as if you had visited an existing empty file. If you make any changes and save them, the file is created.

Emacs recognizes from the contents of a file which end-of-line convention it uses to separate lines—newline (used on GNU/Linux and on Unix), carriage-return line-feed (used on Microsoft systems), or just carriage-return (used on the Macintosh)— and automatically converts the contents to the normal Emacs convention, which is that the newline character separates lines. This is a part of the general feature of coding system conversion (see Section 19.7 [Coding Systems], page 193), and makes it possible to edit files imported from different operating systems with equal convenience. If you change the text and save the file, Emacs performs the inverse conversion, changing newlines back into carriage-return linefeed or just carriage-return if appropriate.

If the file you specify is actually a directory, `C-x C-f` invokes Dired, the Emacs directory browser, so that you can "edit" the contents of the directory (see Chapter 29 [Dired], page 339). Dired is a convenient way to view, delete, or operate on the files in the directory. However, if the variable `find-file-run-dired` is `nil`, then it is an error to try to visit a directory.

Files which are actually collections of other files, or *file archives*, are visited in special modes which invoke a Dired-like environment to allow operations on archive members. See Section 15.13 [File Archives], page 151, for more about these features.

If the file name you specify contains shell-style wildcard characters, Emacs visits all the files that match it. (On case-insensitive filesystems, Emacs matches the wildcards disregarding the letter case.) Wildcards include '?', '*', and '[...]' sequences. To enter the wild card '?' in a file name in the minibuffer, you need to type `C-q ?`. See Section 15.15 [Quoted File Names], page 153, for information on how to visit a file whose name actually contains wildcard characters. You can disable the wildcard feature by customizing `find-file-wildcards`.

If you visit a file that the operating system won't let you modify, or that is marked read-only, Emacs makes the buffer read-only too, so that you won't go ahead and make changes that you'll have trouble saving afterward. You can make the buffer writable with `C-x C-q` (`toggle-read-only`). See Section 16.3 [Misc Buffer], page 158.

If you want to visit a file as read-only in order to protect yourself from entering changes accidentally, visit it with the command C-x C-r (find-file-read-only) instead of C-x C-f.

If you visit a nonexistent file unintentionally (because you typed the wrong file name), use the C-x C-v command (find-alternate-file) to visit the file you really wanted. C-x C-v is similar to C-x C-f, but it kills the current buffer (after first offering to save it if it is modified). When C-x C-v reads the file name to visit, it inserts the entire default file name in the buffer, with point just after the directory part; this is convenient if you made a slight error in typing the name.

C-x 4 f (find-file-other-window) is like C-x C-f except that the buffer containing the specified file is selected in another window. The window that was selected before C-x 4 f continues to show the same buffer it was already showing. If this command is used when only one window is being displayed, that window is split in two, with one window showing the same buffer as before, and the other one showing the newly requested file. See Chapter 17 [Windows], page 165.

C-x 5 f (find-file-other-frame) is similar, but opens a new frame, or makes visible any existing frame showing the file you seek. This feature is available only when you are using a window system. See Chapter 18 [Frames], page 171.

If you wish to edit a file as a sequence of ASCII characters with no special encoding or conversion, use the M-x find-file-literally command. It visits a file, like C-x C-f, but does not do format conversion (see Section 22.12 [Formatted Text], page 236), character code conversion (see Section 19.7 [Coding Systems], page 193), or automatic uncompression (see Section 15.12 [Compressed Files], page 151), and does not add a final newline because of require-final-newline. If you already have visited the same file in the usual (non-literal) manner, this command asks you whether to visit it literally instead.

Two special hook variables allow extensions to modify the operation of visiting files. Visiting a file that does not exist runs the functions in the list find-file-not-found-functions; this variable holds a list of functions, and the functions are called one by one (with no arguments) until one of them returns non-nil. This is not a normal hook, and the name ends in '-functions' rather than '-hook' to indicate that fact.

Successful visiting of any file, whether existing or not, calls the functions in the list find-file-hook, with no arguments. This variable is a normal hook. In the case of a nonexistent file, the find-file-not-found-functions are run first. See Section 32.3.2 [Hooks], page 418.

There are several ways to specify automatically the major mode for editing the file (see Section 20.1 [Choosing Modes], page 207), and to specify local variables defined for that file (see Section 32.3.4 [File Variables], page 420).

15.3 Saving Files

Saving a buffer in Emacs means writing its contents back into the file that was visited in the buffer.

15.3.1 Commands for Saving Files

These are the commands that relate to saving and writing files.

C-x C-s   Save the current buffer in its visited file on disk (`save-buffer`).

C-x s   Save any or all buffers in their visited files (`save-some-buffers`).

M-~   Forget that the current buffer has been changed (`not-modified`). With prefix argument (C-u), mark the current buffer as changed.

C-x C-w   Save the current buffer with a specified file name (`write-file`).

M-x set-visited-file-name
             Change the file name under which the current buffer will be saved.

When you wish to save the file and make your changes permanent, type C-x C-s (`save-buffer`). After saving is finished, C-x C-s displays a message like this:

      `Wrote /u/rms/gnu/gnu.tasks`

If the selected buffer is not modified (no changes have been made in it since the buffer was created or last saved), saving is not really done, because it would have no effect. Instead, C-x C-s displays a message like this in the echo area:

     `(No changes need to be saved)`

The command C-x s (`save-some-buffers`) offers to save any or all modified buffers. It asks you what to do with each buffer. The possible responses are analogous to those of `query-replace`:

y   Save this buffer and ask about the rest of the buffers.

n   Don't save this buffer, but ask about the rest of the buffers.

!   Save this buffer and all the rest with no more questions.

RET   Terminate `save-some-buffers` without any more saving.

.   Save this buffer, then exit `save-some-buffers` without even asking about other buffers.

C-r   View the buffer that you are currently being asked about. When you exit View mode, you get back to `save-some-buffers`, which asks the question again.

d   Diff the buffer against its corresponding file, so you can see what changes you would be saving.

C-h   Display a help message about these options.

C-x C-c, the key sequence to exit Emacs, invokes `save-some-buffers` and therefore asks the same questions.

If you have changed a buffer but you do not want to save the changes, you should take some action to prevent it. Otherwise, each time you use C-x s or C-x C-c, you are liable to save this buffer by mistake. One thing you can do is type M-~ (`not-modified`), which clears out the indication that the buffer is modified. If you do this, none of the save commands will believe that the buffer needs to be saved. ('~'

is often used as a mathematical symbol for 'not'; thus M-~ is 'not', metafied.) You could also use `set-visited-file-name` (see below) to mark the buffer as visiting a different file name, one which is not in use for anything important. Alternatively, you can cancel all the changes made since the file was visited or saved, by reading the text from the file again. This is called *reverting*. See Section 15.4 [Reverting], page 131. (You could also undo all the changes by repeating the undo command C-x u until you have undone all the changes; but reverting is easier.) You can also kill the buffer.

M-x `set-visited-file-name` alters the name of the file that the current buffer is visiting. It reads the new file name using the minibuffer. Then it marks the buffer as visiting that file name, and changes the buffer name correspondingly. `set-visited-file-name` does not save the buffer in the newly visited file; it just alters the records inside Emacs in case you do save later. It also marks the buffer as "modified" so that C-x C-s in that buffer *will* save.

If you wish to mark the buffer as visiting a different file and save it right away, use C-x C-w (`write-file`). It is equivalent to `set-visited-file-name` followed by C-x C-s (except that C-x C-w asks for confirmation if the file exists). C-x C-s used on a buffer that is not visiting a file has the same effect as C-x C-w; that is, it reads a file name, marks the buffer as visiting that file, and saves it there. The default file name in a buffer that is not visiting a file is made by combining the buffer name with the buffer's default directory (see Section 15.1 [File Names], page 119).

If the new file name implies a major mode, then C-x C-w switches to that major mode, in most cases. The command `set-visited-file-name` also does this. See Section 20.1 [Choosing Modes], page 207.

If Emacs is about to save a file and sees that the date of the latest version on disk does not match what Emacs last read or wrote, Emacs notifies you of this fact, because it probably indicates a problem caused by simultaneous editing and requires your immediate attention. See Section 15.3.4 [Simultaneous Editing], page 129.

15.3.2 Backup Files

On most operating systems, rewriting a file automatically destroys all record of what the file used to contain. Thus, saving a file from Emacs throws away the old contents of the file—or it would, except that Emacs carefully copies the old contents to another file, called the *backup* file, before actually saving.

For most files, the variable `make-backup-files` determines whether to make backup files. On most operating systems, its default value is `t`, so that Emacs does write backup files.

For files managed by a version control system (see Section 15.7 [Version Control], page 135), the variable `vc-make-backup-files` determines whether to make backup files. By default it is `nil`, since backup files are redundant when you store all the previous versions in a version control system. See section "General VC Options" in *Specialized Emacs Features*.

At your option, Emacs can keep either a single backup for each file, or make a series of numbered backup files for each file that you edit.

The default value of the `backup-enable-predicate` variable prevents backup files being written for files in the directories used for temporary files, specified by `temporary-file-directory` or `small-temporary-file-directory`.

Emacs makes a backup for a file only the first time the file is saved from one buffer. No matter how many times you save a file, its backup file continues to contain the contents from before the file was visited. Normally this means that the backup file contains the contents from before the current editing session; however, if you kill the buffer and then visit the file again, a new backup file will be made by the next save.

You can also explicitly request making another backup file from a buffer even though it has already been saved at least once. If you save the buffer with C-u C-x C-s, the version thus saved will be made into a backup file if you save the buffer again. C-u C-u C-x C-s saves the buffer, but first makes the previous file contents into a new backup file. C-u C-u C-u C-x C-s does both things: it makes a backup from the previous contents, and arranges to make another from the newly saved contents if you save again.

15.3.2.1 Numbered Backups

The choice of single backup file or multiple numbered backup files is controlled by the variable `version-control`. Its possible values are:

t   Make numbered backups.

nil   Make numbered backups for files that have numbered backups already. Otherwise, make single backups.

never   Never make numbered backups; always make single backups.

The usual way to set this variable is globally, through your '.emacs' file or the customization buffer. However, you can set `version-control` locally in an individual buffer to control the making of backups for that buffer's file. For example, Rmail mode locally sets `version-control` to `never` to make sure that there is only one backup for an Rmail file. See Section 32.3.3 [Locals], page 419.

If you set the environment variable VERSION_CONTROL, to tell various GNU utilities what to do with backup files, Emacs also obeys the environment variable by setting the Lisp variable `version-control` accordingly at startup. If the environment variable's value is 't' or 'numbered', then `version-control` becomes t; if the value is 'nil' or 'existing', then `version-control` becomes nil; if it is 'never' or 'simple', then `version-control` becomes never.

15.3.2.2 Single or Numbered Backups

When Emacs makes a single backup file, its name is normally constructed by appending '~' to the file name being edited; thus, the backup file for 'eval.c' would be 'eval.c~'.

You can change this behavior by defining the variable `make-backup-file-name-function` to a suitable function. Alternatively you can customize the variable `backup-directory-alist` to specify that files matching certain patterns should be backed up in specific directories.

A typical use is to add an element (".". *dir*) to make all backups in the directory with absolute name *dir*; Emacs modifies the backup file names to avoid clashes between files with the same names originating in different directories. Alternatively, adding, say, (".". ".~") would make backups in the invisible subdirectory '.~' of the original file's directory. Emacs creates the directory, if necessary, to make the backup.

If access control stops Emacs from writing backup files under the usual names, it writes the backup file as '%backup%~' in your home directory. Only one such file can exist, so only the most recently made such backup is available.

If you choose to have a series of numbered backup files, backup file names contain '.~', the number, and another '~' after the original file name. Thus, the backup files of 'eval.c' would be called 'eval.c.~1~', 'eval.c.~2~', and so on, all the way through names like 'eval.c.~259~' and beyond. The variable backup-directory-alist applies to numbered backups just as usual.

15.3.2.3 Automatic Deletion of Backups

To prevent excessive consumption of disk space, Emacs can delete numbered backup versions automatically. Generally Emacs keeps the first few backups and the latest few backups, deleting any in between. This happens every time a new backup is made.

The two variables kept-old-versions and kept-new-versions control this deletion. Their values are, respectively, the number of oldest (lowest-numbered) backups to keep and the number of newest (highest-numbered) ones to keep, each time a new backup is made. The backups in the middle (excluding those oldest and newest) are the excess middle versions—those backups are deleted. These variables' values are used when it is time to delete excess versions, just after a new backup version is made; the newly made backup is included in the count in kept-new-versions. By default, both variables are 2.

If delete-old-versions is t, Emacs deletes the excess backup files silently. If it is nil, the default, Emacs asks you whether it should delete the excess backup versions. If it has any other value, then Emacs never automatically deletes backups.

Dired's . (Period) command can also be used to delete old versions. See Section 29.3 [Dired Deletion], page 340.

15.3.2.4 Copying vs. Renaming

Backup files can be made by copying the old file or by renaming it. This makes a difference when the old file has multiple names (hard links). If the old file is renamed into the backup file, then the alternate names become names for the backup file. If the old file is copied instead, then the alternate names remain names for the file that you are editing, and the contents accessed by those names will be the new contents.

The method of making a backup file may also affect the file's owner and group. If copying is used, these do not change. If renaming is used, you become the file's owner, and the file's group becomes the default (different operating systems have different defaults for the group).

Having the owner change is usually a good idea, because then the owner always shows who last edited the file. Also, the owners of the backups show who produced those versions. Occasionally there is a file whose owner should not change; it is a good idea for such files to contain local variable lists to set `backup-by-copying-when-mismatch` locally (see Section 32.3.4 [File Variables], page 420).

The choice of renaming or copying is controlled by four variables. Renaming is the default choice. If the variable `backup-by-copying` is non-`nil`, copying is used. Otherwise, if the variable `backup-by-copying-when-linked` is non-`nil`, then copying is used for files that have multiple names, but renaming may still be used when the file being edited has only one name. If the variable `backup-by-copying-when-mismatch` is non-`nil`, then copying is used if renaming would cause the file's owner or group to change. `backup-by-copying-when-mismatch` is `t` by default if you start Emacs as the superuser. The fourth variable, `backup-by-copying-when-privileged-mismatch`, gives the highest numeric user-id for which `backup-by-copying-when-mismatch` will be forced on. This is useful when low-numbered user-ids are assigned to special system users, such as `root`, `bin`, `daemon`, etc., which must maintain ownership of files.

When a file is managed with a version control system (see Section 15.7 [Version Control], page 135), Emacs does not normally make backups in the usual way for that file. But check-in and check-out are similar in some ways to making backups. One unfortunate similarity is that these operations typically break hard links, disconnecting the file name you visited from any alternate names for the same file. This has nothing to do with Emacs—the version control system does it.

15.3.3 Customizing Saving of Files

If the value of the variable `require-final-newline` is `t`, saving or writing a file silently puts a newline at the end if there isn't already one there. If the value is `visit`, Emacs adds a newline at the end of any file that doesn't have one, just after it visits the file. (This marks the buffer as modified, and you can undo it.) If the value is `visit-save`, that means to add newlines both on visiting and on saving. If the value is `nil`, Emacs leaves the end of the file unchanged; if it's neither `nil` nor `t`, Emacs asks you whether to add a newline. The default is `nil`.

Many major modes are designed for specific kinds of files that are always supposed to end in newlines. These major modes set the variable `require-final-newline` according to `mode-require-final-newline`. By setting the latter variable, you can control how these modes handle final newlines.

When Emacs saves a file, it invokes the `fsync` system call to force the data immediately out to disk. This is important for safety if the system crashes or in case of power outage. However, it can be disruptive on laptops using power saving, because it requires the disk to spin up each time you save a file. Setting `write-region-inhibit-fsync` to a non-`nil` value disables this synchronization. Be careful—this means increased risk of data loss.

15.3.4 Protection against Simultaneous Editing

Simultaneous editing occurs when two users visit the same file, both make changes, and then both save them. If nobody were informed that this was happening, whichever user saved first would later find that his changes were lost.

On some systems, Emacs notices immediately when the second user starts to change the file, and issues an immediate warning. On all systems, Emacs checks when you save the file, and warns if you are about to overwrite another user's changes. You can prevent loss of the other user's work by taking the proper corrective action instead of saving the file.

When you make the first modification in an Emacs buffer that is visiting a file, Emacs records that the file is *locked* by you. (It does this by creating a symbolic link in the same directory with a different name.) Emacs removes the lock when you save the changes. The idea is that the file is locked whenever an Emacs buffer visiting it has unsaved changes.

If you begin to modify the buffer while the visited file is locked by someone else, this constitutes a *collision*. When Emacs detects a collision, it asks you what to do, by calling the Lisp function `ask-user-about-lock`. You can redefine this function for the sake of customization. The standard definition of this function asks you a question and accepts three possible answers:

s   Steal the lock. Whoever was already changing the file loses the lock, and you gain the lock.

p   Proceed. Go ahead and edit the file despite its being locked by someone else.

q   Quit. This causes an error (`file-locked`), and the buffer contents remain unchanged—the modification you were trying to make does not actually take place.

Note that locking works on the basis of a file name; if a file has multiple names, Emacs does not realize that the two names are the same file and cannot prevent two users from editing it simultaneously under different names. However, basing locking on names means that Emacs can interlock the editing of new files that will not really exist until they are saved.

Some systems are not configured to allow Emacs to make locks, and there are cases where lock files cannot be written. In these cases, Emacs cannot detect trouble in advance, but it still can detect the collision when you try to save a file and overwrite someone else's changes.

If Emacs or the operating system crashes, this may leave behind lock files which are stale, so you may occasionally get warnings about spurious collisions. When you determine that the collision is spurious, just use p to tell Emacs to go ahead anyway.

Every time Emacs saves a buffer, it first checks the last-modification date of the existing file on disk to verify that it has not changed since the file was last visited or saved. If the date does not match, it implies that changes were made in the file in some other way, and these changes are about to be lost if Emacs actually does save. To prevent this, Emacs displays a warning message and asks for confirmation before saving. Occasionally you will know why the file was changed and know that it does not matter; then you can answer `yes` and proceed. Otherwise, you should cancel the save with `C-g` and investigate the situation.

The first thing you should do when notified that simultaneous editing has already taken place is to list the directory with `C-u C-x C-d` (see Section 15.8 [Directories], page 147). This shows the file's current author. You should attempt to contact him to warn him not to continue editing. Often the next step is to save the contents of your Emacs buffer under a different name, and use `diff` to compare the two files.

15.3.5 Shadowing Files

`M-x shadow-initialize`
> Set up file shadowing.

`M-x shadow-define-literal-group`
> Declare a single file to be shared between sites.

`M-x shadow-define-regexp-group`
> Make all files that match each of a group of files be shared between hosts.

`M-x shadow-define-cluster RET name RET`
> Define a shadow file cluster *name*.

`M-x shadow-copy-files`
> Copy all pending shadow files.

`M-x shadow-cancel`
> Cancel the instruction to shadow some files.

You can arrange to keep identical *shadow* copies of certain files in more than one place—possibly on different machines. To do this, first you must set up a *shadow file group*, which is a set of identically-named files shared between a list of sites. The file group is permanent and applies to further Emacs sessions as well as the current one. Once the group is set up, every time you exit Emacs, it will copy the file you edited to the other files in its group. You can also do the copying without exiting Emacs, by typing `M-x shadow-copy-files`.

To set up a shadow file group, use `M-x shadow-define-literal-group` or `M-x shadow-define-regexp-group`. See their documentation strings for further information.

Before copying a file to its shadows, Emacs asks for confirmation. You can answer "no" to bypass copying of this file, this time. If you want to cancel the shadowing permanently for a certain file, use `M-x shadow-cancel` to eliminate or change the shadow file group.

A *shadow cluster* is a group of hosts that share directories, so that copying to or from one of them is sufficient to update the file on all of them. Each shadow cluster has a name, and specifies the network address of a primary host (the one we copy files to), and a regular expression that matches the host names of all the other hosts in the cluster. You can define a shadow cluster with `M-x shadow-define-cluster`.

15.3.6 Updating Time Stamps Automatically

You can arrange to put a time stamp in a file, so that it will be updated automatically each time you edit and save the file. The time stamp has to be in the first eight lines of the file, and you should insert it like this:

```
Time-stamp: <>
```

or like this:

```
Time-stamp: " "
```

Then add the hook function `time-stamp` to the hook `before-save-hook`; that hook function will automatically update the time stamp, inserting the current date and time when you save the file. You can also use the command `M-x time-stamp` to update the time stamp manually. For other customizations, see the Custom group `time-stamp`. Note that non-numeric fields in the time stamp are formatted according to your locale setting (see Section C.5 [Environment], page 476).

15.4 Reverting a Buffer

If you have made extensive changes to a file and then change your mind about them, you can get rid of them by reading in the previous version of the file. To do this, use `M-x revert-buffer`, which operates on the current buffer. Since reverting a buffer unintentionally could lose a lot of work, you must confirm this command with **yes**.

`revert-buffer` tries to position point in such a way that, if the file was edited only slightly, you will be at approximately the same piece of text after reverting as before. However, if you have made drastic changes, point may wind up in a totally different piece of text.

Reverting marks the buffer as "not modified" until another change is made.

Some kinds of buffers whose contents reflect data bases other than files, such as Dired buffers, can also be reverted. For them, reverting means recalculating their contents from the appropriate data base. Buffers created explicitly with `C-x b` cannot be reverted; `revert-buffer` reports an error when asked to do so.

When you edit a file that changes automatically and frequently—for example, a log of output from a process that continues to run—it may be useful for Emacs to revert the file without querying you, whenever you visit the file again with `C-x C-f`.

To request this behavior, set the variable `revert-without-query` to a list of regular expressions. When a file name matches one of these regular expressions, `find-file` and `revert-buffer` will revert it automatically if it has changed—provided the buffer itself is not modified. (If you have edited the text, it would be wrong to discard your changes.)

You may find it useful to have Emacs revert files automatically when they change. Three minor modes are available to do this.

`M-x global-auto-revert-mode` enables Global Auto-Revert mode, which periodically checks all file buffers and reverts when the corresponding file has changed. `M-x auto-revert-mode` enables a local version, Auto-Revert mode, which applies only to the current buffer.

You can use Auto-Revert mode to "tail" a file such as a system log, so that changes made to that file by other programs are continuously displayed. To do this, just move the point to the end of the buffer, and it will stay there as the file contents change. However, if you are sure that the file will only change by growing at the end, use Auto-Revert Tail mode instead (`auto-revert-tail-mode`). It is more efficient for this.

The variable `auto-revert-interval` controls how often to check for a changed file. Since checking a remote file is too slow, these modes do not check or revert remote files.

See Section 15.7.2 [VC Mode Line], page 137, for Auto Revert peculiarities in buffers that visit files under version control.

15.5 Auto-Saving: Protection Against Disasters

Emacs saves all the visited files from time to time (based on counting your keystrokes) without being asked. This is called *auto-saving*. It prevents you from losing more than a limited amount of work if the system crashes.

When Emacs determines that it is time for auto-saving, it considers each buffer, and each is auto-saved if auto-saving is enabled for it and it has been changed since the last time it was auto-saved. The message '`Auto-saving...`' is displayed in the echo area during auto-saving, if any files are actually auto-saved. Errors occurring during auto-saving are caught so that they do not interfere with the execution of commands you have been typing.

15.5.1 Auto-Save Files

Auto-saving does not normally save in the files that you visited, because it can be very undesirable to save a program that is in an inconsistent state when you have made half of a planned change. Instead, auto-saving is done in a different file called the *auto-save file*, and the visited file is changed only when you request saving explicitly (such as with `C-x C-s`).

Normally, the auto-save file name is made by appending '`#`' to the front and rear of the visited file name. Thus, a buffer visiting file '`foo.c`' is auto-saved in a file '`#foo.c#`'. Most buffers that are not visiting files are auto-saved only if you request it explicitly; when they are auto-saved, the auto-save file name is made by appending '`#`' to the front and rear of buffer name, then adding digits and letters at the end for uniqueness. For example, the '`*mail*`' buffer in which you compose messages to be sent might be auto-saved in a file named '`#*mail*#704juu`'. Auto-save file names are made this way unless you reprogram parts of Emacs to do something different (the functions `make-auto-save-file-name` and `auto-save-file-name-p`). The file name to be used for auto-saving in a buffer is calculated when auto-saving is turned on in that buffer.

The variable `auto-save-file-name-transforms` allows a degree of control over the auto-save file name. It lets you specify a series of regular expressions and replacements to transform the auto save file name. The default value puts the auto-save files for remote files (see Section 15.14 [Remote Files], page 152) into the temporary file directory on the local machine.

When you delete a substantial part of the text in a large buffer, auto save turns off temporarily in that buffer. This is because if you deleted the text unintentionally, you might find the auto-save file more useful if it contains the deleted text. To reenable auto-saving after this happens, save the buffer with C-x C-s, or use C-u 1 M-x auto-save-mode.

If you want auto-saving to be done in the visited file rather than in a separate auto-save file, set the variable auto-save-visited-file-name to a non-nil value. In this mode, there is no real difference between auto-saving and explicit saving.

A buffer's auto-save file is deleted when you save the buffer in its visited file. (You can inhibit this by setting the variable delete-auto-save-files to nil.) Changing the visited file name with C-x C-w or set-visited-file-name renames any auto-save file to go with the new visited name.

15.5.2 Controlling Auto-Saving

Each time you visit a file, auto-saving is turned on for that file's buffer if the variable auto-save-default is non-nil (but not in batch mode; see Chapter 3 [Entering Emacs], page 17). The default for this variable is t, so auto-saving is the usual practice for file-visiting buffers. Auto-saving can be turned on or off for any existing buffer with the command M-x auto-save-mode. Like other minor mode commands, M-x auto-save-mode turns auto-saving on with a positive argument, off with a zero or negative argument; with no argument, it toggles.

Emacs does auto-saving periodically based on counting how many characters you have typed since the last time auto-saving was done. The variable auto-save-interval specifies how many characters there are between auto-saves. By default, it is 300. Emacs doesn't accept values that are too small: if you customize auto-save-interval to a value less than 20, Emacs will behave as if the value is 20.

Auto-saving also takes place when you stop typing for a while. The variable auto-save-timeout says how many seconds Emacs should wait before it does an auto save (and perhaps also a garbage collection). (The actual time period is longer if the current buffer is long; this is a heuristic which aims to keep out of your way when you are editing long buffers, in which auto-save takes an appreciable amount of time.) Auto-saving during idle periods accomplishes two things: first, it makes sure all your work is saved if you go away from the terminal for a while; second, it may avoid some auto-saving while you are actually typing.

Emacs also does auto-saving whenever it gets a fatal error. This includes killing the Emacs job with a shell command such as 'kill %emacs', or disconnecting a phone line or network connection.

You can request an auto-save explicitly with the command M-x do-auto-save.

15.5.3 Recovering Data from Auto-Saves

You can use the contents of an auto-save file to recover from a loss of data with the command M-x recover-file RET file RET. This visits file and then (after your confirmation) restores the contents from its auto-save file '#file#'. You can then save with C-x C-s to put the recovered text into *file* itself. For example, to recover file 'foo.c' from its auto-save file '#foo.c#', do:

```
M-x recover-file RET foo.c RET
yes RET
C-x C-s
```

Before asking for confirmation, M-x recover-file displays a directory listing describing the specified file and the auto-save file, so you can compare their sizes and dates. If the auto-save file is older, M-x recover-file does not offer to read it.

If Emacs or the computer crashes, you can recover all the files you were editing from their auto save files with the command M-x recover-session. This first shows you a list of recorded interrupted sessions. Move point to the one you choose, and type C-c C-c.

Then recover-session asks about each of the files that were being edited during that session, asking whether to recover that file. If you answer y, it calls recover-file, which works in its normal fashion. It shows the dates of the original file and its auto-save file, and asks once again whether to recover that file.

When recover-session is done, the files you've chosen to recover are present in Emacs buffers. You should then save them. Only this—saving them—updates the files themselves.

Emacs records information about interrupted sessions for later recovery in files named '~/.emacs.d/auto-save-list/.saves-*pid-hostname*'. All of this name except the '*pid-hostname*' part comes from the value of auto-save-list-file-prefix. You can record sessions in a different place by customizing that variable. If you set auto-save-list-file-prefix to nil in your '.emacs' file, sessions are not recorded for recovery.

15.6 File Name Aliases

Symbolic links and hard links both make it possible for several file names to refer to the same file. Hard links are alternate names that refer directly to the file; all the names are equally valid, and no one of them is preferred. By contrast, a symbolic link is a kind of defined alias: when 'foo' is a symbolic link to 'bar', you can use either name to refer to the file, but 'bar' is the real name, while 'foo' is just an alias. More complex cases occur when symbolic links point to directories.

Normally, if you visit a file which Emacs is already visiting under a different name, Emacs displays a message in the echo area and uses the existing buffer visiting that file. This can happen on systems that support hard or symbolic links, or if you use a long file name on a system that truncates long file names, or on a case-insensitive file system. You can suppress the message by setting the variable find-file-suppress-same-file-warnings to a non-nil value. You can disable this feature entirely by setting the variable find-file-existing-other-name to nil: then if you visit the same file under two different names, you get a separate buffer for each file name.

If the variable `find-file-visit-truename` is non-`nil`, then the file name recorded for a buffer is the file's *truename* (made by replacing all symbolic links with their target names), rather than the name you specify. Setting `find-file-visit-truename` also implies the effect of `find-file-existing-other-name`.

15.7 Version Control

Version control systems are packages that can record multiple versions of a source file, usually storing the unchanged parts of the file just once. Version control systems also record history information such as the creation time of each version, who created it, and a description of what was changed in that version.

The Emacs version control interface is called VC. Its commands work with different version control systems—currently, it supports CVS, GNU Arch, RCS, Meta-CVS, Subversion, and SCCS. Of these, the GNU project distributes CVS, GNU Arch, and RCS; we recommend that you use either CVS or GNU Arch for your projects, and RCS for individual files. We also have free software to replace SCCS, known as CSSC; if you are using SCCS and don't want to make the incompatible change to RCS or CVS, you can switch to CSSC.

VC is enabled by default in Emacs. To disable it, set the customizable variable `vc-handled-backends` to `nil` (see section "Customizing VC" in *Specialized Emacs Features*).

15.7.1 Introduction to Version Control

VC allows you to use a version control system from within Emacs, integrating the version control operations smoothly with editing. VC provides a uniform interface to version control, so that regardless of which version control system is in use, you can use it the same way.

This section provides a general overview of version control, and describes the version control systems that VC supports. You can skip this section if you are already familiar with the version control system you want to use.

15.7.1.1 Supported Version Control Systems

VC currently works with six different version control systems or "back ends": CVS, GNU Arch, RCS, Meta-CVS, Subversion, and SCCS.

CVS is a free version control system that is used for the majority of free software projects today. It allows concurrent multi-user development either locally or over the network. Some of its shortcomings, corrected by newer systems such as GNU Arch, are that it lacks atomic commits or support for renaming files. VC supports all basic editing operations under CVS, but for some less common tasks you still need to call CVS from the command line. Note also that before using CVS you must set up a repository, which is a subject too complex to treat here.

GNU Arch is a new version control system that is designed for distributed work. It differs in many ways from old well-known systems, such as CVS and RCS. It supports different transports for interoperating between users, offline operations, and it has good branching and merging features. It also supports atomic commits, and history of file renaming and moving. VC does not support all operations provided by GNU Arch, so you must sometimes invoke it from the command line, or use a specialized module.

RCS is the free version control system around which VC was initially built. The VC commands are therefore conceptually closest to RCS. Almost everything you can do with RCS can be done through VC. You cannot use RCS over the network though, and it only works at the level of individual files, rather than projects. You should use it if you want a simple, yet reliable tool for handling individual files.

Subversion is a free version control system designed to be similar to CVS but without CVS's problems. Subversion supports atomic commits, and versions directories, symbolic links, meta-data, renames, copies, and deletes. It can be used via http or via its own protocol.

Meta-CVS is another attempt to solve problems arising in CVS. It supports directory structure versioning, improved branching and merging, and use of symbolic links and meta-data in repositories.

SCCS is a proprietary but widely used version control system. In terms of capabilities, it is the weakest of the six that VC supports. VC compensates for certain features missing in SCCS (snapshots, for example) by implementing them itself, but some other VC features, such as multiple branches, are not available with SCCS. Since SCCS is non-free, not respecting its users freedom, you should not use it; use its free replacement CSSC instead. But you should use CSSC only if for some reason you cannot use RCS, or one of the higher-level systems such as CVS or GNU Arch.

In the following, we discuss mainly RCS, SCCS and CVS. Nearly everything said about CVS applies to GNU Arch, Subversion and Meta-CVS as well.

15.7.1.2 Concepts of Version Control

When a file is under version control, we also say that it is *registered* in the version control system. Each registered file has a corresponding *master file* which represents the file's present state plus its change history—enough to reconstruct the current version or any earlier version. Usually the master file also records a *log entry* for each version, describing in words what was changed in that version.

The file that is maintained under version control is sometimes called the *work file* corresponding to its master file. You edit the work file and make changes in it, as you would with an ordinary file. (With SCCS and RCS, you must *lock* the file before you start to edit it.) After you are done with a set of changes, you *check the file in*, which records the changes in the master file, along with a log entry for them.

With CVS, there are usually multiple work files corresponding to a single master file—often each user has his own copy. It is also possible to use RCS in this way, but this is not the usual way to use RCS.

A version control system typically has some mechanism to coordinate between users who want to change the same file. One method is *locking* (analogous to the locking that Emacs uses to detect simultaneous editing of a file, but distinct from it). The other method is to merge your changes with other people's changes when you check them in.

With version control locking, work files are normally read-only so that you cannot change them. You ask the version control system to make a work file writable for you by locking it; only one user can do this at any given time. When you check in your changes, that unlocks the file, making the work file read-only again. This allows other users to lock the file to make further changes. SCCS always uses locking, and RCS normally does.

The other alternative for RCS is to let each user modify the work file at any time. In this mode, locking is not required, but it is permitted; check-in is still the way to record a new version.

CVS normally allows each user to modify his own copy of the work file at any time, but requires merging with changes from other users at check-in time. However, CVS can also be set up to require locking. (see section "CVS Options" in *Specialized Emacs Features*).

15.7.1.3 Types of Log File

Projects that use a revision control system can have *two* types of log for changes. One is the per-file log maintained by the revision control system: each time you check in a change, you must fill out a *log entry* for the change (see Section 15.7.3.4 [Log Buffer], page 140). This kind of log is called the *version control log*, also the *revision control log*, *RCS log*, or *CVS log*.

The other kind of log is the file 'ChangeLog' (see Section 25.1 [Change Log], page 292). It provides a chronological record of all changes to a large portion of a program—typically one directory and its subdirectories. A small program would use one 'ChangeLog' file; a large program may well merit a 'ChangeLog' file in each major directory. See Section 25.1 [Change Log], page 292.

A project maintained with version control can use just the per-file log, or it can use both kinds of logs. It can handle some files one way and some files the other way. Each project has its policy, which you should follow.

When the policy is to use both, you typically want to write an entry for each change just once, then put it into both logs. You can write the entry in 'ChangeLog', then copy it to the log buffer when you check in the change. Or you can write the entry in the log buffer while checking in the change, and later use the C-x v a command to copy it to 'ChangeLog' (see section "Change Logs and VC" in *Specialized Emacs Features*).

15.7.2 Version Control and the Mode Line

When you visit a file that is under version control, Emacs indicates this on the mode line. For example, 'RCS-1.3' says that RCS is used for that file, and the current version is 1.3.

The character between the back-end name and the version number indicates the version control status of the file. '-' means that the work file is not locked (if locking is in use), or not modified (if locking is not in use). ':' indicates that the file is locked, or that it is modified. If the file is locked by some other user (for instance, 'jim'), that is displayed as 'RCS:jim:1.3'.

When Auto Revert mode (see Section 15.4 [Reverting], page 131) reverts a buffer that is under version control, it updates the version control information in the mode line. However, Auto Revert mode may not properly update this information if the version control status changes without changes to the work file, from outside the current Emacs session. If you set `auto-revert-check-vc-info` to `t`, Auto Revert mode updates the version control status information every `auto-revert-interval` seconds, even if the work file itself is unchanged. The resulting CPU usage depends on the version control system, but is usually not excessive.

15.7.3 Basic Editing under Version Control

The principal VC command is an all-purpose command that performs either locking or check-in, depending on the situation.

C-x v v   Perform the next logical version control operation on this file.

The precise action of this command depends on the state of the file, and whether the version control system uses locking or not. SCCS and RCS normally use locking; CVS normally does not use locking.

As a special convenience that is particularly useful for files with locking, you can let Emacs check a file in or out whenever you change its read-only flag. This means, for example, that you cannot accidentally edit a file without properly checking it out first. To achieve this, bind the key `C-x C-q` to `vc-toggle-read-only` in your '`~/.emacs`' file. (See Section 32.4.6 [Init Rebinding], page 427.)

15.7.3.1 Basic Version Control with Locking

If locking is used for the file (as with SCCS, and RCS in its default mode), `C-x v v` can either lock a file or check it in:

- If the file is not locked, `C-x v v` locks it, and makes it writable so that you can change it.

- If the file is locked by you, and contains changes, `C-x v v` checks in the changes. In order to do this, it first reads the log entry for the new version. See Section 15.7.3.4 [Log Buffer], page 140.

- If the file is locked by you, but you have not changed it since you locked it, `C-x v v` releases the lock and makes the file read-only again.

- If the file is locked by some other user, `C-x v v` asks you whether you want to "steal the lock" from that user. If you say yes, the file becomes locked by you, but a message is sent to the person who had formerly locked the file, to inform him of what has happened.

These rules also apply when you use CVS in locking mode, except that there is no such thing as stealing a lock.

15.7.3.2 Basic Version Control without Locking

When there is no locking—the default for CVS—work files are always writable; you do not need to do anything before you begin to edit a file. The status indicator on the mode line is '-' if the file is unmodified; it flips to ':' as soon as you save any changes in the work file.

Here is what C-x v v does when using CVS:

- If some other user has checked in changes into the master file, Emacs asks you whether you want to merge those changes into your own work file. You must do this before you can check in your own changes. (To pick up any recent changes from the master file *without* trying to commit your own changes, type C-x v m RET.) See Section 15.7.6.3 [Merging], page 145.

- If there are no new changes in the master file, but you have made modifications in your work file, C-x v v checks in your changes. In order to do this, it first reads the log entry for the new version. See Section 15.7.3.4 [Log Buffer], page 140.

- If the file is not modified, the C-x v v does nothing.

These rules also apply when you use RCS in the mode that does not require locking, except that automatic merging of changes from the master file is not implemented. Unfortunately, this means that nothing informs you if another user has checked in changes in the same file since you began editing it, and when this happens, his changes will be effectively removed when you check in your version (though they will remain in the master file, so they will not be entirely lost). You must therefore verify that the current version is unchanged, before you check in your changes. We hope to eliminate this risk and provide automatic merging with RCS in a future Emacs version.

In addition, locking is possible with RCS even in this mode, although it is not required; C-x v v with an unmodified file locks the file, just as it does with RCS in its normal (locking) mode.

15.7.3.3 Advanced Control in C-x v v

When you give a prefix argument to vc-next-action (C-u C-x v v), it still performs the next logical version control operation, but accepts additional arguments to specify precisely how to do the operation.

- If the file is modified (or locked), you can specify the version number to use for the new version that you check in. This is one way to create a new branch (see Section 15.7.6 [Branches], page 144).

- If the file is not modified (and unlocked), you can specify the version to select; this lets you start working from an older version, or on another branch. If you do not enter any version, that takes you to the highest version on the current branch; therefore C-u C-x v v RET is a convenient way to get the latest version of a file from the repository.

- Instead of the version number, you can also specify the name of a version control system. This is useful when one file is being managed with two version control systems at the same time (see section "Local Version Control" in *Specialized Emacs Features*).

15.7.3.4 Features of the Log Entry Buffer

When you check in changes, C-x v v first reads a log entry. It pops up a buffer called '*VC-Log*' for you to enter the log entry.

Sometimes the '*VC-Log*' buffer contains default text when you enter it, typically the last log message entered. If it does, mark and point are set around the entire contents of the buffer so that it is easy to kill the contents of the buffer with C-w.

If you work by writing entries in the 'ChangeLog' (see Section 25.1 [Change Log], page 292) and then commit the change under revision control, you can generate the Log Edit text from the ChangeLog using C-c C-a (log-edit-insert-changelog). This looks for entries for the file(s) concerned in the top entry in the ChangeLog and uses those paragraphs as the log text. This text is only inserted if the top entry was made under your user name on the current date. See section "Change Logs and VC" in *Specialized Emacs Features*, for the opposite way of working—generating ChangeLog entries from the revision control log.

In the '*VC-Log*' buffer, C-c C-f (M-x log-edit-show-files) shows the list of files to be committed in case you need to check that. (This can be a list of more than one file if you use VC Dired mode or PCL-CVS. See section "VC Dired Mode" in *Specialized Emacs Features*, and section "About PCL-CVS" in *PCL-CVS — The Emacs Front-End to CVS*.)

When you have finished editing the log message, type C-c C-c to exit the buffer and commit the change.

To abort check-in, just **don't** type C-c C-c in that buffer. You can switch buffers and do other editing. As long as you don't try to check in another file, the entry you were editing remains in the '*VC-Log*' buffer, and you can go back to that buffer at any time to complete the check-in.

If you change several source files for the same reason, it is often convenient to specify the same log entry for many of the files. To do this, use the history of previous log entries. The commands M-n, M-p, M-s and M-r for doing this work just like the minibuffer history commands (except that these versions are used outside the minibuffer).

Each time you check in a file, the log entry buffer is put into VC Log mode, which involves running two hooks: text-mode-hook and vc-log-mode-hook. See Section 32.3.2 [Hooks], page 418.

15.7.4 Examining And Comparing Old Versions

One of the convenient features of version control is the ability to examine any version of a file, or compare two versions.

C-x v ~ *version* RET

        Examine version *version* of the visited file, in a buffer of its own.

C-x v =   Compare the current buffer contents with the master version from which you started editing.

C-u C-x v = *file* RET *oldvers* RET *newvers* RET

        Compare the specified two versions of *file*.

C-x v g   Display the file with per-line version information and using colors.

To examine an old version in its entirety, visit the file and then type C-x v ~ *version* RET (vc-version-other-window). This puts the text of version *version* in a file named '*filename.~version~*', and visits it in its own buffer in a separate window. (In RCS, you can also select an old version and create a branch from it. See Section 15.7.6 [Branches], page 144.)

It is usually more convenient to compare two versions of the file, with the command C-x v = (vc-diff). Plain C-x v = compares the current buffer contents (saving them in the file if necessary) with the master version from which you started editing the file (this is not necessarily the latest version of the file). C-u C-x v =, with a numeric argument, reads a file name and two version numbers, then compares those versions of the specified file. Both forms display the output in a special buffer in another window.

You can specify a checked-in version by its number; an empty input specifies the current contents of the work file (which may be different from all the checked-in versions). You can also specify a snapshot name (see section "Snapshots" in *Specialized Emacs Features*) instead of one or both version numbers.

If you supply a directory name instead of the name of a registered file, this command compares the two specified versions of all registered files in that directory and its subdirectories.

C-x v - works by running a variant of the diff utility designed to work with the version control system in use. When you invoke diff this way, in addition to the options specified by diff-switches (see Section 15.9 [Comparing Files], page 148), it receives those specified by vc-diff-switches, plus those specified for the specific back end by vc-*backend*-diff-switches. For instance, when the version control back end is RCS, diff uses the options in vc-rcs-diff-switches. The 'vc...diff-switches' variables are nil by default.

The buffer produced by C-x v = supports the commands of Compilation mode (see Section 24.2 [Compilation Mode], page 274), such as C-x ' and C-c C-c, in both the "old" and "new" text, and they always find the corresponding locations in the current work file. (Older versions are not, in general, present as files on your disk.)

For some back ends, you can display the file *annotated* with per-line version information and using colors to enhance the visual appearance, with the command M-x vc-annotate. It creates a new buffer (the "annotate buffer") displaying the file's text, with each part colored to show how old it is. Text colored red is new, blue means old, and intermediate colors indicate intermediate ages. By default, the color is scaled over the full range of ages, such that the oldest changes are blue, and the newest changes are red.

When you give a prefix argument to this command, it uses the minibuffer to read two arguments: which version number to display and annotate (instead of the current file contents), and the time span in days the color range should cover.

From the annotate buffer, these and other color scaling options are available from the 'VC-Annotate' menu. In this buffer, you can also use the following keys to browse the annotations of past revisions, view diffs, or view log entries:

P   Annotate the previous revision, that is to say, the revision before the
             one currently annotated. A numeric prefix argument is a repeat count,
             so `C-u 10 P` would take you back 10 revisions.

N   Annotate the next revision—the one after the revision currently an-
             notated. A numeric prefix argument is a repeat count.

J   Annotate the revision indicated by the current line.

A   Annotate the revision before the one indicated by the current line.
             This is useful to see the state the file was in before the change on the
             current line was made.

D   Display the diff between the current line's revision and the previous
             revision. This is useful to see what the current line's revision actually
             changed in the file.

L   Show the log of the current line's revision. This is useful to see the
             author's description of the changes in the revision on the current line.

W   Annotate the workfile version–the one you are editing. If you used
             P and N to browse to other revisions, use this key to return to your
             current version.

15.7.5 The Secondary Commands of VC

This section explains the secondary commands of VC; those that you might use
once a day.

15.7.5.1 Registering a File for Version Control

You can put any file under version control by simply visiting it, and then typing
`C-x v i` (`vc-register`).

C-x v i   Register the visited file for version control.

    To register the file, Emacs must choose which version control system to use for
it. If the file's directory already contains files registered in a version control system,
Emacs uses that system. If there is more than one system in use for a directory,
Emacs uses the one that appears first in `vc-handled-backends` (see section "Customizing VC" in *Specialized Emacs Features*). On the other hand, if there are no
files already registered, Emacs uses the first system from `vc-handled-backends`
that could register the file (for example, you cannot register a file under CVS if its
directory is not already part of a CVS tree); with the default value of `vc-handled-
backends`, this means that Emacs uses RCS in this situation.

    If locking is in use, `C-x v i` leaves the file unlocked and read-only. Type `C-x
v v` if you wish to start editing it. After registering a file with CVS, you must
subsequently commit the initial version by typing `C-x v v`. Until you do that, the
version appears as '`@@`' in the mode line.

    The initial version number for a newly registered file is 1.1, by default. You can
specify a different default by setting the variable `vc-default-init-version`, or

you can give C-x v i a numeric argument; then it reads the initial version number for this particular file using the minibuffer.

If vc-initial-comment is non-nil, C-x v i reads an initial comment to describe the purpose of this source file. Reading the initial comment works like reading a log entry (see Section 15.7.3.4 [Log Buffer], page 140).

15.7.5.2 VC Status Commands

C-x v l   Display version control state and change history.

To view the detailed version control status and history of a file, type C-x v l (vc-print-log). It displays the history of changes to the current file, including the text of the log entries. The output appears in a separate window. The point is centered at the revision of the file that is currently being visited.

In the change log buffer, you can use the following keys to move between the logs of revisions and of files, to view past revisions, and to view diffs:

p   Move to the previous revision-item in the buffer. (Revision entries in the log buffer are usually in reverse-chronological order, so the previous revision-item usually corresponds to a newer revision.) A numeric prefix argument is a repeat count.

n   Move to the next revision-item (which most often corresponds to the previous revision of the file). A numeric prefix argument is a repeat count.

P   Move to the log of the previous file, when the logs of multiple files are in the log buffer (see section "VC Dired Mode" in *Specialized Emacs Features*). Otherwise, just move to the beginning of the log. A numeric prefix argument is a repeat count, so C-u 10 P would move backward 10 files.

N   Move to the log of the next file, when the logs of multiple files are in the log buffer (see section "VC Dired Mode" in *Specialized Emacs Features*). It also takes a numeric prefix argument as a repeat count.

f   Visit the revision indicated at the current line, like typing C-x v ~ and specifying this revision's number (see Section 15.7.4 [Old Versions], page 140).

d   Display the diff (see Section 15.9 [Comparing Files], page 148) between the revision indicated at the current line and the next earlier revision. This is useful to see what actually changed when the revision indicated on the current line was committed.

15.7.5.3 Undoing Version Control Actions

C-x v u   Revert the buffer and the file to the version from which you started editing the file.

C-x v c   Remove the last-entered change from the master for the visited file.
             This undoes your last check-in.

If you want to discard your current set of changes and revert to the version from which you started editing the file, use C-x v u (vc-revert-buffer). This leaves the file unlocked; if locking is in use, you must first lock the file again before you change it again. C-x v u requires confirmation, unless it sees that you haven't made any changes with respect to the master version.

C-x v u is also the command to unlock a file if you lock it and then decide not to change it.

To cancel a change that you already checked in, use C-x v c (vc-cancel-version). This command discards all record of the most recent checked-in version, but only if your work file corresponds to that version—you cannot use C-x v c to cancel a version that is not the latest on its branch. C-x v c also offers to revert your work file and buffer to the previous version (the one that precedes the version that is deleted).

If you answer no, VC keeps your changes in the buffer, and locks the file. The no-revert option is useful when you have checked in a change and then discover a trivial error in it; you can cancel the erroneous check-in, fix the error, and check the file in again.

When C-x v c does not revert the buffer, it unexpands all version control headers in the buffer instead (see section "Version Headers" in *Specialized Emacs Features*). This is because the buffer no longer corresponds to any existing version. If you check it in again, the check-in process will expand the headers properly for the new version number.

However, it is impossible to unexpand the RCS 'Log' header automatically. If you use that header feature, you have to unexpand it by hand—by deleting the entry for the version that you just canceled.

Be careful when invoking C-x v c, as it is easy to lose a lot of work with it. To help you be careful, this command always requires confirmation with yes. Note also that this command is disabled under CVS, because canceling versions is very dangerous and discouraged with CVS.

15.7.6 Multiple Branches of a File

One use of version control is to maintain multiple "current" versions of a file. For example, you might have different versions of a program in which you are gradually adding various unfinished new features. Each such independent line of development is called a *branch*. VC allows you to create branches, switch between different branches, and merge changes from one branch to another. Please note, however, that branches are not supported for SCCS.

A file's main line of development is usually called the *trunk*. The versions on the trunk are normally numbered 1.1, 1.2, 1.3, etc. At any such version, you can start an independent branch. A branch starting at version 1.2 would have version number 1.2.1.1, and consecutive versions on this branch would have numbers 1.2.1.2, 1.2.1.3, 1.2.1.4, and so on. If there is a second branch also starting at version 1.2, it would consist of versions 1.2.2.1, 1.2.2.2, 1.2.2.3, etc.

If you omit the final component of a version number, that is called a *branch number*. It refers to the highest existing version on that branch—the *head version* of that branch. The branches in the example above have branch numbers 1.2.1 and 1.2.2.

15.7.6.1 Switching between Branches

To switch between branches, type C-u C-x v v and specify the version number you want to select. This version is then visited *unlocked* (write-protected), so you can examine it before locking it. Switching branches in this way is allowed only when the file is not locked.

You can omit the minor version number, thus giving only the branch number; this takes you to the head version on the chosen branch. If you only type RET, Emacs goes to the highest version on the trunk.

After you have switched to any branch (including the main branch), you stay on it for subsequent VC commands, until you explicitly select some other branch.

15.7.6.2 Creating New Branches

To create a new branch from a head version (one that is the latest in the branch that contains it), first select that version if necessary, lock it with C-x v v, and make whatever changes you want. Then, when you check in the changes, use C-u C-x v v. This lets you specify the version number for the new version. You should specify a suitable branch number for a branch starting at the current version. For example, if the current version is 2.5, the branch number should be 2.5.1, 2.5.2, and so on, depending on the number of existing branches at that point.

To create a new branch at an older version (one that is no longer the head of a branch), first select that version (see Section 15.7.6.1 [Switching Branches], page 145), then lock it with C-x v v. You'll be asked to confirm, when you lock the old version, that you really mean to create a new branch—if you say no, you'll be offered a chance to lock the latest version instead.

Then make your changes and type C-x v v again to check in a new version. This automatically creates a new branch starting from the selected version. You need not specially request a new branch, because that's the only way to add a new version at a point that is not the head of a branch.

After the branch is created, you "stay" on it. That means that subsequent check-ins create new versions on that branch. To leave the branch, you must explicitly select a different version with C-u C-x v v. To transfer changes from one branch to another, use the merge command, described in the next section.

15.7.6.3 Merging Branches

When you have finished the changes on a certain branch, you will often want to incorporate them into the file's main line of development (the trunk). This is not a trivial operation, because development might also have proceeded on the trunk, so that you must *merge* the changes into a file that has already been changed otherwise. VC allows you to do this (and other things) with the vc-merge command.

`C-x v m (vc-merge)`
> Merge changes into the work file.

`C-x v m (vc-merge)` takes a set of changes and merges it into the current version of the work file. It firsts asks you in the minibuffer where the changes should come from. If you just type RET, Emacs merges any changes that were made on the same branch since you checked the file out (we call this *merging the news*). This is the common way to pick up recent changes from the repository, regardless of whether you have already changed the file yourself.

You can also enter a branch number or a pair of version numbers in the minibuffer. Then `C-x v m` finds the changes from that branch, or the differences between the two versions you specified, and merges them into the current version of the current file.

As an example, suppose that you have finished a certain feature on branch 1.3.1. In the meantime, development on the trunk has proceeded to version 1.5. To merge the changes from the branch to the trunk, first go to the head version of the trunk, by typing `C-u C-x v v RET`. Version 1.5 is now current. If locking is used for the file, type `C-x v v` to lock version 1.5 so that you can change it. Next, type `C-x v m 1.3.1 RET`. This takes the entire set of changes on branch 1.3.1 (relative to version 1.3, where the branch started, up to the last version on the branch) and merges it into the current version of the work file. You can now check in the changed file, thus creating version 1.6 containing the changes from the branch.

It is possible to do further editing after merging the branch, before the next check-in. But it is usually wiser to check in the merged version, then lock it and make the further changes. This will keep a better record of the history of changes.

When you merge changes into a file that has itself been modified, the changes might overlap. We call this situation a *conflict*, and reconciling the conflicting changes is called *resolving a conflict*.

Whenever conflicts occur during merging, VC detects them, tells you about them in the echo area, and asks whether you want help in merging. If you say yes, it starts an Ediff session (see section "Ediff" in *The Ediff Manual*).

If you say no, the conflicting changes are both inserted into the file, surrounded by *conflict markers*. The example below shows how a conflict region looks; the file is called '`name`' and the current master file version with user B's changes in it is 1.11.

```
<<<<<<< name
  User A's version
=======
  User B's version
>>>>>>> 1.11
```

Then you can resolve the conflicts by editing the file manually. Or you can type `M-x vc-resolve-conflicts` after visiting the file. This starts an Ediff session, as described above. Don't forget to check in the merged version afterwards.

15.7.6.4 Multi-User Branching

It is often useful for multiple developers to work simultaneously on different branches of a file. CVS allows this by default; for RCS, it is possible if you create multiple source directories. Each source directory should have a link named 'RCS' which points to a common directory of RCS master files. Then each source directory can have its own choice of selected versions, but all share the same common RCS records.

This technique works reliably and automatically, provided that the source files contain RCS version headers (see section "Version Headers" in *Specialized Emacs Features*). The headers enable Emacs to be sure, at all times, which version number is present in the work file.

If the files do not have version headers, you must instead tell Emacs explicitly in each session which branch you are working on. To do this, first find the file, then type C-u C-x v v and specify the correct branch number. This ensures that Emacs knows which branch it is using during this particular editing session.

15.8 File Directories

The file system groups files into *directories*. A *directory listing* is a list of all the files in a directory. Emacs provides commands to create and delete directories, and to make directory listings in brief format (file names only) and verbose format (sizes, dates, and authors included). Emacs also includes a directory browser feature called Dired; see Chapter 29 [Dired], page 339.

C-x C-d *dir-or-pattern* RET
> Display a brief directory listing (list-directory).

C-u C-x C-d *dir-or-pattern* RET
> Display a verbose directory listing.

M-x make-directory RET *dirname* RET
> Create a new directory named *dirname*.

M-x delete-directory RET *dirname* RET
> Delete the directory named *dirname*. It must be empty, or you get an error.

The command to display a directory listing is C-x C-d (list-directory). It reads using the minibuffer a file name which is either a directory to be listed or a wildcard-containing pattern for the files to be listed. For example,

    C-x C-d /u2/emacs/etc RET

lists all the files in directory '/u2/emacs/etc'. Here is an example of specifying a file name pattern:

    C-x C-d /u2/emacs/src/*.c RET

Normally, C-x C-d displays a brief directory listing containing just file names. A numeric argument (regardless of value) tells it to make a verbose listing including sizes, dates, and owners (like 'ls -l').

The text of a directory listing is mostly obtained by running `ls` in an inferior process. Two Emacs variables control the switches passed to `ls`: `list-directory-brief-switches` is a string giving the switches to use in brief listings (`"-CF"` by default), and `list-directory-verbose-switches` is a string giving the switches to use in a verbose listing (`"-l"` by default).

In verbose directory listings, Emacs adds information about the amount of free space on the disk that contains the directory. To do this, it runs the program specified by `directory-free-space-program` with arguments `directory-free-space-args`.

15.9 Comparing Files

The command `M-x diff` compares two files, displaying the differences in an Emacs buffer named '`*diff*`'. It works by running the `diff` program, using options taken from the variable `diff-switches`. The value of `diff-switches` should be a string; the default is `"-c"` to specify a context diff. See section "Diff" in *Comparing and Merging Files*, for more information about `diff` output formats.

The command `M-x diff-backup` compares a specified file with its most recent backup. If you specify the name of a backup file, `diff-backup` compares it with the source file that it is a backup of.

The command `M-x compare-windows` compares the text in the current window with that in the next window. (For more information about windows in Emacs, Chapter 17 [Windows], page 165.) Comparison starts at point in each window, after pushing each initial point value on the mark ring in its respective buffer. Then it moves point forward in each window, one character at a time, until it reaches characters that don't match. Then the command exits.

If point in the two windows is followed by non-matching text when the command starts, `M-x compare-windows` tries heuristically to advance up to matching text in the two windows, and then exits. So if you use `M-x compare-windows` repeatedly, each time it either skips one matching range or finds the start of another.

With a numeric argument, `compare-windows` ignores changes in whitespace. If the variable `compare-ignore-case` is non-`nil`, the comparison ignores differences in case as well. If the variable `compare-ignore-whitespace` is non-`nil`, `compare-windows` normally ignores changes in whitespace, and a prefix argument turns that off.

You can use `M-x smerge-mode` to turn on Smerge mode, a minor mode for editing output from the `diff3` program. This is typically the result of a failed merge from a version control system "update" outside VC, due to conflicting changes to a file. Smerge mode provides commands to resolve conflicts by selecting specific changes.

See section "Emerge" in *Specialized Emacs Features*, for the Emerge facility, which provides a powerful interface for merging files.

15.10 Diff Mode

Diff mode is used for the output of M-x diff; it is also useful for editing patches and comparisons produced by the `diff` program. To select Diff mode manually, type M-x diff-mode.

One general feature of Diff mode is that manual edits to the patch automatically correct line numbers, including those in the hunk header, so that you can actually apply the edited patch. Diff mode treats each hunk location as an "error message," so that you can use commands such as C-x ' to visit the corresponding source locations. It also provides the following commands to navigate, manipulate and apply parts of patches:

M-n   Move to the next hunk-start (diff-hunk-next).

M-p   Move to the previous hunk-start (diff-hunk-prev).

M-}   Move to the next file-start, in a multi-file patch (diff-file-next).

M-{   Move to the previous file-start, in a multi-file patch (diff-file-prev).

M-k   Kill the hunk at point (diff-hunk-kill).

M K   In a multi-file patch, kill the current file part. (diff-file-kill).

C-c C-a   Apply this hunk to its target file (diff-apply-hunk). With a prefix argument of C-u, revert this hunk.

C-c C-c   Go to the source corresponding to this hunk (diff-goto-source).

C-c C-e   Start an Ediff session with the patch (diff-ediff-patch). See section "Ediff" in *The Ediff Manual*.

C-c C-n   Restrict the view to the current hunk (diff-restrict-view). See Section 31.9 [Narrowing], page 396. With a prefix argument of C-u, restrict the view to the current patch of a multiple file patch. To widen again, use C-x n w.

C-c C-r   Reverse the direction of comparison for the entire buffer (diff-reverse-direction).

C-c C-s   Split the hunk at point (diff-split-hunk). This is for manually editing patches, and only works with the unified diff format.

C-c C-u   Convert the entire buffer to unified format (diff-context->unified). With a prefix argument, convert unified format to context format. In Transient Mark mode, when the mark is active, this command operates only on the region.

C-c C-w   Refine the current hunk so that it disregards changes in whitespace (diff-refine-hunk).

C-x 4 a in Diff mode operates on behalf of the target file, but gets the function name from the patch itself. See Section 25.1 [Change Log], page 292. This is useful for making log entries for functions that are deleted by the patch.

15.11 Miscellaneous File Operations

Emacs has commands for performing many other operations on files. All operate on one file; they do not accept wildcard file names.

M-x view-file allows you to scan or read a file by sequential screenfuls. It reads a file name argument using the minibuffer. After reading the file into an Emacs buffer, view-file displays the beginning. You can then type SPC to scroll forward one windowful, or DEL to scroll backward. Various other commands are provided for moving around in the file, but none for changing it; type ? while viewing for a list of them. They are mostly the same as normal Emacs cursor motion commands. To exit from viewing, type q. The commands for viewing are defined by a special minor mode called View mode.

A related command, M-x view-buffer, views a buffer already present in Emacs. See Section 16.3 [Misc Buffer], page 158.

M-x insert-file (also C-x i) inserts a copy of the contents of the specified file into the current buffer at point, leaving point unchanged before the contents and the mark after them.

M-x insert-file-literally is like M-x insert-file, except the file is inserted "literally": it is treated as a sequence of ASCII characters with no special encoding or conversion, similar to the M-x find-file-literally command (see Section 15.2 [Visiting], page 120).

M-x write-region is the inverse of M-x insert-file; it copies the contents of the region into the specified file. M-x append-to-file adds the text of the region to the end of the specified file. See Section 9.3 [Accumulating Text], page 60. The variable write-region-inhibit-fsync applies to these commands, as well as saving files; see Section 15.3.3 [Customize Save], page 128.

M-x delete-file deletes the specified file, like the rm command in the shell. If you are deleting many files in one directory, it may be more convenient to use Dired (see Chapter 29 [Dired], page 339).

M-x rename-file reads two file names *old* and *new* using the minibuffer, then renames file *old* as *new*. If the file name *new* already exists, you must confirm with yes or renaming is not done; this is because renaming causes the old meaning of the name *new* to be lost. If *old* and *new* are on different file systems, the file *old* is copied and deleted.

If the argument *new* is just a directory name, the real new name is in that directory, with the same non-directory component as *old*. For example, M-x rename-file RET ~/foo RET /tmp RET renames '~/foo' to '/tmp/foo'. The same rule applies to all the remaining commands in this section. All of them ask for confirmation when the new file name already exists, too.

The similar command M-x add-name-to-file is used to add an additional name to an existing file without removing its old name. The new name is created as a "hard link" to the existing file. The new name must belong on the same file system that the file is on. On MS-Windows, this command works only if the file resides in an NTFS file system. On MS-DOS, it works by copying the file.

M-x copy-file reads the file *old* and writes a new file named *new* with the same contents.

M-x make-symbolic-link reads two file names *target* and *linkname*, then creates a symbolic link named *linkname*, which points at *target*. The effect is that future attempts to open file *linkname* will refer to whatever file is named *target* at the time the opening is done, or will get an error if the name *target* is nonexistent at that time. This command does not expand the argument *target*, so that it allows you to specify a relative name as the target of the link.

Not all systems support symbolic links; on systems that don't support them, this command is not defined.

15.12 Accessing Compressed Files

Emacs automatically uncompresses compressed files when you visit them, and automatically recompresses them if you alter them and save them. Emacs recognizes compressed files by their file names. File names ending in '.gz' indicate a file compressed with gzip. Other endings indicate other compression programs.

Automatic uncompression and compression apply to all the operations in which Emacs uses the contents of a file. This includes visiting it, saving it, inserting its contents into a buffer, loading it, and byte compiling it.

To disable this feature, type the command M-x auto-compression-mode. You can disable it permanently by customizing the variable auto-compression-mode.

15.13 File Archives

A file whose name ends in '.tar' is normally an *archive* made by the tar program. Emacs views these files in a special mode called Tar mode which provides a Dired-like list of the contents (see Chapter 29 [Dired], page 339). You can move around through the list just as you would in Dired, and visit the subfiles contained in the archive. However, not all Dired commands are available in Tar mode.

If Auto Compression mode is enabled (see Section 15.12 [Compressed Files], page 151), then Tar mode is used also for compressed archives—files with extensions '.tgz', .tar.Z and .tar.gz.

The keys e, f and RET all extract a component file into its own buffer. You can edit it there, and if you save the buffer, the edited version will replace the version in the Tar buffer. v extracts a file into a buffer in View mode. o extracts the file and displays it in another window, so you could edit the file and operate on the archive simultaneously. d marks a file for deletion when you later use x, and u unmarks a file, as in Dired. C copies a file from the archive to disk and R renames a file within the archive. g reverts the buffer from the archive on disk.

The keys M, G, and O change the file's permission bits, group, and owner, respectively.

If your display supports colors and the mouse, moving the mouse pointer across a file name highlights that file name, indicating that you can click on it. Clicking Mouse-2 on the highlighted file name extracts the file into a buffer and displays that buffer.

Saving the Tar buffer writes a new version of the archive to disk with the changes you made to the components.

You don't need the `tar` program to use Tar mode—Emacs reads the archives directly. However, accessing compressed archives requires the appropriate uncompression program.

A separate but similar Archive mode is used for archives produced by the programs `arc`, `jar`, `lzh`, `zip`, and `zoo`, which have extensions corresponding to the program names. Archive mode also works for those `exe` files that are self-extracting executables.

The key bindings of Archive mode are similar to those in Tar mode, with the addition of the `m` key which marks a file for subsequent operations, and `M-DEL` which unmarks all the marked files. Also, the `a` key toggles the display of detailed file information, for those archive types where it won't fit in a single line. Operations such as renaming a subfile, or changing its mode or owner, are supported only for some of the archive formats.

Unlike Tar mode, Archive mode runs the archiving program to unpack and repack archives. Details of the program names and their options can be set in the '`Archive`' Customize group. However, you don't need these programs to look at the archive table of contents, only to extract or manipulate the subfiles in the archive.

15.14 Remote Files

You can refer to files on other machines using a special file name syntax:

```
/host:filename
/user@host:filename
/user@host#port:filename
/method:user@host:filename
/method:user@host#port:filename
```

To carry out this request, Emacs uses either the FTP program or a remote-login program such as `ssh`, `rlogin`, or `telnet`. You can always specify in the file name which method to use—for example, '`/ftp:user@host:filename`' uses FTP, whereas '`/ssh:user@host:filename`' uses `ssh`. When you don't specify a method in the file name, Emacs chooses the method as follows:

1. If the host name starts with '`ftp.`' (with dot), then Emacs uses FTP.

2. If the user name is '`ftp`' or '`anonymous`', then Emacs uses FTP.

3. Otherwise, Emacs uses `ssh`.

Remote file access through FTP is handled by the Ange-FTP package, which is documented in the following. Remote file access through the other methods is handled by the Tramp package, which has its own manual. See section "Top" in *The Tramp Manual*.

When the Ange-FTP package is used, Emacs logs in through FTP using your user name or the name *user*. It may ask you for a password from time to time; this is used for logging in on *host*. The form using *port* allows you to access servers running on a non-default TCP port.

If you want to disable backups for remote files, set the variable `ange-ftp-make-backup-files` to `nil`.

By default, the auto-save files (see Section 15.5.1 [Auto Save Files], page 132) for remote files are made in the temporary file directory on the local machine. This is achieved using the variable `auto-save-file-name-transforms`.

Normally, if you do not specify a user name in a remote file name, that means to use your own user name. But if you set the variable `ange-ftp-default-user` to a string, that string is used instead.

To visit files accessible by anonymous FTP, you use special user names 'anonymous' or 'ftp'. Passwords for these user names are handled specially. The variable `ange-ftp-generate-anonymous-password` controls what happens: if the value of this variable is a string, then that string is used as the password; if non-`nil` (the default), then the value of `user-mail-address` is used; if `nil`, then Emacs prompts you for a password as usual.

Sometimes you may be unable to access files on a remote machine because a *firewall* in between blocks the connection for security reasons. If you can log in on a *gateway* machine from which the target files *are* accessible, and whose FTP server supports gatewaying features, you can still use remote file names; all you have to do is specify the name of the gateway machine by setting the variable `ange-ftp-gateway-host`, and set `ange-ftp-smart-gateway` to `t`. Otherwise you may be able to make remote file names work, but the procedure is complex. You can read the instructions by typing `M-x finder-commentary RET ange-ftp RET`.

You can entirely turn off the FTP file name feature by removing the entries `ange-ftp-completion-hook-function` and `ange-ftp-hook-function` from the variable `file-name-handler-alist`. You can turn off the feature in individual cases by quoting the file name with '/:' (see Section 15.15 [Quoted File Names], page 153).

15.15 Quoted File Names

You can *quote* an absolute file name to prevent special characters and syntax in it from having their special effects. The way to do this is to add '/:' at the beginning.

For example, you can quote a local file name which appears remote, to prevent it from being treated as a remote file name. Thus, if you have a directory named '/foo:' and a file named 'bar' in it, you can refer to that file in Emacs as '/:/foo:/bar'.

'/:' can also prevent '~' from being treated as a special character for a user's home directory. For example, '/:/tmp/~hack' refers to a file whose name is '~hack' in directory '/tmp'.

Quoting with '/:' is also a way to enter in the minibuffer a file name that contains '$'. In order for this to work, the '/:' must be at the beginning of the minibuffer contents. (You can also double each '$'; see [File Names with $], page 120.)

You can also quote wildcard characters with '/:', for visiting. For example, '/:/tmp/foo*bar' visits the file '/tmp/foo*bar'.

Another method of getting the same result is to enter '/tmp/foo[*]bar', which is a wildcard specification that matches only '/tmp/foo*bar'. However, in many cases there is no need to quote the wildcard characters because even unquoted they give the right result. For example, if the only file name in '/tmp' that starts with 'foo' and ends with 'bar' is 'foo*bar', then specifying '/tmp/foo*bar' will visit only '/tmp/foo*bar'.

15.16 File Name Cache

You can use the *file name cache* to make it easy to locate a file by name, without having to remember exactly where it is located. When typing a file name in the minibuffer, C-TAB (`file-cache-minibuffer-complete`) completes it using the file name cache. If you repeat C-TAB, that cycles through the possible completions of what you had originally typed. (However, note that the C-TAB character cannot be typed on most text-only terminals.)

The file name cache does not fill up automatically. Instead, you load file names into the cache using these commands:

M-x file-cache-add-directory RET *directory* RET
> Add each file name in *directory* to the file name cache.

M-x file-cache-add-directory-using-find RET *directory* RET
> Add each file name in *directory* and all of its nested subdirectories to the file name cache.

M-x file-cache-add-directory-using-locate RET *directory* RET
> Add each file name in *directory* and all of its nested subdirectories to the file name cache, using `locate` to find them all.

M-x file-cache-add-directory-list RET *variable* RET
> Add each file name in each directory listed in *variable* to the file name cache. *variable* should be a Lisp variable such as `load-path` or `exec-path`, whose value is a list of directory names.

M-x file-cache-clear-cache RET
> Clear the cache; that is, remove all file names from it.

The file name cache is not persistent: it is kept and maintained only for the duration of the Emacs session. You can view the contents of the cache with the `file-cache-display` command.

15.17 Convenience Features for Finding Files

In this section, we introduce some convenient facilities for finding recently-opened files, reading file names from a buffer, and viewing image files.

If you enable Recentf mode, with M-x `recentf-mode`, the 'File' menu includes a submenu containing a list of recently opened files. M-x `recentf-save-list` saves the current `recent-file-list` to a file, and M-x `recentf-edit-list` edits it.

The M-x `ffap` command generalizes `find-file` with more powerful heuristic defaults (see Section 31.15.3 [FFAP], page 403), often based on the text at point. Partial Completion mode offers other features extending `find-file`, which can be used with `ffap`. See Section 5.3.4 [Completion Options], page 35.

Visiting image files automatically selects Image mode. This major mode allows you to toggle between displaying the file as an image in the Emacs buffer, and displaying its underlying text representation, using the command C-c C-c (image-toggle-display). This works only when Emacs can display the specific image type.

See also the Image-Dired package (see Section 29.17 [Image-Dired], page 352) for viewing images as thumbnails.

15.18 Filesets

If you regularly edit a certain group of files, you can define them as a *fileset*. This lets you perform certain operations, such as visiting, query-replace, and shell commands on all the files at once. To make use of filesets, you must first add the expression (filesets-init) to your '.emacs' file (see Section 32.6 [Init File], page 433). This adds a 'Filesets' menu to the menu bar.

The simplest way to define a fileset is by adding files to it one at a time. To add a file to fileset *name*, visit the file and type M-x filesets-add-buffer RET *name* RET. If there is no fileset *name*, this creates a new one, which initially creates only the current file. The command M-x filesets-remove-buffer removes the current file from a fileset.

You can also edit the list of filesets directly, with M-x filesets-edit (or by choosing 'Edit Filesets' from the 'Filesets' menu). The editing is performed in a Customize buffer (see Section 32.2 [Easy Customization], page 408). Filesets need not be a simple list of files—you can also define filesets using regular expression matching file names. Some examples of these more complicated filesets are shown in the Customize buffer. Remember to select 'Save for future sessions' if you want to use the same filesets in future Emacs sessions.

You can use the command M-x filesets-open to visit all the files in a fileset, and M-x filesets-close to close them. Use M-x filesets-run-cmd to run a shell command on all the files in a fileset. These commands are also available from the 'Filesets' menu, where each existing fileset is represented by a submenu.

16 Using Multiple Buffers

The text you are editing in Emacs resides in an object called a *buffer*. Each time you visit a file, a buffer is created to hold the file's text. Each time you invoke Dired, a buffer is created to hold the directory listing. If you send a message with C-x m, a buffer named '*mail*' is used to hold the text of the message. When you ask for a command's documentation, that appears in a buffer called '*Help*'.

At any time, one and only one buffer is *current*. It is also called the *selected buffer*. Often we say that a command operates on "the buffer" as if there were only one; but really this means that the command operates on the current buffer (most commands do).

When Emacs has multiple windows, each window has its own chosen buffer and displays it; at any time, only one of the windows is selected, and its chosen buffer is the current buffer. Each window's mode line normally displays the name of the window's chosen buffer (see Chapter 17 [Windows], page 165).

Each buffer has a name, which can be of any length, and you can select any buffer by giving its name. Most buffers are made by visiting files, and their names are derived from the files' names. But you can also create an empty buffer with any name you want. A newly started Emacs has a buffer named '*scratch*' which can be used for evaluating Lisp expressions in Emacs. The distinction between upper and lower case matters in buffer names.

Each buffer records individually what file it is visiting, whether it is modified, and what major mode and minor modes are in effect in it (see Chapter 20 [Major Modes], page 207). Any Emacs variable can be made *local to* a particular buffer, meaning its value in that buffer can be different from the value in other buffers. See Section 32.3.3 [Locals], page 419.

A buffer's size cannot be larger than some maximum, which is defined by the largest buffer position representable by the *Emacs integer* data type. This is because Emacs tracks buffer positions using that data type. For 32-bit machines, the largest buffer size is 256 megabytes.

16.1 Creating and Selecting Buffers

C-x b *buffer* RET

> Select or create a buffer named *buffer* (switch-to-buffer).

C-x 4 b *buffer* RET

> Similar, but select *buffer* in another window (switch-to-buffer-other-window).

C-x 5 b *buffer* RET

> Similar, but select *buffer* in a separate frame (switch-to-buffer-other-frame).

C-x LEFT   Select the previous buffer in the list of existing buffers.

C-x RIGHT   Select the next buffer in the list of existing buffers.

C-u M-g M-g
C-u M-g g   Read a number *n* and move to line *n* in the most recently selected buffer other than the current buffer.

To select the buffer named *bufname*, type C-x b *bufname* RET. This runs the command **switch-to-buffer** with argument *bufname*. You can use completion to enter the buffer name (see Section 5.3 [Completion], page 33). An empty argument to C-x b specifies the buffer that was current most recently among those not now displayed in any window.

For conveniently switching between a few buffers, use the commands C-x LEFT and C-x RIGHT. C-x RIGHT (**previous-buffer**) selects the previous buffer (following the order of most recent selection in the current frame), while C-x LEFT (**next-buffer**) moves through buffers in the reverse direction.

To select a buffer in a window other than the current one, type C-x 4 b *bufname* RET. This runs the command **switch-to-buffer-other-window** which displays the buffer *bufname* in another window. By default, if displaying the buffer causes two vertically adjacent windows to be displayed, the heights of those windows are evened out; to countermand that and preserve the window configuration, set the variable **even-window-heights** to nil.

Similarly, C-x 5 b *buffer* RET runs the command **switch-to-buffer-other-frame** which selects a buffer in another frame.

You can control how certain buffers are handled by these commands by customizing the variables **special-display-buffer-names**, **special-display-regexps**, **same-window-buffer-names**, and **same-window-regexps**. See Section 17.5 [Force Same Window], page 168, and Section 18.9 [Special Buffer Frames], page 180, for more about these variables. In addition, if the value of **display-buffer-reuse-frames** is non-nil, and the buffer you want to switch to is already displayed in some frame, Emacs will just raise that frame.

Most buffers are created by visiting files, or by Emacs commands that want to display some text, but you can also create a buffer explicitly by typing C-x b *bufname* RET. This makes a new, empty buffer that is not visiting any file, and selects it for editing. Such buffers are used for making notes to yourself. If you try to save one, you are asked for the file name to use. The new buffer's major mode is determined by the value of **default-major-mode** (see Chapter 20 [Major Modes], page 207).

Note that C-x C-f, and any other command for visiting a file, can also be used to switch to an existing file-visiting buffer. See Section 15.2 [Visiting], page 120.

C-u M-g M-g, that is **goto-line** with a prefix argument of just C-u, reads a number *n* using the minibuffer, selects the most recently selected buffer other than the current buffer in another window, and then moves point to the beginning of line number *n* in that buffer. This is mainly useful in a buffer that refers to line numbers in another buffer: if point is on or just after a number, **goto-line** uses that number as the default for *n*. Note that prefix arguments other than just C-u behave differently. C-u 4 M-g M-g goes to line 4 in the *current* buffer, without reading a number from the minibuffer. (Remember that M-g M-g without prefix argument reads a number *n* and then moves to line number *n* in the current buffer.)

Emacs uses buffer names that start with a space for internal purposes. It treats these buffers specially in minor ways—for example, by default they do not record undo information. It is best to avoid using such buffer names yourself.

16.2 Listing Existing Buffers

C-x C-b   List the existing buffers (`list-buffers`).

To display a list of existing buffers, type C-x C-b. Each line in the list shows one buffer's name, major mode and visited file. The buffers are listed in the order that they were current; the buffers that were current most recently come first.

'*' in the first field of a line indicates the buffer is "modified." If several buffers are modified, it may be time to save some with C-x s (see Section 15.3.1 [Save Commands], page 124). '%' indicates a read-only buffer. '.' marks the current buffer. Here is an example of a buffer list:

```
CRM Buffer              Size  Mode              File
 . * .emacs             3294  Emacs-Lisp        ~/.emacs
   % *Help*              101  Help
     search.c          86055  C                 ~/cvs/emacs/src/search.c
   % src               20959  Dired by name     ~/cvs/emacs/src/
   * *mail*               42  Mail
   % HELLO              1607  Fundamental       ~/cvs/emacs/etc/HELLO
   % NEWS             481184  Outline           ~/cvs/emacs/etc/NEWS
     *scratch*           191  Lisp Interaction
   * *Messages*         1554  Fundamental
```

Note that the buffer '*Help*' was made by a help request; it is not visiting any file. The buffer src was made by Dired on the directory '~/cvs/emacs/src/'. You can list only buffers that are visiting files by giving the command a prefix argument, as in C-u C-x C-b.

`list-buffers` omits buffers whose names begin with a space, unless they visit files: such buffers are used internally by Emacs.

16.3 Miscellaneous Buffer Operations

C-x C-q   Toggle read-only status of buffer (`toggle-read-only`).

M-x rename-buffer RET *name* RET
            Change the name of the current buffer.

M-x rename-uniquely
            Rename the current buffer by adding '`<number>`' to the end.

M-x view-buffer RET *buffer* RET
            Scroll through buffer *buffer*.

A buffer can be *read-only*, which means that commands to change its contents are not allowed. The mode line indicates read-only buffers with '%%' or '%*' near the left margin. Read-only buffers are usually made by subsystems such as Dired and Rmail that have special commands to operate on the text; also by visiting a file whose access control says you cannot write it.

If you wish to make changes in a read-only buffer, use the command C-x C-q (`toggle-read-only`). It makes a read-only buffer writable, and makes a writable buffer read-only. This works by setting the variable `buffer-read-only`, which has a local value in each buffer and makes the buffer read-only if its value is non-`nil`. If you have files under version control, you may find it convenient to bind C-x C-q to `vc-toggle-read-only` instead. Then, typing C-x C-q not only changes the read-only flag, but it also checks the file in or out. See Section 15.7 [Version Control], page 135.

M-x `rename-buffer` changes the name of the current buffer. You specify the new name as a minibuffer argument; there is no default. If you specify a name that is in use for some other buffer, an error happens and no renaming is done.

M-x `rename-uniquely` renames the current buffer to a similar name with a numeric suffix added to make it both different and unique. This command does not need an argument. It is useful for creating multiple shell buffers: if you rename the '`*shell*`' buffer, then do M-x `shell` again, it makes a new shell buffer named '`*shell*`'; meanwhile, the old shell buffer continues to exist under its new name. This method is also good for mail buffers, compilation buffers, and most Emacs features that create special buffers with particular names. (With some of these features, such as M-x `compile`, M-x `grep` an M-x `info`, you need to switch to some other buffer before using the command, in order for it to make a different buffer.)

M-x `view-buffer` is much like M-x `view-file` (see Section 15.11 [Misc File Ops], page 150) except that it examines an already existing Emacs buffer. View mode provides commands for scrolling through the buffer conveniently but not for changing it. When you exit View mode with q, that switches back to the buffer (and the position) which was previously displayed in the window. Alternatively, if you exit View mode with e, the buffer and the value of point that resulted from your perusal remain in effect.

The commands M-x `append-to-buffer` and M-x `insert-buffer` can be used to copy text from one buffer to another. See Section 9.3 [Accumulating Text], page 60.

16.4 Killing Buffers

If you continue an Emacs session for a while, you may accumulate a large number of buffers. You may then find it convenient to *kill* the buffers you no longer need. On most operating systems, killing a buffer releases its space back to the operating system so that other programs can use it. Here are some commands for killing buffers:

C-x k *bufname* RET
> Kill buffer *bufname* (`kill-buffer`).

M-x kill-some-buffers
> Offer to kill each buffer, one by one.

C-x k (`kill-buffer`) kills one buffer, whose name you specify in the minibuffer. The default, used if you type just RET in the minibuffer, is to kill the current buffer. If you kill the current buffer, another buffer becomes current: one that was current in the recent past but is not displayed in any window now. If you ask to kill a file-visiting buffer that is modified (has unsaved editing), then you must confirm with `yes` before the buffer is killed.

The command `M-x kill-some-buffers` asks about each buffer, one by one. An answer of `y` means to kill the buffer. Killing the current buffer or a buffer containing unsaved changes selects a new buffer or asks for confirmation just like `kill-buffer`.

The buffer menu feature (see Section 16.5 [Several Buffers], page 160) is also convenient for killing various buffers.

If you want to do something special every time a buffer is killed, you can add hook functions to the hook `kill-buffer-hook` (see Section 32.3.2 [Hooks], page 418).

If you run one Emacs session for a period of days, as many people do, it can fill up with buffers that you used several days ago. The command `M-x clean-buffer-list` is a convenient way to purge them; it kills all the unmodified buffers that you have not used for a long time. An ordinary buffer is killed if it has not been displayed for three days; however, you can specify certain buffers that should never be killed automatically, and others that should be killed if they have been unused for a mere hour.

You can also have this buffer purging done for you, every day at midnight, by enabling Midnight mode. Midnight mode operates each day at midnight; at that time, it runs `clean-buffer-list`, or whichever functions you have placed in the normal hook `midnight-hook` (see Section 32.3.2 [Hooks], page 418).

To enable Midnight mode, use the Customization buffer to set the variable `midnight-mode` to `t`. See Section 32.2 [Easy Customization], page 408.

16.5 Operating on Several Buffers

The *buffer-menu* facility is like a "Dired for buffers"; it allows you to request operations on various Emacs buffers by editing an Emacs buffer containing a list of them. You can save buffers, kill them (here called *deleting* them, for consistency with Dired), or display them.

`M-x buffer-menu`
> Begin editing a buffer listing all Emacs buffers.

`M-x buffer-menu-other-window`.
> Similar, but do it in another window.

The command `buffer-menu` writes a list of all Emacs buffers[1] into the buffer '`*Buffer List*`', and selects that buffer in Buffer Menu mode.

The buffer is read-only, and can be changed only through the special commands described in this section. The usual Emacs cursor motion commands can be used in the '`*Buffer List*`' buffer. The following commands apply to the buffer described on the current line.

`d`
> Request to delete (kill) the buffer, then move down. The request shows as a 'D' on the line, before the buffer name. Requested deletions take place when you type the `x` command.

---

[1] Buffers which don't visit files and whose names begin with a space are omitted: these are used internally by Emacs.

C-d   Like d but move up afterwards instead of down.

s   Request to save the buffer. The request shows as an 'S' on the line. Requested saves take place when you type the x command. You may request both saving and deletion for the same buffer.

x   Perform previously requested deletions and saves.

u   Remove any request made for the current line, and move down.

DEL   Move to previous line and remove any request made for that line.

The d, C-d, s and u commands to add or remove flags also move down (or up) one line. They accept a numeric argument as a repeat count.

These commands operate immediately on the buffer listed on the current line:

~   Mark the buffer "unmodified." The command ~ does this immediately when you type it.

%   Toggle the buffer's read-only flag. The command % does this immediately when you type it.

t   Visit the buffer as a tags table. See Section 25.3.4 [Select Tags Table], page 299.

There are also commands to select another buffer or buffers:

q   Quit the buffer menu—immediately display the most recent formerly visible buffer in its place.

RET
f   Immediately select this line's buffer in place of the '*Buffer List*' buffer.

o   Immediately select this line's buffer in another window as if by C-x 4 b, leaving '*Buffer List*' visible.

C-o   Immediately display this line's buffer in another window, but don't select the window.

1   Immediately select this line's buffer in a full-screen window.

2   Immediately set up two windows, with this line's buffer selected in one, and the previously current buffer (aside from the buffer '*Buffer List*') displayed in the other.

b   Bury the buffer listed on this line.

m   Mark this line's buffer to be displayed in another window if you exit with the v command. The request shows as a '>' at the beginning of the line. (A single buffer may not have both a delete request and a display request.)

v   Immediately select this line's buffer, and also display in other windows any buffers previously marked with the m command. If you have not marked any buffers, this command is equivalent to 1.

There is also a command that affects the entire buffer list:

T   Delete, or reinsert, lines for non-file buffers. This command toggles
                the inclusion of such buffers in the buffer list.

What `buffer-menu` actually does is create and switch to a suitable buffer, and turn on Buffer Menu mode in it. Everything else described above is implemented by the special commands provided in Buffer Menu mode. One consequence of this is that you can switch from the '`*Buffer List*`' buffer to another Emacs buffer, and edit there. You can reselect the '`*Buffer List*`' buffer later, to perform the operations already requested, or you can kill it, or pay no further attention to it.

The list in the '`*Buffer List*`' buffer looks exactly like the buffer list described in Section 16.2 [List Buffers], page 158, because they really are the same. The only difference between `buffer-menu` and `list-buffers` is that `buffer-menu` switches to the '`*Buffer List*`' buffer in the selected window; `list-buffers` displays the same buffer in another window. If you run `list-buffers` (that is, type `C-x C-b`) and select the buffer list manually, you can use all of the commands described here.

Normally, the buffer '`*Buffer List*`' is not updated automatically when buffers are created and killed; its contents are just text. If you have created, deleted or renamed buffers, the way to update '`*Buffer List*`' to show what you have done is to type g (`revert-buffer`). You can make this happen regularly every `auto-revert-interval` seconds if you enable Auto Revert mode in this buffer, as long as it is not marked modified. Global Auto Revert mode applies to the '`*Buffer List*`' buffer only if `global-auto-revert-non-file-buffers` is non-`nil`. See Info file '`emacs-xtra`', node '`Autorevert`', for details.

The command `buffer-menu-other-window` works the same as `buffer-menu`, except that it displays the buffers list in another window.

16.6 Indirect Buffers

An *indirect buffer* shares the text of some other buffer, which is called the *base buffer* of the indirect buffer. In some ways it is the analogue, for buffers, of a symbolic link between files.

`M-x make-indirect-buffer RET` *base-buffer* `RET` *indirect-name* `RET`
                Create an indirect buffer named *indirect-name* whose base buffer is
                base-buffer.

`M-x clone-indirect-buffer RET`
                Create an indirect buffer that is a twin copy of the current buffer.

`C-x 4 c`   Create an indirect buffer that is a twin copy of the current buffer,
                and select it in another window (`clone-indirect-buffer-other-window`).

The text of the indirect buffer is always identical to the text of its base buffer; changes made by editing either one are visible immediately in the other. But in all other respects, the indirect buffer and its base buffer are completely separate. They have different names, different values of point, different narrowing, different markers, different major modes, and different local variables.

An indirect buffer cannot visit a file, but its base buffer can. If you try to save the indirect buffer, that actually works by saving the base buffer. Killing the base buffer effectively kills the indirect buffer, but killing an indirect buffer has no effect on its base buffer.

One way to use indirect buffers is to display multiple views of an outline. See Section 22.8.4 [Outline Views], page 228.

A quick and handy way to make an indirect buffer is with the command M-x clone-indirect-buffer. It creates and selects an indirect buffer whose base buffer is the current buffer. With a numeric argument, it prompts for the name of the indirect buffer; otherwise it uses the name of the current buffer, with a '<n>' suffix added. C-x 4 c (clone-indirect-buffer-other-window) works like M-x clone-indirect-buffer, but it selects the new buffer in another window.

The more general way to make an indirect buffer is with the command M-x make-indirect-buffer. It creates an indirect buffer from buffer *base-buffer*, under the name *indirect-name*. It prompts for both *base-buffer* and *indirect-name* using the minibuffer.

16.7 Convenience Features and Customization of Buffer Handling

This section describes several modes and features that make it more convenient to switch between buffers.

16.7.1 Making Buffer Names Unique

When several buffers visit identically-named files, Emacs must give the buffers distinct names. The usual method for making buffer names unique adds '<2>', '<3>', etc. to the end of the buffer names (all but one of them).

Other methods work by adding parts of each file's directory to the buffer name. To select one, customize the variable uniquify-buffer-name style (see Section 32.2 [Easy Customization], page 408).

To begin with, the forward naming method includes part of the file's directory name at the beginning of the buffer name; using this method, buffers visiting the files '/u/rms/tmp/Makefile' and '/usr/projects/zaphod/Makefile' would be named 'tmp/Makefile' and 'zaphod/Makefile', respectively (instead of 'Makefile' and 'Makefile<2>').

In contrast, the post-forward naming method would call the buffers 'Makefile|tmp' and 'Makefile|zaphod', and the reverse naming method would call them 'Makefile\tmp' and 'Makefile\zaphod'. The nontrivial difference between post-forward and reverse occurs when just one directory name is not enough to distinguish two files; then reverse puts the directory names in reverse order, so that '/top/middle/file' becomes 'file\middle\top', while post-forward puts them in forward order after the file name, as in 'file|top/middle'.

Which rule to follow for putting the directory names in the buffer name is not very important if you are going to *look* at the buffer names before you type one.

But as an experienced user, if you know the rule, you won't have to look. And then you may find that one rule or another is easier for you to remember and apply quickly.

16.7.2 Switching Between Buffers using Substrings

Iswitchb global minor mode provides convenient switching between buffers using substrings of their names. It replaces the normal definitions of C-x b, C-x 4 b, C-x 5 b, and C-x 4 C-o with alternative commands that are somewhat "smarter."

When one of these commands prompts you for a buffer name, you can type in just a substring of the name you want to choose. As you enter the substring, Iswitchb mode continuously displays a list of buffers that match the substring you have typed.

At any time, you can type RET to select the first buffer in the list. So the way to select a particular buffer is to make it the first in the list. There are two ways to do this. You can type more of the buffer name and thus narrow down the list, excluding unwanted buffers above the desired one. Alternatively, you can use C-s and C-r to rotate the list until the desired buffer is first.

TAB while entering the buffer name performs completion on the string you have entered, based on the displayed list of buffers.

To enable Iswitchb mode, type M-x iswitchb-mode, or customize the variable iswitchb-mode to t (see Section 32.2 [Easy Customization], page 408).

16.7.3 Customizing Buffer Menus

M-x bs-show
          Make a list of buffers similarly to M-x list-buffers but customizable.

M-x bs-show pops up a buffer list similar to the one normally displayed by C-x C-b but which you can customize. If you prefer this to the usual buffer list, you can bind this command to C-x C-b. To customize this buffer list, use the bs Custom group (see Section 32.2 [Easy Customization], page 408).

MSB global minor mode ("MSB" stands for "mouse select buffer") provides a different and customizable mouse buffer menu which you may prefer. It replaces the bindings of mouse-buffer-menu, normally on C-Down-Mouse-1, and the menu bar buffer menu. You can customize the menu in the msb Custom group.

17 Multiple Windows

Emacs can split a frame into two or many windows. Multiple windows can display parts of different buffers, or different parts of one buffer. Multiple frames always imply multiple windows, because each frame has its own set of windows. Each window belongs to one and only one frame.

17.1 Concepts of Emacs Windows

Each Emacs window displays one Emacs buffer at any time. A single buffer may appear in more than one window; if it does, any changes in its text are displayed in all the windows where it appears. But these windows can show different parts of the buffer, because each window has its own value of point.

At any time, one Emacs window is the *selected window*; the buffer this window is displaying is the current buffer. The terminal's cursor shows the location of point in this window. Each other window has a location of point as well. On text-only terminals, there is no way to show where those locations are, since the terminal has only one cursor. On a graphical display, the location of point in a non-selected window is indicated by a hollow box; the cursor in the selected window is blinking or solid.

Commands to move point affect the value of point for the selected Emacs window only. They do not change the value of point in other Emacs windows, even those showing the same buffer. The same is true for commands such as C-x b to switch buffers in the selected window; they do not affect other windows at all. However, there are other commands such as C-x 4 b that select a different window and switch buffers in it. Also, all commands that display information in a window, including (for example) C-h f (`describe-function`) and C-x C-b (`list-buffers`), work by switching buffers in a nonselected window without affecting the selected window.

When multiple windows show the same buffer, they can have different regions, because they can have different values of point. However, they all have the same value for the mark, because each buffer has only one mark position.

Each window has its own mode line, which displays the buffer name, modification status and major and minor modes of the buffer that is displayed in the window. The selected window's mode line appears in a different color. See Section 1.3 [Mode Line], page 8, for full details on the mode line.

17.2 Splitting Windows

C-x 2   Split the selected window into two windows, one above the other (`split-window-vertically`).

C-x 3   Split the selected window into two windows positioned side by side (`split-window-horizontally`).

C-Mouse-2   In the mode line or scroll bar of a window, split that window.

The command C-x 2 (`split-window-vertically`) breaks the selected window into two windows, one above the other. Both windows start out displaying the same buffer, with the same value of point. By default the two windows each get half the height of the window that was split; a numeric argument specifies how many lines to give to the top window.

C-x 3 (`split-window-horizontally`) breaks the selected window into two side-by-side windows. A numeric argument specifies how many columns to give the one on the left. If you are not using scrollbars, a vertical line separates the two windows. You can customize its color with the face `vertical-border`. Windows that are not the full width of the screen have mode lines, but they are truncated. On terminals where Emacs does not support highlighting, truncated mode lines sometimes do not appear in inverse video.

You can split a window horizontally or vertically by clicking C-Mouse-2 in the mode line or the scroll bar. The line of splitting goes through the place where you click: if you click on the mode line, the new scroll bar goes above the spot; if you click in the scroll bar, the mode line of the split window is side by side with your click.

When a window is less than the full width, text lines too long to fit are frequent. Continuing all those lines might be confusing, so if the variable `truncate-partial-width-windows` is non-`nil`, that forces truncation in all windows less than the full width of the screen, independent of the buffer being displayed and its value for `truncate-lines`. See Section 11.16 [Line Truncation], page 84.

Horizontal scrolling is often used in side-by-side windows. See Section 11.3 [Horizontal Scrolling], page 71.

If `split-window-keep-point` is non-`nil`, the default, both of the windows resulting from C-x 2 inherit the value of point from the window that was split. This means that scrolling is inevitable. If this variable is `nil`, then C-x 2 tries to avoid scrolling the text currently visible on the screen, by putting point in each window at a position already visible in the window. It also selects whichever window contains the screen line that the cursor was previously on. Some users prefer that mode on slow terminals.

17.3 Using Other Windows

C-x o   Select another window (`other-window`). That is o, not zero.

C-M-v   Scroll the next window (`scroll-other-window`).

M-x compare-windows
               Find next place where the text in the selected window does not match the text in the next window.

Mouse-1   Mouse-1, in a window's mode line, selects that window but does not move point in it (`mouse-select-window`).

To select a different window, click with Mouse-1 on its mode line. With the keyboard, you can switch windows by typing C-x o (`other-window`). That is an o, for "other," not a zero. When there are more than two windows, this command moves through all the windows in a cyclic order, generally top to bottom and left to right. After the rightmost and bottommost window, it goes back to the one at the upper left corner. A numeric argument means to move several steps in the cyclic order of windows. A negative argument moves around the cycle in the opposite order. When the minibuffer is active, the minibuffer is the last window in the cycle; you can switch from the minibuffer window to one of the other windows, and later switch back and finish supplying the minibuffer argument that is requested. See Section 5.2 [Minibuffer Edit], page 32.

The usual scrolling commands (see Chapter 11 [Display], page 69) apply to the selected window only, but there is one command to scroll the next window. C-M-v (`scroll-other-window`) scrolls the window that C-x o would select. It takes arguments, positive and negative, like C-v. (In the minibuffer, C-M-v scrolls the window that contains the minibuffer help display, if any, rather than the next window in the standard cyclic order.)

The command M-x `compare-windows` lets you compare two files or buffers visible in two windows, by moving through them to the next mismatch. See Section 15.9 [Comparing Files], page 148, for details.

If you set `mouse-autoselect-window` to a non-nil value, moving the mouse into a different window selects that window. This feature is off by default.

17.4 Displaying in Another Window

C-x 4 is a prefix key for commands that select another window (splitting the window if there is only one) and select a buffer in that window. Different C-x 4 commands have different ways of finding the buffer to select.

C-x 4 b *bufname* RET

> Select buffer *bufname* in another window. This runs `switch-to-buffer-other-window`.

C-x 4 C-o *bufname* RET

> Display buffer *bufname* in another window, but don't select that buffer or that window. This runs `display-buffer`.

C-x 4 f *filename* RET

> Visit file *filename* and select its buffer in another window. This runs `find-file-other-window`. See Section 15.2 [Visiting], page 120.

C-x 4 d *directory* RET

> Select a Dired buffer for directory *directory* in another window. This runs `dired-other-window`. See Chapter 29 [Dired], page 339.

C-x 4 m

> Start composing a mail message in another window. This runs `mail-other-window`; its same-window analogue is C-x m (see Chapter 27 [Sending Mail], page 310).

C-x 4 .

> Find a tag in the current tags table, in another window. This runs `find-tag-other-window`, the multiple-window variant of M-. (see Section 25.3 [Tags], page 293).

`C-x 4 r` *filename* `RET`
>
> Visit file *filename* read-only, and select its buffer in another window. This runs `find-file-read-only-other-window`. See Section 15.2 [Visiting], page 120.

17.5 Forcing Display in the Same Window

Certain Emacs commands switch to a specific buffer with special contents. For example, `M-x shell` switches to a buffer named '`*shell*`'. By convention, all these commands are written to pop up the buffer in a separate window. But you can specify that certain of these buffers should appear in the selected window.

If you add a buffer name to the list `same-window-buffer-names`, the effect is that such commands display that particular buffer by switching to it in the selected window. For example, if you add the element `"*grep*"` to the list, the `grep` command will display its output buffer in the selected window.

The default value of `same-window-buffer-names` is not `nil`: it specifies buffer names '`*info*`', '`*mail*`' and '`*shell*`' (as well as others used by more obscure Emacs packages). This is why `M-x shell` normally switches to the '`*shell*`' buffer in the selected window. If you delete this element from the value of `same-window-buffer-names`, the behavior of `M-x shell` will change—it will pop up the buffer in another window instead.

You can specify these buffers more generally with the variable `same-window-regexps`. Set it to a list of regular expressions; then any buffer whose name matches one of those regular expressions is displayed by switching to it in the selected window. (Once again, this applies only to buffers that normally get displayed for you in a separate window.) The default value of this variable specifies Telnet and rlogin buffers.

An analogous feature lets you specify buffers which should be displayed in their own individual frames. See Section 18.9 [Special Buffer Frames], page 180.

17.6 Deleting and Rearranging Windows

`C-x 0`   Delete the selected window (`delete-window`). The last character in this key sequence is a zero.

`C-x 1`   Delete all windows in the selected frame except the selected window (`delete-other-windows`).

`C-x 4 0`   Delete the selected window and kill the buffer that was showing in it (`kill-buffer-and-window`). The last character in this key sequence is a zero.

`C-x ^`   Make selected window taller (`enlarge-window`).

`C-x }`   Make selected window wider (`enlarge-window-horizontally`).

`C-x {`   Make selected window narrower (`shrink-window-horizontally`).

C-x -   Shrink this window if its buffer doesn't need so many lines (`shrink-window-if-larger-than-buffer`).

C-x +   Make all windows the same height (`balance-windows`).

To delete a window, type C-x 0 (`delete-window`). (That is a zero.) The space occupied by the deleted window is given to an adjacent window (but not the mini-buffer window, even if that is active at the time). Once a window is deleted, its attributes are forgotten; only restoring a window configuration can bring it back. Deleting the window has no effect on the buffer it used to display; the buffer continues to exist, and you can select it in any window with C-x b.

C-x 4 0 (`kill-buffer-and-window`) is a stronger command than C-x 0; it kills the current buffer and then deletes the selected window.

C-x 1 (`delete-other-windows`) is more powerful in a different way; it deletes all the windows except the selected one (and the minibuffer); the selected window expands to use the whole frame except for the echo area.

To readjust the division of space among vertically adjacent windows, use C-x ^ (`enlarge-window`). It makes the currently selected window one line bigger, or as many lines as is specified with a numeric argument. With a negative argument, it makes the selected window smaller. C-x } (`enlarge-window-horizontally`) makes the selected window wider by the specified number of columns. C-x { (`shrink-window-horizontally`) makes the selected window narrower by the specified number of columns.

When you make a window bigger, the space comes from its peers. If this makes any window too small, it is deleted and its space is given to an adjacent window. The minimum size is specified by the variables `window-min-height` and `window-min-width`.

The command C-x - (`shrink-window-if-larger-than-buffer`) reduces the height of the selected window, if it is taller than necessary to show the whole text of the buffer it is displaying. It gives the extra lines to other windows in the frame.

You can also use C-x + (`balance-windows`) to even out the heights of all the windows in the selected frame.

Mouse clicks on the mode line provide another way to change window heights and to delete windows. See Section 18.4 [Mode Line Mouse], page 176.

17.7 Window Handling Convenience Features and Customization

M-x `winner-mode` is a global minor mode that records the changes in the window configuration (i.e. how the frames are partitioned into windows), so that you can "undo" them. To undo, use C-c left (`winner-undo`). If you change your mind while undoing, you can redo the changes you had undone using C-c right (M-x `winner-redo`). Another way to enable Winner mode is by customizing the variable `winner-mode`.

The Windmove commands move directionally between neighboring windows in a frame. M-x `windmove-right` selects the window immediately to the right of the currently selected one, and similarly for the "left," "up," and "down" counterparts.

`M-x windmove-default-keybindings` binds these commands to `S-right` etc. (Not all terminals support shifted arrow keys, however.)

Follow minor mode (`M-x follow-mode`) synchronizes several windows on the same buffer so that they always display adjacent sections of that buffer. See Section 11.4 [Follow Mode], page 72.

`M-x scroll-all-mode` provides commands to scroll all visible windows together. You can also turn it on by customizing the variable `scroll-all-mode`. The commands provided are `M-x scroll-all-scroll-down-all`, `M-x scroll-all-page-down-all` and their corresponding "up" equivalents. To make this mode useful, you should bind these commands to appropriate keys.

18 Frames and Graphical Displays

When using a graphical display, you can create multiple windows at the system in a single Emacs session. Each system-level window that belongs to Emacs displays a *frame* which can contain one or several Emacs windows. A frame initially contains a single general-purpose Emacs window which you can subdivide vertically or horizontally into smaller windows. A frame normally contains its own echo area and minibuffer, but you can make frames that don't have these—they use the echo area and minibuffer of another frame.

To avoid confusion, we reserve the word "window" for the subdivisions that Emacs implements, and never use it to refer to a frame.

Editing you do in one frame affects the other frames. For instance, if you put text in the kill ring in one frame, you can yank it in another frame. If you exit Emacs through C-x C-c in one frame, it terminates all the frames. To delete just one frame, use C-x 5 0 (that is zero, not o).

Emacs compiled for MS-DOS emulates some windowing functionality, so that you can use many of the features described in this chapter. See section "MS-DOS Mouse" in *Specialized Emacs Features*.

18.1 Killing and Yanking on Graphical Displays

This section describes facilities for selecting a region, killing, and yanking using the mouse.

18.1.1 Mouse Commands for Editing

The mouse commands for selecting and copying a region are mostly compatible with the xterm program. You can use the same mouse commands for copying between Emacs and other window-based programs. Most of these commands also work in Emacs when you run it under an xterm terminal.

If you select a region with any of these mouse commands, and then immediately afterward type the DELETE function key, it deletes the region that you selected. The BACKSPACE function key and the ASCII character DEL do not do this; if you type any other key in between the mouse command and DELETE, it does not do this.

Mouse-1   Move point to where you click (mouse-set-point). This is normally the left button.

Normally, Emacs does not distinguish between ordinary mouse clicks and clicks that select a frame. When you click on a frame to select it, that also changes the selected window and cursor position according to the mouse click position. On the X window system, you can change this behavior by setting the variable x-mouse-click-focus-ignore-position to t. Then the first click selects the frame, but does not affect the selected window or cursor position. If you click again in the same place, since that click will be in the selected frame, it will change the window or cursor position.

`Drag-Mouse-1`

Set the region to the text you select by dragging, and copy it to the kill ring (`mouse-set-region`). You can specify both ends of the region with this single command.

If you move the mouse off the top or bottom of the window while dragging, the window scrolls at a steady rate until you move the mouse back into the window. This way, you can select regions that don't fit entirely on the screen. The number of lines scrolled per step depends on how far away from the window edge the mouse has gone; the variable `mouse-scroll-min-lines` specifies a minimum step size.

If the variable `mouse-drag-copy-region` is `nil`, this mouse command does not copy the selected region into the kill ring.

`Mouse-2`   Yank the last killed text, where you click (`mouse-yank-at-click`). This is normally the middle button.

`Mouse-3`   This command, `mouse-save-then-kill`, has several functions depending on where you click and the status of the region.

The most basic case is when you click `Mouse-1` in one place and then `Mouse-3` in another. This selects the text between those two positions as the region. It also copies the new region to the kill ring, so that you can copy it to someplace else.

If you click `Mouse-1` in the text, scroll with the scroll bar, and then click `Mouse-3`, it remembers where point was before scrolling (where you put it with `Mouse-1`), and uses that position as the other end of the region. This is so that you can select a region that doesn't fit entirely on the screen.

More generally, if you do not have a highlighted region, `Mouse-3` selects the text between point and the click position as the region. It does this by setting the mark where point was, and moving point to where you click.

If you have a highlighted region, or if the region was set just before by dragging button 1, `Mouse-3` adjusts the nearer end of the region by moving it to where you click. The adjusted region's text also replaces the old region's text in the kill ring.

If you originally specified the region using a double or triple `Mouse-1`, so that the region is defined to consist of entire words or lines, then adjusting the region with `Mouse-3` also proceeds by entire words or lines.

If you use `Mouse-3` a second time consecutively, at the same place, that kills the region already selected.

The simplest way to kill text with the mouse is to press `Mouse-1` at one end, then press `Mouse-3` twice at the other end. See Chapter 9 [Killing], page 55. To copy the text into the kill ring without deleting it from the buffer, press `Mouse-3` just once—or just drag across the text with `Mouse-1`. Then you can copy it elsewhere by yanking it.

To yank the killed or copied text somewhere else, move the mouse there and press `Mouse-2`. See Section 9.2 [Yanking], page 58. However, if `mouse-yank-at-point` is non-`nil`, `Mouse-2` yanks at point. Then it does not matter where you click, or even which of the frame's windows you click on. The default value is `nil`. This variable also affects yanking the secondary selection.

Many graphical applications follow the convention that insertion while text is selected deletes the selected text. You can make Emacs behave this way by enabling Delete Selection mode—with `M-x delete-selection-mode` or using Custom. Another effect of this mode is that DEL, `C-d` and some other keys, when a selection exists, will kill the whole selection. It also enables Transient Mark mode (see Section 8.2 [Transient Mark], page 50).

18.1.2 Cut and Paste with Other Window Applications

To copy text to another windowing application, kill it or save it in the kill ring. Then use the "paste" or "yank" command of the other application to insert the text.

To copy text from another windowing application, use its "cut" or "copy" command to select the text you want. Then yank it in Emacs with `C-y` or `Mouse-2`.

When Emacs puts text into the kill ring, or rotates text to the front of the kill ring, it sets the *primary selection* in the window system. This is how other windowing applications can access the text. On the X Window System, emacs also stores the text in the cut buffer, but only if the text is short enough (the value of `x-cut-buffer-max` specifies the maximum number of characters); putting long strings in the cut buffer can be slow.

The commands to yank the first entry in the kill ring actually check first for a primary selection in another program; after that, they check for text in the cut buffer. If neither of those sources provides text to yank, the kill ring contents are used.

The standard coding system for X Window System selections is `compound-text-with-extensions`. To specify another coding system for selections, use `C-x RET x` or `C-x RET X`. See Section 19.12 [Communication Coding], page 200.

18.1.3 Mouse Commands for Words and Lines

These variants of `Mouse-1` select entire words or lines at a time.

`Double-Mouse-1`

> This key sets the region around the word which you click on. If you click on a character with "symbol" syntax (such as underscore, in C mode), it sets the region around the symbol surrounding that character.
>
> If you click on a character with open-parenthesis or close-parenthesis syntax, it sets the region around the parenthetical grouping which that character starts or ends. If you click on a character with string-

delimiter syntax (such as a singlequote or doublequote in C), it sets the region around the string constant (using heuristics to figure out whether that character is the beginning or the end of it).

`Double-Drag-Mouse-1`

This key selects a region made up of the words you drag across.

`Triple-Mouse-1`

This key sets the region around the line you click on.

`Triple-Drag-Mouse-1`

This key selects a region made up of the lines you drag across.

18.1.4 Secondary Selection

The *secondary selection* is another way of selecting text using the X Window System. It does not use point or the mark, so you can use it to kill text without setting point or the mark.

`M-Drag-Mouse-1`

Set the secondary selection, with one end at the place where you press down the button, and the other end at the place where you release it (`mouse-set-secondary`). The highlighting appears and changes as you drag. You can control the appearance of the highlighting by customizing the `secondary-selection` face (see Section 32.2.5 [Face Customization], page 413).

If you move the mouse off the top or bottom of the window while dragging, the window scrolls at a steady rate until you move the mouse back into the window. This way, you can mark regions that don't fit entirely on the screen.

This way of setting the secondary selection does not alter the kill ring.

`M-Mouse-1`   Set one endpoint for the *secondary selection* (`mouse-start-secondary`).

`M-Mouse-3`   Make a secondary selection, using the place specified with `M-Mouse-1` as the other end (`mouse-secondary-save-then-kill`). This also puts the selected text in the kill ring. A second click at the same place kills the secondary selection just made.

`M-Mouse-2`   Insert the secondary selection where you click (`mouse-yank-secondary`). This places point at the end of the yanked text.

Double or triple clicking of `M-Mouse-1` operates on words and lines, much like Mouse-1.

If `mouse-yank-at-point` is non-nil, M-Mouse-2 yanks at point. Then it does not matter precisely where you click, or even which of the frame's windows you click on. See Section 18.1.1 [Mouse Commands], page 171.

18.1.5 Using the Clipboard

Apart from the primary and secondary selection types, Emacs can handle the *clipboard* selection type which is used by some applications, particularly under Open-Windows and Gnome.

The command M-x menu-bar-enable-clipboard makes the Cut, Paste and Copy menu items, as well as the keys of the same names, all use the clipboard.

You can customize the variable x-select-enable-clipboard to make the Emacs yank functions consult the clipboard before the primary selection, and to make the kill functions to store in the clipboard as well as the primary selection. Otherwise they do not access the clipboard at all. Using the clipboard is the default on MS-Windows and Mac, but not on other systems.

18.2 Following References with the Mouse

Some read-only Emacs buffers include references you can follow, or commands you can activate. These include names of files, of buffers, of possible completions, of matches for a pattern, as well as the buttons in Help buffers and customization buffers. You can follow the reference or activate the command by moving point to it and typing RET. You can also do this with the mouse, using either Mouse-1 or Mouse-2.

Since yanking text into a read-only buffer is not allowed, these buffers generally define Mouse-2 to follow a reference or activate a command. For example, if you click Mouse-2 on a file name in a Dired buffer, you visit that file. If you click Mouse-2 on an error message in the '*Compilation*' buffer, you go to the source code for that error message. If you click Mouse-2 on a completion in the '*Completions*' buffer, you choose that completion.

However, most applications use Mouse-1 to do this sort of thing, so Emacs implements this too. If you click Mouse-1 quickly on a reference or button, it follows or activates. If you click slowly, it moves point as usual. Dragging, meaning moving the mouse while it is held down, also has its usual behavior of setting the region.

Normally, the Mouse-1 click behavior is performed on links in any window. The variable mouse-1-click-in-non-selected-windows controls whether Mouse-1 has this behavior even in non-selected windows, or only in the selected window.

You can usually tell when Mouse-1 and Mouse-2 have this special sort of meaning because the sensitive text highlights when you move the mouse over it. The variable mouse-highlight controls whether to do this highlighting always (even when such text appears where the mouse already is), never, or only immediately after you move the mouse.

In Emacs versions before 22, only Mouse-2 follows links and Mouse-1 always sets point. If you prefer this older behavior, set the variable mouse-1-click-follows-link to nil. This variable also lets you choose various other alternatives for following links with the mouse. Type C-h v mouse-1-click-follows-link RET for more details.

18.3 Mouse Clicks for Menus

Several mouse clicks with the CTRL and SHIFT modifiers bring up menus.

C-Mouse-1   This menu is for selecting a buffer.

The MSB ("mouse select buffer") global minor mode makes this menu smarter and more customizable. See Section 16.7.3 [Buffer Menus], page 164.

C-Mouse-2   This menu is for specifying faces and other text properties for editing formatted text. See Section 22.12 [Formatted Text], page 236.

C-Mouse-3   This menu is mode-specific. For most modes if Menu-bar mode is on, this menu has the same items as all the mode-specific menu-bar menus put together. Some modes may specify a different menu for this button.[1] If Menu-bar mode is off, this menu contains all the items which would be present in the menu bar—not just the mode-specific ones—so that you can access them without having to display the menu bar.

S-Mouse-1   This menu is for specifying the frame's default font.

18.4 Mode Line Mouse Commands

You can use mouse clicks on window mode lines to select and manipulate windows.

Some areas of the mode line, such as the buffer name and the major mode name, have their own special mouse bindings. These areas are highlighted when you hold the mouse over them, and information about the special bindings will be displayed (see Section 18.17 [Tooltips], page 184). This section's commands do not apply in those areas.

Mouse-1   Mouse-1 on a mode line selects the window it belongs to. By dragging Mouse-1 on the mode line, you can move it, thus changing the height of the windows above and below. Changing heights with the mouse in this way never deletes windows, it just refuses to make any window smaller than the minimum height.

Mouse-2   Mouse-2 on a mode line expands that window to fill its frame.

Mouse-3   Mouse-3 on a mode line deletes the window it belongs to. If the frame has only one window, it buries the current buffer instead, and switches to another buffer.

C-Mouse-2   C-Mouse-2 on a mode line splits the window above horizontally, above the place in the mode line where you click.

---

[1] Some systems use Mouse-3 for a mode-specific menu. We took a survey of users, and found they preferred to keep Mouse-3 for selecting and killing regions. Hence the decision to use C-Mouse-3 for this menu. To use Mouse-3 instead, do (global-set-key [mouse-3] 'mouse-popup-menubar-stuff).

Using `Mouse-1` on the divider between two side-by-side mode lines, you can move the vertical boundary left or right. Using `C-Mouse-2` on a scroll bar splits the corresponding window vertically. See Section 17.2 [Split Window], page 165.

18.5 Creating Frames

The prefix key `C-x 5` is analogous to `C-x 4`, with parallel subcommands. The difference is that `C-x 5` commands create a new frame rather than just a new window in the selected frame (see Section 17.4 [Pop Up Window], page 167). If an existing visible or iconified frame already displays the requested material, these commands use the existing frame, after raising or deiconifying as necessary.

The various `C-x 5` commands differ in how they find or create the buffer to select:

`C-x 5 2`   Create a new frame (`make-frame-command`).

`C-x 5 b` *bufname* `RET`

> Select buffer *bufname* in another frame. This runs `switch-to-buffer-other-frame`.

`C-x 5 f` *filename* `RET`

> Visit file *filename* and select its buffer in another frame. This runs `find-file-other-frame`. See Section 15.2 [Visiting], page 120.

`C-x 5 d` *directory* `RET`

> Select a Dired buffer for directory *directory* in another frame. This runs `dired-other-frame`. See Chapter 29 [Dired], page 339.

`C-x 5 m`   Start composing a mail message in another frame. This runs `mail-other-frame`. It is the other-frame variant of `C-x m`. See Chapter 27 [Sending Mail], page 310.

`C-x 5 .`   Find a tag in the current tag table in another frame. This runs `find-tag-other-frame`, the multiple-frame variant of `M-.`. See Section 25.3 [Tags], page 293.

`C-x 5 r` *filename* `RET`

> Visit file *filename* read-only, and select its buffer in another frame. This runs `find-file-read-only-other-frame`. See Section 15.2 [Visiting], page 120.

You can control the appearance of new frames you create by setting the frame parameters in `default-frame-alist`. You can use the variable `initial-frame-alist` to specify parameters that affect only the initial frame. See section "Initial Parameters" in *The Emacs Lisp Reference Manual*, for more information.

The easiest way to specify the principal font for all your Emacs frames is with an X resource (see Section C.7 [Font X], page 481), but you can also do it by modifying `default-frame-alist` to specify the `font` parameter, as shown here:

```
(add-to-list 'default-frame-alist '(font . "10x20"))
```

Here's a similar example for specifying a foreground color:

```
       (add-to-list 'default-frame-alist '(foreground-color . "blue"))
```
By putting such customizations in your '~/.emacs' init file, you can control the appearance of all the frames Emacs creates, including the initial one.

18.6 Frame Commands

The following commands let you create, delete and operate on frames:

C-z   Iconify the selected Emacs frame (`iconify-or-deiconify-frame`). When typed on an Emacs frame's icon, deiconify instead.

             The normal meaning of C-z, to suspend Emacs, is not useful under a graphical display that allows multiple applications to operate simultaneously in their own windows, so Emacs gives C-z a different binding in that case.

C-x 5 0   Delete the selected frame (`delete-frame`). This is not allowed if there is only one frame.

C-x 5 o   Select another frame, raise it, and warp the mouse to it so that it stays selected. If you repeat this command, it cycles through all the frames on your terminal.

C-x 5 1   Delete all frames except the selected one.

To make the command C-x 5 o work properly, you must tell Emacs how the system (or the window manager) generally handles focus-switching between windows. There are two possibilities: either simply moving the mouse onto a window selects it (gives it focus), or you have to click on it in a suitable way to do so. On X, this focus policy also affects whether the focus is given to a frame that Emacs raises. Unfortunately there is no way Emacs can find out automatically which way the system handles this, so you have to explicitly say, by setting the variable focus-follows-mouse. If just moving the mouse onto a window selects it, that variable should be t; if a click is necessary, the variable should be nil.

The window manager that is part of MS-Windows always gives focus to a frame that raises, so this variable has no effect in the native MS-Windows build of Emacs.

18.7 Speedbar Frames

The *speedbar* is a special frame for conveniently navigating in or operating on another frame. The speedbar, when it exists, is always associated with a specific frame, called its *attached frame*; all speedbar operations act on that frame.

Type M-x speedbar to create the speedbar and associate it with the current frame. To dismiss the speedbar, type M-x speedbar again, or select the speedbar and type q. (You can also delete the speedbar frame like any other Emacs frame.) If you wish to associate the speedbar with a different frame, dismiss it and call M-x speedbar from that frame.

The speedbar can operate in various modes. Its default mode is *File Display* mode, which shows the files in the current directory of the selected window of the attached frame, one file per line. Clicking on a file name visits that file in the selected window of the attached frame, and clicking on a directory name shows that directory in the speedbar (see Section 18.2 [Mouse References], page 175). Each line also has a box, '[+]' or '<+>', that you can click on to *expand* the contents of that item. Expanding a directory adds the contents of that directory to the speedbar display, underneath the directory's own line. Expanding an ordinary file adds a list of the tags in that file to the speedbar display; you can click on a tag name to jump to that tag in the selected window of the attached frame. When a file or directory is expanded, the '[+]' changes to '[-]'; you can click on that box to *contract* the item, hiding its contents.

You navigate through the speedbar using the keyboard, too. Typing RET while point is on a line in the speedbar is equivalent to clicking the item on the current line, and SPC expands or contracts the item. U displays the parent directory of the current directory. To copy, delete, or rename the file on the current line, type C, D, and R respectively. To create a new directory, type M.

Another general-purpose speedbar mode is *Buffer Display* mode; in this mode, the speedbar displays a list of Emacs buffers. To switch to this mode, type b in the speedbar. To return to File Display mode, type f. You can also change the display mode by clicking mouse-3 anywhere in the speedbar window (or mouse-1 on the mode-line) and selecting 'Displays' in the pop-up menu.

Some major modes, including Rmail mode, Info, and GUD, have specialized ways of putting useful items into the speedbar for you to select. For example, in Rmail mode, the speedbar shows a list of Rmail files, and lets you move the current message to another Rmail file by clicking on its '<M>' box.

For more details on using and programming the speedbar, See section "Top" in *Speedbar Manual*.

18.8 Multiple Displays

A single Emacs can talk to more than one X display. Initially, Emacs uses just one display—the one specified with the DISPLAY environment variable or with the '--display' option (see Section C.2 [Initial Options], page 472). To connect to another display, use the command make-frame-on-display:

M-x make-frame-on-display RET *display* RET
        Create a new frame on display *display*.

A single X server can handle more than one screen. When you open frames on two screens belonging to one server, Emacs knows they share a single keyboard, and it treats all the commands arriving from these screens as a single stream of input.

When you open frames on different X servers, Emacs makes a separate input stream for each server. This way, two users can type simultaneously on the two displays, and Emacs will not garble their input. Each server also has its own selected frame. The commands you enter with a particular X server apply to that server's selected frame.

Despite these features, people using the same Emacs job from different displays can still interfere with each other if they are not careful. For example, if any one types C-x C-c, that exits the Emacs job for all of them!

18.9 Special Buffer Frames

You can make certain chosen buffers, which Emacs normally displays in "another window," appear in special frames of their own. To do this, set the variable `special-display-buffer-names` to a list of buffer names; any buffer whose name is in that list automatically gets a special frame, when an Emacs command wants to display it "in another window."

For example, if you set the variable this way,

```
(setq special-display-buffer-names
      '("*Completions*" "*grep*" "*tex-shell*"))
```

then completion lists, `grep` output and the TEX mode shell buffer get individual frames of their own. These frames, and the windows in them, are never automatically split or reused for any other buffers. They continue to show the buffers they were created for, unless you alter them by hand. Killing the special buffer deletes its frame automatically.

More generally, you can set `special-display-regexps` to a list of regular expressions; then a buffer gets its own frame if its name matches any of those regular expressions. (Once again, this applies only to buffers that normally get displayed for you in "another window.")

The variable `special-display-frame-alist` specifies the frame parameters for these frames. It has a default value, so you don't need to set it.

For those who know Lisp, an element of `special-display-buffer-names` or `special-display-regexps` can also be a list. Then the first element is the buffer name or regular expression; the rest of the list specifies how to create the frame. It can be an association list specifying frame parameter values; these values take precedence over parameter values specified in `special-display-frame-alist`. If you specify the symbol `same-window` as a "frame parameter" in this list, with a non-`nil` value, that means to use the selected window if possible. If you use the symbol `same-frame` as a "frame parameter" in this list, with a non-`nil` value, that means to use the selected frame if possible.

Alternatively, the value can have this form:

```
(function args...)
```

where *function* is a symbol. Then the frame is constructed by calling *function*; its first argument is the buffer, and its remaining arguments are *args*.

An analogous feature lets you specify buffers which should be displayed in the selected window. See Section 17.5 [Force Same Window], page 168. The same-window feature takes precedence over the special-frame feature; therefore, if you add a buffer name to `special-display-buffer-names` and it has no effect, check to see whether that feature is also in use for the same buffer name.

18.10 Setting Frame Parameters

You can specify the font and colors used for text display, and the colors for the frame borders, the cursor, and the mouse cursor, by customizing the faces `default`, `border`, `cursor` and `mouse`. See Section 32.2.5 [Face Customization], page 413.

You can also set a frame's default font through a pop-up menu. Press S-Mouse-1 to activate this menu.

These commands are available for controlling the window management behavior of the selected frame.

M-x auto-raise-mode

> Toggle whether or not the selected frame should auto-raise. Auto-raise means that every time you move the mouse onto the frame, it raises the frame.

> Some window managers also implement auto-raise. If you enable auto-raise for Emacs frames in your window manager, it will work, but it is beyond Emacs' control, so auto-raise-mode has no effect on it.

M-x auto-lower-mode

> Toggle whether or not the selected frame should auto-lower. Auto-lower means that every time you move the mouse off the frame, the frame moves to the bottom of the stack on the screen.

> The command auto-lower-mode has no effect on auto-lower implemented by the window manager. To control that, you must use the appropriate window manager features.

In Emacs versions that use an X toolkit, the color-setting and font-setting functions don't affect menus and the menu bar, since they are displayed by their own widget classes. To change the appearance of the menus and menu bar, you must use X resources (see Section D.1 [Resources], page 489). See Section C.8 [Colors], page 483, regarding colors. See Section C.7 [Font X], page 481, regarding choice of font.

Colors, fonts, and other attributes of the frame's display can also be customized by setting frame parameters in the variable default-frame-alist (see Section 18.5 [Creating Frames], page 177). For a detailed description of frame parameters and customization, see section "Frame Parameters" in The Emacs Lisp Reference Manual.

18.11 Scroll Bars

On graphical displays, Emacs normally makes a *scroll bar* at the left of each Emacs window.[2] The scroll bar runs the height of the window, and shows a moving rectangular inner box which represents the portion of the buffer currently displayed. The entire height of the scroll bar represents the entire length of the buffer.

You can use Mouse-2 (normally, the middle button) in the scroll bar to move or drag the inner box up and down. If you move it to the top of the scroll bar, you see the top of the buffer. If you move it to the bottom of the scroll bar, you see the bottom of the buffer.

The left and right buttons in the scroll bar scroll by controlled increments. Mouse-1 (normally, the left button) moves the line at the level where you click up

---

[2] Placing it at the left is usually more useful with overlapping frames with text starting at the left margin.

to the top of the window. `Mouse-3` (normally, the right button) moves the line at the top of the window down to the level where you click. By clicking repeatedly in the same place, you can scroll by the same distance over and over.

You can also click `C-Mouse-2` in the scroll bar to split a window vertically. The split occurs on the line where you click.

You can enable or disable Scroll Bar mode with the command `M-x scroll-bar-mode`. With no argument, it toggles the use of scroll bars. With an argument, it turns use of scroll bars on if and only if the argument is positive. This command applies to all frames, including frames yet to be created. Customize the variable `scroll-bar-mode` to control the use of scroll bars at startup. You can use it to specify that they are placed at the right of windows if you prefer that. You have to set this variable through the 'Customize' interface (see Section 32.2 [Easy Customization], page 408), or it will not work properly.

You can also use the X resource 'verticalScrollBars' to control the initial setting of Scroll Bar mode. See Section D.1 [Resources], page 489.

To enable or disable scroll bars for just the selected frame, use the command `M-x toggle-scroll-bar`.

You can control the scroll bar width by changing the value of the `scroll-bar-width` frame parameter.

18.12 Scrolling With "Wheeled" Mice

Some mice have a "wheel" instead of a third button. You can usually click the wheel to act as either `Mouse-2` or `Mouse-3`, depending on the setup. You can also use the wheel to scroll windows instead of using the scroll bar or keyboard commands. Mouse wheel support only works if the system generates appropriate events; whenever possible, it is turned on by default. To toggle this feature, use `M-x mouse-wheel-mode`.

The two variables `mouse-wheel-follow-mouse` and `mouse-wheel-scroll-amount` determine where and by how much buffers are scrolled. The variable `mouse-wheel-progressive-speed` determines whether the scroll speed is linked to how fast you move the wheel.

18.13 Drag and Drop

Emacs supports *drag and drop* using the mouse. For instance, dropping text onto an Emacs frame inserts the text where it is dropped. Dropping a file onto an Emacs frame visits that file. As a special case, dropping the file on a Dired buffer moves or copies the file (according to the conventions of the application it came from) into the directory displayed in that buffer.

Dropping a file normally visits it in the window you drop it on. If you prefer to visit the file in a new window in such cases, customize the variable `dnd-open-file-other-window`.

The XDND and Motif drag and drop protocols, and the old KDE 1.x protocol, are currently supported.

18.14 Menu Bars

You can turn display of menu bars on or off with M-x menu-bar-mode or by customizing the variable menu-bar-mode. With no argument, this command toggles Menu Bar mode, a minor mode. With an argument, the command turns Menu Bar mode on if the argument is positive, off if the argument is not positive. You can use the X resource 'menuBarLines' to control the initial setting of Menu Bar mode. See Section D.1 [Resources], page 489.

Expert users often turn off the menu bar, especially on text-only terminals, where this makes one additional line available for text. If the menu bar is off, you can still pop up a menu of its contents with C-Mouse-3 on a display which supports pop-up menus. See Section 18.3 [Menu Mouse Clicks], page 176.

See Section 1.4 [Menu Bar], page 10, for information on how to invoke commands with the menu bar. See Appendix D [X Resources], page 489, for how to customize the menu bar menus' visual appearance.

18.15 Tool Bars

The *tool bar* is a line (or lines) of icons at the top of the Emacs window, just below the menu bar. You can click on these icons with the mouse to do various jobs.

The global tool bar contains general commands. Some major modes define their own tool bars to replace it. A few "special" modes that are not designed for ordinary editing remove some items from the global tool bar.

Tool bars work only on a graphical display. The tool bar uses colored XPM icons if Emacs was built with XPM support. Otherwise, the tool bar uses monochrome icons (PBM or XBM format).

You can turn display of tool bars on or off with M-x tool-bar-mode or by customizing the option tool-bar-mode.

18.16 Using Dialog Boxes

A dialog box is a special kind of menu for asking you a yes-or-no question or some other special question. Many Emacs commands use a dialog box to ask a yes-or-no question, if you used the mouse to invoke the command to begin with.

You can customize the variable use-dialog-box to suppress the use of dialog boxes. This also controls whether to use file selection windows (but those are not supported on all platforms).

A file selection window is a special kind of dialog box for asking for file names. You can customize the variable use-file-dialog to suppress the use of file selection windows, even if you still want other kinds of dialogs. This variable has no effect if you have suppressed all dialog boxes with the variable use-dialog-box.

For Gtk+ version 2.4 and newer, Emacs use the Gtk+ file chooser dialog. Emacs adds a toggle button that enables and disables showing of hidden files (files starting with a dot) in that dialog. The variable x-gtk-show-hidden-files controls whether to show hidden files by default.

For Gtk+ versions 2.4 through 2.10, you can select the old file dialog (`gtk-file-selector`) by setting the variable `x-gtk-use-old-file-dialog` to a non-`nil` value. If it is `nil`, Emacs uses `gtk-file-chooser`. If Emacs is built with a Gtk+ version that has only one file dialog, this variable has no effect.

Emacs adds help text to the Gtk+ file chooser dialog. The variable `x-gtk-file-dialog-help-text` specifies the text to add; if it is `nil`, that disables the added text.

18.17 Tooltips

Tooltips are small windows that display text information at the current mouse position. They activate when there is a pause in mouse movement. There are two types of tooltip: help tooltips and GUD tooltips.

Help tooltips typically display over text—including the mode line—but are also available for other parts of the Emacs frame, such as the tool bar and menu items.

You can toggle display of help tooltips (Tooltip mode) with the command `M-x tooltip-mode`. When Tooltip mode is disabled, the help text is displayed in the echo area instead.

GUD tooltips show values of variables. They are useful when you are debugging a program. See Section 24.6.2 [Debugger Operation], page 279.

The variables `tooltip-delay` specifies how long Emacs should wait before displaying a tooltip. For additional customization options for displaying tooltips, use `M-x customize-group` RET `tooltip` RET. See Appendix D [X Resources], page 489, for information on customizing the windows that display tooltips.

18.18 Mouse Avoidance

Mouse Avoidance mode keeps the mouse pointer away from point, to avoid obscuring text you want to edit. Whenever it moves the mouse, it also raises the frame. To use Mouse Avoidance mode, customize the variable `mouse-avoidance-mode`. You can set this to various values to move the mouse in several ways:

`banish`   Move the mouse to the upper-right corner on any key-press;

`exile`   Move the mouse to the corner only if the cursor gets too close, and allow it to return once the cursor is out of the way;

`jump`   If the cursor gets too close to the mouse, displace the mouse a random distance & direction;

`animate`   As `jump`, but shows steps along the way for illusion of motion;

`cat-and-mouse`
               The same as `animate`;

`proteus`   As `animate`, but changes the shape of the mouse pointer too.

You can also use the command `M-x mouse-avoidance-mode` to enable the mode.

18.19 Non-Window Terminals

On a text-only terminal, Emacs can display only one Emacs frame at a time. However, you can still create multiple Emacs frames, and switch between them. Switching frames on these terminals is much like switching between different window configurations.

Use C-x 5 2 to create a new frame and switch to it; use C-x 5 o to cycle through the existing frames; use C-x 5 0 to delete the current frame.

Each frame has a number to distinguish it. If your terminal can display only one frame at a time, the selected frame's number n appears near the beginning of the mode line, in the form 'Fn'.

'Fn' is in fact the frame's initial name. You can give frames more meaningful names if you wish, and you can select a frame by its name. Use the command M-x set-frame-name RET name RET to specify a new name for the selected frame, and use M-x select-frame-by-name RET name RET to select a frame according to its name. The name you specify appears in the mode line when the frame is selected.

18.20 Using a Mouse in Terminal Emulators

Some terminal emulators support mouse clicks in the terminal window.

In a terminal emulator which is compatible with xterm, you can use M-x xterm-mouse-mode to give Emacs control over simple use of the mouse—basically, only non-modified single clicks are supported. The normal xterm mouse functionality for such clicks is still available by holding down the SHIFT key when you press the mouse button. Xterm Mouse mode is a global minor mode (see Section 32.1 [Minor Modes], page 406). Repeating the command turns the mode off again.

In the console on GNU/Linux, you can use M-x t-mouse-mode. You need to have the gpm package installed and running on your system in order for this to work.

19 International Character Set Support

Emacs supports a wide variety of international character sets, including European and Vietnamese variants of the Latin alphabet, as well as Cyrillic, Devanagari (for Hindi and Marathi), Ethiopic, Greek, Han (for Chinese and Japanese), Hangul (for Korean), Hebrew, IPA, Kannada, Lao, Malayalam, Tamil, Thai, Tibetan, and Vietnamese scripts. Emacs also supports various encodings of these characters used by other internationalized software, such as word processors and mailers.

Emacs allows editing text with international characters by supporting all the related activities:

- You can visit files with non-ASCII characters, save non-ASCII text, and pass non-ASCII text between Emacs and programs it invokes (such as compilers, spell-checkers, and mailers). Setting your language environment (see Section 19.3 [Language Environments], page 188) takes care of setting up the coding systems and other options for a specific language or culture. Alternatively, you can specify how Emacs should encode or decode text for each command; see Section 19.11 [Text Coding], page 198.

- You can display non-ASCII characters encoded by the various scripts. This works by using appropriate fonts on graphics displays (see Section 19.16 [Defining Fontsets], page 203), and by sending special codes to text-only displays (see Section 19.14 [Terminal Coding], page 201). If some characters are displayed incorrectly, refer to Section 19.17 [Undisplayable Characters], page 204, which describes possible problems and explains how to solve them.

- You can insert non-ASCII characters or search for them. To do that, you can specify an input method (see Section 19.5 [Select Input Method], page 191) suitable for your language, or use the default input method set up when you set your language environment. If your keyboard can produce non-ASCII characters, you can select an appropriate keyboard coding system (see Section 19.14 [Terminal Coding], page 201), and Emacs will accept those characters. Latin-1 characters can also be input by using the C-x 8 prefix, see Section 19.18 [Unibyte Mode], page 204.

  On X Window systems, your locale should be set to an appropriate value to make sure Emacs interprets keyboard input correctly; see Section 19.3 [Language Environments], page 188.

The rest of this chapter describes these issues in detail.

19.1 Introduction to International Character Sets

The users of international character sets and scripts have established many more-or-less standard coding systems for storing files. Emacs internally uses a single multibyte character encoding, so that it can intermix characters from all these scripts in a single buffer or string. This encoding represents each non-ASCII character as a sequence of bytes in the range 0200 through 0377. Emacs translates between the multibyte character encoding and various other coding systems when reading and

writing files, when exchanging data with subprocesses, and (in some cases) in the
C-q command (see Section 19.6 [Multibyte Conversion], page 193).

The command C-h h (view-hello-file) displays the file 'etc/HELLO', which
shows how to say "hello" in many languages. This illustrates various scripts. If
some characters can't be displayed on your terminal, they appear as '?' or as hollow
boxes (see Section 19.17 [Undisplayable Characters], page 204).

Keyboards, even in the countries where these character sets are used, generally
don't have keys for all the characters in them. So Emacs supports various *input
methods*, typically one for each script or language, to make it convenient to type
them.

The prefix key C-x RET is used for commands that pertain to multibyte characters, coding systems, and input methods.

19.2 Enabling Multibyte Characters

By default, Emacs starts in multibyte mode, because that allows you to use all the
supported languages and scripts without limitations.

You can enable or disable multibyte character support, either for Emacs as a
whole, or for a single buffer. When multibyte characters are disabled in a buffer,
we call that *unibyte mode*. Then each byte in that buffer represents a character,
even codes 0200 through 0377.

The old features for supporting the European character sets, ISO Latin-1 and
ISO Latin-2, work in unibyte mode as they did in Emacs 19 and also work for the
other ISO 8859 character sets. However, there is no need to turn off multibyte
character support to use ISO Latin; the Emacs multibyte character set includes all
the characters in these character sets, and Emacs can translate automatically to
and from the ISO codes.

To edit a particular file in unibyte representation, visit it using find-file-
literally. See Section 15.2 [Visiting], page 120. To convert a buffer in multibyte
representation into a single-byte representation of the same characters, the easiest
way is to save the contents in a file, kill the buffer, and find the file again with
find-file-literally. You can also use C-x RET c (universal-coding-system-
argument) and specify 'raw-text' as the coding system with which to find or save a
file. See Section 19.11 [Text Coding], page 198. Finding a file as 'raw-text' doesn't
disable format conversion, uncompression and auto mode selection as find-file-
literally does.

To turn off multibyte character support by default, start Emacs with the
'--unibyte' option (see Section C.2 [Initial Options], page 472), or set the environment variable EMACS_UNIBYTE. You can also customize enable-multibyte-
characters or, equivalently, directly set the variable default-enable-multibyte-
characters to nil in your init file to have basically the same effect as '--unibyte'.

To convert a unibyte session to a multibyte session, set default-enable-
multibyte-characters to t. Buffers which were created in the unibyte session
before you turn on multibyte support will stay unibyte. You can turn on multibyte

support in a specific buffer by invoking the command `toggle-enable-multibyte-characters` in that buffer.

With '`--unibyte`', multibyte strings are not created during initialization from the values of environment variables, '`/etc/passwd`' entries etc. that contain non-ASCII 8-bit characters.

Emacs normally loads Lisp files as multibyte, regardless of whether you used '`--unibyte`'. This includes the Emacs initialization file, '`.emacs`', and the initialization files of Emacs packages such as Gnus. However, you can specify unibyte loading for a particular Lisp file, by putting '`-*-unibyte: t;-*-`' in a comment on the first line (see Section 32.3.4 [File Variables], page 420). Then that file is always loaded as unibyte text, even if you did not start Emacs with '`--unibyte`'. The motivation for these conventions is that it is more reliable to always load any particular Lisp file in the same way. However, you can load a Lisp file as unibyte, on any one occasion, by typing `C-x RET c raw-text RET` immediately before loading it.

The mode line indicates whether multibyte character support is enabled in the current buffer. If it is, there are two or more characters (most often two dashes) near the beginning of the mode line, before the indication of the visited file's end-of-line convention (colon, backslash, etc.). When multibyte characters are not enabled, nothing precedes the colon except a single dash. See Section 1.3 [Mode Line], page 8, for more details about this.

19.3 Language Environments

All supported character sets are supported in Emacs buffers whenever multibyte characters are enabled; there is no need to select a particular language in order to display its characters in an Emacs buffer. However, it is important to select a *language environment* in order to set various defaults. The language environment really represents a choice of preferred script (more or less) rather than a choice of language.

The language environment controls which coding systems to recognize when reading text (see Section 19.8 [Recognize Coding], page 195). This applies to files, incoming mail, netnews, and any other text you read into Emacs. It may also specify the default coding system to use when you create a file. Each language environment also specifies a default input method.

To select a language environment, you can customize the variable `current-language-environment` or use the command `M-x set-language-environment`. It makes no difference which buffer is current when you use this command, because the effects apply globally to the Emacs session. The supported language environments include:

> ASCII, Belarusian, Brazilian Portuguese, Bulgarian, Chinese-BIG5, Chinese-CNS, Chinese-EUC-TW, Chinese-GB, Croatian, Cyrillic-ALT, Cyrillic-ISO, Cyrillic-KOI8, Czech, Devanagari, Dutch, English, Esperanto, Ethiopic, French, Georgian, German, Greek, Hebrew, IPA, Italian, Japanese, Kannada, Korean, Lao, Latin-1, Latin-2, Latin-3, Latin-4, Latin-5, Latin-6, Latin-7, Latin-8 (Celtic), Latin-9 (updated

Latin-1 with the Euro sign), Latvian, Lithuanian, Malayalam, Polish, Romanian, Russian, Slovak, Slovenian, Spanish, Swedish, Tajik, Tamil, Thai, Tibetan, Turkish, UTF-8 (for a setup which prefers Unicode characters and files encoded in UTF-8), Ukrainian, Vietnamese, Welsh, and Windows-1255 (for a setup which prefers Cyrillic characters and files encoded in Windows-1255).

To display the script(s) used by your language environment on a graphical display, you need to have a suitable font. If some of the characters appear as empty boxes, you should install the GNU Intlfonts package, which includes fonts for most supported scripts.[1] See Section 19.15 [Fontsets], page 202, for more details about setting up your fonts.

Some operating systems let you specify the character-set locale you are using by setting the locale environment variables LC_ALL, LC_CTYPE, or LANG.[2] During startup, Emacs looks up your character-set locale's name in the system locale alias table, matches its canonical name against entries in the value of the variables locale-charset-language-names and locale-language-names, and selects the corresponding language environment if a match is found. (The former variable overrides the latter.) It also adjusts the display table and terminal coding system, the locale coding system, the preferred coding system as needed for the locale, and—last but not least—the way Emacs decodes non-ASCII characters sent by your keyboard.

If you modify the LC_ALL, LC_CTYPE, or LANG environment variables while running Emacs, you may want to invoke the set-locale-environment function afterwards to readjust the language environment from the new locale.

The set-locale-environment function normally uses the preferred coding system established by the language environment to decode system messages. But if your locale matches an entry in the variable locale-preferred-coding-systems, Emacs uses the corresponding coding system instead. For example, if the locale 'ja_JP.PCK' matches japanese-shift-jis in locale-preferred-coding-systems, Emacs uses that encoding even though it might normally use japanese-iso-8bit.

You can override the language environment chosen at startup with explicit use of the command set-language-environment, or with customization of current-language-environment in your init file.

To display information about the effects of a certain language environment *lang-env*, use the command C-h L *lang-env* RET (describe-language-environment). This tells you which languages this language environment is useful for, and lists the character sets, coding systems, and input methods that go with it. It also

---

[1] If you run Emacs on X, you need to inform the X server about the location of the newly installed fonts with the following commands:

```
xset fp+ /usr/local/share/emacs/fonts
xset fp rehash
```

[2] If more than one of these is set, the first one that is nonempty specifies your locale for this purpose.

shows some sample text to illustrate scripts used in this language environment. If you give an empty input for *lang-env*, this command describes the chosen language environment.

You can customize any language environment with the normal hook `set-language-environment-hook`. The command `set-language-environment` runs that hook after setting up the new language environment. The hook functions can test for a specific language environment by checking the variable `current-language-environment`. This hook is where you should put non-default settings for specific language environment, such as coding systems for keyboard input and terminal output, the default input method, etc.

Before it starts to set up the new language environment, `set-language-environment` first runs the hook `exit-language-environment-hook`. This hook is useful for undoing customizations that were made with `set-language-environment-hook`. For instance, if you set up a special key binding in a specific language environment using `set-language-environment-hook`, you should set up `exit-language-environment-hook` to restore the normal binding for that key.

19.4 Input Methods

An *input method* is a kind of character conversion designed specifically for interactive input. In Emacs, typically each language has its own input method; sometimes several languages which use the same characters can share one input method. A few languages support several input methods.

The simplest kind of input method works by mapping ASCII letters into another alphabet; this allows you to use one other alphabet instead of ASCII. The Greek and Russian input methods work this way.

A more powerful technique is composition: converting sequences of characters into one letter. Many European input methods use composition to produce a single non-ASCII letter from a sequence that consists of a letter followed by accent characters (or vice versa). For example, some methods convert the sequence a' into a single accented letter. These input methods have no special commands of their own; all they do is compose sequences of printing characters.

The input methods for syllabic scripts typically use mapping followed by composition. The input methods for Thai and Korean work this way. First, letters are mapped into symbols for particular sounds or tone marks; then, sequences of these which make up a whole syllable are mapped into one syllable sign.

Chinese and Japanese require more complex methods. In Chinese input methods, first you enter the phonetic spelling of a Chinese word (in input method `chinese-py`, among others), or a sequence of portions of the character (input methods `chinese-4corner` and `chinese-sw`, and others). One input sequence typically corresponds to many possible Chinese characters. You select the one you mean using keys such as `C-f`, `C-b`, `C-n`, `C-p`, and digits, which have special meanings in this situation.

The possible characters are conceptually arranged in several rows, with each row holding up to 10 alternatives. Normally, Emacs displays just one row at a time, in the echo area; (*i*/*j*) appears at the beginning, to indicate that this is the *i*th row out of a total of *j* rows. Type C-n or C-p to display the next row or the previous row.

Type C-f and C-b to move forward and backward among the alternatives in the current row. As you do this, Emacs highlights the current alternative with a special color; type C-SPC to select the current alternative and use it as input. The alternatives in the row are also numbered; the number appears before the alternative. Typing a digit *n* selects the *n*th alternative of the current row and uses it as input.

TAB in these Chinese input methods displays a buffer showing all the possible characters at once; then clicking Mouse-2 on one of them selects that alternative. The keys C-f, C-b, C-n, C-p, and digits continue to work as usual, but they do the highlighting in the buffer showing the possible characters, rather than in the echo area.

In Japanese input methods, first you input a whole word using phonetic spelling; then, after the word is in the buffer, Emacs converts it into one or more characters using a large dictionary. One phonetic spelling corresponds to a number of different Japanese words; to select one of them, use C-n and C-p to cycle through the alternatives.

Sometimes it is useful to cut off input method processing so that the characters you have just entered will not combine with subsequent characters. For example, in input method latin-1-postfix, the sequence e ' combines to form an 'e' with an accent. What if you want to enter them as separate characters?

One way is to type the accent twice; this is a special feature for entering the separate letter and accent. For example, e ' ' gives you the two characters 'e''. Another way is to type another letter after the e—something that won't combine with that—and immediately delete it. For example, you could type e e DEL ' to get separate 'e' and '''.

Another method, more general but not quite as easy to type, is to use C-\ C-\ between two characters to stop them from combining. This is the command C-\ (toggle-input-method) used twice.

C-\ C-\ is especially useful inside an incremental search, because it stops waiting for more characters to combine, and starts searching for what you have already entered.

To find out how to input the character after point using the current input method, type C-u C-x =. See Section 4.9 [Position Info], page 26.

The variables input-method-highlight-flag and input-method-verbose-flag control how input methods explain what is happening. If input-method-highlight-flag is non-nil, the partial sequence is highlighted in the buffer (for most input methods—some disable this feature). If input-method-verbose-flag is non-nil, the list of possible characters to type next is displayed in the echo area (but not when you are in the minibuffer).

19.5 Selecting an Input Method

C-\   Enable or disable use of the selected input method.

C-x RET C-\ *method* RET
           Select a new input method for the current buffer.

C-h I *method* RET
C-h C-\ *method* RET
           Describe the input method *method* (describe-input-method). By default, it describes the current input method (if any). This description should give you the full details of how to use any particular input method.

M-x list-input-methods
           Display a list of all the supported input methods.

To choose an input method for the current buffer, use C-x RET C-\ (set-input-method). This command reads the input method name from the minibuffer; the name normally starts with the language environment that it is meant to be used with. The variable current-input-method records which input method is selected.

Input methods use various sequences of ASCII characters to stand for non-ASCII characters. Sometimes it is useful to turn off the input method temporarily. To do this, type C-\ (toggle-input-method). To reenable the input method, type C-\ again.

If you type C-\ and you have not yet selected an input method, it prompts for you to specify one. This has the same effect as using C-x RET C-\ to specify an input method.

When invoked with a numeric argument, as in C-u C-\, toggle-input-method always prompts you for an input method, suggesting the most recently selected one as the default.

Selecting a language environment specifies a default input method for use in various buffers. When you have a default input method, you can select it in the current buffer by typing C-\. The variable default-input-method specifies the default input method (nil means there is none).

In some language environments, which support several different input methods, you might want to use an input method different from the default chosen by set-language-environment. You can instruct Emacs to select a different default input method for a certain language environment, if you wish, by using set-language-environment-hook (see Section 19.3 [Language Environments], page 188). For example:

```
(defun my-chinese-setup ()
  "Set up my private Chinese environment."
  (if (equal current-language-environment "Chinese-GB")
      (setq default-input-method "chinese-tonepy")))
(add-hook 'set-language-environment-hook 'my-chinese-setup)
```

This sets the default input method to be chinese-tonepy whenever you choose a Chinese-GB language environment.

Some input methods for alphabetic scripts work by (in effect) remapping the keyboard to emulate various keyboard layouts commonly used for those scripts. How to do this remapping properly depends on your actual keyboard layout. To specify which layout your keyboard has, use the command M-x quail-set-keyboard-layout.

You can use the command M-x quail-show-key to show what key (or key sequence) to type in order to input the character following point, using the selected keyboard layout. The command C-u C-x = also shows that information in addition to the other information about the character.

To see a list of all the supported input methods, type M-x list-input-methods. The list gives information about each input method, including the string that stands for it in the mode line.

19.6 Unibyte and Multibyte Non-ASCII characters

When multibyte characters are enabled, character codes 0240 (octal) through 0377 (octal) are not really legitimate in the buffer. The valid non-ASCII printing characters have codes that start from 0400.

If you type a self-inserting character in the range 0240 through 0377, or if you use C-q to insert one, Emacs assumes you intended to use one of the ISO Latin-n character sets, and converts it to the Emacs code representing that Latin-n character. You select which ISO Latin character set to use through your choice of language environment (see above). If you do not specify a choice, the default is Latin-1.

If you insert a character in the range 0200 through 0237, which forms the eight-bit-control character set, it is inserted literally. You should normally avoid doing this since buffers containing such characters have to be written out in either the emacs-mule or raw-text coding system, which is usually not what you want.

19.7 Coding Systems

Users of various languages have established many more-or-less standard coding systems for representing them. Emacs does not use these coding systems internally; instead, it converts from various coding systems to its own system when reading data, and converts the internal coding system to other coding systems when writing data. Conversion is possible in reading or writing files, in sending or receiving from the terminal, and in exchanging data with subprocesses.

Emacs assigns a name to each coding system. Most coding systems are used for one language, and the name of the coding system starts with the language name. Some coding systems are used for several languages; their names usually start with 'iso'. There are also special coding systems no-conversion, raw-text and emacs-mule which do not convert printing characters at all.

A special class of coding systems, collectively known as codepages, is designed to support text encoded by MS-Windows and MS-DOS software. The names of these coding systems are cpnnnn, where nnnn is a 3- or 4-digit number of the codepage.

You can use these encodings just like any other coding system; for example, to visit a file encoded in codepage 850, type C-x RET c cp850 RET C-x C-f *filename* RET[3].

In addition to converting various representations of non-ASCII characters, a coding system can perform end-of-line conversion. Emacs handles three different conventions for how to separate lines in a file: newline, carriage-return linefeed, and just carriage-return.

C-h C *coding* RET
> Describe coding system *coding*.

C-h C RET   Describe the coding systems currently in use.

M-x list-coding-systems
> Display a list of all the supported coding systems.

The command C-h C (describe-coding-system) displays information about particular coding systems, including the end-of-line conversion specified by those coding systems. You can specify a coding system name as the argument; alternatively, with an empty argument, it describes the coding systems currently selected for various purposes, both in the current buffer and as the defaults, and the priority list for recognizing coding systems (see Section 19.8 [Recognize Coding], page 195).

To display a list of all the supported coding systems, type M-x list-coding-systems. The list gives information about each coding system, including the letter that stands for it in the mode line (see Section 1.3 [Mode Line], page 8).

Each of the coding systems that appear in this list—except for no-conversion, which means no conversion of any kind—specifies how and whether to convert printing characters, but leaves the choice of end-of-line conversion to be decided based on the contents of each file. For example, if the file appears to use the sequence carriage-return linefeed to separate lines, DOS end-of-line conversion will be used.

Each of the listed coding systems has three variants which specify exactly what to do for end-of-line conversion:

...-unix   Don't do any end-of-line conversion; assume the file uses newline to separate lines. (This is the convention normally used on Unix and GNU systems.)

...-dos   Assume the file uses carriage-return linefeed to separate lines, and do the appropriate conversion. (This is the convention normally used on Microsoft systems.[4])

...-mac   Assume the file uses carriage-return to separate lines, and do the appropriate conversion. (This is the convention normally used on the Macintosh system.)

---

[3]   In the MS-DOS port of Emacs, you need to create a cp*nnn* coding system with M-x codepage-setup, before you can use it. See section "MS-DOS and MULE" in *Specialized Emacs Features*.

[4]   It is also specified for MIME 'text/*' bodies and in other network transport contexts. It is different from the SGML reference syntax record-start/record-end format which Emacs doesn't support directly.

These variant coding systems are omitted from the `list-coding-systems` display for brevity, since they are entirely predictable. For example, the coding system `iso-latin-1` has variants `iso-latin-1-unix`, `iso-latin-1-dos` and `iso-latin-1-mac`.

The coding systems `unix`, `dos`, and `mac` are aliases for `undecided-unix`, `undecided-dos`, and `undecided-mac`, respectively. These coding systems specify only the end-of-line conversion, and leave the character code conversion to be deduced from the text itself.

The coding system `raw-text` is good for a file which is mainly ASCII text, but may contain byte values above 127 which are not meant to encode non-ASCII characters. With `raw-text`, Emacs copies those byte values unchanged, and sets `enable-multibyte-characters` to `nil` in the current buffer so that they will be interpreted properly. `raw-text` handles end-of-line conversion in the usual way, based on the data encountered, and has the usual three variants to specify the kind of end-of-line conversion to use.

In contrast, the coding system `no-conversion` specifies no character code conversion at all—none for non-ASCII byte values and none for end of line. This is useful for reading or writing binary files, tar files, and other files that must be examined verbatim. It, too, sets `enable-multibyte-characters` to `nil`.

The easiest way to edit a file with no conversion of any kind is with the `M-x find-file-literally` command. This uses `no-conversion`, and also suppresses other Emacs features that might convert the file contents before you see them. See Section 15.2 [Visiting], page 120.

The coding system `emacs-mule` means that the file contains non ASCII characters stored with the internal Emacs encoding. It handles end-of-line conversion based on the data encountered, and has the usual three variants to specify the kind of end-of-line conversion.

The *character translation* feature can modify the effect of various coding systems, by changing the internal Emacs codes that decoding produces. For instance, the command `unify-8859-on-decoding-mode` enables a mode that "unifies" the Latin alphabets when decoding text. This works by converting all non-ASCII Latin-*n* characters to either Latin-1 or Unicode characters. This way it is easier to use various Latin-*n* alphabets together. (In a future Emacs version we hope to move towards full Unicode support and complete unification of character sets.)

If you set the variable `enable-character-translation` to `nil`, that disables all character translation (including `unify-8859-on-decoding-mode`).

19.8 Recognizing Coding Systems

Emacs tries to recognize which coding system to use for a given text as an integral part of reading that text. (This applies to files being read, output from subprocesses, text from X selections, etc.) Emacs can select the right coding system automatically most of the time—once you have specified your preferences.

Some coding systems can be recognized or distinguished by which byte sequences appear in the data. However, there are coding systems that cannot be distinguished, not even potentially. For example, there is no way to distinguish between Latin-1 and Latin-2; they use the same byte values with different meanings.

Emacs handles this situation by means of a priority list of coding systems. Whenever Emacs reads a file, if you do not specify the coding system to use, Emacs checks the data against each coding system, starting with the first in priority and working down the list, until it finds a coding system that fits the data. Then it converts the file contents assuming that they are represented in this coding system.

The priority list of coding systems depends on the selected language environment (see Section 19.3 [Language Environments], page 188). For example, if you use French, you probably want Emacs to prefer Latin-1 to Latin-2; if you use Czech, you probably want Latin-2 to be preferred. This is one of the reasons to specify a language environment.

However, you can alter the coding system priority list in detail with the command `M-x prefer-coding-system`. This command reads the name of a coding system from the minibuffer, and adds it to the front of the priority list, so that it is preferred to all others. If you use this command several times, each use adds one element to the front of the priority list.

If you use a coding system that specifies the end-of-line conversion type, such as `iso-8859-1-dos`, what this means is that Emacs should attempt to recognize `iso-8859-1` with priority, and should use DOS end-of-line conversion when it does recognize `iso-8859-1`.

Sometimes a file name indicates which coding system to use for the file. The variable `file-coding-system-alist` specifies this correspondence. There is a special function `modify-coding-system-alist` for adding elements to this list. For example, to read and write all '.txt' files using the coding system `chinese-iso-8bit`, you can execute this Lisp expression:

```
(modify-coding-system-alist 'file "\\.txt\\'" 'chinese-iso-8bit)
```

The first argument should be `file`, the second argument should be a regular expression that determines which files this applies to, and the third argument says which coding system to use for these files.

Emacs recognizes which kind of end-of-line conversion to use based on the contents of the file: if it sees only carriage-returns, or only carriage-return linefeed sequences, then it chooses the end-of-line conversion accordingly. You can inhibit the automatic use of end-of-line conversion by setting the variable `inhibit-eol-conversion` to non-`nil`. If you do that, DOS-style files will be displayed with the '^M' characters visible in the buffer; some people prefer this to the more subtle '(DOS)' end-of-line type indication near the left edge of the mode line (see Section 1.3 [Mode Line], page 8).

By default, the automatic detection of coding system is sensitive to escape sequences. If Emacs sees a sequence of characters that begin with an escape character, and the sequence is valid as an ISO-2022 code, that tells Emacs to use one of the ISO-2022 encodings to decode the file.

However, there may be cases that you want to read escape sequences in a file as is. In such a case, you can set the variable `inhibit-iso-escape-detection` to non-`nil`. Then the code detection ignores any escape sequences, and never uses an

ISO-2022 encoding. The result is that all escape sequences become visible in the buffer.

The default value of `inhibit-iso-escape-detection` is `nil`. We recommend that you not change it permanently, only for one specific operation. That's because many Emacs Lisp source files in the Emacs distribution contain non-ASCII characters encoded in the coding system `iso-2022-7bit`, and they won't be decoded correctly when you visit those files if you suppress the escape sequence detection.

The variables `auto-coding-alist`, `auto-coding-regexp-alist` and `auto-coding-functions` are the strongest way to specify the coding system for certain patterns of file names, or for files containing certain patterns; these variables even override '`-*-coding:-*-`' tags in the file itself. Emacs uses `auto-coding-alist` for tar and archive files, to prevent it from being confused by a '`-*-coding:-*-`' tag in a member of the archive and thinking it applies to the archive file as a whole. Likewise, Emacs uses `auto-coding-regexp-alist` to ensure that RMAIL files, whose names in general don't match any particular pattern, are decoded correctly. One of the builtin `auto-coding-functions` detects the encoding for XML files.

When you get new mail in Rmail, each message is translated automatically from the coding system it is written in, as if it were a separate file. This uses the priority list of coding systems that you have specified. If a MIME message specifies a character set, Rmail obeys that specification, unless `rmail-decode-mime-charset` is `nil`.

For reading and saving Rmail files themselves, Emacs uses the coding system specified by the variable `rmail-file-coding-system`. The default value is `nil`, which means that Rmail files are not translated (they are read and written in the Emacs internal character code).

19.9 Specifying a File's Coding System

If Emacs recognizes the encoding of a file incorrectly, you can reread the file using the correct coding system by typing `C-x RET r` coding-system `RET`. To see what coding system Emacs actually used to decode the file, look at the coding system mnemonic letter near the left edge of the mode line (see Section 1.3 [Mode Line], page 8), or type `C-h C RET`.

You can specify the coding system for a particular file in the file itself, using the '`-*-...-*-`' construct at the beginning, or a local variables list at the end (see Section 32.3.4 [File Variables], page 420). You do this by defining a value for the "variable" named `coding`. Emacs does not really have a variable `coding`; instead of setting a variable, this uses the specified coding system for the file. For example, '`-*-mode: C; coding: latin-1;-*-`' specifies use of the Latin-1 coding system, as well as C mode. When you specify the coding explicitly in the file, that overrides `file-coding-system-alist`.

If you add the character '`!`' at the end of the coding system name in `coding`, it disables any character translation (see [Character Translation], page 195) while decoding the file. This is useful when you need to make sure that the character codes in the Emacs buffer will not vary due to changes in user settings; for instance, for the sake of strings in Emacs Lisp source files.

19.10 Choosing Coding Systems for Output

Once Emacs has chosen a coding system for a buffer, it stores that coding system in `buffer-file-coding-system`. That makes it the default for operations that write from this buffer into a file, such as `save-buffer` and `write-region`. You can specify a different coding system for further file output from the buffer using `set-buffer-file-coding-system` (see Section 19.11 [Text Coding], page 198).

You can insert any character Emacs supports into any Emacs buffer, but most coding systems can only handle a subset of these characters. Therefore, you can insert characters that cannot be encoded with the coding system that will be used to save the buffer. For example, you could start with an ASCII file and insert a few Latin-1 characters into it, or you could edit a text file in Polish encoded in `iso-8859-2` and add some Russian words to it. When you save that buffer, Emacs cannot use the current value of `buffer-file-coding-system`, because the characters you added cannot be encoded by that coding system.

When that happens, Emacs tries the most-preferred coding system (set by M-x `prefer-coding-system` or M-x `set-language-environment`), and if that coding system can safely encode all of the characters in the buffer, Emacs uses it, and stores its value in `buffer-file-coding-system`. Otherwise, Emacs displays a list of coding systems suitable for encoding the buffer's contents, and asks you to choose one of those coding systems.

If you insert the unsuitable characters in a mail message, Emacs behaves a bit differently. It additionally checks whether the most-preferred coding system is recommended for use in MIME messages; if not, Emacs tells you that the most-preferred coding system is not recommended and prompts you for another coding system. This is so you won't inadvertently send a message encoded in a way that your recipient's mail software will have difficulty decoding. (You can still use an unsuitable coding system if you type its name in response to the question.)

When you send a message with Mail mode (see Chapter 27 [Sending Mail], page 310), Emacs has four different ways to determine the coding system to use for encoding the message text. It tries the buffer's own value of `buffer-file-coding-system`, if that is non-`nil`. Otherwise, it uses the value of `sendmail-coding-system`, if that is non-`nil`. The third way is to use the default coding system for new files, which is controlled by your choice of language environment, if that is non-`nil`. If all of these three values are `nil`, Emacs encodes outgoing mail using the Latin-1 coding system.

19.11 Specifying a Coding System for File Text

In cases where Emacs does not automatically choose the right coding system for a file's contents, you can use these commands to specify one:

C-x RET f *coding* RET

> Use coding system *coding* for saving or revisiting the visited file in the current buffer.

C-x RET c *coding* RET

> Specify coding system *coding* for the immediately following command.

C-x RET r *coding* RET
> Revisit the current file using the coding system *coding*.

M-x recode-region RET *right* RET *wrong* RET
> Convert a region that was decoded using coding system *wrong*, decoding it using coding system *right* instead.

The command C-x RET f (set-buffer-file-coding-system) sets the file coding system for the current buffer—in other words, it says which coding system to use when saving or reverting the visited file. You specify which coding system using the minibuffer. If you specify a coding system that cannot handle all of the characters in the buffer, Emacs warns you about the troublesome characters when you actually save the buffer.

You can also use this command to specify the end-of-line conversion (see Section 19.7 [Coding Systems], page 193) for encoding the current buffer. For example, C-x RET f dos RET will cause Emacs to save the current buffer's text with DOS-style CRLF line endings.

Another way to specify the coding system for a file is when you visit the file. First use the command C-x RET c (universal-coding-system-argument); this command uses the minibuffer to read a coding system name. After you exit the minibuffer, the specified coding system is used for *the immediately following command*.

So if the immediately following command is C-x C-f, for example, it reads the file using that coding system (and records the coding system for when you later save the file). Or if the immediately following command is C-x C-w, it writes the file using that coding system. When you specify the coding system for saving in this way, instead of with C-x RET f, there is no warning if the buffer contains characters that the coding system cannot handle.

Other file commands affected by a specified coding system include C-x i and C-x C-v, as well as the other-window variants of C-x C-f. C-x RET c also affects commands that start subprocesses, including M-x shell (see Section 31.2 [Shell], page 378). If the immediately following command does not use the coding system, then C-x RET c ultimately has no effect.

An easy way to visit a file with no conversion is with the M-x find-file-literally command. See Section 15.2 [Visiting], page 120.

The variable default-buffer-file-coding-system specifies the choice of coding system to use when you create a new file. It applies when you find a new file, and when you create a buffer and then save it in a file. Selecting a language environment typically sets this variable to a good choice of default coding system for that language environment.

If you visit a file with a wrong coding system, you can correct this with C-x RET r (revert-buffer-with-coding-system). This visits the current file again, using a coding system you specify.

If a piece of text has already been inserted into a buffer using the wrong coding system, you can redo the decoding of it using M-x recode-region. This prompts you for the proper coding system, then for the wrong coding system that was actually used, and does the conversion. It first encodes the region using the wrong coding system, then decodes it again using the proper coding system.

19.12 Coding Systems for Interprocess Communication

This section explains how to specify coding systems for use in communication with other processes.

C-x RET x *coding* RET

> Use coding system *coding* for transferring selections to and from other window-based applications.

C-x RET X *coding* RET

> Use coding system *coding* for transferring *one* selection—the next one—to or from another window-based application.

C-x RET p *input-coding* RET *output-coding* RET

> Use coding systems *input-coding* and *output-coding* for subprocess input and output in the current buffer.

C-x RET c *coding* RET

> Specify coding system *coding* for the immediately following command.

The command C-x RET x (set-selection-coding-system) specifies the coding system for sending selected text to other windowing applications, and for receiving the text of selections made in other applications. This command applies to all subsequent selections, until you override it by using the command again. The command C-x RET X (set-next-selection-coding-system) specifies the coding system for the next selection made in Emacs or read by Emacs.

The command C-x RET p (set-buffer-process-coding-system) specifies the coding system for input and output to a subprocess. This command applies to the current buffer; normally, each subprocess has its own buffer, and thus you can use this command to specify translation to and from a particular subprocess by giving the command in the corresponding buffer.

You can also use C-x RET c just before the command that runs or starts a subprocess, to specify the coding system to use for communication with that subprocess.

The default for translation of process input and output depends on the current language environment.

The variable locale-coding-system specifies a coding system to use when encoding and decoding system strings such as system error messages and format-time-string formats and time stamps. That coding system is also used for decoding non-ASCII keyboard input on X Window systems. You should choose a coding system that is compatible with the underlying system's text representation, which is normally specified by one of the environment variables LC_ALL, LC_CTYPE, and LANG. (The first one, in the order specified above, whose value is nonempty is the one that determines the text representation.)

19.13 Coding Systems for File Names

`C-x RET F` *coding* `RET`
>   Use coding system *coding* for encoding and decoding file *names*.

The variable `file-name-coding-system` specifies a coding system to use for encoding file names. It has no effect on reading and writing the *contents* of files.

If you set the variable to a coding system name (as a Lisp symbol or a string), Emacs encodes file names using that coding system for all file operations. This makes it possible to use non-ASCII characters in file names—or, at least, those non-ASCII characters which the specified coding system can encode. Use `C-x RET F` (`set-file-name-coding-system`) to specify this interactively.

If `file-name-coding-system` is `nil`, Emacs uses a default coding system determined by the selected language environment. In the default language environment, any non-ASCII characters in file names are not encoded specially; they appear in the file system using the internal Emacs representation.

Warning: if you change `file-name-coding-system` (or the language environment) in the middle of an Emacs session, problems can result if you have already visited files whose names were encoded using the earlier coding system and cannot be encoded (or are encoded differently) under the new coding system. If you try to save one of these buffers under the visited file name, saving may use the wrong file name, or it may get an error. If such a problem happens, use `C-x C-w` to specify a new file name for that buffer.

If a mistake occurs when encoding a file name, use the command `M-x recode-file-name` to change the file name's coding system. This prompts for an existing file name, its old coding system, and the coding system to which you wish to convert.

19.14 Coding Systems for Terminal I/O

`C-x RET k` *coding* `RET`
>   Use coding system *coding* for keyboard input.

`C-x RET t` *coding* `RET`
>   Use coding system *coding* for terminal output.

The command `C-x RET t` (`set-terminal-coding-system`) specifies the coding system for terminal output. If you specify a character code for terminal output, all characters output to the terminal are translated into that coding system.

This feature is useful for certain character-only terminals built to support specific languages or character sets—for example, European terminals that support one of the ISO Latin character sets. You need to specify the terminal coding system when using multibyte text, so that Emacs knows which characters the terminal can actually handle.

By default, output to the terminal is not translated at all, unless Emacs can deduce the proper coding system from your terminal type or your locale specification (see Section 19.3 [Language Environments], page 188).

The command `C-x RET k` (`set-keyboard-coding-system`) or the variable `keyboard-coding-system` specifies the coding system for keyboard input.

Character-code translation of keyboard input is useful for terminals with keys that send non-ASCII graphic characters—for example, some terminals designed for ISO Latin-1 or subsets of it.

By default, keyboard input is translated based on your system locale setting. If your terminal does not really support the encoding implied by your locale (for example, if you find it inserts a non-ASCII character if you type M-i), you will need to set `keyboard-coding-system` to `nil` to turn off encoding. You can do this by putting

```
(set-keyboard-coding-system nil)
```

in your '`~/.emacs`' file.

There is a similarity between using a coding system translation for keyboard input, and using an input method: both define sequences of keyboard input that translate into single characters. However, input methods are designed to be convenient for interactive use by humans, and the sequences that are translated are typically sequences of ASCII printing characters. Coding systems typically translate sequences of non-graphic characters.

19.15 Fontsets

A font typically defines shapes for a single alphabet or script. Therefore, displaying the entire range of scripts that Emacs supports requires a collection of many fonts. In Emacs, such a collection is called a *fontset*. A fontset is defined by a list of fonts, each assigned to handle a range of character codes.

Each fontset has a name, like a font. However, while fonts are stored in the system and the available font names are defined by the system, fontsets are defined within Emacs itself. Once you have defined a fontset, you can use it within Emacs by specifying its name, anywhere that you could use a single font. Of course, Emacs fontsets can use only the fonts that the system supports; if certain characters appear on the screen as hollow boxes, this means that the fontset in use for them has no font for those characters.[5]

Emacs creates two fontsets automatically: the *standard fontset* and the *startup fontset*. The standard fontset is most likely to have fonts for a wide variety of non-ASCII characters; however, this is not the default for Emacs to use. (By default, Emacs tries to find a font that has bold and italic variants.) You can specify use of the standard fontset with the '`-fn`' option. For example,

```
emacs -fn fontset-standard
```

You can also specify a fontset with the '`Font`' resource (see Appendix D [X Resources], page 489).

A fontset does not necessarily specify a font for every character code. If a fontset specifies no font for a certain character, or if it specifies a font that does not exist on your system, then it cannot display that character properly. It will display that character as an empty box instead.

---

[5] The Emacs installation instructions have information on additional font support.

19.16 Defining fontsets

Emacs creates a standard fontset automatically according to the value of `standard-fontset-spec`. This fontset's name is

    -*-fixed-medium-r-normal-*-16-*-*-*-*-*-fontset-standard

or just 'fontset-standard' for short.

Bold, italic, and bold-italic variants of the standard fontset are created automatically. Their names have 'bold' instead of 'medium', or 'i' instead of 'r', or both.

If you specify a default ASCII font with the 'Font' resource or the '-fn' argument, Emacs generates a fontset from it automatically. This is the *startup fontset* and its name is `fontset-startup`. It does this by replacing the *foundry*, *family*, *add_style*, and *average_width* fields of the font name with '*', replacing *charset_registry* field with 'fontset', and replacing *charset_encoding* field with 'startup', then using the resulting string to specify a fontset.

For instance, if you start Emacs this way,

    emacs -fn "*courier-medium-r-normal--14-140-*-iso8859-1"

Emacs generates the following fontset and uses it for the initial X window frame:

    -*-*-medium-r-normal-*-14-140-*-*-*-*-fontset-startup

With the X resource 'Emacs.Font', you can specify a fontset name just like an actual font name. But be careful not to specify a fontset name in a wildcard resource like 'Emacs*Font'—that wildcard specification matches various other resources, such as for menus, and menus cannot handle fontsets.

You can specify additional fontsets using X resources named 'Fontset-*n*', where *n* is an integer starting from 0. The resource value should have this form:

    fontpattern, [charset:font]...

fontpattern should have the form of a standard X font name, except for the last two fields. They should have the form 'fontset-alias'.

The fontset has two names, one long and one short. The long name is *fontpattern*. The short name is 'fontset-alias'. You can refer to the fontset by either name.

The construct '*charset*:*font*' specifies which font to use (in this fontset) for one particular character set. Here, *charset* is the name of a character set, and *font* is the font to use for that character set. You can use this construct any number of times in defining one fontset.

For the other character sets, Emacs chooses a font based on *fontpattern*. It replaces 'fontset-alias' with values that describe the character set. For the ASCII character font, 'fontset-alias' is replaced with 'ISO8859-1'.

In addition, when several consecutive fields are wildcards, Emacs collapses them into a single wildcard. This is to prevent use of auto-scaled fonts. Fonts made by scaling larger fonts are not usable for editing, and scaling a smaller font is not useful because it is better to use the smaller font in its own size, which is what Emacs does.

Thus if *fontpattern* is this,

    -*-fixed-medium-r-normal-*-24-*-*-*-*-*-fontset-24

the font specification for ASCII characters would be this:

```
-*-fixed-medium-r-normal-*-24-*-IS08859-1
```

and the font specification for Chinese GB2312 characters would be this:

```
-*-fixed-medium-r-normal-*-24-*-gb2312*-*
```

You may not have any Chinese font matching the above font specification. Most X distributions include only Chinese fonts that have 'song ti' or 'fangsong ti' in *family* field. In such a case, 'Fontset-*n*' can be specified as below:

```
Emacs.Fontset-0: -*-fixed-medium-r-normal-*-24-*-*-*-*-*-fontset-24,\
         chinese-gb2312:-*-*-medium-r-normal-*-24-*-gb2312*-*
```

Then, the font specifications for all but Chinese GB2312 characters have 'fixed' in the *family* field, and the font specification for Chinese GB2312 characters has a wild card '*' in the *family* field.

The function that processes the fontset resource value to create the fontset is called `create-fontset-from-fontset-spec`. You can also call this function explicitly to create a fontset.

See Section C.7 [Font X], page 481, for more information about font naming in X.

19.17 Undisplayable Characters

There may be a some non-ASCII characters that your terminal cannot display. Most text-only terminals support just a single character set (use the variable `default-terminal-coding-system` (see Section 19.14 [Terminal Coding], page 201) to tell Emacs which one); characters which can't be encoded in that coding system are displayed as '?' by default.

Graphical displays can display a broader range of characters, but you may not have fonts installed for all of them; characters that have no font appear as a hollow box.

If you use Latin-1 characters but your terminal can't display Latin-1, you can arrange to display mnemonic ASCII sequences instead, e.g. '"o' for o-umlaut. Load the library 'iso-ascii' to do this.

If your terminal can display Latin-1, you can display characters from other European character sets using a mixture of equivalent Latin-1 characters and ASCII mnemonics. Customize the variable `latin1-display` to enable this. The mnemonic ASCII sequences mostly correspond to those of the prefix input methods.

19.18 Unibyte Editing Mode

The ISO 8859 Latin-*n* character sets define character codes in the range 0240 to 0377 octal (160 to 255 decimal) to handle the accented letters and punctuation needed by various European languages (and some non-European ones). If you disable multibyte characters, Emacs can still handle *one* of these character codes at a time. To specify *which* of these codes to use, invoke `M-x set-language-environment` and specify a suitable language environment such as 'Latin-*n*'.

For more information about unibyte operation, see Section 19.2 [Enabling Multi-byte], page 187. Note particularly that you probably want to ensure that your initialization files are read as unibyte if they contain non-ASCII characters.

Emacs can also display those characters, provided the terminal or font in use supports them. This works automatically. Alternatively, on a graphical display, Emacs can also display single-byte characters through fontsets, in effect by displaying the equivalent multibyte characters according to the current language environment. To request this, set the variable `unibyte-display-via-language-environment` to a non-`nil` value.

If your terminal does not support display of the Latin-1 character set, Emacs can display these characters as ASCII sequences which at least give you a clear idea of what the characters are. To do this, load the library `iso-ascii`. Similar libraries for other Latin-n character sets could be implemented, but we don't have them yet.

Normally non-ISO-8859 characters (decimal codes between 128 and 159 inclusive) are displayed as octal escapes. You can change this for non-standard "extended" versions of ISO-8859 character sets by using the function `standard-display-8bit` in the `disp-table` library.

There are two ways to input single-byte non-ASCII characters:

- You can use an input method for the selected language environment. See Section 19.4 [Input Methods], page 190. When you use an input method in a unibyte buffer, the non-ASCII character you specify with it is converted to unibyte.

- If your keyboard can generate character codes 128 (decimal) and up, representing non-ASCII characters, you can type those character codes directly.

  On a graphical display, you should not need to do anything special to use these keys; they should simply work. On a text-only terminal, you should use the command `M-x set-keyboard-coding-system` or the variable `keyboard-coding-system` to specify which coding system your keyboard uses (see Section 19.14 [Terminal Coding], page 201). Enabling this feature will probably require you to use ESC to type Meta characters; however, on a console terminal or in `xterm`, you can arrange for Meta to be converted to ESC and still be able type 8-bit characters present directly on the keyboard or using Compose or AltGr keys. See Section 2.1 [User Input], page 12.

- For Latin-1 only, you can use the key `C-x 8` as a "compose character" prefix for entry of non-ASCII Latin-1 printing characters. `C-x 8` is good for insertion (in the minibuffer as well as other buffers), for searching, and in any other context where a key sequence is allowed.

  `C-x 8` works by loading the `iso-transl` library. Once that library is loaded, the ALT modifier key, if the keyboard has one, serves the same purpose as `C-x 8`: use ALT together with an accent character to modify the following letter. In addition, if the keyboard has keys for the Latin-1 "dead accent characters," they too are defined to compose with the following character, once `iso-transl` is loaded.

  Use `C-x 8 C-h` to list all the available `C-x 8` translations.

19.19 Charsets

Emacs groups all supported characters into disjoint *charsets*. Each character code belongs to one and only one charset. For historical reasons, Emacs typically divides an 8-bit character code for an extended version of ASCII into two charsets: ASCII, which covers the codes 0 through 127, plus another charset which covers the "right-hand part" (the codes 128 and up). For instance, the characters of Latin-1 include the Emacs charset `ascii` plus the Emacs charset `latin-iso8859-1`.

Emacs characters belonging to different charsets may look the same, but they are still different characters. For example, the letter 'o' with acute accent in charset `latin-iso8859-1`, used for Latin-1, is different from the letter 'o' with acute accent in charset `latin-iso8859-2`, used for Latin-2.

There are two commands for obtaining information about Emacs charsets. The command `M-x list-charset-chars` prompts for a name of a character set, and displays all the characters in that character set. The command `M-x describe-character-set` prompts for a charset name and displays information about that charset, including its internal representation within Emacs.

To find out which charset a character in the buffer belongs to, put point before it and type `C-u C-x =`.

20 Major Modes

Emacs provides many alternative *major modes*, each of which customizes Emacs for editing text of a particular sort. The major modes are mutually exclusive, and each buffer has one major mode at any time. The mode line normally shows the name of the current major mode, in parentheses (see Section 1.3 [Mode Line], page 8).

The least specialized major mode is called *Fundamental mode*. This mode has no mode-specific redefinitions or variable settings, so that each Emacs command behaves in its most general manner, and each user option variable is in its default state. For editing text of a specific type that Emacs knows about, such as Lisp code or English text, you should switch to the appropriate major mode, such as Lisp mode or Text mode.

Selecting a major mode changes the meanings of a few keys to become more specifically adapted to the language being edited. The ones that are changed frequently are TAB, DEL, and C-j. The prefix key C-c normally contains mode-specific commands. In addition, the commands which handle comments use the mode to determine how comments are to be delimited. Many major modes redefine the syntactical properties of characters appearing in the buffer. See Section 32.5 [Syntax], page 433.

The major modes fall into three major groups. The first group contains modes for normal text, either plain or with mark-up. It includes Text mode, HTML mode, SGML mode, TEX mode and Outline mode. The second group contains modes for specific programming languages. These include Lisp mode (which has several variants), C mode, Fortran mode, and others. The remaining major modes are not intended for use on users' files; they are used in buffers created for specific purposes by Emacs, such as Dired mode for buffers made by Dired (see Chapter 29 [Dired], page 339), Mail mode for buffers made by C-x m (see Chapter 27 [Sending Mail], page 310), and Shell mode for buffers used for communicating with an inferior shell process (see Section 31.2.2 [Interactive Shell], page 380).

Most programming-language major modes specify that only blank lines separate paragraphs. This is to make the paragraph commands useful. (See Section 22.3 [Paragraphs], page 215.) They also cause Auto Fill mode to use the definition of TAB to indent the new lines it creates. This is because most lines in a program are usually indented (see Chapter 21 [Indentation], page 210).

20.1 How Major Modes are Chosen

You can select a major mode explicitly for the current buffer, but most of the time Emacs determines which mode to use based on the file name or on special text in the file.

To explicitly select a new major, you use an M-x command. Take the name of a major mode and add -mode to get the name of the command to select that mode. Thus, you can enter Lisp mode by executing M-x lisp-mode.

When you visit a file, Emacs usually chooses the right major mode based on the file's name. For example, files whose names end in '.c' are edited in C mode. The correspondence between file names and major modes is controlled by the variable `auto-mode-alist`. Its value is a list in which each element has this form,

> (*regexp* . *mode-function*)

or this form,

> (*regexp* *mode-function* *flag*)

For example, one element normally found in the list has the form `("\\.c\\'" . c-mode)`, and it is responsible for selecting C mode for files whose names end in '.c'. (Note that '\\' is needed in Lisp syntax to include a '\' in the string, which must be used to suppress the special meaning of '.' in regexps.) If the element has the form (*regexp* *mode-function* *flag*) and *flag* is non-nil, then after calling *mode-function*, Emacs discards the suffix that matched *regexp* and searches the list again for another match.

Sometimes the major mode is determined from the way the file's text begins. The variable `magic-mode-alist` controls this. Its value is a list of elements of these forms:

> (*regexp* . *mode-function*)
> (*match-function* . *mode-function*)

The first form looks like an element of `auto-mode-alist`, but it doesn't work the same: this *regexp* is matched against the text at the start of the buffer, not against the file name. Likewise, the second form calls *match-function* at the beginning of the buffer, and if the function returns non-`nil`, the *mode-function* is called. `magic-mode-alist` takes priority over `auto-mode-alist`.

You can specify the major mode to use for editing a certain file by special text in the first nonblank line of the file. The mode name should appear in this line both preceded and followed by '`-*-`'. Other text may appear on the line as well. For example,

> `;-*-Lisp-*-`

tells Emacs to use Lisp mode. Such an explicit specification overrides any defaults based on the file name. Note how the semicolon is used to make Lisp treat this line as a comment.

Another format of mode specification is

> `-*- mode:` *modename*`;-*-`

which allows you to specify local variables as well, like this:

> `-*- mode:` *modename*`;` *var*`:` *value*`; ... -*-`

See Section 32.3.4 [File Variables], page 420, for more information about this.

On systems with case-insensitive file names, only a single case-insensitive search through the `auto-mode-alist` is made. On other systems, Emacs normally performs a single case-sensitive search through the alist, but if you set this variable to a non-`nil` value, Emacs will perform a second case-insensitive search if the first search fails.

When a file's contents begin with '`#!`', it can serve as an executable shell command, which works by running an interpreter named on the file's first line. The rest of the file is used as input to the interpreter.

When you visit such a file in Emacs, if the file's name does not specify a major mode, Emacs uses the interpreter name on the first line to choose a mode. If the first line is the name of a recognized interpreter program, such as 'perl' or 'tcl', Emacs uses a mode appropriate for programs for that interpreter. The variable interpreter-mode-alist specifies the correspondence between interpreter program names and major modes.

When the first line starts with '#!', you cannot (on many systems) use the '-*-' feature on the first line, because the system would get confused when running the interpreter. So Emacs looks for '-*-' on the second line in such files as well as on the first line.

When you visit a file that does not specify a major mode to use, or when you create a new buffer with C-x b, the variable default-major-mode specifies which major mode to use. Normally its value is the symbol fundamental-mode, which specifies Fundamental mode. If default-major-mode is nil, the major mode is taken from the previously current buffer.

If you change the major mode of a buffer, you can go back to the major mode Emacs would choose automatically: use the command M-x normal-mode to do this. This is the same function that find-file calls to choose the major mode. It also processes the file's '-*-' line or local variables list (if any). See Section 32.3.4 [File Variables], page 420.

The commands C-x C-w and set-visited-file-name change to a new major mode if the new file name implies a mode (see Section 15.3 [Saving], page 123). (C-x C-s does this too, if the buffer wasn't visiting a file.) However, this does not happen if the buffer contents specify a major mode, and certain "special" major modes do not allow the mode to change. You can turn off this mode-changing feature by setting change-major-mode-with-file-name to nil.

21 Indentation

This chapter describes the Emacs commands that add, remove, or adjust indentation.

TAB	Indent the current line "appropriately" in a mode-dependent fashion.
C-j	Perform RET followed by TAB (newline-and-indent).
M-^	Merge the previous and the current line (delete-indentation). This would cancel the effect of a preceding C-j.
C-M-o	Split the current line at point; text on the line after point becomes a new line indented to the same column where point is located (split-line).
M-m	Move (forward or back) to the first nonblank character on the current line (back-to-indentation).
C-M-\	Indent lines in the region to the same column (indent-region).
C-x TAB	Shift lines in the region rigidly right or left (indent-rigidly).
M-i	Indent from point to the next prespecified tab stop column (tab-to-tab-stop).

M-x indent-relative

       Indent from point to under an indentation point in the previous line.

Emacs supports four general categories of operations that could all be called 'indentation':

1. Insert a tab character. You can type C-q TAB to do this.

   A tab character is displayed as a stretch of whitespace which extends to the next display tab stop position, and the default width of a tab stop is eight. See Section 11.14 [Text Display], page 82, for more details.

2. Insert whitespace up to the next tab stop. You can set tab stops at your choice of column positions, then type M-i to advance to the next tab stop. The default tab stop settings have a tab stop every eight columns, which means by default M-i inserts a tab character. To set the tab stops, use M-x edit-tab-stops.

3. Align a line with the previous line. More precisely, the command M-x indent-relative indents the current line under the beginning of some word in the previous line. In Fundamental mode and in Text mode, TAB runs the command indent-relative.

4. The most sophisticated method is *syntax-driven indentation*. Most programming languages have an indentation convention. For Lisp code, lines are indented according to their nesting in parentheses. C code uses the same general idea, but many details are different.

   Type TAB to do syntax-driven indentation, in a mode that supports it. It realigns the current line according with the syntax of the preceding lines. No matter where in the line you are when you type TAB, it aligns the line as a whole.

Normally, most of the above methods insert an optimal mix of tabs and spaces to align to the desired column. See Section 21.3 [Just Spaces], page 212, for how to disable use of tabs. However, C-q TAB always inserts a tab, even when tabs are disabled for the indentation commands.

21.1 Indentation Commands and Techniques

To move over the indentation on a line, do M-m (back-to-indentation). This command, given anywhere on a line, positions point at the first nonblank character on the line, if any, or else at the end of the line.

To insert an indented line before the current line, do C-a C-o TAB. To make an indented line after the current line, use C-e C-j.

If you just want to insert a tab character in the buffer, you can type C-q TAB.

C-M-o (split-line) moves the text from point to the end of the line vertically down, so that the current line becomes two lines. C-M-o first moves point forward over any spaces and tabs. Then it inserts after point a newline and enough indentation to reach the same column point is on. Point remains before the inserted newline; in this regard, C-M-o resembles C-o.

To join two lines cleanly, use the M-^ (delete-indentation) command. It deletes the indentation at the front of the current line, and the line boundary as well, replacing them with a single space. As a special case (useful for Lisp code) the single space is omitted if the characters to be joined are consecutive open parentheses or closing parentheses, or if the junction follows another newline. To delete just the indentation of a line, go to the beginning of the line and use M-\ (delete-horizontal-space), which deletes all spaces and tabs around the cursor.

If you have a fill prefix, M-^ deletes the fill prefix if it appears after the newline that is deleted. See Section 22.5.3 [Fill Prefix], page 219.

There are also commands for changing the indentation of several lines at once. They apply to all the lines that begin in the region. C-M-\ (indent-region) indents each line in the "usual" way, as if you had typed TAB at the beginning of the line. A numeric argument specifies the column to indent to, and each line is shifted left or right so that its first nonblank character appears in that column. C-x TAB (indent-rigidly) moves all of the lines in the region right by its argument (left, for negative arguments). The whole group of lines moves rigidly sideways, which is how the command gets its name.

To remove all indentation from all of the lines in the region, invoke C-x TAB with a large negative argument, such as -1000.

M-x indent-relative indents at point based on the previous line (actually, the last nonempty line). It inserts whitespace at point, moving point, until it is underneath the next indentation point in the previous line. An indentation point is the end of a sequence of whitespace or the end of the line. If point is farther right than any indentation point in the previous line, indent-relative runs tab-to-tab-stop (see next section), unless it is called with a numeric argument, in which case it does nothing.

See Section 22.12.6 [Format Indentation], page 239, for another way of specifying the indentation for part of your text.

21.2 Tab Stops

For typing in tables, you can use M-i (tab-to-tab-stop). This command inserts indentation before point, enough to reach the next tab stop column.

You can specify the tab stops used by M-i. They are stored in a variable called tab-stop-list, as a list of column-numbers in increasing order.

The convenient way to set the tab stops is with M-x edit-tab-stops, which creates and selects a buffer containing a description of the tab stop settings. You can edit this buffer to specify different tab stops, and then type C-c C-c to make those new tab stops take effect. The buffer uses Overwrite mode (see Section 32.1 [Minor Modes], page 406). edit-tab-stops records which buffer was current when you invoked it, and stores the tab stops back in that buffer; normally all buffers share the same tab stops and changing them in one buffer affects all, but if you happen to make tab-stop-list local in one buffer then edit-tab-stops in that buffer will edit the local settings.

Here is what the text representing the tab stops looks like for ordinary tab stops every eight columns.

```
        :       :       :       :       :       :
0       1       2       3       4
012345678901234567890123456789012345678901234567890123456789012345678
To install changes, type C-c C-c
```

The first line contains a colon at each tab stop. The remaining lines are present just to help you see where the colons are and know what to do.

Note that the tab stops that control tab-to-tab-stop have nothing to do with displaying tab characters in the buffer. See Section 11.14 [Text Display], page 82, for more information on that.

21.3 Tabs vs. Spaces

Emacs normally uses both tabs and spaces to indent lines. If you prefer, all indentation can be made from spaces only. To request this, set indent-tabs-mode to nil. This is a per-buffer variable, so altering the variable affects only the current buffer, but there is a default value which you can change as well. See Section 32.3.3 [Locals], page 419.

A tab is not always displayed in the same way. By default, tabs are eight columns wide, but some people like to customize their tools to use a different tab width. So by using spaces only, you can make sure that your file looks the same regardless of the tab width setting.

There are also commands to convert tabs to spaces or vice versa, always preserving the columns of all nonblank text. M-x tabify scans the region for sequences of spaces, and converts sequences of at least two spaces to tabs if that can be done without changing indentation. M-x untabify changes all tabs in the region to appropriate numbers of spaces.

22 Commands for Human Languages

The term *text* has two widespread meanings in our area of the computer field. One is data that is a sequence of characters. Any file that you edit with Emacs is text, in this sense of the word. The other meaning is more restrictive: a sequence of characters in a human language for humans to read (possibly after processing by a text formatter), as opposed to a program or binary data. This chapter is concerned with editing text in the narrower sense.

Human languages have syntactic/stylistic conventions that can be supported or used to advantage by editor commands: conventions involving words, sentences, paragraphs, and capital letters. This chapter describes Emacs commands for all of these things. There are also commands for *filling*, which means rearranging the lines of a paragraph to be approximately equal in length. The commands for moving over and killing words, sentences and paragraphs, while intended primarily for editing text, are also often useful for editing programs.

Emacs has several major modes for editing human-language text. If the file contains text pure and simple, use Text mode, which customizes Emacs in small ways for the syntactic conventions of text. Outline mode provides special commands for operating on text with an outline structure. See Section 22.8 [Outline Mode], page 224.

For text which contains embedded commands for text formatters, Emacs has other major modes, each for a particular formatter. Thus, for input to TeX, you would use TeX mode (see Section 22.9 [TeX Mode], page 230). For input to groff or nroff, use Nroff mode.

Instead of using a text formatter, you can edit formatted text in WYSIWYG style ("what you see is what you get"), with Enriched mode. Then the formatting appears on the screen in Emacs while you edit. See Section 22.12 [Formatted Text], page 236.

If you need to edit pictures made out of text characters (commonly referred to as "ASCII art"), use `M-x edit-picture` to enter Picture mode, a special major mode for editing such pictures. See section "Picture Mode" in *Specialized Emacs Features*.

The "automatic typing" features may be useful when writing text. See Info file `autotype`, node `Top`.

22.1 Words

Emacs has commands for moving over or operating on words. By convention, the keys for them are all Meta characters.

M-f   Move forward over a word (`forward-word`).

M-b   Move backward over a word (`backward-word`).

M-d   Kill up to the end of a word (`kill-word`).

M-DEL   Kill back to the beginning of a word (`backward-kill-word`).

M-@   Mark the end of the next word (mark-word).

M-t   Transpose two words or drag a word across others (transpose-words).

Notice how these keys form a series that parallels the character-based C-f, C-b, C-d, DEL and C-t. M-@ is cognate to C-@, which is an alias for C-SPC.

The commands M-f (forward-word) and M-b (backward-word) move forward and backward over words. These Meta characters are thus analogous to the corresponding control characters, C-f and C-b, which move over single characters in the text. The analogy extends to numeric arguments, which serve as repeat counts. M-f with a negative argument moves backward, and M-b with a negative argument moves forward. Forward motion stops right after the last letter of the word, while backward motion stops right before the first letter.

M-d (kill-word) kills the word after point. To be precise, it kills everything from point to the place M-f would move to. Thus, if point is in the middle of a word, M-d kills just the part after point. If some punctuation comes between point and the next word, it is killed along with the word. (If you wish to kill only the next word but not the punctuation before it, simply do M-f to get the end, and kill the word backwards with M-DEL.) M-d takes arguments just like M-f.

M-DEL (backward-kill-word) kills the word before point. It kills everything from point back to where M-b would move to. For instance, if point is after the space in 'FOO, BAR', it kills 'FOO, '. If you wish to kill just 'FOO', and not the comma and the space, use M-b M-d instead of M-DEL.

M-t (transpose-words) exchanges the word before or containing point with the following word. The delimiter characters between the words do not move. For example, 'FOO, BAR' transposes into 'BAR, FOO' rather than 'BAR FOO,'. See Section 13.3 [Transpose], page 107, for more on transposition.

To operate on the next n words with an operation which applies between point and mark, you can either set the mark at point and then move over the words, or you can use the command M-@ (mark-word) which does not move point, but sets the mark where M-f would move to. M-@ accepts a numeric argument that says how many words to scan for the place to put the mark. In Transient Mark mode, this command activates the mark.

The word commands' understanding of word boundaries is controlled by the syntax table. Any character can, for example, be declared to be a word delimiter. See Section 32.5 [Syntax], page 433.

22.2 Sentences

The Emacs commands for manipulating sentences and paragraphs are mostly on Meta keys, so as to be like the word-handling commands.

M-a   Move back to the beginning of the sentence (backward-sentence).

M-e   Move forward to the end of the sentence (forward-sentence).

M-k   Kill forward to the end of the sentence (kill-sentence).

C-x DEL   Kill back to the beginning of the sentence (backward-kill-sentence).

The commands M-a and M-e (backward-sentence and forward-sentence) move to the beginning and end of the current sentence, respectively. They were chosen to resemble C-a and C-e, which move to the beginning and end of a line. Unlike them, M-a and M-e move over successive sentences if repeated.

Moving backward over a sentence places point just before the first character of the sentence; moving forward places point right after the punctuation that ends the sentence. Neither one moves over the whitespace at the sentence boundary.

Just as C-a and C-e have a kill command, C-k, to go with them, so M-a and M-e have a corresponding kill command M-k (kill-sentence) which kills from point to the end of the sentence. With minus one as an argument it kills back to the beginning of the sentence. Larger arguments serve as a repeat count. There is also a command, C-x DEL (backward-kill-sentence), for killing back to the beginning of a sentence. This command is useful when you change your mind in the middle of composing text.

The sentence commands assume that you follow the American typist's convention of putting two spaces at the end of a sentence; they consider a sentence to end wherever there is a '.', '?' or '!' followed by the end of a line or two spaces, with any number of ')', ']', '"', or '"' characters allowed in between. A sentence also begins or ends wherever a paragraph begins or ends. It is useful to follow this convention, because it makes a distinction between periods that end a sentence and periods that indicate abbreviations; that enables the Emacs sentence commands to distinguish, too. These commands do not stop for periods that indicate abbreviations.

If you want to use just one space between sentences, you can set the variable sentence-end-double-space to nil to make the sentence commands stop for single spaces. However, this mode has a drawback: there is no way to distinguish between periods that end sentences and those that indicate abbreviations. For convenient and reliable editing, we therefore recommend you follow the two-space convention. The variable sentence-end-double-space also affects filling (see Section 22.5.2 [Fill Commands], page 218) in related ways.

The variable sentence-end controls how to recognize the end of a sentence. If non-nil, it is a regexp that matches the last few characters of a sentence, together with the whitespace following the sentence. If the value is nil, the default, then Emacs computes the regexp according to various criteria such as the value of sentence-end-double-space. See Section 12.7 [Regexp Example], page 98, for a detailed explanation of one of the regular expressions Emacs uses for this purpose.

Some languages do not use periods to indicate the end of a sentence. For example, sentences in Thai end with a double space but without a period. Set the variable sentence-end-without-period to t in such cases.

22.3 Paragraphs

The Emacs commands for manipulating paragraphs are also on Meta keys.

M-{   Move back to previous paragraph beginning (backward-paragraph).

M-}   Move forward to next paragraph end (forward-paragraph).

M-h   Put point and mark around this or next paragraph (mark-paragraph).

M-{ moves to the beginning of the current or previous paragraph, while M-} moves to the end of the current or next paragraph. Blank lines and text-formatter command lines separate paragraphs and are not considered part of any paragraph. If there is a blank line before the paragraph, M-{ moves to the blank line, because that is convenient in practice.

In Text mode, an indented line is not a paragraph break. If you want indented lines to have this effect, use Paragraph-Indent Text mode instead. See Section 22.7 [Text Mode], page 224.

In major modes for programs, paragraphs begin and end only at blank lines. This makes the paragraph commands useful, even though there are no paragraphs as such in a program.

When you have set a fill prefix, then paragraphs are delimited by all lines which don't start with the fill prefix. See Section 22.5 [Filling], page 217.

When you wish to operate on a paragraph, you can use the command M-h (mark-paragraph) to set the region around it. Thus, for example, M-h C-w kills the paragraph around or after point. The M-h command puts point at the beginning and mark at the end of the paragraph point was in. In Transient Mark mode, it activates the mark. If point is between paragraphs (in a run of blank lines, or at a boundary), the paragraph following point is surrounded by point and mark. If there are blank lines preceding the first line of the paragraph, one of these blank lines is included in the region.

The precise definition of a paragraph boundary is controlled by the variables paragraph-separate and paragraph-start. The value of paragraph-start is a regexp that should match any line that either starts or separates paragraphs. The value of paragraph-separate is another regexp that should match only lines that separate paragraphs without being part of any paragraph (for example, blank lines). Lines that start a new paragraph and are contained in it must match only paragraph-start, not paragraph-separate. Each regular expression must match at the left margin. For example, in Fundamental mode, paragraph-start is "\f\\|[\t]*$", and paragraph-separate is "[\t\f]*$".

Normally it is desirable for page boundaries to separate paragraphs. The default values of these variables recognize the usual separator for pages.

22.4 Pages

Files are often thought of as divided into *pages* by the *formfeed* character (ASCII control-L, octal code 014). When you print hardcopy for a file, this character forces a page break; thus, each page of the file goes on a separate page on paper. Most Emacs commands treat the page-separator character just like any other character: you can insert it with C-q C-l, and delete it with DEL. Thus, you are free to paginate your file or not. However, since pages are often meaningful divisions of the file, Emacs provides commands to move over them and operate on them.

C-x [Move point to previous page boundary (backward-page).

C-x]   Move point to next page boundary (forward-page).

C-x C-p   Put point and mark around this page (or another page) (mark-page).

C-x l   Count the lines in this page (`count-lines-page`).

The `C-x [` (`backward-page`) command moves point to immediately after the previous page delimiter. If point is already right after a page delimiter, it skips that one and stops at the previous one. A numeric argument serves as a repeat count. The `C-x ]` (`forward-page`) command moves forward past the next page delimiter.

The `C-x C-p` command (`mark-page`) puts point at the beginning of the current page and the mark at the end. The page delimiter at the end is included (the mark follows it). The page delimiter at the front is excluded (point follows it). In Transient Mark mode, this command activates the mark.

`C-x C-p C-w` is a handy way to kill a page to move it elsewhere. If you move to another page delimiter with `C-x [` and `C-x ]`, then yank the killed page, all the pages will be properly delimited once again. The reason `C-x C-p` includes only the following page delimiter in the region is to ensure that.

A numeric argument to `C-x C-p` is used to specify which page to go to, relative to the current one. Zero means the current page. One means the next page, and −1 means the previous one.

The `C-x l` command (`count-lines-page`) is good for deciding where to break a page in two. It displays in the echo area the total number of lines in the current page, and then divides it up into those preceding the current line and those following, as in

    Page has 96 (72+25) lines

Notice that the sum is off by one; this is correct if point is not at the beginning of a line.

The variable `page-delimiter` controls where pages begin. Its value is a regexp that matches the beginning of a line that separates pages. The normal value of this variable is `"^\f"`, which matches a formfeed character at the beginning of a line.

22.5 Filling Text

Filling text means breaking it up into lines that fit a specified width. Emacs does filling in two ways. In Auto Fill mode, inserting text with self-inserting characters also automatically fills it. There are also explicit fill commands that you can use when editing text leaves it unfilled. When you edit formatted text, you can specify a style of filling for each portion of the text (see Section 22.12 [Formatted Text], page 236).

22.5.1 Auto Fill Mode

Auto Fill mode is a minor mode in which lines are broken automatically when they become too wide. Breaking happens only when you type a SPC or RET.

M-x auto-fill-mode
               Enable or disable Auto Fill mode.

SPC
RET   In Auto Fill mode, break lines when appropriate.

M-x auto-fill-mode turns Auto Fill mode on if it was off, or off if it was on. With a positive numeric argument it always turns Auto Fill mode on, and with a negative argument always turns it off. You can see when Auto Fill mode is in effect by the presence of the word 'Fill' in the mode line, inside the parentheses. Auto Fill mode is a minor mode which is enabled or disabled for each buffer individually. See Section 32.1 [Minor Modes], page 406.

In Auto Fill mode, lines are broken automatically at spaces when they get longer than the desired width. Line breaking and rearrangement takes place only when you type SPC or RET. If you wish to insert a space or newline without permitting line-breaking, type C-q SPC or C-q C-j (recall that a newline is really a control-J). Also, C-o inserts a newline without line breaking.

Auto Fill mode works well with programming-language modes, because it indents new lines with TAB. If a line ending in a comment gets too long, the text of the comment is split into two comment lines. Optionally, new comment delimiters are inserted at the end of the first line and the beginning of the second so that each line is a separate comment; the variable comment-multi-line controls the choice (see Section 23.5 [Comments], page 260).

Adaptive filling (see Section 22.5.4 [Adaptive Fill], page 221) works for Auto Filling as well as for explicit fill commands. It takes a fill prefix automatically from the second or first line of a paragraph.

Auto Fill mode does not refill entire paragraphs; it can break lines but cannot merge lines. So editing in the middle of a paragraph can result in a paragraph that is not correctly filled. The easiest way to make the paragraph properly filled again is usually with the explicit fill commands.

Many users like Auto Fill mode and want to use it in all text files. The section on init files says how to arrange this permanently for yourself. See Section 32.6 [Init File], page 433.

22.5.2 Explicit Fill Commands

M-q   Fill current paragraph (fill-paragraph).

C-x f   Set the fill column (set-fill-column).

M-x fill-region
             Fill each paragraph in the region (fill-region).

M-x fill-region-as-paragraph
             Fill the region, considering it as one paragraph.

M-s   Center a line.

To refill a paragraph, use the command M-q (fill-paragraph). This operates on the paragraph that point is inside, or the one after point if point is between paragraphs. Refilling works by removing all the line-breaks, then inserting new ones where necessary.

To refill many paragraphs, use M-x fill-region, which finds the paragraphs in the region and fills each of them.

M-q and `fill-region` use the same criteria as M-h for finding paragraph boundaries (see Section 22.3 [Paragraphs], page 215). For more control, you can use M-x `fill-region-as-paragraph`, which refills everything between point and mark as a single paragraph. This command deletes any blank lines within the region, so separate blocks of text end up combined into one block.

A numeric argument to M-q tells it to *justify* the text as well as filling it. This means that extra spaces are inserted to make the right margin line up exactly at the fill column. To remove the extra spaces, use M-q with no argument. (Likewise for `fill-region`.) Another way to control justification, and choose other styles of filling, is with the `justification` text property; see Section 22.12.7 [Format Justification], page 240.

The command M-s (`center-line`) centers the current line within the current fill column. With an argument *n*, it centers *n* lines individually and moves past them. This binding is made by Text mode and is available only in that and related modes (see Section 22.7 [Text Mode], page 224).

The maximum line width for filling is in the variable `fill-column`. Altering the value of `fill-column` makes it local to the current buffer; until that time, the default value is in effect. The default is initially 70. See Section 32.3.3 [Locals], page 419. The easiest way to set `fill-column` is to use the command C-x f (`set-fill-column`). With a numeric argument, it uses that as the new fill column. With just C-u as argument, it sets `fill-column` to the current horizontal position of point.

Emacs commands normally consider a period followed by two spaces or by a newline as the end of a sentence; a period followed by just one space indicates an abbreviation and not the end of a sentence. To preserve the distinction between these two ways of using a period, the fill commands do not break a line after a period followed by just one space.

If the variable `sentence-end-double-space` is `nil`, the fill commands expect and leave just one space at the end of a sentence. Ordinarily this variable is `t`, so the fill commands insist on two spaces for the end of a sentence, as explained above. See Section 22.2 [Sentences], page 214.

If the variable `colon-double-space` is non-`nil`, the fill commands put two spaces after a colon.

The variable `fill-nobreak-predicate` is a hook (an abnormal hook, see Section 32.3.2 [Hooks], page 418) specifying additional conditions where line-breaking is not allowed. Each function is called with no arguments, with point at a place where Emacs is considering breaking the line. If a function returns a non-`nil` value, then that's a bad place to break the line. Two standard functions you can use are `fill-single-word-nobreak-p` (don't break after the first word of a sentence or before the last) and `fill-french-nobreak-p` (don't break after '(' or before ')', ':' or '?').

22.5.3 The Fill Prefix

To fill a paragraph in which each line starts with a special marker (which might be a few spaces, giving an indented paragraph), you can use the *fill prefix* feature. The fill prefix is a string that Emacs expects every line to start with, and which is not included in filling. You can specify a fill prefix explicitly; Emacs can also deduce the fill prefix automatically (see Section 22.5.4 [Adaptive Fill], page 221).

C-x .   Set the fill prefix (`set-fill-prefix`).

M-q   Fill a paragraph using current fill prefix (`fill-paragraph`).

`M-x fill-individual-paragraphs`

> Fill the region, considering each change of indentation as starting a new paragraph.

`M-x fill-nonuniform-paragraphs`

> Fill the region, considering only paragraph-separator lines as starting a new paragraph.

To specify a fill prefix for the current buffer, move to a line that starts with the desired prefix, put point at the end of the prefix, and type C-x . (`set-fill-prefix`). (That's a period after the C-x.) To turn off the fill prefix, specify an empty prefix: type C-x . with point at the beginning of a line.

When a fill prefix is in effect, the fill commands remove the fill prefix from each line of the paragraph before filling and insert it on each line after filling. (The beginning of the first line of the paragraph is left unchanged, since often that is intentionally different.) Auto Fill mode also inserts the fill prefix automatically when it makes a new line. The C-o command inserts the fill prefix on new lines it creates, when you use it at the beginning of a line (see Section 4.7 [Blank Lines], page 25). Conversely, the command M-^ deletes the prefix (if it occurs) after the newline that it deletes (see Chapter 21 [Indentation], page 210).

For example, if `fill-column` is 40 and you set the fill prefix to ';; ', then M-q in the following text

```
;; This is an
;; example of a paragraph
;; inside a Lisp-style comment.
```

produces this:

```
;; This is an example of a paragraph
;; inside a Lisp-style comment.
```

Lines that do not start with the fill prefix are considered to start paragraphs, both in M-q and the paragraph commands; this gives good results for paragraphs with hanging indentation (every line indented except the first one). Lines which are blank or indented once the prefix is removed also separate or start paragraphs; this is what you want if you are writing multi-paragraph comments with a comment delimiter on each line.

You can use `M-x fill-individual-paragraphs` to set the fill prefix for each paragraph automatically. This command divides the region into paragraphs, treating every change in the amount of indentation as the start of a new paragraph, and fills each of these paragraphs. Thus, all the lines in one "paragraph" have the same amount of indentation. That indentation serves as the fill prefix for that paragraph.

M-x fill-nonuniform-paragraphs is a similar command that divides the region into paragraphs in a different way. It considers only paragraph-separating lines (as defined by paragraph-separate) as starting a new paragraph. Since this means that the lines of one paragraph may have different amounts of indentation, the fill prefix used is the smallest amount of indentation of any of the lines of the paragraph. This gives good results with styles that indent a paragraph's first line more or less that the rest of the paragraph.

The fill prefix is stored in the variable fill-prefix. Its value is a string, or nil when there is no fill prefix. This is a per-buffer variable; altering the variable affects only the current buffer, but there is a default value which you can change as well. See Section 32.3.3 [Locals], page 419.

The indentation text property provides another way to control the amount of indentation paragraphs receive. See Section 22.12.6 [Format Indentation], page 239.

22.5.4 Adaptive Filling

The fill commands can deduce the proper fill prefix for a paragraph automatically in certain cases: either whitespace or certain punctuation characters at the beginning of a line are propagated to all lines of the paragraph.

If the paragraph has two or more lines, the fill prefix is taken from the paragraph's second line, but only if it appears on the first line as well.

If a paragraph has just one line, fill commands *may* take a prefix from that line. The decision is complicated because there are three reasonable things to do in such a case:

- Use the first line's prefix on all the lines of the paragraph.

- Indent subsequent lines with whitespace, so that they line up under the text that follows the prefix on the first line, but don't actually copy the prefix from the first line.

- Don't do anything special with the second and following lines.

All three of these styles of formatting are commonly used. So the fill commands try to determine what you would like, based on the prefix that appears and on the major mode. Here is how.

If the prefix found on the first line matches adaptive-fill-first-line-regexp, or if it appears to be a comment-starting sequence (this depends on the major mode), then the prefix found is used for filling the paragraph, provided it would not act as a paragraph starter on subsequent lines.

Otherwise, the prefix found is converted to an equivalent number of spaces, and those spaces are used as the fill prefix for the rest of the lines, provided they would not act as a paragraph starter on subsequent lines.

In Text mode, and other modes where only blank lines and page delimiters separate paragraphs, the prefix chosen by adaptive filling never acts as a paragraph starter, so it can always be used for filling.

The variable adaptive-fill-regexp determines what kinds of line beginnings can serve as a fill prefix: any characters at the start of the line that match this regular expression are used. If you set the variable `adaptive-fill-mode` to `nil`, the fill prefix is never chosen automatically.

You can specify more complex ways of choosing a fill prefix automatically by setting the variable `adaptive-fill-function` to a function. This function is called with point after the left margin of a line, and it should return the appropriate fill prefix based on that line. If it returns `nil`, `adaptive-fill-regexp` gets a chance to find a prefix.

22.5.5 Refill Mode

Refill minor mode provides support for keeping paragraphs filled as you type or modify them in other ways. It provides an effect similar to typical word processor behavior. This works by running a paragraph-filling command at suitable times.

To toggle the use of Refill mode in the current buffer, type `M-x refill-mode`. When you are typing text, only characters which normally trigger auto filling, like the space character, will trigger refilling. This is to avoid making it too slow. Apart from self-inserting characters, other commands which modify the text cause refilling.

The current implementation is preliminary and not robust. You can get better "line wrapping" behavior using Longlines mode. See Section 22.5.6 [Longlines], page 222. However, Longlines mode has an important side-effect: the newlines that it inserts for you are not saved to disk, so the files that you make with Longlines mode will appear to be completely unfilled if you edit them without Longlines mode.

22.5.6 Long Lines Mode

Long Lines mode is a minor mode for *word wrapping*; it lets you edit "unfilled" text files, which Emacs would normally display as a bunch of extremely long lines. Many text editors, such as those built into many web browsers, normally do word wrapping.

To enable Long Lines mode, type `M-x longlines-mode`. If the text is full of long lines, this will "wrap" them immediately—i.e., break up to fit in the window. As you edit the text, Long Lines mode automatically re-wraps lines by inserting or deleting *soft newlines* as necessary (see Section 22.12.2 [Hard and Soft Newlines], page 237.) These soft newlines won't show up when you save the buffer into a file, or when you copy the text into the kill ring, clipboard, or a register.

Word wrapping is *not* the same as ordinary filling (see Section 22.5.2 [Fill Commands], page 218). It does not contract multiple spaces into a single space, recognize fill prefixes (see Section 22.5.3 [Fill Prefix], page 219), or perform adaptive filling (see Section 22.5.4 [Adaptive Fill], page 221). The reason for this is that a wrapped line is still, conceptually, a single line. Each soft newline is equivalent to exactly one space in that long line, and vice versa. However, you can still call filling functions such as `M-q`, and these will work as expected, inserting soft newlines that won't show up on disk or when the text is copied. You can even rely entirely on the normal fill commands by turning off automatic line wrapping, with `C-u M-x longlines-auto-wrap`. To turn automatic line wrapping back on, type `M-x longlines-auto-wrap`.

Type RET to insert a hard newline, one which automatic refilling will not remove. If you want to see where all the hard newlines are, type M-x longlines-show-hard-newlines. This will mark each hard newline with a special symbol. The same command with a prefix argument turns this display off.

Long Lines mode does not change normal text files that are already filled, since the existing newlines are considered hard newlines. Before Long Lines can do anything, you need to transform each paragraph into a long line. One way is to set fill-column to a large number (e.g., C-u 9999 C-x f), re-fill all the paragraphs, and then set fill-column back to its original value.

22.6 Case Conversion Commands

Emacs has commands for converting either a single word or any arbitrary range of text to upper case or to lower case.

M-l   Convert following word to lower case (downcase-word).

M-u   Convert following word to upper case (upcase-word).

M-c   Capitalize the following word (capitalize-word).

C-x C-l   Convert region to lower case (downcase-region).

C-x C-u   Convert region to upper case (upcase-region).

The word conversion commands are the most useful. M-l (downcase-word) converts the word after point to lower case, moving past it. Thus, repeating M-l converts successive words. M-u (upcase-word) converts to all capitals instead, while M-c (capitalize-word) puts the first letter of the word into upper case and the rest into lower case. All these commands convert several words at once if given an argument. They are especially convenient for converting a large amount of text from all upper case to mixed case, because you can move through the text using M-l, M-u or M-c on each word as appropriate, occasionally using M-f instead to skip a word.

When given a negative argument, the word case conversion commands apply to the appropriate number of words before point, but do not move point. This is convenient when you have just typed a word in the wrong case: you can give the case conversion command and continue typing.

If a word case conversion command is given in the middle of a word, it applies only to the part of the word which follows point. (This is comparable to what M-d (kill-word) does.) With a negative argument, case conversion applies only to the part of the word before point.

The other case conversion commands are C-x C-u (upcase-region) and C-x C-l (downcase-region), which convert everything between point and mark to the specified case. Point and mark do not move.

The region case conversion commands upcase-region and downcase-region are normally disabled. This means that they ask for confirmation if you try to use them. When you confirm, you may enable the command, which means it will not ask for confirmation again. See Section 32.4.10 [Disabling], page 432.

22.7 Text Mode

When you edit files of text in a human language, it's more convenient to use Text mode rather than Fundamental mode. To enter Text mode, type `M-x text-mode`.

In Text mode, only blank lines and page delimiters separate paragraphs. As a result, paragraphs can be indented, and adaptive filling determines what indentation to use when filling a paragraph. See Section 22.5.4 [Adaptive Fill], page 221.

Text mode defines TAB to run `indent-relative` (see Chapter 21 [Indentation], page 210), so that you can conveniently indent a line like the previous line.

Text mode turns off the features concerned with comments except when you explicitly invoke them. It changes the syntax table so that single-quotes are considered part of words. However, if a word starts with single-quotes, these are treated as a prefix for purposes such as capitalization. That is, `M-c` will convert `''hello''` into `''Hello''`, as expected.

If you indent the first lines of paragraphs, then you should use Paragraph-Indent Text mode rather than Text mode. In this mode, you do not need to have blank lines between paragraphs, because the first-line indentation is sufficient to start a paragraph; however paragraphs in which every line is indented are not supported. Use `M-x paragraph-indent-text-mode` to enter this mode. Use `M-x paragraph-indent-minor-mode` to enable an equivalent minor mode in situations where you can't change the major mode—in mail composition, for instance.

Text mode, and all the modes based on it, define `M-TAB` as the command `ispell-complete-word`, which performs completion of the partial word in the buffer before point, using the spelling dictionary as the space of possible words. See Section 13.5 [Spelling], page 108. If your window manager defines `M-TAB` to switch windows, you can type `ESC TAB` or `C-M-i`.

Entering Text mode runs the hook `text-mode-hook`. Other major modes related to Text mode also run this hook, followed by hooks of their own; this includes Paragraph-Indent Text mode, Nroff mode, TeX mode, Outline mode, and Mail mode. Hook functions on `text-mode-hook` can look at the value of `major-mode` to see which of these modes is actually being entered. See Section 32.3.2 [Hooks], page 418.

22.8 Outline Mode

Outline mode is a major mode much like Text mode but intended for editing outlines. It allows you to make parts of the text temporarily invisible so that you can see the outline structure. Type `M-x outline-mode` to switch to Outline mode as the major mode of the current buffer.

When Outline mode makes a line invisible, the line does not appear on the screen. The screen appears exactly as if the invisible line were deleted, except that an ellipsis (three periods in a row) appears at the end of the previous visible line. (Multiple consecutive invisible lines produce just one ellipsis.)

Editing commands that operate on lines, such as `C-n` and `C-p`, treat the text of the invisible line as part of the previous visible line. Killing the ellipsis at the end of a visible line really kills all the following invisible lines.

Outline minor mode provides the same commands as the major mode, Outline mode, but you can use it in conjunction with other major modes. Type M-x `outline-minor-mode` to enable the Outline minor mode in the current buffer. You can also specify this in the text of a file, with a file local variable of the form 'mode: outline-minor' (see Section 32.3.4 [File Variables], page 420).

The major mode, Outline mode, provides special key bindings on the C-c prefix. Outline minor mode provides similar bindings with C-c @ as the prefix; this is to reduce the conflicts with the major mode's special commands. (The variable `outline-minor-mode-prefix` controls the prefix used.)

Entering Outline mode runs the hook `text-mode-hook` followed by the hook `outline-mode-hook` (see Section 32.3.2 [Hooks], page 418).

22.8.1 Format of Outlines

Outline mode assumes that the lines in the buffer are of two types: *heading lines* and *body lines*. A heading line represents a topic in the outline. Heading lines start with one or more stars; the number of stars determines the depth of the heading in the outline structure. Thus, a heading line with one star is a major topic; all the heading lines with two stars between it and the next one-star heading are its subtopics; and so on. Any line that is not a heading line is a body line. Body lines belong with the preceding heading line. Here is an example:

```
* Food
This is the body,
which says something about the topic of food.

** Delicious Food
This is the body of the second-level header.

** Distasteful Food
This could have
a body too, with
several lines.

*** Dormitory Food

* Shelter
Another first-level topic with its header line.
```

A heading line together with all following body lines is called collectively an *entry*. A heading line together with all following deeper heading lines and their body lines is called a *subtree*.

You can customize the criterion for distinguishing heading lines by setting the variable `outline-regexp`. (The recommended ways to do this are in a major mode function or with a file local variable.) Any line whose beginning has a match for this regexp is considered a heading line. Matches that start within a line (not at the left margin) do not count.

The length of the matching text determines the level of the heading; longer matches make a more deeply nested level. Thus, for example, if a text formatter has commands '@chapter', '@section' and '@subsection' to divide the document into chapters and sections, you could make those lines count as heading lines by setting `outline-regexp` to '"@chap\\|@\\(sub\\)*section"'. Note the trick: the two words 'chapter' and 'section' are equally long, but by defining the regexp to match only 'chap' we ensure that the length of the text matched on a chapter heading is shorter, so that Outline mode will know that sections are contained in chapters. This works as long as no other command starts with '@chap'.

You can explicitly specify a rule for calculating the level of a heading line by setting the variable `outline-level`. The value of `outline-level` should be a function that takes no arguments and returns the level of the current heading. The recommended ways to set this variable are in a major mode command or with a file local variable.

22.8.2 Outline Motion Commands

Outline mode provides special motion commands that move backward and forward to heading lines.

C-c C-n   Move point to the next visible heading line (`outline-next-visible-heading`).

C-c C-p   Move point to the previous visible heading line (`outline-previous-visible-heading`).

C-c C-f   Move point to the next visible heading line at the same level as the one point is on (`outline-forward-same-level`).

C-c C-b   Move point to the previous visible heading line at the same level (`outline-backward-same-level`).

C-c C-u   Move point up to a lower-level (more inclusive) visible heading line (`outline-up-heading`).

C-c C-n (`outline-next-visible-heading`) moves down to the next heading line. C-c C-p (`outline-previous-visible-heading`) moves similarly backward. Both accept numeric arguments as repeat counts. The names emphasize that invisible headings are skipped, but this is not really a special feature. All editing commands that look for lines ignore the invisible lines automatically.

More powerful motion commands understand the level structure of headings. C-c C-f (`outline-forward-same-level`) and C-c C-b (`outline-backward-same-level`) move from one heading line to another visible heading at the same depth in the outline. C-c C-u (`outline-up-heading`) moves backward to another heading that is less deeply nested.

22.8.3 Outline Visibility Commands

The other special commands of outline mode are used to make lines visible or invisible. Their names all start with `hide` or `show`. Most of them fall into pairs of opposites. They are not undoable; instead, you can undo right past them. Making lines visible or invisible is simply not recorded by the undo mechanism.

Many of these commands act on the "current" heading line. If point is on a heading line, that is the current heading line; if point is on a body line, the current heading line is the nearest preceding header line.

C-c C-c   Make the current heading line's body invisible (hide-entry).

C-c C-e   Make the current heading line's body visible (show-entry).

C-c C-d   Make everything under the current heading invisible, not including the heading itself (hide-subtree).

C-c C-s   Make everything under the current heading visible, including body, subheadings, and their bodies (show-subtree).

C-c C-l   Make the body of the current heading line, and of all its subheadings, invisible (hide-leaves).

C-c C-k   Make all subheadings of the current heading line, at all levels, visible (show-branches).

C-c C-i   Make immediate subheadings (one level down) of the current heading line visible (show-children).

C-c C-t   Make all body lines in the buffer invisible (hide-body).

C-c C-a   Make all lines in the buffer visible (show-all).

C-c C-q   Hide everything except the top n levels of heading lines (hide-sublevels).

C-c C-o   Hide everything except for the heading or body that point is in, plus the headings leading up from there to the top level of the outline (hide-other).

Two commands that are exact opposites are C-c C-c (hide-entry) and C-c C-e (show-entry). They apply to the body lines directly following the current heading line. Subheadings and their bodies are not affected.

Two more powerful opposites are C-c C-d (hide-subtree) and C-c C-s (show-subtree). Both apply to the current heading line's *subtree*: its body, all its subheadings, both direct and indirect, and all of their bodies. In other words, the subtree contains everything following the current heading line, up to and not including the next heading of the same or higher rank.

Intermediate between a visible subtree and an invisible one is having all the subheadings visible but none of the body. There are two commands for doing this, depending on whether you want to hide the bodies or make the subheadings visible. They are C-c C-l (hide-leaves) and C-c C-k (show-branches).

A little weaker than show-branches is C-c C-i (show-children). It makes just the direct subheadings visible—those one level down. Deeper subheadings remain invisible, if they were invisible.

Two commands have a blanket effect on the whole file. C-c C-t (hide-body) makes all body lines invisible, so that you see just the outline structure (as a special exception, it will not hide lines at the top of the file, preceding the first header line, even though these are technically body lines). C-c C-a (show-all) makes all lines visible. These commands can be thought of as a pair of opposites even though C-c C-a applies to more than just body lines.

The command C-c C-q (hide-sublevels) hides all but the top level headings. With a numeric argument n, it hides everything except the top n levels of heading lines.

The command C-c C-o (hide-other) hides everything except the heading and body text that point is in, plus its parents (the headers leading up from there to top level in the outline) and the top level headings.

When incremental search finds text that is hidden by Outline mode, it makes that part of the buffer visible. If you exit the search at that position, the text remains visible. You can also automatically make text visible as you navigate in it by using M-x reveal-mode.

22.8.4 Viewing One Outline in Multiple Views

You can display two views of a single outline at the same time, in different windows. To do this, you must create an indirect buffer using M-x make-indirect-buffer. The first argument of this command is the existing outline buffer name, and its second argument is the name to use for the new indirect buffer. See Section 16.6 [Indirect Buffers], page 162.

Once the indirect buffer exists, you can display it in a window in the normal fashion, with C-x 4 b or other Emacs commands. The Outline mode commands to show and hide parts of the text operate on each buffer independently; as a result, each buffer can have its own view. If you want more than two views on the same outline, create additional indirect buffers.

22.8.5 Folding Editing

The Foldout package extends Outline mode and Outline minor mode with "folding" commands. The idea of folding is that you zoom in on a nested portion of the outline, while hiding its relatives at higher levels.

Consider an Outline mode buffer with all the text and subheadings under level-1 headings hidden. To look at what is hidden under one of these headings, you could use C-c C-e (M-x show-entry) to expose the body, or C-c C-i to expose the child (level-2) headings.

With Foldout, you use C-c C-z (M-x foldout-zoom-subtree). This exposes the body and child subheadings, and narrows the buffer so that only the level-1 heading, the body and the level-2 headings are visible. Now to look under one of the level-2 headings, position the cursor on it and use C-c C-z again. This exposes the level-2 body and its level-3 child subheadings and narrows the buffer again. Zooming in on successive subheadings can be done as much as you like. A string in the mode line shows how deep you've gone.

When zooming in on a heading, to see only the child subheadings specify a numeric argument: C-u C-c C-z. The number of levels of children can be specified too (compare M-x show-children), e.g. M-2 C-c C-z exposes two levels of child subheadings. Alternatively, the body can be specified with a negative argument: M-- C-c C-z. The whole subtree can be expanded, similarly to C-c C-s (M-x show-subtree), by specifying a zero argument: M-0 C-c C-z.

While you're zoomed in, you can still use Outline mode's exposure and hiding functions without disturbing Foldout. Also, since the buffer is narrowed, "global" editing actions will only affect text under the zoomed-in heading. This is useful for restricting changes to a particular chapter or section of your document.

To unzoom (exit) a fold, use C-c C-x (M-x foldout-exit-fold). This hides all the text and subheadings under the top-level heading and returns you to the previous view of the buffer. Specifying a numeric argument exits that many levels of folds. Specifying a zero argument exits all folds.

To cancel the narrowing of a fold without hiding the text and subheadings, specify a negative argument. For example, M--2 C-c C-x exits two folds and leaves the text and subheadings exposed.

Foldout mode also provides mouse commands for entering and exiting folds, and for showing and hiding text:

C-M-Mouse-1 zooms in on the heading clicked on

> single click: expose body.
>
> double click: expose subheadings.
>
> triple click: expose body and subheadings.
>
> quad click: expose entire subtree.

C-M-Mouse-2 exposes text under the heading clicked on

> single click: expose body.
>
> double click: expose subheadings.
>
> triple click: expose body and subheadings.
>
> quad click: expose entire subtree.

C-M-Mouse-3 hides text under the heading clicked on or exits fold

> single click: hide subtree.
>
> double click: exit fold and hide text.
>
> triple click: exit fold without hiding text.
>
> quad click: exit all folds and hide text.

You can specify different modifier keys (instead of Control-Meta-) by setting foldout-mouse-modifiers; but if you have already loaded the 'foldout.el' library, you must reload it in order for this to take effect.

To use the Foldout package, you can type M-x load-library RET foldout RET; or you can arrange for to do that automatically by putting this in your '.emacs' file:

```
(eval-after-load "outline" '(require 'foldout))
```

22.9 TEX Mode

TEX is a powerful text formatter written by Donald Knuth; it is also free software, like GNU Emacs. LaTEX is a simplified input format for TEX, implemented by TEX macros; it comes with TEX. SliTEX is a special form of LaTEX.[1] DocTEX ('.dtx') is a special file format in which the LaTEX sources are written, combining sources with documentation.

Emacs has a special TEX mode for editing TEX input files. It provides facilities for checking the balance of delimiters and for invoking TEX on all or part of the file.

TEX mode has four variants: Plain TEX mode, LaTEX mode, SliTEX mode, and DocTEX mode (these distinct major modes differ only slightly). They are designed for editing the four different formats. The command `M-x tex-mode` looks at the contents of the buffer to determine whether the contents appear to be either LaTEX input, SliTEX, or DocTEX input; if so, it selects the appropriate mode. If the file contents do not appear to be LaTEX, SliTEX or DocTEX, it selects Plain TEX mode. If the contents are insufficient to determine this, the variable `tex-default-mode` controls which mode is used.

When `M-x tex-mode` does not guess right, you can use the commands `M-x plain-tex-mode`, `M-x latex-mode`, `M-x slitex-mode`, and `doctex-mode` to select explicitly the particular variants of TEX mode.

22.9.1 TEX Editing Commands

Here are the special commands provided in TEX mode for editing the text of the file.

"
: Insert, according to context, either '''' or '"' or '''' (`tex-insert-quote`).

C-j
: Insert a paragraph break (two newlines) and check the previous paragraph for unbalanced braces or dollar signs (`tex-terminate-paragraph`).

M-x tex-validate-region
: Check each paragraph in the region for unbalanced braces or dollar signs.

C-c {
: Insert '{}' and position point between them (`tex-insert-braces`).

C-c }
: Move forward past the next unmatched close brace (`up-list`).

In TEX, the character '"' is not normally used; we use '''' to start a quotation and '''' to end one. To make editing easier under this formatting convention, TEX mode overrides the normal meaning of the key " with a command that inserts a pair of single-quotes or backquotes (`tex-insert-quote`). To be precise, this command inserts '''' after whitespace or an open brace, '"' after a backslash, and '''' after any other character.

---

[1] SliTEX is obsoleted by the '`slides`' document class and other alternative packages in recent LaTEX versions.

If you need the character '"' itself in unusual contexts, use C-q to insert it. Also, " with a numeric argument always inserts that number of '"' characters. You can turn off the feature of " expansion by eliminating that binding in the local map (see Section 32.4 [Key Bindings], page 423).

In TEX mode, '$' has a special syntax code which attempts to understand the way TEX math mode delimiters match. When you insert a '$' that is meant to exit math mode, the position of the matching '$' that entered math mode is displayed for a second. This is the same feature that displays the open brace that matches a close brace that is inserted. However, there is no way to tell whether a '$' enters math mode or leaves it; so when you insert a '$' that enters math mode, the previous '$' position is shown as if it were a match, even though they are actually unrelated.

TEX uses braces as delimiters that must match. Some users prefer to keep braces balanced at all times, rather than inserting them singly. Use C-c { (tex-insert-braces) to insert a pair of braces. It leaves point between the two braces so you can insert the text that belongs inside. Afterward, use the command C-c } (up-list) to move forward past the close brace.

There are two commands for checking the matching of braces. C-j (tex-terminate-paragraph) checks the paragraph before point, and inserts two newlines to start a new paragraph. It outputs a message in the echo area if any mismatch is found. M-x tex-validate-region checks a region, paragraph by paragraph. The errors are listed in the '*Occur*' buffer, and you can use C-c C-c or Mouse-2 in that buffer to go to a particular mismatch.

Note that Emacs commands count square brackets and parentheses in TEX mode, not just braces. This is not strictly correct for the purpose of checking TEX syntax. However, parentheses and square brackets are likely to be used in text as matching delimiters and it is useful for the various motion commands and automatic match display to work with them.

22.9.2 LaTEX Editing Commands

LaTEX mode, and its variant, SliTEX mode, provide a few extra features not applicable to plain TEX.

C-c C-o   Insert '\begin' and '\end' for LaTEX block and position point on a
             line between them (tex-latex-block).

C-c C-e   Close the innermost LaTEX block not yet closed (tex-close-latex-
             block).

In LaTEX input, '\begin' and '\end' commands are used to group blocks of text. To insert a '\begin' and a matching '\end' (on a new line following the '\begin'), use C-c C-o (tex-latex-block). A blank line is inserted between the two, and point is left there. You can use completion when you enter the block type; to specify additional block type names beyond the standard list, set the variable latex-block-names. For example, here's how to add 'theorem', 'corollary', and 'proof':

    (setq latex-block-names '("theorem" "corollary" "proof"))

In LaTeX input, '\begin' and '\end' commands must balance. You can use C-c C-e (tex-close-latex-block) to insert automatically a matching '\end' to match the last unmatched '\begin'. It indents the '\end' to match the corresponding '\begin'. It inserts a newline after '\end' if point is at the beginning of a line.

22.9.3 TeX Printing Commands

You can invoke TeX as an inferior of Emacs on either the entire contents of the buffer or just a region at a time. Running TeX in this way on just one chapter is a good way to see what your changes look like without taking the time to format the entire file.

C-c C-r   Invoke TeX on the current region, together with the buffer's header (tex-region).

C-c C-b   Invoke TeX on the entire current buffer (tex-buffer).

C-c TAB   Invoke BibTeX on the current file (tex-bibtex-file).

C-c C-f   Invoke TeX on the current file (tex-file).

C-c C-l   Recenter the window showing output from the inferior TeX so that the last line can be seen (tex-recenter-output-buffer).

C-c C-k   Kill the TeX subprocess (tex-kill-job).

C-c C-p   Print the output from the last C-c C-r, C-c C-b, or C-c C-f command (tex-print).

C-c C-v   Preview the output from the last C-c C-r, C-c C-b, or C-c C-f command (tex-view).

C-c C-q   Show the printer queue (tex-show-print-queue).

C-c C-c   Invoke some other compilation command on the entire current buffer (tex-compile).

You can pass the current buffer through an inferior TeX by means of C-c C-b (tex-buffer). The formatted output appears in a temporary file; to print it, type C-c C-p (tex-print). Afterward, you can use C-c C-q (tex-show-print-queue) to view the progress of your output towards being printed. If your terminal has the ability to display TeX output files, you can preview the output on the terminal with C-c C-v (tex-view).

You can specify the directory to use for running TeX by setting the variable tex-directory. "." is the default value. If your environment variable TEXINPUTS contains relative directory names, or if your files contains '\input' commands with relative file names, then tex-directory *must* be "." or you will get the wrong results. Otherwise, it is safe to specify some other directory, such as "/tmp".

If you want to specify which shell commands are used in the inferior TeX, you can do so by setting the values of the variables tex-run-command, latex-run-command, slitex-run-command, tex-dvi-print-command, tex-dvi-view-command, and tex-show-queue-command. The default values may (or may not) be appropriate for your system.

Normally, the file name given to these commands comes at the end of the command string; for example, '`latex filename`'. In some cases, however, the file name needs to be embedded in the command; an example is when you need to provide the file name as an argument to one command whose output is piped to another. You can specify where to put the file name with '`*`' in the command string. For example,

>   (setq tex-dvi-print-command "dvips -f * | lpr")

The terminal output from TEX, including any error messages, appears in a buffer called '`*tex-shell*`'. If TEX gets an error, you can switch to this buffer and feed it input (this works as in Shell mode; see Section 31.2.2 [Interactive Shell], page 380). Without switching to this buffer you can scroll it so that its last line is visible by typing `C-c C-l`.

Type `C-c C-k` (`tex-kill-job`) to kill the TEX process if you see that its output is no longer useful. Using `C-c C-b` or `C-c C-r` also kills any TEX process still running.

You can also pass an arbitrary region through an inferior TEX by typing `C-c C-r` (`tex-region`). This is tricky, however, because most files of TEX input contain commands at the beginning to set parameters and define macros, without which no later part of the file will format correctly. To solve this problem, `C-c C-r` allows you to designate a part of the file as containing essential commands; it is included before the specified region as part of the input to TEX. The designated part of the file is called the *header*.

To indicate the bounds of the header in Plain TEX mode, you insert two special strings in the file. Insert '`%**start of header`' before the header, and '`%**end of header`' after it. Each string must appear entirely on one line, but there may be other text on the line before or after. The lines containing the two strings are included in the header. If '`%**start of header`' does not appear within the first 100 lines of the buffer, `C-c C-r` assumes that there is no header.

In LaTEX mode, the header begins with '`\documentclass`' or '`\documentstyle`' and ends with '`\begin{document}`'. These are commands that LaTEX requires you to use in any case, so nothing special needs to be done to identify the header.

The commands (`tex-buffer`) and (`tex-region`) do all of their work in a temporary directory, and do not have available any of the auxiliary files needed by TEX for cross-references; these commands are generally not suitable for running the final copy in which all of the cross-references need to be correct.

When you want the auxiliary files for cross references, use `C-c C-f` (`tex-file`) which runs TEX on the current buffer's file, in that file's directory. Before running TEX, it offers to save any modified buffers. Generally, you need to use (`tex-file`) twice to get the cross-references right.

The value of the variable `tex-start-options` specifies options for the TEX run.

The value of the variable `tex-start-commands` specifies TEX commands for starting TEX. The default value causes TEX to run in nonstop mode. To run TEX interactively, set the variable to `""`.

Large TEX documents are often split into several files—one main file, plus subfiles. Running TEX on a subfile typically does not work; you have to run it on the main file. In order to make `tex-file` useful when you are editing a subfile, you can set the variable `tex-main-file` to the name of the main file. Then `tex-file` runs TeX on that file.

The most convenient way to use `tex-main-file` is to specify it in a local variable list in each of the subfiles. See Section 32.3.4 [File Variables], page 420.

For LaTeX files, you can use BibTeX to process the auxiliary file for the current buffer's file. BibTeX looks up bibliographic citations in a data base and prepares the cited references for the bibliography section. The command C-c TAB (`tex-bibtex-file`) runs the shell command (`tex-bibtex-command`) to produce a '`.bbl`' file for the current buffer's file. Generally, you need to do C-c C-f (`tex-file`) once to generate the '`.aux`' file, then do C-c TAB (`tex-bibtex-file`), and then repeat C-c C-f (`tex-file`) twice more to get the cross-references correct.

To invoke some other compilation program on the current TeX buffer, type C-c C-c (`tex-compile`). This command knows how to pass arguments to many common programs, including '`pdflatex`', '`yap`', '`xdvi`', and '`dvips`'. You can select your desired compilation program using the standard completion keys (see Section 5.3 [Completion], page 33).

22.9.4 TeX Mode Miscellany

Entering any variant of TeX mode runs the hooks `text-mode-hook` and `tex-mode-hook`. Then it runs either `plain-tex-mode-hook`, `latex-mode-hook`, or `slitex-mode-hook`, whichever is appropriate. Starting the TeX shell runs the hook `tex-shell-hook`. See Section 32.3.2 [Hooks], page 418.

The commands M-x iso-iso2tex, M-x iso-tex2iso, M-x iso-iso2gtex and M-x iso-gtex2iso can be used to convert between Latin-1 encoded files and TeX-encoded equivalents.

For managing all kinds of references for LaTeX, you can use RefTeX. See Info file '`reftex`', node 'Top'.

22.10 SGML, XML, and HTML Modes

The major modes for SGML and HTML include indentation support and commands to operate on tags. This section describes the special commands of these modes. (HTML mode is a slightly customized variant of SGML mode.)

C-c C-n   Interactively specify a special character and insert the SGML '&'-command for that character.

C-c C-t   Interactively specify a tag and its attributes (`sgml-tag`). This command asks you for a tag name and for the attribute values, then inserts both the opening tag and the closing tag, leaving point between them.

With a prefix argument n, the command puts the tag around the n words already present in the buffer after point. With -1 as argument, it puts the tag around the region. (In Transient Mark mode, it does this whenever a region is active.)

C-c C-a   Interactively insert attribute values for the current tag (`sgml-attributes`).

C-c C-f   Skip across a balanced tag group (which extends from an opening tag through its corresponding closing tag) (`sgml-skip-tag-forward`). A numeric argument acts as a repeat count.

C-c C-b   Skip backward across a balanced tag group (which extends from an opening tag through its corresponding closing tag) (`sgml-skip-tag-forward`). A numeric argument acts as a repeat count.

C-c C-d   Delete the tag at or after point, and delete the matching tag too (`sgml-delete-tag`). If the tag at or after point is an opening tag, delete the closing tag too; if it is a closing tag, delete the opening tag too.

C-c ? tag RET
           Display a description of the meaning of tag *tag* (`sgml-tag-help`). If the argument *tag* is empty, describe the tag at point.

C-c /   Insert a close tag for the innermost unterminated tag (`sgml-close-tag`). If called from within a tag or a comment, close this element instead of inserting a close tag.

C-c 8   Toggle a minor mode in which Latin-1 characters insert the corresponding SGML commands that stand for them, instead of the characters themselves (`sgml-name-8bit-mode`).

C-c C-v   Run a shell command (which you must specify) to validate the current buffer as SGML (`sgml-validate`).

C-c TAB   Toggle the visibility of existing tags in the buffer. This can be used as a cheap preview.

SGML mode and HTML mode support XML also. In XML, every opening tag must have an explicit closing tag. When `sgml-xml-mode` is non-`nil`, SGML mode and HTML mode always insert explicit closing tags. When you visit a file, these modes determine from the file contents whether it is XML or not, and set `sgml-xml-mode` accordingly, so that they do the right thing for the file in either case.

22.11 Nroff Mode

Nroff mode is a mode like Text mode but modified to handle nroff commands present in the text. Invoke `M-x nroff-mode` to enter this mode. It differs from Text mode in only a few ways. All nroff command lines are considered paragraph separators, so that filling will never garble the nroff commands. Pages are separated by '.bp' commands. Comments start with backslash-doublequote. Also, three special commands are provided that are not in Text mode:

M-n   Move to the beginning of the next line that isn't an nroff command (`forward-text-line`). An argument is a repeat count.

M-p   Like M-n but move up (`backward-text-line`).

M-?   Displays in the echo area the number of text lines (lines that are not nroff commands) in the region (`count-text-lines`).

The other feature of Nroff mode is that you can turn on Electric Nroff mode. This is a minor mode that you can turn on or off with M-x electric-nroff-mode (see Section 32.1 [Minor Modes], page 406). When the mode is on, each time you use RET to end a line that contains an nroff command that opens a kind of grouping, the matching nroff command to close that grouping is automatically inserted on the following line. For example, if you are at the beginning of a line and type . (b RET, this inserts the matching command '.)b' on a new line following point.

If you use Outline minor mode with Nroff mode (see Section 22.8 [Outline Mode], page 224), heading lines are lines of the form '.H' followed by a number (the header level).

Entering Nroff mode runs the hook text-mode-hook, followed by the hook nroff-mode-hook (see Section 32.3.2 [Hooks], page 418).

22.12 Editing Formatted Text

Enriched mode is a minor mode for editing files that contain formatted text in WYSIWYG fashion, as in a word processor. Currently, formatted text in Enriched mode can specify fonts, colors, underlining, margins, and types of filling and justification. In the future, we plan to implement other formatting features as well.

Enriched mode is a minor mode (see Section 32.1 [Minor Modes], page 406). It is typically used in conjunction with Text mode (see Section 22.7 [Text Mode], page 224), but you can also use it with other major modes such as Outline mode and Paragraph-Indent Text mode.

Potentially, Emacs can store formatted text files in various file formats. Currently, only one format is implemented: *text/enriched* format, which is defined by the MIME protocol. See section "Format Conversion" in *the Emacs Lisp Reference Manual*, for details of how Emacs recognizes and converts file formats.

The Emacs distribution contains a formatted text file that can serve as an example. Its name is 'etc/enriched.doc'. It contains samples illustrating all the features described in this section. It also contains a list of ideas for future enhancements.

22.12.1 Requesting to Edit Formatted Text

Whenever you visit a file that Emacs saved in the text/enriched format, Emacs automatically converts the formatting information in the file into Emacs's own internal format (known as *text properties*), and turns on Enriched mode.

To create a new file of formatted text, first visit the nonexistent file, then type M-x enriched-mode before you start inserting text. This command turns on Enriched mode. Do this before you begin inserting text, to ensure that the text you insert is handled properly.

More generally, the command enriched-mode turns Enriched mode on if it was off, and off if it was on. With a prefix argument, this command turns Enriched mode on if the argument is positive, and turns the mode off otherwise.

When you save a buffer while Enriched mode is enabled in it, Emacs automatically converts the text to text/enriched format while writing it into the file. When you visit the file again, Emacs will automatically recognize the format, reconvert the text, and turn on Enriched mode again.

You can add annotations for saving additional text properties, which Emacs normally does not save, by adding to `enriched-translations`. Note that the text/enriched standard requires any non-standard annotations to have names starting with 'x-', as in 'x-read-only'. This ensures that they will not conflict with standard annotations that may be added later.

See section "Text Properties" in *the Emacs Lisp Reference Manual*, for more information about text properties.

22.12.2 Hard and Soft Newlines

In formatted text, Emacs distinguishes between two different kinds of newlines, *hard* newlines and *soft* newlines. (You can enable or disable this feature separately in any buffer with the command `use-hard-newlines`.)

Hard newlines are used to separate paragraphs, or items in a list, or anywhere that there should always be a line break regardless of the margins. The RET command (`newline`) and C-o (`open-line`) insert hard newlines.

Soft newlines are used to make text fit between the margins. All the fill commands, including Auto Fill, insert soft newlines—and they delete only soft newlines.

Although hard and soft newlines look the same, it is important to bear the difference in mind. Do not use RET to break lines in the middle of filled paragraphs, or else you will get hard newlines that are barriers to further filling. Instead, let Auto Fill mode break lines, so that if the text or the margins change, Emacs can refill the lines properly. See Section 22.5.1 [Auto Fill], page 217.

On the other hand, in tables and lists, where the lines should always remain as you type them, you can use RET to end lines. For these lines, you may also want to set the justification style to `unfilled`. See Section 22.12.7 [Format Justification], page 240.

22.12.3 Editing Format Information

There are two ways to alter the formatting information for a formatted text file: with keyboard commands, and with the mouse.

The easiest way to add properties to your document is with the Text Properties menu. You can get to this menu in two ways: from the Edit menu in the menu bar (use F10 e t if you have no mouse), or with C-Mouse-2 (hold the CTRL key and press the middle mouse button). There are also keyboard commands described in the following section.

Most of the items in the Text Properties menu lead to other submenus. These are described in the sections that follow. Some items run commands directly:

Remove Face Properties
> Delete from the region all face and color text properties (`facemenu-remove-face-props`).

Remove Text Properties
> Delete *all* text properties from the region (`facemenu-remove-all`).

Describe Properties
> List all the text properties, widgets, buttons, and overlays of the character following point (`describe-text-properties`).

Display Faces
> Display a list of all the defined faces (`list-faces-display`).

Display Colors
> Display a list of all the defined colors (`list-colors-display`).

22.12.4 Faces in Formatted Text

The Faces submenu lists various Emacs faces including **bold**, *italic*, and underline (see Section 11.5 [Faces], page 72). These menu items operate on the region if it is active and nonempty. Otherwise, they specify to use that face for an immediately following self-inserting character. Instead of the menu, you can use these keyboard commands:

M-o d
> Remove all `face` properties from the region (which includes specified colors), or force the following inserted character to have no `face` property (`facemenu-set-default`).

M-o b
> Add the face **bold** to the region or to the following inserted character (`facemenu-set-bold`).

M-o i
> Add the face *italic* to the region or to the following inserted character (`facemenu-set-italic`).

M-o l
> Add the face ***bold-italic*** to the region or to the following inserted character (`facemenu-set-bold-italic`).

M-o u
> Add the face underline to the region or to the following inserted character (`facemenu-set-underline`).

M-o o *face* RET
> Add the face *face* to the region or to the following inserted character (`facemenu-set-face`).

With a prefix argument, all these commands apply to an immediately following self-inserting character, disregarding the region.

A self-inserting character normally inherits the `face` property (and most other text properties) from the preceding character in the buffer. If you use the above commands to specify face for the next self-inserting character, or the next section's commands to specify a foreground or background color for it, then it does not inherit the `face` property from the preceding character; instead it uses whatever you specified. It will still inherit other text properties, though.

Strictly speaking, these commands apply only to the first following self-inserting character that you type. But if you insert additional characters after it, they will inherit from the first one. So it appears that these commands apply to all of them.

Enriched mode defines two additional faces: `excerpt` and `fixed`. These correspond to codes used in the text/enriched file format.

The `excerpt` face is intended for quotations. This face is the same as `italic` unless you customize it (see Section 32.2.5 [Face Customization], page 413).

The `fixed` face means, "Use a fixed-width font for this part of the text." Applying the `fixed` face to a part of the text will cause that part of the text to appear in a fixed-width font, even if the default font is variable-width. This applies to Emacs and to other systems that display text/enriched format. So if you specifically want a certain part of the text to use a fixed-width font, you should specify the `fixed` face for that part.

By default, the `fixed` face looks the same as `bold`. This is an attempt to distinguish it from `default`. You may wish to customize `fixed` to some other fixed-width medium font. See Section 32.2.5 [Face Customization], page 413.

If your terminal cannot display different faces, you will not be able to see them, but you can still edit documents containing faces, and even add faces and colors to documents. The faces you specify will be visible when the file is viewed on a terminal that can display them.

22.12.5 Colors in Formatted Text

You can specify foreground and background colors for portions of the text. There is a menu for specifying the foreground color and a menu for specifying the background color. Each color menu lists all the colors that you have used in Enriched mode in the current Emacs session.

If you specify a color with a prefix argument—or, in Transient Mark mode, if the region is not active—then it applies to any immediately following self-inserting input. Otherwise, the command applies to the region.

Each color menu contains one additional item: 'Other'. You can use this item to specify a color that is not listed in the menu; it reads the color name with the minibuffer. To display a list of available colors and their names, use the 'Display Colors' menu item in the Text Properties menu (see Section 22.12.3 [Editing Format Info], page 237).

Any color that you specify in this way, or that is mentioned in a formatted text file that you read in, is added to the corresponding color menu for the duration of the Emacs session.

There are no predefined key bindings for specifying colors, but you can do so with the extended commands `M-x facemenu-set-foreground` and `M-x facemenu-set-background`. Both of these commands read the name of the color with the minibuffer.

22.12.6 Indentation in Formatted Text

When editing formatted text, you can specify different amounts of indentation for the right or left margin of an entire paragraph or a part of a paragraph. The margins you specify automatically affect the Emacs fill commands (see Section 22.5 [Filling], page 217) and line-breaking commands.

The Indentation submenu provides a convenient interface for specifying these properties. The submenu contains four items:

Indent More

> Indent the region by 4 columns (`increase-left-margin`). In Enriched mode, this command is also available on `C-x TAB`; if you supply a numeric argument, that says how many columns to add to the margin (a negative argument reduces the number of columns).

Indent Less

> Remove 4 columns of indentation from the region.

Indent Right More

> Make the text narrower by indenting 4 columns at the right margin.

Indent Right Less

> Remove 4 columns of indentation from the right margin.

You can use these commands repeatedly to increase or decrease the indentation.

The most common way to use them is to change the indentation of an entire paragraph. For other uses, the effects of refilling can be hard to predict, except in some special cases like the one described next.

The most common other use is to format paragraphs with *hanging indents*, which means that the first line is indented less than subsequent lines. To set up a hanging indent, increase the indentation of the region starting after the first word of the paragraph and running until the end of the paragraph.

Indenting the first line of a paragraph is easier. Set the margin for the whole paragraph where you want it to be for the body of the paragraph, then indent the first line by inserting extra spaces or tabs.

The variable `standard-indent` specifies how many columns these commands should add to or subtract from the indentation. The default value is 4. The overall default right margin for Enriched mode is controlled by the variable `fill-column`, as usual.

There are also two commands for setting the left or right margin of the region absolutely: `set-left-margin` and `set-right-margin`. Enriched mode binds these commands to `C-c [` and `C-c ]`, respectively. You can specify the margin width either with a numeric argument or in the minibuffer.

Sometimes, as a result of editing, the filling of a paragraph becomes messed up—parts of the paragraph may extend past the left or right margins. When this happens, use `M-q` (`fill-paragraph`) to refill the paragraph.

The fill prefix, if any, works in addition to the specified paragraph indentation: `C-x .` does not include the specified indentation's whitespace in the new value for the fill prefix, and the fill commands look for the fill prefix after the indentation on each line. See Section 22.5.3 [Fill Prefix], page 219.

22.12.7 Justification in Formatted Text

When editing formatted text, you can specify various styles of justification for a paragraph. The style you specify automatically affects the Emacs fill commands.

The Justification submenu provides a convenient interface for specifying the style. The submenu contains five items:

Left   This is the most common style of justification (at least for English). Lines are aligned at the left margin but left uneven at the right.

Right   This aligns each line with the right margin. Spaces and tabs are added on the left, if necessary, to make lines line up on the right.

Full   This justifies the text, aligning both edges of each line. Justified text looks very nice in a printed book, where the spaces can all be adjusted equally, but it does not look as nice with a fixed-width font on the screen. Perhaps a future version of Emacs will be able to adjust the width of spaces in a line to achieve elegant justification.

Center   This centers every line between the current margins.

Unfilled   This turns off filling entirely. Each line will remain as you wrote it; the fill and auto-fill functions will have no effect on text which has this setting. You can, however, still indent the left margin. In unfilled regions, all newlines are treated as hard newlines (see Section 22.12.2 [Hard and Soft Newlines], page 237) .

In Enriched mode, you can also specify justification from the keyboard using the M-j prefix character:

M-j l   Make the region left-filled (set-justification-left).

M-j r   Make the region right-filled (set-justification-right).

M-j b   Make the region fully justified (set-justification-full).

M-j c
M S   Make the region centered (set-justification-center).

M-j u   Make the region unfilled (set-justification-none).

Justification styles apply to entire paragraphs. All the justification-changing commands operate on the paragraph containing point, or, if the region is active, on all paragraphs which overlap the region.

The default justification style is specified by the variable default-justification. Its value should be one of the symbols left, right, full, center, or none. This is a per-buffer variable. Setting the variable directly affects only the current buffer. However, customizing it in a Custom buffer sets (as always) the default value for buffers that do not override it. See Section 32.3.3 [Locals], page 419, and Section 32.2 [Easy Customization], page 408.

22.12.8 Setting Other Text Properties

The Special Properties menu lets you add or remove three other useful text properties: read-only, invisible and intangible. The intangible property disallows moving point within the text, the invisible text property hides text from display, and the read-only property disallows alteration of the text.

Each of these special properties has a menu item to add it to the region. The last menu item, 'Remove Special', removes all of these special properties from the text in the region.

Currently, the `invisible` and `intangible` properties are *not* saved in the text/enriched format. The `read-only` property is saved, but it is not a standard part of the text/enriched format, so other editors may not respect it.

22.12.9 Forcing Enriched Mode

Normally, Emacs knows when you are editing formatted text because it recognizes the special annotations used in the file that you visited. However, sometimes you must take special actions to convert file contents or turn on Enriched mode:

- When you visit a file that was created with some other editor, Emacs may not recognize the file as being in the text/enriched format. In this case, when you visit the file you will see the formatting commands rather than the formatted text. Type `M-x format-decode-buffer` to translate it. This also automatically turns on Enriched mode.

- When you *insert* a file into a buffer, rather than visiting it, Emacs does the necessary conversions on the text which you insert, but it does not enable Enriched mode. If you wish to do that, type `M-x enriched-mode`.

The command `format-decode-buffer` translates text in various formats into Emacs's internal format. It asks you to specify the format to translate from; however, normally you can type just RET, which tells Emacs to guess the format.

If you wish to look at a text/enriched file in its raw form, as a sequence of characters rather than as formatted text, use the `M-x find-file-literally` command. This visits a file, like `find-file`, but does not do format conversion. It also inhibits character code conversion (see Section 19.7 [Coding Systems], page 193) and automatic uncompression (see Section 15.12 [Compressed Files], page 151). To disable format conversion but allow character code conversion and/or automatic uncompression if appropriate, use `format-find-file` with suitable arguments.

22.13 Editing Text-based Tables

Table mode provides an easy and intuitive way to create and edit WYSIWYG text-based tables. Here is an example of such a table:

```
+-----------------+-------------------------------+-----------------+
|    Command      |          Description          |  Key Binding    |
+-----------------+-------------------------------+-----------------+
|  forward-char   |Move point right N characters  |      C-f        |
|                 |(left if N is negative).       |                 |
|                 |                               |                 |
|                 |On reaching end of buffer, stop|                 |
|                 |and signal error.              |                 |
+-----------------+-------------------------------+-----------------+
|  backward-char  |Move point left N characters   |      C-b        |
|                 |(right if N is negative).      |                 |
|                 |                               |                 |
|                 |On attempt to pass beginning or|                 |
|                 |end of buffer, stop and signal |                 |
|                 |error.                         |                 |
+-----------------+-------------------------------+-----------------+
```

Table mode allows the contents of the table such as this one to be easily manipulated by inserting or deleting characters inside a cell. A cell is effectively a localized rectangular edit region and edits to a cell do not affect the contents of the surrounding cells. If the contents do not fit into a cell, then the cell is automatically expanded in the vertical and/or horizontal directions and the rest of the table is restructured and reformatted in accordance with the growth of the cell.

22.13.1 What is a Text-based Table?

Keep the following examples of valid tables in mind as a reference while you read this section:

```
+--+----+---+        +-+        +--+-----+
|  |    |   |        | |        |  |     |
+--+----+---+        +-+        |  +--+--+
|  |    |   |                   |  |  |  |
+--+----+---+                   +--+--+  |
                                |     |  |
                                +-----+--+
```

A table consists of a rectangular frame whose inside is divided into cells. Each cell must be at least one character wide and one character high, not counting its border lines. A cell can be subdivided into multiple rectangular cells, but cells cannot overlap.

The table frame and cell border lines are made of three special characters. These variables specify those characters:

`table-cell-vertical-char`
> Holds the character used for vertical lines. The default value is '|'.

`table-cell-horizontal-char`
> Holds the character used for horizontal lines. The default value is '-'.

`table-cell-intersection-char`
> Holds the character used at where horizontal line and vertical line meet. The default value is '+'.

Based on this definition, the following five tables are examples of invalid tables:

```
+-----+     +-----+       +--+      +-++--+     ++
|     |     |     |       |  |      | ||  |     ++
| +-+ |     |     |       |  |      | ||  |
| | | |     +--+  |       +--+--+   +-++--+
| +-+ |     |  |  |       |  |  |   +-++--+
|     |     |  |  |       |  |  |   | ||  |
+-----+     +--+--+       +--+--+   +-++--+
   a           b             c         d        e
```

From left to right:

a. Overlapped cells or non-rectangular cells are not allowed.

b. Same as a.

c. The border must be rectangular.

d. Cells must have a minimum width/height of one character.

e. Same as d.

22.13.2 How to Create a Table?

The command to create a table is `table-insert`. When called interactively, it asks for the number of columns, number of rows, cell width and cell height. The number of columns is the number of cells horizontally side by side. The number of rows is the number of cells vertically within the table's height. The cell width is a number of characters that each cell holds, left to right. The cell height is a number of lines each cell holds. The cell width and the cell height can be either an integer (when the value is constant across the table) or a series of integer, separated by spaces or commas, where each number corresponds to the next cell within a row from left to right, or the next cell within a column from top to bottom.

22.13.3 Table Recognition

Table mode maintains special text properties in the buffer to allow editing in a convenient fashion. When a buffer with tables is saved to its file, these text properties are lost, so when you visit this file again later, Emacs does not see a table, but just formatted text. To resurrect the table text properties, issue the `M-x table-recognize` command. It scans the current buffer, recognizes valid table cells, and attaches appropriate text properties to allow for table editing. The converse command, `table-unrecognize`, is used to remove the special text properties and convert the buffer back to plain text.

Special commands exist to enable or disable tables within a region, enable or disable individual tables, and enable/disable individual cells. These commands are:

`M-x table-recognize-region`
> Recognize tables within the current region and activate them.

`M-x table-unrecognize-region`
> Deactivate tables within the current region.

`M-x table-recognize-table`
> Recognize the table under point and activate it.

`M-x table-unrecognize-table`
> Deactivate the table under point.

`M-x table-recognize-cell`
> Recognize the cell under point and activate it.

`M-x table-unrecognize-cell`
> Deactivate the cell under point.

For another way of converting text into tables, see Section 22.13.9 [Table Conversion], page 247.

22.13.4 Commands for Table Cells

The commands `table-forward-cell` and `table-backward-cell` move point from the current cell to an adjacent cell forward and backward respectively. The order of the cells is cyclic: when point is in the last cell of a table, typing `M-x table-forward-cell` moves to the first cell in the table. Likewise `M-x table-backward-cell` from the first cell in a table moves to the last cell.

The command `table-span-cell` merges the current cell with the adjacent cell in a specified direction—right, left, above or below. You specify the direction with the minibuffer. It does not allow merges which don't result in a legitimate cell layout.

The command `table-split-cell` splits the current cell vertically or horizontally. This command is a wrapper to the direction specific commands `table-split-cell-vertically` and `table-split-cell-horizontally`. You specify the direction with a minibuffer argument.

The command `table-split-cell-vertically` splits the current cell vertically and creates a pair of cells above and below where point is located. The content in the original cell is split as well.

The command `table-split-cell-horizontally` splits the current cell horizontally and creates a pair of cells right and left of where point is located. If the cell being split is not empty, this asks you how to handle the cell contents. The three options are: `split`, `left`, or `right`. `split` splits the contents at point literally, while the `left` and `right` options move the entire contents into the left or right cell respectively.

The next four commands enlarge or shrink a cell. They use numeric arguments (see Section 4.10 [Arguments], page 28) to specify how many columns or rows to enlarge or shrink a particular table.

`M-x table-heighten-cell`
> Enlarge the current cell vertically.

`M-x table-shorten-cell`
> Shrink the current cell vertically.

`M-x table-widen-cell`
> Enlarge the current cell horizontally.

`M-x table-narrow-cell`
> Shrink the current cell horizontally.

22.13.5 Cell Justification

You can specify text justification for each cell. The justification is remembered independently for each cell and the subsequent editing of cell contents is subject to the specified justification.

The command `table-justify` ask you to specify what to justify: a cell, a column, or a row. If you select cell justification, this command sets the justification only for the current cell. Selecting column or row justification sets the justification for all the cells within a column or row respectively. The command then ask you which kind of justification to apply: `left`, `center`, `right`, `top`, `middle`, `bottom`, or `none`. Horizontal justification and vertical justification are specified independently. The options `left`, `center`, and `right` specify horizontal justification while the options `top`, `middle`, `bottom`, and `none` specify vertical justification. The vertical justification `none` effectively removes vertical justification. Horizontal justification must be one of `left`, `center`, or `right`.

Justification information is stored in the buffer as a part of text property. Therefore, this information is ephemeral and does not survive through the loss of the buffer (closing the buffer and revisiting the buffer erase any previous text properties). To countermand for this, the command `table-recognize` and other recognition commands (see Section 22.13.3 [Table Recognition], page 244) are equipped with a convenience feature (turned on by default). During table recognition, the contents of a cell are examined to determine which justification was originally applied to the cell and then applies this justification to the cell. This is a speculative algorithm and is therefore not perfect, however, the justification is deduced correctly most of the time. To disable this feature, customize the variable `table-detect-cell-alignment` and set it to `nil`.

22.13.6 Commands for Table Rows

The command `table-insert-row` inserts a row of cells before the current row in a table. The current row where point is located is pushed down after the newly inserted row. A numeric prefix argument specifies the number of rows to insert. Note that in order to insert rows *after* the last row at the bottom of a table, you must place point below the table—that is, outside the table—prior to invoking this command.

The command `table-delete-row` deletes a row of cells at point. A numeric prefix argument specifies the number of rows to delete.

22.13.7 Commands for Table Columns

The command `table-insert-column` inserts a column of cells to the left of the current row in a table. This pushes the current column to the right. To insert a column to the right side of the rightmost column, place point to the right of the rightmost column, which is outside of the table, prior to invoking this command. A numeric prefix argument specifies the number of columns to insert.

A command `table-delete-column` deletes a column of cells at point. A numeric prefix argument specifies the number of columns to delete.

22.13.8 Fix Width of Cells

The command `table-fixed-width-mode` toggles fixed width mode on and off. When fixed width mode is turned on, editing inside a cell never changes the cell width; when it is off, the cell width expands automatically in order to prevent a word from being folded into multiple lines. By default, fixed width mode is disabled.

22.13.9 Conversion Between Plain Text and Tables

The command `table-capture` captures plain text in a region and turns it into a table. Unlike `table-recognize` (see Section 22.13.3 [Table Recognition], page 244), the original text does not have a table appearance but may hold a logical table structure. For example, some elements separated by known patterns form a two dimensional structure which can be turned into a table.

Here's an example of data that `table-capture` can operate on. The numbers are horizontally separated by a comma and vertically separated by a newline character.

```
1, 2, 3, 4
5, 6, 7, 8
, 9, 10
```

Invoking `M-x table-capture` on that text produces this table:

```
+-----+-----+-----+-----+
|1    |2    |3    |4    |
+-----+-----+-----+-----+
|5    |6    |7    |8    |
+-----+-----+-----+-----+
|     |9    |10   |     |
+-----+-----+-----+-----+
```

The conversion uses ',' for the column delimiter and newline for a row delimiter, cells are left justified, and minimum cell width is 5.

The command `table-release` does the opposite of `table-capture`. It releases a table by removing the table frame and cell borders. This leaves the table contents as plain text. One of the useful applications of `table-capture` and `table-release` is to edit a text in layout. Look at the following three paragraphs (the latter two are indented with header lines):

```
'table-capture' is a powerful command, but mastering its
power requires some practice.  Here are some things it can do:

Parse Cell Items        By using column delimiter regular
                        expression and raw delimiter regular
                        expression, it parses the specified text
                        area and extracts cell items from
                        non-table text and then forms a table out
                        of them.

Capture Text Area       When no delimiters are specified it
                        creates a single cell table.  The text in
                        the specified region is placed in that
                        cell.
```

Applying `table-capture` to a region containing the above three paragraphs, with empty strings for column delimiter regexp and row delimiter regexp, creates a table with a single cell like the following one.

```
+-----------------------------------------------------------------------+
|'table-capture' is a powerful command, but mastering its               |
|power requires some practice.  Here are some things it can do:          |
|                                                                        |
|Parse Cell Items         By using column delimiter regular             |
|                         expression and raw delimiter regular          |
|                         expression, it parses the specified text      |
|                         area and extracts cell items from             |
|                         non-table text and then forms a table out     |
|                         of them.                                       |
|                                                                        |
|Capture Text Area        When no delimiters are specified it           |
|                         creates a single cell table.  The text in     |
|                         the specified region is placed in that        |
|                         cell.                                          |
+-----------------------------------------------------------------------+
```

By splitting the cell appropriately we now have a table consisting of paragraphs occupying its own cell. Each cell can now be edited independently without affecting the layout of other cells.

```
+-----------------------------------------------------------------------+
|'table-capture' is a powerful command, but mastering its               |
|power requires some practice.  Here are some things it can do:          |
+--------------------+--------------------------------------------------+
|Parse Cell Items    |By using column delimiter regular                 |
|                    |expression and raw delimiter regular              |
|                    |expression, it parses the specified text          |
|                    |area and extracts cell items from                 |
|                    |non-table text and then forms a table out         |
|                    |of them.                                          |
+--------------------+--------------------------------------------------+
|Capture Text Area   |When no delimiters are specified it               |
|                    |creates a single cell table.  The text in         |
|                    |the specified region is placed in that            |
|                    |cell.                                             |
+--------------------+--------------------------------------------------+
```

By applying `table-release`, which does the opposite process, the contents become once again plain text. `table-release` works as a companion command to `table-capture`.

22.13.10 Analyzing Table Dimensions

The command `table-query-dimension` analyzes a table structure and reports information regarding its dimensions. In case of the above example table, the `table-query-dimension` command displays in echo area:

```
Cell: (21w, 6h), Table: (67w, 16h), Dim: (2c, 3r), Total Cells: 5
```

This indicates that the current cell is 21 character wide and 6 lines high, the entire table is 67 characters wide and 16 lines high. The table has 2 columns and 3 rows. It has a total of 5 cells, since the first row has a spanned cell.

22.13.11 Table Miscellany

The command `table-insert-sequence` inserts a string into each cell. Each string is a part of a sequence i.e. a series of increasing integer numbers.

The command `table-generate-source` generates a table formatted for a specific markup language. It asks for a language (which must be one of `html`, `latex`, or `cals`), a destination buffer where to put the result, and the table caption (a string), and then inserts the generated table in the proper syntax into the destination buffer. The default destination buffer is `table.lang`, where *lang* is the language you specified.

23 Editing Programs

Emacs provides many features to facilitate editing programs. Some of these features can

- Find or move over top-level definitions (see Section 23.2 [Defuns], page 251).
- Apply the usual indentation conventions of the language (see Section 23.3 [Program Indent], page 253).
- Balance parentheses (see Section 23.4 [Parentheses], page 257).
- Insert, kill or align comments (see Section 23.5 [Comments], page 260).
- Highlight program syntax (see Section 11.7 [Font Lock], page 76).

This chapter describes these features and many more.

23.1 Major Modes for Programming Languages

Emacs has specialized major modes for various programming languages. See Chapter 20 [Major Modes], page 207. A programming language major mode typically specifies the syntax of expressions, the customary rules for indentation, how to do syntax highlighting for the language, and how to find the beginning of a function definition. It often customizes or provides facilities for compiling and debugging programs as well.

Ideally, Emacs should provide a major mode for each programming language that you might want to edit; if it doesn't have a mode for your favorite language, you can contribute one. But often the mode for one language can serve for other syntactically similar languages. The major mode for language l is called l-mode, and you can select it by typing M-x l-mode RET. See Section 20.1 [Choosing Modes], page 207.

The existing programming language major modes include Lisp, Scheme (a variant of Lisp) and the Scheme-based DSSSL expression language, Ada, ASM, AWK, C, C++, Delphi (Object Pascal), Fortran (free format and fixed format), Icon, IDL (CORBA), IDLWAVE, Java, Metafont (TEX's companion for font creation), Modula2, Objective-C, Octave, Pascal, Perl, Pike, PostScript, Prolog, Python, Simula, Tcl, and VHDL. An alternative mode for Perl is called CPerl mode. Modes are available for the scripting languages of the common GNU and Unix shells, VMS DCL, and MS-DOS/MS-Windows 'BAT' files. There are also major modes for editing makefiles, DNS master files, and various sorts of configuration files.

In most programming languages, indentation should vary from line to line to illustrate the structure of the program. So the major modes for programming languages arrange for TAB to update the indentation of the current line. They also rebind DEL to treat a tab as if it were the equivalent number of spaces; this lets you delete one column of indentation without worrying whether the whitespace consists of spaces or tabs. Use C-b C-d to delete a tab character before point, in these modes.

Separate manuals are available for the modes for Ada (see section "Ada Mode" in *Ada Mode*), C/C++/Objective C/Java/Corba IDL/Pike/AWK (see section "CC

Mode" in *CC Mode*) and the IDLWAVE modes (see section "IDLWAVE" in *IDL-WAVE User Manual*). For Fortran mode, see section "Fortran" in *Specialized Emacs Features*.

Turning on a major mode runs a normal hook called the *mode hook*, which is the value of a Lisp variable. Each major mode has a mode hook, and the hook's name is always made from the mode command's name by adding '-hook'. For example, turning on C mode runs the hook `c-mode-hook`, while turning on Lisp mode runs the hook `lisp-mode-hook`. The purpose of the mode hook is to give you a place to set up customizations for that major mode. See Section 32.3.2 [Hooks], page 418.

23.2 Top-Level Definitions, or Defuns

In Emacs, a major definition at the top level in the buffer, something like a function, is called a *defun*. The name comes from Lisp, but in Emacs we use it for all languages.

23.2.1 Left Margin Convention

Emacs assumes by default that any opening delimiter found at the left margin is the start of a top-level definition, or defun. Therefore, **don't put an opening delimiter at the left margin unless it should have that significance**. For instance, never put an open-parenthesis at the left margin in a Lisp file unless it is the start of a top-level list.

If you don't follow this convention, not only will you have trouble when you explicitly use the commands for motion by defuns; other features that use them will also give you trouble. This includes the indentation commands (see Section 23.3 [Program Indent], page 253) and Font Lock mode (see Section 11.7 [Font Lock], page 76).

The most likely problem case is when you want an opening delimiter at the start of a line inside a string. To avoid trouble, put an escape character ('\', in C and Emacs Lisp, '/' in some other Lisp dialects) before the opening delimiter. This will not affect the contents of the string, but will prevent that opening delimiter from starting a defun. Here's an example:

```
    (insert "Foo:
 \(bar)
  ")
```

To help you catch violations of this convention, Font Lock mode highlights confusing opening delimiters (those that ought to be quoted) in bold red.

If you need to override this convention, you can so by setting this user option:

`open-paren-in-column-0-is-defun-start`   [Variable]
    If this user option is set to `t` (the default), opening parentheses or braces at column zero always start defuns. When it's `nil`, defuns are found by searching for parens or braces at the outermost level.

Usually, you shouldn't need to set `open-paren-in-column-0-is-defun-start` to `nil`. However, if your buffer contains parentheses or braces in column zero which don't start defuns and this confuses Emacs, it sometimes helps to set the option to `nil`. Be aware, though, that this will make scrolling and display in large buffers quite sluggish, and that parentheses and braces must be correctly matched throughout the buffer for it to work properly.

In the earliest days, the original Emacs found defuns by moving upward a level of parentheses or braces until there were no more levels to go up. This always required scanning all the way back to the beginning of the buffer, even for a small function. To speed up the operation, we changed Emacs to assume that any opening delimiter at the left margin is the start of a defun. This heuristic is nearly always right, and avoids the need to scan back to the beginning of the buffer. However, now that modern computers are so powerful, this scanning is rarely slow enough to annoy, so we've provided a way to disable the heuristic.

23.2.2 Moving by Defuns

These commands move point or set up the region based on top-level major definitions, also called *defuns*.

C-M-a   Move to beginning of current or preceding defun (`beginning-of-defun`).

C-M-e   Move to end of current or following defun (`end-of-defun`).

C-M-h   Put region around whole current or following defun (`mark-defun`).

The commands to move to the beginning and end of the current defun are `C-M-a` (`beginning-of-defun`) and `C-M-e` (`end-of-defun`). If you repeat one of these commands, or use a positive numeric argument, each repetition moves to the next defun in the direction of motion.

`C-M-a` with a negative argument $-n$ moves forward n times to the next beginning of a defun. This is not exactly the same place that `C-M-e` with argument n would move to; the end of this defun is not usually exactly the same place as the beginning of the following defun. (Whitespace, comments, and perhaps declarations can separate them.) Likewise, `C-M-e` with a negative argument moves back to an end of a defun, which is not quite the same as `C-M-a` with a positive argument.

To operate on the current defun, use `C-M-h` (`mark-defun`) which puts point at the beginning and mark at the end of the current defun. This is the easiest way to get ready to kill the defun in order to move it to a different place in the file. If you use the command while point is between defuns, it uses the following defun. Successive uses of `C-M-h`, or using it in Transient Mark mode when the mark is active, extends the end of the region to include one more defun each time.

In C mode, `C-M-h` runs the function `c-mark-function`, which is almost the same as `mark-defun`; the difference is that it backs up over the argument declarations, function name and returned data type so that the entire C function is inside the region. This is an example of how major modes adjust the standard key bindings so that they do their standard jobs in a way better fitting a particular language. Other major modes may replace any or all of these key bindings for that purpose.

23.2.3 Imenu

The Imenu facility offers a way to find the major definitions in a file by name. It is also useful in text formatter major modes, where it treats each chapter, section, etc., as a definition. (See Section 25.3 [Tags], page 293, for a more powerful feature that handles multiple files together.)

If you type M-x imenu, it reads the name of a definition using the minibuffer, then moves point to that definition. You can use completion to specify the name; the command always displays the whole list of valid names.

Alternatively, you can bind the command imenu to a mouse click. Then it displays mouse menus for you to select a definition name. You can also add the buffer's index to the menu bar by calling imenu-add-menubar-index. If you want to have this menu bar item available for all buffers in a certain major mode, you can do this by adding imenu-add-menubar-index to its mode hook. But if you have done that, you will have to wait a little while each time you visit a file in that mode, while Emacs finds all the definitions in that buffer.

When you change the contents of a buffer, if you add or delete definitions, you can update the buffer's index based on the new contents by invoking the '*Rescan*' item in the menu. Rescanning happens automatically if you set imenu-auto-rescan to a non-nil value. There is no need to rescan because of small changes in the text.

You can customize the way the menus are sorted by setting the variable imenu-sort-function. By default, names are ordered as they occur in the buffer; if you want alphabetic sorting, use the symbol imenu--sort-by-name as the value. You can also define your own comparison function by writing Lisp code.

Imenu provides the information to guide Which Function mode (see below). The Speedbar can also use it (see Section 18.7 [Speedbar], page 178).

23.2.4 Which Function Mode

Which Function mode is a minor mode that displays the current function name in the mode line, updating it as you move around in a buffer.

To either enable or disable Which Function mode, use the command M-x which-function-mode. This command is global; it applies to all buffers, both existing ones and those yet to be created. However, it takes effect only in certain major modes, those listed in the value of which-func-modes. If the value is t, then Which Function mode applies to all major modes that know how to support it—in other words, all the major modes that support Imenu.

23.3 Indentation for Programs

The best way to keep a program properly indented is to use Emacs to reindent it as you change it. Emacs has commands to indent properly either a single line, a specified number of lines, or all of the lines inside a single parenthetical grouping.

Emacs also provides a Lisp pretty-printer in the library pp. This program reformats a Lisp object with indentation chosen to look nice.

23.3.1 Basic Program Indentation Commands

The basic indentation commands indent a single line according to the usual conventions of the language you are editing.

TAB   Adjust indentation of current line.

C-j   Insert a newline, then adjust indentation of following line (newline-and-indent).

The basic indentation command is TAB, which gives the current line the correct indentation as determined from the previous lines. The function that TAB runs depends on the major mode; it is lisp-indent-line in Lisp mode, c-indent-command in C mode, etc. These functions understand the syntax and conventions of different languages, but they all do conceptually the same job: TAB in any programming-language major mode inserts or deletes whitespace at the beginning of the current line, independent of where point is in the line. If point was inside the whitespace at the beginning of the line, TAB puts it at the end of that whitespace; otherwise, TAB keeps point fixed with respect to the characters around it.

Use C-q TAB to insert a tab character at point.

When entering lines of new code, use C-j (newline-and-indent), which inserts a newline and then adjusts indentation after it. (It also deletes any trailing whitespace which remains before the new newline.) Thus, C-j at the end of a line creates a blank line with appropriate indentation. In programming language modes, it is equivalent to RET TAB.

TAB indents a line that starts within a parenthetical grouping under the preceding line within the grouping, or the text after the parenthesis. Therefore, if you manually give one of these lines a nonstandard indentation, the lines below will tend to follow it. This behavior is convenient in cases where you have overridden the standard result of TAB because you find it unaesthetic for a particular line.

In some modes, an open-parenthesis, open-brace or other opening delimiter at the left margin is assumed by Emacs (including the indentation routines) to be the start of a function. This speeds up indentation commands. If you will be editing text which contains opening delimiters in column zero that aren't the beginning of a functions, even inside strings or comments, you must set open-paren-in-column-0-is-defun-start. See Section 23.2.1 [Left Margin Paren], page 251, for more information on this.

Normally, lines are indented with tabs and spaces. If you want Emacs to use spaces only, set indent-tabs-mode (see Section 21.3 [Just Spaces], page 212).

23.3.2 Indenting Several Lines

When you wish to reindent several lines of code which have been altered or moved to a different level in the parenthesis structure, you have several commands available.

C-M-q   Reindent all the lines within one parenthetical grouping (indent-pp-sexp).

C-M-\   Reindent all lines in the region (indent-region).

C-u TAB   Shift an entire parenthetical grouping rigidly sideways so that its first
            line is properly indented.

M-x indent-code-rigidly
            Shift all the lines in the region rigidly sideways, but do not alter lines
            that start inside comments and strings.

You can reindent the contents of a single parenthetical grouping by positioning
point before the beginning of it and typing C-M-q (indent-pp-sexp in Lisp mode,
c-indent-exp in C mode; also bound to other suitable commands in other modes).
The indentation of the line where the grouping starts is not changed; therefore this
changes only the relative indentation within the grouping, not its overall indentation. To correct that as well, type TAB first.

Another way to specify the range to be reindented is with the region. The
command C-M-\ (indent-region) applies TAB to every line whose first character
is between point and mark.

If you like the relative indentation within a grouping, but not the indentation
of its first line, you can type C-u TAB to reindent the whole grouping as a rigid
unit. (This works in Lisp modes and C and related modes.) TAB with a numeric
argument reindents the current line as usual, then reindents by the same amount
all the lines in the parenthetical grouping starting on the current line. It is clever,
though, and does not alter lines that start inside strings. Neither does it alter C
preprocessor lines when in C mode, but it does reindent any continuation lines that
may be attached to them.

You can also perform this operation on the region, using the command M-x
indent-code-rigidly. It rigidly shifts all the lines in the region sideways, like
indent-rigidly does (see Section 21.1 [Indentation Commands], page 211). It
doesn't alter the indentation of lines that start inside a string, unless the region
also starts inside that string. The prefix arg specifies the number of columns to
indent.

23.3.3 Customizing Lisp Indentation

The indentation pattern for a Lisp expression can depend on the function called by
the expression. For each Lisp function, you can choose among several predefined
patterns of indentation, or define an arbitrary one with a Lisp program.

The standard pattern of indentation is as follows: the second line of the expression is indented under the first argument, if that is on the same line as the beginning
of the expression; otherwise, the second line is indented underneath the function
name. Each following line is indented under the previous line whose nesting depth
is the same.

If the variable lisp-indent-offset is non-nil, it overrides the usual indentation pattern for the second line of an expression, so that such lines are always
indented lisp-indent-offset more columns than the containing list.

Certain functions override the standard pattern. Functions whose names start
with def treat the second lines as the start of a *body*, by indenting the second line

`lisp-body-indent` additional columns beyond the open-parenthesis that starts the expression.

You can override the standard pattern in various ways for individual functions, according to the `lisp-indent-function` property of the function name. Normally you would use this for macro definitions and specify it using the `declare` construct (see section "Defining Macros" in *the Emacs Lisp Reference Manual*).

23.3.4 Commands for C Indentation

Here are special features for indentation in C mode and related modes:

C-c C-q
: Reindent the current top-level function definition or aggregate type declaration (`c-indent-defun`).

C-M-q
: Reindent each line in the balanced expression that follows point (`c-indent-exp`). A prefix argument inhibits warning messages about invalid syntax.

TAB
: Reindent the current line, and/or in some cases insert a tab character (`c-indent-command`).

> If `c-tab-always-indent` is `t`, this command always reindents the current line and does nothing else. This is the default.
>
> If that variable is `nil`, this command reindents the current line only if point is at the left margin or in the line's indentation; otherwise, it inserts a tab (or the equivalent number of spaces, if `indent-tabs-mode` is `nil`).
>
> Any other value (not `nil` or `t`) means always reindent the line, and also insert a tab if within a comment or a string.

To reindent the whole current buffer, type `C-x h C-M-\`. This first selects the whole buffer as the region, then reindents that region.

To reindent the current block, use `C-M-u C-M-q`. This moves to the front of the block and then reindents it all.

23.3.5 Customizing C Indentation

C mode and related modes use a flexible mechanism for customizing indentation. C mode indents a source line in two steps: first it classifies the line syntactically according to its contents and context; second, it determines the indentation offset associated by your selected *style* with the syntactic construct and adds this onto the indentation of the *anchor statement*.

C-c . RET *style* RET
: Select a predefined style *style* (`c-set-style`).

A *style* is a named collection of customizations that can be used in C mode and the related modes. section "Styles" in *The CC Mode Manual*, for a complete description. Emacs comes with several predefined styles, including **gnu**, **k&r**, **bsd**, **stroustrup**, **linux**, **python**, **java**, **whitesmith**, **ellemtel**, and **awk**. Some of these styles are primarily intended for one language, but any of them can be used with any of the languages supported by these modes. To find out what a style looks like, select it and reindent some code, e.g., by typing C-M-Q at the start of a function definition.

To choose a style for the current buffer, use the command C-c .. Specify a style name as an argument (case is not significant). This command affects the current buffer only, and it affects only future invocations of the indentation commands; it does not reindent the code already in the buffer. To reindent the whole buffer in the new style, you can type C-x h C-M-\.

You can also set the variable c-default-style to specify the default style for various major modes. Its value should be either the style's name (a string) or an alist, in which each element specifies one major mode and which indentation style to use for it. For example,

```
(setq c-default-style
       '((java-mode . "java") (awk-mode . "awk") (other . "gnu")))
```

specifies explicit choices for Java and AWK modes, and the default 'gnu' style for the other C-like modes. (These settings are actually the defaults.) This variable takes effect when you select one of the C-like major modes; thus, if you specify a new default style for Java mode, you can make it take effect in an existing Java mode buffer by typing M-x java-mode there.

The gnu style specifies the formatting recommended by the GNU Project for C; it is the default, so as to encourage use of our recommended style.

See section "Indentation Engine Basics" in *the CC Mode Manual*, and section "Customizing Indentation" in *the CC Mode Manual*, for more information on customizing indentation for C and related modes, including how to override parts of an existing style and how to define your own styles.

23.4 Commands for Editing with Parentheses

This section describes the commands and features that take advantage of the parenthesis structure in a program, or help you keep it balanced.

When talking about these facilities, the term "parenthesis" also includes braces, brackets, or whatever delimiters are defined to match in pairs. The major mode controls which delimiters are significant, through the syntax table (see Section 32.5 [Syntax], page 433). In Lisp, only parentheses count; in C, these commands apply to braces and brackets too.

You can use M-x check-parens to find any unbalanced parentheses and unbalanced string quotes in the buffer.

23.4.1 Expressions with Balanced Parentheses

These commands deal with balanced expressions, also called *sexps*[1].

C-M-f   Move forward over a balanced expression (forward-sexp).

C-M-b   Move backward over a balanced expression (backward-sexp).

---

[1] The word "sexp" is used to refer to an expression in Lisp.

C-M-k   Kill balanced expression forward (`kill-sexp`).

C-M-t   Transpose expressions (`transpose-sexps`).

C-M-@
C-M-SPC   Put mark after following expression (`mark-sexp`).

Each programming language major mode customizes the definition of balanced expressions to suit that language. Balanced expressions typically include symbols, numbers, and string constants, as well as any pair of matching delimiters and their contents. Some languages have obscure forms of expression syntax that nobody has bothered to implement in Emacs.

By convention, the keys for these commands are all Control-Meta characters. They usually act on expressions just as the corresponding Meta characters act on words. For instance, the command C-M-b moves backward over a balanced expression, just as M-b moves back over a word.

To move forward over a balanced expression, use C-M-f (`forward-sexp`). If the first significant character after point is an opening delimiter ('(' in Lisp; '(', '[' or '{' in C), C-M-f moves past the matching closing delimiter. If the character begins a symbol, string, or number, C-M-f moves over that.

The command C-M-b (`backward-sexp`) moves backward over a balanced expression. The detailed rules are like those above for C-M-f, but with directions reversed. If there are prefix characters (single-quote, backquote and comma, in Lisp) preceding the expression, C-M-b moves back over them as well. The balanced expression commands move across comments as if they were whitespace, in most modes.

C-M-f or C-M-b with an argument repeats that operation the specified number of times; with a negative argument, it moves in the opposite direction.

Killing a whole balanced expression can be done with C-M-k (`kill-sexp`). C-M-k kills the characters that C-M-f would move over.

A somewhat random-sounding command which is nevertheless handy is C-M-t (`transpose-sexps`), which drags the previous balanced expression across the next one. An argument serves as a repeat count, moving the previous expression over that many following ones. A negative argument drags the previous balanced expression backwards across those before it (thus canceling out the effect of C-M-t with a positive argument). An argument of zero, rather than doing nothing, transposes the balanced expressions ending at or after point and the mark.

To set the region around the next balanced expression in the buffer, use C-M-@ (`mark-sexp`), which sets mark at the same place that C-M-f would move to. C-M-@ takes arguments like C-M-f. In particular, a negative argument is useful for putting the mark at the beginning of the previous balanced expression. The alias C-M-SPC is equivalent to C-M-@. When you repeat this command, or use it in Transient Mark mode when the mark is active, it extends the end of the region by one sexp each time.

In languages that use infix operators, such as C, it is not possible to recognize all balanced expressions as such because there can be multiple possibilities at a given position. For example, C mode does not treat 'foo + bar' as a single expression, even though it *is* one C expression; instead, it recognizes 'foo' as one expression and 'bar' as another, with the '+' as punctuation between them. Both 'foo + bar' and 'foo' are legitimate choices for "the expression following point" when point is at the 'f', so the expression commands must perforce choose one or the other to operate on. Note that '(foo + bar)' is recognized as a single expression in C mode, because of the parentheses.

23.4.2 Moving in the Parenthesis Structure

The Emacs commands for handling parenthetical groupings see nothing except parentheses (or whatever characters must balance in the language you are working with), and the escape characters that might be used to quote those. They are mainly intended for editing programs, but can be useful for editing any text that has parentheses. They are sometimes called "list" commands because in Lisp these groupings are lists.

C-M-n   Move forward over a parenthetical group (forward-list).

C-M-p   Move backward over a parenthetical group (backward-list).

C-M-u   Move up in parenthesis structure (backward-up-list).

C-M-d   Move down in parenthesis structure (down-list).

The "list" commands C-M-n (forward-list) and C-M-p (backward-list) move over one (or n) parenthetical groupings, skipping blithely over any amount of text that doesn't include meaningful parentheses (symbols, strings, etc.).

C-M-n and C-M-p try to stay at the same level in the parenthesis structure. To move *up* one (or n) levels, use C-M-u (backward-up-list). C-M-u moves backward up past one unmatched opening delimiter. A positive argument serves as a repeat count; a negative argument reverses the direction of motion, so that the command moves forward and up one or more levels.

To move *down* in the parenthesis structure, use C-M-d (down-list). In Lisp mode, where '(' is the only opening delimiter, this is nearly the same as searching for a '('. An argument specifies the number of levels to go down.

23.4.3 Automatic Display Of Matching Parentheses

The Emacs parenthesis-matching feature is designed to show automatically how parentheses (and other matching delimiters) match in the text. Whenever you type a self-inserting character that is a closing delimiter, the cursor moves momentarily to the location of the matching opening delimiter, provided that is on the screen. If it is not on the screen, Emacs displays some of the text near it in the echo area. Either way, you can tell which grouping you are closing off.

If the opening delimiter and closing delimiter are mismatched—such as in '[x)'— a warning message is displayed in the echo area.

Three variables control parenthesis match display:

blink-matching-paren turns the feature on or off: nil disables it, but the default is t to enable match display.

`blink-matching-delay` says how many seconds to leave the cursor on the matching opening delimiter, before bringing it back to the real location of point; the default is 1, but on some systems it is useful to specify a fraction of a second.

`blink-matching-paren-distance` specifies how many characters back to search to find the matching opening delimiter. If the match is not found in that distance, scanning stops, and nothing is displayed. This is to prevent the scan for the matching delimiter from wasting lots of time when there is no match. The default is 25600.

Show Paren mode provides a more powerful kind of automatic matching. Whenever point is after a closing delimiter, that delimiter and its matching opening delimiter are both highlighted; otherwise, if point is before an opening delimiter, the matching closing delimiter is highlighted. (There is no need to highlight the opening delimiter in that case, because the cursor appears on top of that character.) Use the command `M-x show-paren-mode` to enable or disable this mode.

Show Paren mode uses the faces `show-paren-match` and `show-paren-mismatch` to highlight parentheses; you can customize them to control how highlighting looks. See Section 32.2.5 [Face Customization], page 413.

23.5 Manipulating Comments

Because comments are such an important part of programming, Emacs provides special commands for editing and inserting comments. It can also do spell checking on comments with Flyspell Prog mode (see Section 13.5 [Spelling], page 108).

23.5.1 Comment Commands

The comment commands in this table insert, kill and align comments. They are described in this section and following sections.

`M-;`   Insert or realign comment on current line; alternatively, comment or uncomment the region (`comment-dwim`).

`C-u M-;`   Kill comment on current line (`comment-kill`).

`C-x ;`   Set comment column (`comment-set-column`).

`C-M-j`
`M-j`   Like RET followed by inserting and aligning a comment (`comment-indent-new-line`). See Section 23.5.2 [Multi-Line Comments], page 262.

`M-x comment-region`
`C-c C-c` (in C-like modes)
             Add or remove comment delimiters on all the lines in the region.

The command to create or align a comment is `M-;` (`comment-dwim`). The word "dwim" is an acronym for "Do What I Mean"; it indicates that this command can be used for many different jobs relating to comments, depending on the situation where you use it.

If there is no comment already on the line, M-; inserts a new comment, aligned at a specific column called the *comment column*. The new comment begins with the string Emacs thinks comments should start with (the value of comment-start; see below). Point is after that string, so you can insert the text of the comment right away. If the major mode has specified a string to terminate comments, M-; inserts that after point, to keep the syntax valid.

If the text of the line extends past the comment column, this command aligns the comment start string to a suitable boundary (usually, at least one space is inserted).

You can also use M-; to align an existing comment. If a line already contains the comment-start string, M-; realigns it to the conventional alignment and moves point after it. (Exception: comments starting in column 0 are not moved.) Even when an existing comment is properly aligned, M-; is still useful for moving directly to the start of the text inside the comment.

C-u M-; kills any comment on the current line, along with the whitespace before it. To reinsert the comment on another line, move to the end of that line, do C-y, and then do M-; to realign it.

Note that C-u M-; is not a distinct key; it is M-; (comment-dwim) with a prefix argument. That command is programmed so that when it receives a prefix argument it calls comment-kill. However, comment-kill is a valid command in its own right, and you can bind it directly to a key if you wish.

M-; does two other jobs when used with an active region in Transient Mark mode (see Section 8.2 [Transient Mark], page 50). Then it either adds or removes comment delimiters on each line of the region. (If every line is a comment, it removes comment delimiters from each; otherwise, it adds comment delimiters to each.) If you are not using Transient Mark mode, then you should use the commands comment-region and uncomment-region to do these jobs (see Section 23.5.2 [Multi-Line Comments], page 262), or else enable Transient Mark mode momentarily (see Section 8.3 [Momentary Mark], page 52). A prefix argument used in these circumstances specifies how many comment delimiters to add or how many to delete.

Some major modes have special rules for aligning certain kinds of comments in certain contexts. For example, in Lisp code, comments which start with two semicolons are indented as if they were lines of code, instead of at the comment column. Comments which start with three semicolons are supposed to start at the left margin and are often used for sectioning purposes. Emacs understands these conventions by indenting a double-semicolon comment using TAB, and by not changing the indentation of a triple-semicolon comment at all.

```
;; This function is just an example.
;;; Here either two or three semicolons are appropriate.
(defun foo (x)
;;;  And now, the first part of the function:
  ;; The following line adds one.
  (1+ x))              ; This line adds one.
```

For C-like modes, you can configure the exact effect of M-; more flexibly than for most buffers by setting the variables c-indent-comment-alist and c-indent-

comments-syntactically-p. For example, on a line ending in a closing brace, M-;
puts the comment one space after the brace rather than at comment-column. For
full details see section "Comment Commands" in *The CC Mode Manual*.

23.5.2 Multiple Lines of Comments

If you are typing a comment and wish to continue it on another line, you can use
the command C-M-j or M-j (comment-indent-new-line). If comment-multi-line
(see Section 23.5.3 [Options for Comments], page 262) is non-nil, it moves to a
new line within the comment. Otherwise it closes the comment and starts a new
comment on a new line. When Auto Fill mode is on, going past the fill column
while typing a comment causes the comment to be continued in just this fashion.

To turn existing lines into comment lines, use the M-x comment-region command (or type C-c C-c in C-like modes). It adds comment delimiters to the lines
that start in the region, thus commenting them out. With a negative argument, it
does the opposite—it deletes comment delimiters from the lines in the region.

With a positive argument, comment-region duplicates the last character of the
comment start sequence it adds; the argument specifies how many copies of the
character to insert. Thus, in Lisp mode, C-u 2 M-x comment-region adds ';;' to
each line. Duplicating the comment delimiter is a way of calling attention to the
comment. It can also affect how the comment is aligned or indented. In Lisp, for
proper indentation, you should use an argument of two or three, if between defuns;
if within a defun, it must be three.

You can configure C Mode such that when you type a '/' at the start of a line in
a multi-line block comment, this closes the comment. Enable the comment-close-
slash clean-up for this. See section "Clean-ups" in *The CC Mode Manual*.

23.5.3 Options Controlling Comments

The *comment column*, the column at which Emacs tries to place comments, is stored
in the variable comment-column. You can set it to a number explicitly. Alternatively, the command C-x ; (comment-set-column) sets the comment column to the
column point is at. C-u C-x ; sets the comment column to match the last comment
before point in the buffer, and then does a M-; to align the current line's comment
under the previous one.

The variable comment-column is per-buffer: setting the variable in the normal
fashion affects only the current buffer, but there is a default value which you can
change with setq-default. See Section 32.3.3 [Locals], page 419. Many major
modes initialize this variable for the current buffer.

The comment commands recognize comments based on the regular expression
that is the value of the variable comment-start-skip. Make sure this regexp does
not match the null string. It may match more than the comment starting delimiter
in the strictest sense of the word; for example, in C mode the value of the variable
is "/*+ *\\|//+ *", which matches extra stars and spaces after the '/*' itself,
and accepts C++ style comments also. (Note that '\\' is needed in Lisp syntax to
include a '\' in the string, which is needed to deny the first star its special meaning
in regexp syntax. See Section 12.6 [Regexp Backslash], page 95.)

When a comment command makes a new comment, it inserts the value of `comment-start` to begin it. The value of `comment-end` is inserted after point, so that it will follow the text that you will insert into the comment. When `comment-end` is non-empty, it should start with a space. For example, in C mode, `comment-start` has the value `"/* "` and `comment-end` has the value `" */"`.

The variable `comment-padding` specifies how many spaces `comment-region` should insert on each line between the comment delimiter and the line's original text. The default is 1, to insert one space. `nil` means 0. Alternatively, `comment-padding` can hold the actual string to insert.

The variable `comment-multi-line` controls how C-M-j (`indent-new-comment-line`) behaves when used inside a comment. Specifically, when `comment-multi-line` is `nil`, the command inserts a comment terminator, begins a new line, and finally inserts a comment starter. Otherwise it does not insert the terminator and starter, so it effectively continues the current comment across multiple lines. In languages that allow multi-line comments, the choice of value for this variable is a matter of taste. The default for this variable depends on the major mode.

The variable `comment-indent-function` should contain a function that will be called to compute the alignment for a newly inserted comment or for aligning an existing comment. It is set differently by various major modes. The function is called with no arguments, but with point at the beginning of the comment, or at the end of a line if a new comment is to be inserted. It should return the column in which the comment ought to start. For example, in Lisp mode, the indent hook function bases its decision on how many semicolons begin an existing comment, and on the code in the preceding lines.

23.6 Documentation Lookup

Emacs provides several features you can use to look up the documentation of functions, variables and commands that you plan to use in your program.

23.6.1 Info Documentation Lookup

For many major modes, that apply to languages that have documentation in Info, you can use C-h S (`info-lookup-symbol`) to view the Info documentation for a symbol used in the program. You specify the symbol with the minibuffer; the default is the symbol appearing in the buffer at point. For example, in C mode this looks for the symbol in the C Library Manual. The command only works if the appropriate manual's Info files are installed.

The major mode determines where to look for documentation for the symbol— which Info files to look in, and which indices to search. You can also use M-x `info-lookup-file` to look for documentation for a file name.

If you use C-h S in a major mode that does not support it, it asks you to specify the "symbol help mode." You should enter a command such as `c-mode` that would select a major mode which C-h S does support.

23.6.2 Man Page Lookup

On Unix, the main form of on-line documentation was the *manual page* or *man page*. In the GNU operating system, we aim to replace man pages with better-organized manuals that you can browse with Info (see Section 7.7 [Misc Help], page 47). This process is not finished, so it is still useful to read manual pages.

You can read the man page for an operating system command, library function, or system call, with the M-x man command. It runs the man program to format the man page; if the system permits, it runs man asynchronously, so that you can keep on editing while the page is being formatted. (On MS-DOS and MS-Windows 3, you cannot edit while Emacs waits for man to finish.) The result goes in a buffer named '*Man *topic**'. These buffers use a special major mode, Man mode, that facilitates scrolling and jumping to other manual pages. For details, type C-h m while in a man page buffer.

Each man page belongs to one of ten or more *sections*, each named by a digit or by a digit and a letter. Sometimes there are multiple man pages with the same name in different sections. To read a man page from a specific section, type '*topic*(*section*)' or '*section* *topic*' when M-x manual-entry prompts for the topic. For example, to read the man page for the C library function chmod (as opposed to a command of the same name), type M-x manual-entry RET chmod(2) RET. (chmod is a system call, so it is in section '2'.)

If you do not specify a section, the results depend on how the man program works on your system. Some of them display only the first man page they find. Others display all man pages that have the specified name, so you can move between them with the M-n and M-p keys[2]. The mode line shows how many manual pages are present in the Man buffer.

By default, Emacs highlights the text in man pages. For a long man page, highlighting can take substantial time. You can turn off highlighting of man pages by setting the variable Man-fontify-manpage-flag to nil.

If you insert the text of a man page into an Emacs buffer in some other fashion, you can use the command M-x Man-fontify-manpage to perform the same conversions that M-x manual-entry does.

An alternative way of reading manual pages is the M-x woman command[3]. Unlike M-x man, it does not run any external programs to format and display the man pages; instead it does the job in Emacs Lisp, so it works on systems such as MS-Windows, where the man program (and other programs it uses) are not generally available.

M-x woman prompts for a name of a manual page, and provides completion based on the list of manual pages that are installed on your machine; the list of available manual pages is computed automatically the first time you invoke woman. The word

---

[2] On some systems, the man program accepts a '-a' command-line option which tells it to display all the man pages for the specified topic. If you want this behavior, you can add this option to the value of the variable Man-switches.

[3] The name of the command, woman, is an acronym for "w/o (without) man," since it doesn't use the man program.

at point in the current buffer is used to suggest the default for the name the manual page.

With a numeric argument, M-x woman recomputes the list of the manual pages used for completion. This is useful if you add or delete manual pages.

If you type a name of a manual page and M-x woman finds that several manual pages by the same name exist in different sections, it pops up a window with possible candidates asking you to choose one of them.

For more information about setting up and using M-x woman, see section "Browse UN*X Manual Pages WithOut Man" in *The WoMan Manual*.

23.6.3 Emacs Lisp Documentation Lookup

As you edit Lisp code to be run in Emacs, you can use the commands C-h f (describe-function) and C-h v (describe-variable) to view documentation of functions and variables that you want to use. These commands use the minibuffer to read the name of a function or variable to document, and display the documentation in a window. Their default arguments are based on the code in the neighborhood of point. For C-h f, the default is the function called in the innermost list containing point. C-h v uses the symbol name around or adjacent to point as its default.

A more automatic but less powerful method is Eldoc mode. This minor mode constantly displays in the echo area the argument list for the function being called at point. (In other words, it finds the function call that point is contained in, and displays the argument list of that function.) If point is over a documented variable, it shows the first line of the variable's docstring. Eldoc mode applies in Emacs Lisp and Lisp Interaction modes, and perhaps a few others that provide special support for looking up doc strings. Use the command M-x eldoc-mode to enable or disable this feature.

23.7 Hideshow minor mode

Hideshow minor mode provides selective display of portions of a program, known as *blocks*. You can use M-x hs-minor-mode to enable or disable this mode, or add hs-minor-mode to the mode hook for certain major modes in order to enable it automatically for those modes.

Just what constitutes a block depends on the major mode. In C mode or C++ mode, they are delimited by braces, while in Lisp mode and similar modes they are delimited by parentheses. Multi-line comments also count as blocks.

C-c @ C-h   Hide the current block (hs-hide-block).

C-c @ C-s   Show the current block (hs-show-block).

C-c @ C-c   Either hide or show the current block (hs-toggle-hiding).

S-Mouse-2   Either hide or show the block you click on (hs-mouse-toggle-hiding).

C-c @ C-M-h
              Hide all top-level blocks (hs-hide-all).

`C-c @ C-M-s`
> Show everything in the buffer (`hs-show-all`).

`C-c @ C-l`   Hide all blocks *n* levels below this block (`hs-hide-level`).

These variables exist for customizing Hideshow mode.

`hs-hide-comments-when-hiding-all`
> Non-`nil` says that `hs-hide-all` should hide comments too.

`hs-isearch-open`
> Specifies what kind of hidden blocks incremental search should make visible. The value should be one of these four symbols:
>
> `code`   Open only code blocks.
>
> `comment`   Open only comments.
>
> `t`   Open both code blocks and comments.
>
> `nil`   Open neither code blocks nor comments.

`hs-special-modes-alist`
> A list of elements, each specifying how to initialize Hideshow variables for one major mode. See the variable's documentation string for more information.

23.8 Completion for Symbol Names

In Emacs, completion is something you normally do in the minibuffer. But one kind of completion is available in all buffers: completion for symbol names.

The character `M-TAB` runs a command to complete the partial symbol before point against the set of meaningful symbol names. This command inserts at point any additional characters that it can determine from the partial name.

If your window manager defines `M-TAB` to switch windows, you can type `ESC TAB` or `C-M-i` instead. However, most window managers let you customize these shortcuts, and we recommend that you change any that get in the way of use of Emacs.

If the partial name in the buffer has multiple possible completions that differ in the very next character, so that it is impossible to complete even one more character, `M-TAB` displays a list of all possible completions in another window.

In most programming language major modes, `M-TAB` runs the command `complete-symbol`, which provides two kinds of completion. Normally it does completion based on a tags table (see Section 25.3 [Tags], page 293); with a numeric argument (regardless of the value), it does completion based on the names listed in the Info file indexes for your language. Thus, to complete the name of a symbol defined in your own program, use `M-TAB` with no argument; to complete the name of a standard library function, use `C-u M-TAB`. Of course, Info-based completion works only if there is an Info file for the standard library functions of your language, and only if it is installed at your site.

In Emacs-Lisp mode, the name space for completion normally consists of non-trivial symbols present in Emacs—those that have function definitions, values or properties. However, if there is an open-parenthesis immediately before the beginning of the partial symbol, only symbols with function definitions are considered as completions. The command which implements this is `lisp-complete-symbol`.

In Text mode and related modes, M-TAB completes words based on the spell-checker's dictionary. See Section 13.5 [Spelling], page 108.

23.9 Glasses minor mode

Glasses minor mode makes 'unreadableIdentifiersLikeThis' readable by altering the way they display. It knows two different ways to do this: by displaying underscores between a lower-case letter and the following capital letter, and by emboldening the capital letters. It does not alter the buffer text, only the way they display, so you can use it even on read-only buffers. You can use the command M-x glasses-mode to enable or disable the mode in the current buffer; you can also add glasses mode to the mode hook of the programming language major modes in which you normally want to use Glasses mode.

23.10 Other Features Useful for Editing Programs

A number of Emacs commands that aren't designed specifically for editing programs are useful for that nonetheless.

The Emacs commands that operate on words, sentences and paragraphs are useful for editing code. Most symbols names contain words (see Section 22.1 [Words], page 213); sentences can be found in strings and comments (see Section 22.2 [Sentences], page 214). Paragraphs in the strict sense can be found in program code (in long comments), but the paragraph commands are useful in other places too, because programming language major modes define paragraphs to begin and end at blank lines (see Section 22.3 [Paragraphs], page 215). Judicious use of blank lines to make the program clearer will also provide useful chunks of text for the paragraph commands to work on. Auto Fill mode, if enabled in a programming language major mode, indents the new lines which it creates.

The selective display feature is useful for looking at the overall structure of a function (see Section 11.12 [Selective Display], page 80). This feature hides the lines that are indented more than a specified amount. Programming modes often support Outline minor mode (see Section 22.8 [Outline Mode], page 224). The Foldout package provides folding-editor features (see Section 22.8.5 [Foldout], page 228).

The "automatic typing" features may be useful for writing programs. See section "Autotyping" in *Autotyping*.

23.11 C and Related Modes

This section gives a brief description of the special features available in C, C++, Objective-C, Java, CORBA IDL, Pike and AWK modes. (These are called "C mode and related modes.") See section "CC Mode" in *CC Mode*, for a more extensive description of these modes and their special features.

23.11.1 C Mode Motion Commands

This section describes commands for moving point, in C mode and related modes.

`M-x c-beginning-of-defun`
`M-x c-end-of-defun`

> Move point to the beginning or end of the current function or top-level definition. These are found by searching for the least enclosing braces. (By contrast, `beginning-of-defun` and `end-of-defun` search for braces in column zero.) If you are editing code where the opening brace of a function isn't placed in column zero, you may wish to bind `C-M-a` and `C-M-e` to these commands. See Section 23.2.2 [Moving by Defuns], page 252.

`C-c C-u`

> Move point back to the containing preprocessor conditional, leaving the mark behind. A prefix argument acts as a repeat count. With a negative argument, move point forward to the end of the containing preprocessor conditional.
>
> '#elif' is equivalent to '#else' followed by '#if', so the function will stop at a '#elif' when going backward, but not when going forward.

`C-c C-p`

> Move point back over a preprocessor conditional, leaving the mark behind. A prefix argument acts as a repeat count. With a negative argument, move forward.

`C-c C-n`

> Move point forward across a preprocessor conditional, leaving the mark behind. A prefix argument acts as a repeat count. With a negative argument, move backward.

`M-a`

> Move point to the beginning of the innermost C statement (`c-beginning-of-statement`). If point is already at the beginning of a statement, move to the beginning of the preceding statement. With prefix argument *n*, move back *n* − 1 statements.
>
> In comments or in strings which span more than one line, this command moves by sentences instead of statements.

`M-e`

> Move point to the end of the innermost C statement or sentence; like `M-a` except that it moves in the other direction (`c-end-of-statement`).

23.11.2 Electric C Characters

In C mode and related modes, certain printing characters are *electric*—in addition to inserting themselves, they also reindent the current line, and optionally also insert newlines. The "electric" characters are {, }, :, #, ;, ,, <, >, /, *, (, and).

You might find electric indentation inconvenient if you are editing chaotically indented code. If you are new to CC Mode, you might find it disconcerting. You can toggle electric action with the command C-c C-l; when it is enabled, '/l' appears in the mode line after the mode name:

C-c C-l   Toggle electric action (c-toggle-electric-state). With a prefix argument, this command enables electric action if the argument is positive, disables it if it is negative.

Electric characters insert newlines only when, in addition to the electric state, the *auto-newline* feature is enabled (indicated by '/la' in the mode line after the mode name). You can turn this feature on or off with the command C-c C-a:

C-c C-a   Toggle the auto-newline feature (c-toggle-auto-newline). With a prefix argument, this command turns the auto-newline feature on if the argument is positive, and off if it is negative.

Usually the CC Mode style configures the exact circumstances in which Emacs inserts auto-newlines. You can also configure this directly. See section "Custom Auto-newlines" in *The CC Mode Manual*.

23.11.3 Hungry Delete Feature in C

If you want to delete an entire block of whitespace at point, you can use *hungry deletion*. This deletes all the contiguous whitespace either before point or after point in a single operation. *Whitespace* here includes tabs and newlines, but not comments or preprocessor commands.

C-c C-DEL
C-c DEL   c-hungry-delete-backwards—Delete the entire block of whitespace preceding point.

C-c C-d
C-c C-DELETE
C-c DELETE c-hungry-delete-forward—Delete the entire block of whitespace following point.

As an alternative to the above commands, you can enable *hungry delete mode*. When this feature is enabled (indicated by '/h' in the mode line after the mode name), a single DEL deletes all preceding whitespace, not just one space, and a single C-c C-d (but *not* plain DELETE) deletes all following whitespace.

M-x c-toggle-hungry-state
            Toggle the hungry-delete feature (c-toggle-hungry-state)[4]. With a prefix argument, this command turns the hungry-delete feature on if the argument is positive, and off if it is negative.

The variable c-hungry-delete-key controls whether the hungry-delete feature is enabled.

---

[4] This command had the binding C-c C-d in earlier versions of Emacs. C-c C-d is now bound to c-hungry-delete-forward.

23.11.4 Other Commands for C Mode

```
C-c C-w
M-x c-subword-mode
```
> Enable (or disable) *subword mode*. In subword mode, Emacs's word commands recognize upper case letters in 'StudlyCapsIdentifiers' as word boundaries. This is indicated by the flag '/w' on the mode line after the mode name (e.g. 'C/law'). You can even use M-x c-subword-mode in non-CC Mode buffers.
>
> In the GNU project, we recommend using underscores to separate words within an identifier in C or C++, rather than using case distinctions.

`M-x c-context-line-break`
> This command inserts a line break and indents the new line in a manner appropriate to the context. In normal code, it does the work of C-j (newline-and-indent), in a C preprocessor line it additionally inserts a '\' at the line break, and within comments it's like M-j (c-indent-new-comment-line).
>
> c-context-line-break isn't bound to a key by default, but it needs a binding to be useful. The following code will bind it to C-j. We use c-initialization-hook here to make sure the keymap is loaded before we try to change it.
>
> ```
> (defun my-bind-clb ()
>   (define-key c-mode-base-map "\C-j" 'c-context-line-break))
> (add-hook 'c-initialization-hook 'my-bind-clb)
> ```

`C-M-h`
> Put mark at the end of a function definition, and put point at the beginning (c-mark-function).

`M-q`
> Fill a paragraph, handling C and C++ comments (c-fill-paragraph). If any part of the current line is a comment or within a comment, this command fills the comment or the paragraph of it that point is in, preserving the comment indentation and comment delimiters.

`C-c C-e`
> Run the C preprocessor on the text in the region, and show the result, which includes the expansion of all the macro calls (c-macro-expand). The buffer text before the region is also included in preprocessing, for the sake of macros defined there, but the output from this part isn't shown.
>
> When you are debugging C code that uses macros, sometimes it is hard to figure out precisely how the macros expand. With this command, you don't have to figure it out; you can see the expansions.

`C-c C-\`
> Insert or align '\' characters at the ends of the lines of the region (c-backslash-region). This is useful after writing or editing a C macro definition.
>
> If a line already ends in '\', this command adjusts the amount of whitespace before it. Otherwise, it inserts a new '\'. However, the

last line in the region is treated specially; no '\' is inserted on that line, and any '\' there is deleted.

M-x cpp-highlight-buffer

> Highlight parts of the text according to its preprocessor conditionals. This command displays another buffer named '*CPP Edit*', which serves as a graphic menu for selecting how to display particular kinds of conditionals and their contents. After changing various settings, click on '[A]pply these settings' (or go to that buffer and type a) to rehighlight the C mode buffer accordingly.

C-c C-s
> Display the syntactic information about the current source line (c-show-syntactic-information). This information directs how the line is indented.

M-x cwarn-mode
M-x global-cwarn-mode

> CWarn minor mode highlights certain suspicious C and C++ constructions:

> - Assignments inside expressions.
> - Semicolon following immediately after 'if', 'for', and 'while' (except after a 'do ... while' statement);
> - C++ functions with reference parameters.

> You can enable the mode for one buffer with the command M-x cwarn-mode, or for all suitable buffers with the command M-x global-cwarn-mode or by customizing the variable global-cwarn-mode. You must also enable Font Lock mode to make it work.

M-x hide-ifdef-mode
> Hide-ifdef minor mode hides selected code within '#if' and '#ifdef' preprocessor blocks. See the documentation string of hide-ifdef-mode for more information.

M-x ff-find-related-file
> Find a file "related" in a special way to the file visited by the current buffer. Typically this will be the header file corresponding to a C/C++ source file, or vice versa. The variable ff-related-file-alist specifies how to compute related file names.

23.12 Asm Mode

Asm mode is a major mode for editing files of assembler code. It defines these commands:

TAB   tab-to-tab-stop.

C-j   Insert a newline and then indent using tab-to-tab-stop.

:   Insert a colon and then remove the indentation from before the label preceding colon. Then do `tab-to-tab-stop`.

;   Insert or align a comment.

The variable `asm-comment-char` specifies which character starts comments in assembler syntax.

24 Compiling and Testing Programs

The previous chapter discusses the Emacs commands that are useful for making changes in programs. This chapter deals with commands that assist in the larger process of compiling and testing programs.

24.1 Running Compilations under Emacs

Emacs can run compilers for noninteractive languages such as C and Fortran as inferior processes, feeding the error log into an Emacs buffer. It can also parse the error messages and show you the source lines where compilation errors occurred.

M-x compile

> Run a compiler asynchronously under Emacs, with error messages going to the '*compilation*' buffer.

M-x recompile

> Invoke a compiler with the same command as in the last invocation of M-x compile.

M-x kill-compilation

> Kill the running compilation subprocess.

To run make or another compilation command, do M-x compile. This command reads a shell command line using the minibuffer, and then executes the command in an inferior shell, putting output in the buffer named '*compilation*'. The current buffer's default directory is used as the working directory for the execution of the command; normally, therefore, the compilation happens in this directory.

The default for the compilation command is normally 'make -k', which is correct most of the time for nontrivial programs. (See section "Make" in *GNU Make Manual*.) If you have done M-x compile before, the default each time is the command you used the previous time. compile stores this command in the variable compile-command, so setting that variable specifies the default for the next use of M-x compile. If a file specifies a file local value for compile-command, that provides the default when you type M-x compile in that file's buffer. See Section 32.3.4 [File Variables], page 420.

Starting a compilation displays the buffer '*compilation*' in another window but does not select it. The buffer's mode line tells you whether compilation is finished, with the word 'run', 'signal' or 'exit' inside the parentheses. You do not have to keep this buffer visible; compilation continues in any case. While a compilation is going on, the string 'Compiling' appears in the mode lines of all windows. When this string disappears, the compilation is finished.

If you want to watch the compilation transcript as it appears, switch to the '*compilation*' buffer and move point to the end of the buffer. When point is at the end, new compilation output is inserted above point, which remains at the end. If point is not at the end of the buffer, it remains fixed while more compilation output is added at the end of the buffer.

If you set the variable compilation-scroll-output to a non-nil value, then the compilation buffer always scrolls to follow output as it comes in.

To rerun the last compilation with the same command, type M-x recompile. This automatically reuses the compilation command from the last invocation of M-x compile. It also reuses the '*compilation*' buffer and starts the compilation in its default directory, which is the directory in which the previous compilation was started.

When the compiler process terminates, for whatever reason, the mode line of the '*compilation*' buffer changes to say 'exit' (followed by the exit code, '[0]' for a normal exit), or 'signal' (if a signal terminated the process), instead of 'run'.

Starting a new compilation also kills any compilation already running in '*compilation*', as the buffer can only handle one compilation at any time. However, M-x compile asks for confirmation before actually killing a compilation that is running. You can also kill the compilation process with M-x kill-compilation.

If you want to run two compilations at once, you should start the first one, then rename the '*compilation*' buffer (perhaps using rename-uniquely; see Section 16.3 [Misc Buffer], page 158), and start the other compilation. That will create a new '*compilation*' buffer.

Emacs does not expect a compiler process to launch asynchronous subprocesses; if it does, and they keep running after the main compiler process has terminated, Emacs may kill them or their output may not arrive in Emacs. To avoid this problem, make the main process wait for its subprocesses to finish. In a shell script, you can do this using '$!' and 'wait', like this:

```
(sleep 10; echo 2nd)& pid=$!   # Record pid of subprocess
echo first message
wait $pid                       # Wait for subprocess
```

If the background process does not output to the compilation buffer, so you only need to prevent it from being killed when the main compilation process terminates, this is sufficient:

```
nohup command; sleep 1
```

You can control the environment passed to the compilation command with the variable compilation-environment. Its value is a list of environment variable settings; each element should be a string of the form "envvarname=value". These environment variable settings override the usual ones.

24.2 Compilation Mode

The '*compilation*' buffer uses a special major mode, Compilation mode, whose main feature is to provide a convenient way to visit the source line corresponding to an error message. These commands are also available in other special buffers that list locations in files, including those made by M-x grep and M-x occur.

M-g M-n
M-g n
C-x `   Visit the locus of the next error message or match.

M-g M-p
M-g p   Visit the locus of the previous error message or match.

RET   Visit the locus of the error message that point is on. This command
           is used in the compilation buffer.

Mouse-2   Visit the locus of the error message that you click on.

M-n   Find and highlight the locus of the next error message, without select-
           ing the source buffer.

M-p   Find and highlight the locus of the previous error message, without
           selecting the source buffer.

M-}   Move point to the next error for a different file than the current one.

M-{   Move point to the previous error for a different file than the current
           one.

C-c C-f   Toggle Next Error Follow minor mode, which makes cursor motion in
           the compilation buffer produce automatic source display.

You can visit the source for any particular error message by moving point in the
'*compilation*' buffer to that error message and typing RET (compile-goto-error). Alternatively, you can click Mouse-2 on the error message; you need not
switch to the '*compilation*' buffer first.

To parse the compiler error messages sequentially, type C-x ' (next-error).
The character following the C-x is the backquote or "grave accent," not the single-quote. This command is available in all buffers, not just in '*compilation*'; it
displays the next error message at the top of one window and source location of the
error in another window. It also temporarily highlights the relevant source line, for
a period controlled by the variable next-error-highlight.

The first time C-x ' is used after the start of a compilation, it moves to the first
error's location. Subsequent uses of C-x ' advance down to subsequent errors. If you
visit a specific error message with RET or Mouse-2, subsequent C-x ' commands
advance from there. When C-x ' gets to the end of the buffer and finds no more
error messages to visit, it fails and signals an Emacs error. C-u C-x ' starts scanning
from the beginning of the compilation buffer, and goes to the first error's location.

By default, C-x ' skips less important messages. The variable compilation-skip-threshold controls this. If its value is 2, C-x ' skips anything less than error,
1 skips anything less than warning, and 0 doesn't skip any messages. The default
is 1.

When the window has a left fringe, an arrow in the fringe points to the current
message in the compilation buffer. The variable compilation-context-lines controls the number of lines of leading context to display before the current message.
Going to an error message location scrolls the '*compilation*' buffer to put the
message that far down from the top. The value nil is special: if there's a left fringe,
the window doesn't scroll at all if the message is already visible. If there is no left
fringe, nil means display the message at the top of the window.

If you're not in the compilation buffer when you run next-error, Emacs will
look for a buffer that contains error messages. First, it looks for one displayed in the
selected frame, then for one that previously had next-error called on it, and then

at the current buffer. Finally, Emacs looks at all the remaining buffers. `next-error` signals an error if it can't find any such buffer.

To parse messages from the compiler, Compilation mode uses the variable `compilation-error-regexp-alist` which lists various formats of error messages and tells Emacs how to extract the source file and the line number from the text of a message. If your compiler isn't supported, you can tailor Compilation mode to it by adding elements to that list. A similar variable `grep-regexp-alist` tells Emacs how to parse output of a `grep` command.

Compilation mode also redefines the keys SPC and DEL to scroll by screenfuls, and M-n (`compilation-next-error`) and M-p (`compilation-previous-error`) to move to the next or previous error message. You can also use M-{ (`compilation-next-file` and M-} (`compilation-previous-file`) to move up or down to an error message for a different source file.

You can type C-c C-f to toggle Next Error Follow mode. In this minor mode, ordinary cursor motion in the compilation buffer automatically updates the source buffer. For instance, moving the cursor to the next error message causes the location of that error to be displayed immediately.

The features of Compilation mode are also available in a minor mode called Compilation Minor mode. This lets you parse error messages in any buffer, not just a normal compilation output buffer. Type M-x `compilation-minor-mode` to enable the minor mode. This defines the keys RET and `Mouse-2`, as in the Compilation major mode.

Compilation minor mode works in any buffer, as long as the contents are in a format that it understands. In an Rlogin buffer (see Section 31.2.11 [Remote Host], page 388), Compilation minor mode automatically accesses remote source files by FTP (see Section 15.1 [File Names], page 119).

24.3 Subshells for Compilation

Emacs uses a shell to run the compilation command, but specifies the option for a noninteractive shell. This means, in particular, that the shell should start with no prompt. If you find your usual shell prompt making an unsightly appearance in the '*compilation*' buffer, it means you have made a mistake in your shell's init file by setting the prompt unconditionally. (This init file's name may be '.bashrc', '.profile', '.cshrc', '.shrc', or various other things, depending on the shell you use.) The shell init file should set the prompt only if there already is a prompt. Here's how to do it in bash:

```
if [ "${PS1+set}" = set ]
then PS1=...
fi
```

And here's how to do it in csh:

```
if ($?prompt) set prompt = ...
```

There may well be other things that your shell's init file ought to do only for an interactive shell. You can use the same method to conditionalize them.

The MS-DOS "operating system" does not support asynchronous subprocesses; to work around this lack, M-x compile runs the compilation command synchronously on MS-DOS. As a consequence, you must wait until the command finishes before you can do anything else in Emacs. See Info file 'emacs-xtra', node 'MS-DOS'.

24.4 Searching with Grep under Emacs

Just as you can run a compiler from Emacs and then visit the lines with compilation errors, you can also run grep and then visit the lines on which matches were found. This works by treating the matches reported by grep as if they were "errors." The buffer of matches uses Grep mode, which is a variant of Compilation mode (see Section 24.2 [Compilation Mode], page 274).

M-x grep

M-x lgrep   Run grep asynchronously under Emacs, with matching lines listed in the buffer named '*grep*'.

M-x grep-find
M-x find-grep
M-x rgrep   Run grep via find, with user-specified arguments, and collect output in the buffer named '*grep*'.

M-x kill-grep
              Kill the running grep subprocess.

To run grep, type M-x grep, then enter a command line that specifies how to run grep. Use the same arguments you would give grep when running it normally: a grep-style regexp (usually in single-quotes to quote the shell's special characters) followed by file names, which may use wildcards. If you specify a prefix argument for M-x grep, it finds the tag (see Section 25.3 [Tags], page 293) in the buffer around point, and puts that into the default grep command.

Your command need not simply run grep; you can use any shell command that produces output in the same format. For instance, you can chain grep commands, like this:

    grep -nH -e foo *.el | grep bar | grep toto

The output from grep goes in the '*grep*' buffer. You can find the corresponding lines in the original files using C-x ', RET, and so forth, just like compilation errors.

Some grep programs accept a '--color' option to output special markers around matches for the purpose of highlighting. You can make use of this feature by setting grep-highlight-matches to t. When displaying a match in the source buffer, the exact match will be highlighted, instead of the entire source line.

The command M-x grep-find (also available as M-x find-grep) is similar to M-x grep, but it supplies a different initial default for the command—one that runs both find and grep, so as to search every file in a directory tree. See also the find-grep-dired command, in Section 29.15 [Dired and Find], page 351.

The commands M-x lgrep (local grep) and M-x rgrep (recursive grep) are more user-friendly versions of grep and grep-find, which prompt separately for the regular expression to match, the files to search, and the base directory for the search. Case sensitivity of the search is controlled by the current value of case-fold-search.

These commands build the shell commands based on the variables grep-template (for lgrep) and grep-find-template (for rgrep).

The files to search can use aliases defined in the variable grep-files-aliases.

Subdirectories listed in the variable grep-find-ignored-directories such as those typically used by various version control systems, like CVS and arch, are automatically skipped by rgrep.

24.5 Finding Syntax Errors On The Fly

Flymake mode is a minor mode that performs on-the-fly syntax checking for many programming and markup languages, including C, C++, Perl, HTML, and TeX/LaTeX. It is somewhat analogous to Flyspell mode, which performs spell checking for ordinary human languages in a similar fashion (see Section 13.5 [Spelling], page 108). As you edit a file, Flymake mode runs an appropriate syntax checking tool in the background, using a temporary copy of the buffer. It then parses the error and warning messages, and highlights the erroneous lines in the buffer. The syntax checking tool used depends on the language; for example, for C/C++ files this is usually the C compiler. Flymake can also use build tools such as make for checking complicated projects.

To activate Flymake mode, type M-x flymake-mode. You can move to the errors spotted by Flymake mode with M-x flymake-goto-next-error and M-x flymake-goto-prev-error. To display any error messages associated with the current line, use M-x flymake-display-err-menu-for-current-line.

For more details about using Flymake, see section "Flymake" in *The Flymake Manual*.

24.6 Running Debuggers Under Emacs

The GUD (Grand Unified Debugger) library provides an interface to various symbolic debuggers from within Emacs. We recommend the debugger GDB, which is free software, but GUD can also run DBX, SDB or XDB. GUD can also serve as an interface to Perl's debugging mode, the Python debugger PDB, and to JDB, the Java Debugger. See section "The Lisp Debugger" in *the Emacs Lisp Reference Manual*, for information on debugging Emacs Lisp programs.

24.6.1 Starting GUD

There are several commands for starting a debugger, each corresponding to a particular debugger program.

`M-x gdb RET` *file* `RET`

> Run GDB as a subprocess of Emacs. By default, this uses an IDE-like graphical interface; see Section 24.6.5 [GDB Graphical Interface], page 283. Only GDB works with the graphical interface.

`M-x dbx RET` *file* `RET`

> Run DBX as a subprocess of Emacs. Since Emacs does not implement a graphical interface for DBX, communication with DBX works by typing commands in the GUD interaction buffer. The same is true for all the other supported debuggers.

`M-x xdb RET` *file* `RET`

> Similar, but run XDB. Use the variable `gud-xdb-directories` to specify directories to search for source files.

`M-x sdb RET` *file* `RET`

> Similar, but run SDB.

> Some versions of SDB do not mention source file names in their messages. When you use them, you need to have a valid tags table (see Section 25.3 [Tags], page 293) in order for GUD to find functions in the source code. If you have not visited a tags table or the tags table doesn't list one of the functions, you get a message saying 'The sdb support requires a valid tags table to work'. If this happens, generate a valid tags table in the working directory and try again.

`M-x perldb RET` *file* `RET`

> Run the Perl interpreter in debug mode to debug *file*, a Perl program.

`M-x jdb RET` *file* `RET`

> Run the Java debugger to debug *file*.

`M-x pdb RET` *file* `RET`

> Run the Python debugger to debug *file*.

Each of these commands takes one argument: a command line to invoke the debugger. In the simplest case, specify just the name of the executable file you want to debug. You may also use options that the debugger supports. However, shell wildcards and variables are not allowed. GUD assumes that the first argument not starting with a '-' is the executable file name.

24.6.2 Debugger Operation

Generally when you run a debugger with GUD, the debugger uses an Emacs buffer for its ordinary input and output. This is called the GUD buffer. Input and output from the program you are debugging also use this buffer. We call this *text command mode*. The GDB Graphical Interface can use further buffers (see Section 24.6.5 [GDB Graphical Interface], page 283).

The debugger displays the source files of the program by visiting them in Emacs buffers. An arrow in the left fringe indicates the current execution line.[1] Moving point in this buffer does not move the arrow. The arrow is not part of the file's text; it appears only on the screen.

You can start editing these source files at any time in the buffers that display them. If you do modify a source file, keep in mind that inserting or deleting lines will throw off the arrow's positioning; GUD has no way of figuring out which line corresponded before your changes to the line number in a debugger message. Also, you'll typically have to recompile and restart the program for your changes to be reflected in the debugger's tables.

The Tooltip facility (see Section 18.17 [Tooltips], page 184) provides support for GUD. You activate this feature by turning on the minor mode `gud-tooltip-mode`. Then you can display a variable's value in a tooltip simply by pointing at it with the mouse. This operates in the GUD buffer and in source buffers with major modes in the list `gud-tooltip-modes`. If the variable `gud-tooltip-echo-area` is non-`nil` then the variable's value is displayed in the echo area. When debugging a C program using the GDB Graphical Interface, you can also display macro definitions associated with an identifier when the program is not executing.

GUD tooltips are disabled when you use GDB in text command mode (see Section 24.6.5 [GDB Graphical Interface], page 283), because displaying an expression's value in GDB can sometimes expand a macro and result in a side effect that interferes with the program's operation. The GDB graphical interface supports GUD tooltips and assures they will not cause side effects.

24.6.3 Commands of GUD

The GUD interaction buffer uses a variant of Shell mode, so the Emacs commands of Shell mode are available (see Section 31.2.3 [Shell Mode], page 380). All the usual commands for your debugger are available, and you can use the Shell mode history commands to repeat them. If you wish, you can control your debugger process entirely through this buffer.

GUD mode also provides commands for setting and clearing breakpoints, for selecting stack frames, and for stepping through the program. These commands are available both in the GUD buffer and globally, but with different key bindings. It also has its own tool bar from which you can invoke the more common commands by clicking on the appropriate icon. This is particularly useful for repetitive commands like `gud-next` and `gud-step`, and allows you to keep the GUD buffer hidden.

The breakpoint commands are normally used in source file buffers, because that is the easiest way to specify where to set or clear the breakpoint. Here's the global command to set a breakpoint:

C-x SPC   Set a breakpoint on the source line that point is on.

Here are the other special commands provided by GUD. The keys starting with C-c are available only in the GUD interaction buffer. The key bindings that start

---

[1] On a text-only terminal, the arrow appears as '=>' and overlays the first two text columns.

with C-x C-a are available in the GUD interaction buffer and also in source files. Some of these commands are not available to all the supported debuggers.

C-c C-l
C-x C-a C-l

>Display in another window the last line referred to in the GUD buffer (that is, the line indicated in the last location message). This runs the command **gud-refresh**.

C-c C-s
C-x C-a C-s

>Execute a single line of code (**gud-step**). If the line contains a function call, execution stops after entering the called function.

C-c C-n
C-x C-a C-n

>Execute a single line of code, stepping across entire function calls at full speed (**gud-next**).

C-c C-i
C-x C-a C-i

>Execute a single machine instruction (**gud-stepi**).

C-c C-p
C-x C-a C-p

>Evaluate the expression at point (**gud-print**). If Emacs does not print the exact expression that you want, mark it as a region first.

C-c C-r
C-x C-a C-r

>Continue execution without specifying any stopping point. The program will run until it hits a breakpoint, terminates, or gets a signal that the debugger is checking for (**gud-cont**)

C-c C-d
C-x C-a C-d

>Delete the breakpoint(s) on the current source line, if any (**gud-remove**). If you use this command in the GUD interaction buffer, it applies to the line where the program last stopped.

C-c C-t
C-x C-a C-t

>Set a temporary breakpoint on the current source line, if any (**gud-tbreak**). If you use this command in the GUD interaction buffer, it applies to the line where the program last stopped.

C-c <
C-x C-a <   Select the next enclosing stack frame (**gud-up**). This is equivalent to the GDB command 'up'.

C-c >
C-x C-a >   Select the next inner stack frame (**gud-down**). This is equivalent to the GDB command 'down'.

```
C-c C-u
C-x C-a C-u
```

> Continue execution to the current line (`gud-until`). The program will run until it hits a breakpoint, terminates, gets a signal that the debugger is checking for, or reaches the line on which the cursor currently sits.

```
C-c C-f
C-x C-a C-f
```

> Run the program until the selected stack frame returns or stops for some other reason (`gud-finish`).

If you are using GDB, these additional key bindings are available:

```
C-x C-a C-j
```

> Only useful in a source buffer, `gud-jump` transfers the program's execution point to the current line. In other words, the next line that the program executes will be the one where you gave the command. If the new execution line is in a different function from the previously one, GDB prompts for confirmation since the results may be bizarre. See the GDB manual entry regarding `jump` for details.

TAB

> With GDB, complete a symbol name (`gud-gdb-complete-command`). This key is available only in the GUD interaction buffer.

These commands interpret a numeric argument as a repeat count, when that makes sense.

Because TAB serves as a completion command, you can't use it to enter a tab as input to the program you are debugging with GDB. Instead, type `C-q TAB` to enter a tab.

24.6.4 GUD Customization

On startup, GUD runs one of the following hooks: `gdb-mode-hook`, if you are using GDB; `dbx-mode-hook`, if you are using DBX; `sdb-mode-hook`, if you are using SDB; `xdb-mode-hook`, if you are using XDB; `perldb-mode-hook`, for Perl debugging mode; `pdb-mode-hook`, for PDB; `jdb-mode-hook`, for JDB. You can use these hooks to define custom key bindings for the debugger interaction buffer. See Section 32.3.2 [Hooks], page 418.

Here is a convenient way to define a command that sends a particular command string to the debugger, and set up a key binding for it in the debugger interaction buffer:

```
(gud-def function cmdstring binding docstring)
```

This defines a command named *function* which sends *cmdstring* to the debugger process, and gives it the documentation string *docstring*. You can then use the command *function* in any buffer. If *binding* is non-`nil`, `gud-def` also binds the command to `C-c binding` in the GUD buffer's mode and to `C-x C-a binding` generally.

The command string *cmdstring* may contain certain '%'-sequences that stand for data to be filled in at the time *function* is called:

'%f'   The name of the current source file. If the current buffer is the GUD
            buffer, then the "current source file" is the file that the program
            stopped in.

'%l'   The number of the current source line. If the current buffer is the
            GUD buffer, then the "current source line" is the line that the program
            stopped in.

'%e'   In transient-mark-mode the text in the region, if it is active. Otherwise
            the text of the C lvalue or function-call expression at or adjacent to
            point.

'%a'   The text of the hexadecimal address at or adjacent to point.

'%p'   The numeric argument of the called function, as a decimal number. If
            the command is used without a numeric argument, '%p' stands for the
            empty string.

            If you don't use '%p' in the command string, the command you define
            ignores any numeric argument.

'%d'   The name of the directory of the current source file.

'%c'   Fully qualified class name derived from the expression surrounding
            point (jdb only).

24.6.5 GDB Graphical Interface

By default, the command **gdb** starts GDB using a graphical interface, using Emacs
windows for display program state information. In effect, this makes Emacs into
an IDE (interactive development environment). With it, you do not need to use
textual GDB commands; you can control the debugging session with the mouse.
For example, you can click in the fringe of a source buffer to set a breakpoint there,
or on a stack frame in the stack buffer to select that frame.

This mode requires telling GDB that its "screen size" is unlimited, so it sets
the height and width accordingly. For correct operation you must not change these
values during the GDB session.

You can also run GDB in text command mode, like other debuggers. To do
this, replace the GDB "--annotate=3" option with "--fullname" either in the
minibuffer for the current Emacs session, or the custom variable **gud-gdb-command-
name** for all future sessions. You need to use text command mode to debug multiple
programs within one Emacs session. If you have customized **gud-gdb-command-
name** in this way, you can use M-x gdba to invoke GDB in graphical mode.

24.6.5.1 GDB User Interface Layout

If the variable **gdb-many-windows** is **nil** (the default value) then M-x gdb normally
displays only the GUD buffer. However, if the variable **gdb-show-main** is also non-
nil, it starts with two windows: one displaying the GUD buffer, and the other
showing the source for the **main** function of the program you are debugging.

If **gdb-many-windows** is non-**nil**, then M-x gdb displays the following frame
layout:

```
+-----------------------------------+-----------------------------------+
|   GUD buffer (I/O of GDB)          |   Locals buffer                   |
|-----------------------------------+-----------------------------------|
|   Primary Source buffer            |   I/O buffer for debugged pgm     |
|-----------------------------------+-----------------------------------|
|   Stack buffer                     |   Breakpoints buffer              |
+-----------------------------------+-----------------------------------+
```

However, if `gdb-use-separate-io-buffer` is `nil`, the I/O buffer does not appear and the primary source buffer occupies the full width of the frame.

If you change the window layout, for example, while editing and re-compiling your program, then you can restore this standard window layout with the command `gdb-restore-windows`.

To switch between this standard layout and a simple layout containing just the GUD buffer and a source file, type `M-x gdb-many-windows`.

You may also specify additional GDB-related buffers to display, either in the same frame or a different one. Select the buffers you want with the 'GUD->GDB-windows' and 'GUD->GDB-Frames' sub-menus. If the menu-bar is unavailable, type `M-x gdb-display-buffertype-buffer` or `M-x gdb-frame-buffertype-buffer` respectively, where *buffertype* is the relevant buffer type, such as '`breakpoints`'. Most of these buffers are read-only, and typing `q` in them kills them.

When you finish debugging, kill the GUD buffer with `C-x k`, which will also kill all the buffers associated with the session. However you need not do this if, after editing and re-compiling your source code within Emacs, you wish continue debugging. When you restart execution, GDB will automatically find your new executable. Keeping the GUD buffer has the advantage of keeping the shell history as well as GDB's breakpoints. You do need to check that the breakpoints in recently edited source files are still in the right places.

24.6.5.2 Source Buffers

Many GDB commands can be entered using keybindings or the tool bar but sometimes it is quicker to use the fringe. These commands either manipulate breakpoints or control program execution. When there is no fringe, you can use the margin but this is only present when the source file already has a breakpoint.

You can click `Mouse-1` in the fringe or display margin of a source buffer to set a breakpoint there and, on a graphical display, a red bullet will appear on that line. If a breakpoint already exists on that line, the same click will remove it. You can also enable or disable a breakpoint by clicking `C-Mouse-1` on the bullet.

A solid arrow in the left fringe of a source buffer indicates the line of the innermost frame where the debugged program has stopped. A hollow arrow indicates the current execution line of higher level frames.

If you drag the arrow in the fringe with `Mouse-1` (`gdb-mouse-until`), execution will continue to the line where you release the button, provided it is still in the same frame. Alternatively, you can click `Mouse-3` at some point in the fringe of this buffer and execution will advance to there. A similar command (`gdb-mouse-jump`) allows you to jump to a source line without executing the intermediate lines by clicking

C-Mouse-3. This command allows you to go backwards which can be useful for running through code that has already executed, in order to examine its execution in more detail.

Mouse-1   Set or clear a breakpoint.

C-Mouse-1   Enable or disable a breakpoint.

Mouse-3   Continue execution to here.

C-Mouse-3   Jump to here.

If the variable `gdb-find-source-frame` is non-`nil` and execution stops in a frame for which there is no source code e.g after an interrupt, then Emacs finds and displays the first frame further up stack for which there is source. If it is `nil` then the source buffer continues to display the last frame which maybe more useful, for example, when re-setting a breakpoint.

24.6.5.3 Breakpoints Buffer

The breakpoints buffer shows the existing breakpoints, watchpoints and catchpoints (see section "Breakpoints" in *The GNU debugger*). It has these special commands, which mostly apply to the *current breakpoint*, the breakpoint which point is on.

SPC   Enable/disable the current breakpoint (`gdb-toggle-breakpoint`). On a graphical display, this changes the color of a bullet in the margin of a source buffer at the relevant line. This is red when the breakpoint is enabled and grey when it is disabled. Text-only terminals correspondingly display a 'B' or 'b'.

D   Delete the current breakpoint (`gdb-delete-breakpoint`).

RET   Visit the source line for the current breakpoint (`gdb-goto-breakpoint`).

Mouse-2   Visit the source line for the breakpoint you click on.

24.6.5.4 Stack Buffer

The stack buffer displays a *call stack*, with one line for each of the nested subroutine calls (*stack frames*) now active in the program. See section "Backtraces" in *The GNU debugger*.

An arrow in the fringe points to the selected frame or, if the fringe is not present, the number of the selected frame is displayed in reverse contrast. To select a frame in GDB, move point in the stack buffer to that stack frame and type RET (`gdb-frames-select`), or click Mouse-2 on a stack frame. If the locals buffer is visible, selecting a stack frame updates it to display the local variables of the new frame.

24.6.5.5 Other Buffers

Input/Output Buffer

If the variable `gdb-use-separate-io-buffer` is non-`nil`, the program being debugged takes its input and displays its output here. Otherwise it uses the GUD buffer for that. To toggle whether GUD mode uses this buffer, do M-x gdb-use-separate-io-buffer. This takes effect when you next restart the program you are debugging.

The history and replay commands from Shell mode are available here, as are the commands to send signals to the debugged program. See Section 31.2.3 [Shell Mode], page 380.

Locals Buffer

The locals buffer displays the values of local variables of the current frame for simple data types (see section "Information on a frame" in *The GNU debugger*). Press RET or click Mouse-2 on the value if you want to edit it.

Arrays and structures display their type only. With GDB 6.4 or later, move point to their name and press RET, or alternatively click Mouse-2 there, to examine their values. With earlier versions of GDB, use Mouse-2 or RET on the type description ('[struct/union]' or '[array]'). See Section 24.6.5.6 [Watch Expressions], page 287.

Registers Buffer

The registers buffer displays the values held by the registers (see section "Registers" in *The GNU debugger*). Press RET or click Mouse-2 on a register if you want to edit its value. With GDB 6.4 or later, recently changed register values display with font-lock-warning-face. With earlier versions of GDB, you can press SPC to toggle the display of floating point registers (toggle-gdb-all-registers).

Assembler Buffer

The assembler buffer displays the current frame as machine code. An arrow points to the current instruction, and you can set and remove breakpoints as in a source buffer. Breakpoint icons also appear in the fringe or margin.

Threads Buffer

The threads buffer displays a summary of all threads currently in your program (see section "Debugging programs with multiple threads" in *The GNU debugger*). Move point to any thread in the list and press RET to select it (gdb-threads-select) and display the associated source in the primary source buffer. Alternatively, click Mouse-2 on a thread to select it. If the locals buffer is visible, its contents update to display the variables that are local in the new thread.

Memory Buffer

The memory buffer lets you examine sections of program memory (see section "Examining memory" in *The GNU debugger*). Click Mouse-1 on the appropriate part of the header line to change the starting address or number of data items that the buffer displays. Click Mouse-3 on the header line to select the display format or unit size for these data items.

24.6.5.6 Watch Expressions

If you want to see how a variable changes each time your program stops, move point into the variable name and click on the watch icon in the tool bar (gud-watch) or type C-x C-a C-w. If you specify a prefix argument, you can enter the variable name in the minibuffer.

Each watch expression is displayed in the speedbar. Complex data types, such as arrays, structures and unions are represented in a tree format. Leaves and simple data types show the name of the expression and its value and, when the speedbar frame is selected, display the type as a tooltip. Higher levels show the name, type and address value for pointers and just the name and type otherwise. Root expressions also display the frame address as a tooltip to help identify the frame in which they were defined.

To expand or contract a complex data type, click Mouse-2 or press SPC on the tag to the left of the expression. Emacs asks for confirmation before expanding the expression if its number of immediate children exceeds the value of the variable gdb-max-children.

To delete a complex watch expression, move point to the root expression in the speedbar and type D (gdb-var-delete).

To edit a variable with a simple data type, or a simple element of a complex data type, move point there in the speedbar and type RET (gdb-edit-value). Or you can click Mouse-2 on a value to edit it. Either way, this reads the new value using the minibuffer.

If you set the variable gdb-show-changed-values to non-nil (the default value), Emacs uses font-lock-warning-face to highlight values that have recently changed and shadow face to make variables which have gone out of scope less noticeable. When a variable goes out of scope you can't edit its value.

If the variable gdb-use-colon-colon-notation is non-nil, Emacs uses the 'function::variable' format. This allows the user to display watch expressions which share the same variable name. The default value is nil.

To automatically raise the speedbar every time the display of watch expressions updates, set gdb-speedbar-auto-raise to non-nil. This can be useful if you are debugging with a full screen Emacs frame.

24.7 Executing Lisp Expressions

Emacs has several different major modes for Lisp and Scheme. They are the same in terms of editing commands, but differ in the commands for executing Lisp expressions. Each mode has its own purpose.

Emacs-Lisp mode

        The mode for editing source files of programs to run in Emacs Lisp. This mode defines C-M-x to evaluate the current defun. See Section 24.8 [Lisp Libraries], page 288.

Lisp Interaction mode

> The mode for an interactive session with Emacs Lisp. It defines C-j to evaluate the sexp before point and insert its value in the buffer. See Section 24.10 [Lisp Interaction], page 290.

Lisp mode   The mode for editing source files of programs that run in Lisps other than Emacs Lisp. This mode defines C-M-x to send the current defun to an inferior Lisp process. See Section 24.11 [External Lisp], page 291.

Inferior Lisp mode

> The mode for an interactive session with an inferior Lisp process. This mode combines the special features of Lisp mode and Shell mode (see Section 31.2.3 [Shell Mode], page 380).

Scheme mode

> Like Lisp mode but for Scheme programs.

Inferior Scheme mode

> The mode for an interactive session with an inferior Scheme process.

Most editing commands for working with Lisp programs are in fact available globally. See Chapter 23 [Programs], page 250.

24.8 Libraries of Lisp Code for Emacs

Lisp code for Emacs editing commands is stored in files whose names conventionally end in '.el'. This ending tells Emacs to edit them in Emacs-Lisp mode (see Section 24.7 [Executing Lisp], page 287).

Emacs Lisp code can be compiled into byte-code, which loads faster, takes up less space, and executes faster. See section "Byte Compilation" in *the Emacs Lisp Reference Manual*. By convention, the compiled code for a library goes in a separate file whose name ends in '.elc'. Thus, the compiled code for 'foo.el' goes in 'foo.elc'.

To execute a file of Emacs Lisp code, use M-x load-file. This command reads a file name using the minibuffer and then executes the contents of that file as Lisp code. It is not necessary to visit the file first; in any case, this command reads the file as found on disk, not text in an Emacs buffer.

Once a file of Lisp code is installed in the Emacs Lisp library directories, users can load it using M-x load-library. Programs can load it by calling load, a more primitive function that is similar but accepts some additional arguments.

M-x load-library differs from M-x load-file in that it searches a sequence of directories and tries three file names in each directory. Suppose your argument is *lib*; the three names are '*lib*.elc', '*lib*.el', and lastly just '*lib*'. If '*lib*.elc' exists, it is by convention the result of compiling '*lib*.el'; it is better to load the compiled file, since it will load and run faster.

If load-library finds that '*lib*.el' is newer than '*lib*.elc' file, it issues a warning, because it's likely that somebody made changes to the '.el' file and forgot to recompile it. Nonetheless, it loads '*lib*.elc'. This is because people often leave unfinished edits the source file, and don't recompile it until they think it is ready to use.

Because the argument to `load-library` is usually not in itself a valid file name, file name completion is not available. Indeed, when using this command, you usually do not know exactly what file name will be used.

The sequence of directories searched by `M-x load-library` is specified by the variable `load-path`, a list of strings that are directory names. The default value of the list contains the directories where the Lisp code for Emacs itself is stored. If you have libraries of your own, put them in a single directory and add that directory to `load-path`. `nil` in this list stands for the current default directory, but it is probably not a good idea to put `nil` in the list. If you find yourself wishing that `nil` were in the list, most likely what you really want to do is use `M-x load-file` this once.

Often you do not have to give any command to load a library, because the commands defined in the library are set up to *autoload* that library. Trying to run any of those commands calls `load` to load the library; this replaces the autoload definitions with the real ones from the library.

By default, Emacs refuses to load compiled Lisp files which were compiled with XEmacs, a modified versions of Emacs—they can cause Emacs to crash. Set the variable `load-dangerous-libraries` to `t` if you want to try loading them.

24.9 Evaluating Emacs Lisp Expressions

Lisp programs intended to be run in Emacs should be edited in Emacs-Lisp mode; this happens automatically for file names ending in '`.el`'. By contrast, Lisp mode itself is used for editing Lisp programs intended for other Lisp systems. To switch to Emacs-Lisp mode explicitly, use the command `M-x emacs-lisp-mode`.

For testing of Lisp programs to run in Emacs, it is often useful to evaluate part of the program as it is found in the Emacs buffer. For example, after changing the text of a Lisp function definition, evaluating the definition installs the change for future calls to the function. Evaluation of Lisp expressions is also useful in any kind of editing, for invoking noninteractive functions (functions that are not commands).

`M-:`   Read a single Lisp expression in the minibuffer, evaluate it, and print the value in the echo area (`eval-expression`).

`C-x C-e`   Evaluate the Lisp expression before point, and print the value in the echo area (`eval-last-sexp`).

`C-M-x`   Evaluate the defun containing or after point, and print the value in the echo area (`eval-defun`).

`M-x eval-region`
            Evaluate all the Lisp expressions in the region.

`M-x eval-buffer`
            Evaluate all the Lisp expressions in the buffer.

`M-:` (`eval-expression`) is the most basic command for evaluating a Lisp expression interactively. It reads the expression using the minibuffer, so you can execute any expression on a buffer regardless of what the buffer contains. When the expression is evaluated, the current buffer is once again the buffer that was current when `M-:` was typed.

In Emacs-Lisp mode, the key `C-M-x` is bound to the command `eval-defun`, which parses the defun containing or following point as a Lisp expression and evaluates it. The value is printed in the echo area. This command is convenient for installing in the Lisp environment changes that you have just made in the text of a function definition.

`C-M-x` treats `defvar` expressions specially. Normally, evaluating a `defvar` expression does nothing if the variable it defines already has a value. But `C-M-x` unconditionally resets the variable to the initial value specified in the `defvar` expression. `defcustom` expressions are treated similarly. This special feature is convenient for debugging Lisp programs. Typing `C-M-x` on a `defface` expression reinitializes the face according to the `defface` specification.

The command `C-x C-e` (`eval-last-sexp`) evaluates the Lisp expression preceding point in the buffer, and displays the value in the echo area. It is available in all major modes, not just Emacs-Lisp mode. It does not treat `defvar` specially.

When the result of an evaluation is an integer, you can type `C-x C-e` a second time to display the value of the integer result in additional formats (octal, hexadecimal, and character).

If `C-x C-e`, or `M-:` is given a numeric argument, it inserts the value into the current buffer at point, rather than displaying it in the echo area. The argument's value does not matter. `C-M-x` with a numeric argument instruments the function definition for Edebug (see section "Instrumenting" in *the Emacs Lisp Reference Manual*).

The most general command for evaluating Lisp expressions from a buffer is `eval-region`. `M-x eval-region` parses the text of the region as one or more Lisp expressions, evaluating them one by one. `M-x eval-buffer` is similar but evaluates the entire buffer. This is a reasonable way to install the contents of a file of Lisp code that you are ready to test. Later, as you find bugs and change individual functions, use `C-M-x` on each function that you change. This keeps the Lisp world in step with the source file.

The two customizable variables `eval-expression-print-level` and `eval-expression-print-length` control the maximum depth and length of lists to print in the result of the evaluation commands before abbreviating them. `eval-expression-debug-on-error` controls whether evaluation errors invoke the debugger when these commands are used; its default is `t`.

24.10 Lisp Interaction Buffers

The buffer '`*scratch*`' which is selected when Emacs starts up is provided for evaluating Lisp expressions interactively inside Emacs.

The simplest way to use the '`*scratch*`' buffer is to insert Lisp expressions and type `C-j` after each expression. This command reads the Lisp expression before point, evaluates it, and inserts the value in printed representation before point.

The result is a complete typescript of the expressions you have evaluated and their values.

The '*scratch*' buffer's major mode is Lisp Interaction mode, which is the same as Emacs-Lisp mode except for the binding of C-j.

The rationale for this feature is that Emacs must have a buffer when it starts up, but that buffer is not useful for editing files since a new buffer is made for every file that you visit. The Lisp interpreter typescript is the most useful thing I can think of for the initial buffer to do. Type M-x lisp-interaction-mode to put the current buffer in Lisp Interaction mode.

An alternative way of evaluating Emacs Lisp expressions interactively is to use Inferior Emacs-Lisp mode, which provides an interface rather like Shell mode (see Section 31.2.3 [Shell Mode], page 380) for evaluating Emacs Lisp expressions. Type M-x ielm to create an '*ielm*' buffer which uses this mode. For more information see that command's documentation.

24.11 Running an External Lisp

Emacs has facilities for running programs in other Lisp systems. You can run a Lisp process as an inferior of Emacs, and pass expressions to it to be evaluated. You can also pass changed function definitions directly from the Emacs buffers in which you edit the Lisp programs to the inferior Lisp process.

To run an inferior Lisp process, type M-x run-lisp. This runs the program named lisp, the same program you would run by typing lisp as a shell command, with both input and output going through an Emacs buffer named '*lisp*'. That is to say, any "terminal output" from Lisp will go into the buffer, advancing point, and any "terminal input" for Lisp comes from text in the buffer. (You can change the name of the Lisp executable file by setting the variable inferior-lisp-program.)

To give input to Lisp, go to the end of the buffer and type the input, terminated by RET. The '*lisp*' buffer is in Inferior Lisp mode, which combines the special characteristics of Lisp mode with most of the features of Shell mode (see Section 31.2.3 [Shell Mode], page 380). The definition of RET to send a line to a subprocess is one of the features of Shell mode.

For the source files of programs to run in external Lisps, use Lisp mode. You can switch to this mode with M-x lisp-mode, and it is used automatically for files whose names end in '.l', '.lsp', or '.lisp'.

When you edit a function in a Lisp program you are running, the easiest way to send the changed definition to the inferior Lisp process is the key C-M-x. In Lisp mode, this runs the function lisp-eval-defun, which finds the defun around or following point and sends it as input to the Lisp process. (Emacs can send input to any inferior process regardless of what buffer is current.)

Contrast the meanings of C-M-x in Lisp mode (for editing programs to be run in another Lisp system) and Emacs-Lisp mode (for editing Lisp programs to be run in Emacs; see see Section 24.9 [Lisp Eval], page 289): in both modes it has the effect of installing the function definition that point is in, but the way of doing so is different according to where the relevant Lisp environment is found.

25 Maintaining Large Programs

This chapter describes Emacs features for maintaining large programs. The version control features (see Section 15.7 [Version Control], page 135) are also particularly useful for this purpose.

25.1 Change Logs

A change log file contains a chronological record of when and why you have changed a program, consisting of a sequence of entries describing individual changes. Normally it is kept in a file called 'ChangeLog' in the same directory as the file you are editing, or one of its parent directories. A single 'ChangeLog' file can record changes for all the files in its directory and all its subdirectories.

The Emacs command C-x 4 a adds a new entry to the change log file for the file you are editing (add-change-log-entry-other-window). If that file is actually a backup file, it makes an entry appropriate for the file's parent—that is useful for making log entries for functions that have been deleted in the current version.

C-x 4 a visits the change log file and creates a new entry unless the most recent entry is for today's date and your name. It also creates a new item for the current file. For many languages, it can even guess the name of the function or other object that was changed.

When the variable add-log-keep-changes-together is non-nil, C-x 4 a adds to any existing item for the file rather than starting a new item.

If add-log-always-start-new-record is non-nil, C-x 4 a always makes a new entry, even if the last entry was made by you and on the same date.

If the value of the variable change-log-version-info-enabled is non-nil, C-x 4 a adds the file's version number to the change log entry. It finds the version number by searching the first ten percent of the file, using regular expressions from the variable change-log-version-number-regexp-list.

The change log file is visited in Change Log mode. In this major mode, each bunch of grouped items counts as one paragraph, and each entry is considered a page. This facilitates editing the entries. C-j and auto-fill indent each new line like the previous line; this is convenient for entering the contents of an entry.

You can use the command M-x change-log-merge to merge other log files into a buffer in Change Log Mode, preserving the date ordering of entries.

Version control systems are another way to keep track of changes in your program and keep a change log. See Section 15.7.3.4 [Log Buffer], page 140.

25.2 Format of ChangeLog

A change log entry starts with a header line that contains the current date, your name, and your email address (taken from the variable add-log-mailing-address). Aside from these header lines, every line in the change log starts with a space or a tab. The bulk of the entry consists of *items*, each of which starts with a line starting with whitespace and a star. Here are two entries, both dated in May 1993, with two items and one item respectively.

```
1993-05-25  Richard Stallman  <rms@gnu.org>

        * man.el: Rename symbols 'man-*' to 'Man-*'.
        (manual-entry): Make prompt string clearer.

        * simple.el (blink-matching-paren-distance):
        Change default to 12,000.

1993-05-24  Richard Stallman  <rms@gnu.org>

        * vc.el (minor-mode-map-alist): Don't use it if it's void.
        (vc-cancel-version): Doc fix.
```

One entry can describe several changes; each change should have its own item, or its own line in an item. Normally there should be a blank line between items. When items are related (parts of the same change, in different places), group them by leaving no blank line between them.

You should put a copyright notice and permission notice at the end of the change log file. Here is an example:

```
Copyright 1997, 1998 Free Software Foundation, Inc.
Copying and distribution of this file, with or without modification, are
permitted provided the copyright notice and this notice are preserved.
```

Of course, you should substitute the proper years and copyright holder.

25.3 Tags Tables

A *tags table* is a description of how a multi-file program is broken up into files. It lists the names of the component files and the names and positions of the functions (or other named subunits) in each file. Grouping the related files makes it possible to search or replace through all the files with one command. Recording the function names and positions makes possible the M-. command which finds the definition of a function by looking up which of the files it is in.

Tags tables are stored in files called *tags table files*. The conventional name for a tags table file is 'TAGS'.

Each entry in the tags table records the name of one tag, the name of the file that the tag is defined in (implicitly), and the position in that file of the tag's definition. When a file parsed by etags is generated from a different source file, like a C file generated from a Cweb source file, the tags of the parsed file reference the source file.

Just what names from the described files are recorded in the tags table depends on the programming language of the described file. They normally include all file names, functions and subroutines, and may also include global variables, data types, and anything else convenient. Each name recorded is called a *tag*.

See also the Ebrowse facility, which is tailored for C++. See section "Ebrowse" in *Ebrowse User's Manual*.

25.3.1 Source File Tag Syntax

Here is how tag syntax is defined for the most popular languages:

- In C code, any C function or typedef is a tag, and so are definitions of `struct`, `union` and `enum`. `#define` macro definitions, `#undef` and `enum` constants are also tags, unless you specify '`--no-defines`' when making the tags table. Similarly, global variables are tags, unless you specify '`--no-globals`', and so are struct members, unless you specify '`--no-members`'. Use of '`--no-globals`', '`--no-defines`' and '`--no-members`' can make the tags table file much smaller.

  You can tag function declarations and external variables in addition to function definitions by giving the '`--declarations`' option to `etags`.

- In C++ code, in addition to all the tag constructs of C code, member functions are also recognized; member variables are also recognized, unless you use the '`--no-members`' option. Tags for variables and functions in classes are named '*class*::*variable*' and '*class*::*function*'. `operator` definitions have tag names like '`operator+`'.

- In Java code, tags include all the constructs recognized in C++, plus the `interface`, `extends` and `implements` constructs. Tags for variables and functions in classes are named '*class.variable*' and '*class.function*'.

- In LaTeX text, the argument of any of the commands \chapter, \section, \subsection, \subsubsection, \eqno, \label, \ref, \cite, \bibitem, \part, \appendix, \entry, \index, \def, \newcommand, \renewcommand, \newenvironment or \renewenvironment is a tag.

  Other commands can make tags as well, if you specify them in the environment variable `TEXTAGS` before invoking `etags`. The value of this environment variable should be a colon-separated list of command names. For example,

  ```
  TEXTAGS="mycommand:myothercommand"
  export TEXTAGS
  ```

  specifies (using Bourne shell syntax) that the commands '\mycommand' and '\myothercommand' also define tags.

- In Lisp code, any function defined with `defun`, any variable defined with `defvar` or `defconst`, and in general the first argument of any expression that starts with '`(def`' in column zero is a tag.

- In Scheme code, tags include anything defined with `def` or with a construct whose name starts with '`def`'. They also include variables set with `set!` at top level in the file.

Several other languages are also supported:

- In Ada code, functions, procedures, packages, tasks and types are tags. Use the '`--packages-only`' option to create tags for packages only.

  In Ada, the same name can be used for different kinds of entity (e.g., for a procedure and for a function). Also, for things like packages, procedures and functions, there is the spec (i.e. the interface) and the body (i.e. the implementation). To make it easier to pick the definition you want, Ada tag name have suffixes indicating the type of entity:

  '/b'   package body.

'/f'   function.

'/k'   task.

'/p'   procedure.

'/s'   package spec.

'/t'   type.

Thus, `M-x find-tag RET bidule/b RET` will go directly to the body of the package `bidule`, while `M-x find-tag RET bidule RET` will just search for any tag `bidule`.

- In assembler code, labels appearing at the beginning of a line, followed by a colon, are tags.

- In Bison or Yacc input files, each rule defines as a tag the nonterminal it constructs. The portions of the file that contain C code are parsed as C code.

- In Cobol code, tags are paragraph names; that is, any word starting in column 8 and followed by a period.

- In Erlang code, the tags are the functions, records and macros defined in the file.

- In Fortran code, functions, subroutines and block data are tags.

- In HTML input files, the tags are the title and the h1, h2, h3 headers. Also, tags are `name=` in anchors and all occurrences of `id=`.

- In Lua input files, all functions are tags.

- In makefiles, targets are tags; additionally, variables are tags unless you specify '`--no-globals`'.

- In Objective C code, tags include Objective C definitions for classes, class categories, methods and protocols. Tags for variables and functions in classes are named '`class::variable`' and '`class::function`'.

- In Pascal code, the tags are the functions and procedures defined in the file.

- In Perl code, the tags are the packages, subroutines and variables defined by the `package`, `sub`, `my` and `local` keywords. Use '`--globals`' if you want to tag global variables. Tags for subroutines are named '`package::sub`'. The name for subroutines defined in the default package is '`main::sub`'.

- In PHP code, tags are functions, classes and defines. Vars are tags too, unless you use the '`--no-members`' option.

- In PostScript code, the tags are the functions.

- In Prolog code, tags are predicates and rules at the beginning of line.

- In Python code, `def` or `class` at the beginning of a line generate a tag.

You can also generate tags based on regexp matching (see Section 25.3.3 [Etags Regexps], page 297) to handle other formats and languages.

25.3.2 Creating Tags Tables

The `etags` program is used to create a tags table file. It knows the syntax of several languages, as described in the previous section. Here is how to run `etags`:

```
etags inputfiles ...
```

The `etags` program reads the specified files, and writes a tags table named 'TAGS' in the current working directory.

If the specified files don't exist, `etags` looks for compressed versions of them and uncompresses them to read them. Under MS-DOS, `etags` also looks for file names like 'mycode.cgz' if it is given 'mycode.c' on the command line and 'mycode.c' does not exist.

`etags` recognizes the language used in an input file based on its file name and contents. You can specify the language with the '--language=name' option, described below.

If the tags table data become outdated due to changes in the files described in the table, the way to update the tags table is the same way it was made in the first place. If the tags table fails to record a tag, or records it for the wrong file, then Emacs cannot possibly find its definition until you update the tags table. However, if the position recorded in the tags table becomes a little bit wrong (due to other editing), the worst consequence is a slight delay in finding the tag. Even if the stored position is very far wrong, Emacs will still find the tag, after searching most of the file for it. That delay is hardly noticeable with today's computers.

Thus, there is no need to update the tags table after each edit. You should update a tags table when you define new tags that you want to have listed, or when you move tag definitions from one file to another, or when changes become substantial.

One tags table can virtually include another. Specify the included tags file name with the '--include=file' option when creating the file that is to include it. The latter file then acts as if it covered all the source files specified in the included file, as well as the files it directly contains.

If you specify the source files with relative file names when you run `etags`, the tags file will contain file names relative to the directory where the tags file was initially written. This way, you can move an entire directory tree containing both the tags file and the source files, and the tags file will still refer correctly to the source files. If the tags file is in '/dev', however, the file names are made relative to the current working directory. This is useful, for example, when writing the tags to '/dev/stdout'.

When using a a relative file name, it should not be a symbolic link pointing to a tags file in a different directory, because this would generally render the file names invalid.

If you specify absolute file names as arguments to `etags`, then the tags file will contain absolute file names. This way, the tags file will still refer to the same files even if you move it, as long as the source files remain in the same place. Absolute file names start with '/', or with 'device:/' on MS-DOS and MS-Windows.

When you want to make a tags table from a great number of files, you may have problems listing them on the command line, because some systems have a limit on its length. The simplest way to circumvent this limit is to tell **etags** to read the file names from its standard input, by typing a dash in place of the file names, like this:

```
find . -name "*.[chCH]" -print | etags -
```

Use the option '**--language=**_name_' to specify the language explicitly. You can intermix these options with file names; each one applies to the file names that follow it. Specify '**--language=auto**' to tell **etags** to resume guessing the language from the file names and file contents. Specify '**--language=none**' to turn off language-specific processing entirely; then **etags** recognizes tags by regexp matching alone (see Section 25.3.3 [Etags Regexps], page 297).

The option '**--parse-stdin=**_file_' is mostly useful when calling **etags** from programs. It can be used (only once) in place of a file name on the command line. **Etags** will read from standard input and mark the produced tags as belonging to the file _file_.

'**etags --help**' outputs the list of the languages **etags** knows, and the file name rules for guessing the language. It also prints a list of all the available **etags** options, together with a short explanation. If followed by one or more '**--language=**_lang_' options, it outputs detailed information about how tags are generated for _lang_.

25.3.3 Etags Regexps

The '**--regex**' option provides a general way of recognizing tags based on regexp matching. You can freely intermix this option with file names, and each one applies to the source files that follow it. If you specify multiple '**--regex**' options, all of them are used in parallel. The syntax is:

```
--regex=[{language}]/tagregexp/[nameregexp/]modifiers
```

The essential part of the option value is _tagregexp_, the regexp for matching tags. It is always used anchored, that is, it only matches at the beginning of a line. If you want to allow indented tags, use a regexp that matches initial whitespace; start it with '**[\t]****'.

In these regular expressions, '\' quotes the next character, and all the GCC character escape sequences are supported ('\a' for bell, '\b' for back space, '\d' for delete, '\e' for escape, '\f' for formfeed, '\n' for newline, '\r' for carriage return, '\t' for tab, and '\v' for vertical tab).

Ideally, _tagregexp_ should not match more characters than are needed to recognize what you want to tag. If the syntax requires you to write _tagregexp_ so it matches more characters beyond the tag itself, you should add a _nameregexp_, to pick out just the tag. This will enable Emacs to find tags more accurately and to do completion on tag names more reliably. You can find some examples below.

The _modifiers_ are a sequence of zero or more characters that modify the way **etags** does the matching. A regexp with no modifiers is applied sequentially to each line of the input file, in a case-sensitive way. The modifiers and their meanings are:

'**i**'   Ignore case when matching this regexp.

'm'   Match this regular expression against the whole file, so that multi-line matches are possible.

's'   Match this regular expression against the whole file, and allow '.' in *tagregexp* to match newlines.

The '-R' option cancels all the regexps defined by preceding '--regex' options. It too applies to the file names following it. Here's an example:

```
etags --regex=/reg1/i voo.doo --regex=/reg2/m \
    bar.ber -R --lang=lisp los.er
```

Here etags chooses the parsing language for 'voo.doo' and 'bar.ber' according to their contents. etags also uses *reg1* to recognize additional tags in 'voo.doo', and both *reg1* and *reg2* to recognize additional tags in 'bar.ber'. *reg1* is checked against each line of 'voo.doo' and 'bar.ber', in a case-insensitive way, while *reg2* is checked against the whole 'bar.ber' file, permitting multi-line matches, in a case-sensitive way. etags uses only the Lisp tags rules, with no user-specified regexp matching, to recognize tags in 'los.er'.

You can restrict a '--regex' option to match only files of a given language by using the optional prefix {*language*}. ('etags --help' prints the list of languages recognized by etags.) This is particularly useful when storing many predefined regular expressions for etags in a file. The following example tags the DEFVAR macros in the Emacs source files, for the C language only:

```
--regex='{c}/[ \t]*DEFVAR_[A-Z_ \t(]+"\([^"]+\)"/'
```

When you have complex regular expressions, you can store the list of them in a file. The following option syntax instructs etags to read two files of regular expressions. The regular expressions contained in the second file are matched without regard to case.

```
--regex=@case-sensitive-file --ignore-case-regex=@ignore-case-file
```

A regex file for etags contains one regular expression per line. Empty lines, and lines beginning with space or tab are ignored. When the first character in a line is '@', etags assumes that the rest of the line is the name of another file of regular expressions; thus, one such file can include another file. All the other lines are taken to be regular expressions. If the first non-whitespace text on the line is '--', that line is a comment.

For example, we can create a file called 'emacs.tags' with the following contents:

```
                -- This is for GNU Emacs C source files
    {c}/[ \t]*DEFVAR_[A-Z_ \t(]+"\([^"]+\)"/\1/
```

and then use it like this:

```
etags --regex=@emacs.tags *.[ch] */*.[ch]
```

Here are some more examples. The regexps are quoted to protect them from shell interpretation.

- Tag Octave files:

```
    etags --language=none \
        --regex='/[ \t]*function.*=[ \t]*\([^ \t]*\)[ \t]*(/\1/' \
        --regex='/###key \(.*\)/\1/' \
        --regex='/[ \t]*global[ \t].*/' \
        *.m
```

Note that tags are not generated for scripts, so that you have to add a line by yourself of the form '###key *scriptname*' if you want to jump to it.

- Tag Tcl files:

```
etags --language=none --regex='/proc[ \t]+\([^ \t]+\)/\1/' *.tcl
```

- Tag VHDL files:

```
etags --language=none \
  --regex='/[ \t]*\(ARCHITECTURE\|CONFIGURATION\) +[^ ]* +OF/' \
  --regex='/[ \t]*\(ATTRIBUTE\|ENTITY\|FUNCTION\|PACKAGE\
  \( BODY\)?\|PROCEDURE\|PROCESS\|TYPE\)[ \t]+\([^ \t(]+\)/\3/'
```

25.3.4 Selecting a Tags Table

Emacs has at any time one *selected* tags table, and all the commands for working with tags tables use the selected one. To select a tags table, type M-x visit-tags-table, which reads the tags table file name as an argument, with 'TAGS' in the default directory as the default.

Emacs does not actually read in the tags table contents until you try to use them; all visit-tags-table does is store the file name in the variable tags-file-name, and setting the variable yourself is just as good. The variable's initial value is nil; that value tells all the commands for working with tags tables that they must ask for a tags table file name to use.

Using visit-tags-table when a tags table is already loaded gives you a choice: you can add the new tags table to the current list of tags tables, or start a new list. The tags commands use all the tags tables in the current list. If you start a new list, the new tags table is used *instead* of others. If you add the new table to the current list, it is used *as well as* the others.

You can specify a precise list of tags tables by setting the variable tags-table-list to a list of strings, like this:

```
(setq tags-table-list
      '("~/emacs" "/usr/local/lib/emacs/src"))
```

This tells the tags commands to look at the 'TAGS' files in your '~/emacs' directory and in the '/usr/local/lib/emacs/src' directory. The order depends on which file you are in and which tags table mentions that file, as explained above.

Do not set both tags-file-name and tags-table-list.

25.3.5 Finding a Tag

The most important thing that a tags table enables you to do is to find the definition of a specific tag.

M-. *tag* RET

Find first definition of *tag* (find-tag).

C-u M-.   Find next alternate definition of last tag specified.

C-u - M-.   Go back to previous tag found.

C-M-. *pattern* RET

Find a tag whose name matches *pattern* (find-tag-regexp).

C-u C-M-.   Find the next tag whose name matches the last pattern used.

C-x 4 . *tag* RET
> Find first definition of *tag*, but display it in another window (`find-tag-other-window`).

C-x 5 . *tag* RET
> Find first definition of *tag*, and create a new frame to select the buffer (`find-tag-other-frame`).

M-*   Pop back to where you previously invoked M-. and friends.

M-. (`find-tag`) is the command to find the definition of a specified tag. It searches through the tags table for that tag, as a string, and then uses the tags table info to determine the file that the definition is in and the approximate character position in the file of the definition. Then `find-tag` visits that file, moves point to the approximate character position, and searches ever-increasing distances away to find the tag definition.

If an empty argument is given (just type RET), the balanced expression in the buffer before or around point is used as the *tag* argument. See Section 23.4.1 [Expressions], page 257.

You don't need to give M-. the full name of the tag; a part will do. This is because M-. finds tags in the table which contain *tag* as a substring. However, it prefers an exact match to a substring match. To find other tags that match the same substring, give `find-tag` a numeric argument, as in C-u M-.; this does not read a tag name, but continues searching the tags table's text for another tag containing the same substring last used. If you have a real META key, M-0 M-. is an easier alternative to C-u M-..

Like most commands that can switch buffers, `find-tag` has a variant that displays the new buffer in another window, and one that makes a new frame for it. The former is C-x 4 ., which invokes the command `find-tag-other-window`. The latter is C-x 5 ., which invokes `find-tag-other-frame`.

To move back to places you've found tags recently, use C-u - M-.; more generally, M-. with a negative numeric argument. This command can take you to another buffer. C-x 4 . with a negative argument finds the previous tag location in another window.

As well as going back to places you've found tags recently, you can go back to places *from where* you found them. Use M-*, which invokes the command `pop-tag-mark`, for this. Typically you would find and study the definition of something with M-. and then return to where you were with M-*.

Both C-u - M-. and M-* allow you to retrace your steps to a depth determined by the variable `find-tag-marker-ring-length`.

The command C-M-. (`find-tag-regexp`) visits the tags that match a specified regular expression. It is just like M-. except that it does regexp matching instead of substring matching.

25.3.6 Searching and Replacing with Tags Tables

The commands in this section visit and search all the files listed in the selected tags table, one by one. For these commands, the tags table serves only to specify a sequence of files to search. These commands scan the list of tags tables starting with the first tags table (if any) that describes the current file, proceed from there to the end of the list, and then scan from the beginning of the list until they have covered all the tables in the list.

M-x tags-search RET *regexp* RET

> Search for *regexp* through the files in the selected tags table.

M-x tags-query-replace RET *regexp* RET *replacement* RET

> Perform a `query-replace-regexp` on each file in the selected tags table.

M-,

> Restart one of the commands above, from the current location of point (`tags-loop-continue`).

M-x `tags-search` reads a regexp using the minibuffer, then searches for matches in all the files in the selected tags table, one file at a time. It displays the name of the file being searched so you can follow its progress. As soon as it finds an occurrence, `tags-search` returns.

Having found one match, you probably want to find all the rest. To find one more match, type M-, (`tags-loop-continue`) to resume the `tags-search`. This searches the rest of the current buffer, followed by the remaining files of the tags table.

M-x `tags-query-replace` performs a single `query-replace-regexp` through all the files in the tags table. It reads a regexp to search for and a string to replace with, just like ordinary M-x `query-replace-regexp`. It searches much like M-x `tags-search`, but repeatedly, processing matches according to your input. See Section 12.9 [Replace], page 99, for more information on query replace.

You can control the case-sensitivity of tags search commands by customizing the value of the variable `tags-case-fold-search`. The default is to use the same setting as the value of `case-fold-search` (see Section 12.8 [Search Case], page 98).

It is possible to get through all the files in the tags table with a single invocation of M-x `tags-query-replace`. But often it is useful to exit temporarily, which you can do with any input event that has no special query replace meaning. You can resume the query replace subsequently by typing M-,; this command resumes the last tags search or replace command that you did.

The commands in this section carry out much broader searches than the `find-tag` family. The `find-tag` commands search only for definitions of tags that match your substring or regexp. The commands `tags-search` and `tags-query-replace` find every occurrence of the regexp, as ordinary search commands and replace commands do in the current buffer.

These commands create buffers only temporarily for the files that they have to search (those which are not already visited in Emacs buffers). Buffers in which no match is found are quickly killed; the others continue to exist.

It may have struck you that `tags-search` is a lot like `grep`. You can also run `grep` itself as an inferior of Emacs and have Emacs show you the matching lines one by one. See Section 24.4 [Grep Searching], page 277.

25.3.7 Tags Table Inquiries

`M-x list-tags RET` *file* `RET`
> Display a list of the tags defined in the program file *file*.

`M-x tags-apropos RET` *regexp* `RET`
> Display a list of all tags matching *regexp*.

`M-x list-tags` reads the name of one of the files described by the selected tags table, and displays a list of all the tags defined in that file. The "file name" argument is really just a string to compare against the file names recorded in the tags table; it is read as a string rather than as a file name. Therefore, completion and defaulting are not available, and you must enter the file name the same way it appears in the tags table. Do not include a directory as part of the file name unless the file name recorded in the tags table includes a directory.

`M-x tags-apropos` is like `apropos` for tags (see Section 7.3 [Apropos], page 43). It finds all the tags in the selected tags table whose entries match *regexp*, and displays them. If the variable `tags-apropos-verbose` is non-`nil`, it displays the names of the tags files together with the tag names.

You can customize the appearance of the output by setting the variable `tags-tag-face` to a face. You can display additional output with `M-x tags-apropos` by customizing the variable `tags-apropos-additional-actions`—see its documentation for details.

You can also use the collection of tag names to complete a symbol name in the buffer. See Section 23.8 [Symbol Completion], page 266.

26 Abbrevs

A defined *abbrev* is a word which *expands*, if you insert it, into some different text. Abbrevs are defined by the user to expand in specific ways. For example, you might define 'foo' as an abbrev expanding to 'find outer otter'. Then you could insert 'find outer otter ' into the buffer by typing f o o SPC.

A second kind of abbreviation facility is called *dynamic abbrev expansion*. You use dynamic abbrev expansion with an explicit command to expand the letters in the buffer before point by looking for other words in the buffer that start with those letters. See Section 26.6 [Dynamic Abbrevs], page 307.

"Hippie" expansion generalizes abbreviation expansion. See section "Hippie Expansion" in *Features for Automatic Typing*.

26.1 Abbrev Concepts

An *abbrev* is a word which has been defined to *expand* into a specified *expansion*. When you insert a word-separator character following the abbrev, that expands the abbrev—replacing the abbrev with its expansion. For example, if 'foo' is defined as an abbrev expanding to 'find outer otter', then you can insert 'find outer otter.' into the buffer by typing f o o ..

Abbrevs expand only when Abbrev mode (a minor mode) is enabled. Disabling Abbrev mode does not cause abbrev definitions to be forgotten, but they do not expand until Abbrev mode is enabled again. The command M-x abbrev-mode toggles Abbrev mode; with a numeric argument, it turns Abbrev mode on if the argument is positive, off otherwise. See Section 32.1 [Minor Modes], page 406. abbrev-mode is also a variable; Abbrev mode is on when the variable is non-nil. The variable abbrev-mode automatically becomes local to the current buffer when it is set.

Abbrevs can have *mode-specific* definitions, active only in one major mode. Abbrevs can also have *global* definitions that are active in all major modes. The same abbrev can have a global definition and various mode-specific definitions for different major modes. A mode-specific definition for the current major mode overrides a global definition.

You can define abbrevs interactively during the editing session. You can also save lists of abbrev definitions in files for use in later sessions. Some users keep extensive lists of abbrevs that they load in every session.

26.2 Defining Abbrevs

C-x a g   Define an abbrev, using one or more words before point as its expansion (add-global-abbrev).

C-x a l   Similar, but define an abbrev specific to the current major mode (add-mode-abbrev).

C-x a i g   Define a word in the buffer as an abbrev (inverse-add-global-abbrev).

C-x a i l   Define a word in the buffer as a mode-specific abbrev (`inverse-add-mode-abbrev`).

`M-x define-global-abbrev RET` *abbrev* `RET` *exp* `RET`
  Define *abbrev* as an abbrev expanding into *exp*.

`M-x define-mode-abbrev RET` *abbrev* `RET` *exp* `RET`
  Define *abbrev* as a mode-specific abbrev expanding into *exp*.

`M-x kill-all-abbrevs`
  Discard all abbrev definitions, leaving a blank slate.

The usual way to define an abbrev is to enter the text you want the abbrev to expand to, position point after it, and type `C-x a g` (`add-global-abbrev`). This reads the abbrev itself using the minibuffer, and then defines it as an abbrev for one or more words before point. Use a numeric argument to say how many words before point should be taken as the expansion. For example, to define the abbrev 'foo' as mentioned above, insert the text 'find outer otter' and then type `C-u 3 C-x a g f o o RET`.

An argument of zero to `C-x a g` means to use the contents of the region as the expansion of the abbrev being defined.

The command `C-x a l` (`add-mode-abbrev`) is similar, but defines a mode-specific abbrev. Mode-specific abbrevs are active only in a particular major mode. `C-x a l` defines an abbrev for the major mode in effect at the time `C-x a l` is typed. The arguments work the same as for `C-x a g`.

If the abbrev text itself is already in the buffer, you can use the commands `C-x a i g` (`inverse-add-global-abbrev`) and `C-x a i l` (`inverse-add-mode-abbrev`) to define it as an abbrev by specify the expansion in the minibuffer. These commands are called "inverse" because they invert the meaning of the two text strings they use (one from the buffer and one read with the minibuffer).

You can define an abbrev without inserting either the abbrev or its expansion in the buffer using the command `define-global-abbrev`. It reads two arguments— the abbrev, and its expansion. The command `define-mode-abbrev` does likewise for a mode-specific abbrev.

To change the definition of an abbrev, just define a new definition. When the abbrev has a prior definition, the abbrev definition commands ask for confirmation before replacing it.

To remove an abbrev definition, give a negative argument to the abbrev definition command: `C-u - C-x a g` or `C-u - C-x a l`. The former removes a global definition, while the latter removes a mode-specific definition. `M-x kill-all-abbrevs` removes all abbrev definitions, both global and local.

26.3 Controlling Abbrev Expansion

When Abbrev mode is enabled, an abbrev expands whenever it is present in the buffer just before point and you type a self-inserting whitespace or punctuation character (SPC, comma, etc.). More precisely, any character that is not a word constituent expands an abbrev, and any word-constituent character can be part of an abbrev. The most common way to use an abbrev is to insert it and then insert a punctuation or whitespace character to expand it.

Abbrev expansion preserves case; thus, 'foo' expands into 'find outer otter'; 'Foo' into 'Find outer otter', and 'FOO' into 'FIND OUTER OTTER' or 'Find Outer Otter' according to the variable abbrev-all-caps (setting it non-nil specifies 'FIND OUTER OTTER').

These commands are used to control abbrev expansion:

M-'   Separate a prefix from a following abbrev to be expanded (abbrev-prefix-mark).

C-x a e   Expand the abbrev before point (expand-abbrev). This is effective even when Abbrev mode is not enabled.

M-x expand-region-abbrevs
             Expand some or all abbrevs found in the region.

You may wish to expand an abbrev and attach a prefix to the expansion; for example, if 'cnst' expands into 'construction', you might want to use it to enter 'reconstruction'. It does not work to type recnst, because that is not necessarily a defined abbrev. What you can do is use the command M-' (abbrev-prefix-mark) in between the prefix 're' and the abbrev 'cnst'. First, insert 're'. Then type M-'; this inserts a hyphen in the buffer to indicate that it has done its work. Then insert the abbrev 'cnst'; the buffer now contains 're-cnst'. Now insert a non-word character to expand the abbrev 'cnst' into 'construction'. This expansion step also deletes the hyphen that indicated M-' had been used. The result is the desired 'reconstruction'.

If you actually want the text of the abbrev in the buffer, rather than its expansion, you can accomplish this by inserting the following punctuation with C-q. Thus, foo C-q , leaves 'foo,' in the buffer, not expanding it.

If you expand an abbrev by mistake, you can undo the expansion and bring back the abbrev itself by typing C-_ to undo (see Section 13.1 [Undo], page 105). This also undoes the insertion of the non-word character that expanded the abbrev. If the result you want is the terminating non-word character plus the unexpanded abbrev, you must reinsert the terminating character, quoting it with C-q. You can also use the command M-x unexpand-abbrev to cancel the last expansion without deleting the terminating character.

M-x expand-region-abbrevs searches through the region for defined abbrevs, and for each one found offers to replace it with its expansion. This command is useful if you have typed in text using abbrevs but forgot to turn on Abbrev mode first. It may also be useful together with a special set of abbrev definitions for making several global replacements at once. This command is effective even if Abbrev mode is not enabled.

Expanding any abbrev first runs the hook pre-abbrev-expand-hook (see Section 32.3.2 [Hooks], page 418).

26.4 Examining and Editing Abbrevs

M-x list-abbrevs
> Display a list of all abbrev definitions. With a numeric argument, list only local abbrevs.

M-x edit-abbrevs
> Edit a list of abbrevs; you can add, alter or remove definitions.

The output from M-x list-abbrevs looks like this:

```
various other tables...
(lisp-mode-abbrev-table)
"dk"        0    "define-key"
(global-abbrev-table)
"dfn"        0    "definition"
```

(Some blank lines of no semantic significance, and some other abbrev tables, have been omitted.)

A line containing a name in parentheses is the header for abbrevs in a particular abbrev table; global-abbrev-table contains all the global abbrevs, and the other abbrev tables that are named after major modes contain the mode-specific abbrevs.

Within each abbrev table, each nonblank line defines one abbrev. The word at the beginning of the line is the abbrev. The number that follows is the number of times the abbrev has been expanded. Emacs keeps track of this to help you see which abbrevs you actually use, so that you can eliminate those that you don't use often. The string at the end of the line is the expansion.

Some abbrevs are marked with '(sys)'. These "system" abbrevs (see section "Abbrevs" in *The Emacs Lisp Reference Manual*) are pre-defined by various modes, and are not saved to your abbrev file. To disable a "system" abbrev, define an abbrev of the same name that expands to itself, and save it to your abbrev file.

M-x edit-abbrevs allows you to add, change or kill abbrev definitions by editing a list of them in an Emacs buffer. The list has the same format described above. The buffer of abbrevs is called '*Abbrevs*', and is in Edit-Abbrevs mode. Type C-c C-c in this buffer to install the abbrev definitions as specified in the buffer—and delete any abbrev definitions not listed.

The command edit-abbrevs is actually the same as list-abbrevs except that it selects the buffer '*Abbrevs*' whereas list-abbrevs merely displays it in another window.

26.5 Saving Abbrevs

These commands allow you to keep abbrev definitions between editing sessions.

M-x write-abbrev-file RET *file* RET
> Write a file *file* describing all defined abbrevs.

M-x read-abbrev-file RET *file* RET
> Read the file *file* and define abbrevs as specified therein.

M-x quietly-read-abbrev-file RET *file* RET
> Similar but do not display a message about what is going on.

M-x define-abbrevs
> Define abbrevs from definitions in current buffer.

M-x insert-abbrevs
> Insert all abbrevs and their expansions into current buffer.

M-x write-abbrev-file reads a file name using the minibuffer and then writes a description of all current abbrev definitions into that file. This is used to save abbrev definitions for use in a later session. The text stored in the file is a series of Lisp expressions that, when executed, define the same abbrevs that you currently have.

M-x read-abbrev-file reads a file name using the minibuffer and then reads the file, defining abbrevs according to the contents of the file. The function quietly-read-abbrev-file is similar except that it does not display a message in the echo area; you cannot invoke it interactively, and it is used primarily in the '.emacs' file. If either of these functions is called with nil as the argument, it uses the file name specified in the variable abbrev-file-name, which is by default "~/.abbrev_defs". That file is your standard abbrev definition file, and Emacs loads abbrevs from it automatically when it starts up.

Emacs will offer to save abbrevs automatically if you have changed any of them, whenever it offers to save all files (for C-x s or C-x C-c). It saves them in the file specified by abbrev-file-name. This feature can be inhibited by setting the variable save-abbrevs to nil.

The commands M-x insert-abbrevs and M-x define-abbrevs are similar to the previous commands but work on text in an Emacs buffer. M-x insert-abbrevs inserts text into the current buffer after point, describing all current abbrev definitions; M-x define-abbrevs parses the entire current buffer and defines abbrevs accordingly.

26.6 Dynamic Abbrev Expansion

The abbrev facility described above operates automatically as you insert text, but all abbrevs must be defined explicitly. By contrast, *dynamic abbrevs* allow the meanings of abbreviations to be determined automatically from the contents of the buffer, but dynamic abbrev expansion happens only when you request it explicitly.

M-/
> Expand the word in the buffer before point as a *dynamic abbrev*, by searching in the buffer for words starting with that abbreviation (dabbrev-expand).

C-M-/
> Complete the word before point as a dynamic abbrev (dabbrev-completion).

For example, if the buffer contains 'does this follow' and you type f o M-/, the effect is to insert 'follow' because that is the last word in the buffer that starts with 'fo'. A numeric argument to M-/ says to take the second, third, etc.

distinct expansion found looking backward from point. Repeating M-/ searches for an alternative expansion by looking farther back. After scanning all the text before point, it searches the text after point. The variable dabbrev-limit, if non-nil, specifies how far away in the buffer to search for an expansion.

After scanning the current buffer, M-/ normally searches other buffers, unless you have set dabbrev-check-all-buffers to nil.

For finer control over which buffers to scan, customize the variable dabbrev-ignored-buffer-regexps. Its value is a list of regular expressions. If a buffer's name matches any of these regular expressions, dynamic abbrev expansion skips that buffer.

A negative argument to M-/, as in C-u - M-/, says to search first for expansions after point, then other buffers, and consider expansions before point only as a last resort. If you repeat the M-/ to look for another expansion, do not specify an argument. Repeating M-/ cycles through all the expansions after point and then the expansions before point.

After you have expanded a dynamic abbrev, you can copy additional words that follow the expansion in its original context. Simply type SPC M-/ for each additional word you want to copy. The spacing and punctuation between words is copied along with the words.

The command C-M-/ (dabbrev-completion) performs completion of a dynamic abbrev. Instead of trying the possible expansions one by one, it finds all of them, then inserts the text that they have in common. If they have nothing in common, C-M-/ displays a list of completions, from which you can select a choice in the usual manner. See Section 5.3 [Completion], page 33.

Dynamic abbrev expansion is completely independent of Abbrev mode; the expansion of a word with M-/ is completely independent of whether it has a definition as an ordinary abbrev.

26.7 Customizing Dynamic Abbreviation

Normally, dynamic abbrev expansion ignores case when searching for expansions. That is, the expansion need not agree in case with the word you are expanding.

This feature is controlled by the variable dabbrev-case-fold-search. If it is t, case is ignored in this search; if it is nil, the word and the expansion must match in case. If the value of dabbrev-case-fold-search is case-fold-search, which is true by default, then the variable case-fold-search controls whether to ignore case while searching for expansions.

Normally, dynamic abbrev expansion preserves the case pattern *of the dynamic abbrev you are expanding*, by converting the expansion to that case pattern.

The variable dabbrev-case-replace controls whether to preserve the case pattern of the dynamic abbrev. If it is t, the dynamic abbrev's case pattern is preserved in most cases; if it is nil, the expansion is always copied verbatim. If the value of dabbrev-case-replace is case-replace, which is true by default, then the variable case-replace controls whether to copy the expansion verbatim.

However, if the expansion contains a complex mixed case pattern, and the dynamic abbrev matches this pattern as far as it goes, then the expansion is always copied verbatim, regardless of those variables. Thus, for example, if the buffer contains `variableWithSillyCasePattern`, and you type v a M-/, it copies the expansion verbatim including its case pattern.

The variable `dabbrev-abbrev-char-regexp`, if non-`nil`, controls which characters are considered part of a word, for dynamic expansion purposes. The regular expression must match just one character, never two or more. The same regular expression also determines which characters are part of an expansion. The value `nil` has a special meaning: dynamic abbrevs are made of word characters, but expansions are made of word and symbol characters.

In shell scripts and makefiles, a variable name is sometimes prefixed with '$' and sometimes not. Major modes for this kind of text can customize dynamic abbrev expansion to handle optional prefixes by setting the variable `dabbrev-abbrev-skip-leading-rogexp`. Its value should be a regular expression that matches the optional prefix that dynamic abbrev expression should ignore.

27 Sending Mail

To send a message in Emacs, you start by typing a command (C-x m) to select and initialize the '*mail*' buffer. Then you edit the text and headers of the message in this buffer, and type another command (C-c C-s or C-c C-c) to send the message.

C-x m   Begin composing a message to send (compose-mail).

C-x 4 m   Likewise, but display the message in another window (compose-mail-other-window).

C-x 5 m   Likewise, but make a new frame (compose-mail-other-frame).

C-c C-s   In Mail mode, send the message (mail-send).

C-c C-c   Send the message and bury the mail buffer (mail-send-and-exit).

The command C-x m (compose-mail) selects a buffer named '*mail*' and initializes it with the skeleton of an outgoing message. C-x 4 m (compose-mail-other-window) selects the '*mail*' buffer in a different window, leaving the previous current buffer visible. C-x 5 m (compose-mail-other-frame) creates a new frame to select the '*mail*' buffer.

Because the mail-composition buffer is an ordinary Emacs buffer, you can switch to other buffers while in the middle of composing mail, and switch back later (or never). If you use the C-x m command again when you have been composing another message but have not sent it, you are asked to confirm before the old message is erased. If you answer n, the '*mail*' buffer remains selected with its old contents, so you can finish the old message and send it. C-u C-x m is another way to do this. Sending the message marks the '*mail*' buffer "unmodified," which avoids the need for confirmation when C-x m is next used.

If you are composing a message in the '*mail*' buffer and want to send another message before finishing the first, rename the '*mail*' buffer using M-x rename-uniquely (see Section 16.3 [Misc Buffer], page 158). Then you can use C-x m or its variants described above to make a new '*mail*' buffer. Once you've done that, you can work with each mail buffer independently.

The variable mail-default-directory controls the default directory for mail buffers, and also says where to put their auto-save files.

27.1 The Format of the Mail Buffer

In addition to the *text* or *body*, a message has *header fields* which say who sent it, when, to whom, why, and so on. Some header fields, such as 'Date' and 'Sender', are created automatically when you send the message. Others, such as the recipient names, must be specified by you in order to send the message properly.

In the mail buffer, you can insert and edit header fields using ordinary editing commands. Mail mode provides a commands to help you edit some header fields, and some are preinitialized in the buffer automatically when appropriate.

The line in the buffer that says

```
--text follows this line--
```
is a special delimiter that separates the headers you have specified from the text. Whatever follows this line is the text of the message; the headers precede it. The delimiter line itself does not appear in the message actually sent. The text used for the delimiter line is controlled by the variable `mail-header-separator`.

Here is an example of what the headers and text in the mail buffer might look like.

```
To: gnu@gnu.org
CC: lungfish@spam.org, byob@spam.org
Subject: The Emacs Manual
--Text follows this line--
Please ignore this message.
```

27.2 Mail Header Fields

A header field in the mail buffer starts with a field name at the beginning of a line, terminated by a colon. Upper and lower case are equivalent in field names (and in mailing addresses also). After the colon and optional whitespace comes the contents of the field.

You can use any name you like for a header field, but normally people use only standard field names with accepted meanings. Here is a table of fields commonly used in outgoing messages.

‘To’   This field contains the mailing addresses to which the message is addressed. If you list more than one address, use commas, not spaces, to separate them.

‘Subject’   The contents of the ‘Subject’ field should be a piece of text that says what the message is about. The reason ‘Subject’ fields are useful is that most mail-reading programs can provide a summary of messages, listing the subject of each message but not its text.

‘CC’   This field contains additional mailing addresses to send the message to, like ‘To’ except that these readers should not regard the message as directed at them.

‘BCC’   This field contains additional mailing addresses to send the message to, which should not appear in the header of the message actually sent. Copies sent this way are called *blind carbon copies*.

              To send a blind carbon copy of every outgoing message to yourself, set the variable `mail-self-blind` to `t`. To send a blind carbon copy of every message to some other *address*, set the variable `mail-default-headers` to `"Bcc: address\n"`.

‘FCC’   This field contains the name of one file and directs Emacs to append a copy of the message to that file when you send the message. If the file is in Rmail format, Emacs writes the message in Rmail format; otherwise, Emacs writes the message in system mail file format. To specify more than one file, use several 'FCC' fields, with one file name in each field.

To put a fixed file name in the 'FCC' field each time you start editing an outgoing message, set the variable `mail-archive-file-name` to that file name. Unless you remove the 'FCC' field before sending, the message will be written into that file when it is sent.

'From'   Use the 'From' field to say who you are, when the account you are using to send the mail is not your own. The contents of the 'From' field should be a valid mailing address, since replies will normally go there. If you don't specify the 'From' field yourself, Emacs uses the value of `user-mail-address` as the default.

'Reply-to'   Use this field to direct replies to a different address. Most mail-reading programs (including Rmail) automatically send replies to the 'Reply-to' address in preference to the 'From' address. By adding a 'Reply-to' field to your header, you can work around any problems your 'From' address may cause for replies.

To put a fixed 'Reply-to' address into every outgoing message, set the variable `mail-default-reply-to` to that address (as a string). Then `mail` initializes the message with a 'Reply-to' field as specified. You can delete or alter that header field before you send the message, if you wish. When Emacs starts up, if the environment variable REPLYTO is set, `mail-default-reply-to` is initialized from that environment variable.

'In-reply-to'
This field contains a piece of text describing the message you are replying to. Some mail systems can use this information to correlate related pieces of mail. Normally this field is filled in by Rmail when you reply to a message in Rmail, and you never need to think about it (see Chapter 28 [Rmail], page 319).

'References'
This field lists the message IDs of related previous messages. Rmail sets up this field automatically when you reply to a message.

The 'To', 'CC', and 'BCC' header fields can appear any number of times, and each such header field can contain multiple addresses, separated by commas. This way, you can specify any number of places to send the message. These fields can also have continuation lines: one or more lines starting with whitespace, following the starting line of the field, are considered part of the field. Here's an example of a 'To' field with a continuation line:

```
To: foo@here.net, this@there.net,
    me@gnu.cambridge.mass.usa.earth.spiral3281
```

When you send the message, if you didn't write a 'From' field yourself, Emacs puts in one for you. The variable `mail-from-style` controls the format:

nil   Use just the email address, as in 'king@grassland.com'.

parens   Use both email address and full name, as in:
                'king@grassland.com (Elvis Parsley)'.

angles   Use both email address and full name, as in:
                'Elvis Parsley <king@grassland.com>'.

system-default
                Allow the system to insert the 'From' field.

You can direct Emacs to insert certain default headers into the outgoing message
by setting the variable `mail-default-headers` to a string. Then C-x m inserts this
string into the message headers. If the default header fields are not appropriate for
a particular message, edit them as appropriate before sending the message.

27.3 Mail Aliases

You can define *mail aliases* in a file named '~/.mailrc'. These are short mnemonic
names which stand for mail addresses or groups of mail addresses. Like many other
mail programs, Emacs expands aliases when they occur in the 'To', 'From', 'CC',
'BCC', and 'Reply-to' fields, plus their 'Resent-' variants.

To define an alias in '~/.mailrc', write a line in the following format:

    alias *shortaddress fulladdresses*

Here *fulladdresses* stands for one or more mail addresses for *shortaddress* to expand
into. Separate multiple addresses with spaces; if an address contains a space, quote
the whole address with a pair of double-quotes.

For instance, to make `maingnu` stand for gnu@gnu.org plus a local address of
your own, put in this line:

    alias maingnu gnu@gnu.org local-gnu

Addresses specified in this way should use doublequotes around an entire address
when the address contains spaces. But you need not include doublequotes around
parts of the address, such as the person's full name. Emacs puts them in if they
are needed. For example,

    alias chief-torturer "George W. Bush <bush@whitehouse.gov>"

is correct in '.mailrc'. Emacs will insert the address as '"George W. Bush"
<bush@whitehouse.gov>'.

Emacs also recognizes "include" commands in '.mailrc' files. They look like
this:

    source *filename*

The file '~/.mailrc' is used primarily by other mail-reading programs; it can contain
various other commands. Emacs ignores everything in it except for alias definitions
and include commands.

Another way to define a mail alias, within Emacs alone, is with the **define-mail-alias** command. It prompts for the alias and then the full address. You can
use it to define aliases in your '.emacs' file, like this:

    (define-mail-alias "maingnu" "gnu@gnu.org")

define-mail-alias records aliases by adding them to a variable named **mail-aliases**. If you are comfortable with manipulating Lisp lists, you can set **mail-**

aliases directly. The initial value of `mail-aliases` is `t`, which means that Emacs should read '`.mailrc`' to get the proper value.

You can specify a different file name to use instead of '`~/.mailrc`' by setting the variable `mail-personal-alias-file`.

Normally, Emacs expands aliases when you send the message. You do not need to expand mail aliases before sending the message, but you can expand them if you want to see where the mail will actually go. To do this, use the command `M-x expand-mail-aliases`; it expands all mail aliases currently present in the mail headers that hold addresses.

If you like, you can have mail aliases expand as abbrevs, as soon as you type them in (see Chapter 26 [Abbrevs], page 303). To enable this feature, execute the following:

```
(add-hook 'mail-mode-hook 'mail-abbrevs-setup)
```

This can go in your '`.emacs`' file. See Section 32.3.2 [Hooks], page 418. If you use this feature, you must use `define-mail-abbrev` instead of `define-mail-alias`; the latter does not work with this package. Note that the mail abbreviation package uses the variable `mail-abbrevs` instead of `mail-aliases`, and that all alias names are converted to lower case.

The mail abbreviation package also provides the `C-c C-a` (`mail-interactive-insert-alias`) command, which reads an alias name (with completion) and inserts its definition at point. This is useful when editing the message text itself or a header field such as '`Subject`' in which Emacs does not normally expand aliases.

Note that abbrevs expand only if you insert a word-separator character afterward. However, you can rebind `C-n` and `M->` to cause expansion as well. Here's how to do that:

```
(add-hook 'mail-mode-hook
    (lambda ()
      (define-key
        mail-mode-map [remap next-line] 'mail-abbrev-next-line)
      (define-key
        mail-mode-map [remap end-of-buffer] 'mail-abbrev-end-of-buffer)))
```

27.4 Mail Mode

The major mode used in the mail buffer is Mail mode, which is much like Text mode except that various special commands are provided on the `C-c` prefix. These commands all have to do specifically with editing or sending the message. In addition, Mail mode defines the character '`%`' as a word separator; this is helpful for using the word commands to edit mail addresses.

Mail mode is normally used in buffers set up automatically by the `mail` command and related commands. However, you can also switch to Mail mode in a file-visiting buffer. This is a useful thing to do if you have saved the text of a draft message in a file.

27.4.1 Mail Sending

Mail mode has two commands for sending the message you have been editing:

C-c C-s   Send the message, and leave the mail buffer selected (`mail-send`).

C-c C-c   Send the message, and select some other buffer (`mail-send-and-exit`).

C-c C-s (`mail-send`) sends the message and marks the mail buffer unmodified, but leaves that buffer selected so that you can modify the message (perhaps with new recipients) and send it again. C-c C-c (`mail-send-and-exit`) sends and then deletes the window or switches to another buffer. It puts the mail buffer at the lowest priority for reselection by default, since you are finished with using it. This is the usual way to send the message.

In a file-visiting buffer, sending the message does not clear the modified flag, because only saving the file should do that. Also, you don't get a warning if you try to send the same message twice.

When you send a message that contains non ASCII characters, they need to be encoded with a coding system (see Section 19.7 [Coding Systems], page 193). Usually the coding system is specified automatically by your chosen language environment (see Section 19.3 [Language Environments], page 188). You can explicitly specify the coding system for outgoing mail by setting the variable **sendmail-coding-system** (see Section 19.8 [Recognize Coding], page 195).

If the coding system thus determined does not handle the characters in a particular message, Emacs asks you to select the coding system to use, showing a list of possible coding systems.

The variable **send-mail-function** controls how the default mail user agent sends mail. It should be set to a function. The default is sendmail send it, which delivers mail using the Sendmail installation on the local host. To send mail through a SMTP server, set it to `smtpmail-send-it` and set up the Emacs SMTP library (see section "Emacs SMTP Library" in *Sending mail via SMTP*). A third option is `feedmail-send-it`, see the commentary section of the 'feedmail.el' package for more information.

27.4.2 Mail Header Editing

Mail mode provides special commands to move to particular header fields and to complete addresses in headers.

C-c C-f C-t
        Move to the 'To' header field, creating one if there is none (`mail-to`).

C-c C-f C-s
        Move to the 'Subject' header field, creating one if there is none (`mail-subject`).

C-c C-f C-c
        Move to the 'CC' header field, creating one if there is none (`mail-cc`).

C-c C-f C-b
        Move to the 'BCC' header field, creating one if there is none (`mail-bcc`).

C-c C-f C-f
        Move to the 'FCC' header field, creating one if there is none (`mail-fcc`).

M-TAB   Complete a mailing address (`mail-complete`).

There are five commands to move point to particular header fields, all based on the prefix `C-c C-f` ('C-f' is for "field"). They are listed in the table above. If the field in question does not exist, these commands create one. We provide special motion commands for these particular fields because they are the fields users most often want to edit.

While editing a header field that contains mailing addresses, such as 'To:', 'CC:' and 'BCC:', you can complete a mailing address by typing M-TAB (`mail-complete`). It inserts the full name corresponding to the address, if it can determine the full name. The variable `mail-complete-style` controls whether to insert the full name, and what style to use, as in `mail-from-style` (see Section 27.2 [Mail Headers], page 311). (If your window manager defines M-TAB to switch windows, you can type ESC TAB or C-M-i.)

For completion purposes, the valid mailing addresses are taken to be the local users' names plus your personal mail aliases. You can specify additional sources of valid addresses; see the customization group 'mailalias' to see the variables for customizing this feature (see Section 32.2.1 [Customization Groups], page 408).

If you type M-TAB in the body of the message, `mail-complete` invokes `ispell-complete-word`, as in Text mode.

27.4.3 Citing Mail

Mail mode also has commands for yanking or *citing* all or part of a message that you are replying to. These commands are active only when you started sending a message using an Rmail command.

C-c C-y   Yank the selected message from Rmail (`mail-yank-original`).

C-c C-r   Yank the region from the Rmail buffer (`mail-yank-region`).

C-c C-q   Fill each paragraph cited from another message (`mail-fill-yanked-message`).

When mail sending is invoked from the Rmail mail reader using an Rmail command, `C-c C-y` can be used inside the mail buffer to insert the text of the message you are replying to. Normally it indents each line of that message three spaces and eliminates most header fields. A numeric argument specifies the number of spaces to indent. An argument of just `C-u` says not to indent at all and not to eliminate anything. `C-c C-y` always uses the current message from the Rmail buffer, so you can insert several old messages by selecting one in Rmail, switching to '*mail*' and yanking it, then switching back to Rmail to select another.

You can specify the text for `C-c C-y` to insert at the beginning of each line: set `mail-yank-prefix` to the desired string. (A value of `nil` means to use indentation; this is the default.) However, `C-u C-c C-y` never adds anything at the beginning of the inserted lines, regardless of the value of `mail-yank-prefix`.

To yank just a part of an incoming message, set the region in Rmail to the part you want; then go to the '*Mail*' message and type `C-c C-r` (`mail-yank-region`). Each line that is copied is indented or prefixed according to `mail-yank-prefix`.

After using C-c C-y or C-c C-r, you can type C-c C-q (mail-fill-yanked-message) to fill the paragraphs of the yanked old message or messages. One use of C-c C-q fills all such paragraphs, each one individually. To fill a single paragraph of the quoted message, use M-q. If filling does not automatically handle the type of citation prefix you use, try setting the fill prefix explicitly. See Section 22.5 [Filling], page 217.

27.4.4 Mail Mode Miscellany

C-c C-t   Move to the beginning of the message body text (mail-text).

C-c C-w   Insert the file '~/.signature' at the end of the message text (mail-signature).

C-c C-i *file* RET
             Insert the contents of *file* at the end of the outgoing message (mail-attach-file).

M-x ispell-message
             Perform spelling correction on the message text, but not on citations from other messages.

C-c C-t (mail-text) moves point to just after the header separator line —that is, to the beginning of the message body text.

C-c C-w (mail-signature) adds a standard piece of text at the end of the message to say more about who you are. The text comes from the file '~/.signature' in your home directory. To insert your signature automatically, set the variable mail-signature to t; after that, starting a mail message automatically inserts the contents of your '~/.signature' file. If you want to omit your signature from a particular message, delete it from the buffer before you send the message.

You can also set mail-signature to a string; then that string is inserted automatically as your signature when you start editing a message to send. If you set it to some other Lisp expression, the expression is evaluated each time, and its value (which should be a string) specifies the signature.

You can do spelling correction on the message text you have written with the command M-x ispell-message. If you have yanked an incoming message into the outgoing draft, this command skips what was yanked, but it checks the text that you yourself inserted. (It looks for indentation or mail-yank-prefix to distinguish the cited lines from your input.) See Section 13.5 [Spelling], page 108.

To include a file in the outgoing message, you can use C-x i, the usual command to insert a file in the current buffer. But it is often more convenient to use a special command, C-c C-i (mail-attach-file). This command inserts the file contents at the end of the buffer, after your signature if any, with a delimiter line that includes the file name. Note that this is not a MIME attachment.

Turning on Mail mode (which C-x m does automatically) runs the normal hooks text-mode-hook and mail-mode-hook. Initializing a new outgoing message runs the normal hook mail-setup-hook; if you want to add special fields to your mail header or make other changes to the appearance of the mail buffer, use that hook. See Section 32.3.2 [Hooks], page 418.

The main difference between these hooks is just when they are invoked. Whenever you type M-x mail, mail-mode-hook runs as soon as the '*mail*' buffer is created. Then the mail-setup function inserts the default contents of the buffer. After these default contents are inserted, mail-setup-hook runs.

27.5 Mail Amusements

M-x spook adds a line of randomly chosen keywords to an outgoing mail message. The keywords are chosen from a list of words that suggest you are discussing something subversive.

The idea behind this feature is the suspicion that the NSA[1] snoops on all electronic mail messages that contain keywords suggesting they might find them interesting. (The NSA says they don't, but that's what they *would* say.) The idea is that if lots of people add suspicious words to their messages, the NSA will get so busy with spurious input that they will have to give up reading it all.

Here's how to insert spook keywords automatically whenever you start entering an outgoing message:

```
(add-hook 'mail-setup-hook 'spook)
```

Whether or not this confuses the NSA, it at least amuses people.

You can use the fortune program to put a "fortune cookie" message into outgoing mail. To do this, add fortune-to-signature to mail-setup-hook:

```
(add-hook 'mail-setup-hook 'fortune-to-signature)
```

27.6 Mail-Composition Methods

In this chapter we have described the usual Emacs mode for editing and sending mail—Mail mode. Emacs has alternative facilities for editing and sending mail, including MH-E and Message mode, not documented in this manual. See section "MH-E" in *The Emacs Interface to MH*. See section "Message" in *Message Manual*. You can choose any of them as your preferred method. The commands C-x m, C-x 4 m and C-x 5 m use whichever agent you have specified, as do various other Emacs commands and facilities that send mail.

To specify your mail-composition method, customize the variable mail-user-agent. Currently legitimate values include sendmail-user-agent (Mail mode), mh-e-user-agent, message-user-agent and gnus-user-agent.

If you select a different mail-composition method, the information in this chapter about the '*mail*' buffer and Mail mode does not apply; the other methods use a different format of text in a different buffer, and their commands are different as well.

---

[1] The US National Security Agency.

28 Reading Mail with Rmail

Rmail is an Emacs subsystem for reading and disposing of mail that you receive. Rmail stores mail messages in files called Rmail files which use a special format. Reading the message in an Rmail file is done in a special major mode, Rmail mode, which redefines most letters to run commands for managing mail.

28.1 Basic Concepts of Rmail

Using Rmail in the simplest fashion, you have one Rmail file '~/RMAIL' in which all of your mail is saved. It is called your *primary Rmail file*. The command M-x rmail reads your primary Rmail file, merges new mail in from your inboxes, displays the first message you haven't read yet, and lets you begin reading. The variable rmail-file-name specifies the name of the primary Rmail file.

Rmail uses narrowing to hide all but one message in the Rmail file. The message that is shown is called the *current message*. Rmail mode's special commands can do such things as delete the current message, copy it into another file, send a reply, or move to another message. You can also create multiple Rmail files and use Rmail to move messages between them.

Within the Rmail file, messages are normally arranged sequentially in order of receipt; you can specify other ways to sort them. Messages are identified by consecutive integers which are their *message numbers*. The number of the current message is displayed in Rmail's mode line, followed by the total number of messages in the file. You can move to a message by specifying its message number with the j key (see Section 28.3 [Rmail Motion], page 320).

Following the usual conventions of Emacs, changes in an Rmail file become permanent only when you save the file. You can save it with s (rmail-expunge-and-save), which also expunges deleted messages from the file first (see Section 28.4 [Rmail Deletion], page 321). To save the file without expunging, use C-x C-s. Rmail also saves the Rmail file after merging new mail from an inbox file (see Section 28.5 [Rmail Inbox], page 322).

You can exit Rmail with q (rmail-quit); this expunges and saves the Rmail file, then buries the Rmail buffer as well as its summary buffer, if present (see Section 28.11 [Rmail Summary], page 329). But there is no need to "exit" formally. If you switch from Rmail to editing in other buffers, and never switch back, you have exited. Just make sure to save the Rmail file eventually (like any other file you have changed). C-x s is a suitable way to do this (see Section 15.3.1 [Save Commands], page 124). The Rmail command b, rmail-bury, buries the Rmail buffer and its summary buffer without expunging and saving the Rmail file.

28.2 Scrolling Within a Message

When Rmail displays a message that does not fit on the screen, you must scroll through it to read the rest. You could do this with C-v, M-v and M-<, but in Rmail scrolling is so frequent that it deserves to be easier.

SPC   Scroll forward (scroll-up).

DEL   Scroll backward (`scroll-down`).

.   Scroll to start of message (`rmail-beginning-of-message`).

/   Scroll to end of message (`rmail-end-of-message`).

Since the most common thing to do while reading a message is to scroll through it by screenfuls, Rmail makes SPC and DEL synonyms of C-v (`scroll-up`) and M-v (`scroll-down`)

The command . (`rmail-beginning-of-message`) scrolls back to the beginning of the selected message. This is not quite the same as M-<: for one thing, it does not set the mark; for another, it resets the buffer boundaries to the current message if you have changed them. Similarly, the command / (`rmail-end-of-message`) scrolls forward to the end of the selected message.

28.3 Moving Among Messages

The most basic thing to do with a message is to read it. The way to do this in Rmail is to make the message current. The usual practice is to move sequentially through the file, since this is the order of receipt of messages. When you enter Rmail, you are positioned at the first message that you have not yet made current (that is, the first one that has the 'unseen' attribute; see Section 28.9 [Rmail Attributes], page 326). Move forward to see the other new messages; move backward to re-examine old messages.

n   Move to the next nondeleted message, skipping any intervening deleted messages (`rmail-next-undeleted-message`).

p   Move to the previous nondeleted message (`rmail-previous-undeleted-message`).

M-n   Move to the next message, including deleted messages (`rmail-next-message`).

M-p   Move to the previous message, including deleted messages (`rmail-previous-message`).

j   Move to the first message. With argument *n*, move to message number *n* (`rmail-show-message`).

>   Move to the last message (`rmail-last-message`).

<   Move to the first message (`rmail-first-message`).

M-s *regexp* RET
                 Move to the next message containing a match for *regexp* (`rmail-search`).

- M-s *regexp* RET
                 Move to the previous message containing a match for *regexp*.

n and p are the usual way of moving among messages in Rmail. They move through the messages sequentially, but skip over deleted messages, which is usually what you want to do. Their command definitions are named `rmail-next-undeleted-message` and `rmail-previous-undeleted-message`. If you do not want to skip deleted messages—for example, if you want to move to a message to undelete it—use the variants M-n and M-p (rmail-next-message and rmail-previous-message). A numeric argument to any of these commands serves as a repeat count.

In Rmail, you can specify a numeric argument by typing just the digits. You don't need to type C-u first.

The M-s (rmail-search) command is Rmail's version of search. The usual incremental search command C-s works in Rmail, but it searches only within the current message. The purpose of M-s is to search for another message. It reads a regular expression (see Section 12.5 [Regexps], page 92) nonincrementally, then searches starting at the beginning of the following message for a match. It then selects that message. If *regexp* is empty, M-s reuses the regexp used the previous time.

To search backward in the file for another message, give M-s a negative argument. In Rmail you can do this with - M-s.

It is also possible to search for a message based on labels. See Section 28.8 [Rmail Labels], page 325.

To move to a message specified by absolute message number, use j (rmail-show-message) with the message number as argument. With no argument, j selects the first message. < (rmail-first-message) also selects the first message. > (rmail-last-message) selects the last message.

28.1 Deleting Messages

When you no longer need to keep a message, you can *delete* it. This flags it as ignorable, and some Rmail commands pretend it is no longer present; but it still has its place in the Rmail file, and still has its message number.

Expunging the Rmail file actually removes the deleted messages. The remaining messages are renumbered consecutively. Expunging is the only action that changes the message number of any message, except for undigestifying (see Section 28.16 [Rmail Digest], page 334).

d   Delete the current message, and move to the next nondeleted message (rmail-delete-forward).

C-d   Delete the current message, and move to the previous nondeleted message (rmail-delete-backward).

u   Undelete the current message, or move back to a deleted message and undelete it (rmail-undelete-previous-message).

x   Expunge the Rmail file (rmail-expunge).

There are two Rmail commands for deleting messages. Both delete the current message and select another message. d (rmail-delete-forward) moves to the following message, skipping messages already deleted, while C-d (rmail-delete-backward) moves to the previous nondeleted message. If there is no nondeleted message to move to in the specified direction, the message that was just deleted remains current. d with a numeric argument is equivalent to C-d.

Whenever Rmail deletes a message, it runs the hook `rmail-delete-message-hook`. When the hook functions are invoked, the message has been marked deleted, but it is still the current message in the Rmail buffer.

To make all the deleted messages finally vanish from the Rmail file, type x (`rmail-expunge`). Until you do this, you can still *undelete* the deleted messages. The undeletion command, u (`rmail-undelete-previous-message`), is designed to cancel the effect of a d command in most cases. It undeletes the current message if the current message is deleted. Otherwise it moves backward to previous messages until a deleted message is found, and undeletes that message.

You can usually undo a d with a u because the u moves back to and undeletes the message that the d deleted. But this does not work when the d skips a few already-deleted messages that follow the message being deleted; then the u command undeletes the last of the messages that were skipped. There is no clean way to avoid this problem. However, by repeating the u command, you can eventually get back to the message that you intend to undelete. You can also select a particular deleted message with the M-p command, then type u to undelete it.

A deleted message has the '`deleted`' attribute, and as a result '`deleted`' appears in the mode line when the current message is deleted. In fact, deleting or undeleting a message is nothing more than adding or removing this attribute. See Section 28.9 [Rmail Attributes], page 326.

28.5 Rmail Files and Inboxes

When you receive mail locally, the operating system places incoming mail for you in a file that we call your *inbox*. When you start up Rmail, it runs a C program called `movemail` to copy the new messages from your local inbox into your primary Rmail file, which also contains other messages saved from previous Rmail sessions. It is in this file that you actually read the mail with Rmail. This operation is called *getting new mail*. You can get new mail at any time in Rmail by typing g.

The variable `rmail-primary-inbox-list` contains a list of the files which are inboxes for your primary Rmail file. If you don't set this variable explicitly, it is initialized from the `MAIL` environment variable, or, as a last resort, set to `nil`, which means to use the default inbox. The default inbox file depends on your operating system; often it is '`/var/mail/username`', '`/usr/spool/mail/username`', or '`/usr/mail/username`'.

You can specify the inbox file(s) for any Rmail file with the command `set-rmail-inbox-list`; see Section 28.6 [Rmail Files], page 323.

There are two reasons for having separate Rmail files and inboxes.

1. The inbox file format varies between operating systems and according to the other mail software in use. Only one part of Rmail needs to know about the alternatives, and it need only understand how to convert all of them to Rmail's own format.

2. It is very cumbersome to access an inbox file without danger of losing mail, because it is necessary to interlock with mail delivery. Moreover, different operating systems use different interlocking techniques. The strategy of moving

mail out of the inbox once and for all into a separate Rmail file avoids the need for interlocking in all the rest of Rmail, since only Rmail operates on the Rmail file.

Rmail was written to use Babyl format as its internal format. Since then, we have recognized that the usual inbox format on Unix and GNU systems is adequate for the job, and we plan to change Rmail to use that as its internal format. However, the Rmail file will still be separate from the inbox file, even when their format is the same.

When getting new mail, Rmail first copies the new mail from the inbox file to the Rmail file; then it saves the Rmail file; then it clears out the inbox file. This way, a system crash may cause duplication of mail between the inbox and the Rmail file, but cannot lose mail. If `rmail-preserve-inbox` is non-`nil`, then Rmail does not clear out the inbox file when it gets new mail. You may wish to set this, for example, on a portable computer you use to check your mail via POP while traveling, so that your mail will remain on the server and you can save it later on your workstation.

In some cases, Rmail copies the new mail from the inbox file indirectly. First it runs the `movemail` program to move the mail from the inbox to an intermediate file called '`~/.newmail-inboxname`'. Then Rmail merges the new mail from that file, saves the Rmail file, and only then deletes the intermediate file. If there is a crash at the wrong time, this file continues to exist, and Rmail will use it again the next time it gets new mail from that inbox.

If Rmail is unable to convert the data in '`~/.newmail-inboxname`' into Babyl format, it renames the file to '`~/RMAILOSE.n`' (n is an integer chosen to make the name unique) so that Rmail will not have trouble with the data again. You should look at the file, find whatever message confuses Rmail (probably one that includes the control-underscore character, octal code 037), and delete it. Then you can use `1 g` to get new mail from the corrected file.

28.6 Multiple Rmail Files

Rmail operates by default on your *primary Rmail file*, which is named '`~/RMAIL`' and receives your incoming mail from your system inbox file. But you can also have other Rmail files and edit them with Rmail. These files can receive mail through their own inboxes, or you can move messages into them with explicit Rmail commands (see Section 28.7 [Rmail Output], page 324).

`i file RET`   Read *file* into Emacs and run Rmail on it (`rmail-input`).

`M-x set-rmail-inbox-list RET files RET`
              Specify inbox file names for current Rmail file to get mail from.

`g`   Merge new mail from current Rmail file's inboxes (`rmail-get-new-mail`).

`C-u g file RET`
              Merge new mail from inbox file *file*.

To run Rmail on a file other than your primary Rmail file, you can use the `i` (`rmail-input`) command in Rmail. This visits the file in Rmail mode. You can use

`M-x rmail-input` even when not in Rmail, but it is easier to type `C-u M-x rmail`, which does the same thing.

The file you read with `i` should normally be a valid Rmail file. If it is not, Rmail tries to decompose it into a stream of messages in various known formats. If it succeeds, it converts the whole file to an Rmail file. If you specify a file name that doesn't exist, `i` initializes a new buffer for creating a new Rmail file.

You can also select an Rmail file from a menu. In the Classify menu, choose the Input Rmail File item; then choose the Rmail file you want. The variables `rmail-secondary-file-directory` and `rmail-secondary-file-regexp` specify which files to offer in the menu: the first variable says which directory to find them in; the second says which files in that directory to offer (all those that match the regular expression). These variables also apply to choosing a file for output (see Section 28.7 [Rmail Output], page 324).

Each Rmail file can contain a list of inbox file names; you can specify this list with `M-x set-rmail-inbox-list RET` *files* `RET`. The argument can contain any number of file names, separated by commas. It can also be empty, which specifies that this file should have no inboxes. Once you specify a list of inboxes in an Rmail file, the Rmail file remembers it permanently until you specify a different list.

As a special exception, if your primary Rmail file does not specify any inbox files, it uses your standard system inbox.

The `g` command (`rmail-get-new-mail`) merges mail into the current Rmail file from its inboxes. If the Rmail file has no inboxes, `g` does nothing. The command `M-x rmail` also merges new mail into your primary Rmail file.

To merge mail from a file that is not the usual inbox, give the `g` key a numeric argument, as in `C-u g`. Then it reads a file name and merges mail from that file. The inbox file is not deleted or changed in any way when `g` with an argument is used. This is, therefore, a general way of merging one file of messages into another.

28.7 Copying Messages Out to Files

These commands copy messages from an Rmail file into another file.

`o` *file* `RET`   Append a copy of the current message to the file *file*, using Rmail file format by default (`rmail-output-to-rmail-file`).

`C-o` *file* `RET`

       Append a copy of the current message to the file *file*, using system inbox file format by default (`rmail-output`).

`w` *file* `RET` Output just the message body to the file *file*, taking the default file name from the message 'Subject' header.

The commands `o` and `C-o` copy the current message into a specified file. This file may be an Rmail file or it may be in system inbox format; the output commands ascertain the file's format and write the copied message in that format.

The `o` and `C-o` commands differ in two ways: each has its own separate default file name, and each specifies a choice of format to use when the file does not already exist. The `o` command uses Rmail format when it creates a new file, while `C-o` uses system inbox format for a new file. The default file name for o is the file name used last with o, and the default file name for C-o is the file name used last with C-o.

If the output file is an Rmail file currently visited in an Emacs buffer, the output commands copy the message into that buffer. It is up to you to save the buffer eventually in its file.

Sometimes you may receive a message whose body holds the contents of a file. You can save the body to a file (excluding the message header) with the w command (rmail-output-body-to-file). Often these messages contain the intended file name in the 'Subject' field, so the w command uses the 'Subject' field as the default for the output file name. However, the file name is read using the minibuffer, so you can specify a different name if you wish.

You can also output a message to an Rmail file chosen with a menu. In the Classify menu, choose the Output Rmail File menu item; then choose the Rmail file you want. This outputs the current message to that file, like the o command. The variables rmail-secondary-file directory and rmail-secondary-file-regexp specify which files to offer in the menu: the first variable says which directory to find them in; the second says which files in that directory to offer (all those that match the regular expression).

Copying a message with o or C-o gives the original copy of the message the 'filed' attribute, so that 'filed' appears in the mode line when such a message is current. w gives it the 'stored' attribute. If you like to keep just a single copy of every mail message, set the variable rmail-delete-after-output to t; then the o, C-o and w commands delete the original message after copying it. (You can undelete the original afterward if you wish.)

Copying messages into files in system inbox format uses the header fields that are displayed in Rmail at the time. Thus, if you use the t command to view the entire header and then copy the message, the entire header is copied. See Section 28.13 [Rmail Display], page 332.

The variable rmail-output-file-alist lets you specify intelligent defaults for the output file, based on the contents of the current message. The value should be a list whose elements have this form:

(regexp . name-exp)

If there's a match for regexp in the current message, then the default file name for output is name-exp. If multiple elements match the message, the first matching element decides the default file name. The subexpression name-exp may be a string constant giving the file name to use, or more generally it may be any Lisp expression that returns a file name as a string. rmail-output-file-alist applies to both o and C-o.

28.8 Labels

Each message can have various *labels* assigned to it as a means of classification. Each label has a name; different names are different labels. Any given label is either present or absent on a particular message. A few label names have standard meanings and are given to messages automatically by Rmail when appropriate; these special labels are called *attributes*. All other labels are assigned only by users.

a *label* RET
>   Assign the label *label* to the current message (`rmail-add-label`).

k *label* RET
>   Remove the label *label* from the current message (`rmail-kill-label`).

C-M-n *labels* RET
>   Move to the next message that has one of the labels *labels* (`rmail-next-labeled-message`).

C-M-p *labels* RET
>   Move to the previous message that has one of the labels *labels* (`rmail-previous-labeled-message`).

l *labels* RET
C-M-l *labels* RET
>   Make a summary of all messages containing any of the labels *labels* (`rmail-summary-by-labels`).

The a (`rmail-add-label`) and k (`rmail-kill-label`) commands allow you to assign or remove any label on the current message. If the *label* argument is empty, it means to assign or remove the same label most recently assigned or removed.

Once you have given messages labels to classify them as you wish, there are two ways to use the labels: in moving and in summaries.

The command C-M-n *labels* RET (`rmail-next-labeled-message`) moves to the next message that has one of the labels *labels*. The argument *labels* specifies one or more label names, separated by commas. C-M-p (`rmail-previous-labeled-message`) is similar, but moves backwards to previous messages. A numeric argument to either command serves as a repeat count.

The command C-M-l *labels* RET (`rmail-summary-by-labels`) displays a summary containing only the messages that have at least one of a specified set of labels. The argument *labels* is one or more label names, separated by commas. See Section 28.11 [Rmail Summary], page 329, for information on summaries.

If the *labels* argument to C-M-n, C-M-p or C-M-l is empty, it means to use the last set of labels specified for any of these commands.

28.9 Rmail Attributes

Some labels such as 'deleted' and 'filed' have built-in meanings, and Rmail assigns them to messages automatically at appropriate times; these labels are called *attributes*. Here is a list of Rmail attributes:

'unseen'   Means the message has never been current. Assigned to messages when they come from an inbox file, and removed when a message is made current. When you start Rmail, it initially shows the first message that has this attribute.

'deleted'   Means the message is deleted. Assigned by deletion commands and removed by undeletion commands (see Section 28.4 [Rmail Deletion], page 321).

'filed'   Means the message has been copied to some other file. Assigned by the o and C-o file output commands (see Section 28.7 [Rmail Output], page 324).

'stored'   Assigned by the w file output command (see Section 28.7 [Rmail Output], page 324).

'answered'   Means you have mailed an answer to the message. Assigned by the r command (rmail-reply). See Section 28.10 [Rmail Reply], page 327.

'forwarded'
                Means you have forwarded the message. Assigned by the f command (rmail-forward). See Section 28.10 [Rmail Reply], page 327.

'edited'   Means you have edited the text of the message within Rmail. See Section 28.15 [Rmail Editing], page 334.

'resent'   Means you have resent the message. Assigned by the command M-x rmail-resend. See Section 28.10 [Rmail Reply], page 327.

All other labels are assigned or removed only by users, and have no standard meaning.

28.10 Sending Replies

Rmail has several commands that use Mail mode to send outgoing mail. See Chapter 27 [Sending Mail], page 310, for information on using Mail mode, including certain features meant to work with Rmail. What this section documents are the special commands of Rmail for entering Mail mode. Note that the usual keys for sending mail—C-x m, C-x 4 m, and C-x 5 m—also work normally in Rmail mode.

m   Send a message (rmail mail).

c   Continue editing the already started outgoing message (rmail continue).

r   Send a reply to the current Rmail message (rmail-reply).

f   Forward the current message to other users (rmail-forward).

C-u f   Resend the current message to other users (rmail-resend).

M-m   Try sending a bounced message a second time (rmail-retry-failure).

The most common reason to send a message while in Rmail is to reply to the message you are reading. To do this, type r (rmail-reply). This displays the '*mail*' buffer in another window, much like C-x 4 m, but preinitializes the 'Subject', 'To', 'CC', 'In-reply-to' and 'References' header fields based on the message you are replying to. The 'To' field starts out as the address of the person who sent the message you received, and the 'CC' field starts out with all the other recipients of that message.

You can exclude certain recipients from being placed automatically in the 'CC', using the variable `rmail-dont-reply-to-names`. Its value should be a regular expression (as a string); any recipient that the regular expression matches, is excluded from the 'CC' field. The default value matches your own name, and any name starting with 'info-'. (Those names are excluded because there is a convention of using them for large mailing lists to broadcast announcements.)

To omit the 'CC' field completely for a particular reply, enter the reply command with a numeric argument: `C-u r` or `1 r`. This means to reply only to the sender of the original message.

Once the '*mail*' buffer has been initialized, editing and sending the mail goes as usual (see Chapter 27 [Sending Mail], page 310). You can edit the presupplied header fields if they are not what you want. You can also use the commands of Mail mode (see Section 27.4 [Mail Mode], page 314), including `C-c C-y` which yanks in the message that you are replying to. You can also switch to the Rmail buffer, select a different message there, switch back, and yank the new current message.

Sometimes a message does not reach its destination. Mailers usually send the failed message back to you, enclosed in a *failure message*. The Rmail command `M-m` (`rmail-retry-failure`) prepares to send the same message a second time: it sets up a '*mail*' buffer with the same text and header fields as before. If you type `C-c C-c` right away, you send the message again exactly the same as the first time. Alternatively, you can edit the text or headers and then send it. The variable `rmail-retry-ignored-headers`, in the same format as `rmail-ignored-headers` (see Section 28.13 [Rmail Display], page 332), controls which headers are stripped from the failed message when retrying it.

Another frequent reason to send mail in Rmail is to *forward* the current message to other users. `f` (`rmail-forward`) makes this easy by preinitializing the '*mail*' buffer with the current message as the text, and a subject designating a forwarded message. All you have to do is fill in the recipients and send. When you forward a message, recipients get a message which is "from" you, and which has the original message in its contents.

Forwarding a message encloses it between two delimiter lines. It also modifies every line that starts with a dash, by inserting '- ' at the start of the line. When you receive a forwarded message, if it contains something besides ordinary text—for example, program source code—you might find it useful to undo that transformation. You can do this by selecting the forwarded message and typing `M-x unforward-rmail-message`. This command extracts the original forwarded message, deleting the inserted '- ' strings, and inserts it into the Rmail file as a separate message immediately following the current one.

Resending is an alternative similar to forwarding; the difference is that resending sends a message that is "from" the original sender, just as it reached you—with a few added header fields 'Resent-From' and 'Resent-To' to indicate that it came via you. To resend a message in Rmail, use `C-u f`. (`f` runs `rmail-forward`, which is programmed to invoke `rmail-resend` if you provide a numeric argument.)

The **m** (`rmail-mail`) command is used to start editing an outgoing message that is not a reply. It leaves the header fields empty. Its only difference from C-x 4 m is that it makes the Rmail buffer accessible for C-c C-y, just as r does. Thus, m can be used to reply to or forward a message; it can do anything r or f can do.

The **c** (`rmail-continue`) command resumes editing the '*mail*' buffer, to finish editing an outgoing message you were already composing, or to alter a message you have sent.

If you set the variable `rmail-mail-new-frame` to a non-`nil` value, then all the Rmail commands to start sending a message create a new frame to edit it in. This frame is deleted when you send the message, or when you use the 'Cancel' item in the 'Mail' menu.

All the Rmail commands to send a message use the mail-composition method that you have chosen (see Section 27.6 [Mail Methods], page 318).

28.11 Summaries

A *summary* is a buffer containing one line per message to give you an overview of the mail in an Rmail file. Each line shows the message number and date, the sender, the line count, the labels, and the subject. Moving point in the summary buffer selects messages as you move to their summary lines. Almost all Rmail commands are valid in the summary buffer also; when used there, they apply to the message described by the current line of the summary.

A summary buffer applies to a single Rmail file only; if you are editing multiple Rmail files, each one can have its own summary buffer. The summary buffer name is made by appending '-summary' to the Rmail buffer's name. Normally only one summary buffer is displayed at a time.

28.11.1 Making Summaries

Here are the commands to create a summary for the current Rmail file. Once the Rmail file has a summary buffer, changes in the Rmail file (such as deleting or expunging messages, and getting new mail) automatically update the summary.

h
C-M-h   Summarize all messages (`rmail-summary`).

l *labels* RET
C-M-l *labels* RET
      Summarize messages that have one or more of the specified labels (`rmail-summary-by-labels`).

C-M-r *rcpts* RET
      Summarize messages that have one or more of the specified recipients (`rmail-summary-by-recipients`).

C-M-t *topic* RET
      Summarize messages that have a match for the specified regexp *topic* in their subjects (`rmail-summary-by-topic`).

C-M-s *regexp*
>   Summarize messages whose headers and the subject line match the specified regular expression *regexp* (`rmail-summary-by-regexp`).

The h or C-M-h (`rmail-summary`) command fills the summary buffer for the current Rmail file with a summary of all the messages in the file. It then displays and selects the summary buffer in another window.

C-M-l *labels* RET (`rmail-summary-by-labels`) makes a partial summary mentioning only the messages that have one or more of the labels *labels*. *labels* should contain label names separated by commas.

C-M-r *rcpts* RET (`rmail-summary-by-recipients`) makes a partial summary mentioning only the messages that have one or more of the recipients *rcpts*. *rcpts* should contain mailing addresses separated by commas.

C-M-t *topic* RET (`rmail-summary-by-topic`) makes a partial summary mentioning only the messages whose subjects have a match for the regular expression *topic*.

C-M-s *regexp* RET (`rmail-summary-by-regexp`) makes a partial summary which mentions only the messages whose headers (including the date and the subject lines) match the regular expression *regexp*.

Note that there is only one summary buffer for any Rmail file; making any kind of summary discards any previous summary.

The variable `rmail-summary-window-size` says how many lines to use for the summary window. The variable `rmail-summary-line-count-flag` controls whether the summary line for a message should include the line count of the message.

28.11.2 Editing in Summaries

You can use the Rmail summary buffer to do almost anything you can do in the Rmail buffer itself. In fact, once you have a summary buffer, there's no need to switch back to the Rmail buffer.

You can select and display various messages in the Rmail buffer, from the summary buffer, just by moving point in the summary buffer to different lines. It doesn't matter what Emacs command you use to move point; whichever line point is on at the end of the command, that message is selected in the Rmail buffer.

Almost all Rmail commands work in the summary buffer as well as in the Rmail buffer. Thus, d in the summary buffer deletes the current message, u undeletes, and x expunges. (However, in the summary buffer, a numeric argument to d, C-d and u serves as a repeat count. A negative argument reverses the meaning of d and C-d.) o and C-o output the current message to a file; r starts a reply to it. You can scroll the current message while remaining in the summary buffer using SPC and DEL.

The Rmail commands to move between messages also work in the summary buffer, but with a twist: they move through the set of messages included in the summary. They also ensure the Rmail buffer appears on the screen (unlike cursor motion commands, which update the contents of the Rmail buffer but don't display it in a window unless it already appears). Here is a list of these commands:

n   Move to next line, skipping lines saying 'deleted', and select its message.

p   Move to previous line, skipping lines saying 'deleted', and select its message.

M-n   Move to next line and select its message.

M-p   Move to previous line and select its message.

>   Move to the last line, and select its message.

<   Move to the first line, and select its message.

j
RET   Select the message on the current line (ensuring that the RMAIL buffer appears on the screen). With argument n, select message number n and move to its line in the summary buffer; this signals an error if the message is not listed in the summary buffer.

M-s *pattern* RET
            Search through messages for *pattern* starting with the current message; select the message found, and move point in the summary buffer to that message's line.

Deletion, undeletion, and getting new mail, and even selection of a different message all update the summary buffer when you do them in the Rmail buffer. If the variable `rmail-redisplay-summary` is non-`nil`, these actions also bring the summary buffer back onto the screen.

When you are finished using the summary, type Q (`rmail-summary-wipe`) to delete the summary buffer's window. You can also exit Rmail while in the summary: q (`rmail-summary-quit`) deletes the summary window, then exits from Rmail by saving the Rmail file and switching to another buffer.

28.12 Sorting the Rmail File

M-x rmail-sort-by-date
            Sort messages of current Rmail file by date.

M-x rmail-sort-by-subject
            Sort messages of current Rmail file by subject.

M-x rmail-sort-by-author
            Sort messages of current Rmail file by author's name.

M-x rmail-sort-by-recipient
            Sort messages of current Rmail file by recipient's names.

M-x rmail-sort-by-correspondent
            Sort messages of current Rmail file by the name of the other correspondent.

`M-x rmail-sort-by-lines`

> Sort messages of current Rmail file by size (number of lines).

`M-x rmail-sort-by-keywords RET` *labels* `RET`

> Sort messages of current Rmail file by labels. The argument *labels* should be a comma-separated list of labels. The order of these labels specifies the order of messages; messages with the first label come first, messages with the second label come second, and so on. Messages which have none of these labels come last.

The Rmail sort commands perform a *stable sort*: if there is no reason to prefer either one of two messages, their order remains unchanged. You can use this to sort by more than one criterion. For example, if you use `rmail-sort-by-date` and then `rmail-sort-by-author`, messages from the same author appear in order by date.

With a numeric argument, all these commands reverse the order of comparison. This means they sort messages from newest to oldest, from biggest to smallest, or in reverse alphabetical order.

28.13 Display of Messages

Rmail reformats the header of each message before displaying it for the first time. Reformatting hides uninteresting header fields to reduce clutter. You can use the `t` command to show the entire header or to repeat the header reformatting operation.

`t`

> Toggle display of complete header (`rmail-toggle-header`).

Reformatting the header involves deleting most header fields, on the grounds that they are not interesting. The variable `rmail-ignored-headers` holds a regular expression that specifies which header fields to hide in this way—if it matches the beginning of a header field, that whole field is hidden. However, the variable `rmail-nonignored-headers` provides a further override: a header matching that regular expression is shown even if it matches `rmail-ignored-headers` too.

Rmail saves the complete original header before reformatting; to see it, use the `t` command (`rmail-toggle-header`). This discards the reformatted headers of the current message and displays it with the original header. Repeating `t` reformats the message again, which shows only the interesting headers according to the current values of those variable. Selecting the message again also reformats it if necessary.

One consequence of this is that if you edit the reformatted header (using `e`; see Section 28.15 [Rmail Editing], page 334), subsequent use of `t` will discard your edits. On the other hand, if you use `e` after `t`, to edit the original (unreformatted) header, those changes are permanent.

When the `t` command has a prefix argument, a positive argument means to show the reformatted header, and a zero or negative argument means to show the full header.

When the terminal supports multiple fonts or colors, Rmail highlights certain header fields that are especially interesting—by default, the 'From' and 'Subject' fields. The variable `rmail-highlighted-headers` holds a regular expression that specifies the header fields to highlight; if it matches the beginning of a header field, that whole field is highlighted.

If you specify unusual colors for your text foreground and background, the colors used for highlighting may not go well with them. If so, specify different colors by setting the variable `rmail-highlight-face` to a suitable face. To turn off highlighting entirely in Rmail, set `rmail-highlighted-headers` to `nil`.

You can highlight and activate URLs in incoming messages by adding the function `goto-address` to the hook `rmail-show-message-hook`. Then you can browse these URLs by clicking on them with `Mouse-2` (or `Mouse-1` quickly) or by moving to one and typing `C-c RET`. See Section 31.15.2 [Activating URLs], page 403.

28.14 Rmail and Coding Systems

Rmail automatically decodes messages which contain non-ASCII characters, just as Emacs does with files you visit and with subprocess output. Rmail uses the standard '`charset=charset`' header in the message, if any, to determine how the message was encoded by the sender. It maps *charset* into the corresponding Emacs coding system (see Section 19.7 [Coding Systems], page 193), and uses that coding system to decode message text. If the message header doesn't have the '`charset`' specification, or if *charset* is not recognized, Rmail chooses the coding system with the usual Emacs heuristics and defaults (see Section 19.8 [Recognize Coding], page 195).

Occasionally, a message is decoded incorrectly, either because Emacs guessed the wrong coding system in the absence of the '`charset`' specification, or because the specification was inaccurate. For example, a misconfigured mailer could send a message with a '`charset=iso-8859-1`' header when the message is actually encoded in `koi8-r`. When you see the message text garbled, or some of its characters displayed as empty boxes, this may have happened.

You can correct the problem by decoding the message again using the right coding system, if you can figure out or guess which one is right. To do this, invoke the `M-x rmail-redecode-body` command. It reads the name of a coding system, encodes the message body using whichever coding system was used to decode it before, then redecodes it using the coding system you specified. If you specified the right coding system, the result should be readable.

Decoding and encoding using the wrong coding system is lossless for most encodings, in particular with 8-bit encodings such as iso-8859 or koi8. So, if the initial attempt to redecode the message didn't result in a legible text, you can try other coding systems until you succeed.

With some coding systems, notably those from the iso-2022 family, information can be lost in decoding, so that encoding the message again won't bring back the original incoming text. In such a case, `rmail-redecode-body` cannot work. However, the problems that call for use of `rmail-redecode-body` rarely occur with those coding systems. So in practice the command works when you need it.

28.15 Editing Within a Message

Most of the usual Emacs commands are available in Rmail mode, though a few, such as C-M-n and C-M-h, are redefined by Rmail for other purposes. However, the Rmail buffer is normally read only, and most of the letters are redefined as Rmail commands. If you want to edit the text of a message, you must use the Rmail command e.

e   Edit the current message as ordinary text.

The e command (`rmail-edit-current-message`) switches from Rmail mode into Rmail Edit mode, another major mode which is nearly the same as Text mode. The mode line indicates this change.

In Rmail Edit mode, letters insert themselves as usual and the Rmail commands are not available. When you are finished editing the message and are ready to go back to Rmail, type C-c C-c, which switches back to Rmail mode. Alternatively, you can return to Rmail mode but cancel all the editing that you have done, by typing C-c C-].

Entering Rmail Edit mode runs the hook `text-mode-hook`; then it runs the hook `rmail-edit-mode-hook` (see Section 32.3.2 [Hooks], page 418). It adds the attribute 'edited' to the message. It also displays the full headers of the message, so that you can edit the headers as well as the body of the message, and your changes in the headers will be permanent.

28.16 Digest Messages

A *digest message* is a message which exists to contain and carry several other messages. Digests are used on some moderated mailing lists; all the messages that arrive for the list during a period of time such as one day are put inside a single digest which is then sent to the subscribers. Transmitting the single digest uses much less computer time than transmitting the individual messages even though the total size is the same, because the per-message overhead in network mail transmission is considerable.

When you receive a digest message, the most convenient way to read it is to *undigestify* it: to turn it back into many individual messages. Then you can read and delete the individual messages as it suits you. To do this, select the digest message and type the command M-x `undigestify-rmail-message`. This extracts the submessages as separate Rmail messages, and inserts them following the digest. The digest message itself is flagged as deleted.

28.17 Converting an Rmail File to Inbox Format

The command M-x `unrmail` converts a file in Rmail format to inbox format (also known as the system mailbox, or mbox, format), so that you can use it with other mail-editing tools. You must specify two arguments, the name of the Rmail file and the name to use for the converted file. M-x `unrmail` does not alter the Rmail file itself.

M-x unrmail is useful if you can run Emacs on the machine where the Rmail file resides, or can access the Rmail file remotely (see Section 15.14 [Remote Files], page 152) from a machine where Emacs is installed. If accessing Rmail files from Emacs is impossible, you can use the b2m program instead. b2m is part of the Emacs distribution, it is installed into the same directory where all the other auxiliary programs (etags etc.) are installed, and its source is available in the Emacs source distribution, so that you could copy the source to the target machine and compile it there.

To convert a file '*babyl-file*' into '*mbox-file*', invoke b2m like this:

```
b2m < babyl-file > mbox-file
```

28.18 Reading Rot13 Messages

Mailing list messages that might offend some readers are sometimes encoded in a simple code called *rot13*—so named because it rotates the alphabet by 13 letters. This code is not for secrecy, as it provides none; rather, it enables those who might be offended to avoid seeing the real text of the message.

To view a buffer which uses the rot13 code, use the command M-x rot13-other-window. This displays the current buffer in another window which applies the code when displaying the text.

28.19 movemail program

When invoked for the first time, Rmail attempts to locate the movemail program and determine its version. There are two versions of movemail program: the native one, shipped with GNU Emacs (the "emacs version") and the one included in GNU mailutils (the "mailutils version," see section "movemail" in *GNU mailutils*). They support the same command line syntax and the same basic subset of options. However, the Mailutils version offers additional features.

The Emacs version of movemail is able to retrieve mail from usual UNIX mailbox formats and from remote mailboxes using the POP3 protocol.

The Mailutils version is able to handle a wide set of mailbox formats, such as plain UNIX mailboxes, maildir and MH mailboxes, etc. It is able to retrieve remote mail using POP3 or IMAP4 protocol, and can retrieve mail from them using a TLS encrypted channel. It also accepts mailbox argument in the URL form. The detailed description of mailbox URLs can be found in section "URL" in *Mailbox URL Formats*. In short, a URL is:

```
proto://[user[:password]@]host-or-file-name
```

where square brackets denote optional elements.

proto   Specifies the *mailbox protocol*, or *format* to use. The exact semantics of the rest of URL elements depends on the actual value of *proto* (see below).

user   User name to access the remote mailbox.

password   User password to access the remote mailbox.

host-or-file-name
> Hostname of the remote server for remote mailboxes or file name of a local mailbox.

Proto can be one of:

mbox
> Usual UNIX mailbox format. In this case, neither *user* nor *pass* are used, and *host-or-file-name* denotes the file name of the mailbox file, e.g., `mbox://var/spool/mail/smith`.

mh
> A local mailbox in the MH format. *User* and *pass* are not used. *Host-or-file-name* denotes the name of MH folder, e.g., `mh://Mail/inbox`.

maildir
> A local mailbox in the maildir format. *User* and *pass* are not used, and *host-or-file-name* denotes the name of `maildir` mailbox, e.g., `maildir://mail/inbox`.

file
> Any local mailbox format. Its actual format is detected automatically by `movemail`.

pop
> A remote mailbox to be accessed via POP3 protocol. *User* specifies the remote user name to use, *pass* may be used to specify the user password, *host-or-file-name* is the name or IP address of the remote mail server to connect to; e.g., `pop://smith:guessme@remote.server.net`.

imap
> A remote mailbox to be accessed via IMAP4 protocol. *User* specifies the remote user name to use, *pass* may be used to specify the user password, *host-or-file-name* is the name or IP address of the remote mail server to connect to; e.g., `imap://smith:guessme@remote.server.net`.

Alternatively, you can specify the file name of the mailbox to use. This is equivalent to specifying the '`file`' protocol:

> `/var/spool/mail/user` ≡ `file://var/spool/mail/user`

The variable `rmail-movemail-program` controls which version of `movemail` to use. If that is a string, it specifies the absolute file name of the `movemail` executable. If it is `nil`, Rmail searches for `movemail` in the directories listed in `rmail-movemail-search-path` and `exec-path`, then in `exec-directory`.

28.20 Retrieving Mail from Remote Mailboxes

Some sites use a method called POP for accessing users' inbox data instead of storing the data in inbox files. The Emacs `movemail` can work with POP if you compile it with the macro `MAIL_USE_POP` defined. (You can achieve that by specifying '`--with-pop`' when you run `configure` during the installation of Emacs.)

The Mailutils `movemail` by default supports POP, unless it was configured with '`--disable-pop`' option.

Both versions of `movemail` only work with POP3, not with older versions of POP.

No matter which flavor of `movemail` you use, you can specify POP inbox by using POP *URL* (see Section 28.19 [Movemail], page 335). A POP URL is a "file name" of the form 'pop://*username*@*hostname*', where *hostname* is the host name or IP address of the remote mail server and *username* is the user name on that server. Additionally, you may specify the password in the mailbox URL: 'pop://*username*:*password*@*hostname*'. In this case, *password* takes preference over the one set by `rmail-remote-password`. This is especially useful if you have several remote mailboxes with different passwords.

For backward compatibility, Rmail also supports two alternative ways of specifying remote POP mailboxes. First, specifying an inbox name in the form 'po:*username*:*hostname*' is equivalent to 'pop://*username*@*hostname*'. Alternatively, you may set a "file name" of 'po:*username*' in the inbox list of an Rmail file. `movemail` will handle such a name by opening a connection to the POP server. In this case, the `MAILHOST` environment variable specifies the machine on which to look for the POP server.

Another method for accessing remote mailboxes is IMAP. This method is supported only by the Mailutils `movemail`. To specify an IMAP mailbox in the inbox list, use the following mailbox URL: 'imap://*username*[:*password*]@*hostname*'. The *password* part is optional, as described above.

Accessing a remote mailbox may require a password. Rmail uses the following algorithm to retrieve it:

1. If the *password* is present in mailbox URL (see above), it is used.

2. If the variable `rmail-remote-password` is non-nil, its value is used.

3. Otherwise, if `rmail-remote-password-required` is non-nil, then Rmail will ask you for the password to use.

4. Otherwise, Rmail assumes no password is required.

For compatibility with previous versions, the variables `rmail-pop-password` and `rmail-pop-password-required` may be used instead of `rmail-remote-password` and `rmail-remote-password-required`.

If you need to pass additional command-line flags to `movemail`, set the variable `rmail-movemail-flags` a list of the flags you wish to use. Do not use this variable to pass the '-p' flag to preserve your inbox contents; use `rmail-preserve-inbox` instead.

The `movemail` program installed at your site may support Kerberos authentication. If it is supported, it is used by default whenever you attempt to retrieve POP mail when `rmail-pop-password` and `rmail-pop-password-required` are unset.

Some POP servers store messages in reverse order. If your server does this, and you would rather read your mail in the order in which it was received, you can tell `movemail` to reverse the order of downloaded messages by adding the '-r' flag to `rmail-movemail-flags`.

Mailutils `movemail` supports TLS encryption. If you wish to use it, add the '--tls' flag to `rmail-movemail-flags`.

28.21 Retrieving Mail from Local Mailboxes in Various Formats

If your incoming mail is stored on a local machine in a format other than UNIX mailbox, you will need the Mailutils `movemail` to retrieve it. See Section 28.19 [Movemail], page 335, for the detailed description of `movemail` versions. For example, to access mail from a inbox in `maildir` format located in '/var/spool/mail/in', you would include the following in the Rmail inbox list:

```
maildir://var/spool/mail/in
```

29 Dired, the Directory Editor

Dired makes an Emacs buffer containing a listing of a directory, and optionally some of its subdirectories as well. You can use the normal Emacs commands to move around in this buffer, and special Dired commands to operate on the files listed.

The Dired buffer is "read-only," and inserting text in it is not useful, so ordinary printing characters such as d and x are redefined for special Dired commands. Some Dired commands *mark* or *flag* the *current file* (that is, the file on the current line); other commands operate on the marked files or on the flagged files. You first mark certain files in order to operate on all of them with on command.

The Dired-X package provides various extra features for Dired mode. See section "Top" in *Dired Extra Version 2 User's Manual*.

29.1 Entering Dired

To invoke Dired, do C-x d or M-x dired. The command reads a directory name or wildcard file name pattern as a minibuffer argument to specify the files to list. C-x C-f given a directory name also invokes Dired. Where dired differs from list-directory is that it puts the buffer into Dired mode, so that the special commands of Dired are available.

The variable dired-listing-switches specifies the options to give to ls for listing the directory; this string *must* contain '-l'. If you use a numeric prefix argument with the dired command, you can specify the ls switches with the minibuffer before you enter the directory specification. No matter how they are specified, the ls switches can include short options (that is, single characters) requiring no arguments, and long options (starting with '—') whose arguments are specified with '='.

On MS Windows and MS-DOS systems, Emacs *emulates* ls; see Section G.3 [ls in Lisp], page 508, for options and peculiarities of that emulation.

To display the Dired buffer in another window rather than in the selected window, use C-x 4 d (dired-other-window) instead of C-x d. C-x 5 d (dired-other-frame) uses a separate frame to display the Dired buffer.

29.2 Navigation in the Dired Buffer

All the usual Emacs cursor motion commands are available in Dired buffers. The keys C-n and C-p are redefined to put the cursor at the beginning of the file name on the line, rather than at the beginning of the line.

For extra convenience, SPC and n in Dired are equivalent to C-n. p is equivalent to C-p. (Moving by lines is so common in Dired that it deserves to be easy to type.) DEL (move up and unflag) is often useful simply for moving up.

j (dired-goto-file) moves point to the line that describes a specified file or directory.

Some additional navigation commands are available when the Dired buffer includes several directories. See Section 29.12 [Subdirectory Motion], page 349.

29.3 Deleting Files with Dired

One of the most frequent uses of Dired is to first *flag* files for deletion, then delete the files that were flagged.

d   Flag this file for deletion.

u   Remove deletion flag on this line.

DEL   Move point to previous line and remove the deletion flag on that line.

x   Delete the files that are flagged for deletion.

You can flag a file for deletion by moving to the line describing the file and typing d (`dired-flag-file-deletion`). The deletion flag is visible as a 'D' at the beginning of the line. This command moves point to the next line, so that repeated d commands flag successive files. A numeric argument serves as a repeat count.

The reason for flagging files for deletion, rather than deleting files immediately, is to reduce the danger of deleting a file accidentally. Until you direct Dired to delete the flagged files, you can remove deletion flags using the commands u and DEL. u (`dired-unmark`) works just like d, but removes flags rather than making flags. DEL (`dired-unmark-backward`) moves upward, removing flags; it is like u with argument −1.

To delete the flagged files, type x (`dired-do-flagged-delete`). (This is also known as *expunging*.) This command first displays a list of all the file names flagged for deletion, and requests confirmation with yes. If you confirm, Dired deletes the flagged files, then deletes their lines from the text of the Dired buffer. The Dired buffer, with somewhat fewer lines, remains selected.

If you answer no or quit with C-g when asked to confirm, you return immediately to Dired, with the deletion flags still present in the buffer, and no files actually deleted.

You can delete empty directories just like other files, but normally Dired cannot delete directories that are nonempty. If the variable `dired-recursive-deletes` is non-nil, then Dired can delete nonempty directories including all their contents. That can be somewhat risky.

29.4 Flagging Many Files at Once

Flag all auto-save files (files whose names start and end with '#') for deletion (see Section 15.5 [Auto Save], page 132).

~   Flag all backup files (files whose names end with '~') for deletion (see Section 15.3.2 [Backup], page 125).

&   Flag for deletion all files with certain kinds of names which suggest you could easily create those files again.

. (Period) Flag excess numeric backup files for deletion. The oldest and newest few backup files of any one file are exempt; the middle ones are flagged.

% d *regexp* RET

>   Flag for deletion all files whose names match the regular expression
        regexp.

The #, ~, &, and . commands flag many files for deletion, based on their file
names. These commands are useful precisely because they do not themselves delete
any files; you can remove the deletion flags from any flagged files that you really
wish to keep.

& (`dired-flag-garbage-files`) flags files whose names match the regular expression specified by the variable `dired-garbage-files-regexp`. By default, this matches certain files produced by TEX, '.bak' files, and the '.orig' and '.rej' files produced by `patch`.

(`dired-flag-auto-save-files`) flags for deletion all files whose names look like auto-save files—that is, files whose names begin and end with '#'. See Section 15.5 [Auto Save], page 132.

~ (`dired-flag-backup-files`) flags for deletion all files whose names say they are backup files—that is, files whose names end in '~'. See Section 15.3.2 [Backup], page 125.

. (period, `dired-clean-directory`) flags just some of the backup files for deletion: all but the oldest few and newest few backups of any one file. Normally `dired-kept-versions` (**not** `kept-new-versions`; that applies only when saving) specifies the number of newest versions of each file to keep, and `kept-old-versions` specifies the number of oldest versions to keep.

Period with a positive numeric argument, as in C-u 3 ., specifies the number of newest versions to keep, overriding `dired-kept-versions`. A negative numeric argument overrides `kept-old-versions`, using minus the value of the argument to specify the number of oldest versions of each file to keep.

The % d command flags all files whose names match a specified regular expression (`dired-flag-files-regexp`). Only the non-directory part of the file name is used in matching. You can use '^' and '$' to anchor matches. You can exclude certain subdirectories from marking by hiding them while you use % d. See Section 29.13 [Hiding Subdirectories], page 350.

29.5 Visiting Files in Dired

There are several Dired commands for visiting or examining the files listed in the Dired buffer. All of them apply to the current line's file; if that file is really a directory, these commands invoke Dired on that subdirectory (making a separate Dired buffer).

f
>   Visit the file described on the current line, like typing C-x C-f and supplying that file name (`dired-find-file`). See Section 15.2 [Visiting], page 120.

RET
e
>   Equivalent to f.

o   Like f, but uses another window to display the file's buffer (`dired-find-file-other-window`). The Dired buffer remains visible in the first window. This is like using C-x 4 C-f to visit the file. See Chapter 17 [Windows], page 165.

C-o   Visit the file described on the current line, and display the buffer in another window, but do not select that window (`dired-display-file`).

Mouse-1
Mouse-2   Visit the file named by the line you click on (`dired-mouse-find-file-other-window`). This uses another window to display the file, like the o command.

v   View the file described on the current line, using M-x view-file (`dired-view-file`). Viewing a file with `view-file` is like visiting it, but is slanted toward moving around in the file conveniently and does not allow changing the file. See Section 15.11 [Miscellaneous File Operations], page 150.

^   Visit the parent directory of the current directory (`dired-up-directory`). This is equivalent to moving to the line for '..' and typing f there.

29.6 Dired Marks vs. Flags

Instead of flagging a file with 'D', you can *mark* the file with some other character (usually '*'). Most Dired commands to operate on files use the files marked with '*'. The only command that operates on flagged files is x, which expunges them.

Here are some commands for marking with '*', for unmarking, and for operating on marks. (See Section 29.3 [Dired Deletion], page 340, for commands to flag and unflag files.)

m
* m   Mark the current file with '*' (`dired-mark`). With a numeric argument n, mark the next n files starting with the current file. (If n is negative, mark the previous −n files.)

* *   Mark all executable files with '*' (`dired-mark-executables`). With a numeric argument, unmark all those files.

* @   Mark all symbolic links with '*' (`dired-mark-symlinks`). With a numeric argument, unmark all those files.

* /   Mark with '*' all files which are directories, except for '.' and '..' (`dired-mark-directories`). With a numeric argument, unmark all those files.

* s   Mark all the files in the current subdirectory, aside from '.' and '..' (`dired-mark-subdir-files`).

u
* u   Remove any mark on this line (`dired-unmark`).

DEL
* DEL   Move point to previous line and remove any mark on that line (`dired-unmark-backward`).

* !
U   Remove all marks from all the files in this Dired buffer (`dired-unmark-all-marks`).

* ? *markchar*
M-DEL   Remove all marks that use the character *markchar* (`dired-unmark-all-files`). The argument is a single character—do not use RET to terminate it. See the description of the * c command below, which lets you replace one mark character with another.

                With a numeric argument, this command queries about each marked file, asking whether to remove its mark. You can answer y meaning yes, n meaning no, or ! to remove the marks from the remaining files without asking about them.

* C-n
M-}   Move down to the next marked file (`dired-next-marked-file`) A file is "marked" if it has any kind of mark.

* C-p
M-{   Move up to the previous marked file (`dired-prev-marked-file`)

t
* t   Toggle all marks (`dired-toggle-marks`). files marked with '*' become unmarked, and unmarked files are marked with '*'. Files marked in any other way are not affected.

* c *old-markchar new-markchar*
                Replace all marks that use the character *old-markchar* with marks that use the character *new-markchar* (`dired-change-marks`). This command is the primary way to create or use marks other than '*' or 'D'. The arguments are single characters—do not use RET to terminate them.

                You can use almost any character as a mark character by means of this command, to distinguish various classes of files. If *old-markchar* is a space (' '), then the command operates on all unmarked files; if *new-markchar* is a space, then the command unmarks the files it acts on.

                To illustrate the power of this command, here is how to put 'D' flags on all the files that have no marks, while unflagging all those that already have 'D' flags:

                    * c D t   * c SPC D   * c t SPC

                This assumes that no files were already marked with 't'.

% m *regexp* RET
* % *regexp* RET

> Mark (with '*') all files whose names match the regular expression *regexp* (`dired-mark-files-regexp`). This command is like % d, except that it marks files with '*' instead of flagging with 'D'.
>
> Only the non-directory part of the file name is used in matching. Use '^' and '$' to anchor matches. You can exclude subdirectories by temporarily hiding them (see Section 29.13 [Hiding Subdirectories], page 350).

% g *regexp* RET

> Mark (with '*') all files whose *contents* contain a match for the regular expression *regexp* (`dired-mark-files-containing-regexp`). This command is like % m, except that it searches the file contents instead of the file name.

C-x u
C-_
C-/

> Undo changes in the Dired buffer, such as adding or removing marks (`dired-undo`). *This command does not revert the actual file operations, nor recover lost files!* It just undoes changes in the buffer itself.
>
> In some cases, using this after commands that operate on files can cause trouble. For example, after renaming one or more files, `dired-undo` restores the original names in the Dired buffer, which gets the Dired buffer out of sync with the actual contents of the directory.

29.7 Operating on Files

This section describes the basic Dired commands to operate on one file or several files. All of these commands are capital letters; all of them use the minibuffer, either to read an argument or to ask for confirmation, before they act. All of them let you specify the files to manipulate in these ways:

- If you give the command a numeric prefix argument n, it operates on the next n files, starting with the current file. (If n is negative, the command operates on the $-n$ files preceding the current line.)
- Otherwise, if some files are marked with '*', the command operates on all those files.
- Otherwise, the command operates on the current file only.

Certain other Dired commands, such as ! and the '%' commands, use the same conventions to decide which files to work on.

Commands which ask for a destination directory, such as those which copy and rename files or create links for them, try to guess the default target directory for the operation. Normally, they suggest the Dired buffer's default directory, but if the variable `dired-dwim-target` is non-nil, and if there is another Dired buffer displayed in the next window, that other buffer's directory is suggested instead.

Here are the file-manipulating Dired commands that operate on files.

C *new* RET   Copy the specified files (`dired-do-copy`). The argument *new* is the directory to copy into, or (if copying a single file) the new name. This is like the shell command `cp`.

If `dired-copy-preserve-time` is non-nil, then copying with this command preserves the modification time of the old file in the copy, like 'cp -p'.

The variable `dired-recursive-copies` controls whether to copy directories recursively (like 'cp -r'). The default is nil, which means that directories cannot be copied.

D   Delete the specified files (`dired-do-delete`). This is like the shell command `rm`.

Like the other commands in this section, this command operates on the *marked* files, or the next *n* files. By contrast, x (`dired-do-flagged-delete`) deletes all *flagged* files.

R *new* RET   Rename the specified files (`dired-do-rename`). If you rename a single file, the argument *new* is the new name of the file. If you rename several files, the argument *new* is.the directory into which to move the files (this is like the shell command `mv`).

Dired automatically changes the visited file name of buffers associated with renamed files so that they refer to the new names.

H *new* RET   Make hard links to the specified files (`dired-do-hardlink`). This is like the shell command `ln`. The argument *new* is the directory to make the links in, or (if making just one link) the name to give the link.

S *new* RET   Make symbolic links to the specified files (`dired-do-symlink`). This is like 'ln -s'. The argument *new* is the directory to make the links in, or (if making just one link) the name to give the link.

M *modespec* RET

Change the mode (also called "permission bits") of the specified files (`dired-do-chmod`). This uses the `chmod` program, so *modespec* can be any argument that `chmod` can handle.

G *newgroup* RET

Change the group of the specified files to *newgroup* (`dired-do-chgrp`).

O *newowner* RET

Change the owner of the specified files to *newowner* (`dired-do-chown`). (On most systems, only the superuser can do this.)

The variable `dired-chown-program` specifies the name of the program to use to do the work (different systems put `chown` in different places).

T *timestamp* RET

Touch the specified files (`dired-do-touch`). This means updating their modification times to the present time. This is like the shell command `touch`.

P *command* RET

        Print the specified files (`dired-do-print`). You must specify the command to print them with, but the minibuffer starts out with a suitable guess made using the variables `lpr-command` and `lpr-switches` (the same variables that `lpr-buffer` uses; see Section 31.4 [Printing], page 391).

Z

        Compress the specified files (`dired-do-compress`). If the file appears to be a compressed file already, uncompress it instead.

L

        Load the specified Emacs Lisp files (`dired-do-load`). See Section 24.8 [Lisp Libraries], page 288.

B

        Byte compile the specified Emacs Lisp files (`dired-do-byte-compile`). See section "Byte Compilation" in *The Emacs Lisp Reference Manual*.

A *regexp* RET

        Search all the specified files for the regular expression *regexp* (`dired-do-search`).

        This command is a variant of `tags-search`. The search stops at the first match it finds; use M-, to resume the search and find the next match. See Section 25.3.6 [Tags Search], page 301.

Q *regexp* RET *to* RET

        Perform `query-replace-regexp` on each of the specified files, replacing matches for *regexp* with the string *to* (`dired-do-query-replace-regexp`).

        This command is a variant of `tags-query-replace`. If you exit the query replace loop, you can use M-, to resume the scan and replace more matches. See Section 25.3.6 [Tags Search], page 301.

29.8 Shell Commands in Dired

The Dired command ! (`dired-do-shell-command`) reads a shell command string in the minibuffer and runs that shell command on all the specified files. (X is a synonym for !.) You can specify the files to operate on in the usual ways for Dired commands (see Section 29.7 [Operating on Files], page 344).

    The working directory for the shell command is the top-level directory of the Dired buffer.

    There are two ways of applying a shell command to multiple files:

- If you use '*' surrounded by whitespace in the shell command, then the command runs just once, with the list of file names substituted for the '*'. The order of file names is the order of appearance in the Dired buffer.

      Thus, ! tar cf foo.tar * RET runs `tar` on the entire list of file names, putting them into one tar file 'foo.tar'.

If you want to use '*' as a shell wildcard with whitespace around it, write '*""'. In the shell, this is equivalent to '*'; but since the '*' is not surrounded by whitespace, Dired does not treat it specially.

- If the command string doesn't contain '*' surrounded by whitespace, then it runs once *for each file*. Normally the file name is added at the end.

  For example, ! uudecode RET runs uudecode on each file.

- However, if the command string contains '?' surrounded by whitespace, the current file name is substituted for '?' (rather than added at the end). You can use '?' this way more than once in the command, and the same file name replaces each occurrence.

To iterate over the file names in a more complicated fashion, use an explicit shell loop. For example, here is how to uuencode each file, making the output file name by appending '.uu' to the input file name:

```
for file in * ; do uuencode "$file" "$file" >"$file".uu; done
```

The ! command does not attempt to update the Dired buffer to show new or modified files, because it doesn't understand shell commands, and does not know what files the shell command changed. Use the g command to update the Dired buffer (see Section 29.14 [Dired Updating], page 350).

29.9 Transforming File Names in Dired

This section describes Dired commands which alter file names in a systematic way. Each command operates on some or all of the marked files, using a new name made by transforming the existing name.

Like the basic Dired file-manipulation commands (see Section 29.7 [Operating on Files], page 344), the commands described here operate either on the next *n* files, or on all files marked with '*', or on the current file. (To mark files, use the commands described in Section 29.6 [Marks vs Flags], page 342.)

All of the commands described in this section work *interactively*: they ask you to confirm the operation for each candidate file. Thus, you can select more files than you actually need to operate on (e.g., with a regexp that matches many files), and then filter the selected names by typing y or n when the command prompts for confirmation.

% u   Rename each of the selected files to an upper-case name (dired-upcase). If the old file names are 'Foo' and 'bar', the new names are 'FOO' and 'BAR'.

% l   Rename each of the selected files to a lower-case name (dired-downcase). If the old file names are 'Foo' and 'bar', the new names are 'foo' and 'bar'.

% R *from* RET *to* RET
% C *from* RET *to* RET
% H *from* RET *to* RET
% S *from* RET *to* RET

> These four commands rename, copy, make hard links and make soft links, in each case computing the new name by regular-expression substitution from the name of the old file.

The four regular-expression substitution commands effectively perform a search-and-replace on the selected file names. They read two arguments: a regular expression *from*, and a substitution pattern *to*; they match each "old" file name against *from*, and then replace the matching part with *to*. You can use '\&' and '\digit' in *to* to refer to all or part of what the pattern matched in the old file name, as in `replace-regexp` (see Section 12.9.2 [Regexp Replace], page 100). If the regular expression matches more than once in a file name, only the first match is replaced.

For example, % R `^.*$` RET `x-\&` RET renames each selected file by prepending 'x-' to its name. The inverse of this, removing 'x-' from the front of each file name, is also possible: one method is % R `^x-\(.*\)$` RET `\1` RET; another is % R `^x-` RET RET. (Use '`^`' and '`$`' to anchor matches that should span the whole file name.)

Normally, the replacement process does not consider the files' directory names; it operates on the file name within the directory. If you specify a numeric argument of zero, then replacement affects the entire absolute file name including directory name. (A non-zero argument specifies the number of files to operate on.)

You may want to select the set of files to operate on using the same regexp *from* that you will use to operate on them. To do this, mark those files with % m *from* RET, then use the same regular expression in the command to operate on the files. To make this more convenient, the % commands to operate on files use the last regular expression specified in any % command as a default.

29.10 File Comparison with Dired

Here are two Dired commands that compare specified files using `diff`. They show the output in a buffer using Diff mode (see Section 15.9 [Comparing Files], page 148).

=
> Compare the current file (the file at point) with another file (the file at the mark) using the `diff` program (`dired-diff`). The file at the mark is the first argument of `diff`, and the file at point is the second argument. This refers to the ordinary Emacs mark, not Dired marks; use C-SPC (`set-mark-command`) to set the mark at the first file's line (see Section 8.1 [Setting Mark], page 49).

M-=
> Compare the current file with its latest backup file (`dired-backup-diff`). If the current file is itself a backup, compare it with the file it is a backup of; this way, you can compare a file with any one of its backups.
>
> The backup file is the first file given to `diff`.

29.11 Subdirectories in Dired

A Dired buffer displays just one directory in the normal case; but you can optionally include its subdirectories as well.

The simplest way to include multiple directories in one Dired buffer is to specify the options '-lR' for running ls. (If you give a numeric argument when you run Dired, then you can specify these options in the minibuffer.) That produces a recursive directory listing showing all subdirectories at all levels.

More often, you will want to show only specific subdirectories. You can do this with the i command:

i   Insert the contents of a subdirectory later in the buffer.

Use the i (dired-maybe-insert-subdir) command on a line that describes a file which is a directory. It inserts the contents of that directory into the same Dired buffer, and moves there. Inserted subdirectory contents follow the top-level directory of the Dired buffer, just as they do in 'ls -lR' output.

If the subdirectory's contents are already present in the buffer, the i command just moves to it.

In either case, i sets the Emacs mark before moving, so C-u C-SPC takes you back to the old position in the buffer (the line describing that subdirectory).

Use the l command (dired-do-redisplay) to update the subdirectory's contents. Use C-u k on the subdirectory header line to delete the subdirectory. See Section 29.14 [Dired Updating], page 350.

29.12 Moving Over Subdirectories

When a Dired buffer lists subdirectories, you can use the page motion commands C-x [and C-x] to move by entire directories (see Section 22.4 [Pages], page 216).

The following commands move across, up and down in the tree of directories within one Dired buffer. They move to *directory header lines*, which are the lines that give a directory's name, at the beginning of the directory's contents.

C-M-n   Go to next subdirectory header line, regardless of level (dired-next-subdir).

C-M-p   Go to previous subdirectory header line, regardless of level (dired-prev-subdir).

C-M-u   Go up to the parent directory's header line (dired-tree-up).

C-M-d   Go down in the directory tree, to the first subdirectory's header line (dired-tree-down).

<   Move up to the previous directory-file line (dired-prev-dirline). These lines are the ones that describe a directory as a file in its parent directory.

>   Move down to the next directory-file line (dired-prev-dirline).

29.13 Hiding Subdirectories

Hiding a subdirectory means to make it invisible, except for its header line.

$ Hide or reveal the subdirectory that point is in, and move point to the next subdirectory (`dired-hide-subdir`). A numeric argument serves as a repeat count.

M-$ Hide all subdirectories in this Dired buffer, leaving only their header lines (`dired-hide-all`). Or, if any subdirectory is currently hidden, make all subdirectories visible again. You can use this command to get an overview in very deep directory trees or to move quickly to subdirectories far away.

Ordinary Dired commands never consider files inside a hidden subdirectory. For example, the commands to operate on marked files ignore files in hidden directories even if they are marked. Thus you can use hiding to temporarily exclude subdirectories from operations without having to remove the Dired marks on files in those subdirectories.

29.14 Updating the Dired Buffer

This section describes commands to update the Dired buffer to reflect outside (non-Dired) changes in the directories and files, and to delete part of the Dired buffer.

g Update the entire contents of the Dired buffer (`revert-buffer`).

l Update the specified files (`dired-do-redisplay`). You specify the files for l in the same way as for file operations.

k Delete the specified *file lines*—not the files, just the lines (`dired-do-kill-lines`).

s Toggle between alphabetical order and date/time order (`dired-sort-toggle-or-edit`).

C-u s *switches* RET
   Refresh the Dired buffer using *switches* as `dired-listing-switches`.

Type g (`revert-buffer`) to update the contents of the Dired buffer, based on changes in the files and directories listed. This preserves all marks except for those on files that have vanished. Hidden subdirectories are updated but remain hidden.

To update only some of the files, type l (`dired-do-redisplay`). Like the Dired file-operating commands, this command operates on the next *n* files (or previous −*n* files), or on the marked files if any, or on the current file. Updating the files means reading their current status, then updating their lines in the buffer to indicate that status.

If you use l on a subdirectory header line, it updates the contents of the corresponding subdirectory.

To delete the specified *file lines* from the buffer—not delete the files—type k (`dired-do-kill-lines`). Like the file-operating commands, this command operates on the next *n* files, or on the marked files if any; but it does not operate on the current file as a last resort.

If you use k with a numeric prefix argument to kill the line for a file that is a directory, which you have inserted in the Dired buffer as a subdirectory, it deletes that subdirectory from the buffer as well. Typing C-u k on the header line for a subdirectory also deletes the subdirectory from the Dired buffer.

The g command brings back any individual lines that you have killed in this way, but not subdirectories—you must use i to reinsert a subdirectory.

The files in a Dired buffers are normally listed in alphabetical order by file names. Alternatively Dired can sort them by date/time. The Dired command s (dired-sort-toggle-or-edit) switches between these two sorting modes. The mode line in a Dired buffer indicates which way it is currently sorted—by name, or by date.

C-u s *switches* RET lets you specify a new value for dired-listing-switches.

29.15 Dired and find

You can select a set of files for display in a Dired buffer more flexibly by using the find utility to choose the files.

To search for files with names matching a wildcard pattern use M-x find-name-dired. It reads arguments *directory* and *pattern*, and chooses all the files in *directory* or its subdirectories whose individual names match *pattern*.

The files thus chosen are displayed in a Dired buffer, in which the ordinary Dired commands are available.

If you want to test the contents of files, rather than their names, use M-x find-grep-dired. This command reads two minibuffer arguments, *directory* and *regexp*; it chooses all the files in *directory* or its subdirectories that contain a match for *regexp*. It works by running the programs find and grep. See also M-x grep-find, in Section 24.4 [Grep Searching], page 277. Remember to write the regular expression for grep, not for Emacs. (An alternative method of showing files whose contents match a given regexp is the % g *regexp* command, see Section 29.6 [Marks vs Flags], page 342.)

The most general command in this series is M-x find-dired, which lets you specify any condition that find can test. It takes two minibuffer arguments, *directory* and *find-args*; it runs find in *directory*, passing *find-args* to tell find what condition to test. To use this command, you need to know how to use find.

The format of listing produced by these commands is controlled by the variable find-ls-option, whose default value specifies using options '-ld' for ls. If your listings are corrupted, you may need to change the value of this variable.

The command M-x locate provides a similar interface to the locate program. M-x locate-with-filter is similar, but keeps only files whose names match a given regular expression.

These buffers don't work entirely like ordinary Dired buffers: file operations work, but do not always automatically update the buffer. Reverting the buffer with g deletes all inserted subdirectories, and erases all flags and marks.

29.16 Editing the Dired Buffer

Wdired is a special mode that allows you to perform file operations by editing the Dired buffer directly (the "W" in "Wdired" stands for "writable.") To enter Wdired mode, type `M-x wdired-change-to-wdired-mode` while in a Dired buffer. Alternatively, use 'Edit File Names' in the 'Immediate' menu bar menu.

While in Wdired mode, you can rename files by editing the file names displayed in the Dired buffer. All the ordinary Emacs editing commands, including rectangle operations and `query-replace`, are available for this. Once you are done editing, type `C-c C-c` (`wdired-finish-edit`). This applies your changes and switches back to ordinary Dired mode.

Apart from simply renaming files, you can move a file to another directory by typing in the new file name (either absolute or relative). To mark a file for deletion, delete the entire file name. To change the target of a symbolic link, edit the link target name which appears next to the link name.

The rest of the text in the buffer, such as the file sizes and modification dates, is marked read-only, so you can't edit it. However, if you set `wdired-allow-to-change-permissions` to `t`, you can edit the file permissions. For example, you can change '`-rw-r--r--`' to '`-rw-rw-rw-`' to make a file world-writable. These changes also take effect when you type `C-c C-c`.

29.17 Viewing Image Thumbnails in Dired

Image-Dired is a facility for browsing image files. It provides viewing the images either as thumbnails or in full size, either inside Emacs or through an external viewer.

To enter Image-Dired, mark the image files you want to look at in the Dired buffer, using m as usual. Then type `C-t d` (`image-dired-display-thumbs`). This creates and switches to a buffer containing image-dired, corresponding to the marked files.

You can also enter Image-Dired directly by typing `M-x image-dired`. This prompts for a directory; specify one that has image files. This creates thumbnails for all the images in that directory, and displays them all in the "thumbnail buffer." This takes a long time if the directory contains many image files, and it asks for confirmation if the number of image files exceeds `image-dired-show-all-from-dir-max-files`.

With point in the thumbnail buffer, you can type `RET` (`image-dired-display-thumbnail-original-image`) to display a sized version of it in another window. This sizes the image to fit the window. Use the arrow keys to move around in the buffer. For easy browsing, use `SPC` (`image-dired-display-next-thumbnail-original`) to advance and display the next image. Typing `DEL` (`image-dired-display-previous-thumbnail-original`) backs up to the previous thumbnail and displays that instead.

To view and the image in its original size, either provide a prefix argument (`C-u`) before pressing `RET`, or type `C-RET` (`image-dired-thumbnail-display-external`) to display the image in an external viewer. You must first configure `image-dired-external-viewer`.

You can delete images through Image-Dired also. Type `d` (`image-dired-flag-thumb-original-file`) to flag the image file for deletion in the Dired buffer. You can also delete the thumbnail image from the thumbnail buffer with `C-d` (`image-dired-delete-char`).

More advanced features include *image tags*, which are metadata used to categorize image files. The tags are stored in a plain text file configured by `image-dired-db-file`.

To tag image files, mark them in the dired buffer (you can also mark files in Dired from the thumbnail buffer by typing `m`) and type `C-t t` (`image-dired-tag-files`). You will be prompted for a tag. To mark files having a certain tag, type `C-t f` (`image-dired-mark-tagged-files`). After marking image files with a certain tag, you can use `C-t d` to view them.

You can also tag a file directly from the thumbnail buffer by typing `t t` and you can remove a tag by typing `t r`. There is also a special "tag" called "comment" for each file (it is not a tag in the exact same sense as the other tags, it is handled slightly different). That is used to enter a comment or description about the image. You comment a file from the thumbnail buffer by typing `c`. You will be prompted for a comment. Type `C-t c` to add a comment from Dired (`image-dired-dired-comment-files`).

Image-Dired also provides simple image manipulation. In the thumbnail buffer, type `L` to rotate the original image 90 degrees anti clockwise, and `R` to rotate it 90 degrees clockwise. This rotation is lossless, and uses an external utility called JpegTRAN.

29.18 Other Dired Features

An unusual Dired file-operation command is `+` (`dired-create-directory`). This command reads a directory name, and creates the directory if it does not already exist.

The `w` command (`dired-copy-filename-as-kill`) puts the names of the marked (or next *n*) files into the kill ring, as if you had killed them with `C-w`. The names are separated by a space.

With a zero prefix argument, this uses the absolute file name of each marked file. With just `C-u` as the prefix argument, it uses file names relative to the Dired buffer's default directory. (This can still contain slashes if in a subdirectory.) As a special case, if point is on a directory headerline, `w` gives you the absolute name of that directory. Any prefix argument or marked files are ignored in this case.

The main purpose of this command is so that you can yank the file names into arguments for other Emacs commands. It also displays what it added to the kill ring, so you can use it to display the list of currently marked files in the echo area.

The command `M-x dired-compare-directories` is used to compare the current Dired buffer with another directory. It marks all the files that are "different" between the two directories. It puts these marks in all Dired buffers where these files are listed, which of course includes the current buffer.

The default comparison method (used if you type RET at the prompt) is to compare just the file names—each file name that does not appear in the other directory is "different." You can specify more stringent comparisons by entering a Lisp expression, which can refer to the variables `size1` and `size2`, the respective file sizes; `mtime1` and `mtime2`, the last modification times in seconds, as floating point numbers; and `fa1` and `fa2`, the respective file attribute lists (as returned by the function `file-attributes`). This expression is evaluated for each pair of like-named files, and if the expression's value is non-`nil`, those files are considered "different."

For instance, the sequence `M-x dired-compare-directories RET (> mtime1 mtime2) RET` marks files newer in this directory than in the other, and marks files older in the other directory than in this one. It also marks files with no counterpart, in both directories, as always.

On the X window system, Emacs supports the "drag and drop" protocol. You can drag a file object from another program, and drop it onto a Dired buffer; this either moves, copies, or creates a link to the file in that directory. Precisely which action is taken is determined by the originating program. Dragging files out of a Dired buffer is currently not supported.

30 The Calendar and the Diary

Emacs provides the functions of a desk calendar, with a diary of planned or past events. It also has facilities for managing your appointments, and keeping track of how much time you spend working on certain projects.

To enter the calendar, type M-x calendar; this displays a three-month calendar centered on the current month, with point on the current date. With a numeric argument, as in C-u M-x calendar, it prompts you for the month and year to be the center of the three-month calendar. The calendar uses its own buffer, whose major mode is Calendar mode.

Mouse-2 in the calendar brings up a menu of operations on a particular date; Mouse-3 brings up a menu of commonly used calendar features that are independent of any particular date. To exit the calendar, type q.

This chapter describes the basic calendar features. See Info file 'emacs-xtra', node 'Advanced Calendar/Diary Usage', for information about more specialized features.

30.1 Movement in the Calendar

Calendar mode provides commands to move through the calendar in logical units of time such as days, weeks, months, and years. If you move outside the three months originally displayed, the calendar display "scrolls" automatically through time to make the selected date visible. Moving to a date lets you view its holidays or diary entries, or convert it to other calendars; moving by long time periods is also useful simply to scroll the calendar.

30.1.1 Motion by Standard Lengths of Time

The commands for movement in the calendar buffer parallel the commands for movement in text. You can move forward and backward by days, weeks, months, and years.

C-f	Move point one day forward (`calendar-forward-day`).
C-b	Move point one day backward (`calendar-backward-day`).
C-n	Move point one week forward (`calendar-forward-week`).
C-p	Move point one week backward (`calendar-backward-week`).
M-}	Move point one month forward (`calendar-forward-month`).
M-{	Move point one month backward (`calendar-backward-month`).
C-x]	Move point one year forward (`calendar-forward-year`).
C-x [	Move point one year backward (`calendar-backward-year`).

The day and week commands are natural analogues of the usual Emacs commands for moving by characters and by lines. Just as C-n usually moves to the same column in the following line, in Calendar mode it moves to the same day in the following week. And C-p moves to the same day in the previous week.

The arrow keys are equivalent to C-f, C-b, C-n and C-p, just as they normally are in other modes.

The commands for motion by months and years work like those for weeks, but move a larger distance. The month commands M-} and M-{ move forward or backward by an entire month. The year commands C-x] and C-x [move forward or backward a whole year.

The easiest way to remember these commands is to consider months and years analogous to paragraphs and pages of text, respectively. But the commands themselves are not quite analogous. The ordinary Emacs paragraph commands move to the beginning or end of a paragraph, whereas these month and year commands move by an entire month or an entire year, keeping the same date within the month or year.

All these commands accept a numeric argument as a repeat count. For convenience, the digit keys and the minus sign specify numeric arguments in Calendar mode even without the Meta modifier. For example, 100 C-f moves point 100 days forward from its present location.

30.1.2 Beginning or End of Week, Month or Year

A week (or month, or year) is not just a quantity of days; we think of weeks (months, years) as starting on particular dates. So Calendar mode provides commands to move to the beginning or end of a week, month or year:

C-a   Move point to start of week (calendar-beginning-of-week).

C-e   Move point to end of week (calendar-end-of-week).

M-a   Move point to start of month (calendar-beginning-of-month).

M-e   Move point to end of month (calendar-end-of-month).

M-<   Move point to start of year (calendar-beginning-of-year).

M->   Move point to end of year (calendar-end-of-year).

These commands also take numeric arguments as repeat counts, with the repeat count indicating how many weeks, months, or years to move backward or forward.

By default, weeks begin on Sunday. To make them begin on Monday instead, set the variable calendar-week-start-day to 1.

30.1.3 Specified Dates

Calendar mode provides commands for moving to a particular date specified in various ways.

g d   Move point to specified date (calendar-goto-date).

g D   Move point to specified day of year (calendar-goto-day-of-year).

g w   Move point to specified week of year (calendar-goto-iso-week).

o   Center calendar around specified month (calendar-other-month).

.   Move point to today's date (`calendar-goto-today`).

  g d (`calendar-goto-date`) prompts for a year, a month, and a day of the month, and then moves to that date. Because the calendar includes all dates from the beginning of the current era, you must type the year in its entirety; that is, type '1990', not '90'.

  g D (`calendar-goto-day-of-year`) prompts for a year and day number, and moves to that date. Negative day numbers count backward from the end of the year. g w (`calendar-goto-iso-week`) prompts for a year and week number, and moves to that week.

  o (`calendar-other-month`) prompts for a month and year, then centers the three-month calendar around that month.

  You can return to today's date with . (`calendar-goto-today`).

30.2 Scrolling in the Calendar

The calendar display scrolls automatically through time when you move out of the visible portion. You can also scroll it manually. Imagine that the calendar window contains a long strip of paper with the months on it. Scrolling the calendar means moving the strip horizontally, so that new months become visible in the window.

>   Scroll calendar one month forward (`scroll-calendar-left`).

<   Scroll calendar one month backward (`scroll-calendar-right`).

C-v
NEXT   Scroll calendar three months forward (`scroll-calendar-left-three-months`).

M-v
PRIOR   Scroll calendar three months backward (`scroll-calendar-right-three-months`).

  The most basic calendar scroll commands scroll by one month at a time. This means that there are two months of overlap between the display before the command and the display after. > scrolls the calendar contents one month forward in time. < scrolls the contents one month backwards in time.

  The commands C-v and M-v scroll the calendar by an entire "screenful"—three months—in analogy with the usual meaning of these commands. C-v makes later dates visible and M-v makes earlier dates visible. These commands take a numeric argument as a repeat count; in particular, since C-u multiplies the next command by four, typing C-u C-v scrolls the calendar forward by a year and typing C-u M-v scrolls the calendar backward by a year.

  The function keys NEXT and PRIOR are equivalent to C-v and M-v, just as they are in other modes.

30.3 Counting Days

M-=   Display the number of days in the current region (`calendar-count-days-region`).

To determine the number of days in the region, type M-= (`calendar-count-days-region`). The numbers of days shown is *inclusive*; that is, it includes the days specified by mark and point.

30.4 Miscellaneous Calendar Commands

p d   Display day-in-year (`calendar-print-day-of-year`).

C-c C-l   Regenerate the calendar window (`redraw-calendar`).

SPC   Scroll the next window up (`scroll-other-window`).

DEL   Scroll the next window down (`scroll-other-window-down`).

q   Exit from calendar (`exit-calendar`).

To display the number of days elapsed since the start of the year, or the number of days remaining in the year, type the p d command (`calendar-print-day-of-year`). This displays both of those numbers in the echo area. The count of days elapsed includes the selected date. The count of days remaining does not include that date.

If the calendar window text gets corrupted, type C-c C-l (`redraw-calendar`) to redraw it. (This can only happen if you use non-Calendar-mode editing commands.)

In Calendar mode, you can use SPC (`scroll-other-window`) and DEL (`scroll-other-window-down`) to scroll the other window up or down, respectively. This is handy when you display a list of holidays or diary entries in another window.

To exit from the calendar, type q (`exit-calendar`). This buries all buffers related to the calendar, selecting other buffers. (If a frame contains a dedicated calendar window, exiting from the calendar iconifies that frame.)

30.5 Writing Calendar Files

These packages produce files of various formats containing calendar and diary entries, for display purposes.

The Calendar HTML commands produce files of HTML code that contain calendar and diary entries. Each file applies to one month, and has a name of the format '*yyyy-mm*.html', where *yyyy* and *mm* are the four-digit year and two-digit month, respectively. The variable `cal-html-directory` specifies the default output directory for the HTML files.

Diary entries enclosed by < and > are interpreted as HTML tags (for example: this is a diary entry with <font color="red">some red text</font>). You can change the overall appearance of the displayed HTML pages (for example, the color of various page elements, header styles) via a stylesheet 'cal.css' in the directory containing the HTML files (see the value of the variable `cal-html-css-default` for relevant style settings).

H m   Generate a one-month calendar (`cal-html-cursor-month`).

H y   Generate a calendar file for each month of a year, as well as an index page (`cal-html-cursor-year`). By default, this command writes files to a *yyyy* subdirectory - if this is altered some hyperlinks between years will not work.

If the variable `cal-html-print-day-number-flag` is non-nil, then the monthly calendars show the day-of-the-year number. The variable `cal-html-year-index-cols` specifies the number of columns in the yearly index page.

The Calendar LaTeX commands produce a buffer of LaTeX code that prints as a calendar. Depending on the command you use, the printed calendar covers the day, week, month or year that point is in.

t m   Generate a one-month calendar (`cal-tex-cursor-month`).

t M   Generate a sideways printing one-month calendar (`cal-tex-cursor-month-landscape`).

t d   Generate a one-day calendar (`cal-tex-cursor-day`).

t w 1   Generate a one-page calendar for one week (`cal-tex-cursor-week`).

t w 2   Generate a two-page calendar for one week (`cal-tex-cursor-week2`).

t w 3   Generate an ISO-style calendar for one week (`cal-tex-cursor-week-iso`).

t w 4   Generate a calendar for one Monday-starting week (`cal-tex-cursor-week-monday`).

t f w   Generate a Filofax-style two-weeks-at-a-glance calendar (`cal-tex-cursor-filofax-2week`).

t f W   Generate a Filofax-style one-week-at-a-glance calendar (`cal-tex-cursor-filofax-week`).

t y   Generate a calendar for one year (`cal-tex-cursor-year`).

t Y   Generate a sideways-printing calendar for one year (`cal-tex-cursor-year-landscape`).

t f y   Generate a Filofax-style calendar for one year (`cal-tex-cursor-filofax-year`).

Some of these commands print the calendar sideways (in "landscape mode"), so it can be wider than it is long. Some of them use Filofax paper size (3.75in x 6.75in). All of these commands accept a prefix argument which specifies how many days, weeks, months or years to print (starting always with the selected one).

If the variable `cal-tex-holidays` is non-nil (the default), then the printed calendars show the holidays in `calendar-holidays`. If the variable `cal-tex-diary` is non-nil (the default is `nil`), diary entries are included also (in weekly and monthly calendars only). If the variable `cal-tex-rules` is non-nil (the default is `nil`), the calendar displays ruled pages in styles that have sufficient room. You can use the variable `cal-tex-preamble-extra` to insert extra LaTeX commands in the preamble of the generated document if you need to.

30.6 Holidays

The Emacs calendar knows about all major and many minor holidays, and can display them.

h   Display holidays for the selected date (`calendar-cursor-holidays`).

Mouse-2 Holidays
                     Display any holidays for the date you click on.

x   Mark holidays in the calendar window (`mark-calendar-holidays`).

u   Unmark calendar window (`calendar-unmark`).

a   List all holidays for the displayed three months in another window
                     (`list-calendar-holidays`).

M-x holidays
                     List all holidays for three months around today's date in another win-
                     dow.

M-x list-holidays
                     List holidays in another window for a specified range of years.

To see if any holidays fall on a given date, position point on that date in the calendar window and use the h command. Alternatively, click on that date with Mouse-2 and then choose Holidays from the menu that appears. Either way, this displays the holidays for that date, in the echo area if they fit there, otherwise in a separate window.

To view the distribution of holidays for all the dates shown in the calendar, use the x command. This displays the dates that are holidays in a different face (or places a '*' after these dates, if display with multiple faces is not available). See Info file 'emacs-xtra', node 'Calendar Customizing'. The command applies both to the currently visible months and to other months that subsequently become visible by scrolling. To turn marking off and erase the current marks, type u, which also erases any diary marks (see Section 30.10 [Diary], page 367). If the variable `mark-holidays-in-calendar` is non-nil, creating or updating the calendar marks holidays automatically.

To get even more detailed information, use the a command, which displays a separate buffer containing a list of all holidays in the current three-month range. You can use SPC and DEL in the calendar window to scroll that list up and down, respectively.

The command M-x holidays displays the list of holidays for the current month and the preceding and succeeding months; this works even if you don't have a calendar window. If the variable `view-calendar-holidays-initially` is non-nil, creating the calendar displays holidays in this way. If you want the list of holidays centered around a different month, use C-u M-x holidays, which prompts for the month and year.

The holidays known to Emacs include United States holidays and the major Christian, Jewish, and Islamic holidays; also the solstices and equinoxes.

The command `M-x list-holidays` displays the list of holidays for a range of years. This function asks you for the starting and stopping years, and allows you to choose all the holidays or one of several categories of holidays. You can use this command even if you don't have a calendar window.

The dates used by Emacs for holidays are based on *current practice*, not historical fact. For example Veteran's Day began in 1919, but is shown in earlier years.

30.7 Times of Sunrise and Sunset

Special calendar commands can tell you, to within a minute or two, the times of sunrise and sunset for any date.

S
>Display times of sunrise and sunset for the selected date (`calendar-sunrise-sunset`).

`Mouse-2 Sunrise/sunset`
>Display times of sunrise and sunset for the date you click on.

`M-x sunrise-sunset`
>Display times of sunrise and sunset for today's date.

`C-u M-x sunrise-sunset`
>Display times of sunrise and sunset for a specified date.

Within the calendar, to display the *local times* of sunrise and sunset in the echo area, move point to the date you want, and type S. Alternatively, click `Mouse-2` on the date, then choose 'Sunrise/sunset' from the menu that appears. The command `M-x sunrise-sunset` is available outside the calendar to display this information for today's date or a specified date. To specify a date other than today, use `C-u M-x sunrise-sunset`, which prompts for the year, month, and day.

You can display the times of sunrise and sunset for any location and any date with `C-u C-u M-x sunrise-sunset`. This asks you for a longitude, latitude, number of minutes difference from Coordinated Universal Time, and date, and then tells you the times of sunrise and sunset for that location on that date.

Because the times of sunrise and sunset depend on the location on earth, you need to tell Emacs your latitude, longitude, and location name before using these commands. Here is an example of what to set:

```
(setq calendar-latitude 40.1)
(setq calendar-longitude -88.2)
(setq calendar-location-name "Urbana, IL")
```

Use one decimal place in the values of `calendar-latitude` and `calendar-longitude`.

Your time zone also affects the local time of sunrise and sunset. Emacs usually gets time zone information from the operating system, but if these values are not what you want (or if the operating system does not supply them), you must set them yourself. Here is an example:

```
(setq calendar-time-zone -360)
```

```
(setq calendar-standard-time-zone-name "CST")
(setq calendar-daylight-time-zone-name "CDT")
```

The value of `calendar-time-zone` is the number of minutes difference between your local standard time and Coordinated Universal Time (Greenwich time). The values of `calendar-standard-time-zone-name` and `calendar-daylight-time-zone-name` are the abbreviations used in your time zone. Emacs displays the times of sunrise and sunset *corrected for daylight saving time*. See Section 30.13 [Daylight Saving], page 374, for how daylight saving time is determined.

As a user, you might find it convenient to set the calendar location variables for your usual physical location in your '.emacs' file. And when you install Emacs on a machine, you can create a 'default.el' file which sets them properly for the typical location of most users of that machine. See Section 32.6 [Init File], page 433.

30.8 Phases of the Moon

These calendar commands display the dates and times of the phases of the moon (new moon, first quarter, full moon, last quarter). This feature is useful for debugging problems that "depend on the phase of the moon."

M   Display the dates and times for all the quarters of the moon for the three-month period shown (`calendar-phases-of-moon`).

`M-x phases-of-moon`
                   Display dates and times of the quarters of the moon for three months around today's date.

Within the calendar, use the M command to display a separate buffer of the phases of the moon for the current three-month range. The dates and times listed are accurate to within a few minutes.

Outside the calendar, use the command `M-x phases-of-moon` to display the list of the phases of the moon for the current month and the preceding and succeeding months. For information about a different month, use `C-u M-x phases-of-moon`, which prompts for the month and year.

The dates and times given for the phases of the moon are given in local time (corrected for daylight saving, when appropriate); but if the variable `calendar-time-zone` is void, Coordinated Universal Time (the Greenwich time zone) is used. See Section 30.13 [Daylight Saving], page 374.

30.9 Conversion To and From Other Calendars

The Emacs calendar displayed is *always* the Gregorian calendar, sometimes called the "new style" calendar, which is used in most of the world today. However, this calendar did not exist before the sixteenth century and was not widely used before the eighteenth century; it did not fully displace the Julian calendar and gain universal acceptance until the early twentieth century. The Emacs calendar can display any month since January, year 1 of the current era, but the calendar displayed is the Gregorian, even for a date at which the Gregorian calendar did not exist.

While Emacs cannot display other calendars, it can convert dates to and from several other calendars.

30.9.1 Supported Calendar Systems

The ISO commercial calendar is used largely in Europe.

The Julian calendar, named after Julius Caesar, was the one used in Europe throughout medieval times, and in many countries up until the nineteenth century.

Astronomers use a simple counting of days elapsed since noon, Monday, January 1, 4713 B.C. on the Julian calendar. The number of days elapsed is called the *Julian day number* or the *Astronomical day number.*

The Hebrew calendar is used by tradition in the Jewish religion. The Emacs calendar program uses the Hebrew calendar to determine the dates of Jewish holidays. Hebrew calendar dates begin and end at sunset.

The Islamic calendar is used in many predominantly Islamic countries. Emacs uses it to determine the dates of Islamic holidays. There is no universal agreement in the Islamic world about the calendar; Emacs uses a widely accepted version, but the precise dates of Islamic holidays often depend on proclamation by religious authorities, not on calculations. As a consequence, the actual dates of observance can vary slightly from the dates computed by Emacs. Islamic calendar dates begin and end at sunset.

The French Revolutionary calendar was created by the Jacobins after the 1789 revolution, to represent a more secular and nature-based view of the annual cycle, and to install a 10-day week in a rationalization measure similar to the metric system. The French government officially abandoned this calendar at the end of 1805.

The Maya of Central America used three separate, overlapping calendar systems, the *long count,* the *tzolkin,* and the *haab.* Emacs knows about all three of these calendars. Experts dispute the exact correlation between the Mayan calendar and our calendar; Emacs uses the Goodman-Martinez-Thompson correlation in its calculations.

The Copts use a calendar based on the ancient Egyptian solar calendar. Their calendar consists of twelve 30-day months followed by an extra five-day period. Once every fourth year they add a leap day to this extra period to make it six days. The Ethiopic calendar is identical in structure, but has different year numbers and month names.

The Persians use a solar calendar based on a design of Omar Khayyam. Their calendar consists of twelve months of which the first six have 31 days, the next five have 30 days, and the last has 29 in ordinary years and 30 in leap years. Leap years occur in a complicated pattern every four or five years. The calendar implemented here is the arithmetical Persian calendar championed by Birashk, based on a 2,820-year cycle. It differs from the astronomical Persian calendar, which is based on astronomical events. As of this writing the first future discrepancy is projected to occur on March 20, 2025. It is currently not clear what the official calendar of Iran will be that far into the future.

The Chinese calendar is a complicated system of lunar months arranged into solar years. The years go in cycles of sixty, each year containing either twelve months in an ordinary year or thirteen months in a leap year; each month has either 29 or 30 days. Years, ordinary months, and days are named by combining one of ten "celestial stems" with one of twelve "terrestrial branches" for a total of sixty names that are repeated in a cycle of sixty.

30.9.2 Converting To Other Calendars

The following commands describe the selected date (the date at point) in various other calendar systems:

`Mouse-2 Other calendars`
Display the date that you click on, expressed in various other calendars.

`p c`   Display ISO commercial calendar equivalent for selected day (`calendar-print-iso-date`).

`p j`   Display Julian date for selected day (`calendar-print-julian-date`).

`p a`   Display astronomical (Julian) day number for selected day (`calendar-print-astro-day-number`).

`p h`   Display Hebrew date for selected day (`calendar-print-hebrew-date`).

`p i`   Display Islamic date for selected day (`calendar-print-islamic-date`).

`p f`   Display French Revolutionary date for selected day (`calendar-print-french-date`).

`p C`   Display Chinese date for selected day (`calendar-print-chinese-date`).

`p k`   Display Coptic date for selected day (`calendar-print-coptic-date`).

`p e`   Display Ethiopic date for selected day (`calendar-print-ethiopic-date`).

`p p`   Display Persian date for selected day (`calendar-print-persian-date`).

`p m`   Display Mayan date for selected day (`calendar-print-mayan-date`).

If you are using X, the easiest way to translate a date into other calendars is to click on it with `Mouse-2`, then choose `Other calendars` from the menu that appears. This displays the equivalent forms of the date in all the calendars Emacs understands, in the form of a menu. (Choosing an alternative from this menu doesn't actually do anything—the menu is used only for display.)

Otherwise, move point to the date you want to convert, then type the appropriate command starting with p from the table above. The prefix p is a mnemonic for "print," since Emacs "prints" the equivalent date in the echo area.

30.9.3 Converting From Other Calendars

You can use the other supported calendars to specify a date to move to. This section describes the commands for doing this using calendars other than Mayan; for the Mayan calendar, see the following section.

g c	Move to a date specified in the ISO commercial calendar (`calendar-goto-iso-date`).
g w	Move to a week specified in the ISO commercial calendar (`calendar-goto-iso-week`).
g j	Move to a date specified in the Julian calendar (`calendar-goto-julian-date`).
g a	Move to a date specified with an astronomical (Julian) day number (`calendar-goto-astro-day-number`).
g h	Move to a date specified in the Hebrew calendar (`calendar-goto-hebrew-date`).
g i	Move to a date specified in the Islamic calendar (`calendar-goto-islamic-date`).
g f	Move to a date specified in the French Revolutionary calendar (`calendar-goto-french-date`).
g C	Move to a date specified in the Chinese calendar (`calendar-goto-chinese-date`).
g p	Move to a date specified in the Persian calendar (`calendar-goto-persian-date`).
g k	Move to a date specified in the Coptic calendar (`calendar-goto-coptic-date`).
g e	Move to a date specified in the Ethiopic calendar (`calendar-goto-ethiopic-date`).

These commands ask you for a date on the other calendar, move point to the Gregorian calendar date equivalent to that date, and display the other calendar's date in the echo area. Emacs uses strict completion (see Section 5.3 [Completion], page 33) whenever it asks you to type a month name, so you don't have to worry about the spelling of Hebrew, Islamic, or French names.

One common question concerning the Hebrew calendar is the computation of the anniversary of a date of death, called a "yahrzeit." The Emacs calendar includes a facility for such calculations. If you are in the calendar, the command M-x list-yahrzeit-dates asks you for a range of years and then displays a list of the yahrzeit dates for those years for the date given by point. If you are not in the calendar, this command first asks you for the date of death and the range of years, and then displays the list of yahrzeit dates.

30.9.4 Converting from the Mayan Calendar

Here are the commands to select dates based on the Mayan calendar:

g m l   Move to a date specified by the long count calendar (`calendar-goto-mayan-long-count-date`).

g m n t   Move to the next occurrence of a place in the tzolkin calendar (`calendar-next-tzolkin-date`).

g m p t   Move to the previous occurrence of a place in the tzolkin calendar (`calendar-previous-tzolkin-date`).

g m n h   Move to the next occurrence of a place in the haab calendar (`calendar-next-haab-date`).

g m p h   Move to the previous occurrence of a place in the haab calendar (`calendar-previous-haab-date`).

g m n c   Move to the next occurrence of a place in the calendar round (`calendar-next-calendar-round-date`).

g m p c   Move to the previous occurrence of a place in the calendar round (`calendar-previous-calendar-round-date`).

To understand these commands, you need to understand the Mayan calendars. The *long count* is a counting of days with these units:

1 kin = 1 day   1 uinal = 20 kin   1 tun = 18 uinal
1 katun = 20 tun   1 baktun = 20 katun

Thus, the long count date 12.16.11.16.6 means 12 baktun, 16 katun, 11 tun, 16 uinal, and 6 kin. The Emacs calendar can handle Mayan long count dates as early as 7.17.18.13.3, but no earlier. When you use the g m l command, type the Mayan long count date with the baktun, katun, tun, uinal, and kin separated by periods.

The Mayan tzolkin calendar is a cycle of 260 days formed by a pair of independent cycles of 13 and 20 days. Since this cycle repeats endlessly, Emacs provides commands to move backward and forward to the previous or next point in the cycle. Type g m p t to go to the previous tzolkin date; Emacs asks you for a tzolkin date and moves point to the previous occurrence of that date. Similarly, type g m n t to go to the next occurrence of a tzolkin date.

The Mayan haab calendar is a cycle of 365 days arranged as 18 months of 20 days each, followed a 5-day monthless period. Like the tzolkin cycle, this cycle repeats endlessly, and there are commands to move backward and forward to the previous or next point in the cycle. Type g m p h to go to the previous haab date; Emacs asks you for a haab date and moves point to the previous occurrence of that date. Similarly, type g m n h to go to the next occurrence of a haab date.

The Maya also used the combination of the tzolkin date and the haab date. This combination is a cycle of about 52 years called a *calendar round*. If you type g m p c, Emacs asks you for both a haab and a tzolkin date and then moves point to the previous occurrence of that combination. Use **g m n c** to move point to the next occurrence of a combination. These commands signal an error if the haab/tzolkin date combination you have typed is impossible.

Emacs uses strict completion (see Section 5.3.3 [Strict Completion], page 34) whenever it asks you to type a Mayan name, so you don't have to worry about spelling.

30.10 The Diary

The Emacs diary keeps track of appointments or other events on a daily basis, in conjunction with the calendar. To use the diary feature, you must first create a *diary file* containing a list of events and their dates. Then Emacs can automatically pick out and display the events for today, for the immediate future, or for any specified date.

The name of the diary file is specified by the variable `diary-file`; '~/diary' is the default. A sample diary file is (note that the file format is essentially the same as that used by the external shell utility 'calendar'):

```
12/22/1988   Twentieth wedding anniversary!!
&1/1.        Happy New Year!
10/22        Ruth's birthday.
* 21, *:     Payday
Tuesday--weekly meeting with grad students at 10am
        Supowit, Shen, Bitner, and Kapoor to attend.
1/13/89      Friday the thirteenth!!
&thu 4pm     squash game with Lloyd.
mar 16       Dad's birthday
April 15, 1989 Income tax due.
&* 15        time cards due.
```

This example uses extra spaces to align the event descriptions of most of the entries. Such formatting is purely a matter of taste.

Although you probably will start by creating a diary manually, Emacs provides a number of commands to let you view, add, and change diary entries.

30.10.1 Displaying the Diary

Once you have created a diary file, you can use the calendar to view it. You can also view today's events outside of Calendar mode.

d   Display all diary entries for the selected date (`diary-view-entries`).

Mouse-2 Diary
                Display all diary entries for the date you click on.

s   Display the entire diary file (`diary-show-all-entries`).

m   Mark all visible dates that have diary entries (`mark-diary-entries`).

u   Unmark the calendar window (`calendar-unmark`).

`M-x print-diary-entries`
> Print hard copy of the diary display as it appears.

`M-x diary`   Display all diary entries for today's date.

`M-x diary-mail-entries`
> Mail yourself email reminders about upcoming diary entries.

Displaying the diary entries with `d` shows in a separate window the diary entries for the selected date in the calendar. The mode line of the new window shows the date of the diary entries and any holidays that fall on that date. If you specify a numeric argument with `d`, it shows all the diary entries for that many successive days. Thus, `2 d` displays all the entries for the selected date and for the following day.

Another way to display the diary entries for a date is to click `Mouse-2` on the date, and then choose `Diary entries` from the menu that appears. If the variable `view-diary-entries-initially` is non-`nil`, creating the calendar lists the diary entries for the current date (provided the current date is visible).

To get a broader view of which days are mentioned in the diary, use the `m` command. This displays the dates that have diary entries in a different face (or places a '+' after these dates, if display with multiple faces is not available). See Info file 'emacs-xtra', node 'Calendar Customizing'. The command applies both to the currently visible months and to other months that subsequently become visible by scrolling. To turn marking off and erase the current marks, type `u`, which also turns off holiday marks (see Section 30.6 [Holidays], page 360). If the variable `mark-diary-entries-in-calendar` is non-`nil`, creating or updating the calendar marks diary dates automatically.

To see the full diary file, rather than just some of the entries, use the `s` command.

Display of selected diary entries uses the selective display feature to hide entries that don't apply. The diary buffer as you see it is an illusion, so simply printing the buffer does not print what you see on your screen. There is a special command to print hard copy of the diary buffer *as it appears*; this command is `M-x print-diary-entries`. It sends the data directly to the printer. You can customize it like `lpr-region` (see Section 31.4 [Printing], page 391).

The command `M-x diary` displays the diary entries for the current date, independently of the calendar display, and optionally for the next few days as well; the variable `number-of-diary-entries` specifies how many days to include. See Info file 'emacs-xtra', node 'Diary Customizing'.

If you put `(diary)` in your '.emacs' file, this automatically displays a window with the day's diary entries, when you enter Emacs. The mode line of the displayed window shows the date and any holidays that fall on that date.

Many users like to receive notice of events in their diary as email. To send such mail to yourself, use the command `M-x diary-mail-entries`. A prefix argument specifies how many days (starting with today) to check; otherwise, the variable `diary-mail-days` says how many days.

30.10.2 The Diary File

Your *diary file* is a file that records events associated with particular dates. The name of the diary file is specified by the variable `diary-file`; '~/diary' is the default. The `calendar` utility program supports a subset of the format allowed by the Emacs diary facilities, so you can use that utility to view the diary file, with reasonable results aside from the entries it cannot understand.

Each entry in the diary file describes one event and consists of one or more lines. An entry always begins with a date specification at the left margin. The rest of the entry is simply text to describe the event. If the entry has more than one line, then the lines after the first must begin with whitespace to indicate they continue a previous entry. Lines that do not begin with valid dates and do not continue a preceding entry are ignored.

You can inhibit the marking of certain diary entries in the calendar window; to do this, insert an ampersand ('&') at the beginning of the entry, before the date. This has no effect on display of the entry in the diary window; it affects only marks on dates in the calendar window. Nonmarking entries are especially useful for generic entries that would otherwise mark many different dates.

If the first line of a diary entry consists only of the date or day name with no following blanks or punctuation, then the diary window display doesn't include that line; only the continuation lines appear. For example, this entry:

```
02/11/1989
       Bill B. visits Princeton today
       2pm Cognitive Studies Committee meeting
       2:30-5:30 Liz at Lawrenceville
       4:00pm Dentist appt
       7:30pm Dinner at George's
       8:00-10:00pm concert
```

appears in the diary window without the date line at the beginning. This style of entry looks neater when you display just a single day's entries, but can cause confusion if you ask for more than one day's entries.

You can edit the diary entries as they appear in the window, but it is important to remember that the buffer displayed contains the *entire* diary file, with portions of it concealed from view. This means, for instance, that the `C-f` (`forward-char`) command can put point at what appears to be the end of the line, but what is in reality the middle of some concealed line.

Be careful when editing the diary entries! Inserting additional lines or adding/deleting characters in the middle of a visible line cannot cause problems, but editing at the end of a line may not do what you expect. Deleting a line may delete other invisible entries that follow it. Before editing the diary, it is best to display the entire file with `s` (`diary-show-all-entries`).

30.10.3 Date Formats

Here are some sample diary entries, illustrating different ways of formatting a date. The examples all show dates in American order (month, day, year), but Calendar mode supports European order (day, month, year) as an option.

```
4/20/93  Switch-over to new tabulation system
apr. 25  Start tabulating annual results
4/30  Results for April are due
*/25  Monthly cycle finishes
Friday  Don't leave without backing up files
```

The first entry appears only once, on April 20, 1993. The second and third appear every year on the specified dates, and the fourth uses a wildcard (asterisk) for the month, so it appears on the 25th of every month. The final entry appears every week on Friday.

You can use just numbers to express a date, as in '`month/day`' or '`month/day/year`'. This must be followed by a nondigit. In the date itself, *month* and *day* are numbers of one or two digits. The optional *year* is also a number, and may be abbreviated to the last two digits; that is, you can use '11/12/1989' or '11/12/89'.

Dates can also have the form '`monthname day`' or '`monthname day, year`', where the month's name can be spelled in full or abbreviated (with or without a period). The preferred abbreviations can be controlled using the variables `calendar-abbrev-length`, `calendar-month-abbrev-array`, and `calendar-day-abbrev-array`. The default is to use the first three letters of a name as its abbreviation. Case is not significant.

A date may be *generic*; that is, partially unspecified. Then the entry applies to all dates that match the specification. If the date does not contain a year, it is generic and applies to any year. Alternatively, *month*, *day*, or *year* can be a '*'; this matches any month, day, or year, respectively. Thus, a diary entry '3/*/*' matches any day in March of any year; so does '`march *`'.

If you prefer the European style of writing dates—in which the day comes before the month—type `M-x european-calendar` while in the calendar, or set the variable `european-calendar-style` to t with `M-x customize`, or *before* using any calendar or diary command. This mode interprets all dates in the diary in the European manner, and also uses European style for displaying diary dates. (Note that there is no comma after the *monthname* in the European style.) To go back to the (default) American style of writing dates, type `M-x american-calendar`.

You can use the name of a day of the week as a generic date which applies to any date falling on that day of the week. You can abbreviate the day of the week to three letters (with or without a period) or spell it in full; case is not significant.

30.10.4 Commands to Add to the Diary

While in the calendar, there are several commands to create diary entries:

i d   Add a diary entry for the selected date (`insert-diary-entry`).

i w   Add a diary entry for the selected day of the week (`insert-weekly-diary-entry`).

i m   Add a diary entry for the selected day of the month (`insert-monthly-diary-entry`).

i y   Add a diary entry for the selected day of the year (`insert-yearly-diary-entry`).

You can make a diary entry for a specific date by selecting that date in the calendar window and typing the `i d` command. This command displays the end of your diary file in another window and inserts the date; you can then type the rest of the diary entry.

If you want to make a diary entry that applies to a specific day of the week, select that day of the week (any occurrence will do) and type `i w`. This inserts the day-of-week as a generic date; you can then type the rest of the diary entry. You can make a monthly diary entry in the same fashion: select the day of the month, use the `i m` command, and type the rest of the entry. Similarly, you can insert a yearly diary entry with the `i y` command.

All of the above commands make marking diary entries by default. To make a nonmarking diary entry, give a numeric argument to the command. For example, `C-u i w` makes a nonmarking weekly diary entry.

When you modify the diary file, be sure to save the file before exiting Emacs. Saving the diary file after using any of the above insertion commands will automatically update the diary marks in the calendar window, if appropriate. You can use the command `redraw-calendar` to force an update at any time.

30.10.5 Special Diary Entries

In addition to entries based on calendar dates, the diary file can contain *sexp entries* for regular events such as anniversaries. These entries are based on Lisp expressions (sexps) that Emacs evaluates as it scans the diary file. Instead of a date, a sexp entry contains '%%' followed by a Lisp expression which must begin and end with parentheses. The Lisp expression determines which dates the entry applies to.

Calendar mode provides commands to insert certain commonly used sexp entries:

i a   Add an anniversary diary entry for the selected date (`insert-anniversary-diary-entry`).

i b   Add a block diary entry for the current region (`insert-block-diary-entry`).

i c   Add a cyclic diary entry starting at the date (`insert-cyclic-diary-entry`).

If you want to make a diary entry that applies to the anniversary of a specific date, move point to that date and use the `i a` command. This displays the end of your diary file in another window and inserts the anniversary description; you can then type the rest of the diary entry. The entry looks like this:

`%%(diary-anniversary 10 31 1948) Arthur's birthday`

This entry applies to October 31 in any year after 1948; '10 31 1948' specifies the date. (If you are using the European calendar style, the month and day are interchanged.) The reason this expression requires a beginning year is that advanced diary functions can use it to calculate the number of elapsed years.

A *block* diary entry applies to a specified range of consecutive dates. Here is a block diary entry that applies to all dates from June 24, 1990 through July 10, 1990:

`%%(diary-block 6 24 1990 7 10 1990) Vacation`

The '6 24 1990' indicates the starting date and the '7 10 1990' indicates the stopping date. (Again, if you are using the European calendar style, the month and day are interchanged.)

To insert a block entry, place point and the mark on the two dates that begin and end the range, and type i b. This command displays the end of your diary file in another window and inserts the block description; you can then type the diary entry.

Cyclic diary entries repeat after a fixed interval of days. To create one, select the starting date and use the i c command. The command prompts for the length of interval, then inserts the entry, which looks like this:

`%%(diary-cyclic 50 3 1 1990) Renew medication`

This entry applies to March 1, 1990 and every 50th day following; '3 1 1990' specifies the starting date. (If you are using the European calendar style, the month and day are interchanged.)

All three of these commands make marking diary entries. To insert a nonmarking entry, give a numeric argument to the command. For example, C-u i a makes a nonmarking anniversary diary entry.

Marking sexp diary entries in the calendar is *extremely* time-consuming, since every date visible in the calendar window must be individually checked. So it's a good idea to make sexp diary entries nonmarking (with '&') when possible.

Another sophisticated kind of sexp entry, a *floating* diary entry, specifies a regularly occurring event by offsets specified in days, weeks, and months. It is comparable to a crontab entry interpreted by the cron utility. Here is a nonmarking, floating diary entry that applies to the last Thursday in November:

`&%%(diary-float 11 4 -1) American Thanksgiving`

The 11 specifies November (the eleventh month), the 4 specifies Thursday (the fourth day of the week, where Sunday is numbered zero), and the −1 specifies "last" (1 would mean "first," 2 would mean "second," −2 would mean "second-to-last," and so on). The month can be a single month or a list of months. Thus you could change the 11 above to ''(1 2 3)' and have the entry apply to the last Thursday of January, February, and March. If the month is t, the entry applies to all months of the year.

Each of the standard sexp diary entries takes an optional parameter specifying the name of a face or a single-character string to use when marking the entry in the calendar. Most generally, sexp diary entries can perform arbitrary computations to determine when they apply. See Info file 'emacs-xtra', node 'Sexp Diary Entries'.

30.11 Appointments

If you have a diary entry for an appointment, and that diary entry begins with a recognizable time of day, Emacs can warn you several minutes beforehand that

that appointment is pending. Emacs alerts you to the appointment by displaying a message in your chosen format, as specified by the variable `appt-display-format`. If the value of `appt-audible` is non-nil, the warning includes an audible reminder. In addition, if `appt-display-mode-line` is non-nil, Emacs displays the number of minutes to the appointment on the mode line.

If `appt-display-format` has the value `window`, then the variable `appt-display-duration` controls how long the reminder window is visible for; and the variables `appt-disp-window-function` and `appt-delete-window-function` give the names of functions used to create and destroy the window, respectively.

To enable appointment notification, use the command M-x `appt-activate`. With a positive argument, it enables notification; with a negative argument, it disables notification; with no argument, it toggles. Enabling notification also sets up an appointment list for today from the diary file, giving all diary entries found with recognizable times of day, and reminds you just before each of them.

For example, suppose the diary file contains these lines:

```
Monday
    9:30am Coffee break
    12:00pm Lunch
```

Then on Mondays, you will be reminded at around 9:20am about your coffee break and at around 11:50am about lunch. The variable `appt-message-warning-time` specifies how many minutes in advance to warn you; its default value is 12 (12 minutes).

You can write times in am/pm style (with '`12:00am`' standing for midnight and '`12:00pm`' standing for noon), or 24-hour European/military style. You need not be consistent; your diary file can have a mixture of the two styles. Times must be at the beginning of lines if they are to be recognized.

Emacs updates the appointments list from the diary file automatically just after midnight. You can force an update at any time by re-enabling appointment notification. Both these actions also display the day's diary buffer, unless you set `appt display-diary` to `nil`. The appointments list is also updated whenever the diary file is saved.

You can also use the appointment notification facility like an alarm clock. The command M-x `appt-add` adds entries to the appointment list without affecting your diary file. You delete entries from the appointment list with M-x `appt-delete`.

30.12 Importing and Exporting Diary Entries

You can transfer diary entries between Emacs diary files and a variety of other formats.

You can import diary entries from Outlook-generated appointment messages. While viewing such a message in Rmail or Gnus, do M-x `diary-from-outlook` to import the entry. You can make this command recognize additional appointment message formats by customizing the variable `diary-outlook-formats`.

The icalendar package allows you to transfer data between your Emacs diary file and iCalendar files, which are defined in "RFC 2445—Internet Calendaring and

Scheduling Core Object Specification (iCalendar)" (as well as the earlier vCalendar format).

Importing works for "ordinary" (i.e. non-recurring) events, but (at present) may not work correctly (if at all) for recurring events. Exporting of diary files into iCalendar files should work correctly for most diary entries. This feature is a work in progress, so the commands may evolve in future.

The command `icalendar-import-buffer` extracts iCalendar data from the current buffer and adds it to your (default) diary file. This function is also suitable for automatic extraction of iCalendar data; for example with the Rmail mail client one could use:

```
(add-hook 'rmail-show-message-hook 'icalendar-import-buffer)
```

The command `icalendar-import-file` imports an iCalendar file and adds the results to an Emacs diary file. For example:

```
(icalendar-import-file "/here/is/calendar.ics"
                       "/there/goes/ical-diary")
```

You can use an `#include` directive to add the import file contents to the main diary file, if these are different files. See Info file 'emacs-xtra', node 'Fancy Diary Display'.

Use `icalendar-export-file` to interactively export an entire Emacs diary file to iCalendar format. To export only a part of a diary file, mark the relevant area, and call `icalendar-export-region`. In both cases the result is appended to the target file.

30.13 Daylight Saving Time

Emacs understands the difference between standard time and daylight saving time—the times given for sunrise, sunset, solstices, equinoxes, and the phases of the moon take that into account. The rules for daylight saving time vary from place to place and have also varied historically from year to year. To do the job properly, Emacs needs to know which rules to use.

Some operating systems keep track of the rules that apply to the place where you are; on these systems, Emacs gets the information it needs from the system automatically. If some or all of this information is missing, Emacs fills in the gaps with the rules currently used in Cambridge, Massachusetts. If the resulting rules are not what you want, you can tell Emacs the rules to use by setting certain variables: `calendar-daylight-savings-starts` and `calendar-daylight-savings-ends`.

These values should be Lisp expressions that refer to the variable `year`, and evaluate to the Gregorian date on which daylight saving time starts or (respectively) ends, in the form of a list (*month day year*). The values should be `nil` if your area does not use daylight saving time.

Emacs uses these expressions to determine the starting date of daylight saving time for the holiday list and for correcting times of day in the solar and lunar calculations.

The values for Cambridge, Massachusetts are as follows:

```
(calendar-nth-named-day 2 0 3 year)
```

```
(calendar-nth-named-day 1 0 11 year)
```
That is, the second 0th day (Sunday) of the third month (March) in the year specified by **year**, and the first Sunday of the eleventh month (November) of that year. If daylight saving time were changed to start on October 1, you would set **calendar-daylight-savings-starts** to this:

```
(list 10 1 year)
```
If there is no daylight saving time at your location, or if you want all times in standard time, set **calendar-daylight-savings-starts** and **calendar-daylight-savings-ends** to **nil**.

The variable **calendar-daylight-time-offset** specifies the difference between daylight saving time and standard time, measured in minutes. The value for Cambridge, Massachusetts is 60.

Finally, the two variables **calendar-daylight-savings-starts-time** and **calendar-daylight-savings-ends-time** specify the number of minutes after midnight local time when the transition to and from daylight saving time should occur. For Cambridge, Massachusetts both variables' values are 120.

30.14 Summing Time Intervals

The timeclock feature adds up time intervals, so you can (for instance) keep track of how much time you spend working on particular projects.

Use the M-x **timeclock-in** command when you start working on a project, and M-x **timeclock-out** command when you're done. Each time you do this, it adds one time interval to the record of the project. You can change to working on a different project with M-x **timeclock-change**.

Once you've collected data from a number of time intervals, you can use M-x **timeclock-workday-remaining** to see how much time is left to work today (assuming a typical average of 8 hours a day), and M-x **timeclock-when-to-leave** which will calculate when you're "done."

If you want Emacs to display the amount of time "left" of your workday in the mode line, either customize the **timeclock-modeline-display** variable and set its value to **t**, or invoke the M-x **timeclock-modeline-display** command.

Terminating the current Emacs session might or might not mean that you have stopped working on the project and, by default, Emacs asks you. You can, however, set the value of the variable **timeclock-ask-before-exiting** to **nil** (via M-x **customize**) to avoid the question; then, only an explicit M-x **timeclock-out** or M-x **timeclock-change** will tell Emacs that the current interval is over.

The timeclock functions work by accumulating the data in a file called '**.timelog**' in your home directory. You can specify a different name for this file by customizing the variable **timeclock-file**. If you edit the timeclock file manually, or if you change the value of any of timeclock's customizable variables, you should run the command M-x **timeclock-reread-log** to update the data in Emacs from the file.

31 Miscellaneous Commands

This chapter contains several brief topics that do not fit anywhere else: reading netnews, running shell commands and shell subprocesses, using a single shared Emacs for utilities that expect to run an editor as a subprocess, printing hardcopy, sorting text, narrowing display to part of the buffer, editing double-column files and binary files, saving an Emacs session for later resumption, following hyperlinks, browsing images, emulating other editors, and various diversions and amusements.

31.1 Gnus

Gnus is an Emacs package primarily designed for reading and posting Usenet news. It can also be used to read and respond to messages from a number of other sources— mail, remote directories, digests, and so on.

Here we introduce Gnus and describe several basic features. For full details on Gnus, type `M-x info` and then select the Gnus manual.

To start Gnus, type `M-x gnus RET`.

31.1.1 Gnus Buffers

Unlike most Emacs packages, Gnus uses several buffers to display information and to receive commands. The three Gnus buffers users use most are the *group buffer*, the *summary buffer* and the *article buffer*.

The *group buffer* contains a list of newsgroups. This is the first buffer Gnus displays when it starts up. It normally displays only the groups to which you subscribe and that contain unread articles. Use this buffer to select a specific group.

The *summary buffer* lists one line for each article in a single group. By default, the author, the subject and the line number are displayed for each article, but this is customizable, like most aspects of Gnus display. The summary buffer is created when you select a group in the group buffer, and is killed when you exit the group. Use this buffer to select an article.

The *article buffer* displays the article. In normal Gnus usage, you see this buffer but you don't select it—all useful article-oriented commands work in the summary buffer. But you can select the article buffer, and execute all Gnus commands from that buffer, if you want to.

31.1.2 When Gnus Starts Up

At startup, Gnus reads your '`.newsrc`' news initialization file and attempts to communicate with the local news server, which is a repository of news articles. The news server need not be the same computer you are logged in on.

If you start Gnus and connect to the server, but do not see any newsgroups listed in the group buffer, type `L` or `A k` to get a listing of all the groups. Then type `u` to toggle subscription to groups.

The first time you start Gnus, Gnus subscribes you to a few selected groups. All other groups start out as *killed groups* for you; you can list them with `A k`. All new groups that subsequently come to exist at the news server become *zombie groups* for you; type A z to list them. You can subscribe to a group shown in these lists using the u command.

When you quit Gnus with q, it automatically records in your '.newsrc' and '.newsrc.eld' initialization files the subscribed or unsubscribed status of all groups. You should normally not edit these files manually, but you may if you know how.

31.1.3 Summary of Gnus Commands

Reading news is a two-step process:

1. Choose a group in the group buffer.

2. Select articles from the summary buffer. Each article selected is displayed in the article buffer in a large window, below the summary buffer in its small window.

Each Gnus buffer has its own special commands; the meanings of any given key in the various Gnus buffers are usually analogous, even if not identical. Here are commands for the group and summary buffers:

q   In the group buffer, update your '.newsrc' initialization file and quit Gnus.

         In the summary buffer, exit the current group and return to the group buffer. Thus, typing q twice quits Gnus.

L   In the group buffer, list all the groups available on your news server (except those you have killed). This may be a long list!

l   In the group buffer, list only the groups to which you subscribe and which contain unread articles.

u   In the group buffer, unsubscribe from (or subscribe to) the group listed in the line that point is on. When you quit Gnus by typing q, Gnus lists in your '.newsrc' file which groups you have subscribed to. The next time you start Gnus, you won't see this group, because Gnus normally displays only subscribed-to groups.

C-k   In the group buffer, "kill" the current line's group—don't even list it in '.newsrc' from now on. This affects future Gnus sessions as well as the present session.

         When you quit Gnus by typing q, Gnus writes information in the file '.newsrc' describing all newsgroups except those you have "killed."

SPC   In the group buffer, select the group on the line under the cursor and display the first unread article in that group.

         In the summary buffer,

- Select the article on the line under the cursor if none is selected.

- Scroll the text of the selected article (if there is one).

- Select the next unread article if at the end of the current article.

Thus, you can move through all the articles by repeatedly typing SPC.

DEL   In the group buffer, move point to the previous group containing unread articles.

In the summary buffer, scroll the text of the article backwards.

n   Move point to the next unread group, or select the next unread article.

p   Move point to the previous unread group, or select the previous unread article.

C-n
C-p   Move point to the next or previous item, even if it is marked as read. This does not select the article or group on that line.

s   In the summary buffer, do an incremental search of the current text in the article buffer, just as if you switched to the article buffer and typed C-s.

M-s *regexp* RET

In the summary buffer, search forward for articles containing a match for *regexp*.

31.2 Running Shell Commands from Emacs

Emacs has commands for passing single command lines to inferior shell processes; it can also run a shell interactively with input and output to an Emacs buffer named '*shell*' or run a shell inside a terminal emulator window.

M-! *cmd* RET

Run the shell command line *cmd* and display the output (shell-command).

M-| *cmd* RET

Run the shell command line *cmd* with region contents as input; optionally replace the region with the output (shell-command-on-region).

M-x shell   Run a subshell with input and output through an Emacs buffer. You can then give commands interactively.

M-x term   Run a subshell with input and output through an Emacs buffer. You can then give commands interactively. Full terminal emulation is available.

M-x eshell invokes a shell implemented entirely in Emacs. It is documented in a separate manual. See section "Eshell" in *Eshell: The Emacs Shell*.

31.2.1 Single Shell Commands

M-! (shell-command) reads a line of text using the minibuffer and executes it as a shell command in a subshell made just for that command. Standard input for the command comes from the null device. If the shell command produces any output, the output appears either in the echo area (if it is short), or in an Emacs buffer named '*Shell Command Output*', which is displayed in another window but not selected (if the output is long).

For instance, one way to decompress a file 'foo.gz' from Emacs is to type M-! gunzip foo.gz RET. That shell command normally creates the file 'foo' and produces no terminal output.

A numeric argument, as in M-1 M-!, says to insert terminal output into the current buffer instead of a separate buffer. It puts point before the output, and sets the mark after the output. For instance, M-1 M-! gunzip < foo.gz RET would insert the uncompressed equivalent of 'foo.gz' into the current buffer.

If the shell command line ends in '&', it runs asynchronously. For a synchronous shell command, shell-command returns the command's exit status (0 means success), when it is called from a Lisp program. You do not get any status information for an asynchronous command, since it hasn't finished yet when shell-command returns.

M-| (shell-command-on-region) is like M-! but passes the contents of the region as the standard input to the shell command, instead of no input. With a numeric argument, meaning insert the output in the current buffer, it deletes the old region and the output replaces it as the contents of the region. It returns the command's exit status, like M-!.

One use for M-| is to run gpg to see what keys are in the buffer. For instance, if the buffer contains a GPG key, type C-x h M-| gpg RET to feed the entire buffer contents to the gpg program. That program will ignore everything except the encoded keys, and will output a list of the keys the buffer contains.

Both M-! and M-| use shell-file-name to specify the shell to use. This variable is initialized based on your SHELL environment variable when Emacs is started. If the file name is relative, Emacs searches the directories in the list exec-path; this list is initialized based on the environment variable PATH when Emacs is started. Your '.emacs' file can override either or both of these default initializations.

Both M-! and M-| wait for the shell command to complete, unless you end the command with '&' to make it asynchronous. To stop waiting, type C-g to quit; that terminates the shell command with the signal SIGINT—the same signal that C-c normally generates in the shell. Emacs then waits until the command actually terminates. If the shell command doesn't stop (because it ignores the SIGINT signal), type C-g again; this sends the command a SIGKILL signal which is impossible to ignore.

Asynchronous commands ending in '&' feed their output into the buffer '*Async Shell Command*'. Output arrives in that buffer regardless of whether it is visible in a window.

To specify a coding system for M-! or M-|, use the command C-x RET c immediately beforehand. See Section 19.12 [Communication Coding], page 200.

Error output from these commands is normally intermixed with the regular output. But if the variable shell-command-default-error-buffer has a string as value, and it's the name of a buffer, M-! and M-| insert error output before point in that buffer.

31.2.2 Interactive Inferior Shell

To run a subshell interactively, putting its typescript in an Emacs buffer, use M-x shell. This creates (or reuses) a buffer named '*shell*' and runs a subshell with input coming from and output going to that buffer. That is to say, any "terminal output" from the subshell goes into the buffer, advancing point, and any "terminal input" for the subshell comes from text in the buffer. To give input to the subshell, go to the end of the buffer and type the input, terminated by RET.

Emacs does not wait for the subshell to do anything. You can switch windows or buffers and edit them while the shell is waiting, or while it is running a command. Output from the subshell waits until Emacs has time to process it; this happens whenever Emacs is waiting for keyboard input or for time to elapse.

Input lines, once you submit them, are displayed using the face comint-highlight-input, and prompts are displayed using the face comint-highlight-prompt. This makes it easier to see previous input lines in the buffer. See Section 11.5 [Faces], page 72.

To make multiple subshells, you can invoke M-x shell with a prefix argument (e.g. C-u M-x shell), which will read a buffer name and create (or reuse) a subshell in that buffer. You can also rename the '*shell*' buffer using M-x rename-uniquely, then create a new '*shell*' buffer using plain M-x shell. Subshells in different buffers run independently and in parallel.

The file name used to load the subshell is the value of the variable explicit-shell-file-name, if that is non-nil. Otherwise, the environment variable ESHELL is used, or the environment variable SHELL if there is no ESHELL. If the file name specified is relative, the directories in the list exec-path are searched; this list is initialized based on the environment variable PATH when Emacs is started. Your '.emacs' file can override either or both of these default initializations.

Emacs sends the new shell the contents of the file '~/.emacs_shellname' as input, if it exists, where shellname is the name of the file that the shell was loaded from. For example, if you use bash, the file sent to it is '~/.emacs_bash'. If this file is not found, Emacs tries to fallback on '~/.emacs.d/init_shellname.sh'.

To specify a coding system for the shell, you can use the command C-x RET c immediately before M-x shell. You can also change the coding system for a running subshell by typing C-x RET p in the shell buffer. See Section 19.12 [Communication Coding], page 200.

Emacs sets the envitonment variable INSIDE_EMACS to t in the subshell. Programs can check this variable to determine whether they are running inside an Emacs subshell.

Emacs also sets the EMACS environment variable to t if it is not already defined. **Warning:** This environment variable is deprecated. Programs that check this variable should be changed to check INSIDE_EMACS instead.

31.2.3 Shell Mode

Shell buffers use Shell mode, which defines several special keys attached to the C-c prefix. They are chosen to resemble the usual editing and job control characters present in shells that are not under Emacs, except that you must type C-c first. Here is a complete list of the special key bindings of Shell mode:

RET
    At end of buffer send line as input; otherwise, copy current line to end of buffer and send it (`comint-send-input`). Copying a line in this way omits any prompt at the beginning of the line (text output by programs preceding your input). See Section 31.2.4 [Shell Prompts], page 383, for how Shell mode recognizes prompts.

TAB
    Complete the command name or file name before point in the shell buffer (`comint-dynamic-complete`). TAB also completes history references (see Section 31.2.5.3 [History References], page 386) and environment variable names.

    The variable `shell-completion-fignore` specifies a list of file name extensions to ignore in Shell mode completion. The default setting is `nil`, but some users prefer (`"~" "#" "%"`) to ignore file names ending in '~', '#' or '%'. Other related Comint modes use the variable `comint-completion-fignore` instead.

M-?
    Display temporarily a list of the possible completions of the file name before point in the shell buffer (`comint-dynamic-list-filename-completions`).

C-d
    Either delete a character or send EOF (`comint-delchar-or-maybe-eof`). Typed at the end of the shell buffer, C-d sends EOF to the subshell. Typed at any other position in the buffer, C-d deletes a character as usual.

C-c C-a
    Move to the beginning of the line, but after the prompt if any (`comint-bol-or-process-mark`). If you repeat this command twice in a row, the second time it moves back to the process mark, which is the beginning of the input that you have not yet sent to the subshell. (Normally that is the same place—the end of the prompt on this line—but after C-c SPC the process mark may be in a previous line.)

C-c SPC
    Accumulate multiple lines of input, then send them together. This command inserts a newline before point, but does not send the preceding text as input to the subshell—at least, not yet. Both lines, the one before this newline and the one after, will be sent together (along with the newline that separates them), when you type RET.

C-c C-u
    Kill all text pending at end of buffer to be sent as input (`comint-kill-input`). If point is not at end of buffer, this only kills the part of this text that precedes point.

C-c C-w
    Kill a word before point (`backward-kill-word`).

C-c C-c
    Interrupt the shell or its current subjob if any (`comint-interrupt-subjob`). This command also kills any shell input pending in the shell buffer and not yet sent.

C-c C-z   Stop the shell or its current subjob if any (`comint-stop-subjob`). This command also kills any shell input pending in the shell buffer and not yet sent.

C-c C-\   Send quit signal to the shell or its current subjob if any (`comint-quit-subjob`). This command also kills any shell input pending in the shell buffer and not yet sent.

C-c C-o   Delete the last batch of output from a shell command (`comint-delete-output`). This is useful if a shell command spews out lots of output that just gets in the way. This command used to be called `comint-kill-output`.

C-c C-s   Write the last batch of output from a shell command to a file (`comint-write-output`). With a prefix argument, the file is appended to instead. Any prompt at the end of the output is not written.

C-c C-r
C-M-l   Scroll to display the beginning of the last batch of output at the top of the window; also move the cursor there (`comint-show-output`).

C-c C-e   Scroll to put the end of the buffer at the bottom of the window (`comint-show-maximum-output`).

C-c C-f   Move forward across one shell command, but not beyond the current line (`shell-forward-command`). The variable `shell-command-regexp` specifies how to recognize the end of a command.

C-c C-b   Move backward across one shell command, but not beyond the current line (`shell-backward-command`).

M-x dirs   Ask the shell what its current directory is, so that Emacs can agree with the shell.

M-x send-invisible RET *text* RET

Send *text* as input to the shell, after reading it without echoing. This is useful when a shell command runs a program that asks for a password.

Please note that Emacs will not echo passwords by default. If you really want them to be echoed, evaluate the following Lisp expression:

```
(remove-hook 'comint-output-filter-functions
             'comint-watch-for-password-prompt)
```

M-x comint-continue-subjob

Continue the shell process. This is useful if you accidentally suspend the shell process.[1]

---

[1] You should not suspend the shell process. Suspending a subjob of the shell is a completely different matter—that is normal practice, but you must use the shell to continue the subjob; this command won't do it.

`M-x comint-strip-ctrl-m`

> Discard all control-M characters from the current group of shell output. The most convenient way to use this command is to make it run automatically when you get output from the subshell. To do that, evaluate this Lisp expression:
>
> ```
> (add-hook 'comint-output-filter-functions
>           'comint-strip-ctrl-m)
> ```

`M-x comint-truncate-buffer`

> This command truncates the shell buffer to a certain maximum number of lines, specified by the variable `comint-buffer-maximum-size`. Here's how to do this automatically each time you get output from the subshell:
>
> ```
> (add-hook 'comint-output-filter-functions
>           'comint-truncate-buffer)
> ```

Shell mode is a derivative of Comint mode, a general-purpose mode for communicating with interactive subprocesses. Most of the features of Shell mode actually come from Comint mode, as you can see from the command names listed above. The special features of Shell mode include the directory tracking feature, and a few user commands.

Other Emacs features that use variants of Comint mode include GUD (see Section 24.6 [Debuggers], page 278) and `M-x run-lisp` (see Section 24.11 [External Lisp], page 291).

You can use `M-x comint-run` to execute any program of your choice in a subprocess using unmodified Comint mode—without the specializations of Shell mode.

31.2.4 Shell Prompts

A prompt is text output by a program to show that it is ready to accept new user input. Normally, Comint mode (and thus Shell mode) considers the prompt to be any text output by a program at the beginning of an input line. However, if the variable `comint-use-prompt-regexp` is non-nil, then Comint mode uses a regular expression to recognize prompts. In Shell mode, `shell-prompt-pattern` specifies the regular expression.

The value of `comint-use-prompt-regexp` also affects many motion and paragraph commands. If the value is non-nil, the general Emacs motion commands behave as they normally do in buffers without special text properties. However, if the value is nil, the default, then Comint mode divides the buffer into two types of "fields" (ranges of consecutive characters having the same `field` text property): input and output. Prompts are part of the output. Most Emacs motion commands do not cross field boundaries, unless they move over multiple lines. For instance, when point is in input on the same line as a prompt, `C-a` puts point at the beginning of the input if `comint-use-prompt-regexp` is nil and at the beginning of the line otherwise.

In Shell mode, only shell prompts start new paragraphs. Thus, a paragraph consists of a prompt and the input and output that follow it. However, if `comint-use-`

`prompt-regexp` is `nil`, the default, most paragraph commands do not cross field boundaries. This means that prompts, ranges of input, and ranges of non-prompt output behave mostly like separate paragraphs; with this setting, numeric arguments to most paragraph commands yield essentially undefined behavior. For the purpose of finding paragraph boundaries, Shell mode uses `shell-prompt-pattern`, regardless of `comint-use-prompt-regexp`.

31.2.5 Shell Command History

Shell buffers support three ways of repeating earlier commands. You can use keys like those used for the minibuffer history; these work much as they do in the minibuffer, inserting text from prior commands while point remains always at the end of the buffer. You can move through the buffer to previous inputs in their original place, then resubmit them or copy them to the end. Or you can use a '!'-style history reference.

31.2.5.1 Shell History Ring

`M-p`
`C-UP`　　　　Fetch the next earlier old shell command.

`M-n`
`C-DOWN`　　　Fetch the next later old shell command.

`M-r` *regexp* `RET`
`M-s` *regexp* `RET`
　　　　　　　Search backwards or forwards for old shell commands that match *regexp*.

`C-c C-x`　　　Fetch the next subsequent command from the history.

`C-c .`　　　　Fetch one argument from an old shell command.

`C-c C-l`　　　Display the buffer's history of shell commands in another window (`comint-dynamic-list-input-ring`).

Shell buffers provide a history of previously entered shell commands. To reuse shell commands from the history, use the editing commands `M-p`, `M-n`, `M-r` and `M-s`. These work just like the minibuffer history commands except that they operate on the text at the end of the shell buffer, where you would normally insert text to send to the shell.

`M-p` fetches an earlier shell command to the end of the shell buffer. Successive use of `M-p` fetches successively earlier shell commands, each replacing any text that was already present as potential shell input. `M-n` does likewise except that it finds successively more recent shell commands from the buffer. `C-UP` works like `M-p`, and `C-DOWN` like `M-n`.

The history search commands `M-r` and `M-s` read a regular expression and search through the history for a matching command. Aside from the choice of which command to fetch, they work just like `M-p` and `M-n`. If you enter an empty regexp, these commands reuse the same regexp used last time.

When you find the previous input you want, you can resubmit it by typing RET, or you can edit it first and then resubmit it if you wish. Any partial input you were composing before navigating the history list is restored when you go to the beginning or end of the history ring.

Often it is useful to reexecute several successive shell commands that were previously executed in sequence. To do this, first find and reexecute the first command of the sequence. Then type C-c C-x; that will fetch the following command—the one that follows the command you just repeated. Then type RET to reexecute this command. You can reexecute several successive commands by typing C-c C-x RET over and over.

The command C-c . (comint-input-previous-argument) copies an individual argument from a previous command, like ESC . in Bash. The simplest use copies the last argument from the previous shell command. With a prefix argument n, it copies the nth argument instead. Repeating C-c . copies from an earlier shell command instead, always using the same value of n (don't give a prefix argument when you repeat the C-c . command).

These commands get the text of previous shell commands from a special history list, not from the shell buffer itself. Thus, editing the shell buffer, or even killing large parts of it, does not affect the history that these commands access.

Some shells store their command histories in files so that you can refer to commands from previous shell sessions. Emacs reads the command history file for your chosen shell, to initialize its own command history. The file name is '~/.bash_history' for bash, '~/.sh_history' for ksh, and '~/.history' for other shells.

31.2.5.2 Shell History Copying

C-c C-p   Move point to the previous prompt (comint-previous-prompt).

C-c C-n   Move point to the following prompt (comint-next-prompt).

C-c RET   Copy the input command which point is in, inserting the copy at the end of the buffer (comint-copy-old-input). This is useful if you move point back to a previous command. After you copy the command, you can submit the copy as input with RET. If you wish, you can edit the copy before resubmitting it. If you use this command on an output line, it copies that line to the end of the buffer.

Mouse-2   If comint-use-prompt-regexp is nil (the default), copy the old input command that you click on, inserting the copy at the end of the buffer (comint-insert-input). If comint-use-prompt-regexp is non-nil, or if the click is not over old input, just yank as usual.

Moving to a previous input and then copying it with C-c RET or Mouse-2 produces the same results—the same buffer contents—that you would get by using M-p enough times to fetch that previous input from the history list. However, C-c RET copies the text from the buffer, which can be different from what is in the history list if you edit the input text in the buffer after it has been sent.

31.2.5.3 Shell History References

Various shells including csh and bash support *history references* that begin with '!' and '^'. Shell mode recognizes these constructs, and can perform the history substitution for you.

If you insert a history reference and type TAB, this searches the input history for a matching command, performs substitution if necessary, and places the result in the buffer in place of the history reference. For example, you can fetch the most recent command beginning with 'mv' with ! m v TAB. You can edit the command if you wish, and then resubmit the command to the shell by typing RET.

Shell mode can optionally expand history references in the buffer when you send them to the shell. To request this, set the variable comint-input-autoexpand to input. You can make SPC perform history expansion by binding SPC to the command comint-magic-space.

Shell mode recognizes history references when they follow a prompt. See Section 31.2.4 [Shell Prompts], page 383, for how Shell mode recognizes prompts.

31.2.6 Directory Tracking

Shell mode keeps track of 'cd', 'pushd' and 'popd' commands given to the inferior shell, so it can keep the '*shell*' buffer's default directory the same as the shell's working directory. It recognizes these commands syntactically, by examining lines of input that are sent.

If you use aliases for these commands, you can tell Emacs to recognize them also. For example, if the value of the variable shell-pushd-regexp matches the beginning of a shell command line, that line is regarded as a pushd command. Change this variable when you add aliases for 'pushd'. Likewise, shell-popd-regexp and shell-cd-regexp are used to recognize commands with the meaning of 'popd' and 'cd'. These commands are recognized only at the beginning of a shell command line.

If Emacs gets confused about changes in the current directory of the subshell, use the command M-x dirs to ask the shell what its current directory is. This command works for shells that support the most common command syntax; it may not work for unusual shells.

You can also use M-x dirtrack-mode to enable (or disable) an alternative and more aggressive method of tracking changes in the current directory.

31.2.7 Shell Mode Options

If the variable comint-scroll-to-bottom-on-input is non-nil, insertion and yank commands scroll the selected window to the bottom before inserting. The default is nil.

If comint-scroll-show-maximum-output is non-nil, then arrival of output when point is at the end tries to scroll the last line of text to the bottom line of the window, showing as much useful text as possible. (This mimics the scrolling behavior of most terminals.) The default is t.

By setting `comint-move-point-for-output`, you can opt for having point jump to the end of the buffer whenever output arrives—no matter where in the buffer point was before. If the value is `this`, point jumps in the selected window. If the value is `all`, point jumps in each window that shows the Comint buffer. If the value is `other`, point jumps in all nonselected windows that show the current buffer. The default value is `nil`, which means point does not jump to the end.

If you set `comint-prompt-read-only`, the prompts in the Comint buffer are read-only.

The variable `comint-input-ignoredups` controls whether successive identical inputs are stored in the input history. A non-`nil` value means to omit an input that is the same as the previous input. The default is `nil`, which means to store each input even if it is equal to the previous input.

Three variables customize file name completion. The variable `comint-completion-addsuffix` controls whether completion inserts a space or a slash to indicate a fully completed file or directory name (non-`nil` means do insert a space or slash). `comint-completion-recexact`, if non-`nil`, directs TAB to choose the shortest possible completion if the usual Emacs completion algorithm cannot add even a single character. `comint-completion-autolist`, if non-`nil`, says to list all the possible completions whenever completion is not exact.

Command completion normally considers only executable files. If you set `shell-completion-execonly` to `nil`, it considers nonexecutable files as well.

You can configure the behavior of 'pushd'. Variables control whether 'pushd' behaves like 'cd' if no argument is given (`shell-pushd-tohome`), pop rather than rotate with a numeric argument (`shell-pushd-dextract`), and only add directories to the directory stack if they are not already on it (`shell-pushd-dunique`). The values you choose should match the underlying shell, of course.

If you want Shell mode to handle color output from shell commands, you can enable ANSI Color mode. Here is how to do this:

```
(add-hook 'shell-mode-hook 'ansi-color-for-comint-mode-on)
```

31.2.8 Emacs Terminal Emulator

To run a subshell in a terminal emulator, putting its typescript in an Emacs buffer, use M-x term. This creates (or reuses) a buffer named '*terminal*', and runs a subshell with input coming from your keyboard, and output going to that buffer.

The terminal emulator uses Term mode, which has two input modes. In line mode, Term basically acts like Shell mode; see Section 31.2.3 [Shell Mode], page 380.

In char mode, each character is sent directly to the inferior subshell, as "terminal input." Any "echoing" of your input is the responsibility of the subshell. The sole exception is the terminal escape character, which by default is C-c (see Section 31.2.9 [Term Mode], page 388). Any "terminal output" from the subshell goes into the buffer, advancing point.

Some programs (such as Emacs itself) need to control the appearance on the terminal screen in detail. They do this by sending special control codes. The exact control codes needed vary from terminal to terminal, but nowadays most terminals and terminal emulators (including xterm) understand the ANSI-standard (VT100-

style) escape sequences. Term mode recognizes these escape sequences, and handles each one appropriately, changing the buffer so that the appearance of the window matches what it would be on a real terminal. You can actually run Emacs inside an Emacs Term window.

The file name used to load the subshell is determined the same way as for Shell mode. To make multiple terminal emulators, rename the buffer '*terminal*' to something different using M-x rename-uniquely, just as with Shell mode.

Unlike Shell mode, Term mode does not track the current directory by examining your input. But some shells can tell Term what the current directory is. This is done automatically by bash version 1.15 and later.

31.2.9 Term Mode

The terminal emulator uses Term mode, which has two input modes. In line mode, Term basically acts like Shell mode; see Section 31.2.3 [Shell Mode], page 380. In char mode, each character is sent directly to the inferior subshell, except for the Term escape character, normally C-c.

To switch between line and char mode, use these commands:

C-c C-j   Switch to line mode. Do nothing if already in line mode.

C-c C-k   Switch to char mode. Do nothing if already in char mode.

The following commands are only available in char mode:

C-c C-c   Send a literal C-C to the sub-shell.

C-c char   This is equivalent to C-x char in normal Emacs. For example, C-c o invokes the global binding of C-x o, which is normally 'other-window'.

31.2.10 Page-At-A-Time Output

Term mode has a page-at-a-time feature. When enabled it makes output pause at the end of each screenful.

C-c C-q   Toggle the page-at-a-time feature. This command works in both line and char modes. When page-at-a-time is enabled, the mode-line displays the word 'page'.

With page-at-a-time enabled, whenever Term receives more than a screenful of output since your last input, it pauses, displaying '**MORE**' in the mode-line. Type SPC to display the next screenful of output. Type ? to see your other options. The interface is similar to the more program.

31.2.11 Remote Host Shell

You can login to a remote computer, using whatever commands you would from a regular terminal (e.g. using the telnet or rlogin commands), from a Term window.

A program that asks you for a password will normally suppress echoing of the password, so the password will not show up in the buffer. This will happen just as if you were using a real terminal, if the buffer is in char mode. If it is in line mode, the password is temporarily visible, but will be erased when you hit return. (This happens automatically; there is no special password processing.)

When you log in to a different machine, you need to specify the type of terminal you're using, by setting the TERM environment variable in the environment for the remote login command. (If you use bash, you do that by writing the variable assignment before the remote login command, without separating comma.) Terminal types 'ansi' or 'vt100' will work on most systems.

31.3 Using Emacs as a Server

Various programs such as mail can invoke your choice of editor to edit a particular piece of text, such as a message that you are sending. By convention, most of these programs use the environment variable EDITOR to specify which editor to run. If you set EDITOR to 'emacs', they invoke Emacs—but in an inconvenient fashion, by starting a new, separate Emacs process. This is inconvenient because it takes time and because the new Emacs process doesn't share the buffers with any existing Emacs process.

You can arrange to use your existing Emacs process as the editor for programs like mail by using the Emacs client program and the server that is part of Emacs. Here is how.

First, the preparations. Within Emacs, call the function server-start. (Your '.emacs' init file can do this automatically if you add the expression (server-start) to it, see Section 32.6 [Init File], page 433.) Then, outside Emacs, set the EDITOR environment variable to 'emacsclient'. (Note that some programs use a different environment variable; for example, to make TeX use 'emacsclient', you should set the TEXEDIT environment variable to 'emacsclient +%d %s'.)

As an alternative to using emacsclient, the file 'etc/emacs.bash' defines a Bash command edit which will communicate with a running Emacs session, or start one if none exist.

Now, whenever any program invokes your specified EDITOR program, the effect is to send a message to your principal Emacs telling it to visit a file. (That's what the program emacsclient does.) Emacs displays the buffer immediately and you can immediately begin editing it in the already running Emacs session.

When you've finished editing that buffer, type C-x # (server-edit). This saves the file and sends a message back to the emacsclient program telling it to exit. The programs that use EDITOR wait for the "editor" (actually, emacsclient) to exit. C-x # also checks for other pending external requests to edit various files, and selects the next such file.

You can switch to a server buffer manually if you wish; you don't have to arrive at it with C-x #. But C-x # is the way to say that you are finished with one.

Finishing with a server buffer also kills the buffer, unless it already existed in the Emacs session before the server asked to create it. However, if you set server-kill-new-buffers to nil, then a different criterion is used: finishing with a server buffer kills it if the file name matches the regular expression server-temp-file-regexp. This is set up to distinguish certain "temporary" files.

If you set the variable `server-window` to a window or a frame, `C-x #` displays the server buffer in that window or in that frame.

You can run multiple Emacs servers on the same machine by giving each one a unique "server name", using the variable `server-name`. For example, `M-x set-variable RET server-name RET foo RET` sets the server name to 'foo'. The `emacsclient` program can specify a server by name using the '`-s`' option. See Section 31.3.1 [Invoking emacsclient], page 390.

While `mail` or another application is waiting for `emacsclient` to finish, `emacsclient` does not read terminal input. So the terminal that `mail` was using is effectively blocked for the duration. In order to edit with your principal Emacs, you need to be able to use it without using that terminal. There are three ways to do this:

- Using a window system, run `mail` and the principal Emacs in two separate windows. While `mail` is waiting for `emacsclient`, the window where it was running is blocked, but you can use Emacs by switching windows.

- Using virtual terminals, run `mail` in one virtual terminal and run Emacs in another.

- Use Shell mode or Term mode in Emacs to run the other program such as `mail`; then, `emacsclient` blocks only the subshell under Emacs, and you can still use Emacs to edit the file.

If you run `emacsclient` with the option '`--no-wait`', it returns immediately without waiting for you to "finish" the buffer in Emacs. Note that server buffers created in this way are not killed automatically when you finish with them.

31.3.1 Invoking `emacsclient`

To run the `emacsclient` program, specify file names as arguments, and optionally line numbers as well, like this:

```
emacsclient {[+line[column]] filename}...
```

This tells Emacs to visit each of the specified files; if you specify a line number for a certain file, Emacs moves to that line in the file. If you specify a column number as well, Emacs puts point on that column in the line.

Ordinarily, `emacsclient` does not return until you use the `C-x #` command on each of these buffers. When that happens, Emacs sends a message to the `emacsclient` program telling it to return.

If you invoke `emacsclient` for more than one file, the additional client buffers are buried at the bottom of the buffer list (see Chapter 16 [Buffers], page 156). If you call `C-x #` after you are done editing a client buffer, the next client buffer is automatically selected.

But if you use the option '`-n`' or '`--no-wait`' when running `emacsclient`, then it returns immediately. (You can take as long as you like to edit the files in Emacs.)

The option '`-a command`' or '`--alternate-editor=command`' specifies a command to run if `emacsclient` fails to contact Emacs. This is useful when running `emacsclient` in a script. For example, the following setting for the `EDITOR` environment variable will always give you an editor, even if no Emacs server is running:

```
      EDITOR="emacsclient --alternate-editor emacs +%d %s"
```
The environment variable ALTERNATE_EDITOR has the same effect, with the value of
the '--alternate-editor' option taking precedence.

If you use several displays, you can tell Emacs on which display to open the
given files with the '-d *display*' or '--display=*display*' option to emacsclient.
This is handy when connecting from home to an Emacs session running on your
machine at your workplace.

If there is more than one Emacs server running, you can specify a server name
with the '-s *name*' or '--socket-name=*name*' option to emacsclient. (This option
is not supported on MS-Windows.)

You can also use emacsclient to execute any piece of Emacs Lisp code, using
the '-e' or '--eval' option. When this option is given, the rest of the arguments is
interpreted as a list of expressions to evaluate, not a list of files to visit.

When you start the Emacs server (by calling server-start), Emacs creates a
file with information about TCP connection to the server: the host where Emacs is
running, the port where it is listening, and an authentication string. emacsclient
uses this information if it needs to connect to the server via TCP. By default, the
file goes in the '~/.emacs.d/server/' directory[2]. You can specify the file name
to use with the '-f *file*' or '--server-file=*file*' options, or by setting EMACS_
SERVER_FILE environment variable to the file name.

31.4 Printing Hard Copies

Emacs provides commands for printing hard copies of either an entire buffer or just
part of one, with or without page headers. You can invoke the printing commands
directly, as detailed in the following section, or using the 'File' menu on the menu
bar. See also the hardcopy commands of Dired (see Section 15.11 [Misc File Ops],
page 150) and the diary (see Section 30.10.1 [Displaying the Diary], page 367).

M-x print-buffer
> Print hardcopy of current buffer with page headings containing the file
> name and page number.

M-x lpr-buffer
> Print hardcopy of current buffer without page headings.

M-x print-region
> Like print-buffer but print only the current region.

M-x lpr-region
> Like lpr-buffer but print only the current region.

The hardcopy commands (aside from the PostScript commands) pass extra
switches to the lpr program based on the value of the variable lpr-switches.
Its value should be a list of strings, each string an option starting with '-'. For

---

[2] On MS-Windows, if HOME is not set or the TCP configuration file cannot be found there,
Emacs also looks for the file in the '.emacs.d/server/' subdirectory of the directory
pointed to by the APPDATA environment variable.

example, to specify a line width of 80 columns for all the printing you do in Emacs, set `lpr-switches` like this:

```
(setq lpr-switches '("-w80"))
```

You can specify the printer to use by setting the variable `printer-name`.

The variable `lpr-command` specifies the name of the printer program to run; the default value depends on your operating system type. On most systems, the default is `"lpr"`. The variable `lpr-headers-switches` similarly specifies the extra switches to use to make page headers. The variable `lpr-add-switches` controls whether to supply '-T' and '-J' options (suitable for `lpr`) to the printer program: `nil` means don't add them. `lpr-add-switches` should be `nil` if your printer program is not compatible with `lpr`.

31.5 PostScript Hardcopy

These commands convert buffer contents to PostScript, either printing it or leaving it in another Emacs buffer.

`M-x ps-print-buffer`

> Print hardcopy of the current buffer in PostScript form.

`M-x ps-print-region`

> Print hardcopy of the current region in PostScript form.

`M-x ps-print-buffer-with-faces`

> Print hardcopy of the current buffer in PostScript form, showing the faces used in the text by means of PostScript features.

`M-x ps-print-region-with-faces`

> Print hardcopy of the current region in PostScript form, showing the faces used in the text.

`M-x ps-spool-buffer`

> Generate PostScript for the current buffer text.

`M-x ps-spool-region`

> Generate PostScript for the current region.

`M-x ps-spool-buffer-with-faces`

> Generate PostScript for the current buffer, showing the faces used.

`M-x ps-spool-region-with-faces`

> Generate PostScript for the current region, showing the faces used.

`M-x handwrite`

> Generates/prints PostScript for the current buffer as if handwritten.

The PostScript commands, `ps-print-buffer` and `ps-print-region`, print buffer contents in PostScript form. One command prints the entire buffer; the other, just the region. The corresponding '-with-faces' commands, `ps-print-buffer-with-faces` and `ps-print-region-with-faces`, use PostScript features to show the faces (fonts and colors) in the text properties of the text being printed.

If you are using a color display, you can print a buffer of program code with color highlighting by turning on Font-Lock mode in that buffer, and using `ps-print-buffer-with-faces`.

The commands whose names have 'spool' instead of 'print' generate the Post-Script output in an Emacs buffer instead of sending it to the printer.

`M-x handwrite` is more frivolous. It generates a PostScript rendition of the current buffer as a cursive handwritten document. It can be customized in group `handwrite`. This function only supports ISO 8859-1 characters.

31.6 Variables for PostScript Hardcopy

All the PostScript hardcopy commands use the variables `ps-lpr-command` and `ps-lpr-switches` to specify how to print the output. `ps-lpr-command` specifies the command name to run, `ps-lpr-switches` specifies command line options to use, and `ps-printer-name` specifies the printer. If you don't set the first two variables yourself, they take their initial values from `lpr-command` and `lpr-switches`. If `ps-printer-name` is nil, `printer-name` is used.

The variable `ps-print-header` controls whether these commands add header lines to each page—set it to nil to turn headers off.

If your printer doesn't support colors, you should turn off color processing by setting `ps-print-color-p` to nil. By default, if the display supports colors, Emacs produces hardcopy output with color information; on black-and-white printers, colors are emulated with shades of gray. This might produce illegible output, even if your screen colors only use shades of gray.

By default, PostScript printing ignores the background colors of the faces, unless the variable `ps-use-face-background` is non nil. This is to avoid unwanted interference with the zebra stripes and background image/text.

The variable `ps-paper-type` specifies which size of paper to format for; legitimate values include a4, a3, a4small, b4, b5, executive, ledger, legal, letter, letter-small, statement, tabloid. The default is letter. You can define additional paper sizes by changing the variable `ps-page-dimensions-database`.

The variable `ps-landscape-mode` specifies the orientation of printing on the page. The default is nil, which stands for "portrait" mode. Any non-nil value specifies "landscape" mode.

The variable `ps-number-of-columns` specifies the number of columns; it takes effect in both landscape and portrait mode. The default is 1.

The variable `ps-font-family` specifies which font family to use for printing ordinary text. Legitimate values include Courier, Helvetica, NewCenturySchlbk, Palatino and Times. The variable `ps-font-size` specifies the size of the font for ordinary text. It defaults to 8.5 points.

Emacs supports more scripts and characters than a typical PostScript printer. Thus, some of the characters in your buffer might not be printable using the fonts built into your printer. You can augment the fonts supplied with the printer with those from the GNU Intlfonts package, or you can instruct Emacs to use Intlfonts exclusively. The variable `ps-multibyte-buffer` controls this: the default value, nil, is appropriate for printing ASCII and Latin-1 characters; a value of non-latin-printer is for printers which have the fonts for ASCII, Latin-1, Japanese, and Korean characters built into them. A value of bdf-font arranges for the BDF fonts from the Intlfonts package to be used for *all* characters. Finally, a value of bdf-font-except-latin instructs the printer to use built-in fonts for ASCII and Latin-1 characters, and Intlfonts BDF fonts for the rest.

To be able to use the BDF fonts, Emacs needs to know where to find them. The variable bdf-directory-list holds the list of directories where Emacs should look for the fonts; the default value includes a single directory '/usr/local/share/emacs/fonts/bdf'.

Many other customization variables for these commands are defined and described in the Lisp files 'ps-print.el' and 'ps-mule.el'.

31.7 Printing Package

The basic Emacs facilities for printing hardcopy can be extended using the Printing package. This provides an easy-to-use interface for choosing what to print, previewing PostScript files before printing, and setting various printing options such as print headers, landscape or portrait modes, duplex modes, and so forth. On GNU/Linux or Unix systems, the Printing package relies on the 'gs' and 'gv' utilities, which are distributed as part of the GhostScript program. On MS-Windows, the 'gstools' port of Ghostscript can be used.

To use the Printing package, add (require 'printing) to your init file (see Section 32.6 [Init File], page 433), followed by (pr-update-menus). This function replaces the usual printing commands in the menu bar with a 'Printing' submenu that contains various printing options. You can also type M-x pr-interface RET; this creates a '*Printing Interface*' buffer, similar to a customization buffer, where you can set the printing options. After selecting what and how to print, you start the print job using the 'Print' button (click mouse-2 on it, or move point over it and type RET). For further information on the various options, use the 'Interface Help' button.

31.8 Sorting Text

Emacs provides several commands for sorting text in the buffer. All operate on the contents of the region. They divide the text of the region into many *sort records*, identify a *sort key* for each record, and then reorder the records into the order determined by the sort keys. The records are ordered so that their keys are in alphabetical order, or, for numeric sorting, in numeric order. In alphabetic sorting, all upper-case letters 'A' through 'Z' come before lower-case 'a', in accord with the ASCII character sequence.

The various sort commands differ in how they divide the text into sort records and in which part of each record is used as the sort key. Most of the commands make each line a separate sort record, but some commands use paragraphs or pages as sort records. Most of the sort commands use each entire sort record as its own sort key, but some use only a portion of the record as the sort key.

M-x sort-lines

> Divide the region into lines, and sort by comparing the entire text of a line. A numeric argument means sort into descending order.

M-x sort-paragraphs

> Divide the region into paragraphs, and sort by comparing the entire text of a paragraph (except for leading blank lines). A numeric argument means sort into descending order.

M-x sort-pages

> Divide the region into pages, and sort by comparing the entire text of a page (except for leading blank lines). A numeric argument means sort into descending order.

M-x sort-fields

> Divide the region into lines, and sort by comparing the contents of one field in each line. Fields are defined as separated by whitespace, so the first run of consecutive non-whitespace characters in a line constitutes field 1, the second such run constitutes field 2, etc.
>
> Specify which field to sort by with a numeric argument: 1 to sort by field 1, etc. A negative argument means count fields from the right instead of from the left; thus, minus 1 means sort by the last field. If several lines have identical contents in the field being sorted, they keep the same relative order that they had in the original buffer.

M-x sort-numeric-fields

> Like `M-x sort-fields` except the specified field is converted to an integer for each line, and the numbers are compared. '10' comes before '2' when considered as text, but after it when considered as a number. By default, numbers are interpreted according to `sort-numeric-base`, but numbers beginning with '0x' or '0' are interpreted as hexadecimal and octal, respectively.

M-x sort-columns

> Like `M-x sort-fields` except that the text within each line used for comparison comes from a fixed range of columns. See below for an explanation.

M-x reverse-region

> Reverse the order of the lines in the region. This is useful for sorting into descending order by fields or columns, since those sort commands do not have a feature for doing that.

For example, if the buffer contains this:

```
On systems where clash detection (locking of files being edited) is
implemented, Emacs also checks the first time you modify a buffer
whether the file has changed on disk since it was last visited or
saved.  If it has, you are asked to confirm that you want to change
the buffer.
```

applying `M-x sort-lines` to the entire buffer produces this:

```
On systems where clash detection (locking of files being edited) is
implemented, Emacs also checks the first time you modify a buffer
saved.  If it has, you are asked to confirm that you want to change
the buffer.
whether the file has changed on disk since it was last visited or
```

where the upper-case 'O' sorts before all lower-case letters. If you use C-u 2 M-x
sort-fields instead, you get this:

```
implemented, Emacs also checks the first time you modify a buffer
saved.  If it has, you are asked to confirm that you want to change
the buffer.
On systems where clash detection (locking of files being edited) is
whether the file has changed on disk since it was last visited or
```

where the sort keys were 'Emacs', 'If', 'buffer', 'systems' and 'the'.

M-x sort-columns requires more explanation. You specify the columns by
putting point at one of the columns and the mark at the other column. Because
this means you cannot put point or the mark at the beginning of the first line of
the text you want to sort, this command uses an unusual definition of "region": all
of the line point is in is considered part of the region, and so is all of the line the
mark is in, as well as all the lines in between.

For example, to sort a table by information found in columns 10 to 15, you could
put the mark on column 10 in the first line of the table, and point on column 15 in
the last line of the table, and then run sort-columns. Equivalently, you could run
it with the mark on column 15 in the first line and point on column 10 in the last
line.

This can be thought of as sorting the rectangle specified by point and the mark,
except that the text on each line to the left or right of the rectangle moves along
with the text inside the rectangle. See Section 9.4 [Rectangles], page 61.

Many of the sort commands ignore case differences when comparing, if sort-
fold-case is non-nil.

31.9 Narrowing

Narrowing means focusing in on some portion of the buffer, making the rest temporarily inaccessible. The portion which you can still get to is called the *accessible
portion*. Canceling the narrowing, which makes the entire buffer once again accessible, is called *widening*. The bounds of narrowing in effect in a buffer are called
the buffer's *restriction*.

Narrowing can make it easier to concentrate on a single subroutine or paragraph
by eliminating clutter. It can also be used to limit the range of operation of a replace
command or repeating keyboard macro. .

C-x n n	Narrow down to between point and mark (narrow-to-region).
C-x n w	Widen to make the entire buffer accessible again (widen).
C-x n p	Narrow down to the current page (narrow-to-page).
C-x n d	Narrow down to the current defun (narrow-to-defun).

When you have narrowed down to a part of the buffer, that part appears to be all there is. You can't see the rest, you can't move into it (motion commands won't go outside the accessible part), you can't change it in any way. However, it is not gone, and if you save the file all the inaccessible text will be saved. The word 'Narrow' appears in the mode line whenever narrowing is in effect.

The primary narrowing command is C-x n n (narrow-to-region). It sets the current buffer's restrictions so that the text in the current region remains accessible, but all text before the region or after the region is inaccessible. Point and mark do not change.

Alternatively, use C-x n p (narrow-to-page) to narrow down to the current page. See Section 22.4 [Pages], page 216, for the definition of a page. C-x n d (narrow-to-defun) narrows down to the defun containing point (see Section 23.2 [Defuns], page 251).

The way to cancel narrowing is to widen with C-x n w (widen). This makes all text in the buffer accessible again.

You can get information on what part of the buffer you are narrowed down to using the C-x = command. See Section 4.9 [Position Info], page 26.

Because narrowing can easily confuse users who do not understand it, narrow-to-region is normally a disabled command. Attempting to use this command asks for confirmation and gives you the option of enabling it; if you enable the command, confirmation will no longer be required for it. See Section 32.4.10 [Disabling], page 432.

31.10 Two-Column Editing

Two-column mode lets you conveniently edit two side-by-side columns of text. It uses two side-by-side windows, each showing its own buffer.

There are three ways to enter two-column mode:

F2 2 or C-x 6 2

> Enter two-column mode with the current buffer on the left, and on the right, a buffer whose name is based on the current buffer's name (2C-two-columns). If the right-hand buffer doesn't already exist, it starts out empty; the current buffer's contents are not changed.

> This command is appropriate when the current buffer is empty or contains just one column and you want to add another column.

F2 s or C-x 6 s

> Split the current buffer, which contains two-column text, into two buffers, and display them side by side (2C-split). The current buffer becomes the left-hand buffer, but the text in the right-hand column is moved into the right-hand buffer. The current column specifies the split point. Splitting starts with the current line and continues to the end of the buffer.

> This command is appropriate when you have a buffer that already contains two-column text, and you wish to separate the columns temporarily.

F2 b *buffer* RET
C-x 6 b *buffer* RET

> Enter two-column mode using the current buffer as the left-hand buffer, and using buffer *buffer* as the right-hand buffer (2C-associate-buffer).

F2 s or C-x 6 s looks for a column separator, which is a string that appears on each line between the two columns. You can specify the width of the separator with a numeric argument to F2 s; that many characters, before point, constitute the separator string. By default, the width is 1, so the column separator is the character before point.

When a line has the separator at the proper place, F2 s puts the text after the separator into the right-hand buffer, and deletes the separator. Lines that don't have the column separator at the proper place remain unsplit; they stay in the left-hand buffer, and the right-hand buffer gets an empty line to correspond. (This is the way to write a line that "spans both columns while in two-column mode": write it in the left-hand buffer, and put an empty line in the right-hand buffer.)

The command C-x 6 RET or F2 RET (2C-newline) inserts a newline in each of the two buffers at corresponding positions. This is the easiest way to add a new line to the two-column text while editing it in split buffers.

When you have edited both buffers as you wish, merge them with F2 1 or C-x 6 1 (2C-merge). This copies the text from the right-hand buffer as a second column in the other buffer. To go back to two-column editing, use F2 s.

Use F2 d or C-x 6 d to dissociate the two buffers, leaving each as it stands (2C-dissociate). If the other buffer, the one not current when you type F2 d, is empty, F2 d kills it.

31.11 Editing Binary Files

There is a special major mode for editing binary files: Hexl mode. To use it, use M-x hexl-find-file instead of C-x C-f to visit the file. This command converts the file's contents to hexadecimal and lets you edit the translation. When you save the file, it is converted automatically back to binary.

You can also use M-x hexl-mode to translate an existing buffer into hex. This is useful if you visit a file normally and then discover it is a binary file.

Ordinary text characters overwrite in Hexl mode. This is to reduce the risk of accidentally spoiling the alignment of data in the file. There are special commands for insertion. Here is a list of the commands of Hexl mode:

C-M-d   Insert a byte with a code typed in decimal.

C-M-o   Insert a byte with a code typed in octal.

C-M-x   Insert a byte with a code typed in hex.

C-x [Move to the beginning of a 1k-byte "page."

C-x]   Move to the end of a 1k-byte "page."

M-g   Move to an address specified in hex.

M-j   Move to an address specified in decimal.

C-c C-c   Leave Hexl mode, going back to the major mode this buffer had before
             you invoked `hexl-mode`.

Other Hexl commands let you insert strings (sequences) of binary bytes, move by
`shorts` or `ints`, etc.; type `C-h a hexl-RET` for details.

31.12 Saving Emacs Sessions

Use the desktop library to save the state of Emacs from one session to another. Once
you save the Emacs *desktop*—the buffers, their file names, major modes, buffer
positions, and so on—then subsequent Emacs sessions reload the saved desktop.

You can save the desktop manually with the command `M-x desktop-save`. You
can also enable automatic saving of the desktop when you exit Emacs, and automatic restoration of the last saved desktop when Emacs starts: use the Customization buffer (see Section 32.2 [Easy Customization], page 408) to set `desktop-save-
mode` to t for future sessions, or add this line in your '~/.emacs' file:

    (desktop-save-mode 1)

If you turn on `desktop-save-mode` in your '~/.emacs', then when Emacs starts,
it looks for a saved desktop in the current directory. Thus, you can have separate
saved desktops in different directories, and the starting directory determines which
one Emacs reloads. You can save the current desktop and reload one saved in another directory by typing `M-x desktop-change-dir`. Typing `M-x desktop-revert`
reverts to the desktop previously reloaded.

Specify the option '--no-desktop' on the command line when you don't want
it to reload any saved desktop. This turns off `desktop-save-mode` for the current
session. Starting Emacs with the '--no-init-file' option also disables desktop
reloading, since it bypasses the '.emacs' init file, where `desktop-save-mode` is
usually turned on.

By default, all the buffers in the desktop are restored at one go. However,
this may be slow if there are a lot of buffers in the desktop. You can specify the
maximum number of buffers to restore immediately with the variable `desktop-
restore-eager`; the remaining buffers are restored "lazily," when Emacs is idle.

Type `M-x desktop-clear` to empty the Emacs desktop. This kills all buffers
except for internal ones, and clears the global variables listed in `desktop-globals-
to-clear`. If you want this to preserve certain buffers, customize the variable
`desktop-clear-preserve-buffers-regexp`, whose value is a regular expression
matching the names of buffers not to kill.

If you want to save minibuffer history from one session to another, use the
`savehist` library.

31.13 Recursive Editing Levels

A *recursive edit* is a situation in which you are using Emacs commands to perform
arbitrary editing while in the middle of another Emacs command. For example,
when you type `C-r` inside of a `query-replace`, you enter a recursive edit in which

you can change the current buffer. On exiting from the recursive edit, you go back to the `query-replace`.

Exiting the recursive edit means returning to the unfinished command, which continues execution. The command to exit is `C-M-c` (`exit-recursive-edit`).

You can also *abort* the recursive edit. This is like exiting, but also quits the unfinished command immediately. Use the command `C-]` (`abort-recursive-edit`) to do this. See Section 33.1 [Quitting], page 440.

The mode line shows you when you are in a recursive edit by displaying square brackets around the parentheses that always surround the major and minor mode names. Every window's mode line shows this in the same way, since being in a recursive edit is true of Emacs as a whole rather than any particular window or buffer.

It is possible to be in recursive edits within recursive edits. For example, after typing `C-r` in a `query-replace`, you may type a command that enters the debugger. This begins a recursive editing level for the debugger, within the recursive editing level for `C-r`. Mode lines display a pair of square brackets for each recursive editing level currently in progress.

Exiting the inner recursive edit (such as with the debugger `c` command) resumes the command running in the next level up. When that command finishes, you can then use `C-M-c` to exit another recursive editing level, and so on. Exiting applies to the innermost level only. Aborting also gets out of only one level of recursive edit; it returns immediately to the command level of the previous recursive edit. If you wish, you can then abort the next recursive editing level.

Alternatively, the command `M-x top-level` aborts all levels of recursive edits, returning immediately to the top-level command reader.

The text being edited inside the recursive edit need not be the same text that you were editing at top level. It depends on what the recursive edit is for. If the command that invokes the recursive edit selects a different buffer first, that is the buffer you will edit recursively. In any case, you can switch buffers within the recursive edit in the normal manner (as long as the buffer-switching keys have not been rebound). You could probably do all the rest of your editing inside the recursive edit, visiting files and all. But this could have surprising effects (such as stack overflow) from time to time. So remember to exit or abort the recursive edit when you no longer need it.

In general, we try to minimize the use of recursive editing levels in GNU Emacs. This is because they constrain you to "go back" in a particular order—from the innermost level toward the top level. When possible, we present different activities in separate buffers so that you can switch between them as you please. Some commands switch to a new major mode which provides a command to switch back. These approaches give you more flexibility to go back to unfinished tasks in the order you choose.

31.14 Emulation

GNU Emacs can be programmed to emulate (more or less) most other editors. Standard facilities can emulate these:

CRiSP/Brief (PC editor)

>You can turn on key bindings to emulate the CRiSP/Brief editor with `M-x crisp-mode`. Note that this rebinds M-x to exit Emacs unless you set the variable `crisp-override-meta-x`. You can also use the command `M-x scroll-all-mode` or set the variable `crisp-load-scroll-all` to emulate CRiSP's scroll-all feature (scrolling all windows together).

EDT (DEC VMS editor)

>Turn on EDT emulation with the command `M-x edt-emulation-on`, while `M-x edt-emulation-off` restores normal Emacs command bindings.

>Most of the EDT emulation commands are keypad keys, and most standard Emacs key bindings are still available. The EDT emulation rebindings are done in the global keymap, so there is no problem switching buffers or major modes while in EDT emulation.

TPU (DEC VMS editor)

>`M-x tpu-edt-on` turns on emulation of the TPU editor emulating EDT.

vi (Berkeley editor)

>Viper is the newest emulator for vi. It implements several levels of emulation; level 1 is closest to vi itself, while level 5 departs somewhat from strict emulation to take advantage of the capabilities of Emacs. To invoke Viper, type `M-x viper-mode`; it will guide you the rest of the way and ask for the emulation level. See Info file 'viper', node 'Top'.

vi (another emulator)

>`M-x vi-mode` enters a major mode that replaces the previously established major mode. All of the vi commands that, in real vi, enter "input" mode are programmed instead to return to the previous major mode. Thus, ordinary Emacs serves as vi's "input" mode.

>Because vi emulation works through major modes, it does not work to switch buffers during emulation. Return to normal Emacs first.

>If you plan to use vi emulation much, you probably want to bind a key to the `vi-mode` command.

vi (alternate emulator)

>`M-x vip-mode` invokes another vi emulator, said to resemble real vi more thoroughly than `M-x vi-mode`. "Input" mode in this emulator is changed from ordinary Emacs so you can use ESC to go back to

emulated vi command mode. To get from emulated vi command mode back to ordinary Emacs, type `C-z`.

This emulation does not work through major modes, and it is possible to switch buffers in various ways within the emulator. It is not so necessary to assign a key to the command `vip-mode` as it is with `vi-mode` because terminating insert mode does not use it.

See Info file 'vip', node 'Top', for full information.

WordStar (old wordprocessor)

> `M-x wordstar-mode` provides a major mode with WordStar-like key bindings.

31.15 Hyperlinking and Navigation Features

Various modes documented elsewhere have hypertext features so that you can follow links, usually by clicking `Mouse-2` on the link or typing RET while point is on the link. Clicking `Mouse-1` quickly on the link also follows it. (Hold `Mouse-1` for longer if you want to set point instead.)

Info mode, Help mode and the Dired-like modes are examples of modes that have links in the buffer. The Tags facility links between uses and definitions in source files, see Section 25.3 [Tags], page 293. Imenu provides navigation amongst items indexed in the current buffer, see Section 23.2.3 [Imenu], page 253. Info-lookup provides mode-specific lookup of definitions in Info indexes, see Section 23.6 [Documentation], page 263. Speedbar maintains a frame in which links to files, and locations in files are displayed, see Section 18.7 [Speedbar], page 178.

Other non-mode-specific facilities described in this section enable following links from the current buffer in a context-sensitive fashion.

31.15.1 Following URLs

`M-x browse-url RET` *url* `RET`

> Load a URL into a Web browser.

The Browse-URL package provides facilities for following URLs specifying links on the World Wide Web. Usually this works by invoking a web browser, but you can, for instance, arrange to invoke `compose-mail` from 'mailto:' URLs.

The general way to use this feature is to type `M-x browse-url`, which displays a specified URL. If point is located near a plausible URL, that URL is used as the default. Other commands are available which you might like to bind to keys, such as `browse-url-at-point` and `browse-url-at-mouse`.

You can customize Browse-URL's behavior via various options in the `browse-url` Customize group, particularly `browse-url-browser-function`. You can invoke actions dependent on the type of URL by defining `browse-url-browser-function` as an association list. The package's commentary available via `C-h p` under the 'hypermedia' keyword provides more information. Packages with facilities for following URLs should always go through Browse-URL, so that the customization options for Browse-URL will affect all browsing in Emacs.

31.15.2 Activating URLs

`M-x goto-address`
>   Activate URLs and e-mail addresses in the current buffer.

You can make URLs in the current buffer active with `M-x goto-address`. This finds all the URLs in the buffer, and establishes bindings for `Mouse-2` and `C-c RET` on them. After activation, if you click on a URL with `Mouse-2`, or move to a URL and type `C-c RET`, that will display the web page that the URL specifies. For a 'mailto' URL, it sends mail instead, using your selected mail-composition method (see Section 27.6 [Mail Methods], page 318).

It can be useful to add `goto-address` to mode hooks and the hooks used to display an incoming message. `rmail-show-message-hook` is the appropriate hook for Rmail, and `mh-show-mode-hook` for MH-E. This is not needed for Gnus, which has a similar feature of its own.

31.15.3 Finding Files and URLs at Point

FFAP mode replaces certain key bindings for finding files, including `C-x C-f`, with commands that provide more sensitive defaults. These commands behave like the ordinary ones when given a prefix argument. Otherwise, they get the default file name or URL from the text around point. If what is found in the buffer has the form of a URL rather than a file name, the commands use `browse-url` to view it.

This feature is useful for following references in mail or news buffers, 'README' files, 'MANIFEST' files, and so on. The 'ffap' package's commentary available via `C-h p` under the 'files' keyword and the `ffap` Custom group provide details.

You can turn on FFAP minor mode by calling `ffap-bindings` to make the following key bindings and to install hooks for using `ffap` in Rmail, Gnus and VM article buffers.

`C-x C-f` *filename* `RET`
>   Find *filename*, guessing a default from text around point (`find-file-at-point`).

`C-x C-r`   `ffap-read-only`, analogous to `find-file-read-only`.

`C-x C-v`   `ffap-alternate-file`, analogous to `find-alternate-file`.

`C-x d` *directory* `RET`
>   Start Dired on *directory*, defaulting to the directory name at point (`dired-at-point`).

`C-x C-d`   `ffap-list-directory`, analogous to `list-directory`.

`C-x 4 f`   `ffap-other-window`, analogous to `find-file-other-window`.

`C-x 4 r`   `ffap-read-only-other-window`, analogous to `find-file-read-only-other-window`.

`C-x 4 d`   `ffap-dired-other-window`, analogous to `dired-other-window`.

`C-x 5 f`   `ffap-other-frame`, analogous to `find-file-other-frame`.

`C-x 5 r`   `ffap-read-only-other-frame`, analogous to `find-file-read-only-`
              `other-frame`.

`C-x 5 d`   `ffap-dired-other-frame`, analogous to `dired-other-frame`.

`M-x ffap-next`
              Search buffer for next file name or URL, then find that file or URL.

`S-Mouse-3`   `ffap-at-mouse` finds the file guessed from text around the position of
              a mouse click.

`C-S-Mouse-3`
              Display a menu of files and URLs mentioned in current buffer, then
              find the one you select (`ffap-menu`).

31.16 Dissociated Press

`M-x dissociated-press` is a command for scrambling a file of text either word
by word or character by character. Starting from a buffer of straight English, it
produces extremely amusing output. The input comes from the current Emacs
buffer. Dissociated Press writes its output in a buffer named '`*Dissociation*`',
and redisplays that buffer after every couple of lines (approximately) so you can
read the output as it comes out.

Dissociated Press asks every so often whether to continue generating output.
Answer n to stop it. You can also stop at any time by typing `C-g`. The dissociation
output remains in the '`*Dissociation*`' buffer for you to copy elsewhere if you
wish.

Dissociated Press operates by jumping at random from one point in the buffer
to another. In order to produce plausible output rather than gibberish, it insists
on a certain amount of overlap between the end of one run of consecutive words
or characters and the start of the next. That is, if it has just output 'president'
and then decides to jump to a different point in the file, it might spot the 'ent' in
'pentagon' and continue from there, producing 'presidentagon'.[3] Long sample texts
produce the best results.

A positive argument to `M-x dissociated-press` tells it to operate character by
character, and specifies the number of overlap characters. A negative argument tells
it to operate word by word, and specifies the number of overlap words. In this mode,
whole words are treated as the elements to be permuted, rather than characters.
No argument is equivalent to an argument of two. For your againformation, the
output goes only into the buffer '`*Dissociation*`'. The buffer you start with is
not changed.

Dissociated Press produces results fairly like those of a Markov chain based on
a frequency table constructed from the sample text. It is, however, an independent,
ignoriginal invention. Dissociated Press techniquitously copies several consecutive
characters from the sample between random choices, whereas a Markov chain would

---

[3] This dissociword actually appeared during the Vietnam War, when it was very appropriate. Bush has made it appropriate again.

choose randomly for each word or character. This makes for more plausible sounding results, and runs faster.

It is a mustatement that too much use of Dissociated Press can be a developediment to your real work, sometimes to the point of outragedy. And keep dissociwords out of your documentation, if you want it to be well userenced and properbose. Have fun. Your buggestions are welcome.

31.17 Other Amusements

If you are a little bit bored, you can try M-x hanoi. If you are considerably bored, give it a numeric argument. If you are very, very bored, try an argument of 9. Sit back and watch.

If you want a little more personal involvement, try M-x gomoku, which plays the game Go Moku with you.

M-x blackbox, M-x mpuz and M-x 5x5 are puzzles. blackbox challenges you to determine the location of objects inside a box by tomography. mpuz displays a multiplication puzzle with letters standing for digits in a code that you must guess—to guess a value, type a letter and then the digit you think it stands for. The aim of 5x5 is to fill in all the squares.

M-x decipher helps you to cryptanalyze a buffer which is encrypted in a simple monoalphabetic substitution cipher.

M-x dunnet runs an adventure-style exploration game, which is a bigger sort of puzzle.

M-x lm runs a relatively non-participatory game in which a robot attempts to maneuver towards a tree at the center of the window based on unique olfactory cues from each of the four directions.

M-x life runs Conway's "Life" cellular automaton.

M-x morse-region converts text in a region to Morse code and M-x unmorse-region converts it back. No cause for remorse.

M-x pong plays a Pong-like game, bouncing the ball off opposing bats.

M-x solitaire plays a game of solitaire in which you jump pegs across other pegs.

M-x studlify-region studlify-cases the region, producing text like this:

    M-x stUdlIfY-RegioN stUdlIfY-CaSeS thE region.

M-x tetris runs an implementation of the well-known Tetris game. Likewise, M-x snake provides an implementation of Snake.

When you are frustrated, try the famous Eliza program. Just do M-x doctor. End each input by typing RET twice.

When you are feeling strange, type M-x yow.

The command M-x zone plays games with the display when Emacs is idle.

32 Customization

This chapter talks about various topics relevant to adapting the behavior of Emacs in ways we have anticipated. See *The Emacs Lisp Reference Manual* for how to make more far-reaching and open-ended changes. See Appendix D [X Resources], page 489, for information on using X resources to customize Emacs.

Customization that you do within Emacs normally affects only the particular Emacs session that you do it in—it does not persist between sessions unless you save the customization in a file such as your init file ('.emacs') that will affect future sessions. (See Section 32.6 [Init File], page 433.) When you tell the customization buffer to save customizations for future sessions, this actually works by editing '.emacs' for you.

Another means of customization is the keyboard macro, which is a sequence of keystrokes to be replayed with a single command. See Chapter 14 [Keyboard Macros], page 111, for full instruction how to record, manage, and replay sequences of keys.

32.1 Minor Modes

Minor modes are optional features which you can turn on or off. For example, Auto Fill mode is a minor mode in which SPC breaks lines between words as you type. All the minor modes are independent of each other and of the selected major mode. Most minor modes say in the mode line when they are enabled; for example, 'Fill' in the mode line means that Auto Fill mode is enabled.

You should append `-mode` to the name of a minor mode to produce the name of the command that turns the mode on or off. Thus, the command to enable or disable Auto Fill mode is called `auto-fill-mode`. These commands are usually invoked with `M-x`, but you can bind keys to them if you wish.

With no argument, the minor mode function turns the mode on if it was off, and off if it was on. This is known as *toggling*. A positive argument always turns the mode on, and an explicit zero argument or a negative argument always turns it off.

Some minor modes are global: while enabled, they affect everything you do in the Emacs session, in all buffers. Other minor modes are buffer-local; they apply only to the current buffer, so you can enable the mode in certain buffers and not others.

For most minor modes, the command name is also the name of a variable. The variable's value is non-`nil` if the mode is enabled and `nil` if it is disabled. Some minor-mode commands work by just setting the variable. For example, the command `abbrev-mode` works by setting the value of `abbrev-mode` as a variable; it is this variable that directly turns Abbrev mode on and off. You can directly set the variable's value instead of calling the mode function. For other minor modes, you need to either set the variable through the Customize interface or call the mode function to correctly enable or disable the mode. To check which of these two possibilities applies to a given minor mode, use `C-h v` to ask for documentation on the variable name.

For minor mode commands that work by just setting the minor mode variable, that variable provides a good way for Lisp programs to turn minor modes on and off; it is also useful in a file's local variables list (see Section 32.3.4 [File Variables], page 420). But please think twice before setting minor modes with a local variables list, because most minor modes are a matter of user preference—other users editing the same file might not want the same minor modes you prefer.

The most useful buffer-local minor modes include Abbrev mode, Auto Fill mode, Auto Save mode, Font-Lock mode, Glasses mode, Outline minor mode, Overwrite mode, and Binary Overwrite mode.

Abbrev mode allows you to define abbreviations that automatically expand as you type them. For example, 'amd' might expand to 'abbrev mode'. See Chapter 26 [Abbrevs], page 303, for full information.

Auto Fill mode allows you to enter filled text without breaking lines explicitly. Emacs inserts newlines as necessary to prevent lines from becoming too long. See Section 22.5 [Filling], page 217.

Auto Save mode saves the buffer contents periodically to reduce the amount of work you can lose in case of a crash. See Section 15.5 [Auto Save], page 132.

Enriched mode enables editing and saving of formatted text. See Section 22.12 [Formatted Text], page 236.

Flyspell mode automatically highlights misspelled words. See Section 13.5 [Spelling], page 108.

Font Lock mode automatically highlights certain textual units found in programs, such as comments, strings, and function names being defined. This requires a display that can show multiple fonts or colors. See Section 11.5 [Faces], page 72.

Outline minor mode provides the same facilities as the major mode called Outline mode; but since it is a minor mode instead, you can combine it with any major mode. See Section 22.8 [Outline Mode], page 224.

Overwrite mode causes ordinary printing characters to replace existing text instead of shoving it to the right. For example, if point is in front of the 'B' in 'FOOBAR', then in Overwrite mode typing a G changes it to 'FOOGAR', instead of producing 'FOOGBAR' as usual. In Overwrite mode, the command C-q inserts the next character whatever it may be, even if it is a digit—this gives you a way to insert a character instead of replacing an existing character.

The command `overwrite-mode` is an exception to the rule that commands which toggle minor modes are normally not bound to keys: it is bound to the INSERT function key. This is because many other programs bind INSERT to similar functions.

Binary Overwrite mode is a variant of Overwrite mode for editing binary files; it treats newlines and tabs like other characters, so that they overwrite other characters and can be overwritten by them. In Binary Overwrite mode, digits after C-q specify an octal character code, as usual.

Here are some useful minor modes that normally apply to all buffers at once. Since Line Number mode and Transient Mark mode can be enabled or disabled just by setting the value of the minor mode variable, you *can* set them differently for particular buffers, by explicitly making the corresponding variable local in those buffers. See Section 32.3.3 [Locals], page 419.

Icomplete mode displays an indication of available completions when you are in the minibuffer and completion is active. See Section 5.3.4 [Completion Options], page 35.

Line Number mode enables continuous display in the mode line of the line number of point, and Column Number mode enables display of the column number. See Section 1.3 [Mode Line], page 8.

Scroll Bar mode gives each window a scroll bar (see Section 18.11 [Scroll Bars], page 181). Menu Bar mode gives each frame a menu bar (see Section 18.14 [Menu Bars], page 183). Both of these modes are enabled by default when you use the X Window System.

In Transient Mark mode, every change in the buffer contents "deactivates" the mark, so that commands that operate on the region will get an error. This means you must either set the mark, or explicitly "reactivate" it, before each command that uses the region. The advantage of Transient Mark mode is that Emacs can display the region highlighted. See Chapter 8 [Mark], page 49.

32.2 Easy Customization Interface

Emacs has many *settings* which have values that you can specify in order to customize various commands. Many are documented in this manual. Most settings are *user options*—that is to say, Lisp variables (see Section 32.3 [Variables], page 416)— so their names appear in the Variable Index (see [Variable Index], page 569). The other settings are faces and their attributes (see Section 11.5 [Faces], page 72).

You can browse interactively through settings and change them using M-x customize. This command creates a *customization buffer*, which offers commands to navigate through a logically organized structure of the Emacs settings; you can also use it to edit and set their values, and to save settings permanently in your '~/.emacs' file (see Section 32.6 [Init File], page 433).

The appearance of the example buffers in this section is typically different under a graphical display, since faces are then used to indicate buttons, links and editable fields.

32.2.1 Customization Groups

For customization purposes, settings are organized into *groups* to help you find them. Groups are collected into bigger groups, all the way up to a master group called Emacs.

M-x customize creates a customization buffer that shows the top-level Emacs group and the second-level groups immediately under it. It looks like this, in part:

```
/- Emacs group: --------------------------------------------------\
      [State]: visible group members are all at standard values.
    Customization of the One True Editor.
    See also [Manual].

  Editing group: [Go to Group]
  Basic text editing facilities.

  External group: [Go to Group]
  Interfacing to external utilities.

  more second-level groups

\- Emacs group end --------------------------------------------------/
```

This says that the buffer displays the contents of the Emacs group. The other groups are listed because they are its contents. But they are listed differently, without indentation and dashes, because *their* contents are not included. Each group has a single-line documentation string; the Emacs group also has a '[State]' line.

Most of the text in the customization buffer is read-only, but it typically includes some *editable fields* that you can edit. There are also *buttons* and *links*, which do something when you *invoke* them. To invoke a button or a link, either click on it with Mouse-1, or move point to it and type RET.

For example, the phrase '[State]' that appears in a second-level group is a button. It operates on the same customization buffer. The phrase '[Go to Group]' is a kind of hypertext link to another group. Invoking it creates a new customization buffer, which shows that group and its contents.

The Emacs group includes a few settings, but mainly it contains other groups, which contain more groups, which contain the settings. By browsing the hierarchy of groups, you will eventually find the feature you are interested in customizing. Then you can use the customization buffer to set that feature's settings. You can also go straight to a particular group by name, using the command M-x customize-group.

32.2.2 Browsing and Searching for Options and Faces

M-x customize-browse is another way to browse the available settings. This command creates a special customization buffer which shows only the names of groups and settings, and puts them in a structure.

In this buffer, you can show the contents of a group by invoking the '[+]' button. When the group contents are visible, this button changes to '[-]'; invoking that hides the group contents again.

Each group or setting in this buffer has a link which says '[Group]', '[Option]' or '[Face]'. Invoking this link creates an ordinary customization buffer showing just that group and its contents, just that user option, or just that face. This is the way to change settings that you find with M-x customize-browse.

If you can guess part of the name of the settings you are interested in, M-x customize-apropos is another way to search for settings. However, unlike customize and customize-browse, customize-apropos can only find groups and settings that are loaded in the current Emacs session. See Section 32.2.6 [Customizing Specific Items], page 414.

32.2.3 Changing a Variable

Here is an example of what a variable (a user option) looks like in the customization buffer:

```
Kill Ring Max: [Hide Value] 60
    [State]: STANDARD.
Maximum length of kill ring before oldest elements are thrown away.
```

The text following '[Hide Value]', '60' in this case, indicates the current value of the variable. If you see '[Show Value]' instead of '[Hide Value]', it means that the value is hidden; the customization buffer initially hides values that take up several lines. Invoke '[Show Value]' to show the value.

The line after the variable name indicates the *customization state* of the variable: in the example above, it says you have not changed the option yet. The '[State]' button at the beginning of this line gives you a menu of various operations for customizing the variable.

The line after the '[State]' line displays the beginning of the variable's documentation string. If there are more lines of documentation, this line ends with a '[More]' button; invoke that to show the full documentation string.

To enter a new value for 'Kill Ring Max', move point to the value and edit it textually. For example, you can type M-d, then insert another number. As you begin to alter the text, you will see the '[State]' line change to say that you have edited the value:

```
[State]: EDITED, shown value does not take effect until you set or ...
                                                    save it.
```

Editing the value does not actually set the variable. To do that, you must *set* the variable. To do this, invoke the '[State]' button and choose 'Set for Current Session'.

The state of the variable changes visibly when you set it:

```
[State]: SET for current session only.
```

You don't have to worry about specifying a value that is not valid; the 'Set for Current Session' operation checks for validity and will not install an unacceptable value.

While editing a field that is a file name, directory name, command name, or anything else for which completion is defined, you can type M-TAB (widget-complete) to do completion. (ESC TAB and C-M-i do the same thing.)

Some variables have a small fixed set of possible legitimate values. These variables don't let you edit the value textually. Instead, a '[Value Menu]' button appears before the value; invoke this button to change the value. For a boolean "on or off" value, the button says '[Toggle]', and it changes to the other value. '[Value Menu]' and '[Toggle]' simply edit the buffer; the changes take real effect when you use the 'Set for Current Session' operation.

Some variables have values with complex structure. For example, the value of `file-coding-system-alist` is an association list. Here is how it appears in the customization buffer:

```
File Coding System Alist: [Hide Value]
[INS] [DEL] File regexp: \.elc\'
            Choice: [Value Menu] Encoding/decoding pair:
            Decoding: emacs-mule
            Encoding: emacs-mule
[INS] [DEL] File regexp: \(\'\|/\)loaddefs.el\'
            Choice: [Value Menu] Encoding/decoding pair:
            Decoding: raw-text
            Encoding: raw-text-unix
[INS] [DEL] File regexp: \.tar\'
            Choice: [Value Menu] Encoding/decoding pair:
            Decoding: no-conversion
            Encoding: no-conversion
[INS] [DEL] File regexp:
            Choice: [Value Menu] Encoding/decoding pair:
            Decoding: undecided
            Encoding: nil
[INS]
   [State]: STANDARD.
Alist to decide a coding system to use for a file I/O ...
                           operation. [Hide Rest]
The format is ((PATTERN . VAL.) ...),
where PATTERN is a regular expression matching a file name,
[...more lines of documentation...]
```

Each association in the list appears on four lines, with several editable fields and/or buttons. You can edit the regexps and coding systems using ordinary editing commands. You can also invoke '[Value Menu]' to switch to a different kind of value—for instance, to specify a function instead of a pair of coding systems.

To delete an association from the list, invoke the '[DEL]' button for that item. To add an association, invoke '[INS]' at the position where you want to add it. There is an '[INS]' button between each pair of associations, another at the beginning and another at the end, so you can add a new association at any position in the list.

Two special commands, TAB and S-TAB, are useful for moving through the customization buffer. TAB (`widget-forward`) moves forward to the next button or editable field; S-TAB (`widget-backward`) moves backward to the previous button or editable field.

Typing RET on an editable field also moves forward, just like TAB. We set it up this way because people often type RET when they are finished editing a field. To insert a newline within an editable field, use C-o or C-q C-j.

Setting the variable changes its value in the current Emacs session; *saving* the value changes it for future sessions as well. To save the variable, invoke '[State]' and select the 'Save for Future Sessions' operation. This works by writing code so as to set the variable again, each time you start Emacs (see Section 32.2.4 [Saving Customizations], page 412).

You can also restore the variable to its standard value by invoking '[State]' and selecting the 'Erase Customization' operation. There are actually four reset operations:

'Undo Edits'

> If you have made some modifications and not yet set the variable, this restores the text in the customization buffer to match the actual value.

'Reset to Saved'

> This restores the value of the variable to the last saved value, and updates the text accordingly.

'Erase Customization'

> This sets the variable to its standard value, and updates the text accordingly. This also eliminates any saved value for the variable, so that you will get the standard value in future Emacs sessions.

'Set to Backup Value'

> This sets the variable to a previous value that was set in the customization buffer in this session. If you customize a variable and then reset it, which discards the customized value, you can get the discarded value back again with this operation.

Sometimes it is useful to record a comment about a specific customization. Use the 'Add Comment' item from the '[State]' menu to create a field for entering the comment. The comment you enter will be saved, and displayed again if you again view the same variable in a customization buffer, even in another session.

The state of a group indicates whether anything in that group has been edited, set or saved.

Near the top of the customization buffer there are two lines of buttons:

```
[Set for Current Session] [Save for Future Sessions]
[Undo Edits] [Reset to Saved] [Erase Customization]    [Finish]
```

Invoking '[Finish]' either buries or kills this customization buffer according to the setting of the option custom-buffer-done-kill; the default is to bury the buffer. Each of the other buttons performs an operation—set, save or reset—on each of the settings in the buffer that could meaningfully be set, saved or reset. They do not operate on settings whose values are hidden, nor on subgroups which are hidden or not visible in the buffer.

32.2.4 Saving Customizations

Saving customizations from the customization buffer works by writing code that future sessions will read, code to set up those customizations again.

Normally this saves customizations in your init file, '~/.emacs'. If you wish, you can save customizations in another file instead. To make this work, your '~/.emacs' should set custom-file to the name of that file. Then you should load the file by calling load. For example:

```
(setq custom-file "~/.emacs-custom.el")
(load custom-file)
```

You can use `custom-file` to specify different customization files for different Emacs versions, like this:

```
(cond ((< emacs-major-version 21)
       ;; Emacs 20 customization.
       (setq custom-file "~/.custom-20.el"))
      ((and (= emacs-major-version 21) (< emacs-minor-version 4))
       ;; Emacs 21 customization, before version 21.4.
       (setq custom-file "~/.custom-21.el"))
      ((< emacs-major-version 22)
       ;; Emacs version 21.4 or later.
       (setq custom-file "~/.custom-21.4.el"))
      (t
       ;; Emacs version 22.1 or later.
       (setq custom-file "~/.custom-22.el")))
```

```
(load custom-file)
```

If Emacs was invoked with the '-q' or '--no-init-file' options (see Section C.2 [Initial Options], page 472), it will not let you save your customizations in your '~/.emacs' init file. This is because saving customizations from such a session would wipe out all the other customizations you might have on your init file.

32.2.5 Customizing Faces

In addition to variables, some customization groups also include faces. When you show the contents of a group, both the variables and the faces in the group appear in the customization buffer. Here is an example of how a face looks:

```
Custom Changed Face:(sample) [Hide Face]
    [State]: STANDARD.
Face used when the customize item has been changed.
Parent groups: [Custom Magic Faces]
Attributes: [ ] Font Family: *
            [ ] Width: *
            [ ] Height: *
            [ ] Weight: *
            [ ] Slant: *
            [ ] Underline: *
            [ ] Overline: *
            [ ] Strike-through: *
            [ ] Box around text: *
            [ ] Inverse-video: *
            [X] Foreground: white       (sample)
            [X] Background: blue        (sample)
            [ ] Stipple: *
            [ ] Inherit: *
```

Each face attribute has its own line. The '[x]' button before the attribute name indicates whether the attribute is *enabled*; '[X]' means that it's enabled, and '[ ]' means that it's disabled. You can enable or disable the attribute by clicking that button. When the attribute is enabled, you can change the attribute value in the usual ways.

For the colors, you can specify a color name (use M-x list-colors-display for a list of them) or a hexadecimal color specification of the form '#rrggbb'. ('#000000' is black, '#ff0000' is red, '#00ff00' is green, '#0000ff' is blue, and '#ffffff' is white.) On a black-and-white display, the colors you can use for the background are 'black', 'white', 'gray', 'gray1', and 'gray3'. Emacs supports these shades of gray by using background stipple patterns instead of a color.

Setting, saving and resetting a face work like the same operations for variables (see Section 32.2.3 [Changing a Variable], page 410).

A face can specify different appearances for different types of display. For example, a face can make text red on a color display, but use a bold font on a monochrome display. To specify multiple appearances for a face, select 'For All Kinds of Displays' in the menu you get from invoking '[State]'.

Another more basic way to set the attributes of a specific face is with M-x modify-face. This command reads the name of a face, then reads the attributes one by one. For the color and stipple attributes, the attribute's current value is the default—type just RET if you don't want to change that attribute. Type 'none' if you want to clear out the attribute.

32.2.6 Customizing Specific Items

Instead of finding the setting you want to change by navigating the structure of groups, here are other ways to specify the settings that you want to customize.

M-x customize-option RET *option* RET

> Set up a customization buffer with just one user option variable, *option*.

M-x customize-face RET *face* RET

> Set up a customization buffer with just one face, *face*.

M-x customize-group RET *group* RET

> Set up a customization buffer with just one group, *group*.

M-x customize-apropos RET *regexp* RET

> Set up a customization buffer with all the settings and groups that match *regexp*.

M-x customize-changed RET *version* RET

> Set up a customization buffer with all the settings and groups whose meaning has changed since Emacs version *version*.

M-x customize-saved

> Set up a customization buffer containing all settings that you have saved with customization buffers.

M-x customize-unsaved

> Set up a customization buffer containing all settings that you have set but not saved.

If you want to alter a particular user option with the customization buffer, and you know its name, you can use the command M-x customize-option and specify the user option (variable) name. This sets up the customization buffer with just one user option—the one that you asked for. Editing, setting and saving the value work as described above, but only for the specified user option. Minibuffer completion is handy if you only know part of the name. However, this command can only see options that have been loaded in the current Emacs session.

Likewise, you can modify a specific face, chosen by name, using M-x customize-face. By default it operates on the face used on the character after point.

You can also set up the customization buffer with a specific group, using M-x customize-group. The immediate contents of the chosen group, including settings (user options and faces), and other groups, all appear as well (even if not already loaded). However, the subgroups' own contents are not included.

For a more general way of controlling what to customize, you can use M-x customize-apropos. You specify a regular expression as argument; then all *loaded* settings and groups whose names match this regular expression are set up in the customization buffer. If you specify an empty regular expression, this includes *all* loaded groups and settings—which takes a long time to set up.

When you upgrade to a new Emacs version, you might want to consider customizing new settings, and settings whose meanings or default values have changed. To do this, use M-x customize-changed and specify a previous Emacs version number using the minibuffer. It creates a customization buffer which shows all the settings and groups whose definitions have been changed since the specified version, loading them if necessary.

If you change settings and then decide the change was a mistake, you can use two special commands to revisit your previous changes. Use M-x customize-saved to look at the settings that you have saved. Use M-x customize-unsaved to look at the settings that you have set but not saved.

32.2.7 Customization Themes

Custom themes are collections of settings that can be enabled or disabled as a unit. You can use Custom themes to switch quickly and easily between various collections of settings, and to transfer such collections from one computer to another.

To define a Custom theme, use M-x customize-create-theme, which brings up a buffer named '*New Custom Theme*'. At the top of the buffer is an editable field where you can specify the name of the theme. Click on the button labelled 'Insert Variable' to add a variable to the theme, and click on 'Insert Face' to add a face. You can edit these values in the '*New Custom Theme*' buffer like in an ordinary Customize buffer. To remove an option from the theme, click on its 'State' button and select 'Delete'.

After adding the desired options, click on 'Save Theme' to save the Custom theme. This writes the theme definition to a file '*foo*-theme.el' (where *foo* is the theme name you supplied), in the directory '~/.emacs.d/'. You can specify the directory by setting custom-theme-directory.

You can view and edit the settings of a previously-defined theme by clicking on 'Visit Theme' and specifying the theme name. You can also import the variables and faces that you have set using Customize by visiting the "special" theme named 'user'. This theme, which records all the options that you set in the ordinary customization buffer, is always enabled, and always takes precedence over all other enabled Custom themes. Additionally, the 'user' theme is recorded with code in your '.emacs' file, rather than a 'user-theme.el' file.

Once you have defined a Custom theme, you can use it by customizing the variable custom-enabled-themes. This is a list of Custom themes that are *enabled*, or put into effect. If you set custom-enabled-themes using the Customize interface, the theme definitions are automatically loaded from the theme files, if they aren't already. If you save the value of custom-enabled-themes for future Emacs sessions, those Custom themes will be enabled whenever Emacs is started up.

If two enabled themes specify different values for an option, the theme occurring earlier in custom-enabled-themes takes effect.

You can temporarily enable a Custom theme with M-x enable-theme. This prompts for a theme name in the minibuffer, loads the theme from the theme file if necessary, and enables the theme. You can *disable* any enabled theme with the command M-x disable-theme; this returns the options specified in the theme to their original values. To re-enable the theme, type M-x enable-theme again. If a theme file is changed during your Emacs session, you can reload it by typing M-x load-theme. (This also enables the theme.)

32.3 Variables

A *variable* is a Lisp symbol which has a value. The symbol's name is also called the name of the variable. A variable name can contain any characters that can appear in a file, but conventionally variable names consist of words separated by hyphens. A variable can have a documentation string which describes what kind of value it should have and how the value will be used.

Emacs Lisp allows any variable (with a few exceptions) to have any kind of value, but most variables that Emacs uses expect a value of a certain type. Often the value should always be a string, or should always be a number. Sometimes we say that a certain feature is turned on if a variable is "non-nil," meaning that if the variable's value is nil, the feature is off, but the feature is on for *any* other value. The conventional value to use to turn on the feature—since you have to pick one particular value when you set the variable—is t.

Emacs uses many Lisp variables for internal record keeping, but the most interesting variables for a non-programmer user are those meant for users to change—these are called *user options*.

Each user option that you can set with the customization buffer is in fact a Lisp variable. Emacs does not (usually) change the values of these variables on its own; instead, you set the values in order to control the behavior of certain Emacs commands. Use of the customization buffer is explained above (see Section 32.2 [Easy Customization], page 408); here we describe other aspects of Emacs variables.

32.3.1 Examining and Setting Variables

C-h v var RET

> Display the value and documentation of variable var (describe-variable).

M-x set-variable RET var RET value RET

> Change the value of variable var to value.

To examine the value of a single variable, use C-h v (describe-variable), which reads a variable name using the minibuffer, with completion. It displays both the value and the documentation of the variable. For example,

    C-h v fill-column RET

displays something like this:

```
fill-column is a variable defined in 'C source code'.
fill-column's value is 70
Local in buffer custom.texi; global value is 70
Automatically becomes buffer-local when set in any fashion.

This variable is safe to use as a file local variable only if its value
satisfies the predicate 'integerp'.

Documentation:
*Column beyond which automatic line-wrapping should happen.
Interactively, you can set the buffer local value using C-x f.

You can customize this variable.
```

The line that says you can customize the variable indicates that this variable is a user option. (The star also indicates this, but it is an obsolete indicator that may eventually disappear.) C-h v is not restricted to user options; it allows any variable name.

The most convenient way to set a specific user option variable is with M-x set-variable. This reads the variable name with the minibuffer (with completion), and then reads a Lisp expression for the new value using the minibuffer a second time (you can insert the old value into the minibuffer for editing via M-n). For example,

    M-x set-variable RET fill-column RET 75 RET

sets fill-column to 75.

M-x set-variable is limited to user option variables, but you can set any variable with a Lisp expression, using the function setq. Here is a setq expression to set fill-column:

    (setq fill-column 75)

To execute an expression like this one, go to the '*scratch*' buffer, type in the expression, and then type C-j. See Section 24.10 [Lisp Interaction], page 290.

Setting variables, like all means of customizing Emacs except where otherwise stated, affects only the current Emacs session. The only way to alter the variable in future sessions is to put something in the '~/.emacs' file to set it those sessions (see Section 32.6 [Init File], page 433).

32.3.2 Hooks

Hooks are an important mechanism for customization of Emacs. A hook is a Lisp variable which holds a list of functions, to be called on some well-defined occasion. (This is called *running the hook*.) The individual functions in the list are called the *hook functions* of the hook. With rare exceptions, hooks in Emacs are empty when Emacs starts up, so the only hook functions in any given hook are the ones you explicitly put there as customization.

Most major modes run one or more *mode hooks* as the last step of initialization. This makes it easy for you to customize the behavior of the mode, by setting up a hook function to override the local variable assignments already made by the mode. But hooks are also used in other contexts. For example, the hook `suspend-hook` runs just before Emacs suspends itself (see Section 3.1 [Exiting], page 17).

Most Emacs hooks are *normal hooks*. This means that running the hook operates by calling all the hook functions, unconditionally, with no arguments. We have made an effort to keep most hooks normal so that you can use them in a uniform way. Every variable in Emacs whose name ends in '`-hook`' is a normal hook.

There are also a few *abnormal hooks*. These variables' names end in '`-hooks`' or '`-functions`', instead of '`-hook`'. What makes these hooks abnormal is that there is something peculiar about the way its functions are called—perhaps they are given arguments, or perhaps the values they return are used in some way. For example, `find-file-not-found-functions` (see Section 15.2 [Visiting], page 120) is abnormal because as soon as one hook function returns a non-`nil` value, the rest are not called at all. The documentation of each abnormal hook variable explains in detail what is peculiar about it.

You can set a hook variable with `setq` like any other Lisp variable, but the recommended way to add a hook function to a hook (either normal or abnormal) is by calling `add-hook`. See section "Hooks" in *The Emacs Lisp Reference Manual*.

For example, here's how to set up a hook to turn on Auto Fill mode when entering Text mode and other modes based on Text mode:

```
(add-hook 'text-mode-hook 'turn-on-auto-fill)
```

The next example shows how to use a hook to customize the indentation of C code. (People often have strong personal preferences for one format compared to another.) Here the hook function is an anonymous lambda expression.

```
(setq my-c-style
  '((c-comment-only-line-offset . 4)
    (c-cleanup-list . (scope-operator
       empty-defun-braces
       defun-close-semi))
    (c-offsets-alist . ((arglist-close . c-lineup-arglist)
(substatement-open . 0)))))

(add-hook 'c-mode-common-hook
  '(lambda ()
     (c-add-style "my-style" my-c-style t)))
```

It is best to design your hook functions so that the order in which they are executed does not matter. Any dependence on the order is "asking for trouble." However, the order is predictable: the most recently added hook functions are executed first.

If you play with adding various different versions of a hook function by calling add-hook over and over, remember that all the versions you added will remain in the hook variable together. You can clear out individual functions by calling remove-hook, or do (setq *hook-variable* nil) to remove everything.

32.3.3 Local Variables

M-x make-local-variable RET *var* RET
> Make variable *var* have a local value in the current buffer.

M-x kill-local-variable RET *var* RET
> Make variable *var* use its global value in the current buffer.

M-x make-variable-buffer-local RET *var* RET
> Mark variable *var* so that setting it will make it local to the buffer that is current at that time.

Almost any variable can be made *local* to a specific Emacs buffer. This means that its value in that buffer is independent of its value in other buffers. A few variables are always local in every buffer. Every other Emacs variable has a *global* value which is in effect in all buffers that have not made the variable local

M-x make-local-variable reads the name of a variable and makes it local to the current buffer. Changing its value subsequently in this buffer will not affect others, and changes in its global value will not affect this buffer.

M-x make-variable-buffer-local marks a variable so it will become local automatically whenever it is set. More precisely, once a variable has been marked in this way, the usual ways of setting the variable automatically do make-local-variable first. We call such variables *per-buffer* variables. Many variables in Emacs are normally per-buffer; the variable's document string tells you when this is so. A per-buffer variable's global value is normally never effective in any buffer, but it still has a meaning: it is the initial value of the variable for each new buffer.

Major modes (see Chapter 20 [Major Modes], page 207) always make variables local to the buffer before setting the variables. This is why changing major modes in one buffer has no effect on other buffers. Minor modes also work by setting variables—normally, each minor mode has one controlling variable which is non-nil when the mode is enabled (see Section 32.1 [Minor Modes], page 406). For many minor modes, the controlling variable is per buffer, and thus always buffer-local. Otherwise, you can make it local in a specific buffer like any other variable.

A few variables cannot be local to a buffer because they are always local to each display instead (see Section 18.8 [Multiple Displays], page 179). If you try to make one of these variables buffer-local, you'll get an error message.

M-x kill-local-variable makes a specified variable cease to be local to the current buffer. The global value of the variable henceforth is in effect in this buffer.

Setting the major mode kills all the local variables of the buffer except for a few variables specially marked as *permanent locals*.

To set the global value of a variable, regardless of whether the variable has a local value in the current buffer, you can use the Lisp construct `setq-default`. This construct is used just like `setq`, but it sets variables' global values instead of their local values (if any). When the current buffer does have a local value, the new global value may not be visible until you switch to another buffer. Here is an example:

```
(setq-default fill-column 75)
```

`setq-default` is the only way to set the global value of a variable that has been marked with `make-variable-buffer-local`.

Lisp programs can use `default-value` to look at a variable's default value. This function takes a symbol as argument and returns its default value. The argument is evaluated; usually you must quote it explicitly. For example, here's how to obtain the default value of `fill-column`:

```
(default-value 'fill-column)
```

32.3.4 Local Variables in Files

A file can specify local variable values for use when you edit the file with Emacs. Visiting the file checks for local variable specifications; it automatically makes these variables local to the buffer, and sets them to the values specified in the file.

32.3.4.1 Specifying File Variables

There are two ways to specify file local variable values: in the first line, or with a local variables list. Here's how to specify them in the first line:

```
-*- mode: modename; var: value; ... -*-
```

You can specify any number of variables/value pairs in this way, each pair with a colon and semicolon as shown above. `mode: modename`; specifies the major mode; this should come first in the line. The *values* are not evaluated; they are used literally. Here is an example that specifies Lisp mode and sets two variables with numeric values:

```
;; -*- mode: Lisp; fill-column: 75; comment-column: 50; -*-
```

You can also specify the coding system for a file in this way: just specify a value for the "variable" named `coding`. The "value" must be a coding system name that Emacs recognizes. See Section 19.7 [Coding Systems], page 193. `unibyte: t` specifies unibyte loading for a particular Lisp file. See Section 19.2 [Enabling Multibyte], page 187.

The `eval` pseudo-variable, described below, can be specified in the first line as well.

In shell scripts, the first line is used to identify the script interpreter, so you cannot put any local variables there. To accommodate this, Emacs looks for local variable specifications in the *second* line when the first line specifies an interpreter.

A *local variables list* goes near the end of the file, in the last page. (It is often best to put it on a page by itself.) The local variables list starts with a line containing

the string 'Local Variables:', and ends with a line containing the string 'End:'.
In between come the variable names and values, one set per line, as '*variable:*
value'. The *values* are not evaluated; they are used literally. If a file has both
a local variables list and a '-*-' line, Emacs processes *everything* in the '-*-' line
first, and *everything* in the local variables list afterward.

Here is an example of a local variables list:

```
;; Local Variables: **
;; mode:lisp **
;; comment-column:0 **
;; comment-start: ";; "   **
;; comment-end:"**" **
;; End: **
```

Each line starts with the prefix ';; ' and each line ends with the suffix ' **'.
Emacs recognizes these as the prefix and suffix based on the first line of the list, by
finding them surrounding the magic string 'Local Variables:'; then it automatically discards them from the other lines of the list.

The usual reason for using a prefix and/or suffix is to embed the local variables
list in a comment, so it won't confuse other programs that the file is intended as
input for. The example above is for a language where comment lines start with ';; '
and end with '**'; the local values for comment-start and comment-end customize
the rest of Emacs for this unusual syntax. Don't use a prefix (or a suffix) if you
don't need one.

If you write a multi-line string value, you should put the prefix and suffix on
each line, even lines that start or end within the string. They will be stripped off
for processing the list. If you want to split a long string across multiple lines of
the file, you can use backslash-newline, which is ignored in Lisp string constants.
Here's an example of doing this:

```
# Local Variables:
# compile-command: "cc foo.c -Dfoo=bar -Dhack=whatever \
#    -Dmumble=blaah"
# End:
```

Some "variable names" have special meanings in a local variables list. Specifying
the "variable" mode really sets the major mode, while any value specified for the
"variable" eval is simply evaluated as an expression (its value is ignored). A value
for coding specifies the coding system for character code conversion of this file,
and a value of t for unibyte says to visit the file in a unibyte buffer. These four
"variables" are not really variables; setting them in any other context has no special
meaning.

If mode *is used to set a major mode, it should be the first "variable" in the list.*
Otherwise, the entries that precede it will usually be ignored, since most modes kill
all local variables as part of their initialization.

You can use the mode "variable" to set minor modes as well as the major modes;
in fact, you can use it more than once, first to set the major mode and then to set
minor modes which are specific to particular buffers. But most minor modes should
not be specified in the file at all, because they represent user preferences.

For example, you may be tempted to try to turn on Auto Fill mode with a local variable list. That is a mistake. The choice of Auto Fill mode or not is a matter of individual taste, not a matter of the contents of particular files. If you want to use Auto Fill, set up major mode hooks with your '.emacs' file to turn it on (when appropriate) for you alone (see Section 32.6 [Init File], page 433). Don't use a local variable list to impose your taste on everyone.

The start of the local variables list must be no more than 3000 characters from the end of the file, and must be in the last page if the file is divided into pages. Otherwise, Emacs will not notice it is there. The purpose of this rule is so that a stray 'Local Variables:' not in the last page does not confuse Emacs, and so that visiting a long file that is all one page and has no local variables list need not take the time to search the whole file.

Use the command `normal-mode` to reset the local variables and major mode of a buffer according to the file name and contents, including the local variables list if any. See Section 20.1 [Choosing Modes], page 207.

32.3.4.2 Safety of File Variables

File-local variables can be dangerous; when you visit someone else's file, there's no telling what its local variables list could do to your Emacs. Improper values of the `eval` "variable," and other variables such as `load-path`, could execute Lisp code you didn't intend to run.

Therefore, whenever Emacs encounters file local variable values that are not known to be safe, it displays the file's entire local variables list, and asks you for confirmation before setting them. You can type y or SPC to put the local variables list into effect, or n to ignore it. When Emacs is run in batch mode (see Section C.2 [Initial Options], page 472), it can't really ask you, so it assumes the answer n.

Emacs normally recognizes certain variables/value pairs as safe. For instance, it is safe to give `comment-column` or `fill-column` any integer value. If a file specifies only known-safe variable/value pairs, Emacs does not ask for confirmation before setting them. Otherwise, you can tell Emacs to record all the variable/value pairs in this file as safe, by typing ! at the confirmation prompt. When Emacs encounters these variable/value pairs subsequently, in the same file or others, it will assume they are safe.

Some variables, such as `load-path`, are considered particularly *risky*: there is seldom any reason to specify them as local variables, and changing them can be dangerous. Even if you enter ! at the confirmation prompt, Emacs will not record any values as safe for these variables. If you really want to record safe values for these variables, do it directly by customizing 'safe-local-variable-values' (see Section 32.2 [Easy Customization], page 408).

The variable `enable-local-variables` allows you to change the way Emacs processes local variables. Its default value is `t`, which specifies the behavior described above. If it is `nil`, Emacs simply ignores all file local variables. `:safe` means use only the safe values and ignore the rest. Any other value says to query you about each file that has local variables, without trying to determine whether the values are known to be safe.

The variable `enable-local-eval` controls whether Emacs processes `eval` variables. The three possibilities for the variable's value are `t`, `nil`, and anything else, just as for `enable-local-variables`. The default is `maybe`, which is neither `t` nor `nil`, so normally Emacs does ask for confirmation about processing `eval` variables.

But there is an exception. The `safe-local-eval-forms` is a customizable list of eval forms which are safe. Emacs does not ask for confirmation when it finds these forms for the `eval` variable.

32.4 Customizing Key Bindings

This section describes *key bindings*, which map keys to commands, and *keymaps*, which record key bindings. It also explains how to customize key bindings.

Recall that a command is a Lisp function whose definition provides for interactive use. Like every Lisp function, a command has a function name, which usually consists of lower-case letters and hyphens.

32.4.1 Keymaps

The bindings between key sequences and command functions are recorded in data structures called *keymaps*. Emacs has many of these, each used on particular occasions.

Recall that a *key sequence* (*key*, for short) is a sequence of *input events* that have a meaning as a unit. Input events include characters, function keys and mouse buttons —all the inputs that you can send to the computer with your terminal. A key sequence gets its meaning from its *binding*, which says what command it runs. The function of keymaps is to record these bindings.

The *global* keymap is the most important keymap because it is always in effect. The global keymap defines keys for Fundamental mode; most of these definitions are common to most or all major modes. Each major or minor mode can have its own keymap which overrides the global definitions of some keys.

For example, a self-inserting character such as `g` is self-inserting because the global keymap binds it to the command `self-insert-command`. The standard Emacs editing characters such as `C-a` also get their standard meanings from the global keymap. Commands to rebind keys, such as `M-x global-set-key`, actually work by storing the new binding in the proper place in the global map. See Section 32.4.5 [Rebinding], page 426.

Meta characters work differently; Emacs translates each Meta character into a pair of characters starting with ESC. When you type the character `M-a` in a key sequence, Emacs replaces it with `ESC a`. A meta key comes in as a single input event, but becomes two events for purposes of key bindings. The reason for this is historical, and we might change it someday.

Most modern keyboards have function keys as well as character keys. Function keys send input events just as character keys do, and keymaps can have bindings for them.

On text terminals, typing a function key actually sends the computer a sequence of characters; the precise details of the sequence depends on which function key

and on the model of terminal you are using. (Often the sequence starts with ESC
[.) If Emacs understands your terminal type properly, it recognizes the character
sequences forming function keys wherever they occur in a key sequence (not just at
the beginning). Thus, for most purposes, you can pretend the function keys reach
Emacs directly and ignore their encoding as character sequences.

Mouse buttons also produce input events. These events come with other data—
the window and position where you pressed or released the button, and a time
stamp. But only the choice of button matters for key bindings; the other data
matters only if a command looks at it. (Commands designed for mouse invocation
usually do look at the other data.)

A keymap records definitions for single events. Interpreting a key sequence of
multiple events involves a chain of keymaps. The first keymap gives a definition
for the first event; this definition is another keymap, which is used to look up the
second event in the sequence, and so on.

Key sequences can mix function keys and characters. For example, C-x SELECT
is meaningful. If you make SELECT a prefix key, then SELECT C-n makes sense.
You can even mix mouse events with keyboard events, but we recommend against
it, because such key sequences are inconvenient to use.

As a user, you can redefine any key; but it is usually best to stick to key sequences that consist of C-c followed by a letter (upper or lower case). These keys
are "reserved for users," so they won't conflict with any properly designed Emacs
extension. The function keys F5 through F9 are also reserved for users. If you
redefine some other key, your definition may be overridden by certain extensions or
major modes which redefine the same key.

32.4.2 Prefix Keymaps

A prefix key such as C-x or ESC has its own keymap, which holds the definition for
the event that immediately follows that prefix.

The definition of a prefix key is usually the keymap to use for looking up the
following event. The definition can also be a Lisp symbol whose function definition
is the following keymap; the effect is the same, but it provides a command name for
the prefix key that can be used as a description of what the prefix key is for. Thus,
the binding of C-x is the symbol Control-X-prefix, whose function definition is
the keymap for C-x commands. The definitions of C-c, C-x, C-h and ESC as prefix
keys appear in the global map, so these prefix keys are always available.

Aside from ordinary prefix keys, there is a fictitious "prefix key" which represents
the menu bar; see section "Menu Bar" in *The Emacs Lisp Reference Manual*, for
special information about menu bar key bindings. Mouse button events that invoke
pop-up menus are also prefix keys; see section "Menu Keymaps" in *The Emacs Lisp
Reference Manual*, for more details.

Some prefix keymaps are stored in variables with names:

- ctl-x-map is the variable name for the map used for characters that follow
  C-x.

- help-map is for characters that follow C-h.

- `esc-map` is for characters that follow ESC. Thus, all Meta characters are actually defined by this map.

- `ctl-x-4-map` is for characters that follow C-x 4.

- `mode-specific-map` is for characters that follow C-c.

32.4.3 Local Keymaps

So far we have explained the ins and outs of the global map. Major modes customize Emacs by providing their own key bindings in *local keymaps*. For example, C mode overrides TAB to make it indent the current line for C code. Portions of text in the buffer can specify their own keymaps to substitute for the keymap of the buffer's major mode.

Minor modes can also have local keymaps. Whenever a minor mode is in effect, the definitions in its keymap override both the major mode's local keymap and the global keymap.

A local keymap can locally redefine a key as a prefix key by defining it as a prefix keymap. If the key is also defined globally as a prefix, then its local and global definitions (both keymaps) effectively combine: both of them are used to look up the event that follows the prefix key. Thus, if the mode's local keymap defines C-c as another keymap, and that keymap defines C-z as a command, this provides a local meaning for C-c C-z. This does not affect other sequences that start with C-c; if those sequences don't have their own local bindings, their global bindings remain in effect.

Another way to think of this is that Emacs handles a multi-event key sequence by looking in several keymaps, one by one, for a binding of the whole key sequence. First it checks the minor mode keymaps for minor modes that are enabled, then it checks the major mode's keymap, and then it checks the global keymap. This is not precisely how key lookup works, but it's good enough for understanding the results in ordinary circumstances.

Most major modes construct their keymaps when the mode is used for the first time in a session. If you wish to change one of these keymaps, you must use the major mode's *mode hook* (see Section 32.3.2 [Hooks], page 418).

For example, the command `texinfo-mode` to select Texinfo mode runs the hook `texinfo-mode-hook`. Here's how you can use the hook to add local bindings (not very useful, we admit) for C-c n and C-c p in Texinfo mode:

```
(add-hook 'texinfo-mode-hook
          '(lambda ()
             (define-key texinfo-mode-map "\C-cp"
                         'backward-paragraph)
             (define-key texinfo-mode-map "\C-cn"
                         'forward-paragraph)))
```

32.4.4 Minibuffer Keymaps

The minibuffer has its own set of local keymaps; they contain various completion and exit commands.

- `minibuffer-local-map` is used for ordinary input (no completion).

- `minibuffer-local-ns-map` is similar, except that SPC exits just like RET. This is used mainly for Mocklisp compatibility.

- `minibuffer-local-completion-map` is for permissive completion.

- `minibuffer-local-must-match-map` is for strict completion and for cautious completion.

- Finally, `minibuffer-local-filename-completion-map` and `minibuffer-local-must-match-filename-map` are like the two previous ones, but they are specifically for file name completion. They do not bind SPC.

32.4.5 Changing Key Bindings Interactively

The way to redefine an Emacs key is to change its entry in a keymap. You can change the global keymap, in which case the change is effective in all major modes (except those that have their own overriding local definitions for the same key). Or you can change the current buffer's local map, which affects all buffers using the same major mode.

`M-x global-set-key RET` *key* *cmd* `RET`
> Define *key* globally to run *cmd*.

`M-x local-set-key RET` *key* *cmd* `RET`
> Define *key* locally (in the major mode now in effect) to run *cmd*.

`M-x global-unset-key RET` *key*
> Make *key* undefined in the global map.

`M-x local-unset-key RET` *key*
> Make *key* undefined locally (in the major mode now in effect).

For example, suppose you like to execute commands in a subshell within an Emacs buffer, instead of suspending Emacs and executing commands in your login shell. Normally, `C-z` is bound to the function **suspend-emacs** (when not using the X Window System), but you can change `C-z` to invoke an interactive subshell within Emacs, by binding it to **shell** as follows:

> `M-x global-set-key RET C-z shell RET`

`global-set-key` reads the command name after the key. After you press the key, a message like this appears so that you can confirm that you are binding the key you want:

> `Set key C-z to command:`

You can redefine function keys and mouse events in the same way; just type the function key or click the mouse when it's time to specify the key to rebind.

You can rebind a key that contains more than one event in the same way. Emacs keeps reading the key to rebind until it is a complete key (that is, not a prefix key). Thus, if you type `C-f` for *key*, that's the end; it enters the minibuffer immediately to read *cmd*. But if you type `C-x`, since that's a prefix, it reads another character; if that is `4`, another prefix character, it reads one more character, and so on. For example,

M-x global-set-key RET C-x 4 $ spell-other-window RET

redefines C-x 4 $ to run the (fictitious) command spell-other-window.

The two-character keys consisting of C-c followed by a letter are reserved for user customizations. Lisp programs are not supposed to define these keys, so the bindings you make for them will be available in all major modes and will never get in the way of anything.

You can remove the global definition of a key with global-unset-key. This makes the key *undefined*; if you type it, Emacs will just beep. Similarly, local-unset-key makes a key undefined in the current major mode keymap, which makes the global definition (or lack of one) come back into effect in that major mode.

If you have redefined (or undefined) a key and you subsequently wish to retract the change, undefining the key will not do the job—you need to redefine the key with its standard definition. To find the name of the standard definition of a key, go to a Fundamental mode buffer in a fresh Emacs and use C-h c. The documentation of keys in this manual also lists their command names.

If you want to prevent yourself from invoking a command by mistake, it is better to disable the command than to undefine the key. A disabled command is less work to invoke when you really want to. See Section 32.4.10 [Disabling], page 432.

32.4.6 Rebinding Keys in Your Init File

If you have a set of key bindings that you like to use all the time, you can specify them in your '.emacs' file by using their Lisp syntax. (See Section 32.6 [Init File], page 433.)

The simplest method for doing this works for ASCII characters and Meta-modified ASCII characters only. This method uses a string to represent the key sequence you want to rebind. For example, here's how to bind C-z to shell:

    (global-set-key "\C-z" 'shell)

This example uses a string constant containing one character, C-z. ('\C-' is string syntax for a control character.) The single-quote before the command name, shell, marks it as a constant symbol rather than a variable. If you omit the quote, Emacs would try to evaluate shell immediately as a variable. This probably causes an error; it certainly isn't what you want.

Here is another example that binds the key sequence C-x M-l:

    (global-set-key "\C-x\M-l" 'make-symbolic-link)

To put TAB, RET, ESC, or DEL in the string, you can use the Emacs Lisp escape sequences, '\t', '\r', '\e', and '\d'. Here is an example which binds C-x TAB:

    (global-set-key "\C-x\t" 'indent-rigidly)

These examples show how to write some other special ASCII characters in strings for key bindings:

    (global-set-key "\r" 'newline)   ;; RET
    (global-set-key "\d" 'delete-backward-char)   ;; DEL
    (global-set-key "\C-x\e\e" 'repeat-complex-command)   ;; ESC

When the key sequence includes function keys or mouse button events, or non-ASCII characters such as C-= or H-a, you must use the more general method of rebinding, which uses a vector to specify the key sequence.

The way to write a vector in Emacs Lisp is with square brackets around the vector elements. Use spaces to separate the elements. If an element is a symbol, simply write the symbol's name—no other delimiters or punctuation are needed. If a vector element is a character, write it as a Lisp character constant: '?' followed by the character as it would appear in a string.

Here are examples of using vectors to rebind C-= (a control character not in ASCII), C-M-= (not in ASCII because C-= is not), H-a (a Hyper character; ASCII doesn't have Hyper at all), F7 (a function key), and C-Mouse-1 (a keyboard-modified mouse button):

```
(global-set-key [?\C-=] 'make-symbolic-link)
(global-set-key [?\M-\C-=] 'make-symbolic-link)
(global-set-key [?\H-a] 'make-symbolic-link)
(global-set-key [f7] 'make-symbolic-link)
(global-set-key [C-mouse-1] 'make-symbolic-link)
```

You can use a vector for the simple cases too. Here's how to rewrite the first six examples above to use vectors:

```
(global-set-key [?\C-z] 'shell)
(global-set-key [?\C-x ?l] 'make-symbolic-link)
(global-set-key [?\C-x ?\t] 'indent-rigidly)
(global-set-key [?\r] 'newline)
(global-set-key [?\d] 'delete-backward-char)
(global-set-key [?\C-x ?\e ?\e] 'repeat-complex-command)
```

As you see, you represent a multi-character key sequence with a vector by listing all of the characters, in order, within the square brackets that delimit the vector.

Language and coding systems can cause problems with key bindings for non-ASCII characters. See Section 32.6.5 [Init Non-ASCII], page 438.

32.4.7 Rebinding Function Keys

Key sequences can contain function keys as well as ordinary characters. Just as Lisp characters (actually integers) represent keyboard characters, Lisp symbols represent function keys. If the function key has a word as its label, then that word is also the name of the corresponding Lisp symbol. Here are the conventional Lisp names for common function keys:

left, up, right, down
> Cursor arrow keys.

begin, end, home, next, prior
> Other cursor repositioning keys.

select, print, execute, backtab
insert, undo, redo, clearline
insertline, deleteline, insertchar, deletechar
> Miscellaneous function keys.

f1, f2, ... f35
>   Numbered function keys (across the top of the keyboard).

kp-add, kp-subtract, kp-multiply, kp-divide
kp-backtab, kp-space, kp-tab, kp-enter
kp-separator, kp-decimal, kp-equal
>   Keypad keys (to the right of the regular keyboard), with names or
>   punctuation.

kp-0, kp-1, ... kp-9
>   Keypad keys with digits.

kp-f1, kp-f2, kp-f3, kp-f4
>   Keypad PF keys.

These names are conventional, but some systems (especially when using X) may use different names. To make certain what symbol is used for a given function key on your terminal, type C-h c followed by that key.

A key sequence which contains function key symbols (or anything but ASCII characters) must be a vector rather than a string. Thus, to bind function key 'f1' to the command rmail, write the following:

>   (global-set-key [f1] 'rmail)

To bind the right-arrow key to the command forward-char, you can use this expression:

>   (global-set-key [right] 'forward-char)

This uses the Lisp syntax for a vector containing the symbol right. (This binding is present in Emacs by default.)

See Section 32.4.6 [Init Rebinding], page 427, for more information about using vectors for rebinding.

You can mix function keys and characters in a key sequence. This example binds C-x NEXT to the command forward-page.

>   (global-set-key [?\C-x next] 'forward-page)

where ?\C-x is the Lisp character constant for the character C-x. The vector element next is a symbol and therefore does not take a question mark.

You can use the modifier keys CTRL, META, HYPER, SUPER, ALT and SHIFT with function keys. To represent these modifiers, add the strings 'C-', 'M-', 'H-', 's-', 'A-' and 'S-' at the front of the symbol name. Thus, here is how to make Hyper-Meta-RIGHT move forward a word:

>   (global-set-key [H-M-right] 'forward-word)

Many keyboards have a "numeric keypad" on the right hand side. The numeric keys in the keypad double up as cursor motion keys, toggled by a key labeled 'Num Lock'. By default, Emacs translates these keys to the corresponding keys in the main keyboard. For example, when 'Num Lock' is on, the key labeled '8' on the numeric keypad produces kp-8, which is translated to 8; when 'Num Lock' is off, the same key produces kp-up, which is translated to UP. If you rebind a key such as 8 or UP, it affects the equivalent keypad key too. However, if you rebind a 'kp-' key directly, that won't affect its non-keypad equivalent.

Emacs provides a convenient method for binding the numeric keypad keys, using the variables `keypad-setup`, `keypad-numlock-setup`, `keypad-shifted-setup`, and `keypad-numlock-shifted-setup`. These can be found in the 'keyboard' customization group (see Section 32.2 [Easy Customization], page 408). You can rebind the keys to perform other tasks, such as issuing numeric prefix arguments.

32.4.8 Named ASCII Control Characters

TAB, RET, BS, LFD, ESC and DEL started out as names for certain ASCII control characters, used so often that they have special keys of their own. For instance, TAB was another name for `C-i`. Later, users found it convenient to distinguish in Emacs between these keys and the "same" control characters typed with the CTRL key. Therefore, on most modern terminals, they are no longer the same, and TAB is distinguishable from `C-i`.

Emacs can distinguish these two kinds of input if the keyboard does. It treats the "special" keys as function keys named `tab`, `return`, `backspace`, `linefeed`, `escape`, and `delete`. These function keys translate automatically into the corresponding ASCII characters *if* they have no bindings of their own. As a result, neither users nor Lisp programs need to pay attention to the distinction unless they care to.

If you do not want to distinguish between (for example) TAB and `C-i`, make just one binding, for the ASCII character TAB (octal code 011). If you do want to distinguish, make one binding for this ASCII character, and another for the "function key" `tab`.

With an ordinary ASCII terminal, there is no way to distinguish between TAB and `C-i` (and likewise for other such pairs), because the terminal sends the same character in both cases.

32.4.9 Rebinding Mouse Buttons

Emacs uses Lisp symbols to designate mouse buttons, too. The ordinary mouse events in Emacs are *click* events; these happen when you press a button and release it without moving the mouse. You can also get *drag* events, when you move the mouse while holding the button down. Drag events happen when you finally let go of the button.

The symbols for basic click events are `mouse-1` for the leftmost button, `mouse-2` for the next, and so on. Here is how you can redefine the second mouse button to split the current window:

```
(global-set-key [mouse-2] 'split-window-vertically)
```

The symbols for drag events are similar, but have the prefix 'drag-' before the word 'mouse'. For example, dragging the first button generates a `drag-mouse-1` event.

You can also define bindings for events that occur when a mouse button is pressed down. These events start with 'down-' instead of 'drag-'. Such events are generated only if they have key bindings. When you get a button-down event, a corresponding click or drag event will always follow.

If you wish, you can distinguish single, double, and triple clicks. A double click means clicking a mouse button twice in approximately the same place. The first click generates an ordinary click event. The second click, if it comes soon enough, generates a double-click event instead. The event type for a double-click event starts with 'double-': for example, double-mouse-3.

This means that you can give a special meaning to the second click at the same place, but it must act on the assumption that the ordinary single click definition has run when the first click was received.

This constrains what you can do with double clicks, but user interface designers say that this constraint ought to be followed in any case. A double click should do something similar to the single click, only "more so." The command for the double-click event should perform the extra work for the double click.

If a double-click event has no binding, it changes to the corresponding single-click event. Thus, if you don't define a particular double click specially, it executes the single-click command twice.

Emacs also supports triple-click events whose names start with 'triple-'. Emacs does not distinguish quadruple clicks as event types; clicks beyond the third generate additional triple-click events. However, the full number of clicks is recorded in the event list, so if you know Emacs Lisp you can distinguish if you really want to (see section "Accessing Events" in *The Emacs Lisp Reference Manual*). We don't recommend distinct meanings for more than three clicks, but sometimes it is useful for subsequent clicks to cycle through the same set of three meanings, so that four clicks are equivalent to one click, five are equivalent to two, and six are equivalent to three.

Emacs also records multiple presses in drag and button-down events. For example, when you press a button twice, then move the mouse while holding the button, Emacs gets a 'double-drag-' event. And at the moment when you press it down for the second time, Emacs gets a 'double down-' event (which is ignored, like all button-down events, if it has no binding).

The variable double-click-time specifies how much time can elapse between clicks and still allow them to be grouped as a multiple click. Its value is in units of milliseconds. If the value is nil, double clicks are not detected at all. If the value is t, then there is no time limit. The default is 500.

The variable double-click-fuzz specifies how much the mouse can move between clicks and still allow them to be grouped as a multiple click. Its value is in units of pixels on windowed displays and in units of 1/8 of a character cell on text-mode terminals; the default is 3.

The symbols for mouse events also indicate the status of the modifier keys, with the usual prefixes 'C-', 'M-', 'H-', 's-', 'A-' and 'S-'. These always precede 'double-' or 'triple-', which always precede 'drag-' or 'down-'.

A frame includes areas that don't show text from the buffer, such as the mode line and the scroll bar. You can tell whether a mouse button comes from a special area of the screen by means of dummy "prefix keys." For example, if you click the mouse in the mode line, you get the prefix key mode-line before the ordinary mouse-button symbol. Thus, here is how to define the command for clicking the first button in a mode line to run scroll-up:

```
(global-set-key [mode-line mouse-1] 'scroll-up)
```

Here is the complete list of these dummy prefix keys and their meanings:

`mode-line`   The mouse was in the mode line of a window.

`vertical-line`

> The mouse was in the vertical line separating side-by-side windows. (If you use scroll bars, they appear in place of these vertical lines.)

`vertical-scroll-bar`

> The mouse was in a vertical scroll bar. (This is the only kind of scroll bar Emacs currently supports.)

`menu-bar`   The mouse was in the menu bar.

`header-line`

> The mouse was in a header line.

You can put more than one mouse button in a key sequence, but it isn't usual to do so.

32.4.10 Disabling Commands

Disabling a command means that invoking it interactively asks for confirmation from the user. The purpose of disabling a command is to prevent users from executing it by accident; we do this for commands that might be confusing to the uninitiated.

Attempting to invoke a disabled command interactively in Emacs displays a window containing the command's name, its documentation, and some instructions on what to do immediately; then Emacs asks for input saying whether to execute the command as requested, enable it and execute it, or cancel. If you decide to enable the command, you must then answer another question—whether to do this permanently, or just for the current session. (Enabling permanently works by automatically editing your '.emacs' file.) You can also type ! to enable *all* commands, for the current session only.

The direct mechanism for disabling a command is to put a non-`nil` `disabled` property on the Lisp symbol for the command. Here is the Lisp program to do this:

```
(put 'delete-region 'disabled t)
```

If the value of the `disabled` property is a string, that string is included in the message displayed when the command is used:

```
(put 'delete-region 'disabled
     "It's better to use `kill-region' instead.\n")
```

You can make a command disabled either by editing the '.emacs' file directly, or with the command M-x disable-command, which edits the '.emacs' file for you. Likewise, M-x enable-command edits '.emacs' to enable a command permanently. See Section 32.6 [Init File], page 433.

If Emacs was invoked with the '-q' or '--no-init-file' options (see Section C.2 [Initial Options], page 472), it will not edit your '~/.emacs' init file. Doing so could lose information because Emacs has not read your init file.

Whether a command is disabled is independent of what key is used to invoke it; disabling also applies if the command is invoked using M-x. However, disabling a command has no effect on calling it as a function from Lisp programs.

32.5 The Syntax Table

All the Emacs commands which parse words or balance parentheses are controlled by the *syntax table*. The syntax table says which characters are opening delimiters, which are parts of words, which are string quotes, and so on. It does this by assigning each character to one of fifteen-odd *syntax classes*. In some cases it specifies some additional information also.

Each major mode has its own syntax table (though related major modes sometimes share one syntax table), which it installs in each buffer that uses the mode. The syntax table installed in the current buffer is the one that all commands use, so we call it "the" syntax table.

To display a description of the contents of the current syntax table, type C-h s (describe-syntax). The description of each character includes the string you would have to give to modify-syntax-entry to set up that character's current syntax, starting with the character which designates its syntax class, plus some English text to explain its meaning.

A syntax table is actually a Lisp object, a char-table, whose elements are cons cells. For full information on the syntax table, see section "Syntax Tables" in *The Emacs Lisp Reference Manual*.

32.6 The Init File, '~/.emacs'

When Emacs is started, it normally loads a Lisp program from the file '.emacs' or '.emacs.el' in your home directory (see Section 32.6.4 [Find Init], page 438). We call this file your *init file* because it specifies how to initialize Emacs for you. You can use the command line switch '-q' to prevent loading your init file, and '-u' (or '--user') to specify a different user's init file (see Section C.2 [Initial Options], page 472).

You can also use '~/.emacs.d/init.el' as the init file. Emacs tries this if it cannot find '~/.emacs' or '~/.emacs.el'.

There can also be a *default init file*, which is the library named 'default.el', found via the standard search path for libraries. The Emacs distribution contains no such library; your site may create one for local customizations. If this library exists, it is loaded whenever you start Emacs (except when you specify '-q'). But your init file, if any, is loaded first; if it sets inhibit-default-init non-nil, then 'default' is not loaded.

Your site may also have a *site startup file*; this is named 'site-start.el', if it exists. Like 'default.el', Emacs finds this file via the standard search path for Lisp libraries. Emacs loads this library before it loads your init file. To inhibit loading of this library, use the option '--no-site-file'. See Section C.2 [Initial Options], page 472. We recommend against using 'site-start.el' for changes that some users may not like. It is better to put them in 'default.el', so that users can more easily override them.

You can place 'default.el' and 'site-start.el' in any of the directories which Emacs searches for Lisp libraries. The variable load-path (see Section 24.8 [Lisp Libraries], page 288) specifies these directories. Many sites put these files

in the 'site-lisp' subdirectory of the Emacs installation directory, typically
'/usr/local/share/emacs/site-lisp'.

If you have a large amount of code in your '.emacs' file, you should rename
it to '~/.emacs.el', and byte-compile it. See section "Byte Compilation" in *the
Emacs Lisp Reference Manual*, for more information about compiling Emacs Lisp
programs.

If you are going to write actual Emacs Lisp programs that go beyond minor
customization, you should read the *Emacs Lisp Reference Manual*.

32.6.1 Init File Syntax

The '.emacs' file contains one or more Lisp function call expressions. Each of these
consists of a function name followed by arguments, all surrounded by parentheses.
For example, (setq fill-column 60) calls the function setq to set the variable
fill-column (see Section 22.5 [Filling], page 217) to 60.

You can set any Lisp variable with setq, but with certain variables setq won't
do what you probably want in the '.emacs' file. Some variables automatically
become buffer-local when set with setq; what you want in '.emacs' is to set the
default value, using setq-default. Some customizable minor mode variables do
special things to enable the mode when you set them with Customize, but ordinary
setq won't do that; to enable the mode in your '.emacs' file, call the minor mode
command. The following section has examples of both of these methods.

The second argument to setq is an expression for the new value of the variable.
This can be a constant, a variable, or a function call expression. In '.emacs',
constants are used most of the time. They can be:

Numbers: Numbers are written in decimal, with an optional initial minus sign.

Strings: Lisp string syntax is the same as C string syntax with a few extra
             features. Use a double-quote character to begin and end a string con-
             stant.

             In a string, you can include newlines and special characters literally.
             But often it is cleaner to use backslash sequences for them: '\n' for
             newline, '\b' for backspace, '\r' for carriage return, '\t' for tab, '\f'
             for formfeed (control-L), '\e' for escape, '\\' for a backslash, '\"' for
             a double-quote, or '\ooo' for the character whose octal code is *ooo*.
             Backslash and double-quote are the only characters for which back-
             slash sequences are mandatory.

             '\C-' can be used as a prefix for a control character, as in '\C-s' for
             ASCII control-S, and '\M-' can be used as a prefix for a Meta character,
             as in '\M-a' for Meta-A or '\M-\C-a' for Control-Meta-A.

             See Section 32.6.5 [Init Non-ASCII], page 438, for information about
             including non-ASCII in your init file.

Characters: Lisp character constant syntax consists of a '?' followed by either a
             character or an escape sequence starting with '\'. Examples: ?x, ?\n,
             ?\", ?\). Note that strings and characters are not interchangeable in
             Lisp; some contexts require one and some contexts require the other.

See Section 32.6.5 [Init Non-ASCII], page 438, for information about binding commands to keys which send non-ASCII characters.

True: t stands for 'true'.

False: nil stands for 'false'.

Other Lisp objects:
Write a single-quote (') followed by the Lisp object you want.

32.6.2 Init File Examples

Here are some examples of doing certain commonly desired things with Lisp expressions:

- Make TAB in C mode just insert a tab if point is in the middle of a line.

      (setq c-tab-always-indent nil)

  Here we have a variable whose value is normally t for 'true' and the alternative is nil for 'false'.

- Make searches case sensitive by default (in all buffers that do not override this).

      (setq-default case-fold-search nil)

  This sets the default value, which is effective in all buffers that do not have local values for the variable. Setting case-fold-search with setq affects only the current buffer's local value, which is not what you probably want to do in an init file.

- Specify your own email address, if Emacs can't figure it out correctly.

      (setq user-mail-address "rumsfeld@torture.gov")

  Various Emacs packages that need your own email address use the value of user-mail-address.

- Make Text mode the default mode for new buffers.

      (setq default-major-mode 'text-mode)

  Note that text-mode is used because it is the command for entering Text mode. The single-quote before it makes the symbol a constant; otherwise, text-mode would be treated as a variable name.

- Set up defaults for the Latin-1 character set which supports most of the languages of Western Europe.

      (set-language-environment "Latin-1")

- Turn off Line Number mode, a global minor mode.

      (line-number-mode 0)

- Turn on Auto Fill mode automatically in Text mode and related modes.

```
(add-hook 'text-mode-hook
   '(lambda () (auto-fill-mode 1)))
```

This shows how to add a hook function to a normal hook variable (see Section 32.3.2 [Hooks], page 418). The function we supply is a list starting with `lambda`, with a single-quote in front of it to make it a list constant rather than an expression.

It's beyond the scope of this manual to explain Lisp functions, but for this example it is enough to know that the effect is to execute (`auto-fill-mode 1`) when Text mode is entered. You can replace that with any other expression that you like, or with several expressions in a row.

Emacs comes with a function named `turn-on-auto-fill` whose definition is (`lambda () (auto-fill-mode 1)`). Thus, a simpler way to write the above example is as follows:

```
(add-hook 'text-mode-hook 'turn-on-auto-fill)
```

- Load the installed Lisp library named 'foo' (actually a file 'foo.elc' or 'foo.el' in a standard Emacs directory).

```
(load "foo")
```

When the argument to `load` is a relative file name, not starting with '/' or '~', `load` searches the directories in `load-path` (see Section 24.8 [Lisp Libraries], page 288).

- Load the compiled Lisp file 'foo.elc' from your home directory.

```
(load "~/foo.elc")
```

Here an absolute file name is used, so no searching is done.

- Tell Emacs to find the definition for the function `myfunction` by loading a Lisp library named 'mypackage' (i.e. a file 'mypackage.elc' or 'mypackage.el'):

```
(autoload 'myfunction "mypackage" "Do what I say." t)
```

Here the string `"Do what I say."` is the function's documentation string. You specify it in the `autoload` definition so it will be available for help commands even when the package is not loaded. The last argument, `t`, indicates that this function is interactive; that is, it can be invoked interactively by typing M-x `myfunction` RET or by binding it to a key. If the function is not interactive, omit the `t` or use `nil`.

- Rebind the key C-x l to run the function `make-symbolic-link` (see Section 32.4.6 [Init Rebinding], page 427).

```
(global-set-key "\C-xl" 'make-symbolic-link)
```

or

```
(define-key global-map "\C-xl" 'make-symbolic-link)
```

Note once again the single-quote used to refer to the symbol `make-symbolic-link` instead of its value as a variable.

- Do the same thing for Lisp mode only.

```
(define-key lisp-mode-map "\C-xl" 'make-symbolic-link)
```

- Redefine all keys which now run `next-line` in Fundamental mode so that they run `forward-line` instead.

```
(substitute-key-definition 'next-line 'forward-line
                           global-map)
```

- Make C-x C-v undefined.

```
(global-unset-key "\C-x\C-v")
```

One reason to undefine a key is so that you can make it a prefix. Simply defining C-x C-v *anything* will make C-x C-v a prefix, but C-x C-v must first be freed of its usual non-prefix definition.

- Make '$' have the syntax of punctuation in Text mode. Note the use of a character constant for '$'.

```
(modify-syntax-entry ?\$ "." text-mode-syntax-table)
```

- Enable the use of the command `narrow-to-region` without confirmation.

```
(put 'narrow-to-region 'disabled nil)
```

- Adjusting the configuration to various platforms and Emacs versions.

Users typically want Emacs to behave the same on all systems, so the same init file is right for all platforms. However, sometimes it happens that a function you use for customizing Emacs is not available on some platforms or in older Emacs versions. To deal with that situation, put the customization inside a conditional that tests whether the function or facility is available, like this:

```
(if (fboundp 'blink-cursor-mode)
    (blink-cursor-mode 0))
```

```
(if (boundp 'coding-category-utf-8)
    (set-coding-priority '(coding-category-utf-8)))
```

You can also simply disregard the errors that occur if the function is not defined.

```
(condition case ()
    (set-face-background 'region "grey75")
  (error nil))
```

A `setq` on a variable which does not exist is generally harmless, so those do not need a conditional.

32.6.3 Terminal-specific Initialization

Each terminal type can have a Lisp library to be loaded into Emacs when it is run on that type of terminal. For a terminal type named *termtype*, the library is called 'term/*termtype*' and it is found by searching the directories `load-path` as usual and trying the suffixes '.elc' and '.el'. Normally it appears in the subdirectory 'term' of the directory where most Emacs libraries are kept.

The usual purpose of the terminal-specific library is to map the escape sequences used by the terminal's function keys onto more meaningful names, using `function-key-map`. See the file 'term/lk201.el' for an example of how this is done. Many function keys are mapped automatically according to the information in the Termcap data base; the terminal-specific library needs to map only the function keys that Termcap does not specify.

When the terminal type contains a hyphen, only the part of the name before the first hyphen is significant in choosing the library name. Thus, terminal types 'aaa-48' and 'aaa-30-rv' both use the library 'term/aaa'. The code in the library can use (getenv "TERM") to find the full terminal type name.

The library's name is constructed by concatenating the value of the variable term-file-prefix and the terminal type. Your '.emacs' file can prevent the loading of the terminal-specific library by setting term-file-prefix to nil.

Emacs runs the hook term-setup-hook at the end of initialization, after both your '.emacs' file and any terminal-specific library have been read in. Add hook functions to this hook if you wish to override part of any of the terminal-specific libraries and to define initializations for terminals that do not have a library. See Section 32.3.2 [Hooks], page 418.

32.6.4 How Emacs Finds Your Init File

Normally Emacs uses the environment variable HOME (see Section C.5.1 [General Variables], page 476) to find '.emacs'; that's what '~' means in a file name. If '.emacs' is not found inside '~/' (nor '.emacs.el'), Emacs looks for '~/.emacs.d/init.el' (which, like '~/.emacs.el', can be byte-compiled).

However, if you run Emacs from a shell started by su, Emacs tries to find your own '.emacs', not that of the user you are currently pretending to be. The idea is that you should get your own editor customizations even if you are running as the super user.

More precisely, Emacs first determines which user's init file to use. It gets your user name from the environment variables LOGNAME and USER; if neither of those exists, it uses effective user-ID. If that user name matches the real user-ID, then Emacs uses HOME; otherwise, it looks up the home directory corresponding to that user name in the system's data base of users.

32.6.5 Non-ASCII Characters in Init Files

Language and coding systems may cause problems if your init file contains non-ASCII characters, such as accented letters, in strings or key bindings.

If you want to use non-ASCII characters in your init file, you should put a '-*-coding: *coding-system*-*-' tag on the first line of the init file, and specify a coding system that supports the character(s) in question. See Section 19.8 [Recognize Coding], page 195. This is because the defaults for decoding non-ASCII text might not yet be set up by the time Emacs reads those parts of your init file which use such strings, possibly leading Emacs to decode those strings incorrectly. You should then avoid adding Emacs Lisp code that modifies the coding system in other ways, such as calls to set-language-environment.

To bind non-ASCII keys, you must use a vector (see Section 32.4.6 [Init Rebinding], page 427). The string syntax cannot be used, since the non-ASCII characters will be interpreted as meta keys. For instance:

```
(global-set-key [?char] 'some-function)
```
Type C-q, followed by the key you want to bind, to insert *char*.

Warning: if you change the keyboard encoding, or change between multibyte and unibyte mode, or anything that would alter which code C-q would insert for that character, this keybinding may stop working. It is therefore advisable to use one and only one coding system, for your init file as well as the files you edit. For example, don't mix the 'latin-1' and 'latin-9' coding systems.

33 Dealing with Common Problems

If you type an Emacs command you did not intend, the results are often mysterious. This chapter tells what you can do to cancel your mistake or recover from a mysterious situation. Emacs bugs and system crashes are also considered.

33.1 Quitting and Aborting

`C-g`
`C-BREAK` (MS-DOS only)
>   Quit: cancel running or partially typed command.

`C-]`   Abort innermost recursive editing level and cancel the command which invoked it (`abort-recursive-edit`).

`ESC ESC ESC`
>   Either quit or abort, whichever makes sense (`keyboard-escape-quit`).

`M-x top-level`
>   Abort all recursive editing levels that are currently executing.

`C-x u`   Cancel a previously made change in the buffer contents (`undo`).

There are two ways of canceling a command before it has finished: *quitting* with `C-g`, and *aborting* with `C-]` or `M-x top-level`. Quitting cancels a partially typed command, or one which is still running. Aborting exits a recursive editing level and cancels the command that invoked the recursive edit. (See Section 31.13 [Recursive Edit], page 399.)

Quitting with `C-g` is the way to get rid of a partially typed command, or a numeric argument that you don't want. It also stops a running command in the middle in a relatively safe way, so you can use it if you accidentally give a command which takes a long time. In particular, it is safe to quit out of a kill command; either your text will *all* still be in the buffer, or it will *all* be in the kill ring, or maybe both. Quitting an incremental search does special things, documented under searching; it may take two successive `C-g` characters to get out of a search (see Section 12.1 [Incremental Search], page 86).

On MS-DOS, the character `C-BREAK` serves as a quit character like `C-g`. The reason is that it is not feasible, on MS-DOS, to recognize `C-g` while a command is running, between interactions with the user. By contrast, it *is* feasible to recognize `C-BREAK` at all times. See section "MS-DOS Keyboard" in *Specialized Emacs Features*.

`C-g` works by setting the variable `quit-flag` to `t` the instant `C-g` is typed; Emacs Lisp checks this variable frequently, and quits if it is non-`nil`. `C-g` is only actually executed as a command if you type it while Emacs is waiting for input. In that case, the command it runs is `keyboard-quit`.

On a text terminal, if you quit with `C-g` a second time before the first `C-g` is recognized, you activate the "emergency escape" feature and return to the shell. See Section 33.2.7 [Emergency Escape], page 444.

There are some situations where you cannot quit. When Emacs is waiting for the operating system to do something, quitting is impossible unless special pains are taken for the particular system call within Emacs where the waiting occurs. We have done this for the system calls that users are likely to want to quit from, but it's possible you will a case not handled. In one very common case—waiting for file input or output using NFS—Emacs itself knows how to quit, but many NFS implementations simply do not allow user programs to stop waiting for NFS when the NFS server is hung.

Aborting with C-] (abort-recursive-edit) is used to get out of a recursive editing level and cancel the command which invoked it. Quitting with C-g does not do this, and could not do this, because it is used to cancel a partially typed command *within* the recursive editing level. Both operations are useful. For example, if you are in a recursive edit and type C-u 8 to enter a numeric argument, you can cancel that argument with C-g and remain in the recursive edit.

The sequence ESC ESC ESC (keyboard-escape-quit) can either quit or abort. (We defined it this way because ESC means "get out" in many PC programs.) It can cancel a prefix argument, clear a selected region, or get out of a Query Replace, like C-g. It can get out of the minibuffer or a recursive edit, like C-]. It can also get out of splitting the frame into multiple windows, as with C-x 1. One thing it cannot do, however, is stop a command that is running. That's because it executes as an ordinary command, and Emacs doesn't notice it until it is ready for the next command.

The command M-x top-level is equivalent to "enough" C-] commands to get you out of all the levels of recursive edits that you are in. C-] gets you out one level at a time, but M-x top-level goes out all levels at once. Both C-] and M-x top-level are like all other commands, and unlike C g, in that they take effect only when Emacs is ready for a command. C-] is an ordinary key and has its meaning only because of its binding in the keymap. See Section 31.13 [Recursive Edit], page 399.

C-x u (undo) is not strictly speaking a way of canceling a command, but you can think of it as canceling a command that already finished executing. See Section 13.1 [Undo], page 105, for more information about the undo facility.

33.2 Dealing with Emacs Trouble

This section describes various conditions in which Emacs fails to work normally, and how to recognize them and correct them. For a list of additional problems you might encounter, see section "Bugs and problems" in *GNU Emacs FAQ*, and the file 'etc/PROBLEMS' in the Emacs distribution. Type C-h C-f to read the FAQ; type C-h C-e to read the 'PROBLEMS' file.

33.2.1 If DEL Fails to Delete

Every keyboard has a large key, a little ways above the RET or ENTER key, which you normally use outside Emacs to erase the last character that you typed. We call this key *the usual erasure key*. In Emacs, it is supposed to be equivalent to DEL, and when Emacs is properly configured for your terminal, it translates that key into the character DEL.

When Emacs starts up on a graphical display, it determines automatically which key should be DEL. In some unusual cases Emacs gets the wrong information from the system. If the usual erasure key deletes forwards instead of backwards, that is probably what happened—Emacs ought to be treating the DELETE key as DEL, but it isn't.

On a graphical display, if the usual erasure key is labeled BACKSPACE and there is a DELETE key elsewhere, but the DELETE key deletes backward instead of forward, that too suggests Emacs got the wrong information—but in the opposite sense. It ought to be treating the BACKSPACE key as DEL, and treating DELETE differently, but it isn't.

On a text-only terminal, if you find the usual erasure key prompts for a Help command, like `Control-h`, instead of deleting a character, it means that key is actually sending the BS character. Emacs ought to be treating BS as DEL, but it isn't.

In all of those cases, the immediate remedy is the same: use the command `M-x normal-erase-is-backspace-mode`. This toggles between the two modes that Emacs supports for handling DEL, so if Emacs starts in the wrong mode, this should switch to the right mode. On a text-only terminal, if you want to ask for help when BS is treated as DEL, use F1; `C-?` may also work, if it sends character code 127.

To fix the problem automatically for every Emacs session, you can put one of the following lines into your '.emacs' file (see Section 32.6 [Init File], page 433). For the first case above, where DELETE deletes forwards instead of backwards, use this line to make DELETE act as DEL (resulting in behavior compatible with Emacs 20 and previous versions):

```
(normal-erase-is-backspace-mode 0)
```

For the other two cases, where BACKSPACE ought to act as DEL, use this line:

```
(normal-erase-is-backspace-mode 1)
```

Another way to fix the problem for every Emacs session is to customize the variable `normal-erase-is-backspace`: the value `t` specifies the mode where BS or BACKSPACE is DEL, and `nil` specifies the other mode. See Section 32.2 [Easy Customization], page 408.

On a graphical display, it can also happen that the usual erasure key is labeled BACKSPACE, there is a DELETE key elsewhere, and both keys delete forward. This probably means that someone has redefined your BACKSPACE key as a DELETE key. With X, this is typically done with a command to the `xmodmap` program when you start the server or log in. The most likely motive for this customization was to support old versions of Emacs, so we recommend you simply remove it now.

33.2.2 Recursive Editing Levels

Recursive editing levels are important and useful features of Emacs, but they can seem like malfunctions if you do not understand them.

If the mode line has square brackets '[...]' around the parentheses that contain the names of the major and minor modes, you have entered a recursive editing level. If you did not do this on purpose, or if you don't understand what that means, you should just get out of the recursive editing level. To do so, type M-x top-level. This is called getting back to top level. See Section 31.13 [Recursive Edit], page 399.

33.2.3 Garbage on the Screen

If the text on a text terminal looks wrong, the first thing to do is see whether it is wrong in the buffer. Type C-l to redisplay the entire screen. If the screen appears correct after this, the problem was entirely in the previous screen update. (Otherwise, see the following section.)

Display updating problems often result from an incorrect terminfo entry for the terminal you are using. The file 'etc/TERMS' in the Emacs distribution gives the fixes for known problems of this sort. 'INSTALL' contains general advice for these problems in one of its sections. To investigate the possibility that you have this sort of problem, try Emacs on another terminal made by a different manufacturer. If problems happen frequently on one kind of terminal but not another kind, it is likely to be a bad terminfo entry, though it could also be due to a bug in Emacs that appears for terminals that have or that lack specific features.

33.2.4 Garbage in the Text

If C-l shows that the text is wrong, first type C-h l to see what commands you typed to produce the observed results. Then try undoing the changes step by step using C-x u, until it gets back to a state you consider correct.

If a large portion of text appears to be missing at the beginning or end of the buffer, check for the word 'Narrow' in the mode line. If it appears, the text you don't see is probably still present, but temporarily off-limits. To make it accessible again, type C-x n w. See Section 31.9 [Narrowing], page 396.

33.2.5 Running out of Memory

If you get the error message 'Virtual memory exceeded', save your modified buffers with C-x s. This method of saving them has the smallest need for additional memory. Emacs keeps a reserve of memory which it makes available when this error happens; that should be enough to enable C-x s to complete its work. When the reserve has been used, '!MEM FULL!' appears at the beginning of the mode line, indicating there is no more reserve.

Once you have saved your modified buffers, you can exit this Emacs session and start another, or you can use M-x kill-some-buffers to free space in the current Emacs job. If this frees up sufficient space, Emacs will refill its memory reserve, and '!MEM FULL!' will disappear from the mode line. That means you can safely go on editing in the same Emacs session.

Do not use M-x buffer-menu to save or kill buffers when you run out of memory, because the buffer menu needs a fair amount of memory itself, and the reserve supply may not be enough.

33.2.6 Recovery After a Crash

If Emacs or the computer crashes, you can recover the files you were editing at the time of the crash from their auto-save files. To do this, start Emacs again and type the command M-x recover-session.

This command initially displays a buffer which lists interrupted session files, each with its date. You must choose which session to recover from. Typically the one you want is the most recent one. Move point to the one you choose, and type C-c C-c.

Then recover-session considers each of the files that you were editing during that session; for each such file, it asks whether to recover that file. If you answer y for a file, it shows the dates of that file and its auto-save file, then asks once again whether to recover that file. For the second question, you must confirm with yes. If you do, Emacs visits the file but gets the text from the auto-save file.

When recover-session is done, the files you've chosen to recover are present in Emacs buffers. You should then save them. Only this—saving them—updates the files themselves.

As a last resort, if you had buffers with content which were not associated with any files, or if the autosave was not recent enough to have recorded important changes, you can use the 'etc/emacs-buffer.gdb' script with GDB (the GNU Debugger) to retrieve them from a core dump–provided that a core dump was saved, and that the Emacs executable was not stripped of its debugging symbols.

As soon as you get the core dump, rename it to another name such as 'core.emacs', so that another crash won't overwrite it.

To use this script, run gdb with the file name of your Emacs executable and the file name of the core dump, e.g. 'gdb /usr/bin/emacs core.emacs'. At the (gdb) prompt, load the recovery script: 'source /usr/src/emacs/etc/emacs-buffer.gdb'. Then type the command ybuffer-list to see which buffers are available. For each buffer, it lists a buffer number. To save a buffer, use ysave-buffer; you specify the buffer number, and the file name to write that buffer into. You should use a file name which does not already exist; if the file does exist, the script does not make a backup of its old contents.

33.2.7 Emergency Escape

On text-only terminals, the *emergency escape* feature suspends Emacs immediately if you type C-g a second time before Emacs can actually respond to the first one by quitting. This is so you can always get out of GNU Emacs no matter how badly it might be hung. When things are working properly, Emacs recognizes and handles the first C-g so fast that the second one won't trigger emergency escape. However, if some problem prevents Emacs from handling the first C-g properly, then the second one will get you back to the shell.

When you resume Emacs after a suspension caused by emergency escape, it asks two questions before going back to what it had been doing:

```
Auto-save? (y or n)
Abort (and dump core)? (y or n)
```

Answer each one with y or n followed by RET.

Saying y to 'Auto-save?' causes immediate auto-saving of all modified buffers in which auto-saving is enabled. Saying n skips this.

Saying y to 'Abort (and dump core)?' causes Emacs to crash, dumping core. This is to enable a wizard to figure out why Emacs was failing to quit in the first place. Execution does not continue after a core dump.

If you answer this question n, Emacs execution resumes. With luck, Emacs will ultimately do the requested quit. If not, each subsequent C-g invokes emergency escape again.

If Emacs is not really hung, just slow, you may invoke the double C-g feature without really meaning to. Then just resume and answer n to both questions, and you will get back to the former state. The quit you requested will happen by and by.

Emergency escape is active only for text terminals. On graphical displays, you can use the mouse to kill Emacs or switch to another program.

On MS-DOS, you must type C-BREAK (twice) to cause emergency escape—but there are cases where it won't work, when system call hangs or when Emacs is stuck in a tight loop in C code.

33.2.8 Help for Total Frustration

If using Emacs (or something else) becomes terribly frustrating and none of the techniques described above solve the problem, Emacs can still help you.

First, if the Emacs you are using is not responding to commands, type C-g C-g to get out of it and then start a new one.

Second, type M-x doctor RET.

The Emacs psychotherapist will help you feel better. Each time you say something to the psychotherapist, you must end it by typing RET RET. This indicates you are finished typing.

33.3 Reporting Bugs

Sometimes you will encounter a bug in Emacs. Although we cannot promise we can or will fix the bug, and we might not even agree that it is a bug, we want to hear about problems you encounter. Often we agree they are bugs and want to fix them.

To make it possible for us to fix a bug, you must report it. In order to do so effectively, you must know when and how to do it.

Before reporting a bug, it is a good idea to see if it is already known. You can find the list of known problems in the file 'etc/PROBLEMS' in the Emacs distribution; type C-h C-e to read it. Some additional user-level problems can be found in section "Bugs and problems" in *GNU Emacs FAQ*. Looking up your problem in these two documents might provide you with a solution or a work-around, or give you additional information about related issues.

33.3.1 When Is There a Bug

If Emacs accesses an invalid memory location ("segmentation fault"), or exits with an operating system error message that indicates a problem in the program (as opposed to something like "disk full"), then it is certainly a bug.

If Emacs updates the display in a way that does not correspond to what is in the buffer, then it is certainly a bug. If a command seems to do the wrong thing but the problem corrects itself if you type C-l, it is a case of incorrect display updating.

Taking forever to complete a command can be a bug, but you must make certain that it was really Emacs's fault. Some commands simply take a long time. Type C-g (C-BREAK on MS-DOS) and then C-h l to see whether the input Emacs received was what you intended to type; if the input was such that you *know* it should have been processed quickly, report a bug. If you don't know whether the command should take a long time, find out by looking in the manual or by asking for assistance.

If a command you are familiar with causes an Emacs error message in a case where its usual definition ought to be reasonable, it is probably a bug.

If a command does the wrong thing, that is a bug. But be sure you know for certain what it ought to have done. If you aren't familiar with the command, or don't know for certain how the command is supposed to work, then it might actually be working right. Rather than jumping to conclusions, show the problem to someone who knows for certain.

Finally, a command's intended definition may not be the best possible definition for editing with. This is a very important sort of problem, but it is also a matter of judgment. Also, it is easy to come to such a conclusion out of ignorance of some of the existing features. It is probably best not to complain about such a problem until you have checked the documentation in the usual ways, feel confident that you understand it, and know for certain that what you want is not available. Ask other Emacs users, too. If you are not sure what the command is supposed to do after a careful reading of the manual, check the index and glossary for any terms that may be unclear.

If after careful rereading of the manual you still do not understand what the command should do, that indicates a bug in the manual, which you should report. The manual's job is to make everything clear to people who are not Emacs experts— including you. It is just as important to report documentation bugs as program bugs.

If the on-line documentation string of a function or variable disagrees with the manual, one of them must be wrong; that is a bug.

33.3.2 Understanding Bug Reporting

When you decide that there is a bug, it is important to report it and to report it in a way which is useful. What is most useful is an exact description of what commands you type, starting with the shell command to run Emacs, until the problem happens.

The most important principle in reporting a bug is to report *facts*. Hypotheses and verbal descriptions are no substitute for the detailed raw data. Reporting the facts is straightforward, but many people strain to posit explanations and report them instead of the facts. If the explanations are based on guesses about how Emacs is implemented, they will be useless; meanwhile, lacking the facts, we will have no real information about the bug.

For example, suppose that you type `C-x C-f /glorp/baz.ugh RET`, visiting a file which (you know) happens to be rather large, and Emacs displays 'I feel pretty today'. The best way to report the bug is with a sentence like the preceding one, because it gives all the facts.

A bad way would be to assume that the problem is due to the size of the file and say, "I visited a large file, and Emacs displayed 'I feel pretty today'." This is what we mean by "guessing explanations." The problem is just as likely to be due to the fact that there is a 'z' in the file name. If this is so, then when we got your report, we would try out the problem with some "large file," probably with no 'z' in its name, and not see any problem. There is no way in the world that we could guess that we should try visiting a file with a 'z' in its name.

Alternatively, the problem might be due to the fact that the file starts with exactly 25 spaces. For this reason, you should make sure that you inform us of the exact contents of any file that is needed to reproduce the bug. What if the problem only occurs when you have typed the `C-x C-a` command previously? This is why we ask you to give the exact sequence of characters you typed since starting the Emacs session.

You should not even say "visit a file" instead of `C-x C-f` unless you *know* that it makes no difference which visiting command is used. Similarly, rather than saying "if I have three characters on the line," say "after I type `RET A B C RET C-p`," if that is the way you entered the text.

So please don't guess any explanations when you report a bug. If you want to actually *debug* the problem, and report explanations that are more than guesses, that is useful—but please include the facts as well.

33.3.3 Checklist for Bug Reports

The best way to send a bug report is to mail it electronically to the Emacs maintainers at `bug-gnu-emacs@gnu.org`, or to `emacs-pretest-bug@gnu.org` if you are pretesting an Emacs beta release. (If you want to suggest a change as an improvement, use the same address.)

If you'd like to read the bug reports, you can find them on the newsgroup 'gnu.emacs.bug'; keep in mind, however, that as a spectator you should not criticize anything about what you see there. The purpose of bug reports is to give information to the Emacs maintainers. Spectators are welcome only as long as they do not interfere with this. In particular, some bug reports contain fairly large amounts of data; spectators should not complain about this.

Please do not post bug reports using netnews; mail is more reliable than netnews about reporting your correct address, which we may need in order to ask you for more information. If your data is more than 500,000 bytes, please don't include it directly in the bug report; instead, offer to send it on request, or make it available by ftp and say where.

A convenient way to send a bug report for Emacs is to use the command M-x report-emacs-bug. This sets up a mail buffer (see Chapter 27 [Sending Mail], page 310) and automatically inserts *some* of the essential information. However, it cannot supply all the necessary information; you should still read and follow the guidelines below, so you can enter the other crucial information by hand before you send the message.

To enable maintainers to investigate a bug, your report should include all these things:

- The version number of Emacs. Without this, we won't know whether there is any point in looking for the bug in the current version of GNU Emacs.

  You can get the version number by typing M-x emacs-version RET. If that command does not work, you probably have something other than GNU Emacs, so you will have to report the bug somewhere else.

- The type of machine you are using, and the operating system name and version number. M-x emacs-version RET provides this information too. Copy its output from the '*Messages*' buffer, so that you get it all and get it accurately.

- The operands given to the configure command when Emacs was installed.

- A complete list of any modifications you have made to the Emacs source. (We may not have time to investigate the bug unless it happens in an unmodified Emacs. But if you've made modifications and you don't tell us, you are sending us on a wild goose chase.)

  Be precise about these changes. A description in English is not enough—send a context diff for them.

  Adding files of your own, or porting to another machine, is a modification of the source.

- Details of any other deviations from the standard procedure for installing GNU Emacs.

- The complete text of any files needed to reproduce the bug.

  If you can tell us a way to cause the problem without visiting any files, please do so. This makes it much easier to debug. If you do need files, make sure you arrange for us to see their exact contents. For example, it can matter whether there are spaces at the ends of lines, or a newline after the last line in the buffer (nothing ought to care whether the last line is terminated, but try telling the bugs that).

- The precise commands we need to type to reproduce the bug.

  The easy way to record the input to Emacs precisely is to write a dribble file. To start the file, execute the Lisp expression

      (open-dribble-file "~/dribble")

  using M-: or from the '*scratch*' buffer just after starting Emacs. From then on, Emacs copies all your input to the specified dribble file until the Emacs process is killed.

- For possible display bugs, the terminal type (the value of environment variable TERM), the complete termcap entry for the terminal from '/etc/termcap' (since that file is not identical on all machines), and the output that Emacs actually sent to the terminal.

The way to collect the terminal output is to execute the Lisp expression

```
(open-termscript "~/termscript")
```

using M-: or from the '*scratch*' buffer just after starting Emacs. From then on, Emacs copies all terminal output to the specified termscript file as well, until the Emacs process is killed. If the problem happens when Emacs starts up, put this expression into your '.emacs' file so that the termscript file will be open when Emacs displays the screen for the first time.

Be warned: it is often difficult, and sometimes impossible, to fix a terminal-dependent bug without access to a terminal of the type that stimulates the bug.

- If non-ASCII text or internationalization is relevant, the locale that was current when you started Emacs. On GNU/Linux and Unix systems, or if you use a Posix-style shell such as Bash, you can use this shell command to view the relevant values:

```
echo LC_ALL=$LC_ALL LC_COLLATE=$LC_COLLATE LC_CTYPE=$LC_CTYPE \
     LC_MESSAGES=$LC_MESSAGES LC_TIME=$LC_TIME LANG=$LANG
```

Alternatively, use the `locale` command, if your system has it, to display your locale settings.

You can use the M-! command to execute these commands from Emacs, and then copy the output from the '*Messages*' buffer into the bug report. Alternatively, M-x getenv RET LC_ALL RET will display the value of LC_ALL in the echo area, and you can copy its output from the '*Messages*' buffer.

- A description of what behavior you observe that you believe is incorrect. For example, "The Emacs process gets a fatal signal," or, "The resulting text is as follows, which I think is wrong."

Of course, if the bug is that Emacs gets a fatal signal, then one can't miss it. But if the bug is incorrect text, the maintainer might fail to notice what is wrong. Why leave it to chance?

Even if the problem you experience is a fatal signal, you should still say so explicitly. Suppose something strange is going on, such as, your copy of the source is out of sync, or you have encountered a bug in the C library on your system. (This has happened!) Your copy might crash and the copy here might not. If you *said* to expect a crash, then when Emacs here fails to crash, we would know that the bug was not happening. If you don't say to expect a crash, then we would not know whether the bug was happening—we would not be able to draw any conclusion from our observations.

- If the bug is that the Emacs Manual or the Emacs Lisp Reference Manual fails to describe the actual behavior of Emacs, or that the text is confusing, copy in the text from the online manual which you think is at fault. If the section is small, just the section name is enough.

- If the manifestation of the bug is an Emacs error message, it is important to report the precise text of the error message, and a backtrace showing how the Lisp program in Emacs arrived at the error.

  To get the error message text accurately, copy it from the '*Messages*' buffer into the bug report. Copy all of it, not just part.

  To make a backtrace for the error, use M-x toggle-debug-on-error before the error happens (that is to say, you must give that command and then make the bug happen). This causes the error to start the Lisp debugger, which shows you a backtrace. Copy the text of the debugger's backtrace into the bug report. See section "The Lisp Debugger" in *the Emacs Lisp Reference Manual*, for information on debugging Emacs Lisp programs with the Edebug package.

  This use of the debugger is possible only if you know how to make the bug happen again. If you can't make it happen again, at least copy the whole error message.

- Check whether any programs you have loaded into the Lisp world, including your '.emacs' file, set any variables that may affect the functioning of Emacs. Also, see whether the problem happens in a freshly started Emacs without loading your '.emacs' file (start Emacs with the -q switch to prevent loading the init file). If the problem does *not* occur then, you must report the precise contents of any programs that you must load into the Lisp world in order to cause the problem to occur.

- If the problem does depend on an init file or other Lisp programs that are not part of the standard Emacs system, then you should make sure it is not a bug in those programs by complaining to their maintainers first. After they verify that they are using Emacs in a way that is supposed to work, they should report the bug.

- If you wish to mention something in the GNU Emacs source, show the line of code with a few lines of context. Don't just give a line number.

  The line numbers in the development sources don't match those in your sources. It would take extra work for the maintainers to determine what code is in your version at a given line number, and we could not be certain.

- Additional information from a C debugger such as GDB might enable someone to find a problem on a machine which he does not have available. If you don't know how to use GDB, please read the GDB manual—it is not very long, and using GDB is easy. You can find the GDB distribution, including the GDB manual in online form, in most of the same places you can find the Emacs distribution. To run Emacs under GDB, you should switch to the 'src' subdirectory in which Emacs was compiled, then do 'gdb emacs'. It is important for the directory 'src' to be current so that GDB will read the '.gdbinit' file in this directory.

  However, you need to think when you collect the additional information if you want it to show what causes the bug.

  For example, many people send just a backtrace, but that is not very useful by itself. A simple backtrace with arguments often conveys little about what is happening inside GNU Emacs, because most of the arguments listed in the backtrace are pointers to Lisp objects. The numeric values of these pointers have no significance whatever; all that matters is the contents of the objects they point to (and most of the contents are themselves pointers).

To provide useful information, you need to show the values of Lisp objects in Lisp notation. Do this for each variable which is a Lisp object, in several stack frames near the bottom of the stack. Look at the source to see which variables are Lisp objects, because the debugger thinks of them as integers.

To show a variable's value in Lisp syntax, first print its value, then use the user-defined GDB command `pr` to print the Lisp object in Lisp syntax. (If you must use another debugger, call the function `dobug_print` with the object as an argument.) The `pr` command is defined by the file '.gdbinit', and it works only if you are debugging a running process (not with a core dump).

To make Lisp errors stop Emacs and return to GDB, put a breakpoint at `Fsignal`.

For a short listing of Lisp functions running, type the GDB command `xbacktrace`.

The file '.gdbinit' defines several other commands that are useful for examining the data types and contents of Lisp objects. Their names begin with 'x'. These commands work at a lower level than `pr`, and are less convenient, but they may work even when `pr` does not, such as when debugging a core dump or when Emacs has had a fatal signal.

More detailed advice and other useful techniques for debugging Emacs are available in the file 'etc/DEBUG' in the Emacs distribution. That file also includes instructions for investigating problems whereby Emacs stops responding (many people assume that Emacs is "hung," whereas in fact it might be in an infinite loop)

To find the file 'etc/DEBUG' in your Emacs installation, use the directory name stored in the variable `data-directory`.

Here are some things that are not necessary in a bug report:

- A description of the envelope of the bug—this is not necessary for a reproducible bug.

  Often people who encounter a bug spend a lot of time investigating which changes to the input file will make the bug go away and which changes will not affect it.

  This is often time-consuming and not very useful, because the way we will find the bug is by running a single example under the debugger with breakpoints, not by pure deduction from a series of examples. You might as well save time by not searching for additional examples. It is better to send the bug report right away, go back to editing, and find another bug to report.

  Of course, if you can find a simpler example to report *instead* of the original one, that is a convenience. Errors in the output will be easier to spot, running under the debugger will take less time, etc.

However, simplification is not vital; if you can't do this or don't have time to try, please report the bug with your original test case.

- A core dump file.

  Debugging the core dump might be useful, but it can only be done on your machine, with your Emacs executable. Therefore, sending the core dump file to the Emacs maintainers won't be useful. Above all, don't include the core file in an email bug report! Such a large message can be extremely inconvenient.

- A system-call trace of Emacs execution.

  System-call traces are very useful for certain special kinds of debugging, but in most cases they give little useful information. It is therefore strange that many people seem to think that *the* way to report information about a crash is to send a system-call trace. Perhaps this is a habit formed from experience debugging programs that don't have source code or debugging symbols.

  In most programs, a backtrace is normally far, far more informative than a system-call trace. Even in Emacs, a simple backtrace is generally more informative, though to give full information you should supplement the backtrace by displaying variable values and printing them as Lisp objects with **pr** (see above).

- A patch for the bug.

  A patch for the bug is useful if it is a good one. But don't omit the other information that a bug report needs, such as the test case, on the assumption that a patch is sufficient. We might see problems with your patch and decide to fix the problem another way, or we might not understand it at all. And if we can't understand what bug you are trying to fix, or why your patch should be an improvement, we mustn't install it.

- A guess about what the bug is or what it depends on.

  Such guesses are usually wrong. Even experts can't guess right about such things without first using the debugger to find the facts.

33.3.4 Sending Patches for GNU Emacs

If you would like to write bug fixes or improvements for GNU Emacs, that is very helpful. When you send your changes, please follow these guidelines to make it easy for the maintainers to use them. If you don't follow these guidelines, your information might still be useful, but using it will take extra work. Maintaining GNU Emacs is a lot of work in the best of circumstances, and we can't keep up unless you do your best to help.

- Send an explanation with your changes of what problem they fix or what improvement they bring about. For a bug fix, just include a copy of the bug report, and explain why the change fixes the bug.

  (Referring to a bug report is not as good as including it, because then we will have to look it up, and we have probably already deleted it if we've already fixed the bug.)

- Always include a proper bug report for the problem you think you have fixed. We need to convince ourselves that the change is right before installing it. Even if it is correct, we might have trouble understanding it if we don't have a way to reproduce the problem.

- Include all the comments that are appropriate to help people reading the source in the future understand why this change was needed.

- Don't mix together changes made for different reasons. Send them *individually*.

  If you make two changes for separate reasons, then we might not want to install them both. We might want to install just one. If you send them all jumbled together in a single set of diffs, we have to do extra work to disentangle them— to figure out which parts of the change serve which purpose. If we don't have time for this, we might have to ignore your changes entirely.

  If you send each change as soon as you have written it, with its own explanation, then two changes never get tangled up, and we can consider each one properly without any extra work to disentangle them.

- Send each change as soon as that change is finished. Sometimes people think they are helping us by accumulating many changes to send them all together. As explained above, this is absolutely the worst thing you could do.

  Since you should send each change separately, you might as well send it right away. That gives us the option of installing it immediately if it is important.

- Use 'diff -c' to make your diffs. Diffs without context are hard to install reliably. More than that, they are hard to study; we must always study a patch to decide whether we want to install it. Unidiff format is better than contextless diffs, but not as easy to read as '-c' format.

  If you have GNU diff, use 'diff -c -F'^[_a-zA-Z0-9$]+ *('' when making diffs of C code. This shows the name of the function that each change occurs in.

- Avoid any ambiguity as to which is the old version and which is the new. Please make the old version the first argument to diff, and the new version the second argument. And please give one version or the other a name that indicates whether it is the old version or your new changed one.

- Write the change log entries for your changes. This is both to save us the extra work of writing them, and to help explain your changes so we can understand them.

  The purpose of the change log is to show people where to find what was changed. So you need to be specific about what functions you changed; in large functions, it's often helpful to indicate where within the function the change was.

  On the other hand, once you have shown people where to find the change, you need not explain its purpose in the change log. Thus, if you add a new function, all you need to say about it is that it is new. If you feel that the purpose needs explaining, it probably does—but put the explanation in comments in the code. It will be more useful there.

Please read the 'ChangeLog' files in the 'src' and 'lisp' directories to see what sorts of information to put in, and to learn the style that we use. See Section 25.1 [Change Log], page 292.

- When you write the fix, keep in mind that we can't install a change that would break other systems. Please think about what effect your change will have if compiled on another type of system.

Sometimes people send fixes that *might* be an improvement in general—but it is hard to be sure of this. It's hard to install such changes because we have to study them very carefully. Of course, a good explanation of the reasoning by which you concluded the change was correct can help convince us.

The safest changes are changes to the configuration files for a particular machine. These are safe because they can't create new bugs on other machines.

Please help us keep up with the workload by designing the patch in a form that is clearly safe to install.

33.4 Contributing to Emacs Development

If you would like to help pretest Emacs releases to assure they work well, or if you would like to work on improving Emacs, please contact the maintainers at emacs-devel@gnu.org. A pretester should be prepared to investigate bugs as well as report them. If you'd like to work on improving Emacs, please ask for suggested projects or suggest your own ideas.

If you have already written an improvement, please tell us about it. If you have not yet started work, it is useful to contact emacs-devel@gnu.org before you start; it might be possible to suggest ways to make your extension fit in better with the rest of Emacs.

The development version of Emacs can be downloaded from the CVS repository where it is actively maintained by a group of developers. See the Emacs project page http://savannah.gnu.org/projects/emacs/ for details.

33.5 How To Get Help with GNU Emacs

If you need help installing, using or changing GNU Emacs, there are two ways to find it:

- Send a message to the mailing list help-gnu-emacs@gnu.org, or post your request on newsgroup gnu.emacs.help. (This mailing list and newsgroup interconnect, so it does not matter which one you use.)

- Look in the service directory for someone who might help you for a fee. The service directory is found in the file named 'etc/SERVICE' in the Emacs distribution.

Appendix A GNU GENERAL PUBLIC LICENSE

Version 2, June 1991

Copyright © 1989, 1991 Free Software Foundation, Inc.
51 Franklin Street, Fifth Floor, Boston, MA 02110-1301, USA

Everyone is permitted to copy and distribute verbatim copies
of this license document, but changing it is not allowed.

Preamble

The licenses for most software are designed to take away your freedom to share and change it. By contrast, the GNU General Public License is intended to guarantee your freedom to share and change free software—to make sure the software is free for all its users. This General Public License applies to most of the Free Software Foundation's software and to any other program whose authors commit to using it. (Some other Free Software Foundation software is covered by the GNU Lesser General Public License instead.) You can apply it to your programs, too.

When we speak of free software, we are referring to freedom, not price. Our General Public Licenses are designed to make sure that you have the freedom to distribute copies of free software (and charge for this service if you wish), that you receive source code or can get it if you want it, that you can change the software or use pieces of it in new free programs; and that you know you can do these things.

To protect your rights, we need to make restrictions that forbid anyone to deny you these rights or to ask you to surrender the rights. These restrictions translate to certain responsibilities for you if you distribute copies of the software, or if you modify it.

For example, if you distribute copies of such a program, whether gratis or for a fee, you must give the recipients all the rights that you have. You must make sure that they, too, receive or can get the source code. And you must show them these terms so they know their rights.

We protect your rights with two steps: (1) copyright the software, and (2) offer you this license which gives you legal permission to copy, distribute and/or modify the software.

Also, for each author's protection and ours, we want to make certain that everyone understands that there is no warranty for this free software. If the software is modified by someone else and passed on, we want its recipients to know that what they have is not the original, so that any problems introduced by others will not reflect on the original authors' reputations.

Finally, any free program is threatened constantly by software patents. We wish to avoid the danger that redistributors of a free program will individually obtain patent licenses, in effect making the program proprietary. To prevent this, we have made it clear that any patent must be licensed for everyone's free use or not licensed at all.

The precise terms and conditions for copying, distribution and modification follow.

TERMS AND CONDITIONS FOR COPYING, DISTRIBUTION AND MODIFICATION

0. This License applies to any program or other work which contains a notice placed by the copyright holder saying it may be distributed under the terms of this General Public License. The "Program," below, refers to any such program or work, and a "work based on the Program" means either the Program or any derivative work under copyright law: that is to say, a work containing the Program or a portion of it, either verbatim or with modifications and/or translated into another language. (Hereinafter, translation is included without limitation in the term "modification.") Each licensee is addressed as "you."

    Activities other than copying, distribution and modification are not covered by this License; they are outside its scope. The act of running the Program is not restricted, and the output from the Program is covered only if its contents constitute a work based on the Program (independent of having been made by running the Program). Whether that is true depends on what the Program does.

1. You may copy and distribute verbatim copies of the Program's source code as you receive it, in any medium, provided that you conspicuously and appropriately publish on each copy an appropriate copyright notice and disclaimer of warranty; keep intact all the notices that refer to this License and to the absence of any warranty; and give any other recipients of the Program a copy of this License along with the Program.

    You may charge a fee for the physical act of transferring a copy, and you may at your option offer warranty protection in exchange for a fee.

2. You may modify your copy or copies of the Program or any portion of it, thus forming a work based on the Program, and copy and distribute such modifications or work under the terms of Section 1 above, provided that you also meet all of these conditions:

    a. You must cause the modified files to carry prominent notices stating that you changed the files and the date of any change.

    b. You must cause any work that you distribute or publish, that in whole or in part contains or is derived from the Program or any part thereof, to be licensed as a whole at no charge to all third parties under the terms of this License.

    c. If the modified program normally reads commands interactively when run, you must cause it, when started running for such interactive use in the most ordinary way, to print or display an announcement including an appropriate copyright notice and a notice that there is no warranty (or else, saying that you provide a warranty) and that users may redistribute the program under these conditions, and telling the user how to view a copy of this License. (Exception: if the Program itself is interactive but does not normally print such an announcement, your work based on the Program is not required to print an announcement.)

These requirements apply to the modified work as a whole. If identifiable sections of that work are not derived from the Program, and can be reasonably considered independent and separate works in themselves, then this License, and its terms, do not apply to those sections when you distribute them as separate works. But when you distribute the same sections as part of a whole which is a work based on the Program, the distribution of the whole must be on the terms of this License, whose permissions for other licensees extend to the entire whole, and thus to each and every part regardless of who wrote it.

Thus, it is not the intent of this section to claim rights or contest your rights to work written entirely by you; rather, the intent is to exercise the right to control the distribution of derivative or collective works based on the Program.

In addition, mere aggregation of another work not based on the Program with the Program (or with a work based on the Program) on a volume of a storage or distribution medium does not bring the other work under the scope of this License.

3. You may copy and distribute the Program (or a work based on it, under Section 2) in object code or executable form under the terms of Sections 1 and 2 above provided that you also do one of the following:

   a. Accompany it with the complete corresponding machine-readable source code, which must be distributed under the terms of Sections 1 and 2 above on a medium customarily used for software interchange; or,

   b. Accompany it with a written offer, valid for at least three years, to give any third party, for a charge no more than your cost of physically performing source distribution, a complete machine-readable copy of the corresponding source code, to be distributed under the terms of Sections 1 and 2 above on a medium customarily used for software interchange; or,

   c. Accompany it with the information you received as to the offer to distribute corresponding source code. (This alternative is allowed only for noncommercial distribution and only if you received the program in object code or executable form with such an offer, in accord with Subsection b above.)

The source code for a work means the preferred form of the work for making modifications to it. For an executable work, complete source code means all the source code for all modules it contains, plus any associated interface definition files, plus the scripts used to control compilation and installation of the executable. However, as a special exception, the source code distributed need not include anything that is normally distributed (in either source or binary form) with the major components (compiler, kernel, and so on) of the operating system on which the executable runs, unless that component itself accompanies the executable.

If distribution of executable or object code is made by offering access to copy from a designated place, then offering equivalent access to copy the source code from the same place counts as distribution of the source code, even though third parties are not compelled to copy the source along with the object code.

4. You may not copy, modify, sublicense, or distribute the Program except as expressly provided under this License. Any attempt otherwise to copy, modify, sublicense or distribute the Program is void, and will automatically terminate your rights under this License. However, parties who have received copies, or rights, from you under this License will not have their licenses terminated so long as such parties remain in full compliance.

5. You are not required to accept this License, since you have not signed it. However, nothing else grants you permission to modify or distribute the Program or its derivative works. These actions are prohibited by law if you do not accept this License. Therefore, by modifying or distributing the Program (or any work based on the Program), you indicate your acceptance of this License to do so, and all its terms and conditions for copying, distributing or modifying the Program or works based on it.

6. Each time you redistribute the Program (or any work based on the Program), the recipient automatically receives a license from the original licensor to copy, distribute or modify the Program subject to these terms and conditions. You may not impose any further restrictions on the recipients' exercise of the rights granted herein. You are not responsible for enforcing compliance by third parties to this License.

7. If, as a consequence of a court judgment or allegation of patent infringement or for any other reason (not limited to patent issues), conditions are imposed on you (whether by court order, agreement or otherwise) that contradict the conditions of this License, they do not excuse you from the conditions of this License. If you cannot distribute so as to satisfy simultaneously your obligations under this License and any other pertinent obligations, then as a consequence you may not distribute the Program at all. For example, if a patent license would not permit royalty-free redistribution of the Program by all those who receive copies directly or indirectly through you, then the only way you could satisfy both it and this License would be to refrain entirely from distribution of the Program.

If any portion of this section is held invalid or unenforceable under any particular circumstance, the balance of the section is intended to apply and the section as a whole is intended to apply in other circumstances.

It is not the purpose of this section to induce you to infringe any patents or other property right claims or to contest validity of any such claims; this section has the sole purpose of protecting the integrity of the free software distribution system, which is implemented by public license practices. Many people have made generous contributions to the wide range of software distributed through that system in reliance on consistent application of that system; it is up to the author/donor to decide if he or she is willing to distribute software through any other system and a licensee cannot impose that choice.

This section is intended to make thoroughly clear what is believed to be a consequence of the rest of this License.

8. If the distribution and/or use of the Program is restricted in certain countries either by patents or by copyrighted interfaces, the original copyright holder

who places the Program under this License may add an explicit geographical distribution limitation excluding those countries, so that distribution is permitted only in or among countries not thus excluded. In such case, this License incorporates the limitation as if written in the body of this License.

9. The Free Software Foundation may publish revised and/or new versions of the General Public License from time to time. Such new versions will be similar in spirit to the present version, but may differ in detail to address new problems or concerns.

   Each version is given a distinguishing version number. If the Program specifies a version number of this License which applies to it and "any later version," you have the option of following the terms and conditions either of that version or of any later version published by the Free Software Foundation. If the Program does not specify a version number of this License, you may choose any version ever published by the Free Software Foundation.

10. If you wish to incorporate parts of the Program into other free programs whose distribution conditions are different, write to the author to ask for permission. For software which is copyrighted by the Free Software Foundation, write to the Free Software Foundation; we sometimes make exceptions for this. Our decision will be guided by the two goals of preserving the free status of all derivatives of our free software and of promoting the sharing and reuse of software generally.

NO WARRANTY

11. BECAUSE THE PROGRAM IS LICENSED FREE OF CHARGE, THERE IS NO WARRANTY FOR THE PROGRAM, TO THE EXTENT PERMITTED BY APPLICABLE LAW. EXCEPT WHEN OTHERWISE STATED IN WRITING THE COPYRIGHT HOLDERS AND/OR OTHER PARTIES PROVIDE THE PROGRAM "AS IS" WITHOUT WARRANTY OF ANY KIND, EITHER EXPRESSED OR IMPLIED, INCLUDING, BUT NOT LIMITED TO, THE IMPLIED WARRANTIES OF MERCHANTABILITY AND FITNESS FOR A PARTICULAR PURPOSE. THE ENTIRE RISK AS TO THE QUALITY AND PERFORMANCE OF THE PROGRAM IS WITH YOU. SHOULD THE PROGRAM PROVE DEFECTIVE, YOU ASSUME THE COST OF ALL NECESSARY SERVICING, REPAIR OR CORRECTION.

12. IN NO EVENT UNLESS REQUIRED BY APPLICABLE LAW OR AGREED TO IN WRITING WILL ANY COPYRIGHT HOLDER, OR ANY OTHER PARTY WHO MAY MODIFY AND/OR REDISTRIBUTE THE PROGRAM AS PERMITTED ABOVE, BE LIABLE TO YOU FOR DAMAGES, INCLUDING ANY GENERAL, SPECIAL, INCIDENTAL OR CONSEQUENTIAL DAMAGES ARISING OUT OF THE USE OR INABILITY TO USE THE PROGRAM (INCLUDING BUT NOT LIMITED TO LOSS OF DATA OR DATA BEING RENDERED INACCURATE OR LOSSES SUSTAINED BY YOU OR THIRD PARTIES OR A FAILURE OF THE PROGRAM TO

OPERATE WITH ANY OTHER PROGRAMS), EVEN IF SUCH HOLDER OR OTHER PARTY HAS BEEN ADVISED OF THE POSSIBILITY OF SUCH DAMAGES.

END OF TERMS AND CONDITIONS

How to Apply These Terms to Your New Programs

If you develop a new program, and you want it to be of the greatest possible use to the public, the best way to achieve this is to make it free software which everyone can redistribute and change under these terms.

To do so, attach the following notices to the program. It is safest to attach them to the start of each source file to most effectively convey the exclusion of warranty; and each file should have at least the "copyright" line and a pointer to where the full notice is found.

```
one line to give the program's name and an idea of what it does.
Copyright (C) yyyy  name of author

This program is free software; you can redistribute it and/or
modify it under the terms of the GNU General Public License
as published by the Free Software Foundation; either version 2
of the License, or (at your option) any later version.

This program is distributed in the hope that it will be useful,
but WITHOUT ANY WARRANTY; without even the implied warranty of
MERCHANTABILITY or FITNESS FOR A PARTICULAR PURPOSE.  See the
GNU General Public License for more details.

You should have received a copy of the GNU General Public License along
with this program; if not, write to the Free Software Foundation, Inc.,
51 Franklin Street, Fifth Floor, Boston, MA  02110-1301, USA.
```

Also add information on how to contact you by electronic and paper mail.

If the program is interactive, make it output a short notice like this when it starts in an interactive mode:

```
Gnomovision version 69, Copyright (C) yyyy name of author
Gnomovision comes with ABSOLUTELY NO WARRANTY; for details
type 'show w'.  This is free software, and you are welcome
to redistribute it under certain conditions; type 'show c'
for details.
```

The hypothetical commands 'show w' and 'show c' should show the appropriate parts of the General Public License. Of course, the commands you use may be called something other than 'show w' and 'show c'; they could even be mouse-clicks or menu items—whatever suits your program.

You should also get your employer (if you work as a programmer) or your school, if any, to sign a "copyright disclaimer" for the program, if necessary. Here is a sample; alter the names:

```
Yoyodyne, Inc., hereby disclaims all copyright
interest in the program 'Gnomovision'
(which makes passes at compilers) written
by James Hacker.

signature of Ty Coon, 1 April 1989
Ty Coon, President of Vice
```

This General Public License does not permit incorporating your program into proprietary programs. If your program is a subroutine library, you may consider it more useful to permit linking proprietary applications with the library. If this is what you want to do, use the GNU Lesser General Public License instead of this License.

Appendix B GNU Free Documentation License

Version 1.2, November 2002

Copyright (C) 2000,2001,2002 Free Software Foundation, Inc.

51 Franklin Street, Fifth Floor, Boston, MA 02110-1301 USA

Everyone is permitted to copy and distribute verbatim copies
of this license document, but changing it is not allowed.

0. PREAMBLE

The purpose of this License is to make a manual, textbook, or other functional
and useful document "free" in the sense of freedom: to assure everyone the
effective freedom to copy and redistribute it, with or without modifying it,
either commercially or noncommercially. Secondarily, this License preserves
for the author and publisher a way to get credit for their work, while not being
considered responsible for modifications made by others.

This License is a kind of "copyleft," which means that derivative works of the
document must themselves be free in the same sense. It complements the GNU
General Public License, which is a copyleft license designed for free software.

We have designed this License in order to use it for manuals for free software,
because free software needs free documentation: a free program should come
with manuals providing the same freedoms that the software does. But this
License is not limited to software manuals; it can be used for any textual work,
regardless of subject matter or whether it is published as a printed book. We
recommend this License principally for works whose purpose is instruction or
reference.

1. APPLICABILITY AND DEFINITIONS

This License applies to any manual or other work, in any medium, that contains
a notice placed by the copyright holder saying it can be distributed under the
terms of this License. Such a notice grants a world-wide, royalty-free license,
unlimited in duration, to use that work under the conditions stated herein.
The "Document," below, refers to any such manual or work. Any member of
the public is a licensee, and is addressed as "you." You accept the license if
you copy, modify or distribute the work in a way requiring permission under
copyright law.

A "Modified Version" of the Document means any work containing the Document or a portion of it, either copied verbatim, or with modifications and/or
translated into another language.

A "Secondary Section" is a named appendix or a front-matter section of the
Document that deals exclusively with the relationship of the publishers or authors of the Document to the Document's overall subject (or to related matters) and contains nothing that could fall directly within that overall subject.
(Thus, if the Document is in part a textbook of mathematics, a Secondary Section may not explain any mathematics.) The relationship could be a matter

of historical connection with the subject or with related matters, or of legal, commercial, philosophical, ethical or political position regarding them.

The "Invariant Sections" are certain Secondary Sections whose titles are designated, as being those of Invariant Sections, in the notice that says that the Document is released under this License. If a section does not fit the above definition of Secondary then it is not allowed to be designated as Invariant. The Document may contain zero Invariant Sections. If the Document does not identify any Invariant Sections then there are none.

The "Cover Texts" are certain short passages of text that are listed, as Front-Cover Texts or Back-Cover Texts, in the notice that says that the Document is released under this License. A Front-Cover Text may be at most 5 words, and a Back-Cover Text may be at most 25 words.

A "Transparent" copy of the Document means a machine-readable copy, represented in a format whose specification is available to the general public, that is suitable for revising the document straightforwardly with generic text editors or (for images composed of pixels) generic paint programs or (for drawings) some widely available drawing editor, and that is suitable for input to text formatters or for automatic translation to a variety of formats suitable for input to text formatters. A copy made in an otherwise Transparent file format whose markup, or absence of markup, has been arranged to thwart or discourage subsequent modification by readers is not Transparent. An image format is not Transparent if used for any substantial amount of text. A copy that is not "Transparent" is called "Opaque."

Examples of suitable formats for Transparent copies include plain ASCII without markup, Texinfo input format, LaTeX input format, SGML or XML using a publicly available DTD, and standard-conforming simple HTML, PostScript or PDF designed for human modification. Examples of transparent image formats include PNG, XCF and JPG. Opaque formats include proprietary formats that can be read and edited only by proprietary word processors, SGML or XML for which the DTD and/or processing tools are not generally available, and the machine-generated HTML, PostScript or PDF produced by some word processors for output purposes only.

The "Title Page" means, for a printed book, the title page itself, plus such following pages as are needed to hold, legibly, the material this License requires to appear in the title page. For works in formats which do not have any title page as such, "Title Page" means the text near the most prominent appearance of the work's title, preceding the beginning of the body of the text.

A section "Entitled XYZ" means a named subunit of the Document whose title either is precisely XYZ or contains XYZ in parentheses following text that translates XYZ in another language. (Here XYZ stands for a specific section name mentioned below, such as "Acknowledgements," "Dedications," "Endorsements," or "History.") To "Preserve the Title" of such a section when you modify the Document means that it remains a section "Entitled XYZ" according to this definition.

The Document may include Warranty Disclaimers next to the notice which states that this License applies to the Document. These Warranty Disclaimers are considered to be included by reference in this License, but only as regards disclaiming warranties: any other implication that these Warranty Disclaimers may have is void and has no effect on the meaning of this License.

2. VERBATIM COPYING

You may copy and distribute the Document in any medium, either commercially or noncommercially, provided that this License, the copyright notices, and the license notice saying this License applies to the Document are reproduced in all copies, and that you add no other conditions whatsoever to those of this License. You may not use technical measures to obstruct or control the reading or further copying of the copies you make or distribute. However, you may accept compensation in exchange for copies. If you distribute a large enough number of copies you must also follow the conditions in section 3.

You may also lend copies, under the same conditions stated above, and you may publicly display copies.

3. COPYING IN QUANTITY

If you publish printed copies (or copies in media that commonly have printed covers) of the Document, numbering more than 100, and the Document's license notice requires Cover Texts, you must enclose the copies in covers that carry, clearly and legibly, all these Cover Texts: Front-Cover Texts on the front cover, and Back-Cover Texts on the back cover. Both covers must also clearly and legibly identify you as the publisher of these copies. The front cover must present the full title with all words of the title equally prominent and visible. You may add other material on the covers in addition. Copying with changes limited to the covers, as long as they preserve the title of the Document and satisfy these conditions, can be treated as verbatim copying in other respects.

If the required texts for either cover are too voluminous to fit legibly, you should put the first ones listed (as many as fit reasonably) on the actual cover, and continue the rest onto adjacent pages.

If you publish or distribute Opaque copies of the Document numbering more than 100, you must either include a machine-readable Transparent copy along with each Opaque copy, or state in or with each Opaque copy a computer-network location from which the general network-using public has access to download using public-standard network protocols a complete Transparent copy of the Document, free of added material. If you use the latter option, you must take reasonably prudent steps, when you begin distribution of Opaque copies in quantity, to ensure that this Transparent copy will remain thus accessible at the stated location until at least one year after the last time you distribute an Opaque copy (directly or through your agents or retailers) of that edition to the public.

It is requested, but not required, that you contact the authors of the Document well before redistributing any large number of copies, to give them a chance to provide you with an updated version of the Document.

4. MODIFICATIONS

You may copy and distribute a Modified Version of the Document under the conditions of sections 2 and 3 above, provided that you release the Modified Version under precisely this License, with the Modified Version filling the role of the Document, thus licensing distribution and modification of the Modified Version to whoever possesses a copy of it. In addition, you must do these things in the Modified Version:

A. Use in the Title Page (and on the covers, if any) a title distinct from that of the Document, and from those of previous versions (which should, if there were any, be listed in the History section of the Document). You may use the same title as a previous version if the original publisher of that version gives permission.

B. List on the Title Page, as authors, one or more persons or entities responsible for authorship of the modifications in the Modified Version, together with at least five of the principal authors of the Document (all of its principal authors, if it has fewer than five), unless they release you from this requirement.

C. State on the Title page the name of the publisher of the Modified Version, as the publisher.

D. Preserve all the copyright notices of the Document.

E. Add an appropriate copyright notice for your modifications adjacent to the other copyright notices.

F. Include, immediately after the copyright notices, a license notice giving the public permission to use the Modified Version under the terms of this License, in the form shown in the Addendum below.

G. Preserve in that license notice the full lists of Invariant Sections and required Cover Texts given in the Document's license notice.

H. Include an unaltered copy of this License.

I. Preserve the section Entitled "History," Preserve its Title, and add to it an item stating at least the title, year, new authors, and publisher of the Modified Version as given on the Title Page. If there is no section Entitled "History" in the Document, create one stating the title, year, authors, and publisher of the Document as given on its Title Page, then add an item describing the Modified Version as stated in the previous sentence.

J. Preserve the network location, if any, given in the Document for public access to a Transparent copy of the Document, and likewise the network locations given in the Document for previous versions it was based on. These may be placed in the "History" section. You may omit a network location for a work that was published at least four years before the Document itself, or if the original publisher of the version it refers to gives permission.

K. For any section Entitled "Acknowledgements" or "Dedications," Preserve the Title of the section, and preserve in the section all the substance and tone of each of the contributor acknowledgements and/or dedications given therein.

L. Preserve all the Invariant Sections of the Document, unaltered in their text and in their titles. Section numbers or the equivalent are not considered part of the section titles.

M. Delete any section Entitled "Endorsements." Such a section may not be included in the Modified Version.

N. Do not retitle any existing section to be Entitled "Endorsements" or to conflict in title with any Invariant Section.

O. Preserve any Warranty Disclaimers.

If the Modified Version includes new front-matter sections or appendices that qualify as Secondary Sections and contain no material copied from the Document, you may at your option designate some or all of these sections as Invariant. To do this, add their titles to the list of Invariant Sections in the Modified Version's license notice. These titles must be distinct from any other section titles.

You may add a section Entitled "Endorsements," provided it contains nothing but endorsements of your Modified Version by various parties–for example, statements of peer review or that the text has been approved by an organization as the authoritative definition of a standard.

You may add a passage of up to five words as a Front-Cover Text, and a passage of up to 25 words as a Back-Cover Text, to the end of the list of Cover Texts in the Modified Version. Only one passage of Front-Cover Text and one of Back-Cover Text may be added by (or through arrangements made by) any one entity. If the Document already includes a cover text for the same cover, previously added by you or by arrangement made by the same entity you are acting on behalf of, you may not add another; but you may replace the old one, on explicit permission from the previous publisher that added the old one.

The author(s) and publisher(s) of the Document do not by this License give permission to use their names for publicity for or to assert or imply endorsement of any Modified Version.

5. COMBINING DOCUMENTS

You may combine the Document with other documents released under this License, under the terms defined in section 4 above for modified versions, provided that you include in the combination all of the Invariant Sections of all of the original documents, unmodified, and list them all as Invariant Sections of your combined work in its license notice, and that you preserve all their Warranty Disclaimers.

The combined work need only contain one copy of this License, and multiple identical Invariant Sections may be replaced with a single copy. If there are multiple Invariant Sections with the same name but different contents, make the title of each such section unique by adding at the end of it, in parentheses, the name of the original author or publisher of that section if known, or else a unique number. Make the same adjustment to the section titles in the list of Invariant Sections in the license notice of the combined work.

In the combination, you must combine any sections Entitled "History" in the various original documents, forming one section Entitled "History"; likewise combine any sections Entitled "Acknowledgements," and any sections Entitled "Dedications." You must delete all sections Entitled "Endorsements."

6. COLLECTIONS OF DOCUMENTS

You may make a collection consisting of the Document and other documents released under this License, and replace the individual copies of this License in the various documents with a single copy that is included in the collection, provided that you follow the rules of this License for verbatim copying of each of the documents in all other respects.

You may extract a single document from such a collection, and distribute it individually under this License, provided you insert a copy of this License into the extracted document, and follow this License in all other respects regarding verbatim copying of that document.

7. AGGREGATION WITH INDEPENDENT WORKS

A compilation of the Document or its derivatives with other separate and in-dependent documents or works, in or on a volume of a storage or distribution medium, is called an "aggregate" if the copyright resulting from the compila-tion is not used to limit the legal rights of the compilation's users beyond what the individual works permit. When the Document is included in an aggregate, this License does not apply to the other works in the aggregate which are not themselves derivative works of the Document.

If the Cover Text requirement of section 3 is applicable to these copies of the Document, then if the Document is less than one half of the entire aggre-gate, the Document's Cover Texts may be placed on covers that bracket the Document within the aggregate, or the electronic equivalent of covers if the Document is in electronic form. Otherwise they must appear on printed covers that bracket the whole aggregate.

8. TRANSLATION

Translation is considered a kind of modification, so you may distribute trans-lations of the Document under the terms of section 4. Replacing Invariant Sec-tions with translations requires special permission from their copyright holders, but you may include translations of some or all Invariant Sections in addition to the original versions of these Invariant Sections. You may include a trans-lation of this License, and all the license notices in the Document, and any Warranty Disclaimers, provided that you also include the original English ver-sion of this License and the original versions of those notices and disclaimers. In case of a disagreement between the translation and the original version of this License or a notice or disclaimer, the original version will prevail.

If a section in the Document is Entitled "Acknowledgements," "Dedications," or "History," the requirement (section 4) to Preserve its Title (section 1) will typically require changing the actual title.

9. TERMINATION

You may not copy, modify, sublicense, or distribute the Document except as expressly provided for under this License. Any other attempt to copy, modify, sublicense or distribute the Document is void, and will automatically terminate your rights under this License. However, parties who have received copies, or rights, from you under this License will not have their licenses terminated so long as such parties remain in full compliance.

10. FUTURE REVISIONS OF THIS LICENSE

The Free Software Foundation may publish new, revised versions of the GNU Free Documentation License from time to time. Such new versions will be similar in spirit to the present version, but may differ in detail to address new problems or concerns. See http://www.gnu.org/copyleft/.

Each version of the License is given a distinguishing version number. If the Document specifies that a particular numbered version of this License "or any later version" applies to it, you have the option of following the terms and conditions either of that specified version or of any later version that has been published (not as a draft) by the Free Software Foundation. If the Document does not specify a version number of this License, you may choose any version ever published (not as a draft) by the Free Software Foundation.

ADDENDUM: How to use this License for your documents

To use this License in a document you have written, include a copy of the License in the document and put the following copyright and license notices just after the title page:

```
Copyright (C)  year  your name.
Permission is granted to copy, distribute and/or modify this document
under the terms of the GNU Free Documentation License, Version 1.2
or any later version published by the Free Software Foundation;
with no Invariant Sections, no Front-Cover Texts, and no Back-Cover Texts.
A copy of the license is included in the section entitled ``GNU
Free Documentation License.''
```

If you have Invariant Sections, Front-Cover Texts and Back-Cover Texts, replace the "with...Texts." line with this:

```
with the Invariant Sections being list their titles, with the
Front-Cover Texts being list, and with the Back-Cover Texts being
list.
```

If you have Invariant Sections without Cover Texts, or some other combination of the three, merge those two alternatives to suit the situation.

If your document contains nontrivial examples of program code, we recommend releasing these examples in parallel under your choice of free software license, such as the GNU General Public License, to permit their use in free software.

Appendix C Command Line Arguments for Emacs Invocation

GNU Emacs supports command line arguments to request various actions when invoking Emacs. These are for compatibility with other editors and for sophisticated activities. We don't recommend using them for ordinary editing.

Arguments starting with '-' are *options*, and so is '+*linenum*'. All other arguments specify files to visit. Emacs visits the specified files while it starts up. The last file name on your command line becomes the current buffer; the other files are also visited in other buffers. If there are two files, they are both displayed; otherwise the last file is displayed along with a buffer list that shows what other buffers there are. As with most programs, the special argument '--' says that all subsequent arguments are file names, not options, even if they start with '-'.

Emacs command options can specify many things, such as the size and position of the X window Emacs uses, its colors, and so on. A few options support advanced usage, such as running Lisp functions on files in batch mode. The sections of this chapter describe the available options, arranged according to their purpose.

There are two ways of writing options: the short forms that start with a single '-', and the long forms that start with '--'. For example, '-d' is a short form and '--display' is the corresponding long form.

The long forms with '--' are easier to remember, but longer to type. However, you don't have to spell out the whole option name; any unambiguous abbreviation is enough. When a long option takes an argument, you can use either a space or an equal sign to separate the option name and the argument. Thus, you can write either '--display sugar-bombs:0.0' or '--display=sugar-bombs:0.0'. We recommend an equal sign because it makes the relationship clearer, and the tables below always show an equal sign.

Most options specify how to initialize Emacs, or set parameters for the Emacs session. We call them *initial options*. A few options specify things to do: for example, load libraries, call functions, or terminate Emacs. These are called *action options*. These and file names together are called *action arguments*. Emacs processes all the action arguments in the order they are written. The '.emacs' file can access the values of the action arguments as the elements of a list in the variable `command-line-args`.

C.1 Action Arguments

Here is a table of the action arguments and options:

'*file*'
'--file=*file*'
'--find-file=*file*'
'--visit=*file*'

> Visit *file* using `find-file`. See Section 15.2 [Visiting], page 120. If you visit several files at startup in this way, Emacs also displays a

Buffer Menu buffer to show you what files it has visited. You can inhibit that by setting `inhibit-startup-buffer-menu` to t.

'`+linenum file`'

Visit *file* using `find-file`, then go to line number *linenum* in it.

'`+linenum:columnnum file`'

Visit *file* using `find-file`, then go to line number *linenum* and put point at column number *columnnum*.

'`-l file`'
'`--load=file`'

Load a Lisp library named *file* with the function `load`. See Section 24.8 [Lisp Libraries], page 288. If *file* is not an absolute file name, the library can be found either in the current directory, or in the Emacs library search path as specified with `EMACSLOADPATH` (see Section C.5.1 [General Variables], page 476).

Warning: If previous command-line arguments have visited files, the current directory is the directory of the last file visited.

'`-L dir`'
'`--directory=dir`'

Add directory *dir* to the variable `load-path`.

'`-f function`'
'`--funcall=function`'

Call Lisp function *function*. If it is an interactive function (a command), it reads the arguments interactively just as if you had called the same function with a key sequence. Otherwise, it calls the function with no arguments.

'`--eval=expression`'
'`--execute=expression`'

Evaluate Lisp expression *expression*.

'`--insert=file`'

Insert the contents of *file* into the current buffer. This is like what `M-x insert-file` does. See Section 15.11 [Misc File Ops], page 150.

'`--kill`'   Exit from Emacs without asking for confirmation.

'`--help`'   Print a usage message listing all available options, then exit successfully.

'`--version`'

Print Emacs version, then exit successfully.

C.2 Initial Options

The initial options specify parameters for the Emacs session. This section describes the more general initial options; some other options specifically related to the X Window System appear in the following sections.

Some initial options affect the loading of init files. The normal actions of Emacs are to first load 'site-start.el' if it exists, then your own init file '~/.emacs' if it exists, and finally 'default.el' if it exists. See Section 32.6 [Init File], page 433. Certain options prevent loading of some of these files or substitute other files for them.

'-t *device*'
'--terminal=*device*'

> Use *device* as the device for terminal input and output. '--terminal' implies '--no-window-system'.

'-d *display*'
'--display=*display*'

> Use the X Window System and use the display named *display* to open the initial Emacs frame. See Section C.6 [Display X], page 481, for more details.

'-nw'
'--no-window-system'

> Don't communicate directly with the window system, disregarding the DISPLAY environment variable even if it is set. This means that Emacs uses the terminal from which it was launched for all its display and input.

'-batch'
'--batch'

> Run Emacs in *batch mode*. Batch mode is used for running programs written in Emacs Lisp from shell scripts, makefiles, and so on. You should also use the '-l', '-f' or '--eval' option, to invoke a Lisp program to do batch processing.

> In batch mode, Emacs does not display the text being edited, and the standard terminal interrupt characters such as C-z and C-c continue to have their normal effect. The functions prin1, princ and print output to stdout instead of the echo area, while message and error messages output to stderr. Functions that would normally read from the minibuffer take their input from stdin instead.

> '--batch' implies '-q' (do not load an init file), but 'site-start.el' is loaded nonetheless. It also causes Emacs to exit after processing all the command options. In addition, it disables auto-saving except in buffers for which it has been explicitly requested.

'--script *file*'

> Run Emacs in batch mode, like '--batch', and then read and execute the Lisp code in *file*.

> The normal use of this option is in executable script files that run Emacs. They can start with this text on the first line

>   #!/usr/bin/emacs --script

> which will invoke Emacs with '--script' and supply the name of the script file as *file*. Emacs Lisp then treats '#!' as a comment delimiter.

'-q'
'--no-init-file'

> Do not load your Emacs init file '~/.emacs', or 'default.el' either. Regardless of this switch, 'site-start.el' is still loaded. When invoked like this, Emacs does not allow saving options changed with the M-x customize command and its variants. See Section 32.2 [Easy Customization], page 408.

'--no-site-file'

> Do not load 'site-start.el'. The options '-q', '-u' and '--batch' have no effect on the loading of this file—this option and '-Q' are the only options that block it.

'-Q'
'--quick'   Start emacs with minimum customizations. This is like using '-q' and '--no-site-file', but also disables the startup screen.

'--no-splash'

> Do not display a splash screen on startup. You can also achieve this effect by setting the variable inhibit-splash-screen to non-nil in you personal init file (but *not* in 'site-start.el'). (This variable was called inhibit-startup-message in previous Emacs versions.)

'--no-desktop'

> Do not reload any saved desktop. See Section 31.12 [Saving Emacs Sessions], page 399.

'-u *user*'
'--user=*user*'

> Load *user*'s Emacs init file '~*user*/.emacs' instead of your own[1].

'--debug-init'

> Enable the Emacs Lisp debugger for errors in the init file. See section "Entering the Debugger on an Error" in *The GNU Emacs Lisp Reference Manual*.

'--unibyte'
'--no-multibyte'

> Do almost everything with single-byte buffers and strings. All buffers and strings are unibyte unless you (or a Lisp program) explicitly ask for a multibyte buffer or string. (Note that Emacs always loads Lisp files in multibyte mode, even if '--unibyte' is specified; see Section 19.2 [Enabling Multibyte], page 187.) Setting the environment variable EMACS_UNIBYTE has the same effect (see Section C.5.1 [General Variables], page 476).

---

[1] This option has no effect on MS-Windows.

'--multibyte'
'--no-unibyte'

> Inhibit the effect of EMACS_UNIBYTE, so that Emacs uses multibyte characters by default, as usual.

C.3 Command Argument Example

Here is an example of using Emacs with arguments and options. It assumes you have a Lisp program file called 'hack-c.el' which, when loaded, performs some useful operation on the current buffer, expected to be a C program.

```
emacs --batch foo.c -l hack-c -f save-buffer >& log
```

This says to visit 'foo.c', load 'hack-c.el' (which makes changes in the visited file), save 'foo.c' (note that save-buffer is the function that C-x C-s is bound to), and then exit back to the shell (because of '--batch'). '--batch' also guarantees there will be no problem redirecting output to 'log', because Emacs will not assume that it has a display terminal to work with.

C.4 Resuming Emacs with Arguments

You can specify action arguments for Emacs when you resume it after a suspension. To prepare for this, put the following code in your '.emacs' file (see Section 32.3.2 [Hooks], page 418):

```
(add-hook 'suspend-hook 'resume-suspend-hook)
(add-hook 'suspend-resume-hook 'resume-process-args)
```

As further preparation, you must execute the shell script 'emacs.csh' (if you use csh as your shell) or 'emacs.bash' (if you use bash as your shell). These scripts define an alias named edit, which will resume Emacs giving it new command line arguments such as files to visit. The scripts are found in the 'etc' subdirectory of the Emacs distribution.

Only action arguments work properly when you resume Emacs. Initial arguments are not recognized—it's too late to execute them anyway.

Note that resuming Emacs (with or without arguments) must be done from within the shell that is the parent of the Emacs job. This is why edit is an alias rather than a program or a shell script. It is not possible to implement a resumption command that could be run from other subjobs of the shell; there is no way to define a command that could be made the value of EDITOR, for example. Therefore, this feature does not take the place of the Emacs Server feature (see Section 31.3 [Emacs Server], page 389).

The aliases use the Emacs Server feature if you appear to have a server Emacs running. However, they cannot determine this with complete accuracy. They may think that a server is still running when in actuality you have killed that Emacs, because the file '/tmp/esrv...' still exists. If this happens, find that file and delete it.

C.5 Environment Variables

The *environment* is a feature of the operating system; it consists of a collection of variables with names and values. Each variable is called an *environment variable*; environment variable names are case-sensitive, and it is conventional to use upper case letters only. The values are all text strings.

What makes the environment useful is that subprocesses inherit the environment automatically from their parent process. This means you can set up an environment variable in your login shell, and all the programs you run (including Emacs) will automatically see it. Subprocesses of Emacs (such as shells, compilers, and version-control software) inherit the environment from Emacs, too.

Inside Emacs, the command M-x getenv gets the value of an environment variable. M-x setenv sets a variable in the Emacs environment. (Environment variable substitutions with '$' work in the value just as in file names; see [File Names with $], page 120.)

The way to set environment variables outside of Emacs depends on the operating system, and especially the shell that you are using. For example, here's how to set the environment variable ORGANIZATION to 'not very much' using Bash:

    export ORGANIZATION="not very much"

and here's how to do it in csh or tcsh:

    setenv ORGANIZATION "not very much"

When Emacs is using the X Window System, various environment variables that control X work for Emacs as well. See the X documentation for more information.

C.5.1 General Variables

Here is an alphabetical list of specific environment variables that have special meanings in Emacs, giving the name of each variable and its meaning. Most of these variables are also used by some other programs. Emacs does not require any of these environment variables to be set, but it uses their values if they are set.

CDPATH   Used by the cd command to search for the directory you specify, when you specify a relative directory name.

EMACS_UNIBYTE
                Defining this environment variable with a nonempty value directs Emacs to do almost everything with single-byte buffers and strings. It is equivalent to using the '--unibyte' command-line option on each invocation. See Section C.2 [Initial Options], page 472.

EMACSDATA   Directory for the architecture-independent files that come with Emacs. This is used to initialize the Lisp variable data-directory.

EMACSDOC   Directory for the documentation string file, 'DOC-emacsversion'. This is used to initialize the Lisp variable doc-directory.

`EMACSLOADPATH`
A colon-separated list of directories[2] to search for Emacs Lisp files—used to initialize `load-path`.

`EMACSPATH`   A colon-separated list of directories to search for executable files—used to initialize `exec-path`.

`EMAIL`   Your email address; used to initialize the Lisp variable `user-mail-address`, which the Emacs mail interface puts into the 'From' header of outgoing messages (see Section 27.2 [Mail Headers], page 311).

`ESHELL`   Used for shell-mode to override the `SHELL` environment variable.

`HISTFILE`   The name of the file that shell commands are saved in between logins. This variable defaults to '~/.bash_history' if you use Bash, to '~/.sh_history' if you use ksh, and to '~/.history' otherwise.

`HOME`   The location of your files in the directory tree; used for expansion of file names starting with a tilde ('~'). On MS-DOS, it defaults to the directory from which Emacs was started, with '/bin' removed from the end if it was present. On Windows, the default value of `HOME` is the 'Application Data' subdirectory of the user profile directory (normally, this is 'C:/Documents and Settings/username/Application Data', where username is your user name), though for backwards compatibility 'C:/' will be used instead if a '.emacs' file is found there.

`HOSTNAME`   The name of the machine that Emacs is running on.

`INCPATH`   A colon-separated list of directories. Used by the `complete` package to search for files.

`INFOPATH`   A colon-separated list of directories in which to search for Info files.

`LC_ALL`
`LC_COLLATE`
`LC_CTYPE`
`LC_MESSAGES`
`LC_MONETARY`
`LC_NUMERIC`
`LC_TIME`
`LANG`   The user's preferred locale. The locale has six categories, specified by the environment variables `LC_COLLATE` for sorting, `LC_CTYPE` for character encoding, `LC_MESSAGES` for system messages, `LC_MONETARY` for monetary formats, `LC_NUMERIC` for numbers, and `LC_TIME` for dates and times. If one of these variables is not set, the category defaults to the value of the `LANG` environment variable, or to the default 'C' locale

---

[2]   Here and below, whenever we say "colon-separated list of directories," it pertains to Unix and GNU/Linux systems. On MS-DOS and MS-Windows, the directories are separated by semi-colons instead, since DOS/Windows file names might include a colon after a drive letter.

if `LANG` is not set. But if `LC_ALL` is specified, it overrides the settings of all the other locale environment variables.

On MS-Windows, if `LANG` is not already set in the environment when Emacs starts, Emacs sets it based on the system-wide default language, which you can set in the '`Regional Settings`' Control Panel on some versions of MS-Windows.

The value of the `LC_CTYPE` category is matched against entries in `locale-language-names`, `locale-charset-language-names`, and `locale-preferred-coding-systems`, to select a default language environment and coding system. See Section 19.3 [Language Environments], page 188.

LOGNAME   The user's login name. See also `USER`.

MAIL   The name of your system mail inbox.

MH   Name of setup file for the mh system. (The default is '`~/.mh_profile`'.)

NAME   Your real-world name.

NNTPSERVER
    The name of the news server. Used by the mh and Gnus packages.

ORGANIZATION
    The name of the organization to which you belong. Used for setting the 'Organization:' header in your posts from the Gnus package.

PATH   A colon-separated list of directories in which executables reside. This is used to initialize the Emacs Lisp variable `exec-path`.

PWD   If set, this should be the default directory when Emacs was started.

REPLYTO   If set, this specifies an initial value for the variable `mail-default-reply-to`. See Section 27.2 [Mail Headers], page 311.

SAVEDIR   The name of a directory in which news articles are saved by default. Used by the Gnus package.

SHELL   The name of an interpreter used to parse and execute programs run from inside Emacs.

SMTPSERVER
    The name of the outgoing mail server. Used by the SMTP library (see section "Top" in *Sending mail via SMTP*).

TERM   The type of the terminal that Emacs is using. This variable must be set unless Emacs is run in batch mode. On MS-DOS, it defaults to '`internal`', which specifies a built-in terminal emulation that handles the machine's own display. If the value of `TERM` indicates that Emacs runs in non-windowed mode from `xterm` or a similar terminal emulator, the background mode defaults to '`light`', and Emacs will choose colors that are appropriate for a light background.

TERMCAP   The name of the termcap library file describing how to program the terminal specified by the TERM variable. This defaults to '/etc/termcap'.

TMPDIR   Used by the Emerge package as a prefix for temporary files.

TZ   This specifies the current time zone and possibly also daylight saving time information. On MS-DOS, if TZ is not set in the environment when Emacs starts, Emacs defines a default value as appropriate for the country code returned by DOS. On MS-Windows, Emacs does not use TZ at all.

USER   The user's login name. See also LOGNAME. On MS-DOS, this defaults to 'root'.

VERSION CONTROL
             Used to initialize the version-control variable (see Section 15.3.2.1 [Numbered Backups], page 126).

C.5.2 Miscellaneous Variables

These variables are used only on particular configurations:

COMSPEC   On MS-DOS and MS-Windows, the name of the command interpreter to use when invoking batch files and commands internal to the shell. On MS-DOS this is also used to make a default value for the SHELL environment variable.

NAME   On MS-DOS, this variable defaults to the value of the USER variable.

TEMP
TMP   On MS-DOS and MS-Windows, these specify the name of the directory for storing temporary files in.

EMACSTEST   On MS-DOS, this specifies a file to use to log the operation of the internal terminal emulator. This feature is useful for submitting bug reports.

EMACSCOLORS
             On MS-DOS, this specifies the screen colors. It is useful to set them this way, since otherwise Emacs would display the default colors momentarily when it starts up.

             The value of this variable should be the two-character encoding of the foreground (the first character) and the background (the second character) colors of the default face. Each character should be the hexadecimal code for the desired color on a standard PC text-mode display. For example, to get blue text on a light gray background, specify 'EMACSCOLORS=17', since 1 is the code of the blue color and 7 is the code of the light gray color.

             The PC display usually supports only eight background colors. However, Emacs switches the DOS display to a mode where all 16 colors can be used for the background, so all four bits of the background color are actually used.

WINDOW_GFX

>Used when initializing the Sun windows system.

PRELOAD_WINSOCK

>On MS-Windows, if you set this variable, Emacs will load and initialize the network library at startup, instead of waiting until the first time it is required.

emacs_dir   On MS-Windows, `emacs_dir` is a special environment variable, which indicates the full path of the directory in which Emacs is installed. If Emacs is installed in the standard directory structure, it calculates this value automatically. It is not much use setting this variable yourself unless your installation is non-standard, since unlike other environment variables, it will be overridden by Emacs at startup. When setting other environment variables, such as `EMACSLOADPATH`, you may find it useful to use `emacs_dir` rather than hard-coding an absolute path. This allows multiple versions of Emacs to share the same environment variable settings, and it allows you to move the Emacs installation directory, without changing any environment or registry settings.

C.5.3 The MS-Windows System Registry

Under MS-Windows, the installation program `addpm.exe` adds values for `emacs_dir`, `EMACSLOADPATH`, `EMACSDATA`, `EMACSPATH`, `EMACSDOC`, `SHELL` and `TERM` to the 'HKEY_LOCAL_MACHINE' section of the system registry, under '/Software/GNU/Emacs'. It does this because there is no standard place to set environment variables across different versions of Windows. Running `addpm.exe` is no longer strictly necessary in recent versions of Emacs, but if you are upgrading from an older version, running `addpm.exe` ensures that you do not have older registry entries from a previous installation, which may not be compatible with the latest version of Emacs.

When Emacs starts, as well as checking the environment, it also checks the System Registry for those variables and for `HOME`, `LANG` and `PRELOAD_WINSOCK`.

To determine the value of those variables, Emacs goes through the following procedure. First, the environment is checked. If the variable is not found there, Emacs looks for registry keys by that name under '/Software/GNU/Emacs'; first in the 'HKEY_CURRENT_USER' section of the registry, and if not found there, in the 'HKEY_LOCAL_MACHINE' section. Finally, if Emacs still cannot determine the values, compiled-in defaults are used.

In addition to the environment variables above, you can also add many of the settings which on X belong in the '.Xdefaults' file (see Appendix D [X Resources], page 489) to the '/Software/GNU/Emacs' registry key. Settings you add to the 'HKEY_LOCAL_MACHINE' section will affect all users of the machine. Settings you add to the 'HKEY_CURRENT_USER' section will only affect you, and will override machine wide settings.

C.6 Specifying the Display Name

The environment variable DISPLAY tells all X clients, including Emacs, where to display their windows. Its value is set by default in ordinary circumstances, when you start an X server and run jobs locally. Occasionally you may need to specify the display yourself; for example, if you do a remote login and want to run a client program remotely, displaying on your local screen.

With Emacs, the main reason people change the default display is to let them log into another system, run Emacs on that system, but have the window displayed at their local terminal. You might need to log in to another system because the files you want to edit are there, or because the Emacs executable file you want to run is there.

The syntax of the DISPLAY environment variable is '*host:display.screen*', where *host* is the host name of the X Window System server machine, *display* is an arbitrarily-assigned number that distinguishes your server (X terminal) from other servers on the same machine, and *screen* is a rarely-used field that allows an X server to control multiple terminal screens. The period and the *screen* field are optional. If included, *screen* is usually zero.

For example, if your host is named 'glasperle' and your server is the first (or perhaps the only) server listed in the configuration, your DISPLAY is 'glasperle:0.0'.

You can specify the display name explicitly when you run Emacs, either by changing the DISPLAY variable, or with the option '-d *display*' or '--display=*display*'. Here is an example:

    emacs --display=glasperle:0 &

You can inhibit the direct use of the window system and GUI with the '-nw' option. It tells Emacs to display using ordinary ASCII on its controlling terminal. This is also an initial option.

Sometimes, security arrangements prevent a program on a remote system from displaying on your local system. In this case, trying to run Emacs produces messages like this:

    Xlib: connection to "glasperle:0.0" refused by server

You might be able to overcome this problem by using the xhost command on the local system to give permission for access from your remote machine.

C.7 Font Specification Options

By default, Emacs displays text in a twelve point Courier font (when using X). You can specify a different font on your command line through the option '-fn *name*' (or '--font', which is an alias for '-fn').

'-fn *name*'
'--font=*name*'
            Use font *name* as the default font.

Under X, each font has a long name which consists of fourteen words or numbers, separated by dashes. Some fonts also have shorter nicknames. For instance,

'9x15' is such a nickname. This font makes each character nine pixels wide and fifteen pixels high. You can use either kind of name. Case is insignificant in both kinds. You can use wildcard patterns for the font name; then Emacs lets X choose one of the fonts that match the pattern. The wildcard character '*' matches any sequence of characters (including none) and '?' matches any single character. However, matching is implementation-dependent, and can be inaccurate when wildcards match dashes in a long name. For reliable results, supply all 14 dashes and use wildcards only within a field. Here is an example, which happens to specify the font whose nickname is '6x13':

```
emacs -fn \
   "-misc-fixed-medium-r-semicondensed--13-*-*-*-c-60-iso8859-1" &
```

You can also specify the font in your '.Xdefaults' file:

```
emacs.font: -misc-fixed-medium-r-semicondensed--13-*-*-*-c-60-iso8859-1
```

Note that if you use a wildcard pattern on the command line, you need to enclose it in single or double quotes, to prevent the shell from accidentally expanding it into a list of file names. On the other hand, you should not quote the name in the '.Xdefaults' file.

The default font used by Emacs (under X) is:

```
-adobe-courier-medium-r-*-*-*-120-*-*-*-*-iso8859-1
```

A long font name has the following form:

```
-maker-family-weight-slant-widthtype-style...
...-pixels-height-horiz-vert-spacing-width-registry-encoding
```

maker   This is the name of the font manufacturer.

family   This is the name of the font family—for example, 'courier'.

weight   This is normally 'bold', 'medium' or 'light'. Other words may appear here in some font names.

slant   This is 'r' (roman), 'i' (italic), 'o' (oblique), 'ri' (reverse italic), or 'ot' (other).

widthtype This is normally 'condensed', 'extended', 'semicondensed' or 'normal'. Other words may appear here in some font names.

style   This is an optional additional style name. Usually it is empty—most long font names have two hyphens in a row at this point.

pixels   This is the font height, in pixels.

height   This is the font height on the screen, measured in tenths of a printer's point—approximately 1/720 of an inch. In other words, it is the point size of the font, times ten. For a given vertical resolution, *height* and *pixels* are proportional; therefore, it is common to specify just one of them and use '*' for the other.

horiz   This is the horizontal resolution, in pixels per inch, of the screen for which the font is intended.

vert   This is the vertical resolution, in pixels per inch, of the screen for which the font is intended. Normally the resolution of the fonts on your system is the right value for your screen; therefore, you normally specify '*' for this and *horiz*.

spacing   This is 'm' (monospace), 'p' (proportional) or 'c' (character cell).

width   This is the average character width, in pixels, multiplied by ten.

registry
encoding   These together make up the X font character set that the font depicts. (X font character sets are not the same as Emacs charsets, but they are solutions for the same problem.) You can use the `xfontsel` program to check which choices you have. However, normally you should use 'iso8859' for *registry* and '1' for *encoding*.

You will probably want to use a fixed-width default font—that is, a font in which all characters have the same width. Any font with 'm' or 'c' in the *spacing* field of the long name is a fixed-width font. Here's how to use the `xlsfonts` program to list all the fixed-width fonts available on your system:

```
xlsfonts -fn '*x*' | egrep "^[0-9]+x[0-9]+"
xlsfonts -fn '*-*-*-*-*-*-*-*-*-*-*-m*'
xlsfonts -fn '*-*-*-*-*-*-*-*-*-*-*-c*'
```

To see what a particular font looks like, use the `xfd` command. For example:

```
xfd -fn 6x13
```

displays the entire font '6x13'.

While running Emacs, you can set the font of the current frame (see Section 18.10 [Frame Parameters], page 180) or for a specific kind of text (see Section 11.5 [Faces], page 72).

C.8 Window Color Options

On a color display, you can specify which color to use for various parts of the Emacs display. To find out what colors are available on your system, type M-x `list-colors-display`, or press C-Mouse-2 and select 'Display Colors' from the pop-up menu. (A particular window system might support many more colors, but the list displayed by `list-colors-display` shows their portable subset that can be safely used on any display supported by Emacs.) If you do not specify colors, on windowed displays the default for the background is white and the default for all other colors is black. On a monochrome display, the foreground is black, the background is white, and the border is gray if the display supports that. On terminals, the background is usually black and the foreground is white.

Here is a list of the command-line options for specifying colors:

'-fg *color*'
'--foreground-color=*color*'
          Specify the foreground color. *color* should be a standard color name, or a numeric specification of the color's red, green, and blue components as in '#4682B4' or 'RGB:46/82/B4'.

'-bg *color*'
'--background-color=*color*'
> Specify the background color.

'-bd *color*'
'--border-color=*color*'
> Specify the color of the border of the X window.

'-cr *color*'
'--cursor-color=*color*'
> Specify the color of the Emacs cursor which indicates where point is.

'-ms *color*'
'--mouse-color=*color*'
> Specify the color for the mouse cursor when the mouse is in the Emacs window.

'-r'
'-rv'
'--reverse-video'
> Reverse video—swap the foreground and background colors.

'--color=*mode*'
> For a character terminal only, specify the mode of color support. This option is intended for overriding the number of supported colors that the character terminal advertises in its `termcap` or `terminfo` database. The parameter *mode* can be one of the following:

> 'never'
> 'no'
>> Don't use colors even if the terminal's capabilities specify color support.

> 'default'
> 'auto'
>> Same as when '--color' is not used at all: Emacs detects at startup whether the terminal supports colors, and if it does, turns on colored display.

> 'always'
> 'yes'
> 'ansi8'
>> Turn on the color support unconditionally, and use color commands specified by the ANSI escape sequences for the 8 standard colors.

> '*num*'
>> Use color mode for *num* colors. If *num* is -1, turn off color support (equivalent to 'never'); if it is 0, use the default color support for this terminal (equivalent to 'auto'); otherwise use an appropriate standard mode for *num* colors. Depending on your terminal's capabilities, Emacs might be able to turn on a color mode for 8, 16, 88, or 256 as the value of *num*. If there is no mode that supports *num* colors, Emacs acts as if *num* were 0, i.e. it uses the terminal's default color support mode.

If *mode* is omitted, it defaults to *ansi8*.

For example, to use a coral mouse cursor and a slate blue text cursor, enter:

```
emacs -ms coral -cr 'slate blue' &
```

You can reverse the foreground and background colors through the '-rv' option or with the X resource 'reverseVideo'.

The '-fg', '-bg', and '-rv' options function on text-only terminals as well as on graphical displays.

C.9 Options for Window Size and Position

Here is a list of the command-line options for specifying size and position of the initial Emacs frame:

'-g *widthxheight*[{+-}*xoffset*{+-}*yoffset*]]'
'--geometry=*widthxheight*[{+-}*xoffset*{+-}*yoffset*]]'

Specify the size *width* and *height* (measured in character columns and lines), and positions *xoffset* and *yoffset* (measured in pixels). The *width* and *height* parameters apply to all frames, whereas *xoffset* and *yoffset* only to the initial frame.

'-fs'
'--fullscreen'

Specify that width and height shall be the size of the screen.

'-fh'
'--fullheight'

Specify that the height shall be the height of the screen.

'-fw'
'--fullwidth'

Specify that the width shall be the width of the screen.

In the '--geometry' option, {+-} means either a plus sign or a minus sign. A plus sign before *xoffset* means it is the distance from the left side of the screen; a minus sign means it counts from the right side. A plus sign before *yoffset* means it is the distance from the top of the screen, and a minus sign there indicates the distance from the bottom. The values *xoffset* and *yoffset* may themselves be positive or negative, but that doesn't change their meaning, only their direction.

Emacs uses the same units as xterm does to interpret the geometry. The *width* and *height* are measured in characters, so a large font creates a larger frame than a small font. (If you specify a proportional font, Emacs uses its maximum bounds width as the width unit.) The *xoffset* and *yoffset* are measured in pixels.

You do not have to specify all of the fields in the geometry specification. If you omit both *xoffset* and *yoffset*, the window manager decides where to put the Emacs frame, possibly by letting you place it with the mouse. For example, '164x55' specifies a window 164 columns wide, enough for two ordinary width windows side by side, and 55 lines tall.

The default width for Emacs is 80 characters and the default height is 40 lines. You can omit either the width or the height or both. If you start the geometry with an integer, Emacs interprets it as the width. If you start with an 'x' followed by an integer, Emacs interprets it as the height. Thus, '81' specifies just the width; 'x45' specifies just the height.

If you start with '+' or '-', that introduces an offset, which means both sizes are omitted. Thus, '-3' specifies the *xoffset* only. (If you give just one offset, it is always *xoffset*.) '+3-3' specifies both the *xoffset* and the *yoffset*, placing the frame near the bottom left of the screen.

You can specify a default for any or all of the fields in '.Xdefaults' file, and then override selected fields with a '--geometry' option.

Since the mode line and the echo area occupy the last 2 lines of the frame, the height of the initial text window is 2 less than the height specified in your geometry. In non-X-toolkit versions of Emacs, the menu bar also takes one line of the specified number. But in the X toolkit version, the menu bar is additional and does not count against the specified height. The tool bar, if present, is also additional.

Enabling or disabling the menu bar or tool bar alters the amount of space available for ordinary text. Therefore, if Emacs starts up with a tool bar (which is the default), and handles the geometry specification assuming there is a tool bar, and then your '~/.emacs' file disables the tool bar, you will end up with a frame geometry different from what you asked for. To get the intended size with no tool bar, use an X resource to specify "no tool bar" (see Section D.2 [Table of Resources], page 490); then Emacs will already know there's no tool bar when it processes the specified geometry.

When using one of '--fullscreen', '--fullwidth' or '--fullheight' there may be some space around the frame anyway. That is because Emacs rounds the sizes so they are an even number of character heights and widths.

Some window managers have options that can make them ignore both program-specified and user-specified positions (sawfish is one). If these are set, Emacs fails to position the window correctly.

C.10 Internal and External Borders

An Emacs frame has an internal border and an external border. The internal border is an extra strip of the background color around the text portion of the frame. Emacs itself draws the internal border. The external border is added by the window manager outside the frame; depending on the window manager you use, it may contain various boxes you can click on to move or iconify the window.

'-ib *width*'
'--internal-border=*width*'
> Specify *width* as the width of the internal border (between the text and the main border), in pixels.

'-bw *width*'
'--border-width=*width*'
> Specify *width* as the width of the main border, in pixels.

When you specify the size of the frame, that does not count the borders. The frame's position is measured from the outside edge of the external border.

Use the '-ib *n*' option to specify an internal border *n* pixels wide. The default is 1. Use '-bw *n*' to specify the width of the external border (though the window manager may not pay attention to what you specify). The default width of the external border is 2.

C.11 Frame Titles

An Emacs frame may or may not have a specified title. The frame title, if specified, appears in window decorations and icons as the name of the frame. If an Emacs frame has no specified title, the default title has the form '*invocation-name@machine*' (if there is only one frame) or the selected window's buffer name (if there is more than one frame).

You can specify a title for the initial Emacs frame with a command line option:

'-T *title*'
'--title=*title*'
          Specify *title* as the title for the initial Emacs frame.

The '--name' option (see Section D.1 [Resources], page 489) also specifies the title for the initial Emacs frame.

C.12 Icons

Most window managers allow you to "iconify" a frame, removing it from sight, and leaving a small, distinctive "icon" window in its place. Clicking on the icon window makes the frame itself appear again. If you have many clients running at once, you can avoid cluttering up the screen by iconifying most of the clients.

'-nbi'
'--no-bitmap-icon'
          Do not use a picture of a gnu as the Emacs icon.

'-iconic'
'--iconic'   Start Emacs in iconified state.

By default Emacs uses an icon window containing a picture of the GNU gnu. The '-nbi' or '--no-bitmap-icon' option tells Emacs to let the window manager choose what sort of icon to use—usually just a small rectangle containing the frame's title.

The '-iconic' option tells Emacs to begin running as an icon, rather than showing a frame right away. In this situation, the icon is the only indication that Emacs has started; the text frame doesn't appear until you deiconify it.

C.13 Other Display Options

'-hb'
'--horizontal-scroll-bars'
          Enable horizontal scroll bars. Since horizontal scroll bars are not yet implemented, this actually does nothing.

'-vb'
'--vertical-scroll-bars'
>   Enable vertical scroll bars.

'-lsp *pixels*'
'--line-spacing=*pixels*'
>   Specify *pixels* as additional space to put between lines, in pixels.

'-nbc'
'--no-blinking-cursor'
>   Disable the blinking cursor on graphical displays.

'-D'
'--basic-display'
>   Disable the menu-bar, the tool-bar, the scroll-bars, and tool tips, and
>   turn off the blinking cursor. This can be useful for making a test case
>   that simplifies debugging of display problems.

The '--xrm' option (see Section D.1 [Resources], page 489) specifies additional X resource values.

Appendix D X Options and Resources

You can customize some X-related aspects of Emacs behavior using X resources, as is usual for programs that use X. On MS-Windows, you can customize some of the same aspects using the system registry. See Section C.5.3 [MS-Windows Registry], page 480. Likewise, Emacs on MacOS 'Carbon emulates X resources using the Preferences system. See Section F.3 [Mac Environment Variables], page 502.

When Emacs is built using an "X toolkit", such as Lucid or LessTif, you need to use X resources to customize the appearance of the widgets, including the menubar, scroll-bar, and dialog boxes. This is because the libraries that implement these don't provide for customization through Emacs. GTK+ widgets use a separate system of "GTK resources." In this chapter we describe the most commonly used resource specifications. For full documentation, see the online manual.

D.1 X Resources

Programs running under the X Window System organize their user options under a hierarchy of classes and resources. You can specify default values for these options in your X resources file, usually named '~/.Xdefaults' or '~/.Xresources'. If changes in '~/.Xdefaults' do not take effect, it is because your X server stores its own list of resources; to update them, use the shell command xrdb—for instance, 'xrdb ~/.Xdefaults'.

Each line in the file specifies a value for one option or for a collection of related options, for one program or for several programs (optionally even for all programs).

MS-Windows systems do not support '~/.Xdefaults' files, so instead Emacs compiled for Windows looks for X resources in the Windows Registry, first under the key 'HKEY_CURRENT_USER\SOFTWARE\GNU\Emacs' and then under the key 'HKEY_LOCAL_MACHINE\SOFTWARE\GNU\Emacs'. The menu and scroll bars are native widgets on MS-Windows, so they are only customizable via the system-wide settings in the Display Control Panel. You can also set resources using the '-xrm' command line option (see below.)

Applications such as Emacs look for resources with specific names and their particular meanings. Case distinctions are significant in these names. Each resource specification in '~/.Xdefaults' states the name of the program and the name of the resource. For Emacs, the program name is 'Emacs'. It looks like this:

```
Emacs.borderWidth: 2
```

The order in which the lines appear in the file does not matter. Also, command-line options always override the X resources file.

You can experiment with the effect of different resource settings with the editres program. Select 'Get Tree' from the 'Commands' menu, then click on an Emacs frame. This will display a tree showing the structure of X toolkit widgets used in an Emacs frame. Select one of them, such as 'menubar', then select 'Show Resource Box' from the 'Commands' menu. This displays a list of all the meaningful X resources for that widget, and allows you to edit them. Changes take effect when you click on the 'Apply' button. (See the editres man page for more details.)

D.2 Table of X Resources for Emacs

This table lists the resource names that designate options for Emacs, not counting those for the appearance of the menu bar, each with the class that it belongs to:

`background` (class `Background`)
>   Background color name.

`borderColor` (class `BorderColor`)
>   Color name for the external border.

`cursorColor` (class `Foreground`)
>   Color name for text cursor (point).

`font` (class `Font`)
>   Font name (or fontset name, see Section 19.15 [Fontsets], page 202) for `default` font.

`foreground` (class `Foreground`)
>   Color name for text.

`geometry` (class `Geometry`)
>   Window size and position. Be careful not to specify this resource as 'emacs*geometry', because that may affect individual menus as well as the Emacs frame itself.

>   If this resource specifies a position, that position applies only to the initial Emacs frame (or, in the case of a resource for a specific frame name, only that frame). However, the size, if specified here, applies to all frames.

`iconName` (class `Title`)
>   Name to display in the icon.

`internalBorder` (class `BorderWidth`)
>   Width in pixels of the internal border.

`lineSpacing` (class `LineSpacing`)
>   Additional space (*leading*) between lines, in pixels.

`menuBar` (class `MenuBar`)
>   Give frames menu bars if 'on'; don't have menu bars if 'off'. See Section D.4 [Lucid Resources], page 492, for how to control the appearance of the menu bar if you have one.

`pointerColor` (class `Foreground`)
>   Color of the mouse cursor.

`screenGamma` (class `ScreenGamma`)
>   Gamma correction for colors, equivalent to the frame parameter `screen-gamma`.

`scrollBarWidth` (class `ScrollBarWidth`)
>   The scroll bar width in pixels, equivalent to the frame parameter `scroll-bar-width`.

title (class Title)
>   Name to display in the title bar of the initial Emacs frame.

toolBar (class ToolBar)
>   Number of lines to reserve for the tool bar. A zero value suppresses
>   the tool bar. If the value is non-zero and auto-resize-tool-bars is
>   non-nil, the tool bar's size will be changed automatically so that all
>   tool bar items are visible. If the value of auto-resize-tool-bars is
>   grow-only, the tool bar expands automatically, but does not contract
>   automatically. To contract the tool bar, you must redraw the frame
>   by entering C-l.

useXIM (class UseXIM)
>   Turn off use of X input methods (XIM) if 'false' or 'off'. This is
>   only relevant if your Emacs is actually built with XIM support. It
>   is potentially useful to turn off XIM for efficiency, especially slow X
>   client/server links.

verticalScrollBars (class ScrollBars)
>   Give frames scroll bars if 'on'; don't have scroll bars if 'off'.

D.3 X Resources for Faces

You can use resources to customize the appearance of particular faces (see Section 11.5 [Faces], page 72):

face.attributeForeground
>   Foreground color for face *face*.

face.attributeBackground
>   Background color for face *face*.

face.attributeUnderline
>   Underline flag for face *face*. Use 'on' or 'true' for yes.

face.attributeStrikeThrough
face.attributeOverline
face.attributeBox
face.attributeInverse
>   Likewise, for other boolean font attributes.

face.attributeStipple
>   The name of a pixmap data file to use for the stipple pattern, or false
>   to not use stipple for the face *face*.

face.attributeBackgroundPixmap
>   The background pixmap for the face *face*. Should be a name of a
>   pixmap file or false.

face.attributeFont
>   Font name (full XFD name or valid X abbreviation) for face *face*.
>   Instead of this, you can specify the font through separate attributes.

Instead of using `attributeFont` to specify a font name, you can select a font through these separate attributes:

`face.attributeFamily`
>   Font family for face *face*.

`face.attributeHeight`
>   Height of the font to use for face *face*: either an integer specifying the height in units of 1/10 pt, or a floating point number that specifies a scale factor to scale the underlying face's default font, or a function to be called with the default height which will return a new height.

`face.attributeWidth`
`face.attributeWeight`
`face.attributeSlant`
>   Each of these resources corresponds to a like-named font attribute, and you write the resource value the same as the symbol you would use for the font attribute value.

`face.attributeBold`
>   Bold flag for face *face*—instead of `attributeWeight`. Use 'on' or 'true' for yes.

`face.attributeItalic`
>   Italic flag for face *face*—instead of `attributeSlant`.

D.4 Lucid Menu X Resources

If the Emacs installed at your site was built to use the X toolkit with the Lucid menu widgets, then the menu bar is a separate widget and has its own resources. The resource specifications start with 'Emacs.pane.menubar'—for instance, to specify the font '8x16' for the menu-bar items, write this:

>   `Emacs.pane.menubar.font:  8x16`

Resources for *non-menubar* toolkit pop-up menus have 'menu*' instead of 'pane.menubar'. For example, to specify the font '8x16' for the pop-up menu items, write this:

>   `Emacs.menu*.font:  8x16`

For dialog boxes, use 'dialog*':

>   `Emacs.dialog*.font:  8x16`

The Lucid menus can display multilingual text in your locale. For more information about fontsets see the man page for `XCreateFontSet`. To enable multilingual menu text you specify a `fontSet` resource instead of the font resource. If both `font` and `fontSet` resources are specified, the `fontSet` resource is used.

Thus, to specify '-*-helvetica-medium-r-*--*-120-*-*-*-*-*-*,*' for both the popup and menu bar menus, write this:

>   `Emacs*menu*fontSet:  -*-helvetica-medium-r-*--*-120-*-*-*-*-*-*,*`

The '*menu*' as a wildcard matches 'pane.menubar' and 'menu...'.

Experience shows that on some systems you may need to add 'shell.' before the 'pane.menubar' or 'menu*'. On some other systems, you must not add 'shell.'. The generic wildcard approach should work on both kinds of systems.

Here is a list of the specific resources for menu bars and pop-up menus:

font   Font for menu item text.

fontSet   Fontset for menu item text.

foreground
              Color of the foreground.

background
              Color of the background.

buttonForeground
              In the menu bar, the color of the foreground for a selected item.

margin   The margin of the menu bar, in characters. Default is 1.

D.5 GTK resources

The most common way to customize the GTK widgets Emacs uses (menus, dialogs tool bars and scroll bars) is by choosing an appropriate theme, for example with the GNOME theme selector. You can also do Emacs specific customization by inserting GTK style directives in the file '~/.emacs.d/gtkrc'. Some GTK themes ignore customizations in '~/.emacs.d/gtkrc' so not everything works with all themes. To customize Emacs font, background, faces, etc., use the normal X resources (see Section D.1 [Resources], page 489). We will present some examples of customizations here, but for a more detailed description, see the online manual

The first example is just one line. It changes the font on all GTK widgets to courier with size 12:

```
gtk-font-name = "courier 12"
```

The thing to note is that the font name is not an X font name, like -*-helvetica-medium-r-*-*-120-*-*-*-*-*-*, but a Pango font name. A Pango font name is basically of the format "family style size", where the style is optional as in the case above. A name with a style could be for example:

```
gtk-font-name = "helvetica bold 10"
```

To customize widgets you first define a style and then apply the style to the widgets. Here is an example that sets the font for menus, but not for other widgets:

```
# Define the style 'menufont'.
style "menufont"
{
  font_name = "helvetica bold 14"  # This is a Pango font name
}

# Specify that widget type '*emacs-menuitem*' uses 'menufont'.
widget "*emacs-menuitem*" style "menufont"
```

The widget name in this example contains wildcards, so the style will be applied to all widgets that match "*emacs-menuitem*". The widgets are named by the

way they are contained, from the outer widget to the inner widget. So to apply the
style "my_style" (not shown) with the full, absolute name, for the menubar and the
scroll bar in Emacs we use:

```
widget "Emacs.pane.menubar" style "my_style"
widget "Emacs.pane.emacs.verticalScrollBar" style "my_style"
```

But to avoid having to type it all, wildcards are often used. '*' matches zero or
more characters and '?' matches one character. So "*" matches all widgets.

Each widget has a class (for example GtkMenuItem) and a name (emacs-
menuitem). You can assign styles by name or by class. In this example we have
used the class:

```
style "menufont"
{
  font_name = "helvetica bold 14"
}


widget_class "*GtkMenuBar" style "menufont"
```

The names and classes for the GTK widgets Emacs uses are:

emacs-filedialog	GtkFileSelection
emacs-dialog	GtkDialog
Emacs	GtkWindow
pane	GtkVHbox
emacs	GtkFixed
verticalScrollBar	GtkVScrollbar
emacs-toolbar	GtkToolbar
menubar	GtkMenuBar
emacs-menuitem	anything in menus

GTK absolute names are quite strange when it comes to menus and dialogs.
The names do not start with 'Emacs', as they are free-standing windows and not
contained (in the GTK sense) by the Emacs GtkWindow. To customize the dialogs
and menus, use wildcards like this:

```
widget "*emacs-dialog*" style "my_dialog_style"
widget "*emacs-filedialog* style "my_file_style"
widget "*emacs-menuitem* style "my_menu_style"
```

If you specify a customization in '~/.emacs.d/gtkrc', then it automatically
applies only to Emacs, since other programs don't read that file. For example, the
drop down menu in the file dialog can not be customized by any absolute widget
name, only by an absolute class name. This is because the widgets in the drop down
menu do not have names and the menu is not contained in the Emacs GtkWindow.
To have all menus in Emacs look the same, use this in '~/.emacs.d/gtkrc':

```
widget_class "*Menu*" style "my_menu_style"
```

Here is a more elaborate example, showing how to change the parts of the scroll
bar:

```
style "scroll"
{
  fg[NORMAL] = "red"      # The arrow color.
  bg[NORMAL] = "yellow"   # The thumb and background around the arrow.
  bg[ACTIVE] = "blue"     # The trough color.
```

```
    bg[PRELIGHT] = "white" # The thumb color when the mouse is over it.
}

widget "*verticalScrollBar*" style "scroll"
```

Appendix E Emacs 21 Antinews

For those users who live backwards in time, here is information about downgrading to Emacs version 21.4. We hope you will enjoy the greater simplicity that results from the absence of many Emacs 22 features.

- The buffer position and line number are now displayed at the end of the mode line, where they can be more easily seen.

- The mode line of the selected window is no longer displayed with a special face. All mode lines are created equal. Meanwhile, you can use the variable `mode-line-inverse-video` to control whether mode lines are highlighted at all—`nil` means don't highlight them.

- Clicking on a link with the left mouse button (`mouse-1`) will always set point at the position clicked, instead of following the link. If you want to follow the link, use the middle mouse button (`mouse-2`).

- Emacs is tired of X droppings. If you drop a file or a piece of text onto an Emacs window, nothing will happen.

- On an xterm, even if you enable Xterm Mouse mode, Emacs provides a more convincing simulation of a text terminal by not responding to mouse clicks on the mode line, header line, or display margin.

- For simplicity, windows always have fringes. We wouldn't want to in-fringe anyone's windows. Likewise, horizontal scrolling always works in the same automatic way.

- The horizontal-bar cursor shape has been removed.

- If command line arguments are given, Emacs will not display a splash screen, so that you can immediately get on with your editing. The command-line option '`--no-splash`' is therefore obsolete, and has been removed.

- These command line options have also been removed: '`--color`', '`--fullwidth`', '`--fullheight`', '`--fullscreen`', '`--no-blinking-cursor`', '`--no-desktop`', and '`-Q`'.

- The '`--geometry`' option applies only to the initial frame, and the '`-f`' option will not read arguments for interactive functions.

- We have standardized on one location for the user init file: the file named '`.emacs`' in your home directory. Emacs will not look for the init file in '`~/.emacs.d/init.el`'. Similarly, don't try putting '`.emacs_SHELL`' as '`init_SHELL.sh`' in '`~/.emacs.d`'; Emacs won't find it.

- Emacs will not read '`~/.abbrev_defs`' automatically. If you want to load abbrev definitions from a file, you must always do so explicitly.

- When you are logged in as root, all files now give you writable buffers, reflecting the fact that you can write any files.

- The maximum size of buffers and integer variables has been halved. On 32-bit machines, the maximum buffer size is now 128 megabytes.

- An unquoted '`$`' in a file name is now an error, if the following name is not recognized as an environment variable. Thus, the file name '`foo$bar`' would probably be an error. Meanwhile, the `setenv` command does not expand '$' at all.

- If a single command accumulates too much undo information, Emacs never discards it. If Emacs runs out of memory as a result, it will handle this by crashing.

- Many commands have been removed from the menus or rearranged.

- The `C-h` (help) subcommands have been rearranged—especially those that display specific files. Type `C-h C-h` to see a list of these commands; that will show you what is different.

- The `C-h v` and `C-h f` commands no longer show a hyperlink to the C source code, even if it is available. If you want to find the source code, grep for it.

- The apropos commands will not accept a list of words to match, in order to encourage you to be more specific. Also, the user option `apropos-sort-by-scores` has been removed.

- The minibuffer prompt is now displayed using the default face. The colon is enough to show you what part is the prompt.

- Minibuffer completion commands always complete the entire minibuffer contents, just as if you had typed them at the end of the minibuffer, no matter where point is actually located.

- The command `backward-kill-sexp` is now bound to `C-M-delete` and `C-M-backspace`. Be careful when using these key sequences! It may shut down your X server, or reboot your operating system.

- Commands to set the mark at a place away from point, including `M-@`, `M-h`, etc., don't do anything special when you repeat them. In most cases, typing these commands multiple times is equivalent to typing them once. `M-h` ignores numeric arguments.

- The user option `set-mark-command-repeat-pop` has been removed.

- `C-SPC C-SPC` has no special meaning—it just sets the mark twice. Neither does `C-u C-x C-x`, which simply exchanges point and mark like `C-x C-x`.

- The function `sentence-end` has been eliminated in favor of a more straightforward approach: directly setting the variable `sentence-end`. For example, to end each sentence with a single space, use

      (setq sentence-end "[.?!][]\"')}]*\\($\\|[\t]\\)[\t\n]*")

- The variable `fill-nobreak-predicate` is no longer customizable, and it can only hold a single function.

- Nobreak spaces and hyphens are displayed just like normal characters, and the user option `nobreak-char-display` has been removed.

- `C-w` in an incremental search always grabs an entire word into the search string. More precisely, it grabs text through the next end of a word.

- Yanking now preserves all text properties that were in the killed text. The variable `yank-excluded-properties` has been removed.

- Occur mode, Info mode, and Comint-derived modes now control fontification in their own way, and M-x font-lock-mode has nothing to do with it. To control fontification in Info mode, use the variable Info-fontify.

- 'M-x shell' is now completely standard in regard to scrolling behavior. It no longer has the option of scrolling the input line to the bottom of the window the way a text terminal running a shell does.

- The Grep package has been merged with Compilation mode. Many grep-specific commands and user options have thus been eliminated. Also, M-x grep never tries the GNU grep '-H' option, and instead silently appends '/dev/null' to the command line.

- In Dired's ! command, '*' and '?' now cause substitution of the file names wherever they appear—not only when they are surrounded by whitespace.

- When a file is managed with version control, the command C-x C-q (whose general meaning is to make a buffer read-only or writable) now does so by checking the file in or out. Checking the file out makes the buffer writable; checking it in makes the buffer read-only.

  You can still use C-x v v to do these operations if you wish; its meaning is unchanged. If you want to control the buffer's read-only flag without performing any version control operation, use M-x toggle-read-only.

- SGML mode does not handle XML syntax, and does not have indentation support.

- Many Info mode commands have been removed. Incremental search in Info searches only the current node.

- Many etags features for customizing parsing using regexps have been removed.

- The Emacs server now runs a small C program called 'emacsserver', rather than trying to handle everything in Emacs Lisp. Now there can only be one Emacs server running at a time. The server-mode command and server-name user option have been eliminated.

- The 'emacsclient' program no longer accepts the '--eval', '--display' and '--server-file' command line options, and can only establish local connections using Unix domain sockets.

- The command quail-show-key, for showing how to input a character, has been removed.

- The default value of keyboard-coding-system is always nil, regardless of your locale settings. If you want some other value, set it yourself.

- Unicode support and unification between Latin-n character sets have been removed. Cutting and pasting X selections does not support "extended segments", so there are certain coding systems it cannot handle.

- The input methods for Emacs are included in a separate distribution called "Leim." To use this, you must extract the Leim tar file on top of the Emacs distribution, into the same directory, before you build Emacs.

- The following input methods have been eliminated: belarusian, bulgarian-bds, bulgarian-phonetic, chinese-sisheng, croatian, dutch, georgian, latin-alt-postfix, latin-postfix, latin-prefix, latvian-keyboard, lithuanian-numeric, lithuanian-keyboard, malayalam-inscript, rfc1345, russian-computer, sgml, slovenian, tamil-inscript ucs, ukrainian-computer, vietnamese-telex, and welsh.

- The following language environments have been eliminated: Belarusian, Bulgarian, Chinese-EUC-TW, Croatian, French, Georgian, Italian, Latin-6, Latin-7, Latvian, Lithuanian, Malayalam, Russian, Russian, Slovenian, Swedish, Tajik, Tamil, UTF-8, Ukrainian, Ukrainian, Welsh, and Windows-1255.

- The `code-pages` library, which contained various 8-bit coding systems, has been removed.

- The Kmacro package has been replaced with a simple and elegant keyboard macro system. Use `C-x (` to start a new keyboard macro, `C-x )` to end the macro, and `C-x e` to execute the last macro. Use `M-x name-last-kbd-macro` to name the most recently defined macro.

- Emacs no longer displays your breakpoints in the source buffer, so you have to remember where you left them. It can be difficult to inspect the state of your debugged program from the command line, so Emacs tries to demonstrate this in the GUD buffer.

- The Calc, CUA, Ibuffer, Ido, Password, Printing, Reveal, Ruler-mode, SES, Table, Tramp, and URL packages have been removed. The Benchmark, Cfengine, Conf, Dns, Flymake, Python, Thumbs, and Wdired modes have also been removed.

- The Emacs Lisp Reference Manual and the Introduction to Programming in Emacs Lisp are now distributed separately, not in the Emacs distribution.

- On MS Windows, there is no longer any support for tooltips, images, sound, different mouse pointer shapes, or pointing devices with more than 3 buttons. If you want these features, consider switching to another operating system. But even if you don't want these features, you should still switch—for freedom's sake.

- Emacs will not use Unicode for clipboard operations on MS Windows.

- To keep up with decreasing computer memory capacity and disk space, many other functions and files have been eliminated in Emacs 21.4.

Appendix F Emacs and Mac OS

This section briefly describes the peculiarities of using Emacs under Mac OS with native window system support. For Mac OS X, Emacs can be built either without window system support, with X11, or with Carbon API. This section only applies to the Carbon build. For Mac OS Classic, Emacs can be built with or without Carbon API, and this section applies to either of them because they run on the native window system.

Emacs built on Mac OS X supports most of its major features except display support of PostScript images. The following features of Emacs are not supported on Mac OS Classic: unexec (`dump-emacs`), asynchronous subprocesses (`start-process`), and networking (`open-network-stream`). As a result, packages such as Gnus, GUD, and Comint do not work. Synchronous subprocesses (`call-process`) are supported on non-Carbon build, but specially-crafted external programs are needed. Since external programs to handle commands such as `print-buffer` and `diff` are not available on Mac OS Classic, they are not supported. Non-Carbon build on Mac OS Classic does not support some features such as file dialogs, drag-and-drop, and Unicode menus.

F.1 Keyboard and Mouse Input on Mac

On Mac, Emacs can use CONTROL, COMMAND, OPTION, and laptop FUNCTION keys as any of Emacs modifier keys except SHIFT (i.e., ALT, CTRL, HYPER, META, and SUPER). The assignment is controlled by the variables `mac-control-modifier`, `mac-command-modifier`, `mac-option-modifier`, and `mac-function-modifier`. The value for each of these variables can be one of the following symbols: `alt`, `control`, `hyper`, `meta`, `super`, and `nil` (no particular assignment). By default, the CONTROL key works as CTRL, and the COMMAND key as META.

For the OPTION key, if `mac-option-modifier` is set to `nil`, which is the default, the key works as the normal OPTION key, i.e., dead-key processing will work. This is useful for entering non-ASCII Latin characters directly from the Mac keyboard, for example.

Emacs recognizes the setting in the Keyboard control panel (Mac OS Classic) or the International system preference pane (Mac OS X) and supports international and alternative keyboard layouts (e.g., Dvorak). Selecting one of the layouts from the keyboard layout pull-down menu will affect how the keys typed on the keyboard are interpreted.

Mac OS intercepts and handles certain key combinations (e.g., COMMAND-SPC for switching input languages). These will not be passed to Emacs. One can disable this interception by setting `mac-pass-command-to-system` or `mac-pass-control-to-system` to `nil`.

Especially for one-button mice, the multiple button feature can be emulated by setting `mac-emulate-three-button-mouse` to `t` or `reverse`. If set to `t` (`reverse`, respectively), pressing the mouse button with the OPTION key is recognized as the second (third) button, and that with the COMMAND key is recognized as the third (second) button.

For multi-button mice, the wheel button and the secondary button are recognized as the second and the third button, respectively. If `mac-wheel-button-is-mouse-2` is set to `nil`, their roles are exchanged.

F.2 International Character Set Support on Mac

Mac uses non-standard encodings for the upper 128 single-byte characters. They also deviate from the ISO 2022 standard by using character codes in the range 128-159. The coding systems `mac-roman`, `mac-centraleurroman`, and `mac-cyrillic` are used to represent these Mac encodings.

You can use input methods provided either by LEIM (see Section 19.4 [Input Methods], page 190) or Mac OS to enter international characters. To use the former, see the International Character Set Support section of the manual (see Chapter 19 [International], page 186).

Emacs on Mac OS automatically changes the value of `keyboard-coding-system` according to the current keyboard layout. So users don't need to set it manually, and even if set, it will be changed when the keyboard layout change is detected next time.

The Mac clipboard and the Emacs kill ring (see Chapter 9 [Killing], page 55) are synchronized by default: you can yank a piece of text and paste it into another Mac application, or cut or copy one in another Mac application and yank it into a Emacs buffer. This feature can be disabled by setting `x-select-enable-clipboard` to `nil`. One can still do copy and paste with another application from the Edit menu.

On Mac, the role of the coding system for selection that is set by `set-selection-coding-system` (see Section 19.12 [Communication Coding], page 200) is two-fold. First, it is used as a preferred coding system for the traditional text flavor that does not specify any particular encodings and is mainly used by applications on Mac OS Classic. Second, it specifies the intermediate encoding for the UTF-16 text flavor that is mainly used by applications on Mac OS X.

When pasting UTF-16 text data from the clipboard, it is first converted to the encoding specified by the selection coding system using the converter in the Mac OS system, and then decoded into the Emacs internal encoding using the converter in Emacs. If the first conversion failed, then the UTF-16 data is directly converted to Emacs internal encoding using the converter in Emacs. Copying UTF-16 text to the clipboard goes through the inverse path. The reason for this two-pass decoding is to avoid subtle differences in Unicode mappings between the Mac OS system and Emacs such as various kinds of hyphens, and to minimize users' customization. For example, users that mainly use Latin characters would prefer Greek characters to be decoded into the `mule-unicode-0100-24ff` charset, but Japanese users would prefer them to be decoded into the `japanese-jisx0208` charset. Since the coding system for selection is automatically set according to the system locale setting, users usually don't have to set it manually.

The default language environment (see Section 19.3 [Language Environments], page 188) is set according to the locale setting at the startup time. On Mac OS, the locale setting is consulted in the following order:

1. Environment variables `LC_ALL`, `LC_CTYPE` and `LANG` as in other systems.

2. Preference `AppleLocale` that is set by default on Mac OS X 10.3 and later.

3. Preference `AppleLanguages` that is set by default on Mac OS X 10.1 and later.

4. Variable `mac-system-locale` that is derived from the system language and region codes. This variable is available on all supported Mac OS versions including Mac OS Classic.

The default values of almost all variables about coding systems are also set according to the language environment. So usually you don't have to customize these variables manually.

F.3 Environment Variables and Command Line Arguments.

On Mac OS X, when Emacs is run in a terminal, it inherits the values of environment variables from the shell from which it is invoked. However, when it is run from the Finder as a GUI application, it only inherits environment variable values defined in the file '`~/.MacOSX/environment.plist`' that affects all the applications invoked from the Finder or the `open` command.

Command line arguments are specified like

```
/Applications/Emacs.app/Contents/MacOS/Emacs -g 80x25 &
```

if Emacs is installed at '`/Applications/Emacs.app`'. If Emacs is invoked like this, then it also inherits the values of environment variables from the shell from which it is invoked.

On Mac OS Classic, environment variables and command line arguments for Emacs can be set by modifying the '`STR#`' resources 128 and 129, respectively. A common environment variable that one may want to set is '`HOME`'.

The way to set an environment variable is by adding a string of the form

```
ENV_VAR=VALUE
```

to resource '`STR#`' number 128 using `ResEdit`. To set up the program to use unibyte characters exclusively, for example, add the string

```
EMACS_UNIBYTE=1
```

Although Emacs on Mac does not support X resources (see Appendix D [X Resources], page 489) directly, one can use the Preferences system in place of X resources. For example, adding the line

```
Emacs.cursorType: bar
```

to '`~/.Xresources`' in X11 corresponds to the execution of

```
defaults write org.gnu.Emacs Emacs.cursorType bar
```

on Mac OS X. One can use boolean or numeric values as well as string values as follows:

```
defaults write org.gnu.Emacs Emacs.toolBar -bool false
defaults write org.gnu.Emacs Emacs.lineSpacing -int 3
```

Try M-x man RET defaults RET for the usage of the defaults command. Alternatively, if you have Developer Tools installed on Mac OS X, you can use Property List Editor to edit the file '~/Library/Preferences/org.gnu.Emacs.plist'.

F.4 Volumes and Directories on Mac

This node applies to Mac OS Classic only.

The directory structure in Mac OS Classic is seen by Emacs as

/volumename/filename

So when Emacs requests a file name, doing file name completion on '/' will display all volumes on the system. You can use '..' to go up a directory level.

On Mac OS Classic, to access files and folders on the desktop, look in the folder 'Desktop Folder' in your boot volume (this folder is usually invisible in the Mac Finder).

On Mac OS Classic, Emacs creates the Mac folder ':Preferences:Emacs:' in the 'System Folder' and uses it as the temporary directory. Emacs maps the directory name '/tmp/' to that. Therefore it is best to avoid naming a volume 'tmp'. If everything works correctly, the program should leave no files in it when it exits. You should be able to set the environment variable TMPDIR to use another directory but this folder will still be created.

F.5 Specifying Fonts on Mac

It is rare that you need to specify a font name in Emacs; usually you specify face attributes instead. For example, you can use 14pt Courier by customizing the default face attributes for all frames:

(set-face-attribute 'default nil
                     :family "courier" :height 140)

Alternatively, an interactive one is also available (see Section 32.2.5 [Face Customization], page 413).

But when you do need to specify a font name in Emacs on Mac, use a standard X font name:

-maker-family-weight-slant-widthtype-style...
...-pixels-height-horiz-vert-spacing-width-charset

See Section C.7 [Font X], page 481. Wildcards are supported as they are on X.

Emacs on Mac OS Classic uses QuickDraw Text routines for drawing texts by default. Emacs on Mac OS X uses ATSUI (Apple Type Services for Unicode Imaging) as well as QuickDraw Text, and most of the characters other than Chinese, Japanese, and Korean ones are drawn using the former by default.

ATSUI-compatible fonts have maker name apple and charset iso10646-1. For example, 12-point Monaco can be specified by the name:

-apple-monaco-medium-r-normal--12-*-*-*-*-*-iso10646-1

Note that these names must be specified using a format containing all 14 '-'s (not by '-apple-monaco-medium-r-normal--12-*-iso10646-1', for instance), because every ATSUI-compatible font is a scalable one.

QuickDraw Text fonts have maker name `apple` and various charset names other than `iso10646-1`. Native Apple fonts in Mac Roman encoding has charset `mac-roman`. You can specify a `mac-roman` font for ASCII characters like

```
(add-to-list
 'default-frame-alist
 '(font . "-apple-monaco-medium-r-normal--13-*-*-*-*-*-mac-roman"))
```

but that does not extend to ISO-8859-1: specifying a `mac-roman` font for Latin-1 characters introduces wrong glyphs.

Native Apple Traditional Chinese, Simplified Chinese, Japanese, Korean, Central European, Cyrillic, Symbol, and Dingbats fonts have the charsets 'big5-0', 'gb2312.1980-0', 'jisx0208.1983-sjis' and 'jisx0201.1976-0', 'ksc5601.1989-0', 'mac-centraleurroman', 'mac-cyrillic', 'mac-symbol', and 'mac-dingbats', respectively.

The use of `create-fontset-from-fontset-spec` (see Section 19.16 [Defining Fontsets], page 203) for defining fontsets often results in wrong ones especially when using only OS-bundled QuickDraw Text fonts. The recommended way to use them is to create a fontset using `create-fontset-from-mac-roman-font`:

```
(create-fontset-from-mac-roman-font
 "-apple-courier-medium-r-normal--13-*-*-*-*-*-mac-roman"
 nil "foo")
```

and then optionally specifying Chinese, Japanese, or Korean font families using `set-fontset-font`:

```
(set-fontset-font "fontset-foo"
 'chinese-gb2312 '("song" . "gb2312.1980-0"))
```

Single-byte fonts converted from GNU fonts in BDF format, which are not in the Mac Roman encoding, have foundry, family, and character sets encoded in the names of their font suitcases. E.g., the font suitcase 'ETL-Fixed-ISO8859-1' contains fonts which can be referred to by the name '-ETL-fixed-*-iso8859-1'.

Mac OS X 10.2 or later can use two types of text renderings: Quartz 2D (aka Core Graphics) and QuickDraw. By default, Emacs uses the former on such versions. It can be changed by setting `mac-allow-anti-aliasing` to `t` (Quartz 2D) or `nil` (QuickDraw). Both ATSUI and QuickDraw Text drawings are affected by the value of this variable.

Appearance of text in small sizes will also be affected by the "Turn off text smoothing for font sizes n and smaller" setting in the General pane (Mac OS X 10.1 or 10.2) or in the Appearance pane (10.3 or later) of the System Preferences. This threshold can alternatively be set just for Emacs (i.e., not as the system-wide setting) using the `defaults` command:

```
defaults write org.gnu.Emacs AppleAntiAliasingThreshold n
```

F.6 Mac-Specific Lisp Functions

The function `do-applescript` takes a string argument, executes it as an AppleScript command, and returns the result as a string.

The function `mac-file-name-to-posix` takes a Mac file name and returns the GNU or Unix equivalent. The function `posix-file-name-to-mac` performs the opposite conversion. They are useful for constructing AppleScript commands to be passed to `do-applescript`.

The functions `mac-set-file-creator`, `mac-get-file-creator`, `mac-set-file-type`, and `mac-get-file-type` can be used to set and get creator and file codes.

The function `mac-get-preference` returns the preferences value converted to a Lisp object for a specified key and application.

Appendix G Emacs and Microsoft Windows/MS-DOS

This section describes peculiarities of using Emacs on Microsoft Windows. Some of these peculiarities are also relevant to Microsoft's older MS-DOS "operating system" (also known as "MS-DOG"). However, Emacs features that are relevant *only* to MS-DOS are described in a separate manual (see section "MS-DOS" in *Specialized Emacs Features*).

The behavior of Emacs on MS-Windows is reasonably similar to what is documented in the rest of the manual, including support for long file names, multiple frames, scroll bars, mouse menus, and subprocesses. However, a few special considerations apply, and they are described here.

G.1 Text Files and Binary Files

GNU Emacs uses newline characters to separate text lines. This is the convention used on GNU, Unix, and other Posix-compliant systems.

By contrast, MS-DOS and MS-Windows normally use carriage-return linefeed, a two-character sequence, to separate text lines. (Linefeed is the same character as newline.) Therefore, convenient editing of typical files with Emacs requires conversion of these end-of-line (EOL) sequences. And that is what Emacs normally does: it converts carriage-return linefeed into newline when reading files, and converts newline into carriage-return linefeed when writing files. The same mechanism that handles conversion of international character codes does this conversion also (see Section 19.7 [Coding Systems], page 193).

One consequence of this special format-conversion of most files is that character positions as reported by Emacs (see Section 4.9 [Position Info], page 26) do not agree with the file size information known to the operating system.

In addition, if Emacs recognizes from a file's contents that it uses newline rather than carriage-return linefeed as its line separator, it does not perform EOL conversion when reading or writing that file. Thus, you can read and edit files from GNU and Unix systems on MS-DOS with no special effort, and they will retain their Unix-style end-of-line convention after you edit them.

The mode line indicates whether end-of-line translation was used for the current buffer. If MS-DOS end-of-line translation is in use for the buffer, the MS-Windows build of Emacs displays a backslash '\' after the coding system mnemonic near the beginning of the mode line (see Section 1.3 [Mode Line], page 8). If no EOL translation was performed, the string '(Unix)' is displayed instead of the backslash, to alert you that the file's EOL format is not the usual carriage-return linefeed.

To visit a file and specify whether it uses DOS-style or Unix-style end-of-line, specify a coding system (see Section 19.11 [Text Coding], page 198). For example, C-x RET c unix RET C-x C-f foobar.txt visits the file 'foobar.txt' without converting the EOLs; if some line ends with a carriage-return linefeed pair, Emacs will display '^M' at the end of that line. Similarly, you can direct Emacs to save a buffer in a specified EOL format with the C-x RET f command. For example, to save a buffer with Unix EOL format, type C-x RET f unix RET C-x C-s. If you visit a file with DOS EOL conversion, then save it with Unix EOL format, that effectively converts the file to Unix EOL style, like dos2unix.

When you use NFS, Samba, or some other similar method to access file systems that reside on computers using GNU or Unix systems, Emacs should not perform end-of-line translation on any files in these file systems—not even when you create a new file. To request this, designate these file systems as *untranslated* file systems by calling the function add-untranslated-filesystem. It takes one argument: the file system name, including a drive letter and optionally a directory. For example,

        (add-untranslated-filesystem "Z:")

designates drive Z as an untranslated file system, and

        (add-untranslated-filesystem "Z:\\foo")

designates directory '\foo' on drive Z as an untranslated file system.

Most often you would use add-untranslated-filesystem in your '.emacs' file, or in 'site-start.el' so that all the users at your site get the benefit of it.

To countermand the effect of add-untranslated-filesystem, use the function remove-untranslated-filesystem. This function takes one argument, which should be a string just like the one that was used previously with add-untranslated-filesystem.

Designating a file system as untranslated does not affect character set conversion, only end-of-line conversion. Essentially, it directs Emacs to create new files with the Unix-style convention of using newline at the end of a line. See Section 19.7 [Coding Systems], page 193.

Some kinds of files should not be converted at all, because their contents are not really text. Therefore, Emacs on MS-Windows distinguishes certain files as *binary files*. (This distinction is not part of MS-Windows; it is made by Emacs only.) Binary files include executable programs, compressed archives, etc. Emacs uses the file name to decide whether to treat a file as binary: the variable file-name-buffer-file-type-alist defines the file-name patterns that indicate binary files. If a file name matches one of the patterns for binary files (those whose associations are of the type (*pattern* . t), Emacs reads and writes that file using the no-conversion coding system (see Section 19.7 [Coding Systems], page 193) which turns off *all* coding-system conversions, not only the EOL conversion. file-name-buffer-file-type-alist also includes file-name patterns for files which are known to be Windows-style text files with carriage-return linefeed EOL format, such as 'CONFIG.SYS'; Emacs always writes those files with Windows-style EOLs.

If a file which belongs to an untranslated file system matches one of the file-name patterns in file-name-buffer-file-type-alist, the EOL conversion is determined by file-name-buffer-file-type-alist.

G.2 File Names on MS-Windows

MS-Windows and MS-DOS normally use a backslash, '\', to separate name units within a file name, instead of the slash used on other systems. Emacs on MS-

DOS/MS-Windows permits use of either slash or backslash, and also knows about drive letters in file names.

On MS-DOS/MS-Windows, file names are case-insensitive, so Emacs by default ignores letter-case in file names during completion.

If the variable `w32-get-true-file-attributes` is non-`nil` (the default), Emacs tries to determine the accurate link counts for files. This option is only useful on NTFS volumes, and it considerably slows down Dired and other features, so use it only on fast machines.

G.3 Emulation of `ls` on MS-Windows

Dired normally uses the external program `ls` (or its close work-alike) to produce the directory listing displayed in Dired buffers (see Chapter 29 [Dired], page 339). However, MS-Windows and MS-DOS systems don't come with such a program, although several ports of GNU `ls` are available. Therefore, Emacs on those systems *emulates* `ls` in Lisp, by using the '`ls-lisp.el`' package. While '`ls-lisp.el`' provides a reasonably full emulation of `ls`, there are some options and features peculiar to that emulation; for more details, see the documentation of the variables whose names begin with `ls-lisp`.

G.4 HOME Directory on MS-Windows

The Windows equivalent of the `HOME` directory is the *user-specific application data directory*. The actual location depends on your Windows version and system configuration; typical values are '`C:\Documents and Settings\`*username*`\Application Data`' on Windows 2K/XP and later, and either '`C:\WINDOWS\Application Data`' or '`C:\WINDOWS\Profiles\`*username*`\Application Data`' on the older Windows 9X/ME systems.

The home directory is where your init file '`.emacs`' is stored. When Emacs starts, it first checks whether the environment variable `HOME` is set. If it is, it looks for the init file in the directory pointed by `HOME`. If `HOME` is not defined, Emacs checks for an existing '`.emacs`' file in '`C:\`', the root directory of drive '`C:`'[1]. If there's no such file in '`C:\`', Emacs next uses the Windows system calls to find out the exact location of your application data directory. If that fails as well, Emacs falls back to '`C:\`'.

Whatever the final place is, Emacs sets the value of the `HOME` environment variable to point to it, and it will use that location for other files and directories it normally creates in the user's home directory.

You can always find out where Emacs thinks is your home directory's location by typing `C-x d ~/ RET`. This should present the list of files in the home directory, and show its full name on the first line. Likewise, to visit your init file, type `C-x C-f ~/.emacs RET`.

---

[1] The check in '`C:\`' is in preference to the application data directory for compatibility with older versions of Emacs, which didn't check the application data directory.

Because MS-DOS does not allow file names with leading dots, and because older Windows systems made it hard to create files with such names, the Windows port of Emacs supports an alternative name '_emacs' as a fallback, if such a file exists in the home directory, whereas '.emacs' does not.

G.5 Keyboard Usage on MS-Windows

This section describes the Windows-specific features related to keyboard input in Emacs.

Many key combinations (known as "keyboard shortcuts") that have conventional uses in MS-Windows programs conflict with traditional Emacs key bindings. (These Emacs key bindings were established years before Microsoft was founded.) Examples of conflicts include C-c, C-x, C-z, C-a, and W-SPC. You can redefine some of them with meanings more like the MS-Windows meanings by enabling CUA Mode (see Section 9.5 [CUA Bindings], page 63).

The F10 key on Windows activates the menu bar in a way that makes it possible to use the menus without a mouse. In this mode, the arrow keys traverse the menus, RET selects a highlighted menu item, and ESC closes the menu.

See Info file 'emacs', node 'Windows Keyboard', for information about additional Windows-specific variables in this category.

The variable w32-apps-modifier controls the effect of the APPS key (usually located between the right ALT and the right CTRL keys). Its value can be one of the symbols hyper, super, meta, alt, control, or shift for the respective modifier, or nil to appear as the key apps. The default is nil.

The variable w32-lwindow-modifier determines the effect of the left Windows key (usually labeled with START and the Windows logo). If its value is nil (the default), the key will produce the symbol lwindow. Setting it to one of the symbols hyper, super, meta, alt, control, or shift will produce the respective modifier. A similar variable w32-rwindow-modifier controls the effect of the right Windows key, and w32-scroll-lock-modifier does the same for the SCRLOCK key. If these variables are set to nil, the right Windows key produces the symbol rwindow and SCRLOCK produces the symbol scroll.

Emacs compiled as a native Windows application normally turns off the Windows feature that tapping the ALT key invokes the Windows menu. The reason is that the ALT serves as META in Emacs. When using Emacs, users often press the META key temporarily and then change their minds; if this has the effect of bringing up the Windows menu, it alters the meaning of subsequent commands. Many users find this frustrating.

You can re-enable Windows' default handling of tapping the ALT key by setting w32-pass-alt-to-system to a non-nil value.

G.6 Mouse Usage on MS-Windows

This section describes the Windows-specific variables related to mouse.

The variable w32-mouse-button-tolerance specifies the time interval, in milliseconds, for faking middle mouse button press on 2-button mice. If both mouse buttons are depressed within this time interval, Emacs generates a middle mouse button click event instead of a double click on one of the buttons.

If the variable `w32-pass-extra-mouse-buttons-to-system` is non-nil, Emacs passes the fourth and fifth mouse buttons to Windows.

The variable `w32-swap-mouse-buttons` controls which of the 3 mouse buttons generates the `mouse-2` events. When it is `nil` (the default), the middle button generates `mouse-2` and the right button generates `mouse-3` events. If this variable is non-`nil`, the roles of these two buttons are reversed.

G.7 Subprocesses on Windows 9X/ME and Windows NT/2K/XP

Emacs compiled as a native Windows application (as opposed to the DOS version) includes full support for asynchronous subprocesses. In the Windows version, synchronous and asynchronous subprocesses work fine on both Windows 9X/ME and Windows NT/2K/XP as long as you run only 32-bit Windows applications. However, when you run a DOS application in a subprocess, you may encounter problems or be unable to run the application at all; and if you run two DOS applications at the same time in two subprocesses, you may have to reboot your system.

Since the standard command interpreter (and most command line utilities) on Windows 9X are DOS applications, these problems are significant when using that system. But there's nothing we can do about them; only Microsoft can fix them.

If you run just one DOS application subprocess, the subprocess should work as expected as long as it is "well-behaved" and does not perform direct screen access or other unusual actions. If you have a CPU monitor application, your machine will appear to be 100% busy even when the DOS application is idle, but this is only an artifact of the way CPU monitors measure processor load.

You must terminate the DOS application before you start any other DOS application in a different subprocess. Emacs is unable to interrupt or terminate a DOS subprocess. The only way you can terminate such a subprocess is by giving it a command that tells its program to exit.

If you attempt to run two DOS applications at the same time in separate subprocesses, the second one that is started will be suspended until the first one finishes, even if either or both of them are asynchronous.

If you can go to the first subprocess, and tell it to exit, the second subprocess should continue normally. However, if the second subprocess is synchronous, Emacs itself will be hung until the first subprocess finishes. If it will not finish without user input, then you have no choice but to reboot if you are running on Windows 9X. If you are running on Windows NT/2K/XP, you can use a process viewer application to kill the appropriate instance of NTVDM instead (this will terminate both DOS subprocesses).

If you have to reboot Windows 9X in this situation, do not use the `Shutdown` command on the `Start` menu; that usually hangs the system. Instead, type `CTL-ALT-DEL` and then choose `Shutdown`. That usually works, although it may take a few minutes to do its job.

The variable `w32-quote-process-args` controls how Emacs quotes the process arguments. Non-`nil` means quote with the " character. If the value is a character, use that character to escape any quote characters that appear; otherwise chose a suitable escape character based on the type of the program.

G.8 Printing and MS-Windows

Printing commands, such as `lpr-buffer` (see Section 31.4 [Printing], page 391) and `ps-print-buffer` (see Section 31.5 [PostScript], page 392) work in MS-DOS and MS-Windows by sending the output to one of the printer ports, if a Posix-style `lpr` program is unavailable. The same Emacs variables control printing on all systems, but in some cases they have different default values on MS-DOS and MS-Windows.

Emacs on Windows automatically determines your default printer and sets the variable *printer-name* to that printer's name. But in some rare cases this can fail, or you may wish to use a different printer from within Emacs. The rest of this section explains how to tell Emacs which printer to use.

If you want to use your local printer, then set the Lisp variable `lpr command` to "" (its default value on Windows) and `printer-name` to the name of the printer port—for example, "PRN", the usual local printer port or "LPT2", or "COM1" for a serial printer. You can also set `printer-name` to a file name, in which case "printed" output is actually appended to that file. If you set `printer-name` to "NUL", printed output is silently discarded (sent to the system null device).

You can also use a printer shared by another machine by setting `printer-name` to the UNC share name for that printer—for example, "//joes_pc/hp4si". (It doesn't matter whether you use forward slashes or backslashes here.) To find out the names of shared printers, run the command 'net view' from the command prompt to obtain a list of servers, and 'net view server-name' to see the names of printers (and directories) shared by that server. Alternatively, click the 'Network Neighborhood' icon on your desktop, and look for machines which share their printers via the network.

If the printer doesn't appear in the output of 'net view', or if setting `printer-name` to the UNC share name doesn't produce a hardcopy on that printer, you can use the 'net use' command to connect a local print port such as "LPT2" to the networked printer. For example, typing `net use LPT2: \\joes_pc\hp4si`[2] causes Windows to *capture* the LPT2 port and redirect the printed material to the printer connected to the machine `joes_pc`. After this command, setting `printer-name` to "LPT2" should produce the hardcopy on the networked printer.

With some varieties of Windows network software, you can instruct Windows to capture a specific printer port such as "LPT2", and redirect it to a networked printer via the `Control Panel->Printers` applet instead of 'net use'.

If you set `printer-name` to a file name, it's best to use an absolute file name. Emacs changes the working directory according to the default directory of the cur-

---

[2]   Note that the 'net use' command requires the UNC share name to be typed with the Windows-style backslashes, while the value of `printer-name` can be set with either forward- or backslashes.

rent buffer, so if the file name in `printer-name` is relative, you will end up with several such files, each one in the directory of the buffer from which the printing was done.

If the value of `printer-name` is correct, but printing does not produce the hardcopy on your printer, it is possible that your printer does not support printing plain text (some cheap printers omit this functionality). In that case, try the PostScript print commands, described below.

The commands `print-buffer` and `print-region` call the `pr` program, or use special switches to the `lpr` program, to produce headers on each printed page. MS-DOS and MS-Windows don't normally have these programs, so by default, the variable `lpr-headers-switches` is set so that the requests to print page headers are silently ignored. Thus, `print-buffer` and `print-region` produce the same output as `lpr-buffer` and `lpr-region`, respectively. If you do have a suitable `pr` program (for example, from GNU Coreutils), set `lpr-headers-switches` to `nil`; Emacs will then call `pr` to produce the page headers, and print the resulting output as specified by `printer-name`.

Finally, if you do have an `lpr` work-alike, you can set the variable `lpr-command` to `"lpr"`. Then Emacs will use `lpr` for printing, as on other systems. (If the name of the program isn't `lpr`, set `lpr-command` to specify where to find it.) The variable `lpr-switches` has its standard meaning when `lpr-command` is not `""`. If the variable `printer-name` has a string value, it is used as the value for the `-P` option to `lpr`, as on Unix.

A parallel set of variables, `ps-lpr-command`, `ps-lpr-switches`, and `ps-printer-name` (see Section 31.6 [PostScript Variables], page 393), defines how PostScript files should be printed. These variables are used in the same way as the corresponding variables described above for non-PostScript printing. Thus, the value of `ps-printer-name` is used as the name of the device (or file) to which PostScript output is sent, just as `printer-name` is used for non-PostScript printing. (There are two distinct sets of variables in case you have two printers attached to two different ports, and only one of them is a PostScript printer.)

The default value of the variable `ps-lpr-command` is `""`, which causes PostScript output to be sent to the printer port specified by `ps-printer-name`, but `ps-lpr-command` can also be set to the name of a program which will accept PostScript files. Thus, if you have a non-PostScript printer, you can set this variable to the name of a PostScript interpreter program (such as Ghostscript). Any switches that need to be passed to the interpreter program are specified using `ps-lpr-switches`. (If the value of `ps-printer-name` is a string, it will be added to the list of switches as the value for the `-P` option. This is probably only useful if you are using `lpr`, so when using an interpreter typically you would·set `ps-printer-name` to something other than a string so it is ignored.)

For example, to use Ghostscript for printing on the system's default printer, put this in your '`.emacs`' file:

```
(setq ps-printer-name t)
(setq ps-lpr-command "D:/gs6.01/bin/gswin32c.exe")
(setq ps-lpr-switches '("-q" "-dNOPAUSE" "-dBATCH"
```

```
"-sDEVICE=mswinpr2"
"-sPAPERSIZE=a4"))
```
(This assumes that Ghostscript is installed in the 'D:/gs6.01' directory.)

G.9 Miscellaneous Windows-specific features

This section describes miscellaneous Windows-specific features.

The variable `w32-use-visible-system-caret` is a flag that determines whether to make the system caret visible. The default is `nil`, which means Emacs draws its own cursor to indicate the position of point. A non-`nil` value means Emacs will indicate point location by the system caret; this facilitates use of screen reader software. When this variable is non-`nil`, other variables affecting the cursor display have no effect.

See Info file 'emacs', node 'Windows Misc', for information about additional Windows specific variables in this category.

The GNU Manifesto

The GNU Manifesto which appears below was written by Richard Stallman at the beginning of the GNU project, to ask for participation and support. For the first few years, it was updated in minor ways to account for developments, but now it seems best to leave it unchanged as most people have seen it.

Since that time, we have learned about certain common misunderstandings that different wording could help avoid. Footnotes added in 1993 help clarify these points.

For up-to-date information about available GNU software, please see our web site, `http://www.gnu.org`. For software tasks and other ways to contribute, see `http://www.gnu.org/help`.

What's GNU? Gnu's Not Unix!

GNU, which stands for Gnu's Not Unix, is the name for the complete Unix-compatible software system which I am writing so that I can give it away free to everyone who can use it.[1] Several other volunteers are helping me. Contributions of time, money, programs and equipment are greatly needed.

So far we have an Emacs text editor with Lisp for writing editor commands, a source level debugger, a yacc-compatible parser generator, a linker, and around 35 utilities. A shell (command interpreter) is nearly completed. A new portable optimizing C compiler has compiled itself and may be released this year. An initial kernel exists but many more features are needed to emulate Unix. When the kernel and compiler are finished, it will be possible to distribute a GNU system suitable for program development. We will use TeX as our text formatter, but an nroff is being worked on. We will use the free, portable X window system as well. After this we will add a portable Common Lisp, an Empire game, a spreadsheet, and hundreds of other things, plus on-line documentation. We hope to supply, eventually, everything useful that normally comes with a Unix system, and more.

GNU will be able to run Unix programs, but will not be identical to Unix. We will make all improvements that are convenient, based on our experience with other operating systems. In particular, we plan to have longer file names, file version numbers, a crashproof file system, file name completion perhaps, terminal-independent

---

[1] The wording here was careless. The intention was that nobody would have to pay for *permission* to use the GNU system. But the words don't make this clear, and people often interpret them as saying that copies of GNU should always be distributed at little or no charge. That was never the intent; later on, the manifesto mentions the possibility of companies providing the service of distribution for a profit. Subsequently I have learned to distinguish carefully between "free" in the sense of freedom and "free" in the sense of price. Free software is software that users have the freedom to distribute and change. Some users may obtain copies at no charge, while others pay to obtain copies—and if the funds help support improving the software, so much the better. The important thing is that everyone who has a copy has the freedom to cooperate with others in using it.

display support, and perhaps eventually a Lisp-based window system through which several Lisp programs and ordinary Unix programs can share a screen. Both C and Lisp will be available as system programming languages. We will try to support UUCP, MIT Chaosnet, and Internet protocols for communication.

GNU is aimed initially at machines in the 68000/16000 class with virtual memory, because they are the easiest machines to make it run on. The extra effort to make it run on smaller machines will be left to someone who wants to use it on them.

To avoid horrible confusion, please pronounce the 'G' in the word 'GNU' when it is the name of this project.

Why I Must Write GNU

I consider that the golden rule requires that if I like a program I must share it with other people who like it. Software sellers want to divide the users and conquer them, making each user agree not to share with others. I refuse to break solidarity with other users in this way. I cannot in good conscience sign a nondisclosure agreement or a software license agreement. For years I worked within the Artificial Intelligence Lab to resist such tendencies and other inhospitalities, but eventually they had gone too far: I could not remain in an institution where such things are done for me against my will.

So that I can continue to use computers without dishonor, I have decided to put together a sufficient body of free software so that I will be able to get along without any software that is not free. I have resigned from the AI lab to deny MIT any legal excuse to prevent me from giving GNU away.

Why GNU Will Be Compatible with Unix

Unix is not my ideal system, but it is not too bad. The essential features of Unix seem to be good ones, and I think I can fill in what Unix lacks without spoiling them. And a system compatible with Unix would be convenient for many other people to adopt.

How GNU Will Be Available

GNU is not in the public domain. Everyone will be permitted to modify and redistribute GNU, but no distributor will be allowed to restrict its further redistribution. That is to say, proprietary modifications will not be allowed. I want to make sure that all versions of GNU remain free.

Why Many Other Programmers Want to Help

I have found many other programmers who are excited about GNU and want to help.

Many programmers are unhappy about the commercialization of system software. It may enable them to make more money, but it requires them to feel in conflict with other programmers in general rather than feel as comrades. The fundamental act of friendship among programmers is the sharing of programs; marketing arrangements now typically used essentially forbid programmers to treat others as friends. The purchaser of software must choose between friendship and obeying the law. Naturally, many decide that friendship is more important. But those who believe in law often do not feel at ease with either choice. They become cynical and think that programming is just a way of making money.

By working on and using GNU rather than proprietary programs, we can be hospitable to everyone and obey the law. In addition, GNU serves as an example to inspire and a banner to rally others to join us in sharing. This can give us a feeling of harmony which is impossible if we use software that is not free. For about half the programmers I talk to, this is an important happiness that money cannot replace.

How You Can Contribute

I am asking computer manufacturers for donations of machines and money. I'm asking individuals for donations of programs and work.

One consequence you can expect if you donate machines is that GNU will run on them at an early date. The machines should be complete, ready to use systems, approved for use in a residential area, and not in need of sophisticated cooling or power.

I have found very many programmers eager to contribute part-time work for GNU. For most projects, such part-time distributed work would be very hard to coordinate; the independently-written parts would not work together. But for the particular task of replacing Unix, this problem is absent. A complete Unix system contains hundreds of utility programs, each of which is documented separately. Most interface specifications are fixed by Unix compatibility. If each contributor can write a compatible replacement for a single Unix utility, and make it work properly in place of the original on a Unix system, then these utilities will work right when put together. Even allowing for Murphy to create a few unexpected problems, assembling these components will be a feasible task. (The kernel will require closer communication and will be worked on by a small, tight group.)

If I get donations of money, I may be able to hire a few people full or part time. The salary won't be high by programmers' standards, but I'm looking for people for whom building community spirit is as important as making money. I view this as a way of enabling dedicated people to devote their full energies to working on GNU by sparing them the need to make a living in another way.

Why All Computer Users Will Benefit

Once GNU is written, everyone will be able to obtain good system software free, just like air.[2]

---

[2] This is another place I failed to distinguish carefully between the two different meanings of "free." The statement as it stands is not false—you can get copies of GNU software at no charge, from your friends or over the net. But it does suggest the wrong idea.

This means much more than just saving everyone the price of a Unix license. It means that much wasteful duplication of system programming effort will be avoided. This effort can go instead into advancing the state of the art.

Complete system sources will be available to everyone. As a result, a user who needs changes in the system will always be free to make them himself, or hire any available programmer or company to make them for him. Users will no longer be at the mercy of one programmer or company which owns the sources and is in sole position to make changes.

Schools will be able to provide a much more educational environment by encouraging all students to study and improve the system code. Harvard's computer lab used to have the policy that no program could be installed on the system if its sources were not on public display, and upheld it by actually refusing to install certain programs. I was very much inspired by this.

Finally, the overhead of considering who owns the system software and what one is or is not entitled to do with it will be lifted.

Arrangements to make people pay for using a program, including licensing of copies, always incur a tremendous cost to society through the cumbersome mechanisms necessary to figure out how much (that is, which programs) a person must pay for. And only a police state can force everyone to obey them. Consider a space station where air must be manufactured at great cost: charging each breather per liter of air may be fair, but wearing the metered gas mask all day and all night is intolerable even if everyone can afford to pay the air bill. And the TV cameras everywhere to see if you ever take the mask off are outrageous. It's better to support the air plant with a head tax and chuck the masks.

Copying all or parts of a program is as natural to a programmer as breathing, and as productive. It ought to be as free.

Some Easily Rebutted Objections to GNU's Goals

"Nobody will use it if it is free, because that means they can't rely on any support."

"You have to charge for the program to pay for providing the support."

If people would rather pay for GNU plus service than get GNU free without service, a company to provide just service to people who have obtained GNU free ought to be profitable.[3]

We must distinguish between support in the form of real programming work and mere handholding. The former is something one cannot rely on from a software vendor. If your problem is not shared by enough people, the vendor will tell you to get lost.

If your business needs to be able to rely on support, the only way is to have all the necessary sources and tools. Then you can hire any available person to fix your problem; you are not at the mercy of any individual. With Unix, the price of sources puts this out of consideration for most businesses. With GNU this will

---

[3] Several such companies now exist.

be easy. It is still possible for there to be no available competent person, but this problem cannot be blamed on distribution arrangements. GNU does not eliminate all the world's problems, only some of them.

Meanwhile, the users who know nothing about computers need handholding: doing things for them which they could easily do themselves but don't know how.

Such services could be provided by companies that sell just hand-holding and repair service. If it is true that users would rather spend money and get a product with service, they will also be willing to buy the service having got the product free. The service companies will compete in quality and price; users will not be tied to any particular one. Meanwhile, those of us who don't need the service should be able to use the program without paying for the service.

"You cannot reach many people without advertising, and you must charge for the program to support that."

"It's no use advertising a program people can get free."

There are various forms of free or very cheap publicity that can be used to inform numbers of computer users about something like GNU. But it may be true that one can reach more microcomputer users with advertising. If this is really so, a business which advertises the service of copying and mailing GNU for a fee ought to be successful enough to pay for its advertising and more. This way, only the users who benefit from the advertising pay for it.

On the other hand, if many people get GNU from their friends, and such companies don't succeed, this will show that advertising was not really necessary to spread GNU. Why is it that free market advocates don't want to let the free market decide this?[4]

"My company needs a proprietary operating system to get a competitive edge."

GNU will remove operating system software from the realm of competition. You will not be able to get an edge in this area, but neither will your competitors be able to get an edge over you. You and they will compete in other areas, while benefiting mutually in this one. If your business is selling an operating system, you will not like GNU, but that's tough on you. If your business is something else, GNU can save you from being pushed into the expensive business of selling operating systems.

I would like to see GNU development supported by gifts from many manufacturers and users, reducing the cost to each.[5]

"Don't programmers deserve a reward for their creativity?"

If anything deserves a reward, it is social contribution. Creativity can be a social contribution, but only in so far as society is free to use the results. If programmers

---

[4] The Free Software Foundation raises most of its funds from a distribution service, although it is a charity rather than a company. If *no one* chooses to obtain copies by ordering from the FSF, it will be unable to do its work. But this does not mean that proprietary restrictions are justified to force every user to pay. If a small fraction of all the users order copies from the FSF, that is sufficient to keep the FSF afloat. So we ask users to choose to support us in this way. Have you done your part?

[5] A group of computer companies recently pooled funds to support maintenance of the GNU C Compiler.

deserve to be rewarded for creating innovative programs, by the same token they deserve to be punished if they restrict the use of these programs.

"Shouldn't a programmer be able to ask for a reward for his creativity?"

There is nothing wrong with wanting pay for work, or seeking to maximize one's income, as long as one does not use means that are destructive. But the means customary in the field of software today are based on destruction.

Extracting money from users of a program by restricting their use of it is destructive because the restrictions reduce the amount and the ways that the program can be used. This reduces the amount of wealth that humanity derives from the program. When there is a deliberate choice to restrict, the harmful consequences are deliberate destruction.

The reason a good citizen does not use such destructive means to become wealthier is that, if everyone did so, we would all become poorer from the mutual destructiveness. This is Kantian ethics; or, the Golden Rule. Since I do not like the consequences that result if everyone hoards information, I am required to consider it wrong for one to do so. Specifically, the desire to be rewarded for one's creativity does not justify depriving the world in general of all or part of that creativity.

"Won't programmers starve?"

I could answer that nobody is forced to be a programmer. Most of us cannot manage to get any money for standing on the street and making faces. But we are not, as a result, condemned to spend our lives standing on the street making faces, and starving. We do something else.

But that is the wrong answer because it accepts the questioner's implicit assumption: that without ownership of software, programmers cannot possibly be paid a cent. Supposedly it is all or nothing.

The real reason programmers will not starve is that it will still be possible for them to get paid for programming; just not paid as much as now.

Restricting copying is not the only basis for business in software. It is the most common basis because it brings in the most money. If it were prohibited, or rejected by the customer, software business would move to other bases of organization which are now used less often. There are always numerous ways to organize any kind of business.

Probably programming will not be as lucrative on the new basis as it is now. But that is not an argument against the change. It is not considered an injustice that sales clerks make the salaries that they now do. If programmers made the same, that would not be an injustice either. (In practice they would still make considerably more than that.)

"Don't people have a right to control how their creativity is used?"

"Control over the use of one's ideas" really constitutes control over other people's lives; and it is usually used to make their lives more difficult.

People who have studied the issue of intellectual property rights[6] carefully (such as lawyers) say that there is no intrinsic right to intellectual property. The kinds of supposed intellectual property rights that the government recognizes were created by specific acts of legislation for specific purposes.

For example, the patent system was established to encourage inventors to disclose the details of their inventions. Its purpose was to help society rather than to help inventors. At the time, the life span of 17 years for a patent was short compared with the rate of advance of the state of the art. Since patents are an issue only among manufacturers, for whom the cost and effort of a license agreement are small compared with setting up production, the patents often do not do much harm. They do not obstruct most individuals who use patented products.

The idea of copyright did not exist in ancient times, when authors frequently copied other authors at length in works of non-fiction. This practice was useful, and is the only way many authors' works have survived even in part. The copyright system was created expressly for the purpose of encouraging authorship. In the domain for which it was invented—books, which could be copied economically only on a printing press—it did little harm, and did not obstruct most of the individuals who read the books.

All intellectual property rights are just licenses granted by society because it was thought, rightly or wrongly, that society as a whole would benefit by granting them. But in any particular situation, we have to ask: are we really better off granting such license? What kind of act are we licensing a person to do?

The case of programs today is very different from that of books a hundred years ago. The fact that the easiest way to copy a program is from one neighbor to another, the fact that a program has both source code and object code which are distinct, and the fact that a program is used rather than read and enjoyed, combine to create a situation in which a person who enforces a copyright is harming society as a whole both materially and spiritually; in which a person should not do so regardless of whether the law enables him to.

"Competition makes things get done better."

The paradigm of competition is a race: by rewarding the winner, we encourage everyone to run faster. When capitalism really works this way, it does a good job; but its defenders are wrong in assuming it always works this way. If the runners forget why the reward is offered and become intent on winning, no matter how, they may find other strategies—such as, attacking other runners. If the runners get into a fist fight, they will all finish late.

---

[6] In the 80s I had not yet realized how confusing it was to speak of "the issue" of "intellectual property." That term is obviously biased; more subtle is the fact that it lumps together various disparate laws which raise very different issues. Nowadays I urge people to reject the term "intellectual property" entirely, lest it lead others to suppose that those laws form one coherent issue. The way to be clear is to discuss patents, copyrights, and trademarks separately. See http://www.gnu.org/philosophy/not-ipr.xhtml for more explanation of how this term spreads confusion and bias.

Proprietary and secret software is the moral equivalent of runners in a fist fight. Sad to say, the only referee we've got does not seem to object to fights; he just regulates them ("For every ten yards you run, you can fire one shot"). He really ought to break them up, and penalize runners for even trying to fight.

"Won't everyone stop programming without a monetary incentive?"

Actually, many people will program with absolutely no monetary incentive. Programming has an irresistible fascination for some people, usually the people who are best at it. There is no shortage of professional musicians who keep at it even though they have no hope of making a living that way.

But really this question, though commonly asked, is not appropriate to the situation. Pay for programmers will not disappear, only become less. So the right question is, will anyone program with a reduced monetary incentive? My experience shows that they will.

For more than ten years, many of the world's best programmers worked at the Artificial Intelligence Lab for far less money than they could have had anywhere else. They got many kinds of non-monetary rewards: fame and appreciation, for example. And creativity is also fun, a reward in itself.

Then most of them left when offered a chance to do the same interesting work for a lot of money.

What the facts show is that people will program for reasons other than riches; but if given a chance to make a lot of money as well, they will come to expect and demand it. Low-paying organizations do poorly in competition with high-paying ones, but they do not have to do badly if the high-paying ones are banned.

"We need the programmers desperately. If they demand that we stop helping our neighbors, we have to obey."

You're never so desperate that you have to obey this sort of demand. Remember: millions for defense, but not a cent for tribute!

"Programmers need to make a living somehow."

In the short run, this is true. However, there are plenty of ways that programmers could make a living without selling the right to use a program. This way is customary now because it brings programmers and businessmen the most money, not because it is the only way to make a living. It is easy to find other ways if you want to find them. Here are a number of examples.

A manufacturer introducing a new computer will pay for the porting of operating systems onto the new hardware.

The sale of teaching, hand-holding and maintenance services could also employ programmers.

People with new ideas could distribute programs as freeware[7], asking for donations from satisfied users, or selling hand-holding services. I have met people who
are already working this way successfully.

Users with related needs can form users' groups, and pay dues. A group would
contract with programming companies to write programs that the group's members
would like to use.

All sorts of development can be funded with a Software Tax:

Suppose everyone who buys a computer has to pay x percent of the price
as a software tax. The government gives this to an agency like the NSF
to spend on software development.

But if the computer buyer makes a donation to software development
himself, he can take a credit against the tax. He can donate to the project
of his own choosing—often, chosen because he hopes to use the results
when it is done. He can take a credit for any amount of donation up to
the total tax he had to pay.

The total tax rate could be decided by a vote of the payers of the tax,
weighted according to the amount they will be taxed on.

The consequences:

- The computer-using community supports software development.

- This community decides what level of support is needed.

- Users who care which projects their share is spent on can choose this
  for themselves.

In the long run, making programs free is a step toward the post-scarcity world,
where nobody will have to work very hard just to make a living. People will be
free to devote themselves to activities that are fun, such as programming, after
spending the necessary ten hours a week on required tasks such as legislation, family
counseling, robot repair and asteroid prospecting. There will be no need to be able
to make a living from programming.

We have already greatly reduced the amount of work that the whole society
must do for its actual productivity, but only a little of this has translated itself into
leisure for workers because much nonproductive activity is required to accompany
productive activity. The main causes of this are bureaucracy and isometric struggles
against competition. Free software will greatly reduce these drains in the area of
software production. We must do this, in order for technical gains in productivity
to translate into less work for us.

---

[7] Subsequently we have discovered the need to distinguish between "free software" and
"freeware". The term "freeware" means software you are free to redistribute, but
usually you are not free to study and change the source code, so most of it is not
free software. See http://www.gnu.org/philosophy/words-to-avoid.html for more
explanation.

Glossary

Abbrev　　　An abbrev is a text string which expands into a different text string when present in the buffer. For example, you might define a few letters as an abbrev for a long phrase that you want to insert frequently. See Chapter 26 [Abbrevs], page 303.

Aborting　　Aborting means getting out of a recursive edit (q.v.). The commands C-] and M-x top-level are used for this. See Section 33.1 [Quitting], page 440.

Alt　　　　　Alt is the name of a modifier bit which a keyboard input character may have. To make a character Alt, type it while holding down the ALT key. Such characters are given names that start with Alt- (usually written A- for short). (Note that many terminals have a key labeled ALT which is really a META key.) See Section 2.1 [User Input], page 12.

Argument　　See 'numeric argument.'

ASCII character
　　　　　　　An ASCII character is either an ASCII control character or an ASCII printing character. See Section 2.1 [User Input], page 12.

ASCII control character
　　　　　　　An ASCII control character is the Control version of an upper-case letter, or the Control version of one of the characters '@[\]^_?'.

ASCII printing character
　　　　　　　ASCII printing characters include letters, digits, space, and these punctuation characters: '!@#$%^& *()_-+=|\~` {}[]:;"' <>,.?/'.

Auto Fill Mode
　　　　　　　Auto Fill mode is a minor mode in which text that you insert is automatically broken into lines of a given maximum width. See Section 22.5 [Filling], page 217.

Auto Saving
　　　　　　　Auto saving is the practice of saving the contents of an Emacs buffer in a specially-named file, so that the information will not be lost if the buffer is lost due to a system error or user error. See Section 15.5 [Auto Save], page 132.

Autoloading
　　　　　　　Emacs automatically loads Lisp libraries when a Lisp program requests a function or a variable from those libraries. This is called 'autoloading'. See Section 24.8 [Lisp Libraries], page 288.

Backtrace　　A backtrace is a trace of a series of function calls showing how a program arrived to a certain point. It is used mainly for finding and correcting bugs (q.v.). Emacs can display a backtrace when it signals an error or when you type C-g (see 'quitting'). See Section 33.3.3 [Checklist], page 447.

Backup File

A backup file records the contents that a file had before the current editing session. Emacs makes backup files automatically to help you track down or cancel changes you later regret making. See Section 15.3.2 [Backup], page 125.

Balancing Parentheses

Emacs can balance parentheses (or other matching delimiters) either manually or automatically. You do manual balancing with the commands to move over parenthetical groupings (see Section 23.4.2 [Moving by Parens], page 259). Automatic balancing works by blinking or highlighting the delimiter that matches the one you just inserted (see Section 23.4.3 [Matching Parens], page 259).

Balanced Expressions

A balanced expression is a syntactically recognizable expression, such as a symbol, number, string constant, block, or parenthesized expression in C. See Section 23.4.1 [Expressions], page 257.

Balloon Help

See 'tooltips.'

Base Buffer

A base buffer is a buffer whose text is shared by an indirect buffer (q.v.).

Bind   To bind a key sequence means to give it a binding (q.v.). See Section 32.4.5 [Rebinding], page 426.

Binding   A key sequence gets its meaning in Emacs by having a binding, which is a command (q.v.), a Lisp function that is run when the user types that sequence. See Section 2.3 [Commands], page 14. Customization often involves rebinding a character to a different command function. The bindings of all key sequences are recorded in the keymaps (q.v.). See Section 32.4.1 [Keymaps], page 423.

Blank Lines

Blank lines are lines that contain only whitespace. Emacs has several commands for operating on the blank lines in the buffer.

Bookmark   Bookmarks are akin to registers (q.v.) in that they record positions in buffers to which you can return later. Unlike registers, bookmarks persist between Emacs sessions.

Border   A border is a thin space along the edge of the frame, used just for spacing, not for displaying anything. An Emacs frame has an ordinary external border, outside of everything including the menu bar, plus an internal border that surrounds the text windows and their scroll bars and separates them from the menu bar and tool bar. You can customize both borders with options and resources (see Section C.10 [Borders X], page 486). Borders are not the same as fringes (q.v.).

Buffer   The buffer is the basic editing unit; one buffer corresponds to one text being edited. You can have several buffers, but at any time you are editing only one, the 'current buffer,' though several can be visible when you are using multiple windows (q.v.). Most buffers are visiting (q.v.) some file. See Chapter 16 [Buffers], page 156.

Buffer Selection History
          Emacs keeps a buffer selection history which records how recently each Emacs buffer has been selected. This is used for choosing a buffer to select. See Chapter 16 [Buffers], page 156.

Bug   A bug is an incorrect or unreasonable behavior of a program, or inaccurate or confusing documentation. Emacs developers treat bug reports, both in Emacs code and its documentation, very seriously and ask you to report any bugs you find. See Section 33.3 [Bugs], page 445.

Button Down Event
          A button down event is the kind of input event generated right away when you press down on a mouse button. See Section 32.4.9 [Mouse Buttons], page 430.

By Default See 'default.'

Byte Compilation
          See 'compilation.'

C-   C- in the name of a character is an abbreviation for Control. See Section 2.1 [User Input], page 12.

C-M-   C-M- in the name of a character is an abbreviation for Control-Meta. See Section 2.1 [User Input], page 12.

Case Conversion
          Case conversion means changing text from upper case to lower case or vice versa. See Section 22.6 [Case], page 223, for the commands for case conversion.

Character Characters form the contents of an Emacs buffer; see Section 2.4 [Text Characters], page 15. Also, key sequences (q.v.) are usually made up of characters (though they may include other input events as well). See Section 2.1 [User Input], page 12.

Character Set
          Emacs supports a number of character sets, each of which represents a particular alphabet or script. See Chapter 19 [International], page 186.

Character Terminal
          See 'text-only terminal.'

Click Event

> A click event is the kind of input event generated when you press a mouse button and release it without moving the mouse. See Section 32.4.9 [Mouse Buttons], page 430.

Clipboard

> A clipboard is a buffer provided by the window system for transferring text between applications. On the X Window system, the clipboard is provided in addition to the primary selection (q.v.); on MS-Windows and Mac, the clipboard is used *instead* of the primary selection. See Section 18.1.5 [Clipboard], page 175.

Coding System

> A coding system is an encoding for representing text characters in a file or in a stream of information. Emacs has the ability to convert text to or from a variety of coding systems when reading or writing it. See Section 19.7 [Coding Systems], page 193.

Command

> A command is a Lisp function specially defined to be able to serve as a key binding in Emacs. When you type a key sequence (q.v.), its binding (q.v.) is looked up in the relevant keymaps (q.v.) to find the command to run. See Section 2.3 [Commands], page 14.

Command History

> See 'minibuffer history.'

Command Name

> A command name is the name of a Lisp symbol which is a command (see Section 2.3 [Commands], page 14). You can invoke any command by its name using M-x (see Chapter 6 [Running Commands by Name], page 39).

Comment

> A comment is text in a program which is intended only for humans reading the program, and which is marked specially so that it will be ignored when the program is loaded or compiled. Emacs offers special commands for creating, aligning and killing comments. See Section 23.5 [Comments], page 260.

Common Lisp

> Common Lisp is a dialect of Lisp (q.v.) much larger and more powerful than Emacs Lisp. Emacs provides a subset of Common Lisp in the CL package. See section "Overview" in *Common Lisp Extensions*.

Compilation

> Compilation is the process of creating an executable program from source code. Emacs has commands for compiling files of Emacs Lisp code (see section "Byte Compilation" in *the Emacs Lisp Reference Manual*) and programs in C and other languages (see Section 24.1 [Compilation], page 273).

Complete Key

> A complete key is a key sequence which fully specifies one action to be performed by Emacs. For example, X and C-f and C-x m are complete

keys. Complete keys derive their meanings from being bound (q.v.) to commands (q.v.). Thus, X is conventionally bound to a command to insert 'X' in the buffer; C-x m is conventionally bound to a command to begin composing a mail message. See Section 2.2 [Keys], page 14.

Completion   Completion is what Emacs does when it automatically fills out an abbreviation for a name into the entire name. Completion is done for minibuffer (q.v.) arguments when the set of possible valid inputs is known; for example, on command names, buffer names, and file names. Completion occurs when TAB, SPC or RET is typed. See Section 5.3 [Completion], page 33.

Continuation Line

When a line of text is longer than the width of the window, it takes up more than one screen line when displayed. We say that the text line is continued, and all screen lines used for it after the first are called continuation lines. See Section 4.8 [Continuation Lines], page 25. A related Emacs feature is 'filling' (q.v.).

Control Character

A control character is a character that you type by holding down the CTRL key. Some control characters also have their own keys, so that you can type them without using CTRL. For example, RET, TAB, ESC and DEL are all control characters. See Section 2.1 [User Input], page 12.

Copyleft   A copyleft is a notice giving the public legal permission to redistribute and modify a program or other work of art, but requiring modified versions to carry similar permission. Copyright is normally used to keep users divided and helpless; with copyleft we turn that around to empower users and encourage them to cooperate.

The particular form of copyleft used by the GNU project is called the GNU General Public License. See Appendix A [Copying], page 455.

CTRL   The CTRL or "control" key is what you hold down in order to enter a control character (q.v.).

Current Buffer

The current buffer in Emacs is the Emacs buffer on which most editing commands operate. You can select any Emacs buffer as the current one. See Chapter 16 [Buffers], page 156.

Current Line

The current line is the line that point is on (see Section 1.1 [Point], page 6).

Current Paragraph

The current paragraph is the paragraph that point is in. If point is between two paragraphs, the current paragraph is the one that follows point. See Section 22.3 [Paragraphs], page 215.

Current Defun

> The current defun is the defun (q.v.) that point is in. If point is between defuns, the current defun is the one that follows point. See Section 23.2 [Defuns], page 251.

Cursor

> The cursor is the rectangle on the screen which indicates the position called point (q.v.) at which insertion and deletion takes place. The cursor is on or under the character that follows point. Often people speak of 'the cursor' when, strictly speaking, they mean 'point.' See Section 1.1 [Point], page 6.

Customization

> Customization is making minor changes in the way Emacs works. It is often done by setting variables (see Section 32.3 [Variables], page 416) or faces (see Section 32.2.5 [Face Customization], page 413), or by rebinding key sequences (see Section 32.4.1 [Keymaps], page 423).

Cut and Paste

> See 'killing' and 'yanking.'

Default Argument

> The default for an argument is the value that will be assumed if you do not specify one. When the minibuffer is used to read an argument, the default argument is used if you just type RET. See Chapter 5 [Minibuffer], page 31.

Default

> A default is the value that is used for a certain purpose if and when you do not specify a value to use.

Default Directory

> When you specify a file name that does not start with '/' or '~', it is interpreted relative to the current buffer's default directory. (On MS-Windows and MS-DOS, file names which start with a drive letter 'x :' are treated as absolute, not relative.) See Section 5.1 [Minibuffer File], page 31.

Defun

> A defun is a major definition at the top level in a program. The name 'defun' comes from Lisp, where most such definitions use the construct `defun`. See Section 23.2 [Defuns], page 251.

DEL

> DEL is a character that runs the command to delete one character of text before the cursor. It is typically either the DELETE key or the BACKSPACE key, whichever one is easy to type. See Section 4.3 [Erasing], page 23.

Deletion

> Deletion means erasing text without copying it into the kill ring (q.v.). The alternative is killing (q.v.). See Chapter 9 [Killing], page 55.

Deletion of Files

> Deleting a file means erasing it from the file system. See Section 15.11 [Miscellaneous File Operations], page 150.

Deletion of Messages
: Deleting a message means flagging it to be eliminated from your mail file. Until you expunge (q.v.) the Rmail file, you can still undelete the messages you have deleted. See Section 28.4 [Rmail Deletion], page 321.

Deletion of Windows
: Deleting a window means eliminating it from the screen. Other windows expand to use up the space. The deleted window can never come back, but no actual text is thereby lost. See Chapter 17 [Windows], page 165.

Directory
: File directories are named collections in the file system, within which you can place individual files or subdirectories. See Section 15.8 [Directories], page 147.

Dired
: Dired is the Emacs facility that displays the contents of a file directory and allows you to "edit the directory," performing operations on the files in the directory. See Chapter 29 [Dired], page 339.

Disabled Command
: A disabled command is one that you may not run without special confirmation. The usual reason for disabling a command is that it is confusing for beginning users. See Section 32.4.10 [Disabling], page 432.

Down Event
: Short for 'button down event' (q.v.).

Drag Event
: A drag event is the kind of input event generated when you press a mouse button, move the mouse, and then release the button. See Section 32.1.0 [Mouse Buttons], page 430.

Dribble File
: A dribble file is a file into which Emacs writes all the characters that you type on the keyboard. Dribble files are used to make a record for debugging Emacs bugs. Emacs does not make a dribble file unless you tell it to. See Section 33.3 [Bugs], page 445.

Echo Area
: The echo area is the bottom line of the screen, used for echoing the arguments to commands, for asking questions, and showing brief messages (including error messages). The messages are stored in the buffer '*Messages*' so you can review them later. See Section 1.2 [Echo Area], page 7.

Echoing
: Echoing is acknowledging the receipt of input events by displaying them (in the echo area). Emacs never echoes single-character key sequences; longer key sequences echo only if you pause while typing them.

Electric
: We say that a character is electric if it is normally self-inserting (q.v.), but the current major mode (q.v.) redefines it to do something else as

well. For example, some programming language major modes define
particular delimiter characters to reindent the line or insert one or
more newlines in addition to self-insertion.

End Of Line

End of line is a character or a sequence of characters that indicate
the end of a text line. On GNU and Unix systems, this is a newline
(q.v.), but other systems have other conventions. See Section 19.7
[Coding Systems], page 193. Emacs can recognize several end-of-line
conventions in files and convert between them.

Environment Variable

An environment variable is one of a collection of variables stored by
the operating system, each one having a name and a value. Emacs
can access environment variables set by its parent shell, and it can
set variables in the environment it passes to programs it invokes. See
Section C.5 [Environment], page 476.

EOL   See 'end of line.'

Error   An error occurs when an Emacs command cannot execute in the cur-
             rent circumstances. When an error occurs, execution of the command
             stops (unless the command has been programmed to do otherwise)
             and Emacs reports the error by displaying an error message (q.v.).
             Type-ahead is discarded. Then Emacs is ready to read another edit-
             ing command.

Error Message

An error message is a single line of output displayed by Emacs when
the user asks for something impossible to do (such as, killing text
forward when point is at the end of the buffer). They appear in the
echo area, accompanied by a beep.

ESC   ESC is a character used as a prefix for typing Meta characters on
             keyboards lacking a META key. Unlike the META key (which, like
             the SHIFT key, is held down while another character is typed), you
             press the ESC key as you would press a letter key, and it applies to
             the next character you type.

Expression   See 'balanced expression.'

Expunging   Expunging an Rmail file or Dired buffer or a Gnus newsgroup buffer
             is an operation that truly discards the messages or files you have pre-
             viously flagged for deletion.

Face   A face is a style of displaying characters. It specifies attributes such as
             font family and size, foreground and background colors, underline and
             strike-through, background stipple, etc. Emacs provides features to
             associate specific faces with portions of buffer text, in order to display
             that text as specified by the face attributes. See Section 11.5 [Faces],
             page 72.

File Locking

Emacs uses file locking to notice when two different users start to edit one file at the same time. See Section 15.3.4 [Interlocking], page 129.

File Name A file name is a name that refers to a file. File names may be relative or absolute; the meaning of a relative file name depends on the current directory, but an absolute file name refers to the same file regardless of which directory is current. On GNU and Unix systems, an absolute file name starts with a slash (the root directory) or with '`~/`' or '`~user/`' (a home directory). On MS-Windows/MS-DOS, an absolute file name can also start with a drive letter and a colon '`d:`'.

Some people use the term "pathname" for file names, but we do not; we use the word "path" only in the term "search path" (q.v.).

File-Name Component

A file-name component names a file directly within a particular directory. On GNU and Unix systems, a file name is a sequence of file-name components, separated by slashes. For example, '`foo/bar`' is a file name containing two components, '`foo`' and '`bar`'; it refers to the file named '`bar`' in the directory named '`foo`' in the current directory. MS-DOS/MS-Windows file names can also use backslashes to separate components, as in '`foo\bar`'.

Fill Prefix The fill prefix is a string that should be expected at the beginning of each line when filling is done. It is not regarded as part of the text to be filled. See Section 22.5 [Filling], page 217.

Filling Filling text means shifting text between consecutive lines so that all the lines are approximately the same length. See Section 22.5 [Filling], page 217. Some other editors call this feature 'line wrapping.'

Font Lock Font Lock is a mode that highlights parts of buffer text according to its syntax. See Section 11.7 [Font Lock], page 76.

Fontset A fontset is a named collection of fonts. A fontset specification lists character sets and which font to use to display each of them. Fontsets make it easy to change several fonts at once by specifying the name of a fontset, rather than changing each font separately. See Section 19.15 [Fontsets], page 202.

Formatted Text

Formatted text is text that displays with formatting information while you edit. Formatting information includes fonts, colors, and specified margins. See Section 22.12 [Formatted Text], page 236.

Formfeed Character
See 'page.'

Frame A frame is a rectangular cluster of Emacs windows. Emacs starts out with one frame, but you can create more. You can subdivide each frame into Emacs windows (q.v.). When you are using a window system (q.v.), all the frames can be visible at the same time. See Chapter 18 [Frames], page 171. Some other editors use the term "window" for this, but in Emacs a window means something else.

Fringe   On a graphical display (q.v.), there's a narrow portion of the frame (q.v.) between the text area and the window's border. Emacs displays the fringe using a special face (q.v.) called `fringe`. See Section 11.5 [Faces], page 72.

FTP   FTP is an acronym for File Transfer Protocol. Emacs uses an FTP client program to provide access to remote files (q.v.).

Function Key

A function key is a key on the keyboard that sends input but does not correspond to any character. See Section 32.4.7 [Function Keys], page 428.

Global   Global means "independent of the current environment; in effect throughout Emacs." It is the opposite of local (q.v.). Particular examples of the use of 'global' appear below.

Global Abbrev

A global definition of an abbrev (q.v.) is effective in all major modes that do not have local (q.v.) definitions for the same abbrev. See Chapter 26 [Abbrevs], page 303.

Global Keymap

The global keymap (q.v.) contains key bindings that are in effect except when overridden by local key bindings in a major mode's local keymap (q.v.). See Section 32.4.1 [Keymaps], page 423.

Global Mark Ring

The global mark ring records the series of buffers you have recently set a mark (q.v.) in. In many cases you can use this to backtrack through buffers you have been editing in, or in which you have found tags (see 'tags table'). See Section 8.7 [Global Mark Ring], page 54.

Global Substitution

Global substitution means replacing each occurrence of one string by another string throughout a large amount of text. See Section 12.9 [Replace], page 99.

Global Variable

The global value of a variable (q.v.) takes effect in all buffers that do not have their own local (q.v.) values for the variable. See Section 32.3 [Variables], page 416.

Graphic Character

Graphic characters are those assigned pictorial images rather than just names. All the non-Meta (q.v.) characters except for the Control (q.v.) characters are graphic characters. These include letters, digits, punctuation, and spaces; they do not include RET or ESC. In Emacs, typing a graphic character inserts that character (in ordinary editing modes). See Section 4.1 [Inserting Text], page 20.

Graphical Display

A graphical display is one that can display images and multiple fonts. Usually it also has a window system (q.v.).

Highlighting

Highlighting text means displaying it with a different foreground and/or background color to make it stand out from the rest of the text in the buffer.

Emacs uses highlighting in several ways. When you mark a region with the mouse, the region is always highlighted. Optionally Emacs can also highlight the region whenever it is active (see Section 8.2 [Transient Mark], page 50). Incremental search also highlights matches (see Section 12.1 [Incremental Search], page 86). See also 'font lock'.

Hardcopy   Hardcopy means printed output. Emacs has commands for making printed listings of text in Emacs buffers. See Section 31.4 [Printing], page 391.

HELP   HELP is the Emacs name for C-h or F1. You can type HELP at any time to ask what options you have, or to ask what any command does. See Chapter 7 [Help], page 40.

Help Echo   Help echo is a short message displayed in the echo area when the mouse pointer is located on portions of display that require some explanations. Emacs displays help echo for menu items, parts of the mode line, tool-bar buttons, etc. On graphics displays, the messages can be displayed as tooltips (q.v.). See Section 18.17 [Tooltips], page 184.

Hook   A hook is a list of functions to be called on specific occasions, such as saving a buffer in a file, major mode activation, etc. By customizing the various hooks, you can modify Emacs's behavior without changing any of its code. See Section 32.3.2 [Hooks], page 418.

Hyper   Hyper is the name of a modifier bit which a keyboard input character may have. To make a character Hyper, type it while holding down the HYPER key. Such characters are given names that start with Hyper- (usually written H- for short). See Section 2.1 [User Input], page 12.

Iff   "Iff" means "if and only if." This terminology comes from mathematics.

Inbox   An inbox is a file in which mail is delivered by the operating system. Rmail transfers mail from inboxes to Rmail files (q.v.) in which the mail is then stored permanently or until explicitly deleted. See Section 28.5 [Rmail Inbox], page 322.

Incremental Search

> Emacs provides an incremental search facility, whereby Emacs searches for the string as you type it. See Section 12.1 [Incremental Search], page 86.

Indentation Indentation means blank space at the beginning of a line. Most programming languages have conventions for using indentation to illuminate the structure of the program, and Emacs has special commands to adjust indentation. See Chapter 21 [Indentation], page 210.

Indirect Buffer

> An indirect buffer is a buffer that shares the text of another buffer, called its base buffer (q.v.). See Section 16.6 [Indirect Buffers], page 162.

Info   Info is the hypertext format used by the GNU project for writing documentation.

Input Event

> An input event represents, within Emacs, one action taken by the user on the terminal. Input events include typing characters, typing function keys, pressing or releasing mouse buttons, and switching between Emacs frames. See Section 2.1 [User Input], page 12.

Input Method

> An input method is a system for entering non-ASCII text characters by typing sequences of ASCII characters (q.v.). See Section 19.4 [Input Methods], page 190.

Insertion Insertion means copying text into the buffer, either from the keyboard or from some other place in Emacs.

Interlocking

> Interlocking is a feature for warning when you start to alter a file that someone else is already editing. See Section 15.3.4 [Simultaneous Editing], page 129.

Isearch   See 'incremental search.'

Justification

> Justification means adding extra spaces within lines of text to make them extend exactly to a specified width. See Section 22.12.7 [Format Justification], page 240.

Keybinding See 'binding.'

Keyboard Macro

> Keyboard macros are a way of defining new Emacs commands from sequences of existing ones, with no need to write a Lisp program. See Chapter 14 [Keyboard Macros], page 111.

Keyboard Shortcut

A keyboard shortcut is a key sequence (q.v.) which invokes a command. What some programs call "assigning a keyboard shortcut," Emacs calls "binding a key sequence." See 'binding.'

Key Sequence

A key sequence (key, for short) is a sequence of input events (q.v.) that are meaningful as a single unit. If the key sequence is enough to specify one action, it is a complete key (q.v.); if it is not enough, it is a prefix key (q.v.). See Section 2.2 [Keys], page 14.

Keymap   The keymap is the data structure that records the bindings (q.v.) of key sequences to the commands that they run. For example, the global keymap binds the character C-n to the command function `next-line`. See Section 32.4.1 [Keymaps], page 423.

Keyboard Translation Table

The keyboard translation table is an array that translates the character codes that come from the terminal into the character codes that make up key sequences.

Kill Ring   The kill ring is where all text you have killed recently is saved. You can reinsert any of the killed text still in the ring; this is called yanking (q.v.). See Section 9.2 [Yanking], page 58.

Killing   Killing means erasing text and saving it on the kill ring so it can be yanked (q.v.) later. Some other systems call this "cutting." Most Emacs commands that erase text perform killing, as opposed to deletion (q.v.). See Chapter 9 [Killing], page 55.

Killing a Job

Killing a job (such as, an invocation of Emacs) means making it cease to exist. Any data within it, if not saved in a file, is lost. See Section 3.1 [Exiting], page 17.

Language Environment

Your choice of language environment specifies defaults for the input method (q.v.) and coding system (q.v.). See Section 19.3 [Language Environments], page 188. These defaults are relevant if you edit non-ASCII text (see Chapter 19 [International], page 186).

Line Wrapping

See 'filling.'

Lisp   Lisp is a programming language. Most of Emacs is written in a dialect of Lisp, called Emacs Lisp, that is extended with special features which make it especially suitable for text editing tasks.

List   A list is, approximately, a text string beginning with an open parenthesis and ending with the matching close parenthesis. In C mode and other non-Lisp modes, groupings surrounded by other kinds of matched delimiters appropriate to the language, such as braces, are also considered lists. Emacs has special commands for many operations on lists. See Section 23.4.2 [Moving by Parens], page 259.

Local   Local means "in effect only in a particular context"; the relevant kind of context is a particular function execution, a particular buffer, or a particular major mode. It is the opposite of 'global' (q.v.). Specific uses of 'local' in Emacs terminology appear below.

Local Abbrev

A local abbrev definition is effective only if a particular major mode is selected. In that major mode, it overrides any global definition for the same abbrev. See Chapter 26 [Abbrevs], page 303.

Local Keymap

A local keymap is used in a particular major mode; the key bindings (q.v.) in the current local keymap override global bindings of the same key sequences. See Section 32.4.1 [Keymaps], page 423.

Local Variable

A local value of a variable (q.v.) applies to only one buffer. See Section 32.3.3 [Locals], page 419.

M-   M- in the name of a character is an abbreviation for META, one of the modifier keys that can accompany any character. See Section 2.1 [User Input], page 12.

M-C-   M-C- in the name of a character is an abbreviation for Control-Meta; it means the same thing as C-M-. If your terminal lacks a real META key, you type a Control-Meta character by typing ESC and then typing the corresponding Control character. See Section 2.1 [User Input], page 12.

M-x   M-x is the key sequence which is used to call an Emacs command by name. This is how you run commands that are not bound to key sequences. See Chapter 6 [Running Commands by Name], page 39.

Mail   Mail means messages sent from one user to another through the computer system, to be read at the recipient's convenience. Emacs has commands for composing and sending mail, and for reading and editing the mail you have received. See Chapter 27 [Sending Mail], page 310. See Chapter 28 [Rmail], page 319, for how to read mail.

Mail Composition Method

A mail composition method is a program runnable within Emacs for editing and sending a mail message. Emacs lets you select from several alternative mail composition methods. See Section 27.6 [Mail Methods], page 318.

Major Mode

The Emacs major modes are a mutually exclusive set of options, each of which configures Emacs for editing a certain sort of text. Ideally, each programming language has its own major mode. See Chapter 20 [Major Modes], page 207.

Margin
: The space between the usable part of a window (including the fringe) and the window edge.

Mark
: The mark points to a position in the text. It specifies one end of the region (q.v.), point being the other end. Many commands operate on all the text from point to the mark. Each buffer has its own mark. See Chapter 8 [Mark], page 49.

Mark Ring
: The mark ring is used to hold several recent previous locations of the mark, just in case you want to move back to them. Each buffer has its own mark ring; in addition, there is a single global mark ring (q.v.). See Section 8.6 [Mark Ring], page 54.

Menu Bar
: The menu bar is the line at the top of an Emacs frame. It contains words you can click on with the mouse to bring up menus, or you can use a keyboard interface to navigate it. See Section 18.14 [Menu Bars], page 183.

Message
: See 'mail.'

Meta
: Meta is the name of a modifier bit which you can use in a command character. To enter a meta character, you hold down the META key while typing the character. We refer to such characters with names that start with `Meta-` (usually written `M-` for short). For example, `M-<` is typed by holding down META and at the same time typing `<` (which itself is done, on most terminals, by holding down SHIFT and typing `,`). See Section 2.1 [User Input], page 12.

  On some terminals, the META key is actually labeled ALT or EDIT.

Meta Character
: A Meta character is one whose character code includes the Meta bit.

Minibuffer
: The minibuffer is the window that appears when necessary inside the echo area (q.v.), used for reading arguments to commands. See Chapter 5 [Minibuffer], page 31.

Minibuffer History
: The minibuffer history records the text you have specified in the past for minibuffer arguments, so you can conveniently use the same text again. See Section 5.4 [Minibuffer History], page 36.

Minor Mode
: A minor mode is an optional feature of Emacs which can be switched on or off independently of all other features. Each minor mode has a command to turn it on or off. See Section 32.1 [Minor Modes], page 406.

Minor Mode Keymap

> A minor mode keymap is a keymap that belongs to a minor mode and is active when that mode is enabled. Minor mode keymaps take precedence over the buffer's local keymap, just as the local keymap takes precedence over the global keymap. See Section 32.4.1 [Keymaps], page 423.

Mode Line   The mode line is the line at the bottom of each window (q.v.), giving status information on the buffer displayed in that window. See Section 1.3 [Mode Line], page 8.

Modified Buffer

> A buffer (q.v.) is modified if its text has been changed since the last time the buffer was saved (or since when it was created, if it has never been saved). See Section 15.3 [Saving], page 123.

Moving Text

> Moving text means erasing it from one place and inserting it in another. The usual way to move text is by killing (q.v.) it and then yanking (q.v.) it. See Chapter 9 [Killing], page 55.

MULE   MULE refers to the Emacs features for editing multilingual non-ASCII text using multibyte characters (q.v.). See Chapter 19 [International], page 186.

Multibyte Character

> A multibyte character is a character that takes up several bytes in a buffer. Emacs uses multibyte characters to represent non-ASCII text, since the number of non-ASCII characters is much more than 256. See Section 19.1 [International Chars], page 186.

Named Mark

> A named mark is a register (q.v.) in its role of recording a location in text so that you can move point to that location. See Chapter 10 [Registers], page 65.

Narrowing   Narrowing means creating a restriction (q.v.) that limits editing in the current buffer to only a part of the text in the buffer. Text outside that part is inaccessible for editing until the boundaries are widened again, but it is still there, and saving the file saves it all. See Section 31.9 [Narrowing], page 396.

Newline   Control-J characters in the buffer terminate lines of text and are therefore also called newlines. See Section 2.4 [Text Characters], page 15.

nil   nil is a value usually interpreted as a logical "false." Its opposite is t, interpreted as "true."

Numeric Argument

> A numeric argument is a number, specified before a command, to change the effect of the command. Often the numeric argument serves as a repeat count. See Section 4.10 [Arguments], page 28.

Overwrite Mode
: Overwrite mode is a minor mode. When it is enabled, ordinary text characters replace the existing text after point rather than pushing it to the right. See Section 32.1 [Minor Modes], page 406.

Page
: A page is a unit of text, delimited by formfeed characters (ASCII control-L, code 014) coming at the beginning of a line. Some Emacs commands are provided for moving over and operating on pages. See Section 22.4 [Pages], page 216.

Paragraph
: Paragraphs are the medium-size unit of human-language text. There are special Emacs commands for moving over and operating on paragraphs. See Section 22.3 [Paragraphs], page 215.

Parsing
: We say that certain Emacs commands parse words or expressions in the text being edited. Really, all they know how to do is find the other end of a word or expression. See Section 32.5 [Syntax], page 433.

Point
: Point is the place in the buffer at which insertion and deletion occur. Point is considered to be between two characters, not at one character. The terminal's cursor (q.v.) indicates the location of point. See Section 1.1 [Point], page 6.

Prefix Argument
: See 'numeric argument.'

Prefix Key
: A prefix key is a key sequence (q.v.) whose sole function is to introduce a set of longer key sequences. C-x is an example of prefix key; any two-character sequence starting with C-x is therefore a legitimate key sequence. See Section 2.2 [Keys], page 14.

Primary Rmail File
: Your primary Rmail file is the file named 'RMAIL' in your home directory. That's where Rmail stores your incoming mail, unless you specify a different file name. See Chapter 28 [Rmail], page 319.

Primary Selection
: The primary selection is one particular X selection (q.v.); it is the selection that most X applications use for transferring text to and from other applications.

  The Emacs kill commands set the primary selection and the yank command uses the primary selection when appropriate. See Chapter 9 [Killing], page 55.

Prompt
: A prompt is text used to ask the user for input. Displaying a prompt is called prompting. Emacs prompts always appear in the echo area (q.v.). One kind of prompting happens when the minibuffer is used to read an argument (see Chapter 5 [Minibuffer], page 31); the echoing which happens when you pause in the middle of typing a multi-character key sequence is also a kind of prompting (see Section 1.2 [Echo Area], page 7).

Query-Replace

> Query-replace is an interactive string replacement feature provided by Emacs. See Section 12.9.4 [Query Replace], page 101.

Quitting   Quitting means canceling a partially typed command or a running command, using C-g (or C-BREAK on MS-DOS). See Section 33.1 [Quitting], page 440.

Quoting   Quoting means depriving a character of its usual special significance. The most common kind of quoting in Emacs is with C-q. What constitutes special significance depends on the context and on convention. For example, an "ordinary" character as an Emacs command inserts itself; so in this context, a special character is any character that does not normally insert itself (such as DEL, for example), and quoting it makes it insert itself as if it were not special. Not all contexts allow quoting. See Section 4.1 [Inserting Text], page 20.

Quoting File Names

> Quoting a file name turns off the special significance of constructs such as '$', '~' and ':'. See Section 15.15 [Quoted File Names], page 153.

Read-Only Buffer

> A read-only buffer is one whose text you are not allowed to change. Normally Emacs makes buffers read-only when they contain text which has a special significance to Emacs; for example, Dired buffers. Visiting a file that is write-protected also makes a read-only buffer. See Chapter 16 [Buffers], page 156.

Rectangle   A rectangle consists of the text in a given range of columns on a given range of lines. Normally you specify a rectangle by putting point at one corner and putting the mark at the diagonally opposite corner. See Section 9.4 [Rectangles], page 61.

Recursive Editing Level

> A recursive editing level is a state in which part of the execution of a command involves asking you to edit some text. This text may or may not be the same as the text to which the command was applied. The mode line indicates recursive editing levels with square brackets ('[' and ']'). See Section 31.13 [Recursive Edit], page 399.

Redisplay   Redisplay is the process of correcting the image on the screen to correspond to changes that have been made in the text being edited. See Chapter 1 [Screen], page 6.

Regexp   See 'regular expression.'

Region   The region is the text between point (q.v.) and the mark (q.v.). Many commands operate on the text of the region. See Chapter 8 [Mark], page 49.

Register   Registers are named slots in which text or buffer positions or rectangles can be saved for later use. See Chapter 10 [Registers], page 65. A related Emacs feature is 'bookmarks' (q.v.).

Regular Expression
             A regular expression is a pattern that can match various text strings; for example, 'a[0-9]+' matches 'a' followed by one or more digits. See Section 12.5 [Regexps], page 92.

Remote File
             A remote file is a file that is stored on a system other than your own. Emacs can access files on other computers provided that they are connected to the same network as your machine, and (obviously) that you have a supported method to gain access to those files. See Section 15.14 [Remote Files], page 152.

Repeat Count
             See 'numeric argument.'

Replacement
             See 'global substitution.'

Restriction A buffer's restriction is the amount of text, at the beginning or the end of the buffer, that is temporarily inaccessible. Giving a buffer a nonzero amount of restriction is called narrowing (q.v.); removing a restriction is called widening (q.v.). See Section 31.9 [Narrowing], page 396.

RET   RET is a character that in Emacs runs the command to insert a new-line into the text. It is also used to terminate most arguments read in the minibuffer (q.v.). See Section 2.1 [User Input], page 12.

Reverting   Reverting means returning to the original state. Emacs lets you revert a buffer by re-reading its file from disk. See Section 15.4 [Reverting], page 131.

Rmail File   An Rmail file is a file containing text in a special format used by Rmail for storing mail. See Chapter 28 [Rmail], page 319.

Saving   Saving a buffer means copying its text into the file that was visited (q.v.) in that buffer. This is the way text in files actually gets changed by your Emacs editing. See Section 15.3 [Saving], page 123.

Scroll Bar   A scroll bar is a tall thin hollow box that appears at the side of a window. You can use mouse commands in the scroll bar to scroll the window. The scroll bar feature is supported only under windowing systems. See Section 18.11 [Scroll Bars], page 181.

Scrolling   Scrolling means shifting the text in the Emacs window so as to see a different part of the buffer. See Section 11.1 [Scrolling], page 69.

Searching   Searching means moving point to the next occurrence of a specified
             string or the next match for a specified regular expression. See Chap-
             ter 12 [Search], page 86.

Search Path

             A search path is a list of directory names, to be used for searching
             for files for certain purposes. For example, the variable load-path
             holds a search path for finding Lisp library files. See Section 24.8
             [Lisp Libraries], page 288.

Secondary Selection

             The secondary selection is one particular X selection; some X appli-
             cations can use it for transferring text to and from other applications.
             Emacs has special mouse commands for transferring text using the sec-
             ondary selection. See Section 18.1.4 [Secondary Selection], page 174.

Selected Frame

             The selected frame is the one your input currently operates on. See
             Chapter 18 [Frames], page 171.

Selected Window

             The selected frame is the one your input currently operates on. See
             Section 17.1 [Basic Window], page 165.

Selecting a Buffer

             Selecting a buffer means making it the current (q.v.) buffer. See Sec-
             tion 16.1 [Select Buffer], page 156.

Selection   Windowing systems allow an application program to specify selections
             whose values are text. A program can also read the selections that
             other programs have set up. This is the principal way of transferring
             text between window applications. Emacs has commands to work
             with the primary (q.v.) selection and the secondary (q.v.) selection,
             and also with the clipboard (q.v.).

Self-Documentation

             Self-documentation is the feature of Emacs which can tell you what
             any command does, or give you a list of all commands related to a topic
             you specify. You ask for self-documentation with the help character,
             C-h. See Chapter 7 [Help], page 40.

Self-Inserting Character

             A character is self-inserting if typing that character inserts that char-
             acter in the buffer. Ordinary printing and whitespace characters are
             self-inserting in Emacs, except in certain special major modes.

Sentences   Emacs has commands for moving by or killing by sentences. See Sec-
             tion 22.2 [Sentences], page 214.

Sexp   A sexp (short for "s-expression") is the basic syntactic unit of Lisp
             in its textual form: either a list, or Lisp atom. Sexps are also the

balanced expressions (q.v.) of the Lisp language; this is why the commands for editing balanced expressions have 'sexp' in their name. See Section 23.4.1 [Expressions], page 257.

Simultaneous Editing

Simultaneous editing means two users modifying the same file at once. Simultaneous editing, if not detected, can cause one user to lose his or her work. Emacs detects all cases of simultaneous editing, and warns one of the users to investigate. See Section 15.3.4 [Simultaneous Editing], page 129.

SPC   SPC is the space character, which you enter by pressing the space bar.

Speedbar   The speedbar is a special tall frame that provides fast access to Emacs buffers, functions within those buffers, Info nodes, and other interesting parts of text within Emacs. See Section 18.7 [Speedbar], page 178.

Spell Checking

Spell checking means checking correctness of the written form of each one of the words in a text. Emacs uses the Ispell spelling-checker program to check the spelling of parts of a buffer via a convenient user interface. See Section 13.5 [Spelling], page 108.

String   A string is a kind of Lisp data object which contains a sequence of characters. Many Emacs variables are intended to have strings as values. The Lisp syntax for a string consists of the characters in the string with a '"' before and another '"' after. A '"' that is part of the string must be written as '\"' and a '\' that is part of the string must be written as '\\'. All other characters, including newline, can be included just by writing them inside the string; however, backslash sequences as in C, such as '\n' for newline or '\241' using an octal character code, are allowed as well.

String Substitution

See 'global substitution'.

Syntax Highlighting

See 'font lock.'

Syntax Table

The syntax table tells Emacs which characters are part of a word, which characters balance each other like parentheses, etc. See Section 32.5 [Syntax], page 433.

Super   Super is the name of a modifier bit which a keyboard input character may have. To make a character Super, type it while holding down the SUPER key. Such characters are given names that start with Super- (usually written s- for short). See Section 2.1 [User Input], page 12.

Suspending Suspending Emacs means stopping it temporarily and returning control to its parent process, which is usually a shell. Unlike killing a job (q.v.), you can later resume the suspended Emacs job without losing your buffers, unsaved edits, undo history, etc. See Section 3.1 [Exiting], page 17.

TAB   TAB is the tab character. In Emacs it is typically used for indentation or completion.

Tags Table   A tags table is a file that serves as an index to the function definitions in one or more other files. See Section 25.3 [Tags], page 293.

Termscript File

A termscript file contains a record of all characters sent by Emacs to the terminal. It is used for tracking down bugs in Emacs redisplay. Emacs does not make a termscript file unless you tell it to. See Section 33.3 [Bugs], page 445.

Text   'Text' has two meanings (see Chapter 22 [Text], page 213):

• Data consisting of a sequence of characters, as opposed to binary numbers, executable programs, and the like. The basic contents of an Emacs buffer (aside from the text properties, q.v.) are always text in this sense.

• Data consisting of written human language, as opposed to programs, or following the stylistic conventions of human language.

Text-only Terminal

A text-only terminal is a display that is limited to displaying text in character units. Such a terminal cannot control individual pixels it displays. Emacs supports a subset of display features on text-only terminals.

Text Properties

Text properties are annotations recorded for particular characters in the buffer. Images in the buffer are recorded as text properties; they also specify formatting information. See Section 22.12.3 [Editing Format Info], page 237.

Tool Bar   The tool bar is a line (sometimes multiple lines) of icons at the top of an Emacs frame. Clicking on one of these icons executes a command. You can think of this as a graphical relative of the menu bar (q.v.). See Section 18.15 [Tool Bars], page 183.

Tooltips   Tooltips are small windows displaying a help echo (q.v.) text that explains parts of the display, lists useful options available via mouse clicks, etc. See Section 18.17 [Tooltips], page 184.

Top Level   Top level is the normal state of Emacs, in which you are editing the text of the file you have visited. You are at top level whenever you are not in a recursive editing level (q.v.) or the minibuffer (q.v.), and not in the middle of a command. You can get back to top level by aborting (q.v.) and quitting (q.v.). See Section 33.1 [Quitting], page 440.

Transposition

> Transposing two units of text means putting each one into the place formerly occupied by the other. There are Emacs commands to transpose two adjacent characters, words, balanced expressions (q.v.) or lines (see Section 13.3 [Transpose], page 107).

Truncation   Truncating text lines in the display means leaving out any text on a line that does not fit within the right margin of the window displaying it. See also 'continuation line.' See Section 4.8 [Continuation Lines], page 25.

TTY   See 'text-only terminal.'

Undoing   Undoing means making your previous editing go in reverse, bringing back the text that existed earlier in the editing session. See Section 13.1 [Undo], page 105.

User Option

> A user option is a face (q.v.) or a variable (q.v.) that exists so that you can customize Emacs by setting it to a new value. See Section 32.2 [Easy Customization], page 408.

Variable   A variable is an object in Lisp that can store an arbitrary value. Emacs uses some variables for internal purposes, and has others (known as 'user options' (q.v.)) just so that you can set their values to control the behavior of Emacs. The variables used in Emacs that you are likely to be interested in are listed in the Variables Index in this manual (see [Variable Index], page 569). See Section 32.3 [Variables], page 416, for information on variables.

Version Control

> Version control systems keep track of multiple versions of a source file. They provide a more powerful alternative to keeping backup files (q.v.). See Section 15.7 [Version Control], page 135.

Visiting   Visiting a file means loading its contents into a buffer (q.v.) where they can be edited. See Section 15.2 [Visiting], page 120.

Whitespace   Whitespace is any run of consecutive formatting characters (space, tab, newline, and backspace).

Widening   Widening is removing any restriction (q.v.) on the current buffer; it is the opposite of narrowing (q.v.). See Section 31.9 [Narrowing], page 396.

Window   Emacs divides a frame (q.v.) into one or more windows, each of which can display the contents of one buffer (q.v.) at any time. See Chapter 1 [Screen], page 6, for basic information on how Emacs uses the screen. See Chapter 17 [Windows], page 165, for commands to control the use of windows. Some other editors use the term "window" for what we call a 'frame' (q.v.) in Emacs.

Window System

> A window system is software that operates on a graphical display (q.v.), to subdivide the screen so that multiple applications can have their] own windows at the same time. All modern operating systems include a window system.

Word Abbrev

> See 'abbrev.'

Word Search

> Word search is searching for a sequence of words, considering the punctuation between them as insignificant. See Section 12.3 [Word Search], page 91.

WYSIWYG

> WYSIWYG stands for "What you see is what you get." Emacs generally provides WYSIWYG editing for files of characters; in Enriched mode (see Section 22.12 [Formatted Text], page 236), it provides WYSIWYG editing for files that include text formatting information.

Yanking

> Yanking means reinserting text previously killed. It can be used to undo a mistaken kill, or for copying or moving text. Some other systems call this "pasting." See Section 9.2 [Yanking], page 58.

Key (Character) Index

Command and Function Index

T

Variable Index

Concept Index